MATHEMATICS

Grade 5 • Student Edition

Second Edition

Colorado Springs, Colorado

Printed in the United States of America
23 22 21 20 19 18 17 1 2 3 4 5 6 7

Mathematics, Grade 5 – Student Edition
Purposeful Design Mathematics series
ISBN 978-1-58331-585-9, Catalog #40051

Purposeful Design Publications is the publishing division of the Association of Christian Schools International (ACSI) and is committed to the ministry of Christian school education, to enable Christian educators and schools worldwide to effectively prepare students for life. As the publisher of textbooks, trade books, and other educational resources within ACSI, Purposeful Design Publications strives to produce biblically sound materials that reflect Christian scholarship and stewardship and that address the identified needs of Christian schools around the world.

References to books, computer software, and other ancillary resources in this series are not endorsements by ACSI. These materials were selected to provide teachers with additional resources appropriate to the concepts being taught and to promote student understanding and enjoyment.

Photos of X-36 and *Gossamer Albatross* on page 170 courtesy of NASA.

Photo of Dominic L. Gorie on Student Edition page 216 courtesy of NASA.

Photo of astronaut exercising on Student Edition page 217 courtesy of NASA.

Photo of Valentina Tereshkova on Student Edition page 234 courtesy of NASA.

Photo of PhoneSat 2.4 on Student Edition page 250 courtesy of Ames Research Center/NASA.

NASA does not necessarily sponsor, authorize, or endorse this textbook.

Purposeful Design Publications
A Division of ACSI
PO Box 65130 • Colorado Springs, CO • 80962-5130
Customer Service Department: 800/367-0798 • Website: www.purposefuldesign.com

Table of Contents

Chapter 1: Place Value

1.1 Hundred Thousands....2
1.2 Hundred Billions....4
1.3 Compare Whole Numbers....6
1.4 Round Whole Numbers....8
1.5 Tenths and Hundredths....10
1.6 Thousandths....12
1.7 Compare Decimals....14
1.8 Round Decimals....16
1.9 Problem Solving: Decimals....18
1.10 Chapter 1 Review....20

Chapter 2: Add and Subtract

2.1 Estimate Answers....24
2.2 Larger Numbers....26
2.3 Problem Solving: Add and Subtract....28
2.4 Estimate Decimal Sums....30
2.5 Add Decimals....32
2.6 Properties of Addition....24
2.7 Estimate Decimal Differences....26
2.8 Equivalent Decimals....38
2.9 Subtract Decimals....40
2.10 Problem Solving: 2 Steps....42
2.11 Add and Subtract Thousandths....44
2.12 Chapter 2 Review....46
2.13 Chapters 1–2 Review....48

Chapter 3: Multiply Whole Numbers

3.1 Properties of Multiplication....52
3.2 Mental Math: Multiples....54
3.3 Least Common Multiple....56
3.4 Greatest Common Factor....58
3.5 Multiply by 1-Digit Factors....60
3.6 Multiply Larger Numbers....62
3.7 Estimate Products....64
3.8 Multiply by 2-Digit Factors....66
3.9 Problem Solving: 2-Digit Factors....68
3.10 Multiply by 3-Digit Factors....70
3.11 Practice: 3-Digit Factors....72
3.12 Calculators: Multistep Problems....74
3.13 Explore Exponents....76
3.14 Lattice Multiplication....78
3.15 Chapter 3 Review....80

Chapter 4: 1-Digit Divisors

4.1 Explore Divisibility....84
4.2 Rules of Division....86
4.3 Quotients and Remainders....88
4.4 Estimate Quotients....90
4.5 Divide 2- and 3-Digit Numbers....92
4.6 Find Averages....94
4.7 Zero in the Quotient....96
4.8 Divide Larger Numbers....98
4.9 Problem Solving: 1-Digit Divisors....100
4.10 Chapter 4 Review....102

Chapter 5: 2-Digit Divisors

5.1 Division Patterns....106
5.2 Estimate Quotients....108
5.3 1-Digit Quotients....110
5.4 2-Digit Quotients....112
5.5 Adjust Estimated Quotients....114
5.6 3-Digit Quotients....116
5.7 Zero in the Quotient....118
5.8 Problem Solving: 2-Digit Divisors....120
5.9 Chapter 5 Review....122
5.10 Chapters 3–5 Review....124

Chapter 6: Multiply and Divide Decimals

6.1 Estimate Decimal Products....128
6.2 Multiply by Whole Numbers....130
6.3 Multiply Decimals....132
6.4 Zero in the Product....134
6.5 Problem Solving: Multiply....136
6.6 Divide by Whole Numbers....138
6.7 Zeros in Division....140
6.8 Divide by 10, 100, and 1,000....142

6.9 Order of Operations........................144
6.10 Problem Solving: Divide 146
6.11 Chapter 6 Review 148

Chapter 7: Geometry

7.1 Line Relationships............................152
7.2 Name Rays and Angles.....................154
7.3 Use a Protractor 156
7.4 Classify Triangles 158
7.5 Polygons...160
7.6 Quadrilaterals...................................162
7.7 Solids..164
7.8 Practice: Polygons and Solids...........166
7.9 Circles...168
7.10 Line Symmetry.................................170
7.11 Motion in Geometry 172
7.12 Congruence and Similarity...............174
7.13 Problem Solving: Angles..................176
7.14 Chapter 7 Review 178
7.15 Chapters 6–7 Review.......................180

Chapter 8: Integers and Fractions

8.1 Integers 184
8.2 Compare Integers............................186
8.3 Relate Fractions to Integers 188
8.4 Fraction Review 190
8.5 Equivalent Fractions 192
8.6 Fractions and Decimals....................194
8.7 Prime and Composite Numbers........196
8.8 Greatest Common Factor 198
8.9 Fractions in Simplest Form 200
8.10 Least Common Multiple...................202
8.11 Compare Fractions 204
8.12 Improper Fractions 206
8.13 Problem Solving: Fractions...............208
8.14 Chapter 8 Review 210

Chapter 9: Add and Subtract Fractions

9.1 Like Denominators...........................214
9.2 Mixed Numbers...............................216
9.3 Add and Rename 218
9.4 Subtract from Whole Numbers.........220
9.5 Rename and Subtract 222
9.6 Estimate with Fractions 224
9.7 Least Common Denominator...........226
9.8 Related Denominators......................228
9.9 Add: Unlike Denominators 230
9.10 Subtract: Unlike Denominators.........232
9.11 Add: Mixed Numbers 234
9.12 Subtract: Mixed Numbers 236
9.13 Problem Solving: Use a Map............238
9.14 Chapter 9 Review 240

Chapter 10: Multiply and Divide Fractions

10.1 Multiply Fractions: Models 244
10.2 Multiply by Fractions........................246
10.3 Multiply by Whole Numbers............248
10.4 Multiply by Mixed Numbers............250
10.5 Problem Solving: Multiply 252
10.6 Estimate Products............................254
10.7 Divide Fractions: Models..................256
10.8 Divide by Fractions..........................258
10.9 Problem Solving: Patterns................260
10.10 Chapter 10 Review 262
10.11 Chapters 8–10 Review.....................264

Chapter 11: Ratio, Proportion, and Percent

11.1 Explore Ratios 268
11.2 Find Equal Ratios.............................270

11.3 Explore Proportions 272
11.4 Solve Proportions 274
11.5 Problem Solving: Scale Drawings 276
11.6 Explore Percent 278
11.7 Ratio and Percent 280
11.8 Fractions and Percent 282
11.9 Decimals and Percent 284
11.10 Mental Math: Estimate Percent 286
11.11 Find Percent 288
11.12 Problem Solving: Percent 290
11.13 Chapter 11 Review 292

Chapter 12: Measurement

12.1 Customary Units of Length 296
12.2 Customary Units of Capacity 298
12.3 Customary Units of Weight 300
12.4 Metric Units of Length 302
12.5 Metric Units of Capacity 304
12.6 Metric Units of Mass 306
12.7 Temperature 308
12.8 Elapsed Time 310
12.9 Problem Solving: Time Zones 312
12.10 Chapter 12 Review 314

Chapter 13: Area, Perimeter, and Volume

13.1 Area: Rectangles 318
13.2 Perimeter 320
13.3 Circumference 322
13.4 Coordinate Geometry 324
13.5 Area: Right Triangles 326
13.6 Area: Triangles 328
13.7 Area: Irregular Figures 330
13.8 Surface Area 332
13.9 Understand Volume 334
13.10 Find Volume 336
13.11 Problem Solving: Formulas 338
13.12 Chapter 13 Review 340

Chapter 14: Graphs, Statistics, and Probability

14.1 Collect and Organize Data 344
14.2 Pictographs and Bar Graphs 346
14.3 Histograms 348
14.4 Line Graphs 350
14.5 Circle Graphs 352
14.6 Problem Solving: Graphs 354
14.7 Statistics and Line Plots 356
14.8 Range, Mean, Median, and Mode 358
14.9 Practice: Statistics and Graphs 360
14.10 Probability of Outcomes 362
14.11 More About Probability 364
14.12 Chapter 14 Review 366
14.13 Chapters 11–14 Review 368

Chapter 15: Cumulative Review

15.1 Review: Chapters 1–2 372
15.2 Review: Chapters 3–5 374
15.3 Review: Chapters 6–7 376
15.4 Review: Chapters 8–10 378
15.5 Review: Chapters 11–14 380

Reference 383
Glossary 385
Index 391

Chapter 1
Place Value

In the beginning God created
the heavens and the earth.
Genesis 1:1

Key Ideas:

Place Value: reading and writing whole numbers to hundred billions

Place Value: reading and writing decimals to thousandths

Money: counting and comparing amounts of money

Money: adding and subtracting money

1.1 Hundred Thousands

Construct Meaning

Welcome to the neighborhood—not a house and the streets around it, but the neighborhood in the universe! The solar system consists of the sun, eight planets and their moons, and other objects such as asteroids, meteoroids, and comets.

Earth has one moon. The average distance from Earth to the moon, center to center, is approximately two hundred thirty-nine thousand miles.

thousands period,			ones period		
hundred thousands	ten thousands	thousands	hundreds	tens	ones
2	3	9,	0	0	0

All whole numbers can be written using only the digits 0, 1, 2, 3, 4, 5, 6, 7, 8, and 9. To make large numbers easier to read, commas separate the number into groups of three digits. Each group is called a period. The value of each digit is shown by its place in a number.

	thousands period,			ones period		
periods →	thousands period,			ones period		
place values →	hundred thousands	ten thousands	thousands	hundreds	tens	ones
standard form →	1	7	4,	6	5	1
expanded form →	1 × 100,000 = 100,000	7 × 10,000 = 70,000	4 × 1,000 = 4,000	6 × 100 = 600	5 × 10 = 50	1 × 1 = 1
	100,000 +	**70,000 +**	**4,000 +**	**600 +**	**50 +**	**1**

= **174,651**

word form
one hundred seventy-four thousand, six hundred fifty-one

Check Understanding

a. Write the standard form for 80,000 + 3,000 + 200 + 90 + 4.
b. Write 361,401 in expanded form.

Read each number. Use place value to tell what the orange digit represents.

c. 92,641 **d.** 89,450 **e.** 683,526

Practice

Write the number in expanded form.

	thousands,			ones		
	hundred thousands	ten thousands	thousands	hundreds	tens	ones
1.		6	8,	1	9	7
2.	4	2	1,	5	7	3
3.	9	3	4,	2	0	2

Write the number in standard form.

4. seven hundred fourteen thousand, three hundred sixty-eight
5. four hundred sixty-two thousand, one hundred twelve
6. nine hundred thirty-four thousand, one hundred seventy-nine
7. five hundred nineteen thousand, eight hundred ninety-one
8. 300,000 + 70,000 + 6,000 + 400 + 80 + 2
9. 100,000 + 4,000 + 60
10. 700,000 + 8,000 + 900 + 9
11. 600,000 + 40,000 + 3,000 + 900 + 20 + 5

Use place value to tell what the green digit represents.

12. 89,016
13. 61,721
14. 320,354
15. 754,333

16. **Count by 10s from 64 to 134. Write each number.**
17. **Count by 100s from 827 to 1,427. Write each number.**

Apply

18. The cashier at First Bank gave Mr. Bennett the following bills: 7 tens, 1 one, and 5 hundreds. What was the amount of the check Mr. Bennett cashed?

Review

19. 12 + 3
20. 46 – 9
21. 73 – 8
22. 28 + 14
23. 92 – 6
24. 65 + 37
25. 13 × 2
26. 36 ÷ 6
27. 24 × 4
28. 45 ÷ 9
29. 44 ÷ 4
30. 43 × 8

1.2 Hundred Billions

Construct Meaning

Over six billion people live on Earth. How is this number written? Large numbers are grouped into periods of three digits. Ones, thousands, millions, and billions are periods. Commas separate the periods and show where to use the period name. Six billion is written 6,000,000,000. What does the following number represent?

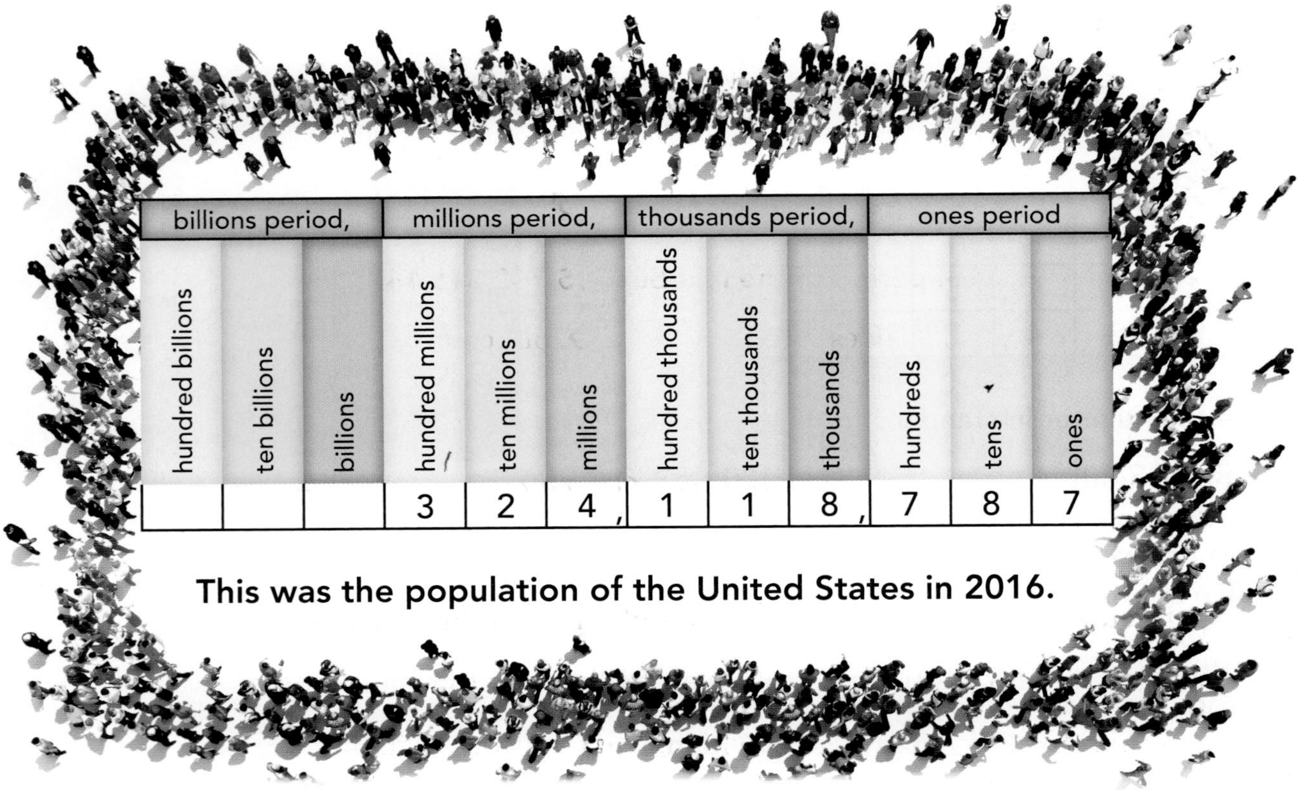

billions period,			millions period,			thousands period,			ones period		
hundred billions	ten billions	billions	hundred millions	ten millions	millions	hundred thousands	ten thousands	thousands	hundreds	tens	ones
			3	2	4,	1	1	8,	7	8	7

This was the population of the United States in 2016.

To read the number, say the number in a period and then the period name: 324 million, 118 thousand, 787.

To write the standard form, use commas to separate the periods: 324,118,787.

To show expanded form, write: 300,000,000 + 20,000,000 + 4,000,000 + 100,000 + 10,000 + 8,000 + 700 + 80 + 7.

To use the word form, write: three hundred twenty-four million, one hundred eighteen thousand, seven hundred eighty-seven.

Check Understanding

Use the number 324,118,787 to complete each exercise.

a. Use place value to write what the 3 represents.
b. Name the period that includes the digits 118.
c. Name the place value position of the digit 2.
d. How did the number above change to the number 324,218,787?

Practice

Perform the stated operation and write the resulting number.

1. Add one hundred billion to 420,512,030,406. What would the new number be?
2. Add fifty million to 43,000,060,010. What would the new number be?
3. Add three thousand to 307,200,000. What would the new number be?

Use place value to tell what the purple digit represents.

4. 338,306,000
5. 870,046,764,597
6. 331,576,832,000

Write the digits for each period of the number 585,742,216,147.

7. millions
8. ones
9. billions
10. thousands

Write the word form.

11. 83,175,000
12. 600,453,281,954
13. 2,067,001,905

Write the expanded form.

14. two hundred forty-two million, seven hundred three thousand, seven hundred
15. forty-four billion, three hundred sixteen million, one thousand, two hundred
16. two hundred billion, sixty-seven million, two thousand, eight hundred three

Apply

17. The solar system is part of the vast Milky Way Galaxy. The spiral-shaped galaxy is about 100,000 light-years across. A light-year is not a measurement of time but of distance—the distance light travels in one year. Light travels at 186,000 miles per second. One light-year is about 5,879,000,000,000 miles.

    In comparison to the galaxy, the solar system seems small. It is about 12 light-hours across or about 8 billion miles. Write 8 billion in standard form.

1.3 Compare Whole Numbers

Construct Meaning

Derrick lives in Ogden, Utah. He is packing for a visit with his aunt and uncle who live in Brainerd, Minnesota. He wants to know which state is larger in area. He learned that Utah has an area of 84,900 square miles (sq mi) and Minnesota has an area of 86,936 sq mi. How can Derrick tell which state is larger?

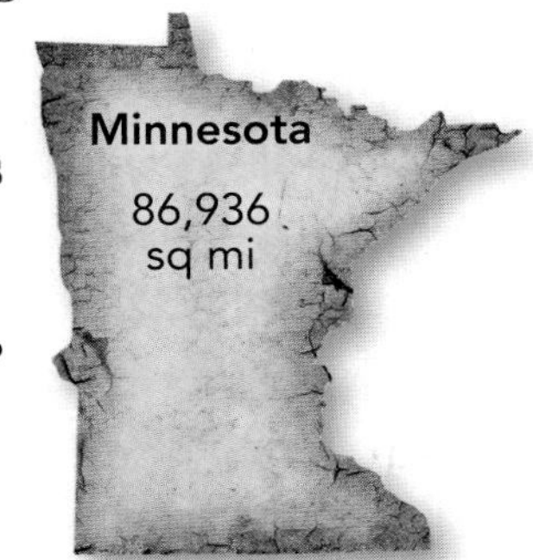

Two numbers can be compared by comparing the digits in each place value position.

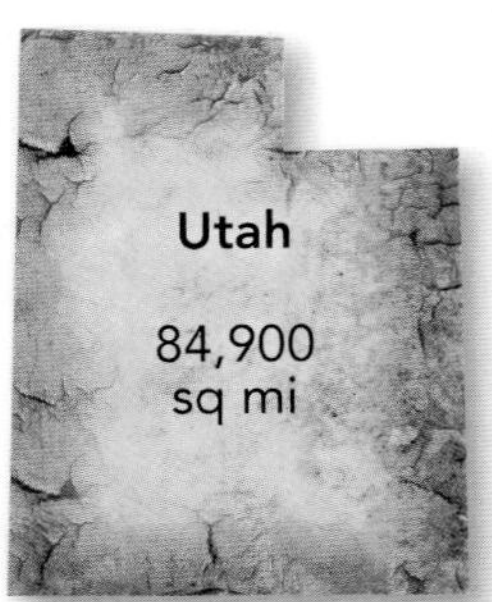

thousands,			ones		
hundred thousands	ten thousands	thousands	hundreds	tens	ones
	8	4,	9	0	0
	8	6,	9	3	6
4 < 6, so 84,900 < 86,936					

- Line up the numbers by place value.
- Start comparing at the left.
- Check each place until the digits are different.

In square miles, Utah is smaller than Minnesota.

Other numbers can be ordered in the same way.

Order the population of these four states from greatest to least:

	millions,	hundred thousands	ten thousands	thousands,	hundreds	tens	ones
Maryland	6,	0	0	6,	4	0	1
Missouri	6,	0	8	3,	6	7	2
Tennessee	6,	6	0	0,	2	9	9
Indiana	6,	6	1	9,	6	8	0

- The digits in the highest place, millions, are the same—6 millions.
- The greatest digit in the hundred thousands place is 6. Both Tennessee and Indiana have a 6.
- A difference in digits is found in the ten thousands place between the two greatest populations. 1 > 0, so 6,619,680 > 6,600,299.
- Compare the remaining numbers: 6,083,672 > 6,006,401.

By population, the four states are ordered Indiana, Tennessee, Missouri, and Maryland.

Check Understanding

a. Order from least to greatest. 56,276 56,343 56,145

b. How is comparing 79,617 and 81,823 different from solving the previous problem?

c. Why start at the left to compare numbers?

Practice

Write >, <, or =.

1. 741 ◯ 471
2. 1,064 ◯ 1,066
3. 6,805 ◯ 6,850
4. 26,765 ◯ 22,886
5. 867,551 ◯ 687,504
6. 503,011 ◯ 503,101

Use the numbers in the chart to answer the following questions.

7. Which numbers are less than 320,000 square kilometers?
8. Which numbers are greater than 335,000 square kilometers?
9. Which numbers are between 310,000 and 325,000 square kilometers?
10. Which number shows a 2 in the ten thousands place?
11. Write the names of the countries in order of their area from the least to the greatest square kilometers.

Areas of Five European Countries	
Finland	338,445 sq km
Germany	357,021 sq km
Italy	301,230 sq km
Norway	324,220 sq km
Poland	312,685 sq km

Apply

12. During a mountain hike, Kaitlyn walked to the sign marking the elevation as 12,877 feet (ft). Her friend Ivy reached 14,110 ft. Write a comparison sentence about the hike.

13. Write three numbers greater than 94,329 and less than 95,006.

Twin Lakes, Colorado, United States

Review

Use commas to separate the periods in the number.

14. 18264
15. 607352
16. 98954321
17. 100100

Use place value to tell what the blue digit represents.

18. 745,197
19. 3,800,620
20. 6,570,432
21. 102,812

Write in expanded form and word form.

22. 40,800,053
23. 905,632
24. 2,071,300,000
25. 60,497

1.4 Round Whole Numbers

Construct Meaning

The students of Courageous Christian School recycled plastic water bottles. At the end of the year, 84,352 bottles had been collected. To report the total in the *Courageous Chronicle*, the school secretary wants to use a rounded number. How could the number 84,352 be rounded to the nearest thousand?

One way to round is to use a number line.

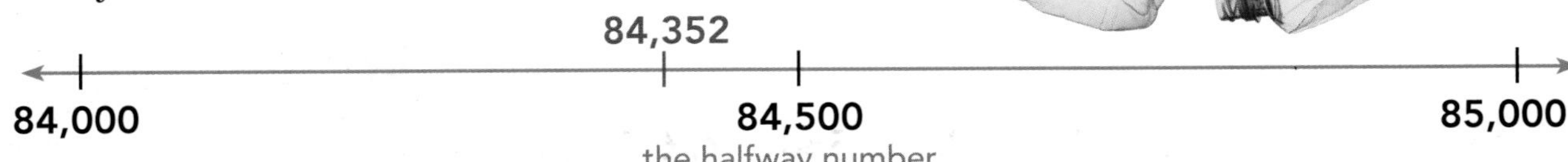

84,352 is closer to 84,000 than to 85,000.

Follow these steps to round to any place value position.

Step 1: Locate the digit in the place to which the number should be rounded. This is the target digit.

84,352

Step 2: Look at the digit to the right of the target digit. If the digit to the right is 5 or greater, round the target digit up. If the digit is less than 5, round down by keeping the target digit the same.

84,352

84,000

Rounded to the nearest thousand, 84,352 is 84,000.

Step 3: Replace all the digits to the right of the target digit with zeros.

Check Understanding

a. Write the number that is halfway between 30,000 and 40,000.
b. Write the thousands that the number 6,520 is between.
c. Round 52,633 to the nearest thousand.
d. Round 184,528 to the nearest ten thousand.
e. Round 8,924,513 to the nearest million.

Practice

Round the number to the greatest place value.

1. 370,764   2. 26,982   3. 52,344   4. 4,327,600

Round to the nearest thousand.

5. 6,670   6. 73,583   7. 9,161   8. 511,482

Round to the nearest hundred thousand.

9. 650,555   10. 8,029,040   11. 1,378,290   12. 216,443

Round to the nearest million.

13. 3,789,500   14. 5,039,784   15. 3,367,580   16. 6,516,443

Complete the chart.

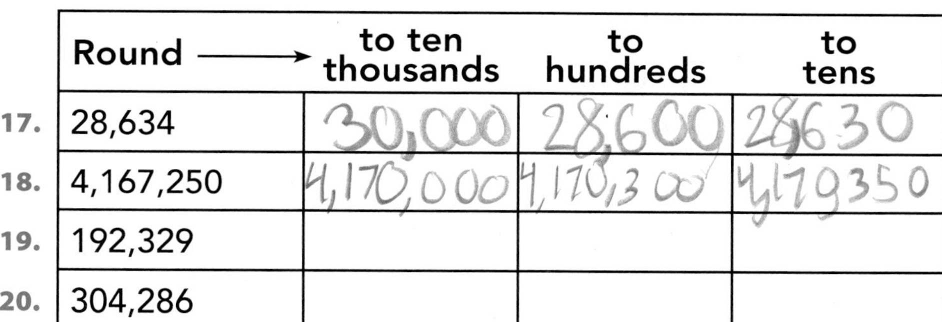

	Round →	to ten thousands	to hundreds	to tens
17.	28,634	30,000	28,600	28630
18.	4,167,250	4,170,000	4,170,300	4,179350
19.	192,329			
20.	304,286			

Challenge

Time can be recorded in minutes, seconds, and hundredths of a second. Use the figures in the chart to answer the questions.

2014 Winter Olympic Games Women's Giant Slalom		
athlete	**country**	**time**
Nadia Fanchini	Italy	2:37.25
Viktoria Rebensburg	Germany	2:37.14
Tina Maze	Slovenia	2:36.87
Anna Fenninger	Austria	2:36.94

21. Who was the winner of this event?
22. List the times in order from least to greatest.
23. Round each time to the nearest second (in the order listed on the chart).

Review

Write >, <, or =.

24. 45 million ◯ 450 thousand
25. 2 billion ◯ 2,000,000,000
26. 7,365,049 ◯ 7,365,094
27. 2,943,052 ◯ 2,953,052

1.5 Tenths and Hundredths

Construct Meaning

At the 0.5 km marker, Ethan was leading in the 1 km race. How much of the race does Ethan still have to run?

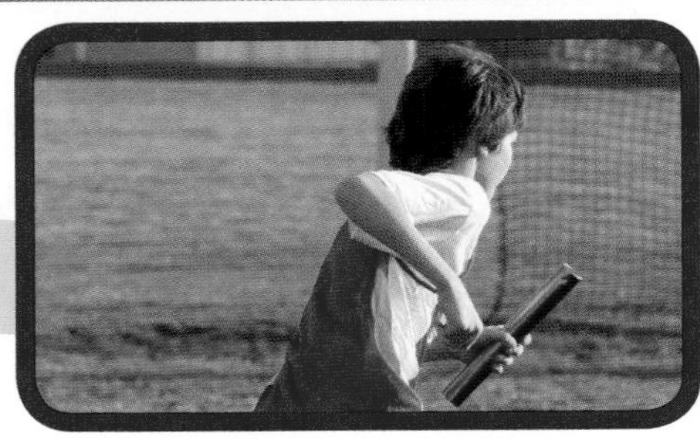

A decimal names part of a whole.

Decimal numbers can be modeled with squares.

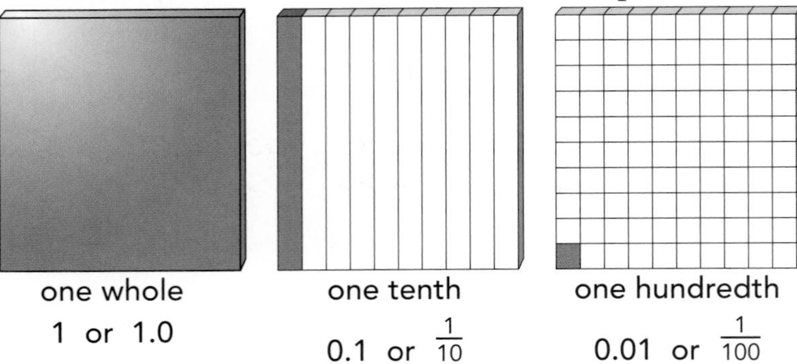

one whole	one tenth	one hundredth
1 or 1.0	0.1 or $\frac{1}{10}$	0.01 or $\frac{1}{100}$

Ethan has run 0.5 of one kilometer.

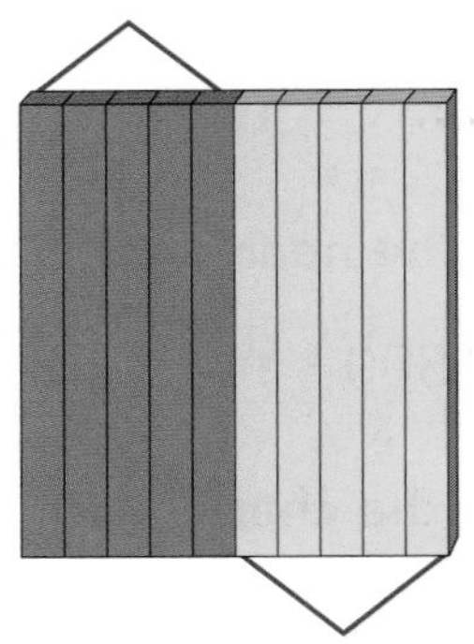

Ethan has 0.5 km left to run.

Decimal numbers can be modeled with money.

one whole dollar
100 cents or $1.00

one dime
10 cents or $0.10

one penny
1 cent or $0.01

$3.54

Decimal numbers can be written on a place value chart.

hundreds	tens	ones .	tenths	hundredths
1	0	2 .	5	6

One hundred two and fifty-six hundredths is written 102.56.
The whole number part of the number is 102.
The decimal part is 0.56.

A decimal point separates the whole number part from the decimal part and is read "and."

Check Understanding

Copy the place value chart. Write the numbers.

a. 3 ones, 2 tenths, 4 hundredths
b. 1 ten, 8 ones, 0 tenths, 9 hundredths
c. five and thirty-eight hundredths
d. nine hundred and two tenths
e. fourteen and seventy hundredths

hundreds	tens	ones .	tenths	hundredths

Practice

Write the decimal number for the shaded parts.

1.  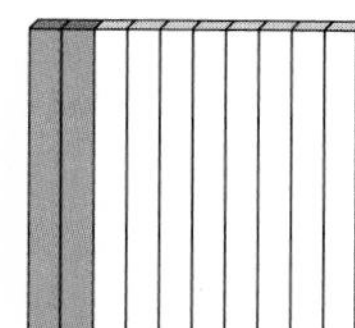 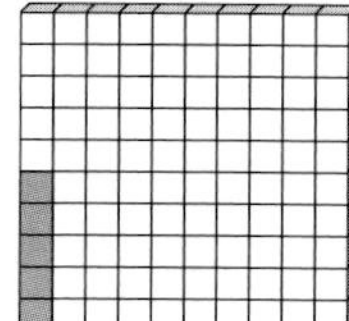

2. 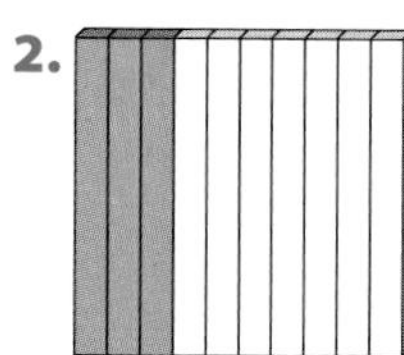 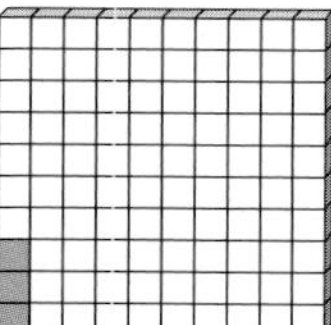

Write the number that matches. Use the Answer Bank.

3. The digit 9 has a value of 9 tens.
4. The digit 7 has a value of 7 ones.
5. The digit 8 has a value of 8 tenths.
6. The digit 4 has a value of 4 hundredths.
7. The decimal parts of the numbers are equal.

Answer Bank

56.28	24.6	85.19	27.36
80.74	76.89	93.72	62.60

Write a decimal to represent the bold words.

8. By the time Brayden reached the **eight tenths** marker in the race, Cody had passed him.
9. The drinking straw measured **twenty hundredths** of a meter.
10. You can see **ninety-nine and ninety-nine hundredths** percent of the mass of the solar system with your own eyes, using no instruments whatsoever.

Write as part of one dollar, expressed as hundredths.

11. 6 dimes
12. 2 quarters
13. 47 pennies
14. 3 dimes
15. 25 pennies
16. 3 quarters

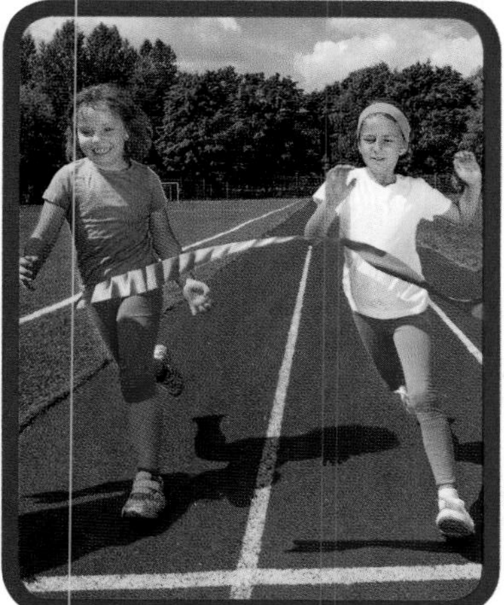

Apply

17. If Hannah completed the race in 3.10 minutes and Latisha crossed the finish line in 3.01 minutes, which girl ran faster?

Review

Write >, <, or =.

18. 156 ◯ 163
19. 8,600 ◯ 8,588
20. 19,820 ◯ 19,820

Round to the nearest ten thousand.

21. 56,614
22. 127,407
23. 430,917
24. 3,685,000

1.6 Thousandths

Construct Meaning

Blake's father works for a company that makes vitamins. He must find the cost of producing various vitamins in order to set the retail price. He made this chart to show the cost of four vitamins.

multiple vitamin	$0.125 per tablet
calcium	$0.053 per tablet
vitamin C	$0.116 per tablet
vitamin E	$0.129 per tablet

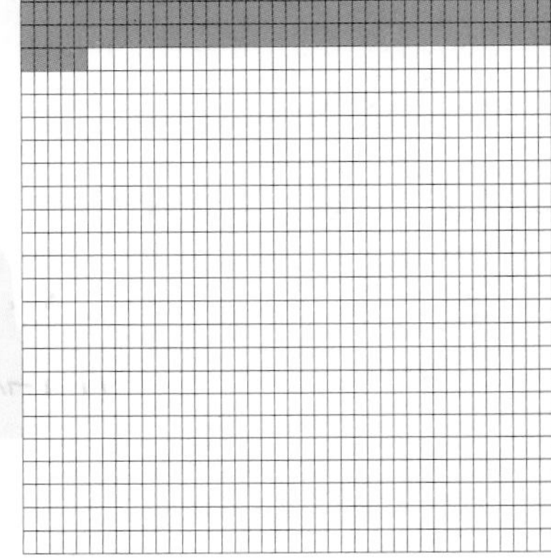

This shape is divided into 1,000 smaller shapes. The colored part represents one hundred twenty-five thousandths of a dollar. Which vitamin pill price would be shown by the colored parts?

The shaded parts show 0.125, the price ($0.125) of one multiple-vitamin pill.

Use a place value chart to write decimal numbers in expanded form. How would you place the digits to show 4.253?

Write: 4.253 Read: four and two hundred fifty-three thousandths Expanded form: 4 + 0.2 + 0.05 + 0.003

tens	ones .	tenths	hundredths	thousandths
	4 .	2	5	3
	4 × 1 .	2 × 0.1	5 × 0.01	3 × 0.001

Check Understanding

a. Write the decimal for one thousandth.
b. How many times greater is the place value of hundredths than thousandths?

Use the number 436.515 for each problem.

c. Write the value of the digit 3.
d. Write the value of the digit 5 in both place value positions.
e. Name the place value position of the digit 1.
f. Write the word form of the number.

Practice

Write the decimal.

1. four tenths
2. thirty-five hundredths
3. forty-two thousandths
4. seven hundred fourteen thousandths
5. one and one thousandth

Write the number from the Answer Bank in which 7 has the value of:

6. 7 hundredths
7. 7 tenths
8. 7 thousandths
9. 7 ones
10. 7 tens

Answer Bank

0.786	4.325
70.122	55.472
2.287	87.324

Write the place value position of each underlined digit.

11. 0.<u>4</u>1
12. 1.2<u>2</u>9
13. 3.<u>0</u>17
14. 9.88<u>3</u>

Write the word form for each decimal number.

15. 0.523
16. 0.374
17. 3.867
18. 8.009

Write the expanded form for each decimal number.

19. 0.813
20. 0.024
21. 0.678
22. 5.43

Apply

23. As Allie and Gabriela are playing in the ultraviolet rays of the sun, their bodies are making vitamin D. God has designed human bodies to manufacture enough vitamin D in summer to last through the winter. To prevent sunburn, they use sunblock. If a bottle of sunblock costs \$0.279 per ounce (oz), would this be more or less than \$0.27 per ounce?

Review

Use mental math and place value to determine how much less a is than b.

24. **a.** 0.27 **b.** 0.28
25. **a.** 4.75 **b.** 4.85
26. **a.** 27.36 **b.** 27.37
27. **a.** 0.8 **b.** 0.81

Write the decimal number in standard form.

28. nineteen and nine hundredths
29. four hundred one and one tenth

1.7 Compare Decimals

Construct Meaning

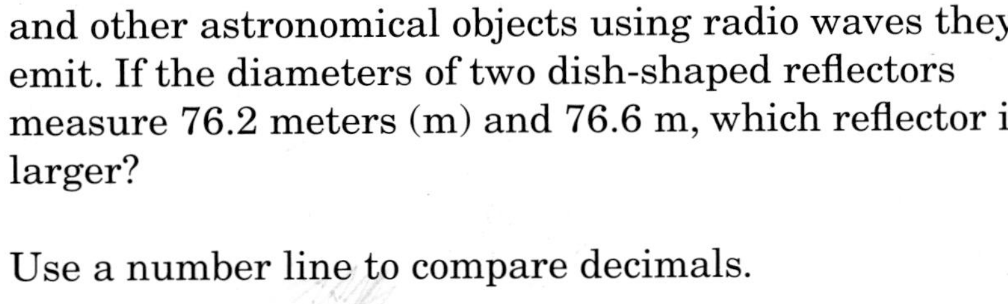

Radio astronomy is the study of planets, stars, galaxies, and other astronomical objects using radio waves they emit. If the diameters of two dish-shaped reflectors measure 76.2 meters (m) and 76.6 m, which reflector is larger?

Use a number line to compare decimals.

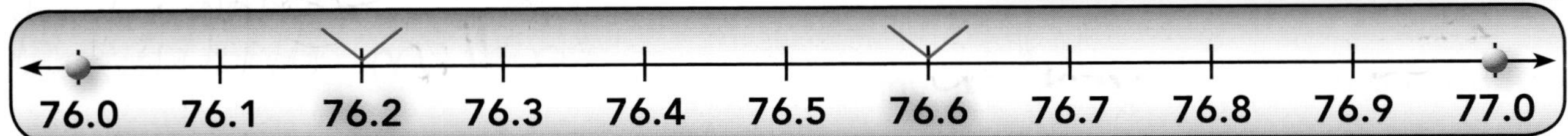

The number 76.6 is to the right of 76.2, therefore, 76.6 is greater than 76.2.

The reflector which has a diameter of 76.6 meters is larger.

As with whole numbers, compare two decimals by comparing the digits in each place value position.

Compare 0.883 and 0.892. Start comparing at the left. Check each place until the digits are different.

hundreds	tens	ones .	tenths	hundredths	thousandths
		0 .	8	8	3
		0 .	8	9	2

8 < 9, so 0.883 < 0.892

Order other decimals the same way.
Order 3.123, 0.312, and 3.120 from greatest to least.

hundreds	tens	ones .	tenths	hundredths	thousandths
		3 .	1	2	3
		0 .	3	1	2
		3 .	1	2	0

- First, line up the numbers by place value.
- Next, compare the numbers two at a time. Because the 3 in the ones place is greater than 0, 3.123 > 0.312 and 3.120 > 0.312.
- Because the 3 in the thousandths place is greater than 0, 3.123 > 3.120.
- Finally, list the numbers from greatest to least: 3.123, 3.120, 0.312.

Check Understanding

Write >, <, or =.

a. 2.40 ◯ 2.04 b. 0.64 ◯ 0.79 c. 1.55 ◯ 1.53 d. 4.000 ◯ 4.001

Order from least to greatest.

e. 66.89 67.91 67.19

f. 88.52 89.78 88.26

Practice

Order from greatest to least.

1. 

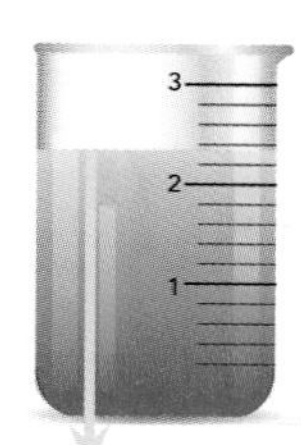

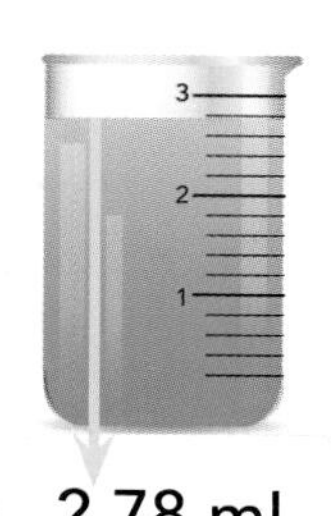

2. 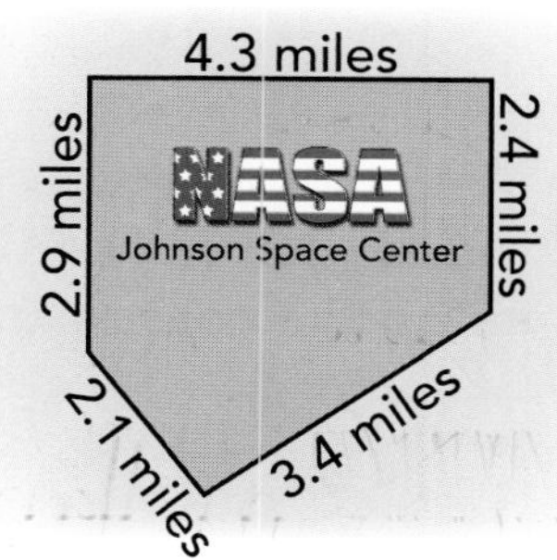

Write >, <, or =.

3. 3.37 ◯ 3.39
4. 0.079 ◯ 0.790
5. 5.510 ◯ 5.50
6. 28.25 ◯ 28.250
7. 40.19 ◯ 40.2
8. 9.06 ◯ 9.6

Use the Answer Bank to solve.

Which numbers are
9. greater than 1.6?
10. less than 0.074?
11. between 0.3 and 1?

Answer Bank

1.328	0.74	0.06
0.566	0.053	1.73
1.006	1.701	0.088
0.5	0.37	1.495

Apply

12. Audrey, Evelyn, and Greyson formed a Future Scientists Club. They used the Internet to research different types of butterflies. They recorded, in centimeters (cm), the following wingspans of three different butterflies: 8.693 cm, 7.035 cm, and 8.093 cm. Order the butterflies' wingspans from least to greatest.

Review

Write the word form of each decimal number.

13. 0.034
14. 0.88
15. 304.601
16. 5.007

Write the standard form.

17. one million, two hundred seventy-two thousand
18. three hundred one billion
19. six hundred twenty thousand, sixteen

1.8 Round Decimals

Construct Meaning

Round the decimals.

Use a number line to locate and round each city's rainfall amount to the nearest inch (in.).

city	September rainfall
Chicago, Illinois, USA	3.6 in.
Milan, Italy	3.2 in.
Zurich, Switzerland	3.9 in.

3.2 3.6 3.9

3 3.5 4

Which of these decimals is closer to 3 in? 3.2 in.
Which of these decimals are closer to 4 in? 3.6 in. and 3.9 in.
What is the number halfway between 3 in. and 4 in? 3.5 in.

In one year, the total rainfall in Forks, Washington, was 160.88 in. Simplify this figure by rounding the number to the nearest tenth of an inch. Apply the steps you learned for rounding whole numbers to rounding decimals.

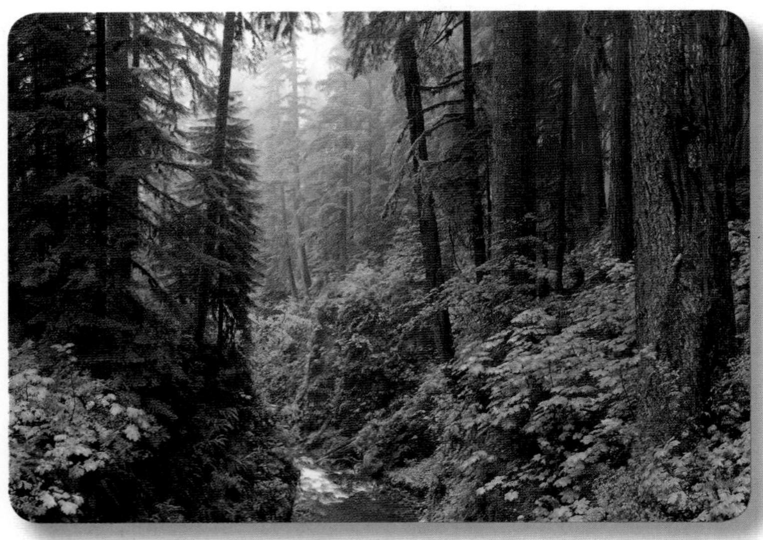

- First, target the digit in the place to which you will round. 160.88
- Look at the digit in the place to the immediate right. 160.88
- If the digit is 5 or more, round up. If it is less than 5, round down, leaving the targeted digit the same. Because 8 > 5, the tenths digit increases by 1.

160.88 in. rounds to 160.9 in.

Check Understanding

Round each number to the place of the blue digit.

a. 12.5 **b.** 6.38 **c.** 4.732 **d.** 8.46 **e.** 2.91

Write the two whole numbers that each decimal falls between. Then, circle the whole number you would round it to.

f. 0.7 **g.** 8.2 **h.** 5.51 **i.** 9.8 **j.** 0.04

Practice

1. Draw a number line with endpoints of 2 and 3. On the line, locate and label 2.1, 2.4, 2.9, 2.2, and 2.7.

2. Which of the decimals round to 3?

3. Which decimals round to 2?

Round to the nearest whole number.

4. 36.4 5. 4.9 6. 13.51 7. 0.7 8. 80.06

Round to the nearest tenth.

9. 61.52 10. 9.763 11. 4.087 12. 55.04 13. 0.11

Round to the nearest hundredth.

14. 23.665 15. 0.942 16. 78.508 17. 39.566 18. 59.610

Round the amount to the nearest dollar.

19. \$3.86 20. \$9.39 21. \$62.73 22. \$1.27 23. \$40.50

Round the number 12.783 to these place values.

24. ones 25. tenths 26. hundredths 27. tens

Apply

28. Katarina is 154.3 cm tall. Her brother Andrew is 150.6 cm tall. Round both figures to the nearest centimeter. Which student's height is closer to 151 cm?

29. Write at least five different decimal numbers with digits in the hundredths place that round to 2.1 when rounded to the nearest tenth.

Review

Write the word form.

30. 0.034 31. 0.88 32. 304.601 33. 99.993

Write >, <, or =.

34. 31.07 ◯ 13.70 35. 1.0 ◯ 0.1 36. 0.56 ◯ 0.560 37. 0.08 ◯ 0.80

1.9 Problem Solving: Decimals

Construct Meaning

Gift Shop Prices						
space pen	Earth key ring	International Space Station model	astronaut mug	rocket water bottle	Mars rover T-shirt	space ice cream
$19.95	$3.45	$19.90	$10.00	$2.95	$12.50	$2.75

Angelina's family is visiting the Johnson Space Center near Houston, Texas. She has $20.00 to spend on items in the gift shop. In addition to buying something for herself, Angelina would like to purchase a gift for her older brother and for her friend Susanna. How would you advise Angelina to spend her money?

Solving a problem is like taking a trip. Angelina's family had to choose the highways to take. Some roads are better than others. Some have higher or lower speed limits. Some might not even lead to the Johnson Space Center. The Problem-Solving Guide is like a road map to help you move toward your destination.

Use the 5-step Problem-Solving Guide to help Angelina make her decisions.

Understand the question. How can Angelina buy appropriate gifts with $20.00?

Analyze the data. Angelina has $20.00 to spend. The gifts she is considering range in price from $2.95 to $19.95.

Plan the strategy. Should Angelina choose her own gift first, or the other two gifts? Should she spend about the same amount for each gift, or unequal amounts? Estimate the total cost.

Solve the problem. Subtract the total cost of the gifts from $20.00.

Evaluate the result. Does Angelina have enough money? If so, she can solve her problem in a reasonable way.

Can you think of a different way to solve the problem?

Check Understanding

Read the problem in the box. Follow each direction.

a. Rewrite the question in your own words.
b. List the data you were given.
c. Write a plan for solving the problem.
d. Find the solution.
e. Explain how you know your results are reasonable.

> Angelina has $1.10 of her $20.00 left. Which three different items from the NASA gift shop did she purchase?

Practice

1. Benjamin is ordering chicken sandwiches and sweet potato fries for his friend and himself. Sandwiches cost $3.55 and fries cost $1.19. Benjamin has $11.00. Estimate the total cost. Does Benjamin have enough money? Would it be better to overestimate or underestimate the total amount needed?

2. Mrs. Campbell is preparing meatloaf for a church dinner. She needs a total of 15 pounds (lb) of hamburger. At the supermarket, she picks up packages weighing 3.5 lb, 3.2 lb, 3.4 lb, and 3.9 lb. She rounds the weight of each package to the nearest pound. Did her estimate meet her need? In this situation, would it be better to overestimate or underestimate the total amount she has?

> The ancient Romans developed a system for writing numbers that was used throughout Europe until the 1500s. Roman numerals can still be found on clockfaces, monuments and public buildings, and introductory pages of books.
>
> The seven symbols are:
>
> | I | V | X | L | C | D | M |
> |---|---|---|---|---|---|---|
> | 1 | 5 | 10 | 50 | 100 | 500 | 1,000 |
>
> Roman numerals do not have place value.
> The symbols are combined, usually by addition, and written from left to right.
>
> XXXIII = 33 (10 + 10 + 10 + 1 + 1 + 1)
>
> DCLXVII = 667 (500 + 100 + 50 + 10 + 5 + 1 + 1)
>
> A symbol of lesser value placed before a symbol of greater value means you subtract and is generally used to represent fours and nines.
>
> IV means 4 (5 – 1) IX means 9 (10 – 1)
>
> XL means 40 (50 – 10) XC means 90 (100 – 10)

Write the number in standard form.

3. XIV **4.** MDLVIII **5.** LXXVI **6.** CXC **7.** MCMIV

Write the Roman numeral.

8. 48 **9.** 117 **10.** 1,730 **11.** 2,039 **12.** 504

1.10 Chapter 1 Review

Write the letter of the correct answer.

1. Which is the standard form for fifteen million, seven?

   a. 15,007 **c.** 15,000,007
   b. 15,000,070 **d.** 15,000,000,007

2. Which is the standard form for 200,000 + 20,000 + 3,000 + 200 + 80 + 5?

   a. 2,232,805 **c.** 220,325
   b. 223,285 **d.** 223,205

3. Which is true?

   a. 64.05 > 64.50 **c.** 64.05 < 64.050
   b. 64.05 = 64.050 **d.** 64.05 < 64.00

4. Which number is greater than 781.70?

   a. 781.7 **c.** 781.77
   b. 781.07 **d.** 781.007

Write the number in expanded form.

5. 4,008
6. 4,782.304
7. 19,680
8. 5,001.009

Write the number in word form.

9. 475,069
10. 6,328.5
11. 0.401
12. 134,965,500

Write in order from least to greatest.

13. 1,350,000 1,040,000 1,003,000 1,020,000
14. 2.632 2.326 2.236
15. 70.721 71.272 71.271

Name the place value of the blue digit.

16. 23.475
17. 134.892
18. 0.132
19. 89.451

Round to the nearest place value given.

20. ten thousands: 75,374
21. millions: 163,248,300
22. tenths: 13.01
23. hundredths: 75.374

Use the chart at the right to answer the questions.

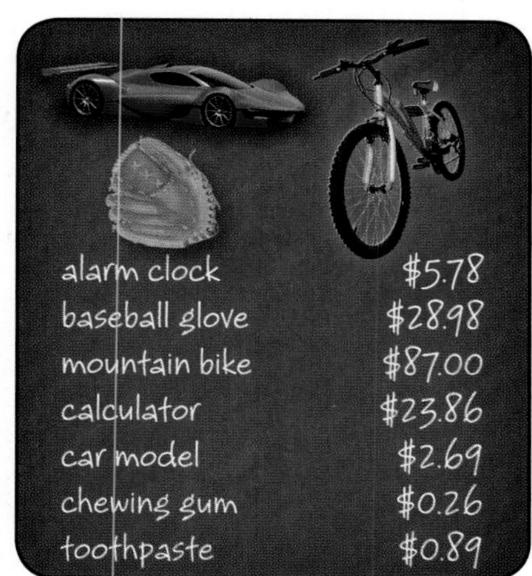

24. Which items are greater than $1.00 and less than $10.00?
25. The price of which item would round to $24.00?

Write >, <, or = to compare the prices.

26. toothpaste ◯ chewing gum
27. car model ◯ alarm clock
28. baseball glove ◯ mountain bike
29. Write the prices of the items in order from least to greatest.
30. Make a list of the items. Beside each name, write the price rounded to the nearest dollar.

Use a calculator to solve.

31. If you purchased the alarm clock, car model, and toothpaste with a $20 bill, how much change would you receive?
32. If the sum of the purchased items from Exercise 31 was changed into pennies, how many pennies would this be?

Solve.

33. The inner four planets of the solar system are Earth, Mars, Venus, and Mercury. Of the four planets, the ones that are the nearest to the sun have no moons. Earth, which is the third farthest from the sun, has one moon. Venus has no moon. Thermometers sometimes contain a liquid with the same name as the planet closest to the sun. A NASA rover bears the name of the planet fourth from the sun. Write the names of the planets in order of distance, beginning with the one nearest the sun.

These sentences about place value are missing terms. Write the correct word(s).

34. Each group of three digits in a number is called a ____.
35. In the number 2,415,867,000, the 1 represents ____.
36. The number 200,415,867,000 could be ____ to 200,000,000,000.
37. Numbers less than one can be written as ____.
38. In the number 9.016, the value of the 6 is six ____.
39. To the nearest ____, the number 9.016 rounds to 9.02.
40. If you were writing 9.016 in ____, you would write "nine and sixteen thousandths."

Chapter 2
Add and Subtract

To the Lord your God belong the heavens,
even the highest heavens,
the earth and everything in it.
Deuteronomy 10:14

Key Ideas:

Addition: adding whole numbers and decimals and estimating sums

Subtraction: subtracting whole numbers and decimals and estimating differences

Money: making change

Algebra: using the commutative and associative properties of addition

2.1 Estimate Answers

Construct Meaning

On December 17, 1903, The Wright brothers' first aircraft, the *Flyer*, flew 120 ft, 175 ft, 200 ft, and 852 ft in four flights before being damaged by a gust of wind. Today, it holds a place of honor in the National Air and Space Museum in Washington, D.C.

Estimate the sum of total miles flown by the *Flyer*.

- Use front-end estimation.
  Add the front-end digits only.

120	→	100
175	→	100
200	→	200
+852	→	800
		1,200

The front-end estimation strategy uses the digits in the greatest place value and replaces the remaining digits with zeros.

The estimated sum is 1200 ft.

- Use rounding to estimate.
  Round to the greatest place value before adding.

120	→	100
175	→	200
200	→	200
+852	→	900
		1,400

The estimated sum is 1400 ft.

The exact sum is 1,347 ft. Which estimate is more precise?

Rounding can also be used to estimate differences. Use rounding to the hundreds place to estimate the difference for the problem below.

One airship traveled 3,670 nautical miles, and another one traveled 2,794 nautical miles.

3,670	→	3,700
−2,794	→	−2,800
		900

Check Understanding

Use front-end estimation to find the sum.

a. 375 + 220

b. 834 + 406

c. 720 + 570

d. 4,603 + 2,706

e. 9,134 + 6,032

Round each number to the nearest thousand before adding or subtracting.

f. 5,389 + 2,272

g. 16,535 + 11,213

h. 22,870 − 11,232

i. 8,672 − 3,457

j. 39,271 − 27,042

Practice

Use front-end estimation to find the sum.

1. 575 + 384
2. 747 + 518
3. 652 + 333
4. 6,832 + 3,204
5. 22,018 + 10,476

Estimate each sum by rounding to the greatest place value. Find the exact sum.

6. 358 + 634
7. 8,619 + 6,322
8. 624 + 892 + 147
9. 12,613 + 44,491 + 26,743
10. 84,132 + 25,450

Round to the greatest place value to find the estimated difference for each.

11. 73 − 37
12. 813 − 584
13. 3,982 − 1,357
14. 62,178 − 38,501

Round each number to nearest thousand to find the estimated difference. Then, find the exact difference.

15. 7,918 − 593
16. 6,230 − 3,956
17. 12,561 − 5,801
18. 47,682 − 23,526

Apply

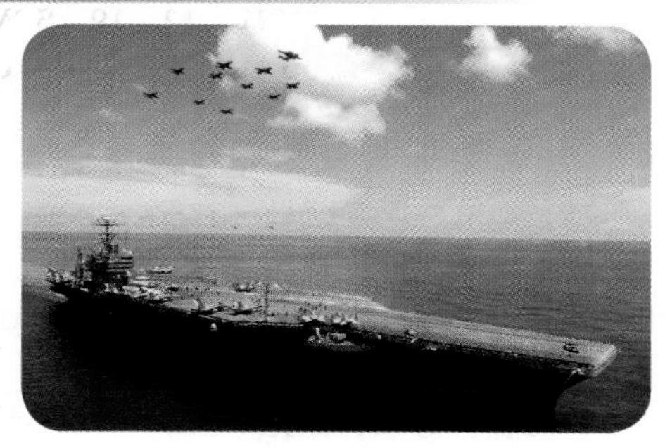

19. If 1,964 people came to the National Air and Space Museum to see the *Flyer* during the month of July, and 2,116 people came during August, about how many visitors came during those two months?

20. Miguel said that 564 airplanes landed on the aircraft carrier for refueling, and 323 airplanes landed for repair. Is an estimate of 400 reasonable when estimating the difference?

21. In a two-week period, 402 of the 766 biplanes flew south. Estimate the number of biplanes that did not fly south.

Review

Write what the 8 represents in each number.

22. 687,312
23. 43,867
24. 298,394
25. 803,469

Write the numbers in order from the least to the greatest.

26. 5,912 5,219 2,519
27. 1,387,248,967 1,837,248,967 1,387,842,967

Round each number to the nearest ten thousand and to the nearest million.

28. 4,376,152
29. 6,841,793
30. 1,931,220

Round each decimal number to the nearest tenth.

31. 5.176
32. 1,762.840

2.2 Larger Numbers

Construct Meaning

From an early age, Charles Lindbergh was interested in flying. After becoming a pilot, he enjoyed the thrill of stunt flying.

A French man offered $25,000 to the first pilot to fly nonstop from New York to Paris. On May 20, 1927, Charles landed the *Spirit of St. Louis* in Paris. His 3,600-mile flight lasted $33\frac{1}{2}$ hours.

How many people knew about his feat if 4,273 people saw it, and 5,619 people heard it on the radio?

Estimate and then use regrouping to add the two addends.

$$\begin{array}{r} \scriptstyle 1 \\ 4{,}273 \\ +5{,}619 \\ \hline 9{,}892 \end{array}$$

9,892 people knew that Charles Lindbergh made the first solo transatlantic flight.

Check the answer against your estimate to make sure it is reasonable.

Compare the number of people who heard about Lindbergh's adventure by radio with the number who watched him land. Find 5,619 – 4,273.

$$\begin{array}{r} \scriptstyle 5\,11 \\ 5{,}\not{6}\not{1}9 \\ -4{,}273 \\ \hline 1{,}346 \end{array}$$

1,346 more people heard the news than saw it.

Addition and subtraction are inverse operations. Use the inverse operation to check your work.

Regroup to add these three addends. 735 + 696 + 595 = ______. Write the addends vertically so the digits in each number are lined up by the same place value.

$$\begin{array}{r} \scriptstyle 1 \\ 735 \\ 696 \\ +595 \\ \hline 6 \end{array}$$

Add the ones. Regroup 16 as 1 ten and 6 ones.

$$\begin{array}{r} \scriptstyle 2\,1 \\ 735 \\ 696 \\ +595 \\ \hline 26 \end{array}$$

Add the tens. Regroup 22 as 2 hundreds and 2 tens.

$$\begin{array}{r} \scriptstyle 2\,1 \\ 735 \\ 696 \\ +595 \\ \hline 2{,}026 \end{array}$$

Add the hundreds. Regroup 20 as 2 thousands and 0 hundreds. 2,026 is the sum.

Check Understanding

Solve. Use inverse operations to check Exercises a and b.

a. 69 + 64

b. 6,872 − 2,493

c. 12,705 − 10,962

d. 347 + 631 + 595

Practice

Solve. Check Exercises 1 and 2.

1. 52,467 − 13,698

2. 9,876,000 + 34,987

3. 706 − 429

4. 4,675 − 1,598

5. 37,638 − 4,729

6. 714 + 77 + 561

7. 354 + 523 + 310

8. 1,736 + 14 + 309

Apply

9. Sterling's family wants to take a flight from New York to France via London. It takes 5 hr and 45 min to travel from New York to London; it takes 2 hr and 15 min to travel from London to France. How many hours will the family spend flying one way? How many hours will the round trip take?

10. Lance received 3,500 frequent flyer miles for a one-way trip from North Carolina to California. He received the same on his return trip. On a round trip from Kentucky to Kansas, he received 900 frequent flyer miles each way. What is the difference in the number of miles each trip earned?

Review

Write addends that match the estimated sum.

11. ____ + ____ = 600

12. ____ + ____ = 300

13. ____ + ____ = 1,200

14. ____ + ____ = 14,000

Write the numbers in order from greatest to least.

15. 5,678 5,768 5,876 8,675

16. 12,710 12,723 12,718 12,719

Estimate by rounding to the greatest place value.

17. 614 + 386

18. 1,940 − 1,242

19. 46,736 + 21,579

20. 3,081 + 974

21. 72,186 − 56,349

2.3 Problem Solving: Add and Subtract

Construct Meaning

People began to fly helicopters in the 1930s. Helicopters have rotor blades that spin to create lift. The pilot can fly forward, backward, or sideways. Helicopters can hover motionless in the air and do not need a runway to land or to take off. They can fly where airplanes cannot. Helicopters can get medical help to injured people and transport objects and people to locations quickly. Some tour companies offer helicopter rides. During the summer months a theme park offered 351 tickets for helicopter rides. In 30 days, 162 tickets were sold. How many tickets are still available?

Use the Problem-Solving Guide to write an equation.

Step 1: Understand the question. How many tickets are still available?

Step 2: Analyze the data.

At the start of summer, 351 tickets were available. Of that number, 162 tickets had been sold. Is the fact that the requests were received in 30 days important for solving this problem? No, only the number of tickets is important.

Step 3: Plan the strategy.

To find the number of tickets left, find the difference between the number of tickets available at the beginning of the summer and the number of tickets that have been sold. Finding the difference is a subtraction problem.

An equation is a number sentence written with an equals sign. The variable, x, represents the unknown number.

$$351 - 162 = x$$

$$\downarrow \quad \downarrow$$

$$400 - 200 = 200$$

Use rounding to estimate the answer.

Step 4: Solve the problem.

$$\begin{array}{r} \overset{2\ \overset{14}{\not 4}\ 11}{\not 3 \not 5 \not 1} \\ -162 \\ \hline 189 \end{array}$$

$351 - 162 = 189$

$x = 189$ tickets

Step 5: Evaluate the result.

Check your answer. Compare it to the estimate.

$$\begin{array}{rl} \overset{1\,1}{189} & \text{tickets available} \\ +162 & \text{tickets sold} \\ \hline 351 & \text{tickets at beginning of sale} \end{array}$$

Is this a reasonable answer compared to the estimate of 200 tickets? Yes, because 200 is close to 189.

There are 189 tickets still available.

Practice

Write an equation. Solve. Check your answer.

1. Miss Sanchez earned $540 in two weeks. She bought a cell phone for $299. How much money did she have left?

2. Pedro worked a total of 79 hours to help his Bible study group clean the yards of some elderly church members. Oliver worked 23 fewer hours than Pedro. How many hours did Oliver work?

3. At Forest Christian School, 578 students gave toys for needy children. At Windsor Academy, 756 students gave toys. How many students in total gave toys at Windsor Academy and Forest Christian School?

4. A salesman delivered fishing poles to four sporting-goods shops. He gave one shop 48, another shop 60, another 72, and the last shop 36. How many fishing poles did he deliver?

5. Lucinda has put in 1,487 hours toward earning her pilot's license. Her license requires a total of 2,000 hours. How many more hours does Lucinda need to get her pilot's license?

6. London paid $120 for license fees, $240 for flight-test fees, $265 for course materials, and $1,175 for a new helmet. How much money did he spend?

7. To get supplies to the mission station, a missionary pilot traveled 1,876 mi on Monday. The next day she traveled 2,004 mi. Everyone rejoiced when the plane circled overhead. How many miles was the trip to the mission station?

8. The most remote village was 225 mi by canoe from the mission station. Levi had canoed 143 mi. How much farther did he have to go?

9. Igor Sikorsky designed the first true production helicopter. His US patent was filed June 27, 1931, and on September 14, 1939, the VS-300 made its first flight. How many years passed between filing the patent and the first flight?

2.4 Estimate Decimal Sums

Construct Meaning

Prior to arrival, the pilot may announce the temperature of your destination.

Destination	Temperature
Portland, Oregon	70.1° Fahrenheit
Washington, D.C.	75.8° Fahrenheit
São Paulo, Brazil	87.5° Fahrenheit

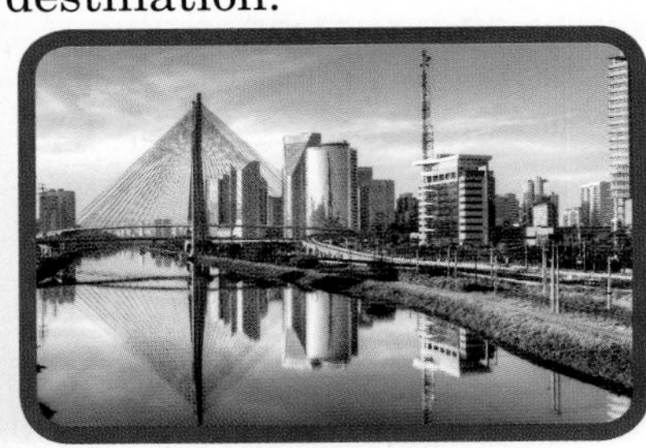

Use the number line to round to the nearest whole number.

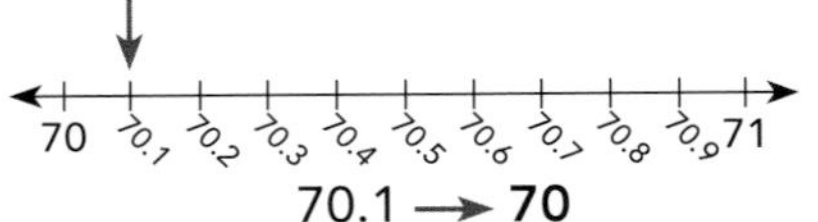

70.1 → **70**

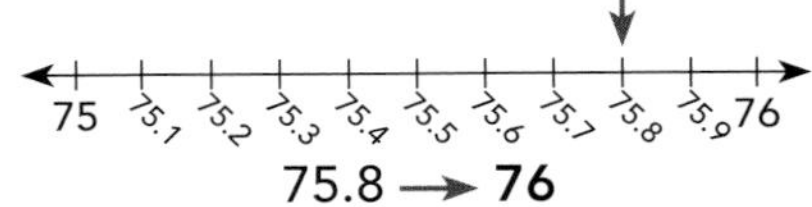

75.8 → **76**

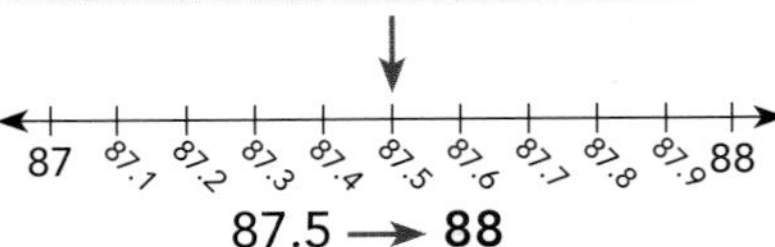

87.5 → **88**

Decimals can be rounded the same way whole numbers are rounded.

Use the place value chart to round 9.787 to the nearest hundredth.

ones	.	tenths	hundredths	thousandths
9	.	7	8	7

Find the target digit in the hundredths place.

Look at the digit in the place to the right.

Because 7 is greater than 5, increase the target digit by 1.

9.	7	9

Drop all digits to the right of the target digit.

9.787 rounds to 9.79.

Use front-end estimation to estimate decimal sums.

Leo saved his money for a new movie. The first week he saved \$6.45 and the second week he saved \$5.32. About how much did he save?

Step 1

$$\begin{array}{r} \$6.45 \\ +\ 5.32 \\ \hline 11. \end{array}$$

Add the front-end digits.

Step 2

$$\begin{array}{r} \$6.45 \\ +\ 5.32 \\ \hline \end{array}$$

Consider the tenths and hundredths.

$\$0.45 + 0.32 \approx \$1.00$

Step 3

$$\begin{array}{r} \$11.00 \\ +\ \ 1.00 \\ \hline \$12.00 \end{array}$$

Adjust the estimate.

Leo saved about \$12.00.

Check Understanding

Round to the nearest whole number. Add to estimate the sum.

a. $\begin{array}{r} 34.27 \\ +12.35 \\ \hline \end{array}$

b. $\begin{array}{r} 7.3 \\ +5.8 \\ \hline \end{array}$

c. $\begin{array}{r} 29.80 \\ +64.76 \\ \hline \end{array}$

d. 4.4 + 3.82 + 7.1

Round to the tenths and then add.

e. $\begin{array}{r} 8.75 \\ +4.66 \\ \hline \end{array}$

f. $\begin{array}{r} 25.16 \\ +17.29 \\ \hline \end{array}$

Round to the hundredths and then add.

g. $\begin{array}{r} 5.666 \\ +4.982 \\ \hline \end{array}$

h. $\begin{array}{r} 43.872 \\ +11.931 \\ \hline \end{array}$

Use front-end estimation to estimate the decimal sum.

Step 1

$\begin{array}{r} \$3.51 \\ +\ \ 5.35 \\ \hline 8.\ \ \ \ \end{array}$

Step 2

$\begin{array}{r} \$3.51 \\ +\ \ 5.35 \\ \hline \end{array}$

$\$0.51 + 0.35 \approx \$1.00$

Step 3

$\begin{array}{r} \$8.00 \\ +\ \ 1.00 \\ \hline \end{array}$

i.

Practice

Round to the nearest whole number to estimate the sum.

1. $\begin{array}{r} 45.32 \\ +17.84 \\ \hline \end{array}$

2. $\begin{array}{r} 72.6 \\ +34.8 \\ \hline \end{array}$

3. $\begin{array}{r} 4.6 \\ +3.3 \\ \hline \end{array}$

4. 21.9 + 46.3 + 82.8

Round to the nearest tenth to estimate the sum.

5. $\begin{array}{r} 8.75 \\ +4.66 \\ \hline \end{array}$

6. $\begin{array}{r} 23.54 \\ +60.17 \\ \hline \end{array}$

7. $\begin{array}{r} 107.42 \\ +218.55 \\ \hline \end{array}$

8. $\begin{array}{r} 76.39 \\ +23.07 \\ \hline \end{array}$

9. $\begin{array}{r} 2.661 \\ +3.543 \\ \hline \end{array}$

Use front-end estimation and adjust your estimate.

10. $\begin{array}{r} \$8.67 \\ +\ \ 4.54 \\ \hline \end{array}$

11. $\begin{array}{r} \$2.06 \\ +\ \ 9.78 \\ \hline \end{array}$

12. $\begin{array}{r} \$3.68 \\ +\ \ 1.33 \\ \hline \end{array}$

13. $\begin{array}{r} \$7.03 \\ +\ \ 1.12 \\ \hline \end{array}$

14. $\begin{array}{r} \$2.12 \\ +\ \ 3.05 \\ \hline \end{array}$

Apply

15. Amelia Earhart saw her first airplane at the age of 11. At 25, she had her pilot's license. In 1932, she became the first woman to fly alone across the Atlantic Ocean. Most of the Atlantic Ocean may be seen on a map between 74.8 degrees and 6.4 degrees longitude. Round each decimal to the nearest whole number.

16. Ruth ran 1.2 mi, Samantha ran 1.4 mi, and Mia ran 1.6 mi of the relay race. Round each number to the nearest whole number to estimate the length of the race.

17. Mason spent $50.95 on a skateboard. He spent $20.99 on a new helmet. Use front-end estimation to estimate how much he spent.

Review

Round each number to the place value in parentheses.

18. 36.06 (tens)
19. 7.54 (tenths)
20. 8.39 (ones)
21. 58.173 (hundredths)

2.5 Add Decimals

Construct Meaning

Mrs. Parker's fifth-grade class held a walkathon to raise money for a field trip to an air show. Geoff walked 1.5 mi and Rob walked 1.7 mi. How many total miles did they walk?

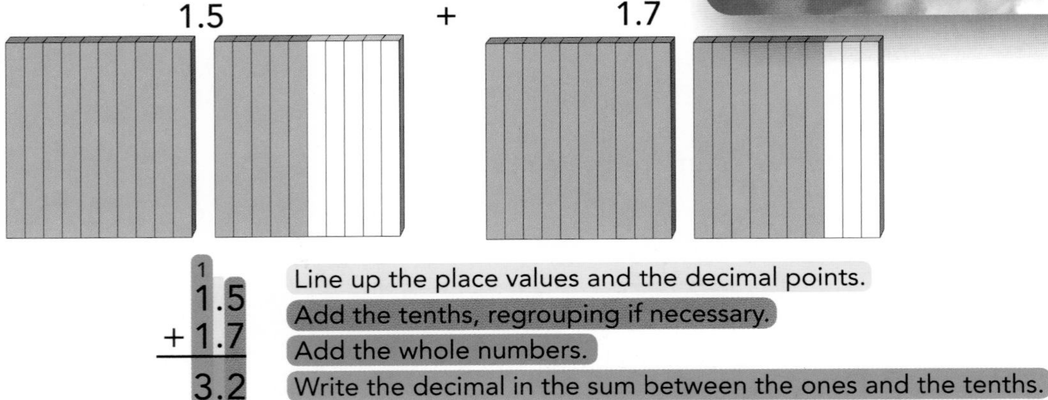

$$\begin{array}{r} {}^{1} \\ 1.5 \\ +\,1.7 \\ \hline 3.2 \end{array}$$

Line up the place values and the decimal points.
Add the tenths, regrouping if necessary.
Add the whole numbers.
Write the decimal in the sum between the ones and the tenths.

Geoff and Rob walked 3.2 mi.

The walkathon was successful, and the students were excited about the air show. The day before the show, they learned about Chuck Yeager. In August 1947, he flew his Bell X-1 to reach Mach 0.85, which is almost the speed of sound, or Mach 1. Two months later, he exceeded the speed of sound. The sonic boom was heard all over the Mojave Desert in California! The X-1 had flown 0.20 Mach more than Mach 0.85. How fast did it go?

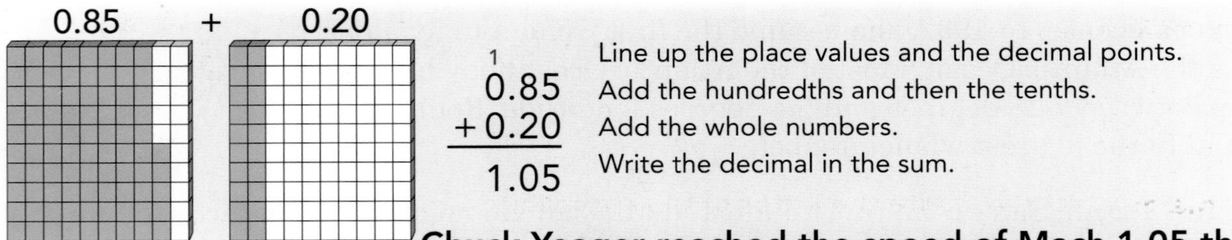

$$\begin{array}{r} {}^{1} \\ 0.85 \\ +\,0.20 \\ \hline 1.05 \end{array}$$

Line up the place values and the decimal points.
Add the hundredths and then the tenths.
Add the whole numbers.
Write the decimal in the sum.

Chuck Yeager reached the speed of Mach 1.05 that day.

When adding or comparing numbers of different place value, use a zero to make an equivalent decimal.

$$\begin{array}{r} 26.30 \\ +\,16.85 \\ \hline \end{array}$$

Check Understanding

Write decimal numbers to match the models. Add.

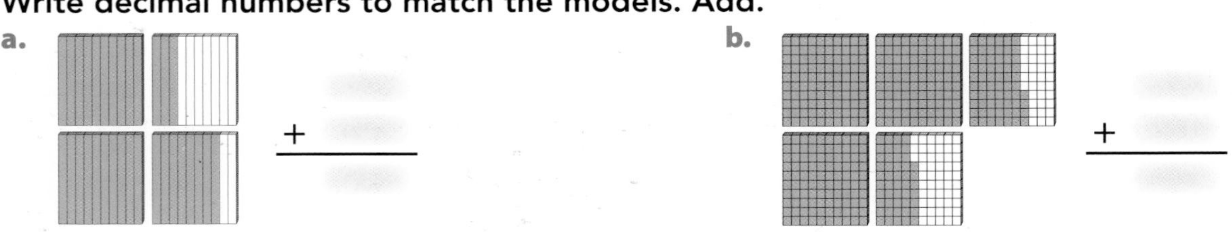

Practice

Line up the decimals and add.

1. 3.6 + 5.9 + 2.7
2. 6.7 + 3.48
3. 53.89 + 49.65
4. 249.71 + 89.3

Draw and shade models to show the value of the decimal number. Add to find the sum.

5. 1.5 + 2.3
6. 1.25 + 2.67

Add.

7. 3.6 + 1.2
8. 7.48 + 5.17
9. 21.39 + 4.51
10. 113.7 + 86.42
11. 55.38 + 7.6

Apply

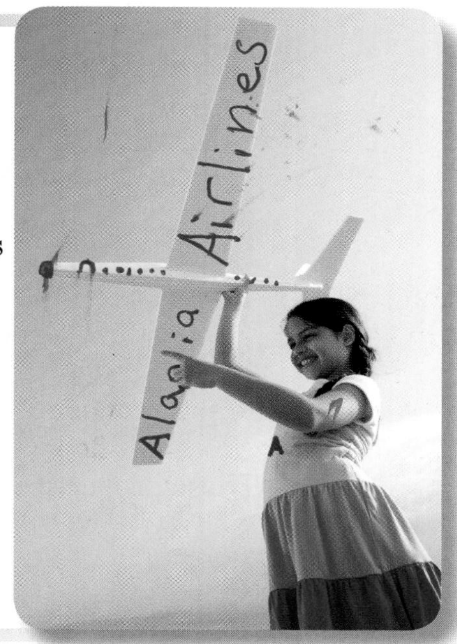

12. Rosie's model airplane flew 19.7 ft, Orlando's airplane flew 21.4 ft, and Sebastian's flew 20.9 ft. What was the combined footage for the three models?

13. Patrick bought several tools before he built shelves for his model airplanes. He bought a hammer for $9.95, pliers for $8.75, a drill for $24.99, and a set of screwdrivers for $16.49. How much did Patrick spend?

14. Madison's radio-controlled glider flew at a speed of 46.25 miles per hour (mph). The next time she flew it, the speed doubled. Was the maximum number of miles per hour greater than or less than 95 mph?

Review

Round to the nearest ten. Write the letter of the estimated sum.

15. 46.31 + 25.74
    - **a.** 60
    - **b.** 80
    - **c.** 70

16. 235.1 + 40.8
    - **a.** 280
    - **b.** 275
    - **c.** 270

17. 14.3 + 26.578
    - **a.** 41
    - **b.** 40
    - **c.** 50

Add and then check.

18. 26,531 + 35,479
19. 184 + 798
20. 3,241 + 5,683
21. 9,764 + 2,843
22. $65.45 + 38.59

2.6 *Properties of Addition*

Construct Meaning

From biplanes to jets to rockets to missiles, aircraft technology had already boomed by the beginning of World War II in 1939. A Soviet military rocket carried the first payload, a 184-pound artificial satellite called *Sputnik I*, into space in 1957. By 1963, the United States had sent an X-15 to 354,200 ft, or 67.08 mi, into space. This achievement involved many people. How many crew members worked on the X-15 if there were 9 technicians and 8 engineers?

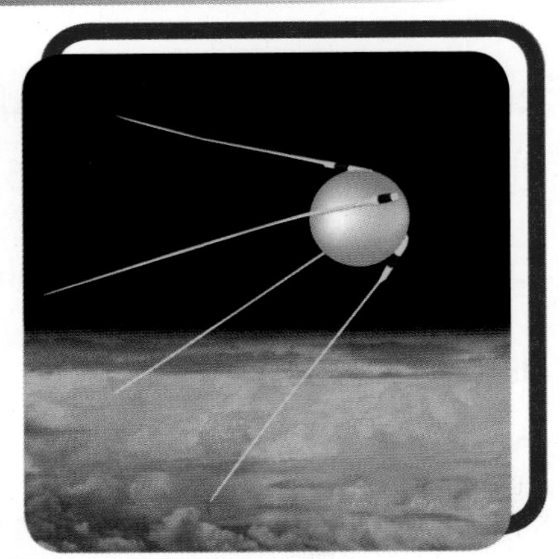

Commutative (Order) Property of Addition

9 + 8 = 17 or 8 + 9 = 17

(9 = addend, 8 = addend, 17 = sum; 8 = addend, 9 = addend, 17 = sum)

Changing the order of the addends does not change the sum.

17 crew members worked on the X-15.

Associative (Grouping) Property of Addition

(1.3 + 2.5) + 43.7 = ▒ or 1.3 + (2.5 + 43.7) = ▒

3.8 + 43.7 = 47.5   1.3 + 46.2 = 47.5

Grouping addends differently does not change the sum.

Zero Property of Addition

136 + 0 = 136 or 0 + 136 = 136

The sum of a number and zero is that number.

These properties use the terms "addend" and "sum." The sum is the result of two or more addends being added together.

Use your calculator to find the sum.

Check Understanding

Identify the property. Write "Commutative Property of Addition," "Associative Property of Addition," or "Zero Property of Addition."

a. (2.6 + 5.2) + 4.8 = 2.6 + (5.2 + 4.8)

b. 17 + 0 = 17

c. 45.6 + 13.1 = 13.1 + 45.6

d. 6 + 8 + 7 = 8 + 6 + 7

Practice

Complete. Identify the property shown.

1. 6.5 + 8.1 = _____ + 6.5
2. 46 + (77 + 33) = (_____ + 77) + 33
3. 156 + _____ = 156
4. (57.9 + 3.4) + 23.6 = 57.9 + (3.4 + _____)
5. _____ + 24.8 = 24.8 + 83.2
6. 14 + 6 + 20 + 9 = 20 + 14 + _____ + 6

Use the Commutative Property of Addition to rewrite each equation. Find the sum.

7. 8.1 + 9.4 = *n*
8. 69 + 37 + 10 = *n*
9. 376 + 13 = *n*
10. 14.8 + 26.5 = *n*

11. Use the Associative Property of Addition to show two different ways to find the sum of the gift prices.

Use the Zero Property of Addition to find the missing addend or sum.

12. 45 + _____ = _____
13. _____ + 0 = 18.3
14. _____ + _____ = 33.3

Use your calculator to find the sum.

15. 9.7 + 6.4 + 35.8
16. 876 + 115 + 4,703

Apply

Use the Associative Property of Addition to solve the problem two different ways.

17. Test pilots flew F-100 and F-104 Starfighter jets to get a feel for how the X-15 would fly. The planes accelerated to 25,000 ft quickly, and then flew 50,000 ft higher. They flew 25,000 additional feet. What was the final altitude the planes reached?

Write the numbers in order from the greatest to the least.

18. 45,791 47,591 41,579 54,179
19. 364,176 365,716 369,617 363,116

Add.

20. 54,971 + 67,487
21. 7.46 + 9.37
22. 89,264 + 37,825
23. 14.9 + 72.3
24. 76,542 + 13,906
25. 65.3 + 8.17
26. 23,476 + 38,924
27. 406.1 + 24.9
28. 54 + 83 + 16
29. 25.4 + 6.01

2.7 Estimate Decimal Differences

Construct Meaning

The Airbus Industrie A320 is a mid-size airliner that carries between 150 and 180 passengers. Technology advancements aid the pilot in flying.

Commuter airliners, however, are smaller and carry only a few passengers a short distance. The Cessna 208B Grand Caravan carries 14 passengers. Commuter airliners are equipped with radar weather sensors to help the pilot detect and avoid bad weather.

Radar detects a thunderstorm 9.65 mi ahead. The pilot's destination is 5.15 mi away. About how many miles is the difference between the destination and the storm?

Estimate the difference with decimals just as with whole numbers.

Round to the greatest place value and then use mental math to subtract.

$$\begin{array}{r} 9.65 \\ -5.15 \\ \hline \end{array} \rightarrow \begin{array}{r} 10 \\ -\ 5 \\ \hline 5 \text{ miles} \end{array}$$

The pilot knows the storm is about 5 miles beyond his destination.

Round to the nearest tenth and then subtract.

$$\begin{array}{r} 9.65 \\ -5.15 \\ \hline \end{array} \rightarrow \begin{array}{r} 9.7 \\ -5.2 \\ \hline 4.5 \text{ miles} \end{array}$$

The pilot knows the storm is about 4.5 miles beyond his destination.

Compare the estimates. Rounding to the nearest whole number estimates the storm to be about 5 mi beyond the pilot's destination. Rounding to the nearest tenth estimates the storm to be about 4.5 mi beyond his destination. The pilot would be wise to make decisions using the shorter distance, so rounding to a smaller place value would be a more precise estimate.

Rounding decimals can give a more precise answer than front-end estimation.

Front-end estimation

$$\begin{array}{r} 4.139 \\ -1.895 \\ \hline 3 \end{array}$$

$$\begin{array}{r} 4.139 \\ -1.895 \\ \hline \end{array} \rightarrow \begin{array}{r} \overset{3}{\cancel{4}}.\overset{11}{\cancel{1}} \\ -1.9 \\ \hline 2.2 \end{array}$$

Rounding to the nearest tenth

2.2 is more precise than 3.

Check Understanding

Round to the nearest whole number and then subtract.

a. $\begin{array}{r} 6.2 \\ -3.4 \\ \hline \end{array}$

b. $\begin{array}{r} 8.37 \\ -6.25 \\ \hline \end{array}$

Round to the nearest tenth and then subtract.

c. $\begin{array}{r} 7.54 \\ -2.71 \\ \hline \end{array}$

d. $\begin{array}{r} 37.824 \\ -23.061 \\ \hline \end{array}$

Practice

Round to the nearest whole number to estimate the difference.

1. $\begin{array}{r} 6.7 \\ -\ 3.9 \\ \hline \end{array}$

2. $\begin{array}{r} 7.8 \\ -\ 5.2 \\ \hline \end{array}$

3. $\begin{array}{r} 33.29 \\ -\ 15.72 \\ \hline \end{array}$

4. $\begin{array}{r} 24.72 \\ -\ 13.86 \\ \hline \end{array}$

5. $\begin{array}{r} 50.61 \\ -\ 25.14 \\ \hline \end{array}$

Round to the nearest tenth to estimate the difference.

6. $\begin{array}{r} 2.86 \\ -\ 1.48 \\ \hline \end{array}$

7. $\begin{array}{r} 30.25 \\ -\ 16.52 \\ \hline \end{array}$

8. $\begin{array}{r} 54.216 \\ -\ 3.890 \\ \hline \end{array}$

9. $\begin{array}{r} 81.259 \\ -\ 19.715 \\ \hline \end{array}$

10. $\begin{array}{r} 134.29 \\ -\ 98.52 \\ \hline \end{array}$

Estimate by rounding to the nearest ten. Subtract mentally.

11. $\begin{array}{r} \$34.62 \\ -\ 15.17 \\ \hline \end{array}$

12. $\begin{array}{r} \$116.98 \\ -\ 45.62 \\ \hline \end{array}$

13. $\begin{array}{r} \$89.16 \\ -\ 43.62 \\ \hline \end{array}$

14. $\begin{array}{r} \$475.49 \\ -\ 93.21 \\ \hline \end{array}$

15. $\begin{array}{r} \$706.84 \\ -\ 19.35 \\ \hline \end{array}$

Apply

16. The Rogers family traveled 236.6 mi on an airliner. Their connecting flights took them 232.1 more miles to their final destination in Florida. Mr. Rogers estimated a difference of 5 mi in traveling the two segments. What place value did he round to?

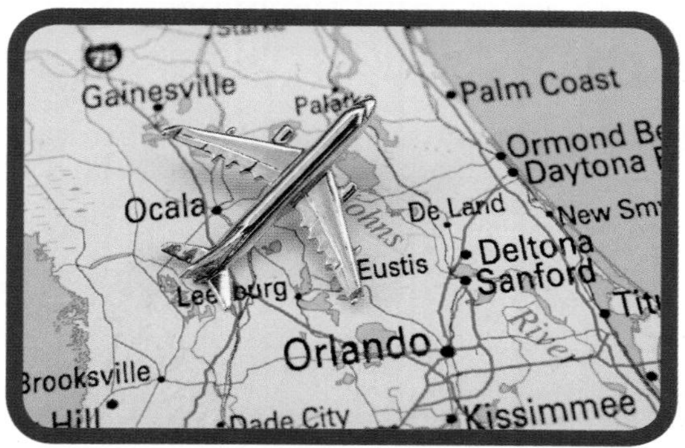

Review

Write what the 2 represents in each number.

17. 6,132
18. 42,576,840
19. 9.2
20. 524
21. 29,073

Write > or <.

22. 387,461 ◯ 389,456
23. 4,873 ◯ 4,983
24. 63,010 ◯ 60,310
25. 52,107 ◯ 52,106
26. 1,365,237 ◯ 1,366,237
27. 708 ◯ 807
28. 924,429 ◯ 904,409
29. 5,771 ◯ 5,762
30. 23,741 ◯ 23,740

Add or subtract.

31. 185 − 93
32. 1,675 − 388
33. 281 + 4,564 + 67
34. 384 + 76

2.8 Equivalent Decimals

Construct Meaning

Writing a zero at the end of a decimal does not change the value of a decimal even though the decimal is given a new name. This allows for writing equivalent decimals because the zero has no value. Equivalent decimals are decimals that represent the same amount.

Decimal squares are helpful in modeling equivalent decimals.

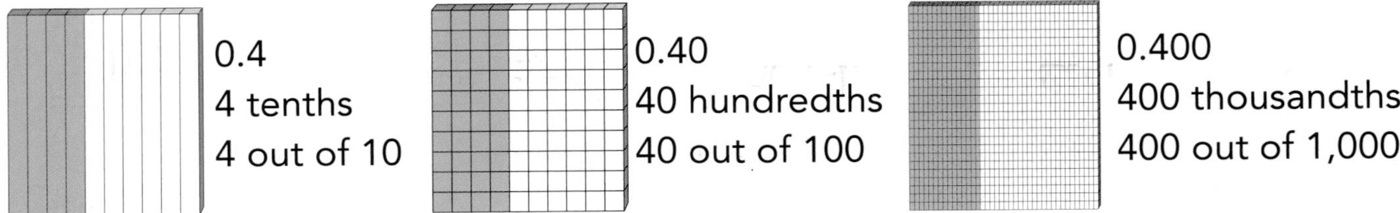

The number 0.4 is read "four tenths." The number 0.40 is read "forty hundredths" because the zero is in the hundredths place. The number 0.400 is read "four hundred thousandths" because zeros are in the hundredths and thousandths places. The zeros must be placed to the right of the number 4 in order to form an equivalent decimal.

Place value charts are also helpful in forming equivalent decimals. Solve $6.7 - 4.13 = n$.

	ones .	tenths	hundredths
	6 .	7	0
−	4 .	1	3

Line up the decimals.
Use zero to make an equivalent decimal.
Subtract.

$$\begin{array}{r} 6.\overset{6}{\not7}\overset{10}{\not0} \\ -\,4.13 \\ \hline 2.57 \end{array}$$

The decimal is read "and."

The zero renamed 6.7 from six and seven tenths to six and seventy hundredths so four and thirteen hundredths could be subtracted.

Solve $5.148 + 3.26 = n$.

	ones .	tenths	hundredths	thousandths
	5 .	1	4	8
+	3 .	2	6	0

Line up the decimals.
Place a zero. 3.26 is equivalent to 3.260.
Add.

$$\begin{array}{r} \overset{1}{5.148} \\ +\,3.260 \\ \hline 8.408 \end{array}$$

Check Understanding

Sophia prepared for the obstacle course by running 1.3 mi as fast as she could.

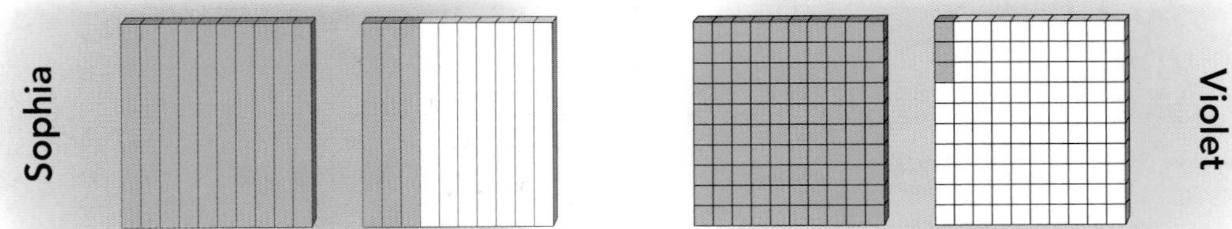

Violet ran 1.03 mi. Did they run the same distance?

a. _____ ran farther than _____.

b. 1.3 and 1.03 are not equivalent decimals. The _____ in 1.03 was not placed to the right of the number 3.

c. Write 0.006 in word form.
d. Write two and fifty-three thousandths in standard form.

Practice

Make a decimal place value chart as shown in the example. Write three equivalent decimals for the colored part of the model.

Example:

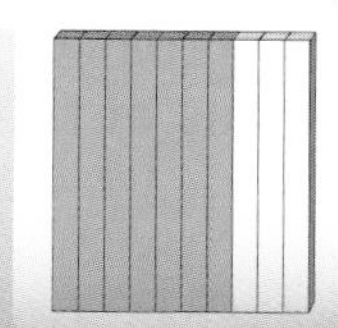

ones .	tenths	hundredths	thousandths
0 .	7		
0 .	7	0	
0 .	7	0	0

1. 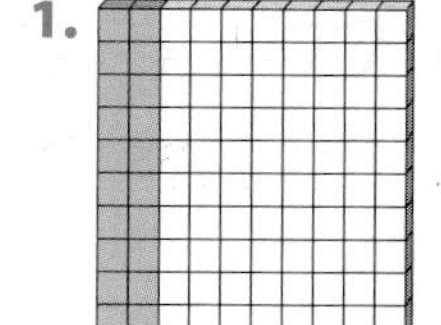

2. 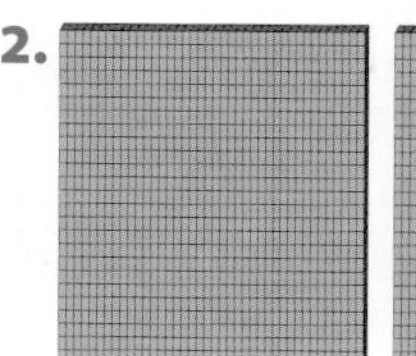 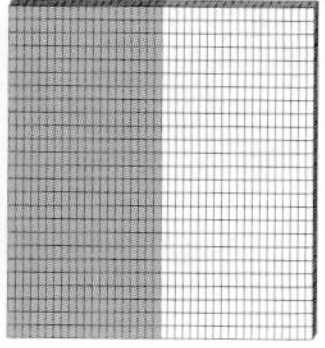

Write an equivalent decimal for each number.

3. 6.3 4. 5.10 5. 9.800 6. 39.6 7. 438.57

Write the word form for each decimal.

8. 3.7 9. 42.03 10. 9.145 11. 6.106 12. 0.001

Write in standard form.

13. forty-five thousandths 14. nine and nine hundred one thousandths

Write what the 7 represents in each number.

15. 3,241.07 16. 8.007 17. 7.245 18. 1.718

Write "yes" or "no" to indicate whether the decimals are equivalent.

19. 9.1 and 9.11 20. 0.80 and 0.08 21. 0.200 and 0.2 22. 0.560 and 0.56

Solve.

23. 5.4 – 3.22 24. 0.032 + 0.1 25. 44.55 – 2.6 26. 13.22 + 11.0

Apply

27. Warren holds a box. Does it weigh 0.25 lb or 0.250 lb? Explain.

28. By deflecting radar signals, a stealth fighter flew 1,450.5 mi before being observed. Write the number in word form.

Review

Write >, <, or =.

29. 3.752 ◯ 3.572 30. 6.252 ◯ 62.52 31. 0.04 ◯ 0.040 32. 17.6 ◯ 1.76

2.9 Subtract Decimals

Construct Meaning

Aerobatic airplanes are small and light. They are customized to allow the pilot to perform daring twists, turns, loops, and rolls in the air. The Pitts Special S-2A is an aerobatic airplane used in air shows. Weighing only 1,000 lb, it is a little over 17 ft long and 6 ft high.

Austin and Rachael attended the Sun and Fun Fly-In. One plane left a trail of smoke 1.3 mi long. Another trail was 0.15 mi long. Find the difference in the lengths of the trails of smoke.

Solve 1.30 – 0.15 = x

- Use a number line.

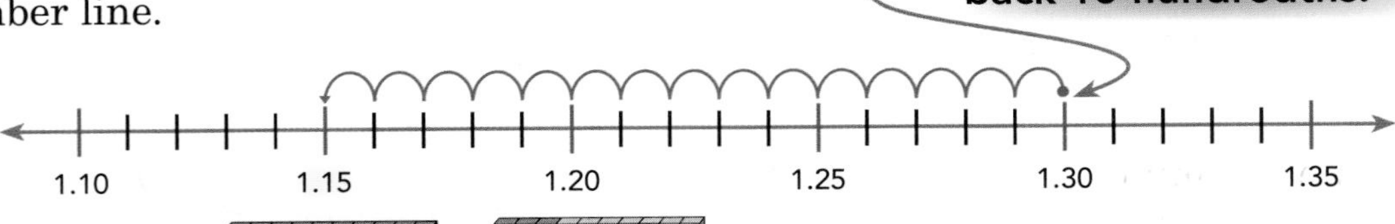

- Use decimal models.

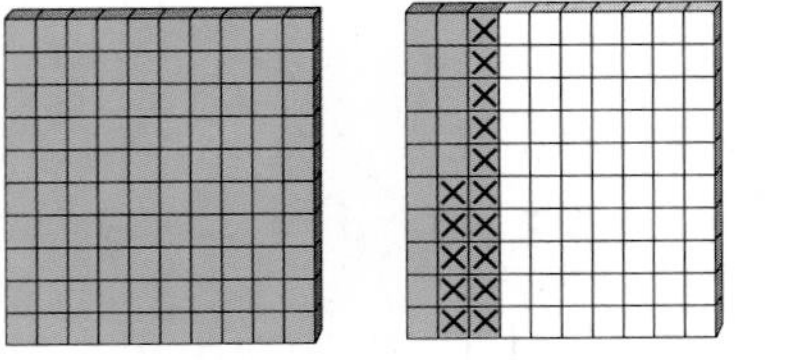

1.30 – 0.15 = 1.15

- Use Base 10 blocks.

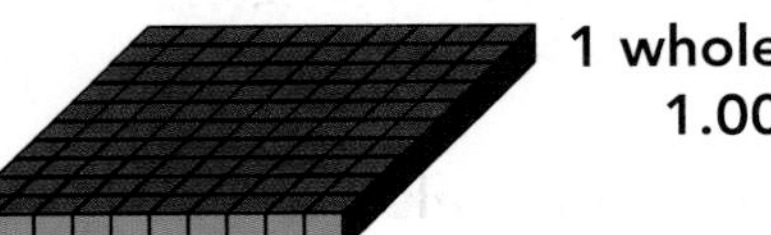

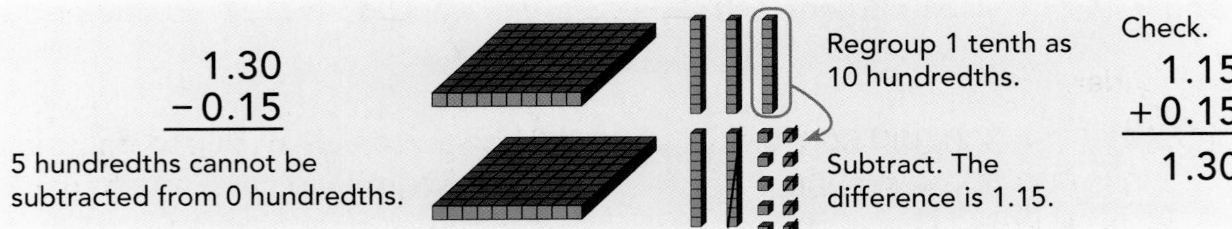

The trails of smoke differ in length by 1.15 mi.

Check Understanding

a. Draw a number line and number it like the one above. Solve 1.24 – 0.05 = x.

b. Write an equation for the decimal model.

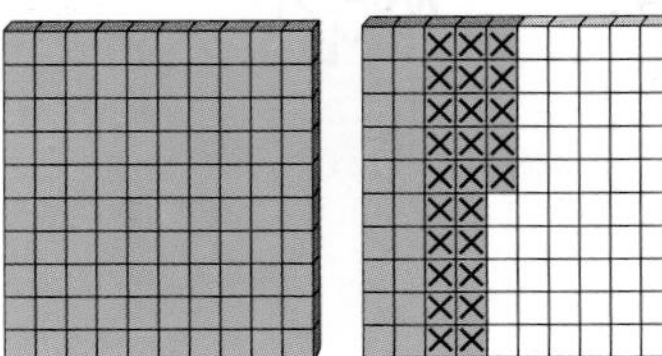

Subtract.

c. 2.7 – 1.4 **d.** 5.1 – 3.8 **e.** 25.18 – 16.19 **f.** 42.91 – 16.37

Practice

Subtract. Place an extra zero where needed.

1. $\begin{array}{r} \$45.31 \\ -\ \ 23.56 \\ \hline \end{array}$
2. $\begin{array}{r} 9.3 \\ -2.5 \\ \hline \end{array}$
3. $\begin{array}{r} 762 \\ -144.15 \\ \hline \end{array}$
4. $\begin{array}{r} \$6.49 \\ -\ \ 1.50 \\ \hline \end{array}$
5. $\begin{array}{r} 4,362.7 \\ -1,784.9 \\ \hline \end{array}$

6. 4.9 – 0.75
7. 9.06 – 8.67
8. 15 – 7.6
9. 24.6 – 9
10. 901.7 – 52.8
11. 37.1 – 29.46
12. $5 – 2.51
13. 479 – 0.3

Apply

14. Austin took $30.00 to the air show. He had $12.50 left after buying tickets. How much money did he spend for the tickets?

15. With the amount of money he had left after purchasing the tickets, he spent $8.75 on refreshments. How much money did Austin take home?

Review

Estimate the sum by rounding to the greatest place value.

16. $\begin{array}{r} 49 \\ +84 \\ \hline \end{array}$
17. $\begin{array}{r} 455 \\ +391 \\ \hline \end{array}$
18. $\begin{array}{r} 1,466 \\ +2,836 \\ \hline \end{array}$
19. $\begin{array}{r} 13,781 \\ +26,147 \\ \hline \end{array}$
20. $\begin{array}{r} 8,247 \\ +6,679 \\ \hline \end{array}$

Write the standard form.

21. 8,000,000,000 + 300,000,000 + 4,000,000 + 900,000 + 20,000 + 1,000 + 600 + 50 + 7

22. Sixty-three billion, three hundred sixty-five million, nine hundred twenty-two thousand, five

Estimate the difference by rounding to the nearest whole number.

23. $\begin{array}{r} 3.4 \\ -1.5 \\ \hline \end{array}$
24. $\begin{array}{r} 4.9 \\ -2.1 \\ \hline \end{array}$
25. $\begin{array}{r} 126.8 \\ -\ \ \ 6.7 \\ \hline \end{array}$
26. $\begin{array}{r} 17.03 \\ -13.39 \\ \hline \end{array}$
27. $\begin{array}{r} 762.68 \\ -144.74 \\ \hline \end{array}$

2.10 Problem Solving: 2 Steps

Construct Meaning

The world's fastest and highest flying aircraft of its type is the SR-71 Blackbird. It can fly 2,200 mph, or 3 times the speed of sound, and at an altitude of over 85,000 ft. One of its uses is to carry out experiments in the area of aerodynamics.

Savannah's first airplane trip alone was to visit her grandparents in Texas. She was aboard an airplane that cruised at a speed of 427.5 mph. It accelerated an additional 68.25 mph during the the flight. Savannah wondered how much faster the fastest plane in the world could travel.

through the steps of the Problem-Solving Guide to solve the problem.

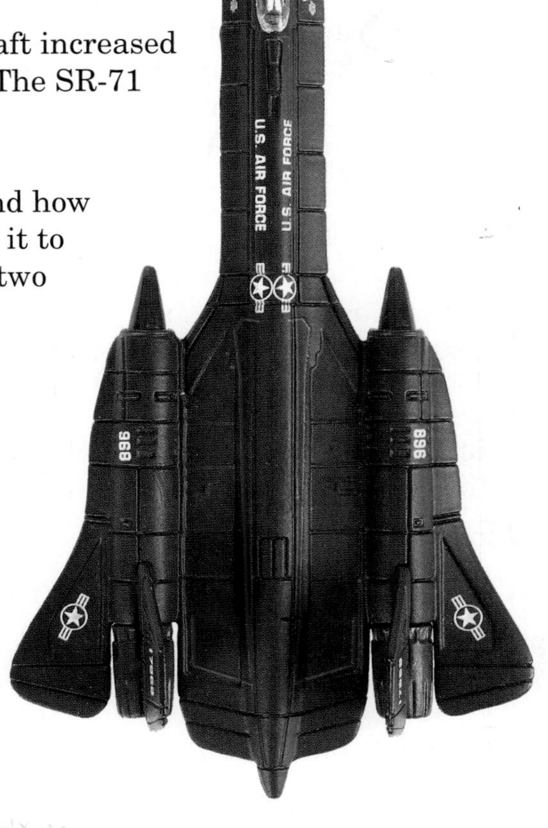

1. Understand the question.
What do you want to know? The difference between the speed of Savannah's airplane and the speed of an SR-71, the fastest plane.

2. Analyze the data.
What information do you have? The pilot of the aircraft increased its speed 68.25 more mph after reaching 427.5 mph. The SR-71 can travel 2,200 mph.

3. Plan the strategy.
What is an efficient method to solve the problem? Find how fast Savannah's aircraft was traveling, then compare it to how fast an SR-71 can travel. This problem requires two operations.

4. Solve the problem.

$$\begin{array}{r} 427.50 \\ +\ 68.25 \\ \hline 495.75 \end{array} \text{ mph}$$

(how fast Savannah's aircraft travels)

$$\begin{array}{r} 2{,}200.00 \\ -\ 495.75 \\ \hline 1{,}704.25 \end{array} \text{ mph}$$

(how much faster the SR-71 travels)

5. Evaluate the result.
Is the answer logical? Since the SR-71 is the world's fastest aircraft, it makes sense that it could travel 1,704.25 mph faster than a commercial aircraft.

Check Understanding

a. Savannah arrived safely at the airport where her grandmother was waiting for her. At a snack shop Savannah bought a slice of pizza for $2.75, a drink for $1.25, and a $1.00 cookie for her grandmother. Savannah paid with a $20 bill. How much change did she receive?

Practice

1. When Savannah arrived in Avalon, Texas, the morning temperature was 88.9°F. The sun was bright, and that afternoon it was 6.7°F warmer. The temperature that evening cooled down 10.4°F. What was the evening low?

2. Grandmother stopped at the grocery store and bought a gallon of milk for $3.29. The cashier also rang up $0.18 tax. How much change did Grandmother receive from a $5 bill?

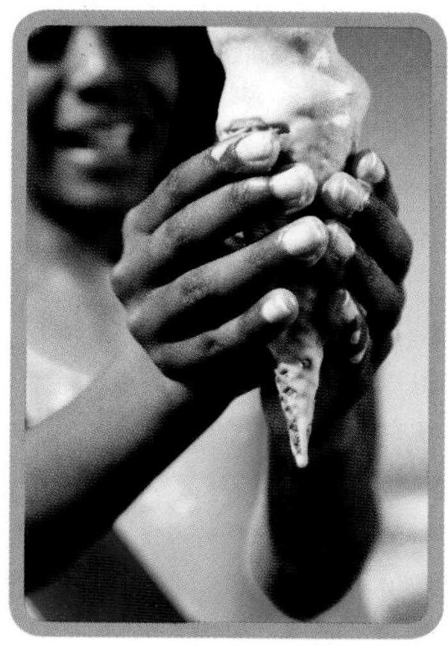

3. One day at the county fair, Savannah bought an ice cream cone that cost $1.45. The waffle cone was an additional $0.25. She had a coupon for $0.75 off the total price. How much did she pay?

4. Savannah attended church on Sunday with her grandparents. There was a report that showed the monthly financial support for a missionary family in Ireland. The offerings received for three Sundays were $17.68, $20.95, and $9.40. What did the fourth offering need to be if the amount pledged to support the missionary family was $60 per month?

5. The average yearly rainfall for Avalon, Texas, is 997.6 mm. The total rainfall for January through March is 212.5 mm. The total for April through June is 359.6 mm. What is the average yearly rainfall for the second half of the year?

6. Savannah earned $15 for a job she did for her grandparents. She gave $2.50 to the missionary family. She bought a souvenir for $4.00 and a T-shirt for $7.98. How much money was left?

Review

Find the missing number.

7. $235 + y = 561$
8. $x + 89 = 101$
9. $z = 4{,}672 + 37$
10. $b + 18.6 = 92.5$
11. $118.32 = t + 38.7$
12. $402.9 + p = 549.2$
13. $1.1 + c = 7.92$
14. $136.93 = 57.13 + f$
15. $42 = m + 3.8$

2.11 Add and Subtract Thousandths

Construct Meaning

Ricardo, a baseball athlete at Peak Christian Preparatory School, hit a record 35 home runs last year. Ricardo's batting average last year was 0.288. The record for highest lifetime batting average from Peak Christian Preparatory School, 0.301, is held by a former student named Owen. What is the difference between Ricardo's record batting average and Owen's lifetime batting average?

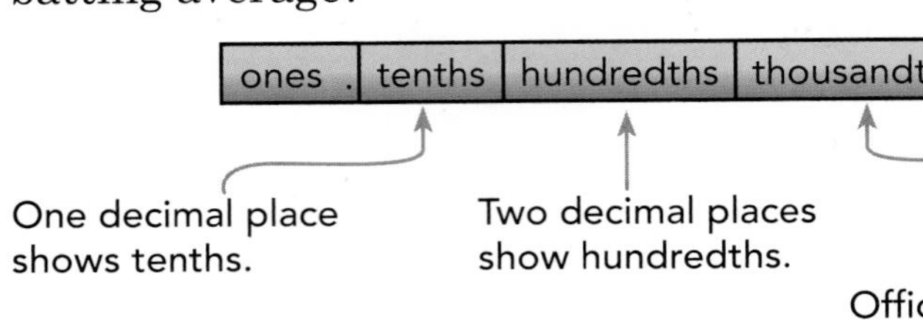

Official batting averages are recorded in the thousandths.

When subtracting decimals, these steps are important:

- Line up each place value and the decimal points.
- Subtract the thousandths, the hundredths, and then the tenths, regrouping if necessary.
- Subtract the whole numbers.
- Write the decimal point between the ones and the tenths.

$$\begin{array}{r} \scriptstyle 2\ 9\ 11 \\ 0.\not{3}\not{0}\not{1} \\ -\,0.288 \\ \hline 0.013 \end{array}$$

The difference between Ricardo's record and Owen's batting average is 0.013, or thirteen thousandths.

When adding or subtracting decimals, it is sometimes necessary to place zeros after the decimal point to make an equivalent decimal.

Solve 1.8 + 4.938.

$$\begin{array}{r} 1.800 \\ +\,4.938 \\ \hline 6.738 \end{array}$$

Read "six **and** seven hundred thirty-eight thousandths."

Check Understanding

Solve.

a. $\begin{array}{r} 0.234 \\ +\,1.782 \\ \hline \end{array}$

b. $\begin{array}{r} 2.71 \\ +\,2.428 \\ \hline \end{array}$

c. $\begin{array}{r} 72.645 \\ -\,39.427 \\ \hline \end{array}$

d. 1.4 − 0.765

e. 3.014 + 2.398

Write the correct number word.

f. 1.654
one and six hundred fifty-four
one and six hundred fifty-four thousandths
one and sixty-five four

g. 0.008
eight thousands
eight hundredths
eight thousandths

Practice

Write a word name for each number.

1. 0.8
2. 0.016
3. 1.72
4. 163.52
5. 4.004

Solve.

6. $\begin{array}{r} 0.425 \\ +1.763 \\ \hline \end{array}$

7. $\begin{array}{r} 2.314 \\ +6.8 \\ \hline \end{array}$

8. $\begin{array}{r} 24.86 \\ -18.275 \\ \hline \end{array}$

9. $4.567 + 16.32$

10. $246.3 - 8.712$

Estimate the difference by rounding to the nearest ten before subtracting.

11. $\begin{array}{r} 76.135 \\ -\ 8.617 \\ \hline \end{array}$

12. $\begin{array}{r} 909.812 \\ -126.742 \\ \hline \end{array}$

Solve.

13. $\begin{array}{r} 97.31 \\ -35.094 \\ \hline \end{array}$

14. $\begin{array}{r} 9.205 \\ +2.167 \\ \hline \end{array}$

15. $66.72 + n = 85.652$

16. $a - 17.064 = 34.126$

17. $s + 53.437 = 64.507$

18. The driver put 30.536 gallons of gasoline in the bus to take the baseball team to the airport. The one-way trip used 14.511 gallons. How many gallons of gasoline remained for the return trip from the airport?

19. The baseball team traveled to Orlando, Florida for a tournament. The first day they traveled 448.645 mi and the second day they traveled 242.789 mi. How many miles did they travel to the tournament in Florida?

2.12 Chapter 2 Review

Estimate the sum by rounding to the greatest place value before adding.

1. $\begin{array}{r} 247 \\ +634 \\ \hline \end{array}$

2. $\begin{array}{r} 13,724 \\ 34,582 \\ +48,031 \\ \hline \end{array}$

Round each number to the nearest thousand to find the estimated difference.

3. $\begin{array}{r} 8,517 \\ -\ \ 593 \\ \hline \end{array}$

4. $\begin{array}{r} 14,651 \\ -\ \ 4,703 \\ \hline \end{array}$

5. $\begin{array}{r} 86,571 \\ -23,613 \\ \hline \end{array}$

Write the letter of the addition property illustrated by each number sentence.

6. (1.4 + 3.6) + 18.2 = 1.4 + (3.6 + 18.2) 7. 9 + 0 = 9 8. 6 + 7 + 4 = 4 + 7 + 6

a. Commutative Property of Addition
b. Associative Property of Addition
c. Zero Property of Addition

Complete.

9. 7.9 + 6.2 = ____ + 7.9 10. 243 + ____ = 243

Write an equivalent decimal for each number.

11. 5.4 12. 6.10 13. 4.700 14. 562.47

Write "yes" or "no" to indicate whether the decimals are equivalent.

15. 8.2 and 8.22 16. 0.300 and 0.3 17. 0.70 and 0.07

18. With decimal models in mind, write an explanation of why 0.5 = 0.50.

Estimate the sum by rounding to the nearest whole number before adding.

19. $\begin{array}{r} 38.27 \\ +13.42 \\ \hline \end{array}$

20. $\begin{array}{r} 347.80 \\ +362.74 \\ \hline \end{array}$

Round to the nearest tenth.
Write the letter of the estimated sum.

21. $\begin{array}{r} 6.71 \\ +3.49 \\ \hline \end{array}$

a. 10.2
b. 10.3
c. 1.02

22. $\begin{array}{r} 23.74 \\ +71.17 \\ \hline \end{array}$

a. 9.49
b. 9.94
c. 94.9

Estimate the difference by rounding to the nearest ten before subtracting.

23. $\begin{array}{r} \$42.51 \\ -\ \ 17.16 \\ \hline \end{array}$

24. $\begin{array}{r} \$113.96 \\ -\ \ \ 35.51 \\ \hline \end{array}$

Solve.

25. $\begin{array}{r} 5.2 \\ +3.4 \\ \hline \end{array}$

26. $\begin{array}{r} \$9.31 \\ -\ 4.75 \\ \hline \end{array}$

Solve.

27. 271 + 576 + 893 + 408
28. 2,716 + 4,892 + 3,947
29. $r + 94 = 123.7$
30. $b + 4{,}372 = 5{,}001$
31. $104 - z = 37.42$
32. $w - 241 = 421$

33. At John F. Kennedy International Airport, 3,247 flights arrived on time. 1,124 flights were behind schedule, and 1,087 flights arrived a few minutes early. Compare the number of flights that arrived on time with those that did not arrive as scheduled.

2.13 Chapters 1–2 Review

Write the number as directed.

1. 7,009 (expanded form)
2. 0.301 (word form)
3. nineteen million, three (standard form)

Write in order from least to greatest.

4. 3,570,000   3,050,000   3,007,000   3,060,000

Write >, <, or =.

5. 0.35 ◯ 0.350
6. 6.381 ◯ 63.81
7. 42.7 ◯ 24.7

Estimate by rounding each number to the greatest place value before adding or subtracting. Then, find the exact sum or difference.

8. $\begin{array}{r} 7{,}436 \\ +\,2{,}241 \\ \hline \end{array}$

9. $\begin{array}{r} 6{,}807 \\ -\quad 403 \\ \hline \end{array}$

10. $\begin{array}{r} 49{,}231 \\ -\,20{,}974 \\ \hline \end{array}$

11. $\begin{array}{r} 874 \\ +\ \ 78 \\ \hline \end{array}$

Solve.

12. 98.7 + 1.64
13. 235 + 1,782 + 49
14. 96.52 – 1.782
15. $x + 417 = 485$
16. $6{,}114 - y = 5$
17. $s + 7.9 = 10.386$

Estimate the sum or difference by rounding to the nearest tenth.

18. $\begin{array}{r} \$5.87 \\ -\ \ 1.42 \\ \hline \end{array}$

19. $\begin{array}{r} 28.168 \\ +\ \ 2.643 \\ \hline \end{array}$

20. $\begin{array}{r} 0.154 \\ +\,0.097 \\ \hline \end{array}$

21. $\begin{array}{r} 479.80 \\ -\ \ 35.753 \\ \hline \end{array}$

Estimate the sum by rounding to the greatest place value before adding.

22. $\begin{array}{r} 8{,}517 \\ +5{,}322 \\ \hline \end{array}$

23. $\begin{array}{r} 514 \\ 773 \\ +276 \\ \hline \end{array}$

Write the correct addition property name illustrated by each equation.

24. 76 + 98 = 98 + 76

25. 23 + (45 + 76) = (23 + 45) + 76

26. 2,350 + 0 = 2,350

Answer Bank

Associative Property | Zero Property | Commutative Property

Complete.

27. 32 + (64 + 23) = (____ + 64) + 23

28. 12 + 16 + 18 = 16 + ____ + 12

Write an equivalent decimal for each number.

29. 8.4

30. 432.77

31. 3.10

32. 8.900

Solve.

33. 64.7 + 2.64

34. 435 + 2,781 + 69

35. $x + 217 = 685$

36. $4{,}114 - y = 5$

37. Stuart and Sheney Salazar traveled 835.7 mi from Lima, Peru to Quito, Ecuador. Then, they traveled 475.5 mi to Bogota, Columbia, to visit Alliance Academy. How many miles did they travel one way? How many miles did they travel round trip?

38. The Tippets family rented an RV for their family road trip. When they left their home, the odometer read 55,635 mi. When they returned one week later, their odometer read 56,664 mi. How many miles did they travel on their family road trip?

Chapter 3
Multiply Whole Numbers

He determines the number of the stars
and calls them each by name.
Psalm 147:4

Key Ideas:

Multiplication: multiplying whole numbers with up to three-digit factors

Algebra: using the commutative and associative properties of multiplication

Algebra: writing equations without variables

Multiplication: estimating products

3.1 Properties of Multiplication

Construct Meaning

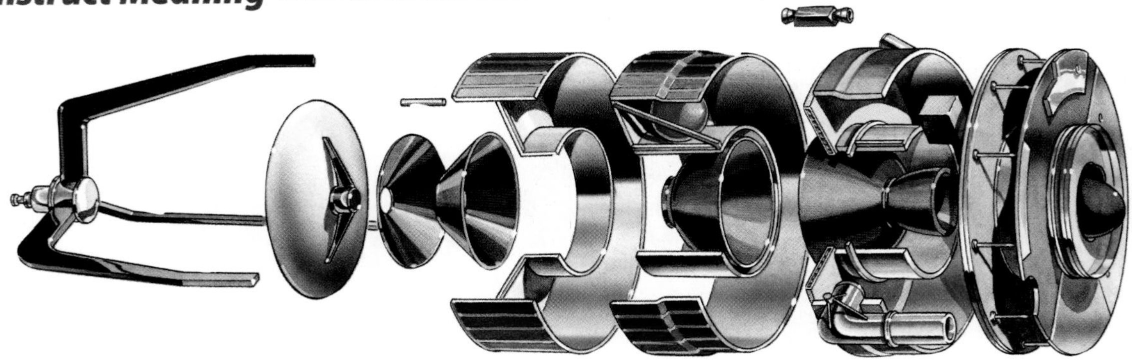

Mike and Joy visited the Kennedy Space Center. They were amazed at the size differences between the space shuttles and the probes. During the tour, they learned that the Giotto space probe, which flew past Halley's comet in 1986, was only 10 ft long. The space shuttles were more than 18 times as long as the Giotto space probe. Mike and Joy used multiplication to find the length of a space shuttle.

One of the uses of multiplication is to compare sizes or amounts to find information.

length of the Giotto probe × 18 = approximate length of a space shuttle
10 feet × 18 = 180 ft

A space shuttle is approximately 180 ft long.

Multiplication is a shortcut to replace repeated addition.

If a bus that holds 40 people makes 5 trips an hour around the launch pad, how many people can take the tour in one hour?

$40 + 40 + 40 + 40 + 40 = 200$
$40 \times 5 = 200$ people

REMEMBER

Multiplication is the operation that finds the **product** of two **factors**. factor × factor = product

1. **Zero Property of Multiplication**
   The product of zero and any other factor is zero. $0 \times 12 = 0$; $0 \times 400 = 0$

2. **Multiplication Identity Property of One**
   The product of one and any other factor is that factor. $1 \times 89 = 89$; $1{,}000 \times 1 = 1{,}000$

3. **Commutative Property of Multiplication**
   Changing the order of the factors does not change the product. $4 \times 5 = 20$; $5 \times 4 = 20$

4. **Associative Property of Multiplication**
   Grouping factors differently does not change the product. $6 \times (5 \times 2) = 60$; $(6 \times 5) \times 2 = 60$

5. **Distributive Property of Multiplication**
   The product remains the same whether a factor is multiplied by the sum of the addends or by each addend. $2 \times (4 + 5) = 18$; $(2 \times 4) + (2 \times 5) = 18$

Check Understanding

Name the multiplication property demonstrated by each number sentence.

a. $2 \times 9 = 9 \times 2$
b. $3 \times (7 \times 4) = (3 \times 7) \times 4$
c. $0 \times 9 = 0$
d. $1 \times 32 = 32$
e. $3 \times (4 + 8) = (3 \times 4) + (3 \times 8)$
f. $11 \times 15 = 15 \times 11$
g. $(8 \times 8) \times 3 = 8 \times (8 \times 3)$
h. $10{,}000 \times 0 = 0$
i. $6 \times (5 + 3) = (6 \times 5) + (6 \times 3)$

Practice

Write the missing number(s) and identify the property of multiplication.

1. $3 \times$ ____ $= 0$
2. $7 \times (6 \times$ ____$) = (7 \times 6) \times 5 =$ ____
3. $1 \times$ ____ $= 9$
4. $6 \times (8 +$ ____$) = (6 \times 8) + ($____ $\times 7) =$ ____
5. $4 \times 5 =$ ____ $\times 4 =$ ____
6. $3 \times (20 + 10) = (3 \times$ ____$) + (3 \times$ ____$) =$ ____
7. $15 \times 2 = 2 \times$ ____ $=$ ____
8. $1{,}245 \times 0 \times 3{,}626 =$ ____

Write a number sentence to illustrate each property.

9. Commutative Property of Multiplication
10. Associative Property of Multiplication
11. Zero Property of Multiplication
12. Multiplication Identity Property of One
13. Distributive Property of Multiplication

Challenge

14. Describe how the Distributive Property of Multiplication could help you solve 4 × 23 using only mental math.

Review

Quickly state each multiplication fact to a partner.

15.	3 × 9	9 × 3	4 × 9	5 × 9
16.	4 × 7	3 × 7	7 × 7	7 × 9
17.	7 × 6	6 × 6	2 × 7	7 × 8
18.	9 × 8	9 × 7	9 × 6	9 × 5
19.	5 × 2	5 × 5	5 × 8	5 × 7
20.	6 × 8	6 × 7	8 × 8	5 x 6
21.	9 × 2	9 × 10	9 × 11	8 × 9
22.	8 × 7	7 × 5	7 × 10	7 × 11

3.2 Mental Math: Multiples

Construct Meaning

In science class, Melissa learned that Jupiter takes 12 times longer to orbit the sun than the earth does. She knows that it takes Earth 365 days to orbit the sun. How can she quickly determine the time it takes for Jupiter to orbit the sun?

Round 365 days to the nearest hundred, which is 400 days, for Earth's orbit. If Jupiter's orbit is 12 times longer, multiply 400 × 12.

If 4 × 12 = 48, then 40 × 12 = 480, and 400 × 12 = 4,800.

It takes Jupiter about 4,800 days to orbit the sun.

A multiple is the product of a given number and another whole number.

Multiples of 10, 100, and 1,000 are easy to remember.

multiples of 10	10	20	30	40	50	60	70	80	90	100
multiples of 100	100	200	300	400	500	600	700	800	900	1,000
multiples of 1,000	1,000	2,000	3,000	4,000	5,000	6,000	7,000	8,000	9,000	10,000

To use these multiples to do mental math, begin with any two factors and their product.

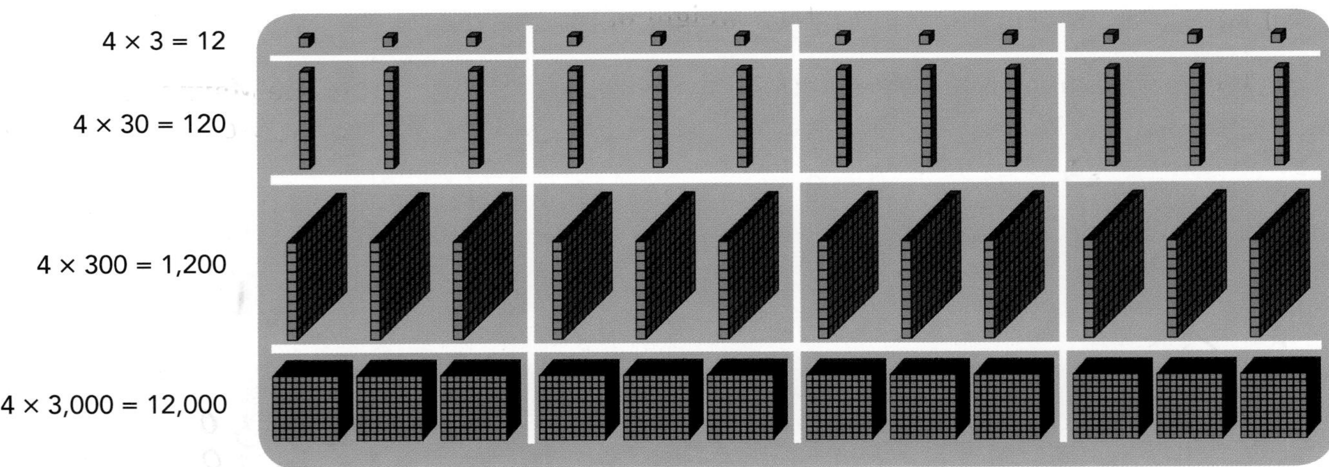

What pattern do you see when you multiply with multiples of 10, 100, and 1,000?

Check Understanding

Complete the pattern.

a.	b.	c.	d.
5 × 3 = ____	7 × 2 = ____	11 × 8 = ____	12 × 6 = ____
5 × 30 = ____	7 × 20 = ____	11 × ____ = 880	12 × 60 = ____
5 × 300 = ____	7 × ____ = 1,400	11 × 800 = ____	12 × ____ = 7,200
5 × 3,000 = ____	7 × 2,000 = ____	11 × ____ = 88,000	12 × 6,000 = ____

Practice

Use mental math to multiply.

1. 60 × 6
2. 400 × 5
3. 3,000 × 4
4. 8,000 × 3
5. 9,000 × 2
6. 800 × 7
7. 90 × 5
8. 200 × 8
9. 700 × 4
10. 30 × 9

Apply

Use mental math.

11. Emmet's father works as a scientist for NASA. His monthly salary is $7,000. What does he earn in one year?

12. A telescope magnifies distant objects, enabling astronomers to study the planets and stars. A reflecting telescope uses bowl-shaped mirrors to gather light and make objects visible. A telescope on Mount Wilson in California has a mirror that is 60 in. across. A telescope in Russia has one that is about four times wider. Approximately how many inches across is it?

13. The students at Faith Christian School are recycling newspapers to raise enough money for a telescope for the school. If there are 12 classes and each class collects about 500 lb of paper, what is the approximate total weight of the newspapers?

14. The W.M. Keck Observatory is located in Hawaii on the summit of the Mauna Kea volcano. Two of the world's largest telescopes, the Keck I and Keck II, are located there. The cost to [illegible]n the Keck Observatory was over $140 million. If four donors each gave $40 million to the Keck Foundation, would that equal or exceed the amount needed?

3.3 Least Common Multiple

Construct Meaning

Esteban's teacher asked him to complete a chart to show the first 10 multiples of 3 and 5. When he had finished, he noticed that some of the numbers were the same.

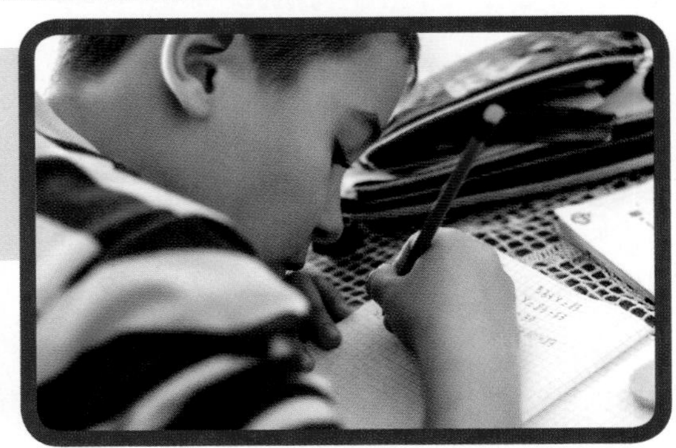

multiples of 3	3	6	9	12	15	18	21	24	27	30
multiples of 5	5	10	15	20	25	30	35	40	45	50

Which multiples are the same?

15 and 30 are multiples of both 3 and 5.

Multiples that are shared by two or more numbers are called common multiples.
The least common multiple (LCM) is the smallest multiple that is common to two or more numbers.

The least common multiple of 3 and 5 is 15.

Use a Calculator:

A calculator is useful for finding the multiples of a number.

Press 7 + 7 = .

Continue to press = to find each multiple of 7.

Check Understanding

Complete.

a. What is the product of a given number and another whole number called?

b. What are the multiples that are shared by two or more numbers called?

c. What is the smallest common multiple of two or more numbers called?

d. What is a strategy to find the LCM of two numbers?

e. What is a strategy to find the LCM of three numbers?

Practice

List the first 10 multiples of each number.

1. 4 2. 6 3. 2 4. 8 5. 9 6. 7 7. 3 8. 5

Compare the first 10 multiples of each pair of numbers. Identify the LCM for each pair.

9. 4 and 6
10. 6 and 8
11. 8 and 9
12. 2 and 5
13. 3 and 4
14. 5 and 7
15. 2 and 3
16. 3 and 7

Apply

17. Alika and her sister, Imani, have soccer practice after school. Alika's team practices every other day, and Imani's team practices every third day. Their mother wishes their practices were on the same day. Alika pointed out that sometimes they do have practice on the same day. If both teams begin practice on September 1, how often will the girls have practice on the same day? Use the calendar to see the dates of each girl's practice.

SEPTEMBER

Sun	Mon	Tue	Wed	Thu	Fri	Sat
	1	2	3	4	5	6
7	8	9	10	11	12	13
14	15	16	17	18	19	20
21	22	23	24	25	26	27
28	29	30				

18. Complete each analogy using the least common multiple.
    a. 15 is to 3 and 5 as ____ is to 4 and 5.
    b. 6 is to 2 and 3 as ____ is to 3 and 4.
    c. 10 is to 2 and 5 as ____ is to 2 and 9.

Review

Find the product. Use mental math when possible.

19. 300×4
20. $7{,}000 \times 10$
21. 500×10
22. $2{,}000 \times 9$
23. 80×7
24. 900×8

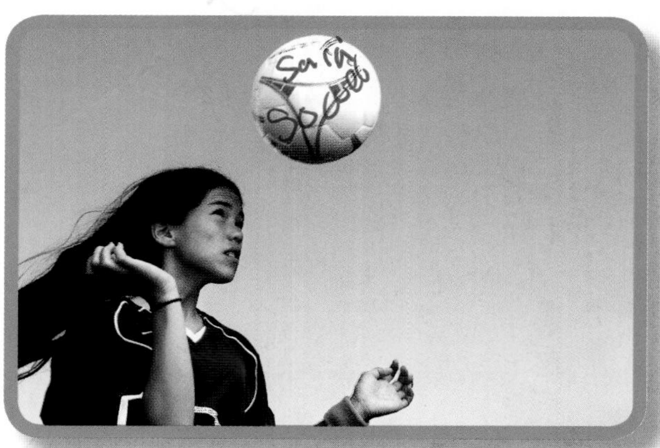

Copy and complete.

25. $7 \times 8 = 8 \times$ ____ $=$ ____
26. $2 \times (8 + 3) = (2 \times$ ____$) + (2 \times 3) =$ ____
27. $9 \times (2 + 5) = ($____ $\times 2) + ($____ $\times 5) =$ ____

3.4 Greatest Common Factor

Construct Meaning

Multiples of a given number are greater than or equal to that number. Some multiples of 6 are 6, 12, 18, 24, and 30.

A factor of a given number divides the number evenly with no remainder. If 6 is the product, what are the possible equations?

$1 \times 6 = 6$	$2 \times 3 = 6$
factor × factor	factor × factor

The factors of 6 are 1, 2, 3, and 6.
Factoring is the process of finding parts of a number by using multiplication and division facts.

Find the factors of 14.

$1 \times 14 = 14$
$2 \times 7 = 14$
Factors of 14 are 1, 2, 7, and 14.

Find the factors of 32.

$1 \times 32 = 32$
$2 \times 16 = 32$
$4 \times 8 = 32$
Factors of 32 are 1, 2, 4, 8, 16, and 32.

Use a Venn diagram to find the common factors of 14 and 32. Common factors are shared by two or more numbers.

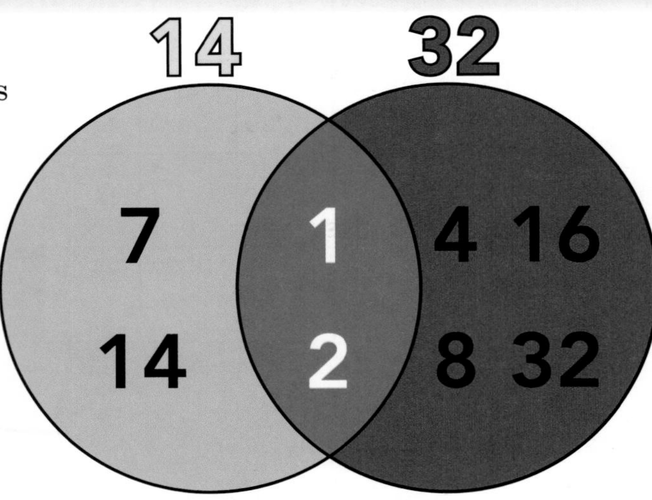

The largest common factor of two or more numbers is the greatest common factor (GCF). What is the GCF of 14 and 32?

The common factors are 1 and 2.

The GCF of 14 and 32 is 2.

Check Understanding

Strategies for Finding Factors

- Factors of a number will evenly divide that number.
- Any number is a factor of itself.
- Use multiplication facts.
- 1 is a factor of all whole numbers.
- 2 is a factor of all even numbers.
- 5 and 10 are factors of all numbers that end with a 0.
- Break down larger factors into smaller factors.

Use a Venn diagram to show the common factors and the greatest common factor of each.

a. 10 and 20 b. 6 and 12 c. 24 and 32

Practice

Find the factors of each number. List the common factors and the greatest common factor of each number pair.

1. 9 and 15
2. 8 and 16
3. 12 and 16
4. 9 and 36
5. 30 and 50
6. 15 and 25
7. 18 and 27
8. 7 and 21
9. 7 and 11

Apply

10. Demarco wants to make ice cream sundaes. He has 12 scoops of vanilla ice cream and 18 spoonfuls of chocolate chips. He decides to divide the ice cream and chocolate chips into portions of equal size with nothing left over. How many sundaes can he make? What is the amount of ice cream and chocolate chips that will be in each sundae?

11. Arianna was listing the factors of a number less than 50. The first five numbers that she wrote were 1, 2, 3, 5, and 6. What number was she factoring?

12. Isabella's teacher gave her a piece of poster board that measured 12 in. by 8 in. She asked her to divide it evenly into squares of the largest size possible. What size will each square be?

Review

Find the LCM (least common multiple) for each pair of numbers.

13. 6 and 9
14. 2 and 6
15. 2 and 7
16. 3 and 6
17. 5 and 6
18. 4 and 10
19. 4 and 5
20. 3 and 11
21. 2 and 9
22. 12 and 30

3.5 Multiply by 1-Digit Factors

Construct Meaning

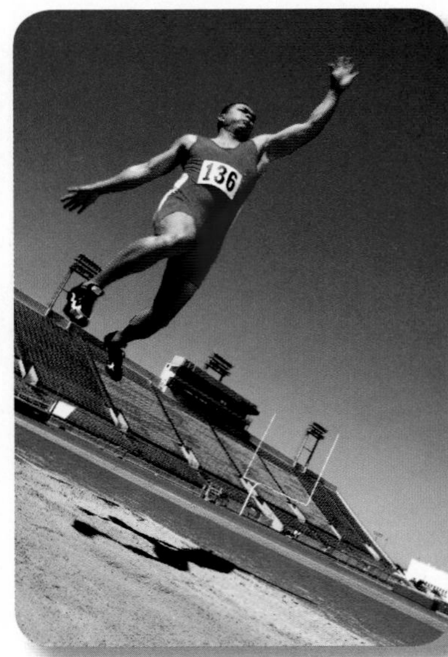

The pull of gravity on the moon is about $\frac{1}{6}$ of the earth's gravitational pull. This means that your best long jump on Earth would be about 6 times longer on the moon. The men's long jump record is a little more than 29 feet. How far could the world-record holder jump on the moon?

29 feet × 6

Step 1

Multiply the ones.
6 × 9 ones = 54 ones.
Regroup 54 ones as 5 tens and 4 ones.

$$\begin{array}{r} {}^{5} \\ 29 \\ \times\ 6 \\ \hline 4 \end{array}$$

Step 2

Multiply the tens.
6 × 2 tens = 12 tens.
Add the regrouped tens as 12 tens + 5 tens = 17 tens.

$$\begin{array}{r} {}^{5} \\ 29 \\ \times\ 6 \\ \hline 174 \end{array}$$

On the moon, the record-setting long jump would be more than 174 ft.

Multiply three-digit numbers the same way. Try 6 × 292.

Multiply the ones.
Regroup 12 ones as 1 ten and 2 ones.

$$\begin{array}{r} {}^{1} \\ 292 \\ \times\ 6 \\ \hline 2 \end{array}$$

Multiply the tens.
6 × 9 tens = 54 tens.
Add the regrouped ten as 54 tens + 1 ten = 55 tens.
Regroup 55 tens as 5 hundreds and 5 tens.

$$\begin{array}{r} {}^{5\,1} \\ 292 \\ \times\ 6 \\ \hline 52 \end{array}$$

Multiply the hundreds.
6 × 2 hundreds = 12 hundreds.
Add the regrouped hundreds.
12 + 5 = 1 thousand and 7 hundreds.

$$\begin{array}{r} {}^{5\,1} \\ 292 \\ \times\ 6 \\ \hline 1{,}752 \end{array}$$

Check Understanding

Multiply to find the product.

a. $\begin{array}{r} 92 \\ \times\ 8 \\ \hline \end{array}$

b. $\begin{array}{r} 72 \\ \times\ 4 \\ \hline \end{array}$

c. $\begin{array}{r} 807 \\ \times\ 6 \\ \hline \end{array}$

d. $\begin{array}{r} 635 \\ \times\ 7 \\ \hline \end{array}$

e. If a crater on the near side of the moon is 188 mi wide, and a basin on the dark side of the moon is three times wider, how wide is the basin?

Practice

Multiply to find the product.

1. 36×5
2. 68×4
3. 241×3
4. 52×4
5. 72×3
6. 84×5
7. 432×6
8. 67×6
9. 98×8
10. 157×7
11. 317×4
12. 657×9
13. 958×3
14. 25×8
15. 401×9

Apply

16. If a canvasback duck flies at a rate of 63 mph, how far could the canvasback duck fly in 4 hours?

17. A sailfish can swim 68 mph. If it could swim from noon until 6:00 PM, how many miles would it travel?

18. In 1958, a tornado struck Wichita Falls, Texas, at a speed of 286 mph. On the planet Neptune, the wind blows more than 4 times faster. Using the speed of the tornado in Wichita Falls for comparison, compute the approximate speed of Neptune's wind.

Review

Find the sum.

19. $3,246 + 4,786$
20. $11,539 + 4,600$
21. $5,785 + 6,941$
22. $23,416 + 18,323$
23. $9,321 + 7,652$
24. $46,630 + 33,758$
25. $18,747 + 2,789$
26. $2,235 + 8,221$

3.6 Multiply Larger Numbers

Construct Meaning

Multiplying larger numbers requires that you understand place value. To find multiplication products, pay attention to place value and work in sequence.

3,428 can be written as:

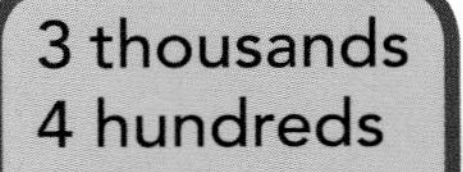

3 thousands
4 hundreds
2 tens
8 ones

OR

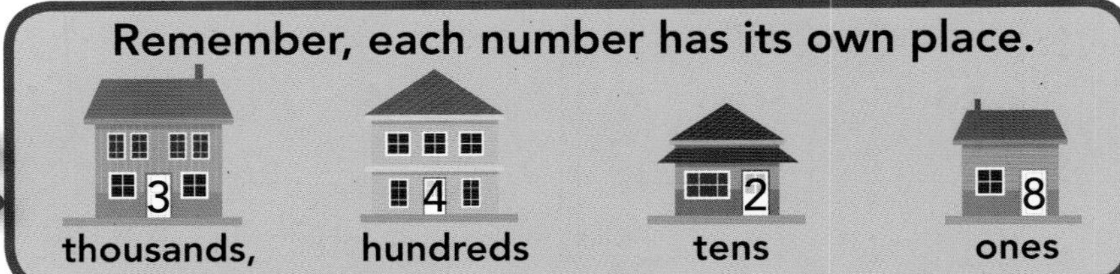

42,759 can be written as:

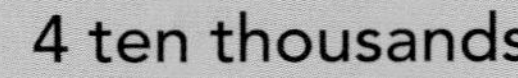

4 ten thousands
2 thousands
7 hundreds
5 tens
9 ones

OR

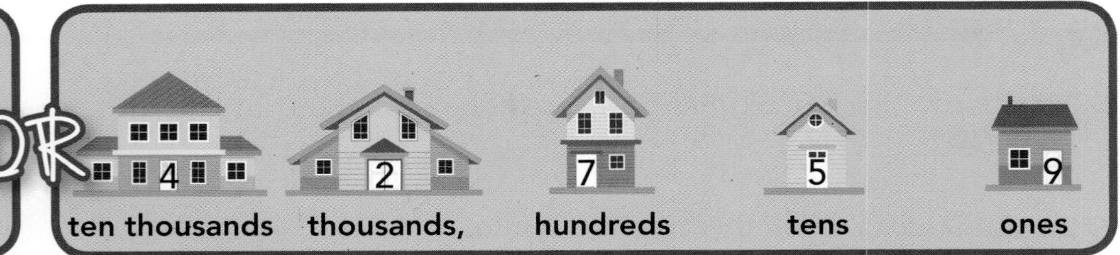

Method 1:
Use the Distributive Property of Multiplication to find the product of 3,428 × 5.

3,000 × 5	=		15,000
400 × 5	=		2,000
20 × 5	=		100
8 × 5	=	+	40
			17,140

Multiply the number in each place.
Add the products.

Method 2:
Use partial products by multiplying ones, tens, hundreds, and thousands. Regroup as needed.

$$\begin{array}{r} {}^{2\ 14} \\ 3{,}428 \\ +\quad 5 \\ \hline 17{,}140 \end{array}$$

Compare the products of each method.
17,140 = 17,140

Check Understanding

a. Copy and complete. Use the Distributive Property of Multiplication to find the product of 42,759 × 6.

40,000 × 6 =
2,000 × 6 =
700 × 6 =
50 × 6 =
9 × 6 = +

b. Regroup as needed.

$$\begin{array}{r} 42{,}759 \\ \times\quad 6 \\ \hline \end{array}$$

c. Compare the products from a and b.

Practice

Find the product.

1. $\begin{array}{r} 7,961 \\ \times \quad 4 \\ \hline \end{array}$

2. $\begin{array}{r} 13,563 \\ \times \quad 7 \\ \hline \end{array}$

3. $\begin{array}{r} 8,124 \\ \times \quad 5 \\ \hline \end{array}$

4. $\begin{array}{r} 6,082 \\ \times \quad 9 \\ \hline \end{array}$

5. $\begin{array}{r} 22,935 \\ \times \quad 3 \\ \hline \end{array}$

6. $\begin{array}{r} 3,136 \\ \times \quad 2 \\ \hline \end{array}$

7. $\begin{array}{r} 56,207 \\ \times \quad 7 \\ \hline \end{array}$

8. $\begin{array}{r} 4,927 \\ \times \quad 8 \\ \hline \end{array}$

9. $\begin{array}{r} 77,898 \\ \times \quad 0 \\ \hline \end{array}$

10. $\begin{array}{r} 9,601 \\ \times \quad 7 \\ \hline \end{array}$

11. $\begin{array}{r} 90,999 \\ \times \quad 3 \\ \hline \end{array}$

12. $\begin{array}{r} 84,611 \\ \times \quad 9 \\ \hline \end{array}$

13. $\begin{array}{r} 1,707 \\ \times \quad 7 \\ \hline \end{array}$

14. $\begin{array}{r} 6,526 \\ \times \quad 5 \\ \hline \end{array}$

15. $\begin{array}{r} 1,888 \\ \times \quad 8 \\ \hline \end{array}$

Apply

Use mental math and the Distributive Property of Multiplication to solve.

16. 4,200 × 5
17. 7,500 × 2
18. 51,000 × 3

19. If an airplane could fly 34,122 mi in a 24-hour period, it would make it to the moon in about one week. What is the approximate distance from Earth to the moon?

20. The diameter of the moon is about 2,155 mi. Earth's diameter is about 4 times that of the moon. What is the approximate diameter of the earth?

21. Nicole knows that 9 × 8,200 = 73,800. How can she compute 8 × 8,200 without using multiplication?

Review

Write the word form for each number.

22. 55,020
23. 849,303
24. 3,126,900
25. Put commas in the number 3262988004, and then write the number in word form.

3.7 Estimate Products

Construct Meaning

Mrs. Garcia's eighth-grade science students want to take a class trip to the Dominion Observatory in Victoria, British Columbia. They will take a ferry from Seattle to Vancouver Island and will pay for their own meals. The approximate cost per student is $185. If there are 22 students, what is the approximate total cost of the class trip?

Estimate

1. Round to the highest place value. Multiply.

$$\begin{array}{r} \$185 \\ \times\ 22 \\ \hline \end{array} \rightarrow \begin{array}{r} \$200 \\ \times\ 20 \\ \hline \$4{,}000 \end{array}$$

OR

2. Use front-end estimation. Multiply.

$$\begin{array}{r} \$185 \\ \times\ 22 \\ \hline \end{array} \rightarrow \begin{array}{r} \$100 \\ \times\ 20 \\ \hline \$2{,}000 \end{array}$$

Which method of estimation is more accurate in this case?

Rounding to the greatest place value is more accurate in this case.

Check Understanding

If the trip to Dominion Observatory is successful, Mrs. Garcia will estimate the projected cost of returning next year. She believes the cost may increase by about $25 per student. There will be 26 students in her class next year. Use both methods of estimation to estimate the total cost for next year's trip.

cost per student:	$185
cost increase:	+ 25
next year's cost:	$210

Estimate using the projected figures for next year.

a. Round to the greatest place value. Multiply.

$$\begin{array}{r} \$210 \\ \times\ 26 \\ \hline \end{array} \qquad \begin{array}{r} \square \\ \times\ \square \\ \hline \square \end{array}$$ **total cost of the trip**

c. Multiply to find the actual cost.

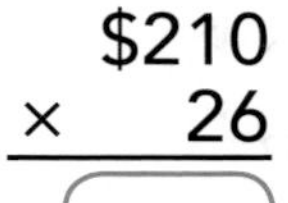

$$\begin{array}{r} \$210 \\ \times\ 26 \\ \hline \square \end{array}$$ **total cost of the trip**

b. Use front-end estimation. Multiply.

$$\begin{array}{r} \$210 \\ \times\ 26 \\ \hline \end{array} \qquad \begin{array}{r} \square \\ \times\ \square \\ \hline \square \end{array}$$ **total cost of the trip**

d. Compare your results.

Practice

Use front-end estimation to estimate the product.

1. 455×62
2. 801×35
3. $1{,}221 \times 82$
4. 337×50
5. $7{,}221 \times 90$
6. 718×42
7. 533×74
8. 122×80
9. 635×91
10. 249×21

Round each factor to the greatest place value. Estimate the product.

11. 491×35
12. 862×48
13. $3{,}200 \times 61$
14. 697×43
15. 998×56
16. 275×68
17. 149×33
18. $5{,}025 \times 50$
19. 382×76
20. 725×29

Apply

Estimate by rounding to the greatest place value.

21. Mrs. Moxness went to the grocery store to buy fruit for a large salad she was preparing for a church picnic. She only had $20, so she estimated the cost as she selected each item. Use mental math to estimate the total cost of the fruit on her list. Is $20 enough to pay for all the fruit?

22. About how much more do 4 lb pounds of grapes cost than 5 lb of apples?

Grocery List

4 lb bananas
$0.60 per lb

5 lb apples
$1.25 per lb

4 lb grapes
$1.75 per lb

3 lb oranges
$0.50 per lb

3.8 Multiply by 2-Digit Factors

Construct Meaning

The moon is Earth's only natural satellite, traveling around the earth in an elliptical path called an orbit. One complete trip of the moon around Earth, called a revolution, takes 27 days. How many days does it take for the moon to make 12 revolutions?

Multiply 27 days × 12.

Multiply by the digit in the ones place. Regroup if necessary.

$$\begin{array}{r} {}^{1} \\ 27 \\ \times 12 \\ \hline 54 \end{array}$$

Multiply by the digit in the tens place.

$$\begin{array}{r} 27 \\ \times 12 \\ \hline 54 \\ +270 \\ \hline \end{array}$$

← Write a zero to show you multiplied by 10.

Add the two partial products.

$$\begin{array}{r} 27 \\ \times 12 \\ \hline 54 \\ +270 \\ \hline 324 \end{array}$$

It takes 324 days for the moon to make 12 revolutions around Earth.

You know that it takes the earth one year, or 365 days, to make one revolution around the sun. How many days are required for Earth to make 12 revolutions?

Multiply 365 × 12.

$$\begin{array}{r} {}^{1\,1} \\ 365 \\ \times\ \ 12 \\ \hline 730 \end{array}$$

Multiply by 2. 730 ← 2 × 365

$$\begin{array}{r} 365 \\ \times\ \ 12 \\ \hline 730 \\ +3\,650 \\ \hline \end{array}$$

Multiply by 10. 3 650 ← 10 × 365

$$\begin{array}{r} 365 \\ \times\ \ 12 \\ \hline 730 \\ +3\,650 \\ \hline 4{,}380 \end{array}$$

Add the partial products. Regroup to add. 4,380 days

Add three days for the three leap years occurring during the 12 revolutions.

4,383 days are required for Earth to make 12 revolutions around the sun.

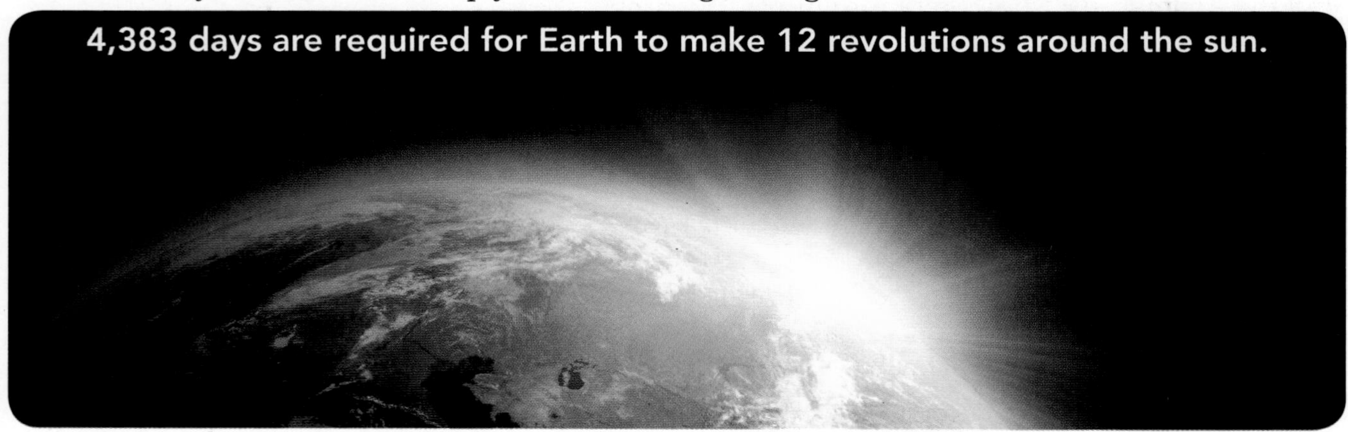

Practice

Find the product.

1. 36×25
2. 28×17
3. 44×56
4. 15×32
5. 43×21
6. 38×19
7. 52×20
8. 45×37
9. 73×33
10. 617×18
11. 412×70
12. 328×75
13. 720×24
14. 639×83

Apply

15. If Earth orbits the sun at an average speed of 18 miles per second, how many miles does the earth travel

a. in 1 minute?
b. in 1 hour?
c. in 1 day?

16. Determine whether each statement is a reasonable estimate or not.

a. The product of 75 and 25 is about 10,000.
b. The product of 122 and 12 is about 400.

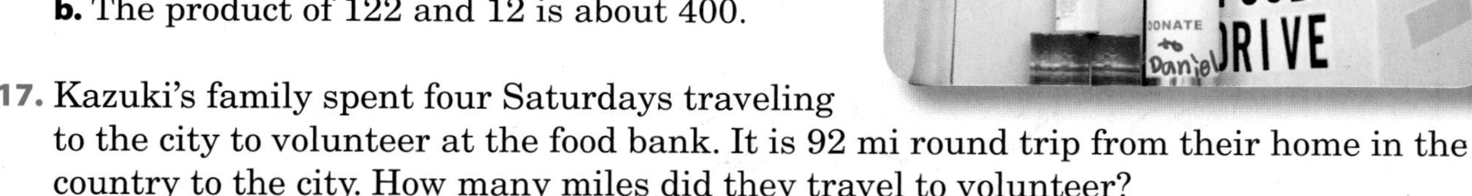

17. Kazuki's family spent four Saturdays traveling to the city to volunteer at the food bank. It is 92 mi round trip from their home in the country to the city. How many miles did they travel to volunteer?

Review

List the multiples of 10, 100, and 1,000 for each number.

18. 7 **19.** 8 **20.** 9

Find the estimated product by rounding to the greatest place value before multiplying.

21. 28×3
22. 41×9
23. 55×8
24. 73×7
25. 69×4

Use front-end digits to find the estimated product.

26. 37×4
27. 82×11
28. 94×7
29. 56×2
30. 25×6

3.9 Problem Solving: 2-Digit Factors

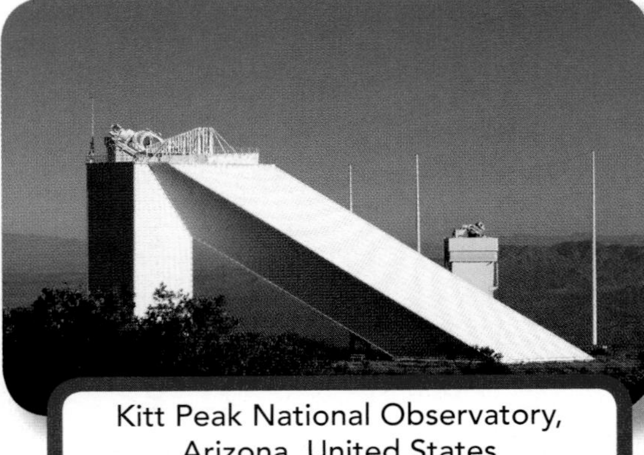

Kitt Peak National Observatory, Arizona, United States

Construct Meaning

Mr. Chambers' fifth graders formed an Astronomy Club to study plants, stars, and other objects in the universe. They plan to visit an observatory that has several large telescopes. If 32 students each bring $18 to cover the cost of the trip, how much money will Mr. Chambers collect?

Problem-Solving Guide

1. Understand the question.
   How much money is needed for all the students to go on the trip?

2. Analyze the data.
   There are 32 students.
   Each student will pay $18.

3. Plan the strategy.
   Multiply to solve.
   $18 × 32 students
   Estimate by rounding to the greatest place value.
   $20 × 30 = $600
   About $600 is needed.

4. Solve the problem.

$$\begin{array}{r} \$18 \\ \times\ 32 \\ \hline 36 \\ +\ 540 \\ \hline \$576 \end{array}$$

$576 will be collected for 32 students to go on the trip.

5. Evaluate the result.
   $576 seems reasonable because the estimate was $600.

Check Understanding

Mr. Chambers' class met at the school at 6:00 AM to travel to the Kitt Peak National Observatory. There were 32 students, 4 teachers, and 5 parents going on the field trip. Three of Mr. Chambers' students brought mini muffins for breakfast. Arturo brought 2 dozen blueberry muffins, Cheyenne brought 3 dozen oatmeal raisin muffins, and Grace brought 1 dozen banana nut muffins.

a. How many total muffins are there?

b. Are there enough muffins for every student to have two muffins? Why or why not?

c. Are there enough muffins for every student and adult to each have two muffins? Why or why not?

Practice

The students in Mr. Chambers' class decided to open membership in their Astronomy Club to other classes at school. At the next meeting, the total attendance was 53 students, 3 teachers, and 4 parent volunteers. Use the Problem-Solving Guide to solve the following problems:

1. Some of Mr. Chambers' students brought cookies for this meeting. Joshua and Kiara each brought 3 dozen. Jesalynn and Darius each brought 4 dozen. Are there enough cookies for each person attending to have 2 cookies?

2. One of the parent volunteers owns a toy store. He gave the Astronomy Club 35 bags of glow-in-the-dark planets and stars to distribute to the members. If each bag contains 19 planets and stars, how many pieces are there altogether?

3. Two of Mr. Chambers' students, Kinsley and Chen, want to group the planets and stars into small bags so each student at the Astronomy Club meeting can take an equal number home. Chen thinks they should put 13 into each bag, but Kinsley says they only have enough to put 12 into each bag. Who is right?

4. After the meeting, Mr. Chambers decided to print packets of information about astronomy for the club members. Each packet requires 27 pieces of paper. How many sheets of paper does Mr. Chambers need to make an information packet for every student who attended the meeting?

5. A ream of paper contains 500 sheets. If Mr. Chambers has 3 reams, does he have enough to print 53 information packets?

3.10 Multiply by 3-Digit Factors

Construct Meaning

There are 374 students enrolled at Hope Academy. This year, the school cafeteria staff prepared 297 lunches per day. If the school year was 176 days long, how many lunches were prepared?

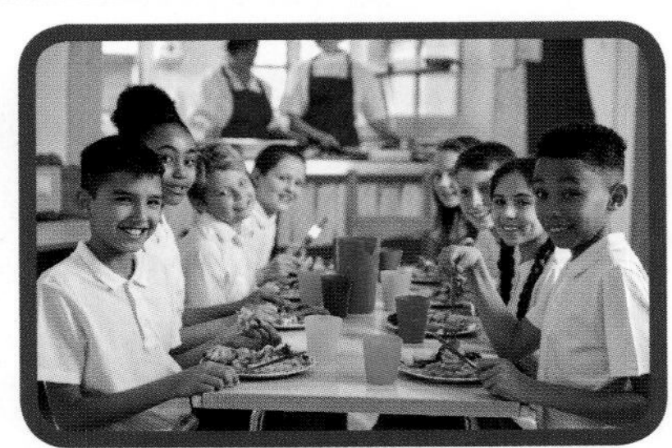

$$\begin{array}{r} 297 \\ \times 176 \\ \hline \end{array}$$

Multiply the ones.

$$\begin{array}{r} {}^{5\,4} \\ 297 \\ \times 176 \\ \hline 1\,782 \end{array}$$

Multiply the tens.

$$\begin{array}{r} {}^{6\,4} \\ 297 \\ \times 176 \\ \hline 1\,782 \\ 20\,790 \end{array}$$

Multiply the hundreds. Add the partial products.

$$\begin{array}{r} {}^{5\,4} \\ 297 \\ \times 176 \\ \hline 1\,782 \\ 20\,790 \\ +29\,700 \\ \hline 52{,}272 \end{array}$$

There were 52,272 lunches prepared.

Another way to look at 297 × 176 is 297 × (100 + 70 + 6).

$$\begin{array}{rl} 297 & \\ \times 176 & \longrightarrow 100 + 70 + 6 \\ \hline 1\,782 & \longleftarrow 6 \times 297 \\ 20\,790 & \longleftarrow 70 \times 297 \\ +29\,700 & \longleftarrow 100 \times 297 \\ \hline 52{,}272 & \end{array}$$

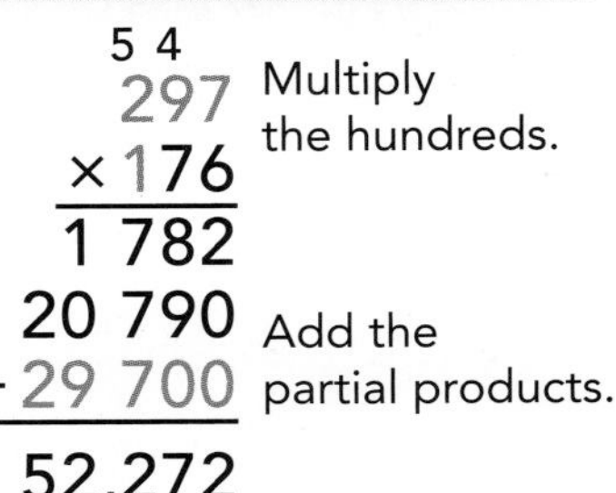

Check your answer by multiplying the rounded factors to see whether the product is reasonable. The answer 52,272 is reasonable because 300 × 200 = 60,000.

Solve 2,312 × 342.

Multiply the ones.

$$\begin{array}{r} 2{,}312 \\ \times \quad 342 \\ \hline 4\,624 \end{array}$$

Multiply the tens.

$$\begin{array}{r} {}^{1} \\ 2{,}312 \\ \times \quad 342 \\ \hline 4\,624 \\ 92\,480 \end{array}$$

Multiply the hundreds. Add the partial products.

$$\begin{array}{r} 2{,}312 \\ \times \quad 342 \\ \hline 4\,624 \\ 92\,480 \\ +693\,600 \\ \hline 790{,}704 \end{array}$$

Check Understanding

Write C if the problem has been solved correctly. If there is an error, write I for incorrect and explain the error.

a. $$\begin{array}{r} 529 \\ \times 384 \\ \hline 2\,016 \\ 42\,320 \\ +158\,700 \\ \hline 203{,}036 \end{array}$$

b. $$\begin{array}{r} 6{,}177 \\ \times \quad 215 \\ \hline 30\,885 \\ 61\,770 \\ +123\,540 \\ \hline 216{,}195 \end{array}$$

c. $$\begin{array}{r} 4{,}000 \\ \times \quad 189 \\ \hline 36\,999 \\ 320\,000 \\ +400\,000 \\ \hline 756{,}999 \end{array}$$

d. $$\begin{array}{r} 303 \\ \times 504 \\ \hline 1\,212 \\ 0\,000 \\ +151\,500 \\ \hline 152{,}712 \end{array}$$

Practice

Find the product. Check your answer using estimation.

1. $\begin{array}{r} 264 \\ \times 327 \\ \hline \end{array}$

2. $\begin{array}{r} 421 \\ \times 271 \\ \hline \end{array}$

3. $\begin{array}{r} 612 \\ \times 494 \\ \hline \end{array}$

4. $\begin{array}{r} 423 \\ \times 325 \\ \hline \end{array}$

5. $\begin{array}{r} 283 \\ \times 846 \\ \hline \end{array}$

6. $\begin{array}{r} 517 \\ \times 716 \\ \hline \end{array}$

7. $\begin{array}{r} 745 \\ \times 281 \\ \hline \end{array}$

8. $\begin{array}{r} 1,485 \\ \times \quad 182 \\ \hline \end{array}$

9. $\begin{array}{r} 2,537 \\ \times \quad 863 \\ \hline \end{array}$

10. $\begin{array}{r} 7,351 \\ \times \quad 545 \\ \hline \end{array}$

Choose the better estimate.

11. 61 × 340
    1,800 or 18,000

12. 90 × 599
    40,000 or 50,000

13. 308 × 3,000
    90,000 or 900,000

Apply

14. In 1970, the crew of *Apollo 13* traveled the farthest distance anyone had ever traveled from Earth. The distance was more than 31 times Earth's diameter, which is about 7,926 miles. About how far away from the earth was the *Apollo 13* crew when they set this record?

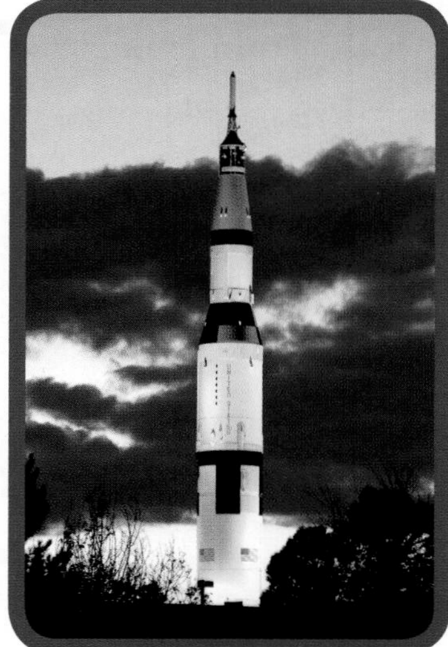

Review

Solve.

15. $\begin{array}{r} 617 \\ -543 \\ \hline \end{array}$

16. $\begin{array}{r} 5,492 \\ -2,843 \\ \hline \end{array}$

17. $\begin{array}{r} 6,918 \\ -3,859 \\ \hline \end{array}$

18. $\begin{array}{r} 26,437 \\ - \quad 5,766 \\ \hline \end{array}$

19. $\begin{array}{r} 493 \\ 668 \\ +285 \\ \hline \end{array}$

20. $\begin{array}{r} 4,720 \\ +5,986 \\ \hline \end{array}$

21. $\begin{array}{r} 78,484 \\ +32,246 \\ \hline \end{array}$

22. $\begin{array}{r} 153,469 \\ +822,383 \\ \hline \end{array}$

Write > or <.

23. 0.625 ◯ 0.652

24. 49.88 ◯ 498.8

25. 0.03 ◯ 0.003

26. 10,000 × 5 ◯ 5,000 × 12

3.11 Practice: 3-Digit Factors

Practice

Solve each problem using the steps in the Problem-Solving Guide.

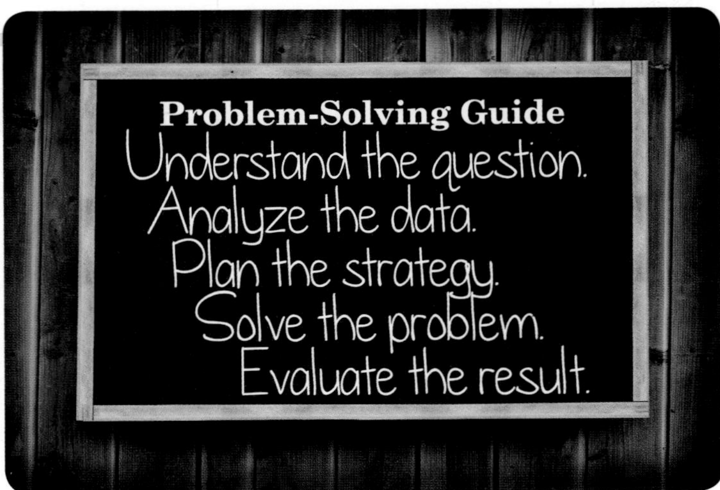

1. The manager of a deli in New Orleans calculated that during the busiest part of the tourist season, 125 lb of meat were used each day to make muffulettas. During 154 days, how many pounds of meat were used?

2. A train travels from New York City to New Orleans and back. The distance between the two cities is 1,380 miles. What is the total mileage if the train makes 85 round trips?

3. A bakery in New York City frequently donates brownies to a nearby Christian school. Last year, students sold the brownies after school to raise money for a summer mission trip to Israel. The bakery made 120 donations, giving 12 dozen brownies each time. What was the total number of brownies the bakery donated?

4. Outside New Orleans, land is being cleared to build new housing. The county will allow only 250 trees to be cut per square mile. If there are 105 sq mi to be developed, what is the maximum number of trees that could be cut?

Write the information that is not needed to solve the problem. Then, find the answer.

5. It takes 5 quarts (qt) of milk to make one pound of cheese and 3 gallons (gal) of milk to make one gallon of ice cream. How many quarts of milk are needed to make 125 pounds of cheese?

Use multiplication to find some interesting statistics.

6. Americans consume between 1 and 3 teaspoons (tsp) of salt daily. This is about twice the recommended amount. If you consume 3 tsp of salt per day, how many teaspoons will you eat in one year? Use a calculator to divide your answer by 48 to find how many cups of salt you would consume per year at this rate. Round the answer to the nearest tenth.

7. A taco salad from a fast food restaurant has 1,620 milligrams (mg) of sodium from salt. If you had a taco salad every day for a week, how many milligrams of sodium would that be?

8. The daily recommended intake of salt is 1,100 to 2,300 mg. What is the maximum amount, in milligrams, of safe salt intake for a week? How does the sodium total from a week of taco salads compare with that figure?

Challenge

9. A salesman bought a box of 115 calendars for $290. He sold 45 of them for $8 each at a teacher convention and sold the rest to a bookstore for $12 each. How much was the salesman's profit?

3.12 Calculators: Multistep Problems

Construct Meaning

Some problems require the use of more than one operation to solve. Carefully analyze the information given. Plan a way to solve the problem one step at a time. Choose the numbers and the operation you will use for the first step—addition, subtraction, multiplication, or division. Then, decide which operation to use next to solve the problem.

Understand the question.
Analyze the data.
Plan the strategy.
Solve the problem.
Evaluate the result.

Mrs. Baker shops for Christmas gifts early so that in December she can be with her family and focus on the birth of Christ. During the October sale at Main Street Christian Bookstore, she bought the following items: Six music CDs at \$12 each, seven devotional books at \$22 each, and two Bibles at \$39 each. If she had \$325 to spend, what will she have left?

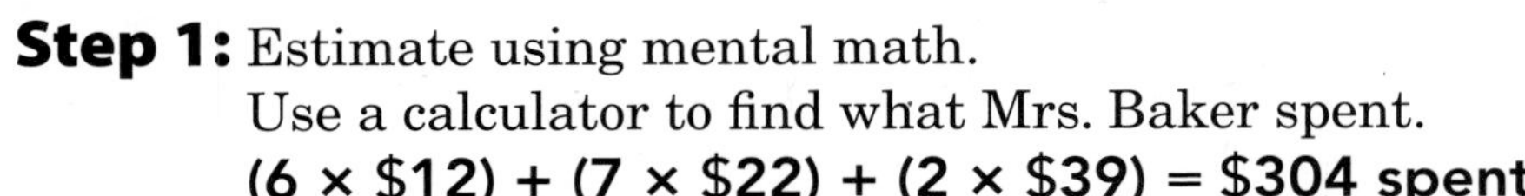

Step 1: Estimate using mental math.
Use a calculator to find what Mrs. Baker spent.
(6 × \$12) + (7 × \$22) + (2 × \$39) = \$304 spent

Step 2: Compute the amount of money remaining.
\$325 – \$304 = \$21 left

Check Understanding

When customers buy items in a store, they pay the retail price. Store owners buy the items from a supplier for a lesser amount called the wholesale price. The chart below shows the wholesale prices for the items Mrs. Baker bought.

Wholesale Prices	CDs	\$6 each	devotional books	\$12 each	Bibles	\$15 each

Use the chart and a calculator to figure how much profit Mr. Hoff, the store owner, made on the items he sold to Mrs. Baker.

a. Figure the total amount that Mr. Hoff paid for the items Mrs. Baker bought.
(6 × 6) + (7 × 12) + (2 × 15) = ____

b. Calculate the profit Mr. Hoff made from the sale by finding the difference between what Mrs. Baker paid and the amount Mr. Hoff paid.

Practice

Use a calculator to solve.

1. Gianna and Elijah each earn $11 per hour at the Main Street Christian Bookstore. Last week, Gianna worked for 24 hours and Brian worked 16 hours. What was the total amount Mr. Hoff paid to Gianna and Elijah last week?

2. Kwan purchased a Christian T-shirt for $16. He also bought a CD priced at $14.97, but a sticker on the CD said "Take $2.49 off." What did Kwan pay for the T-shirt and CD?

3. Jasmine has worked at Mr. Hoff's store for five years and now earns $14 an hour. This week, she and Elijah each worked 32 hours. How much more did Jasmine earn than Elijah?

Apply

Choose a problem-solving strategy that best helps you solve each of the following problems.

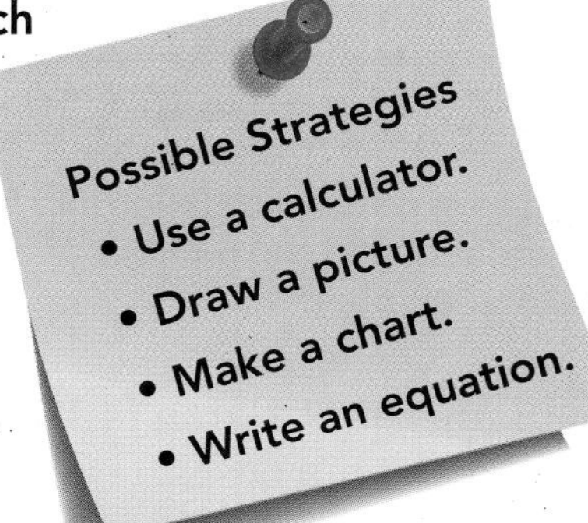

4. Gianna was responsible for setting up a display near the entrance of the bookstore. She used Bibles, calendars, Christian novels, and family picture frames. She placed Bibles on one end. The novels were between the picture frames and the calendars. If the calendars are not next to the Bibles,
what is?

5. During December, the bookstore sells many Scripture calendars for the coming year. They sold a total of 580 calendars during the first two weeks of December. If they sold 179 calendars the first week, how many were sold during the second week?

6. Mr. Hoff usually buys best-selling Christian books for $180 per box. The publisher is now offering a reduced price of $112 per box. Mr. Hoff is going to order 45 boxes of books. How much money will he save?

3.13 Explore Exponents

Construct Meaning

Astronomers often work with very large numbers in their study of objects in the universe. In astronomy, as well as other fields of science, large numbers may be expressed, or shown, in a shorter form using exponents.

Another way to express 100,000 is $10 \times 10 \times 10 \times 10 \times 10$. It can also be written as 10^5 and read "10 to the fifth power." 10 is the base number, and 5 is the exponent.

base number 10^5 exponent

Read the following base numbers and exponents. The exponent tells the number of times the base number is used as a factor.

2^5 5^8 10^7 3^9 4^6

Powers of 10
$10 = 10 \times 1 = 10^1$
$100 = 10 \times 10 = 10^2$
$1{,}000 = 10 \times 10 \times 10 = 10^3$
$10{,}000 = 10 \times 10 \times 10 \times 10 = 10^4$

In each row, note the relationship between the exponent and the number of zeros in the first number.

People from around the world bring their balloons to participate in the Balloon Fiesta held in Albuquerque, New Mexico. Nearly one million spectators enjoy this event each fall. Write this number as a power of ten.

$1{,}000{,}000 = 10^6$

The diameter of Earth is 12,756 kilometers (km). An astronomer would rewrite that figure for scientific purposes.

12,756 km could be rounded to 13,000 km.
$13{,}000 = 13 \times 1{,}000 =$ **13×10^3 km**

Check Understanding

Round to the highest place value and express using exponents.

a. 4,030
b. 65,892
c. 41,738
d. 125,640
e. 38,618
f. 7,955
g. 89,750
h. 192,214

i. The distance from the earth to its moon is 238,613 miles. Round that figure to the highest place value and express using exponents of 10.

Practice

The chart shows the diameter of each planet in the solar system, ordering the planets from smallest to largest. Round the diameter of each planet to the nearest thousand and express using powers of 10. Use your answers to compare the relative sizes of the planets.

Planets in Earth's Solar System

planet	diameter (in km)	rounded figure	expressed with exponents
Mercury	4,879	1.	
Mars	6,792	2.	
Venus	12,104	3.	
Earth	12,756	4.	
Neptune	49,528	5.	
Uranus	51,118	6.	
Saturn	120,536	7.	
Jupiter	142,984	8.	

Review

Write the letter of the correct estimated product.

9. 536 × 120
   - **a.** 6,000
   - **b.** 60,000
   - **c.** 600,000

10. 420 × 277
   - **a.** 120,000
   - **b.** 12,000
   - **c.** 1,200

11. 312 × 702
   - **a.** 2,100,000
   - **b.** 2,100
   - **c.** 210,000

12. 675 × 435
   - **a.** 280,000
   - **b.** 28,000
   - **c.** 2,800

Use the Distributive Property of Multiplication to find the product.

13. 5 × 532
14. 7 × 924
15. 8 × 860
16. 9 × 235

Name the property of multiplication shown by each equation. Solve for Exercises 18–19.

17. 495 × 0 = 0
18. 895 × 42 = 42 × 895
19. 8 × (9 × 7) = (8 × 9) × 7

Find the product.

20. $\begin{array}{r} 498 \\ \times \quad 5 \\ \hline \end{array}$

21. $\begin{array}{r} 4{,}500 \\ \times \quad 22 \\ \hline \end{array}$

22. $\begin{array}{r} 5{,}289 \\ \times \quad 363 \\ \hline \end{array}$

23. $\begin{array}{r} 12{,}630 \\ \times \quad 767 \\ \hline \end{array}$

24. $\begin{array}{r} 898 \\ \times 257 \\ \hline \end{array}$

3.14 *Lattice Multiplication*

Construct Meaning

A lattice is made from wooden or metal strips placed in a diagonal pattern with open spaces between the strips. Often a lattice supports ivy or roses as they grow. In lattice multiplication, a framework resembling a lattice supports the problem as you multiply factors with two or more digits. A lattice box is drawn so the number of boxes matches the number of digits in each factor.

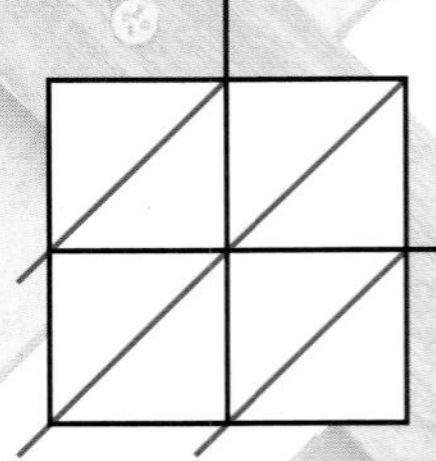

Use lattice multiplication to find the product of 52 × 43. Follow the steps.

1. Draw a lattice. For this example, draw four squares. Then, draw a diagonal line through each square.

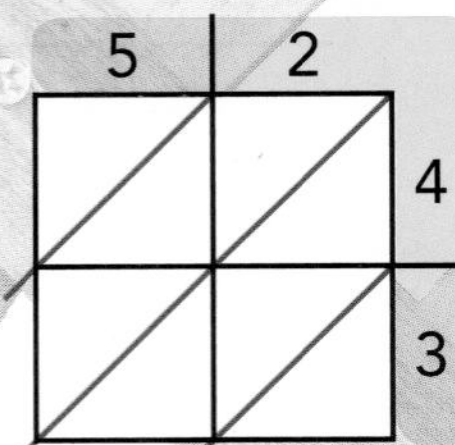

2. Write the digits of one factor across the top edge of the lattice and the digits of the other factor down the right edge.

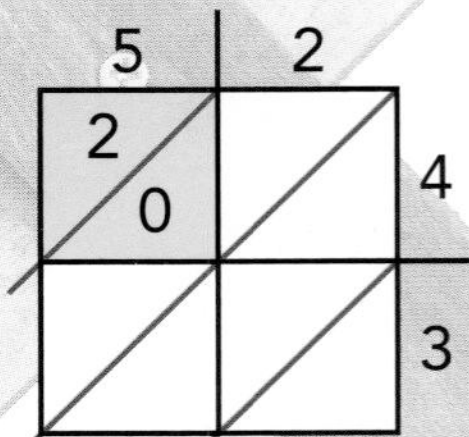

3. Start at the square in the upper left corner and multiply the digit at the top of the column by the digit at the right of the row. Record the product in the square where the two factors meet. Write the tens in the upper half of the square and the ones in the lower half.

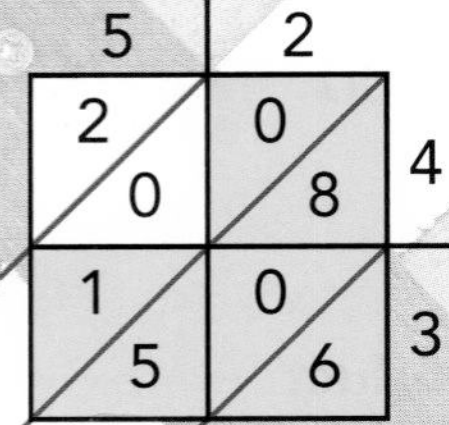

4. Do the same for each square in the lattice. When a product has no tens, write a zero in the upper half of the square.

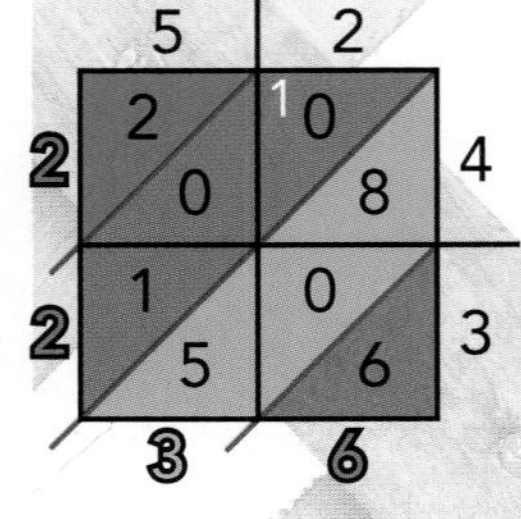

5. Start in the lower right corner and add the digits along each diagonal. Write each sum below each diagonal. Regroup at the top of the next diagonal if necessary.

6. Read the product from the top left edge down and then along the bottom of the lattice.

52 × 43 = 2,236

Check Understanding

Find the product of 756 × 819 using lattice multiplication.

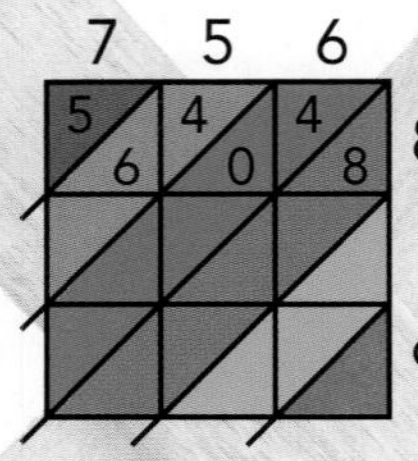

a. Copy and complete the lattice multiplication. Multiply for each box in the lattice. (Start at the upper left.)

b. Add diagonally. (Start at the lower right.)

c. Write the product. (Read from top left to bottom right.)

Practice

Use lattice multiplication to find the product.

1.
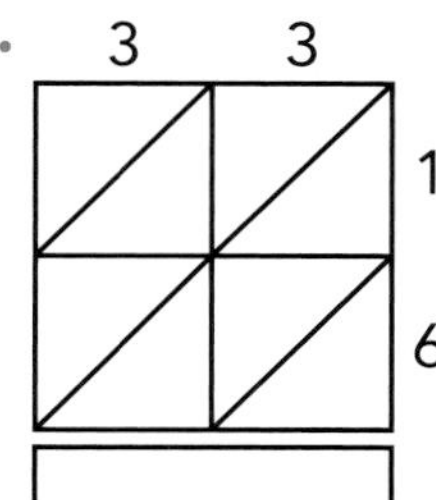

3.
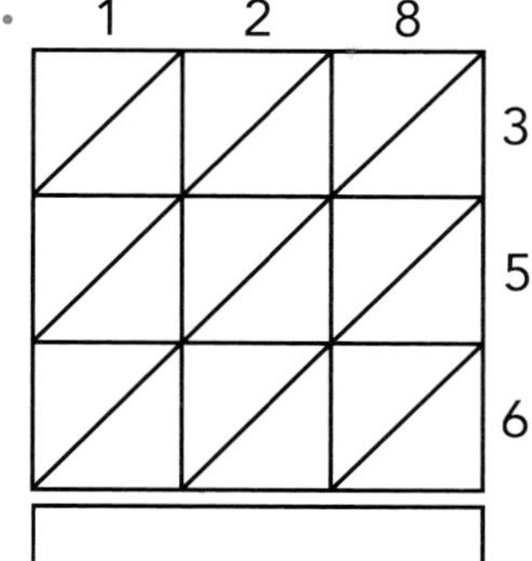

5.
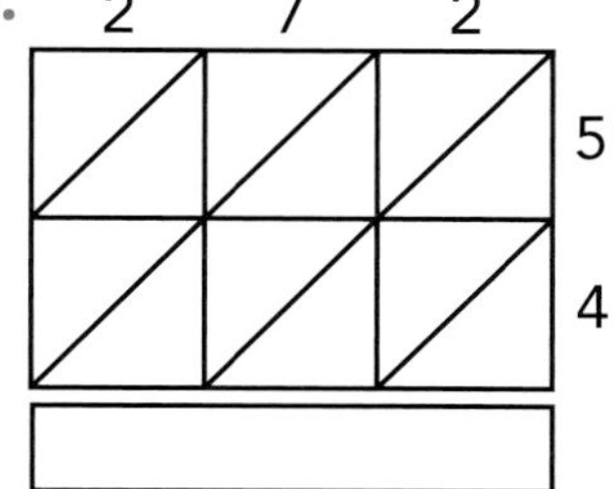

2.
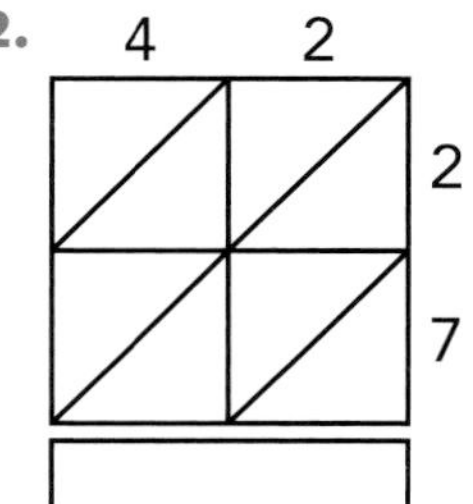

4.
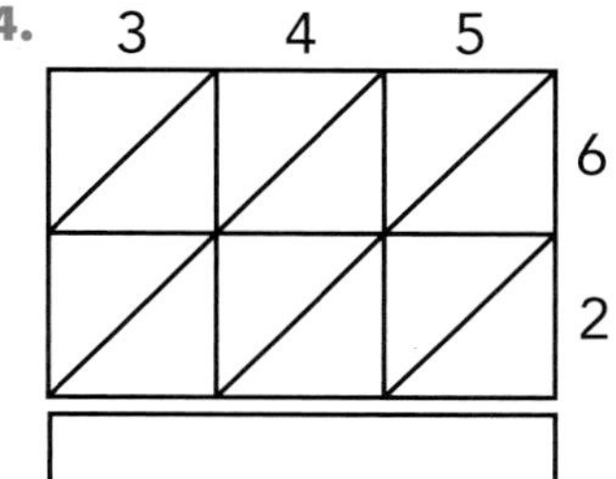

6.
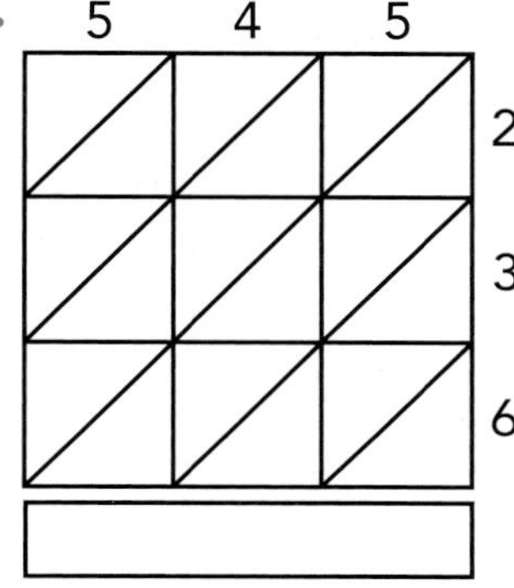

7. 84 × 44
8. 72 × 99

9. 120 × 619
10. 651 × 477

11. 19 × 66
12. 58 × 236

Review

13. Write the next four numbers in the pattern: 3, 3, 6, 9, 15, ___, ___, ___, ___

14. Round 358,789,235 to the nearest hundred million.

15. Find the Least Common Multiple for 7 and 28.

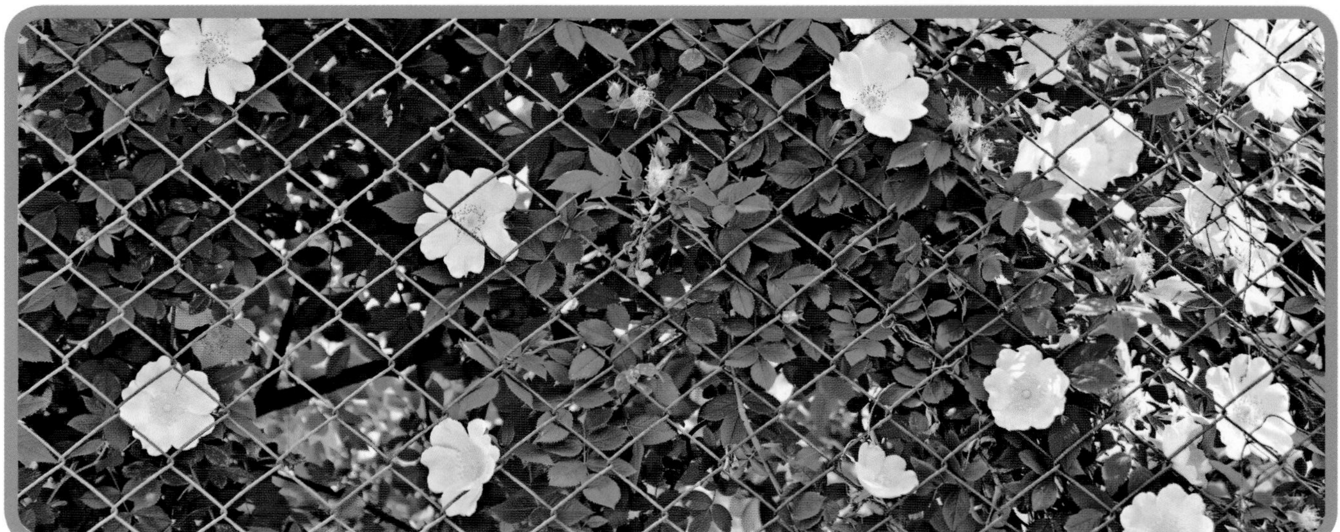

3.15 Chapter 3 Review

Find the product.

1. $\begin{array}{r} 75 \\ \times \;\; 8 \\ \hline \end{array}$
2. $\begin{array}{r} 49 \\ \times 63 \\ \hline \end{array}$
3. $\begin{array}{r} 55 \\ \times 98 \\ \hline \end{array}$
4. $\begin{array}{r} 687 \\ \times \;\; 26 \\ \hline \end{array}$
5. $\begin{array}{r} 354 \\ \times \;\; 79 \\ \hline \end{array}$
6. $\begin{array}{r} 262 \\ \times \;\; 45 \\ \hline \end{array}$
7. $\begin{array}{r} 891 \\ \times 765 \\ \hline \end{array}$
8. $\begin{array}{r} 4,328 \\ \times \;\;\;\; 33 \\ \hline \end{array}$
9. $\begin{array}{r} 539 \\ \times 644 \\ \hline \end{array}$
10. $\begin{array}{r} 7,870 \\ \times \;\;\; 141 \\ \hline \end{array}$
11. $\begin{array}{r} 476 \\ \times 295 \\ \hline \end{array}$
12. $\begin{array}{r} 5,820 \\ \times \;\;\;\; 36 \\ \hline \end{array}$

Use mental math to find the product.

13. 800 × 4,000
14. 900 × 12,000
15. 5,000 × 110
16. 80 × 30,000

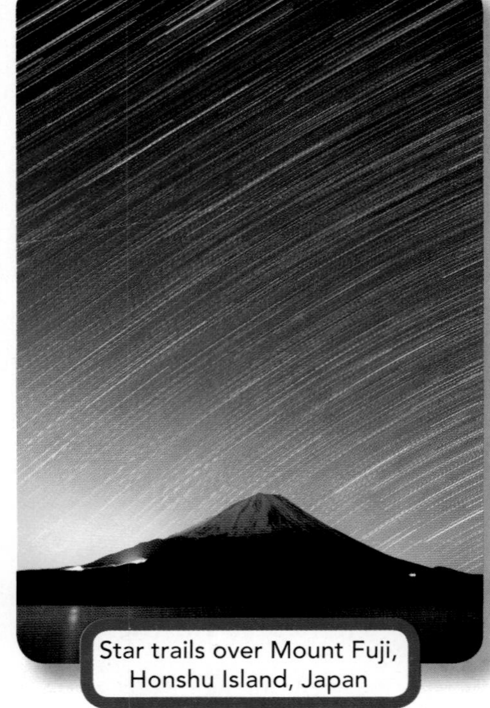

Star trails over Mount Fuji, Honshu Island, Japan

Write the letter of the equivalent equation.

17. 42 × (18 + 69) =
   a. (42 + 18) × 69
   b. (42 × 18) + (42 × 69)
   c. (42 × 18) × (42 × 69)

18. 15 × (850 × 5) =
   a. (15 × 850) × 5
   b. (15 + 850) × 5
   c. 15 + 850 + 5

Solve.

19. Marsha was using a calculator. She had written 27, 36, 45, 54, 63 on her paper. What was she looking for?
   a. factors of 9
   b. multiples of 9
   c. multiples of 7

Find the Least Common Multiple for each pair of numbers.

20. 4 and 3
21. 5 and 8
22. 6 and 9
23. 7 and 12

24. Susana's brother is working to help pay his college tuition. He makes $8 an hour and works 15 hours per week. He also receives $175 a month for helping coach track at the high school. What are his total earnings for one month?

Estimate the product using front-end digits.

25. 46×57

26. 92×39

27. 55×40

28. 81×61

29. 33×28

Estimate the product by rounding both factors to the greatest place value.

30. 482×56

31. $5{,}621 \times 29$

32. 843×81

33. $2{,}650 \times 39$

34. 999×71

35. Isadora decided to read her entire Bible in one year. She thought she could read about 3 pages a day. Her Bible has 1,045 pages. Can she complete reading the Bible in one year? Could she take off one day a week and finish within one year? Explain your answer.

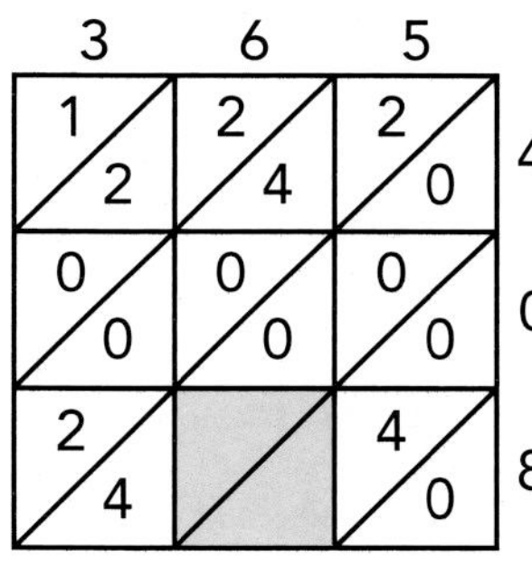

36. What are the missing numbers on the lattice? Use the lattice to find the product of 365 × 408.

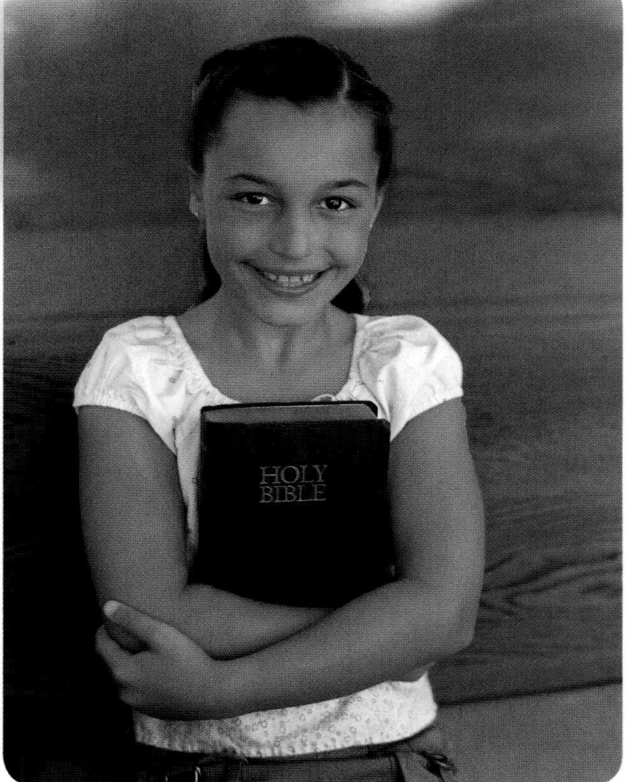

37. Kathryn is making a tile mosaic for an art project at school. It will be 12 in. by 18 in. The tiles are available in the following sizes: 2 in., 3 in., 4 in., and 5 in. The project requires that all the tiles in the mosaic be the same size. Which sizes of tile will work on her mosaic? What is the largest tile she could use?

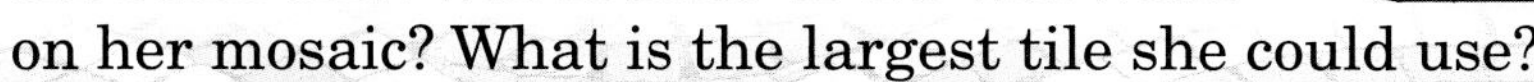

Chapter 4
1-Digit Divisors

Those who are wise will shine like the brightness of the heavens, and those who lead many to righteousness, like the stars for ever and ever.
Daniel 12:3

Key Ideas:

Division: finding averages

Division: dividing five-digit numbers by one-digit divisors

Division: rules of divisibility

Division: two-digit quotients

4.1 Explore Divisibility

Construct Meaning

Mr. Fortini hosts a space camp for fifth-grade students. He wants to divide the students into groups of five. On the first day, 65 students attended the camp. How many groups could Mr. Fortini form?

How many groups of five are in 65?
Use Base 10 blocks to find the answer.

5)65

There are 13 groups of five in 65. Mr. Fortini could form 13 groups.

Check by multiplying. $13 \times 5 = 65$

A number is divisible by another number if it can be divided evenly by that number with no remainder. You can use the rules of divisibility listed below to find whether a number is divisible by another number.

Is 65 divisible by 5?

A number is divisible by 5 if the digit in the ones place is 0 or 5.

Look at the number in the ones place. (tens | ones: 5)6|5)
The digit in the ones place is 5.
There is no remainder, so 65 is divisible by 5. ($5\overline{)65}$ = 13)

Rules of Divisibility

2 The digit in the ones place will be an even number. (0, 2, 4, 6, 8)

3 The sum of the digits will be divisible by 3. (15, 30, 45, 57)

5 The digit in the ones place will be 5 or 0. (15, 20, 25, 30)

6 The number will be divisible by both 2 and 3. (12, 18, 24, 36)

9 The sum of the digits will be divisible by 9. (18, 27, 45, 72)

10 The digit in the ones place will be 0. (20, 30, 50, 60)

Check Understanding

Write the number of the model that shows the correct answer.

a. $6\overline{)36}$

b. $4\overline{)32}$

c. $6\overline{)24}$

d. $8\overline{)80}$

1 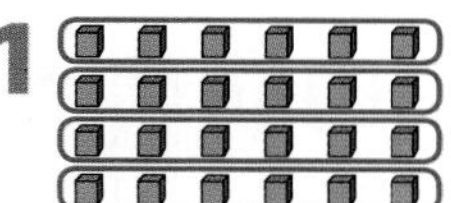

2 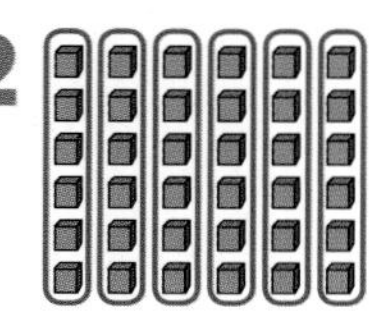

3 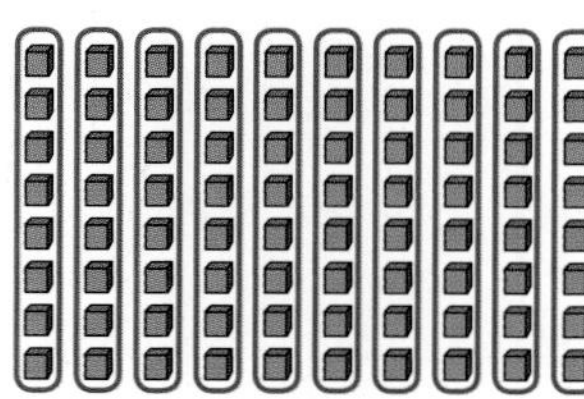

4 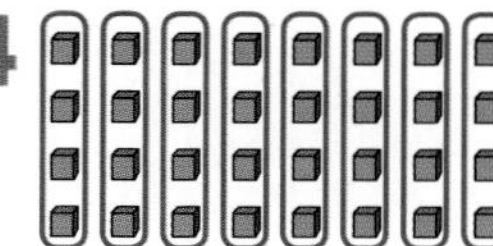

Practice

Write "yes" if the black number is divisible by the orange number. Write "no" if it is not. Use the rules of divisibility to help you.

1. 36 9
2. 24 10
3. 18 3
4. 142 2
5. 54 5
6. 49 6
7. 90 5
8. 700 10
9. 20 3
10. 81 9

Solve. Check by multiplying.

11. $10\overline{)80}$
12. $9\overline{)45}$
13. $5\overline{)60}$
14. $6\overline{)42}$
15. $3\overline{)54}$
16. $2\overline{)96}$
17. $6\overline{)24}$
18. $9\overline{)81}$
19. $10\overline{)110}$
20. $5\overline{)75}$
21. $3\overline{)36}$
22. $2\overline{)48}$
23. $9\overline{)36}$
24. $6\overline{)54}$
25. $2\overline{)44}$

Challenge

By which numbers (2, 3, 5, 6, 9, or 10) is each number divisible?

26. 72
27. 50
28. 78
29. 140
30. 228
31. 45

Review

Write the least common multiple.

32. 2 and 6
33. 3 and 4
34. 3 and 5
35. 4 and 8
36. 3 and 9
37. 5 and 10

4.2 Rules of Division

Construct Meaning

To purchase tickets to the baseball game, Steph, Randy, and Jenna had to save a total of \$36. How much did each ticket cost?

Find $3\overline{)\$36}$. Think: ____ $\times 3 = 36$

$12 \times 3 = 36$, so $36 \div 3 = 12$

The price of each ticket was \$12.

You can write four related multiplication and division sentences using 3, 12, and 36.

$12 \times 3 = 36$	$3 \times 12 = 36$
$36 \div 12 = 3$	$36 \div 3 = 12$

There are three different ways to show division. Each part of a division problem has a name: dividend, divisor, and quotient.

divisor $3\overline{)36}$ dividend, 12 quotient

$36 \div 3 = 12$ (36 dividend, 3 divisor, 12 quotient)

$\frac{36}{3} = 12$ (36 dividend, 3 divisor, 12 quotient)

Every division symbol is read "divided by."

To read $3\overline{)36}$, begin with the number inside the box: "thirty-six divided by three."

To read $36 \div 3$, work from left to right: "thirty-six divided by three."

To read $\frac{36}{3}$, work from top to bottom: "thirty-six divided by three."

At the game, Randy said to his friends, "I can find the quotient for 4,675,892 divided by 1 in one second." Randy knew his division rules. Which rule makes it possible for Randy to find the quotient in one second?

Division Rules to Remember

When any number other than 0 is divided by itself, the quotient will be 1. $9 \div 9 = 1$

When a number is divided by 1, the quotient will be that number. $9 \div 1 = 9$

When zero is divided by any number, the quotient will be 0. $0 \div 9 = 0$

It is impossible to divide by zero! How would you divide \$100 among zero people?

Rule 2 makes it possible for Randy to divide quickly. 4,675,892 ÷ 1 = 4,675,892

Check Understanding

Solve. Label the parts of each problem.

a. $4\overline{)36}$ b. $40 \div 5$ c. $\frac{12}{2}$ d. $6\overline{)48}$

Practice

Solve if possible. Write the number of the division rule you used.

1. $237 \div 0$
2. $360 \div 360$
3. $400 \div 1$
4. $0 \div 50$

Divide.

5. $2\overline{)22}$
6. $5\overline{)15}$
7. $6\overline{)42}$
8. $7\overline{)21}$
9. $4\overline{)16}$
10. $3\overline{)33}$
11. $7\overline{)42}$
12. $9\overline{)27}$
13. $8\overline{)24}$
14. $2\overline{)24}$
15. $36 \div 9$
16. $12 \div 3$
17. $35 \div 7$
18. $70 \div 7$
19. $540 \div 6$
20. $30 \div 3$
21. $32 \div 8$
22. $990 \div 11$
23. $72 \div 12$
24. $0 \div 81$
25. $\frac{45}{5}$
26. $\frac{18}{3}$
27. $\frac{81}{9}$
28. $\frac{72}{8}$
29. $\frac{40}{8}$

Write the related facts for each set of numbers.

30. 6, 9, 54
31. 56, 7, 8
32. 8, 8, 64
33. 9, 63, 7

Apply

34. Madelyn and her dad found 50 golf balls, which she gave away. If she gives an equal number of the golf balls to 10 of her friends, how many will each friend receive?

35. Quentin has 48 marbles. He wants to share them with his three best friends. If Quentin and his friends divide the marbles equally, how many will each boy receive?

Review

36. 204×3
37. 82×6
38. 69×4
39. 42×8
40. 121×2

4.3 Quotients and Remainders

Construct Meaning

The fifth-grade students at Mount Elim Bible Camp are going boating on the river. Before departing, each boat must have three people aboard. If 14 people want to take a ride, how many boats will be needed? Find 14 ÷ 3.

Find the greatest number of 3s in 14.

$3 \times 3 = 9$ too low $3 \times 4 = 12$ close $3 \times 5 = 15$ too high

The greatest number of 3s in 14 is 4.

$$\begin{array}{r} 4 \text{ R2} \\ 3\overline{)14} \\ -12 \\ \hline 2 \end{array}$$

4 R2 quotient; divisor 3; 14 dividend; 2 remainder

Check by multiplying.

$$\begin{array}{r} 4 \\ \times\ 3 \\ \hline 12 \\ +\ 2 \\ \hline 14 \end{array}$$

4 ← quotient; 3 ← divisor; 2 ← remainder; 14 ← dividend

Five boats will be needed to carry 14 people.

Four boats will carry three students each.

The remainder tells you that a fifth boat will be needed.

Large rafts carry nine passengers. How many rafts will be needed for 183 people?

- Divide.
- Multiply.
- Subtract.
- Compare.
- Bring down.

Find 183 ÷ 9.

1 Will the first digit of the quotient be in the hundreds place?

$9\overline{)183}$

No, there are not enough hundreds. 9 > 1

2 Divide the tens.

$$\begin{array}{r} 2 \\ 9\overline{)183} \\ -18 \\ \hline 0 \end{array}$$

Multiply.
Subtract.
Compare. 0 < 9

3 Divide the ones.

$$\begin{array}{r} 20 \text{ R3} \\ 9\overline{)183} \\ -18\downarrow \\ \hline 03 \\ 0 \\ \hline 3 \end{array}$$

Bring down.
Multiply.
Write the remainder.

4 Check by multiplying.

$$\begin{array}{r} 20 \\ \times\ 9 \\ \hline 180 \\ +\ 3 \\ \hline 183 \end{array}$$

There are 20 groups of 9.
The remainder is 3.

Twenty rafts will carry nine passengers each. One additional raft will be used for the remaining three passengers. Twenty-one rafts will be needed.

Check Understanding

Complete.

a. $\begin{array}{r} 4 \text{ R } \_ \\ 8\overline{)34} \\ -32 \\ \hline \end{array}$

b. $\begin{array}{r} \_ \text{ R } \_ \\ 6\overline{)28} \\ -24 \\ \hline \end{array}$

c. $\begin{array}{r} 2\_ \text{ R } \_ \\ 7\overline{)141} \\ -14 \\ \hline \end{array}$

d. $\begin{array}{r} 3\_ \text{ R } \_ \\ 5\overline{)161} \\ -15 \\ \hline \end{array}$

Practice

Divide. Check by multiplying.

1. $6\overline{)44}$
2. $5\overline{)69}$
3. $3\overline{)110}$
4. $2\overline{)175}$
5. $4\overline{)281}$
6. $5\overline{)164}$
7. $9\overline{)211}$
8. $7\overline{)492}$
9. $8\overline{)324}$
10. $3\overline{)124}$

Divide.

11. 162 ÷ 4
12. 89 ÷ 9
13. 76 ÷ 3
14. 122 ÷ 6
15. 380 ÷ 7
16. 430 ÷ 6
17. 131 ÷ 2
18. 332 ÷ 5
19. 510 ÷ 9
20. 321 ÷ 8
21. 132 ÷ 5
22. 289 ÷ 9

Find the quotient.

23. $\frac{37}{5}$
24. $\frac{61}{9}$
25. $\frac{43}{7}$
26. $\frac{440}{9}$
27. $\frac{520}{6}$

Apply

28. Scott, Toby, and Xavier went to a weekend retreat for fathers and sons. A total of 123 people attended the retreat. How many groups of eight can stay in the cabins? How many will make a smaller group?

Review

Write the numbers that are divisible by 8.

29. 36 64 56 16 21 74 32

Write the numbers that are evenly divisible by 7.

30. 50 21 63 15 70 49 44

4.4 Estimate Quotients

Construct Meaning

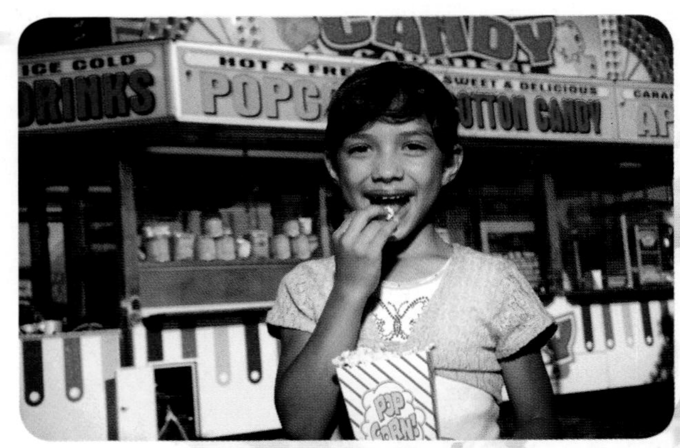

The fifth-grade band students at Harvest Academy hosted a fun fair. Some of the students helped sell popcorn at the concession stand. Maude sold 79 bags of buttered popcorn in four hours. About how many bags of buttered popcorn did she sell per hour?

To estimate the number of bags Maude sold per hour, determine the exact division problem.

$79 \div 4$

Compatible numbers are numbers that can be computed mentally and are near the given numbers. Finding compatible numbers helps you determine the estimated quotient. Find a multiple of 4 that is close to 79.

$4 \times 10 = 40$ too low $4 \times 20 = 80$ close $4 \times 30 = 120$ too high

80 is close to 79, so 80 and 4 are the compatible numbers.

$4\overline{)80}$ = 20

The estimated quotient is 20.
The exact quotient will be less than 20 because 80 > 79.
20 is an overestimate.

Maude sold about 20 bags of buttered popcorn per hour.

Alejandro sold 131 bags of cheddar popcorn in 4 hours.
About how many bags of cheddar popcorn did Alejandro sell per hour? $131 \div 4$
Choose a multiple of 4 that is close to 131.

$4 \times 30 = 120$ $4 \times 40 = 160$

Use $120 \div 4$ as the compatible numbers. The estimated quotient is 30.

$4\overline{)120}$ = 30

The exact quotient will be greater than 30 because 120 < 131.
30 is an underestimate.

Alejandro sold about 30 bags of cheddar popcorn per hour.

Check Understanding

Choose the best estimate. Write "under" or "over" for each estimate.

a. $5\overline{)31}$ b. $3\overline{)149}$ c. $8\overline{)162}$ d. $7\overline{)419}$

50 20 6 60

Practice

Write the letter of the best estimate for each quotient.

1. $4\overline{)250}$	**a.** 70	**b.** 50	**c.** 40	**d.** 60
2. $3\overline{)272}$	**a.** 90	**b.** 70	**c.** 60	**d.** 80
3. $6\overline{)423}$	**a.** 80	**b.** 40	**c.** 70	**d.** 60
4. $7\overline{)200}$	**a.** 20	**b.** 30	**c.** 40	**d.** 70
5. $5\overline{)618}$	**a.** 120	**b.** 130	**c.** 100	**d.** 110
6. $8\overline{)730}$	**a.** 40	**b.** 60	**c.** 70	**d.** 90
7. $9\overline{)350}$	**a.** 30	**b.** 40	**c.** 100	**d.** 70

Estimate. Write "under" or "over" for each estimated quotient.

8. $2\overline{)130}$	10. $5\overline{)390}$	12. $8\overline{)270}$	14. $5\overline{)456}$	16. $8\overline{)170}$
9. $3\overline{)220}$	11. $6\overline{)359}$	13. $4\overline{)430}$	15. $9\overline{)185}$	17. $2\overline{)157}$

Apply

Estimate the answer.

18. Rosette sold 206 pickles in three hours. About how many pickles did she sell per hour?

19. Luke sold 359 cups of lemonade in six hours. About how many cups of lemonade did Luke sell per hour?

Review

Solve.

20. $63 \div 7$ 21. $72 \div 9$ 22. $64 \div 8$ 23. $48 \div 6$

24. Write the numbers that are divisible by 3.

33 22 27 37 9 19

4.5 Divide 2- and 3-Digit Numbers

Construct Meaning

The Vitt family reunion is next weekend. The 42 people attending the reunion will stay in seven cabins. If each cabin holds an equal number, how many people will stay in each cabin?

Draw a picture to show 42 ÷ 7.

$$7\overline{)42} = 6$$

-42 Multiply. Subtract.

0 Compare. 0 < 7

6 people will stay in each cabin.

The cost of each cabin is $396. If six people pay an equal amount for one cabin, how much will each person pay? Divide $396 by six people.

Will the first digit of the quotient be in the hundreds place? $6\overline{)\$396}$ No, there are not enough hundreds. 6 > 3

Divide the tens.

$$\begin{array}{r} \$\ 6 \\ 6\overline{)\$396} \\ -36 \\ \hline 3 \end{array}$$

Multiply. Subtract. Compare. 3 < 6

Divide the ones.

$$\begin{array}{r} \$\ 66 \\ 6\overline{)\$396} \\ -36\downarrow \\ \hline 36 \\ -36 \\ \hline 0 \end{array}$$

Bring down. Multiply. Subtract. Compare. 0 < 6

Multiply to check.

$66 ← quotient
× 6 ← divisor
$396 ← dividend

Each person will pay $66.

Check Understanding

Copy and complete each problem.

a. $5\overline{)75}$ — quotient 1_; -5; 2

b. $2\overline{)96}$ — $-$ ___

c. $4\overline{)324}$ — quotient 8_; -32

d. $7\overline{)637}$ — $-$ ___

e. $9\overline{)594}$ — $-$ ___

Practice

Divide. Check by multiplying.

1. $2\overline{)94}$
2. $4\overline{)88}$
3. $3\overline{)57}$
4. $5\overline{)80}$
5. $6\overline{)78}$
6. $9\overline{)459}$
7. $6\overline{)264}$
8. $2\overline{)796}$
9. $3\overline{)369}$
10. $8\overline{)968}$

Divide.

11. $72 \div 6$
12. $56 \div 2$
13. $81 \div 3$
14. $132 \div 6$
15. $125 \div 5$
16. $176 \div 8$
17. $252 \div 7$
18. $138 \div 6$

Divide.

19. $5\overline{)31}$
20. $7\overline{)46}$
21. $8\overline{)99}$
22. $7\overline{)56}$
23. $6\overline{)156}$
24. $9\overline{)563}$
25. $2\overline{)468}$
26. $3\overline{)478}$
27. $4\overline{)589}$
28. $5\overline{)697}$
29. $8\overline{)963}$
30. $6\overline{)546}$

Apply

31. Ashleigh and Skyler grow lilies in their pond. They sold nine plants for a total of $36. If each plant cost an equal amount, what was the price of one plant?

32. They sold a total of 312 plants in six days. If they sold an equal number each day, how many plants did they sell per day?

Review

33. $34{,}628 - 22{,}819$
34. $3{,}892 - 904$
35. $5{,}768 - 3{,}979$
36. $56{,}934 - 9{,}845$
37. $167{,}284 - 38{,}395$
38. 67,146 – 66,835
39. 7,031 – 5,008
40. 300,002 – 175,934

4.6 Find Averages

Construct Meaning

Have you ever seen a shooting star? Shooting stars are meteors, pieces of rock or metal that produce bright streaks of light as they pass through the earth's atmosphere.

Ron and Diane counted the shooting stars they saw in one month. During the first week, they saw 27 meteors. The second week, they saw 21, the third week, 30, and the fourth week, 38. What was the average number of meteors, or shooting stars, they counted each week?

The average, also called the mean, can be found by adding the number of shooting stars they saw each week and dividing the sum by the number of addends.

Add the numbers.

Week 1	27
Week 2	21
Week 3	30
Week 4	+ 38
	116

Divide the sum by the number of addends.

$$\begin{array}{r} 29 \\ 4\overline{)116} \\ -\ 8 \\ \hline 36 \\ -\ 36 \\ \hline 0 \end{array}$$

Ron and Diane saw an average of 29 shooting stars per week.

The difference between the greatest number and the least number in a set of numerical data is the range. The numbers in the chart are the data. The greatest number is 38; the least number is 21. The difference, 17, is the range of this set of numbers.

Check Understanding

Find the average, or mean, of each set of numbers.

a. 30 46 54 65 10

b. 72 89 272 193 32 44 152

c. 223 66 123 56 25 200 35 40

Practice

Find the average, or mean, of each set of numbers.

1. 126 254 331
2. 260 177 422 105
3. 47 208 144 230 36 325
4. 327 103 255 220 90
5. 75 77 28 56 106 10 75

Find the average of each set of numbers.

6. 105 153 144 110 104 112 120 128
7. 248 177 251 124 150
8. 125 143 102 189 140 147
9. 352 280 367
10. 123 140 204 113 107 118 112

Use a calculator to find the average and the range of each set of numbers.

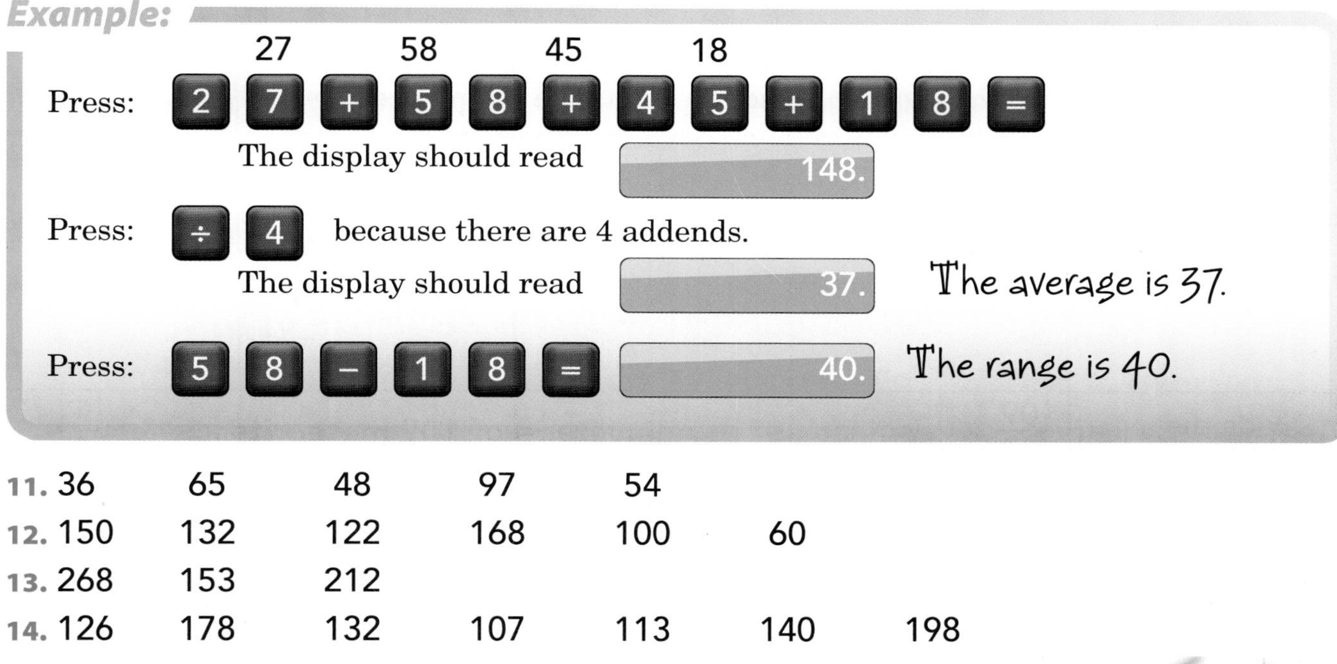

Example:

27 58 45 18

Press: 2 7 + 5 8 + 4 5 + 1 8 =

The display should read 148.

Press: ÷ 4 because there are 4 addends.

The display should read 37. The average is 37.

Press: 5 8 − 1 8 = 40. The range is 40.

11. 36 65 48 97 54
12. 150 132 122 168 100 60
13. 268 153 212
14. 126 178 132 107 113 140 198

Apply

Use pencil and paper or a calculator to find the average. Write the method you used.

15. Omar and Lori spent the afternoon hiking a nature trail. They spotted 56 birds the first hour, 45 birds the second hour, and 22 the third hour. What was the average number of birds they saw in an hour?

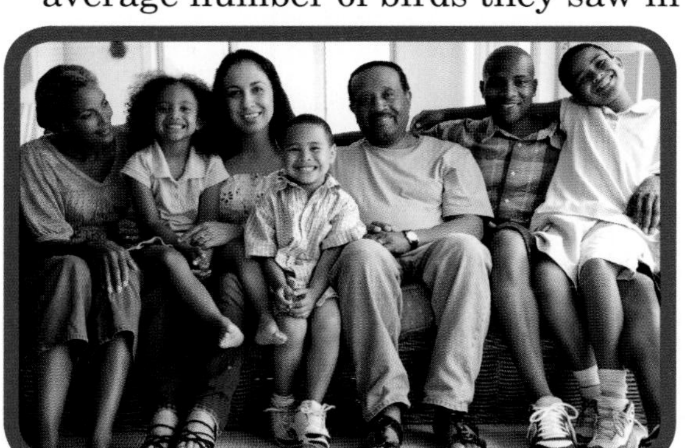

16. Brantley, Hailey, and Ian drove to their grandparents' home in Virginia. They traveled 388 miles the first day and 600 miles the second day. What was the average number of miles they drove per day?

4.7 Zero in the Quotient

Construct Meaning

Did you know that bits of the solar system fall to Earth every day? Chunks of metallic or stony matter that survive a fiery fall through the earth's atmosphere and reach the earth's surface are called meteorites.

If 436 meteorites were to hit the earth in 4 years, what would be the average number in one year?

Estimate the quotient to help find the answer. $4 \times 100 = 400$.
The quotient should be close to 100. Divide to find the exact quotient.

$436 \div 4$
↓ ↓
$400 \div 4$

Divide the hundreds. $4 \div 4 = 1$ $\begin{array}{r} 1 \\ 4\overline{)436} \\ -4 \\ \hline 03 \end{array}$ Multiply. Subtract. Compare. 0 < 4 Bring down the tens.	Divide the tens. There are not enough tens. Write a 0 in the quotient. $\begin{array}{r} 10 \\ 4\overline{)436} \\ -4 \\ \hline 03 \\ -\ 0 \\ \hline 36 \end{array}$ 36 Bring down the ones.
Divide the ones. $36 \div 4 = 9$ $\begin{array}{r} 109 \\ 4\overline{)436} \\ -4 \\ \hline 03 \\ -\ 0 \\ \hline 36 \\ -36 \\ \hline 0 \end{array}$ Multiply. Subtract.	**An average of 109 meteorites would hit the earth in one year.**

Check Understanding

Copy and complete each problem.

a. $\begin{array}{r} 10 \\ 5\overline{)525} \end{array}$

b. $\begin{array}{r} 10 \\ 3\overline{)329} \end{array}$ R

c. $\begin{array}{r} 1 \\ 6\overline{)642} \end{array}$

d. $\begin{array}{r} 1 \\ 8\overline{)852} \end{array}$ R

Practice

Write the letter of the correct quotient.

1. $7\overline{)743}$	**a.** 107 R2	**b.** 106 R1	**c.** 104	**d.** 102
2. $9\overline{)986}$	**a.** 108 R2	**b.** 108	**c.** 109 R5	**d.** 107
3. $4\overline{)422}$	**a.** 105 R2	**b.** 104 R1	**c.** 106 R2	**d.** 107 R3
4. $6\overline{)654}$	**a.** 110	**b.** 109	**c.** 103	**d.** 140

Find the quotient.

5. $7\overline{)707}$
6. $4\overline{)429}$
7. $3\overline{)319}$
8. $2\overline{)212}$
9. $6\overline{)652}$
10. $9\overline{)987}$
11. $8\overline{)864}$
12. $5\overline{)510}$
13. $4\overline{)416}$
14. $7\overline{)714}$
15. $3\overline{)301}$
16. $6\overline{)647}$

17. 876 ÷ 8
18. 924 ÷ 9
19. 535 ÷ 5
20. 411 ÷ 4
21. 754 ÷ 7
22. 327 ÷ 3

Divide. Check by multiplying.

23. 540 ÷ 5
24. 206 ÷ 2
25. 831 ÷ 8
26. 946 ÷ 9
27. 402 ÷ 4
28. 318 ÷ 3

Apply

29. The fifth-grade students at Lake Hills Christian School raised money for a mission trip to Mexico by selling tickets to a school play. Three classes had a total of 312 tickets to sell. If each class had the same number of tickets, how many did one class receive?

30. The fifth-grade students earned $468 from ticket sales. If the play was performed four times, how much money did they earn from each performance?

Review

Use mental math to solve. Remember to first solve inside the parentheses.

31. 45 ÷ 9
32. 50 ÷ 5
33. 66 ÷ 6
34. (56 ÷ 8) × 4
35. (49 ÷ 7) × 6
36. 5 × (35 ÷ 5)
37. 8 × (81 ÷ 9)
38. (12 ÷ 2) × 9
39. (36 ÷ 4) × 3

4.8 Divide Larger Numbers

Construct Meaning

When a large meteorite strikes the earth, a huge crater forms. Meteor Crater near Winslow, Arizona, is 550 ft deep and over 5,000 ft across. Scientists believe that an iron-nickel meteorite 150 ft in diameter struck Earth at 40,000 mph to cause this crater. If you ride your bike 7 mph, how many times faster did the meteorite travel?

40,000 miles per hour ÷ 7 miles per hour

Estimate the quotient of 40,000 miles per hour ÷ 7 miles per hour.

Use a basic fact close to these numbers: 42,000 ÷ 7 = 6,000.

The meteorite traveled about 6,000 times faster.

Because $42{,}000 > 40{,}000$, so 6,000 is an overestimate.

Find the exact quotient.

Will the first digit in the quotient be in the ten thousands place?

```
7)40,000
```

No, $4 < 7$.

Divide the thousands.

Think: 7 × 5 is close to 40, without going over.

```
   5
7)40,000
 -35        Multiply.
  ---       Subtract.
   5        Compare. 5 < 7
```

Divide the hundreds.

Think: 7 × 7 is close to 50, without going over.

```
   5 7
7)40,000
 -35↓
  ---
   5 0      Bring down the hundreds.
  -4 9      Multiply.
  ----      Subtract.
     1      Compare. 1 < 7
```

Divide the tens.

Think: 7 × 1 is close to 10, without going over.

```
   5 71
7)40,000
 -35
  ---
   5 0
  -4 9↓
  ----
     10     Bring down the hundreds.
   -  7     Multiply.
   ----     Subtract.
      3     Compare. 3 < 7
```

Divide the ones.

Think: 7 × 4 is close to 30, without going over.

```
   5 714 R2
7)40,000
 -35
  ---
   5 0
  -4 9
  ----
     10
   -  7↓
   ----
      30
     -28
     ---
       2
```

The meteorite traveled about 5,714 times faster.

Check by multiplying.

```
   5,714 ← quotient
 ×     7 ← divisor
  ------
  39 998
+      2 ← remainder
  ------
  40,000 ← dividend
```

Check Understanding

Copy each problem. Write only the first digit of the quotient in the correct place.

Example:

$$\begin{array}{r} 6 \\ 6\overline{)37,318} \end{array}$$

a. $8\overline{)1,624}$ b. $5\overline{)45,555}$ c. $9\overline{)18,290}$ d. $3\overline{)21,500}$

Practice

Divide. Multiply to check.

1. $4\overline{)1,200}$
2. $2\overline{)2,600}$
3. $7\overline{)2,800}$
4. $4\overline{)3,456}$
5. $9\overline{)6,934}$
6. $6\overline{)5,246}$
7. $4\overline{)1,425}$
8. $2\overline{)7,834}$
9. $8\overline{)48,254}$
10. $7\overline{)64,318}$
11. $3\overline{)27,988}$
12. $5\overline{)25,789}$

Find the quotient.

13. 67,428 ÷ 2
14. 78,565 ÷ 5
15. 38,422 ÷ 4
16. 45,727 ÷ 3
17. 97,516 ÷ 8
18. 56,488 ÷ 7
19. 23,152 ÷ 6
20. 17,369 ÷ 4
21. 82,360 ÷ 9

Review

Find the product.

22. 62 × 73
23. 471 × 653
24. 3,245 × 14

Find the sum.

25. 647 + 745 + 893
26. 1,256 + 3,578 + 701
27. 4,208 + 3,551 + 2,001

Find the quotient.

28. 834 ÷ 9
29. 643 ÷ 3
30. 520 ÷ 5

A crater formed by the collapse of a volcano is called a caldera. This is a picture of Crater Lake, a caldera formed by the eruption and collapse of Mount Mazama. Crater Lake is about 1,932 ft deep, making it the deepest lake in the United States and the seventh deepest lake in the world.

4.9 Problem Solving: 1-Digit Divisors

Construct Meaning

Jill's family has an apple orchard. Each year Jill and her friends help harvest the apples by placing them into produce crates. On Saturday, they picked 173 apples. Jill's dad asked them to distribute an equal number of apples into 8 crates. How many apples were placed in each crate?

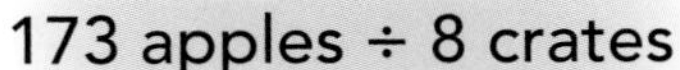

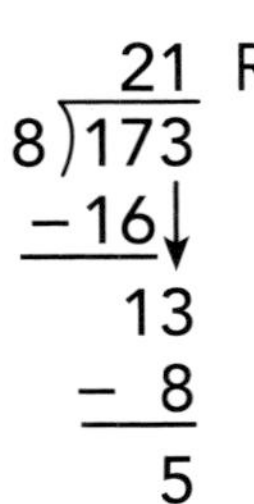

Jill and her friends placed 21 apples into each crate.

What should happen to the remainder?
When solving a word problem that has a remainder, there are 3 choices:

- Round the quotient to the next higher number.
- Drop the remainder.
- Use the remainder as your answer.

Since there were not enough apples for each box to get another apple, the remainder was dropped.

Check Understanding

Solve the problem. Decide if you should round the quotient to the next higher number, drop the remainder, or use the remainder as the answer. Write the correct answer.

a. Nate's family is making gift baskets for the fifth-grade teachers. They have 150 stickers to divide equally into four baskets. How many stickers will be placed in each basket?

b. Tatum's class is having a pool party. The students will ride in cars to the pool. There are 28 students in her class. If each car carries no more than five, how many cars will be needed?

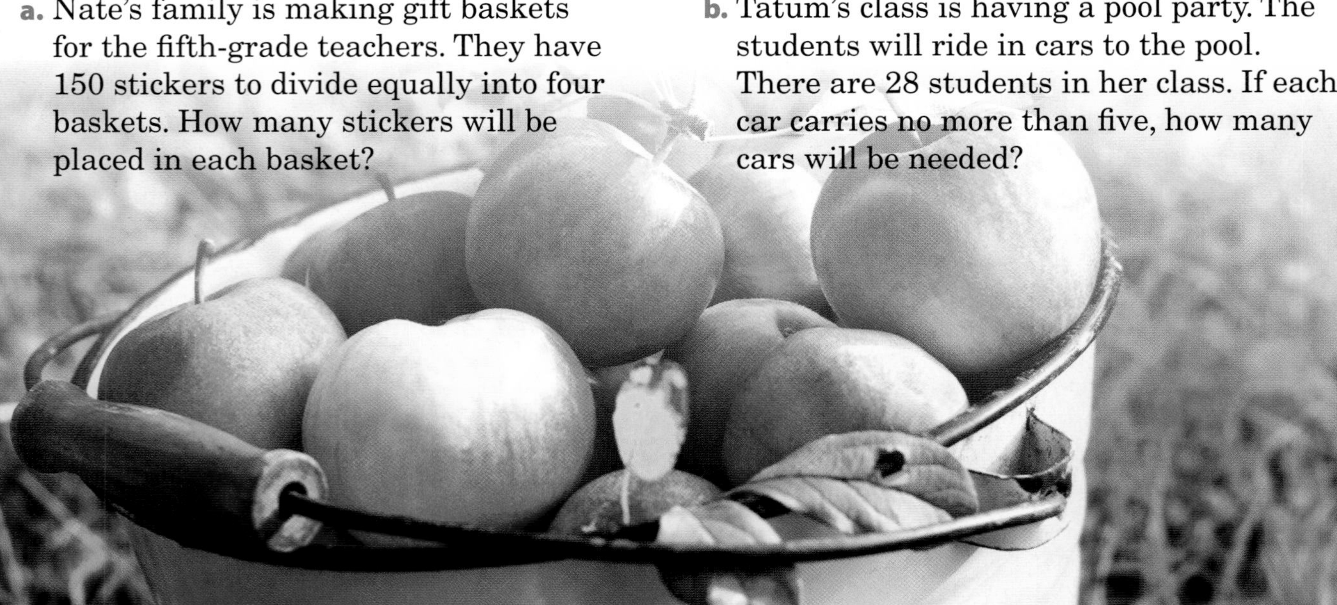

Practice

Write the quotient. Explain how you used the remainder.

1. Micah's class cut 230 sunflowers to give to nine nursing homes. Each home will receive the same number of flowers. Micah and his classmates will be able to keep the extra flowers for their room. How many sunflowers will they keep?

2. Claudia's fifth-grade class is helping the kindergarten students sharpen and organize their pencils. Each pencil basket may contain no more than nine pencils. If there are 58 pencils, how many baskets will they need?

Solve.

3. Morgan and Jamal work at a balloon shop. They fill helium balloons for birthday parties. On Monday, they filled 122 balloons. Tuesday, they filled 153, and on Wednesday they filled 121. What was the average number of balloons they filled each day?

4. At the balloon shop, Morgan and Jamal need to separate 1,899 balloons into 9 groups. How many balloons will be in each group?

5. They inflated 147 balloons for seven parties. If the balloons are divided equally among the parties, how many will be at each party?

Challenge

room accessories		bedding		cooking		personal	
desk lamp	$11	pillow	$10	mini fridge	$108	hair dryer	$26
bulletin board	$11	sheet set	$28	dishes	$32	shower basket	$14
poster	$9	comforter	$45	can opener	$13	laundry bag	$8
shoe storage	$15	throw blanket	$19	microwave	$45	backpack	$49
bookshelf	$15	sleep mask	$9	electric kettle	$23	bath towel	$9

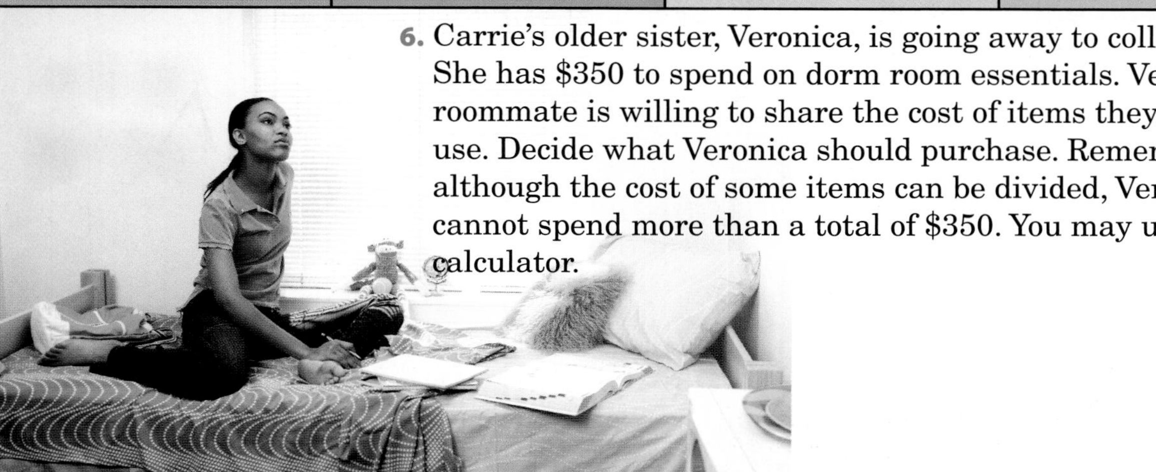

6. Carrie's older sister, Veronica, is going away to college. She has $350 to spend on dorm room essentials. Veronica's roommate is willing to share the cost of items they can both use. Decide what Veronica should purchase. Remember that although the cost of some items can be divided, Veronica cannot spend more than a total of $350. You may use a calculator.

4.10 Chapter 4 Review

1. Which group of numbers is evenly divisible by 5? Write the letter.

   a. 22, 26, 41, 53 **b.** 15, 20, 45, 30 **c.** 62, 74, 86, 98

2. List five numbers evenly divisible by 2.

Write the letter of the correct quotient.

3. $36 \div 4$
   a. 9
   b. 6
   c. 7

4. $42 \div 6$
   a. 8
   b. 9
   c. 7

5. $63 \div 7$
   a. 6
   b. 9
   c. 8

Estimate the quotient by using compatible numbers.

6. $359 \div 4$
7. $640 \div 9$
8. $367 \div 6$
9. $507 \div 5$

Find the average for each set of numbers.

10.	21	36	12	44	32	
11.	56	14	72	99	10	25
12.	110	235	150	484	121	
13.	266	454	164	388		

Complete each problem.

14. $9\overline{)5{,}428}$
15. $6\overline{)33{,}231}$

Write the letter of the correct quotient.

16. 639 ÷ 7
  a. 92
  b. 91 R2
  c. 92 R2
  d. 93 R1

17. 462 ÷ 5
  a. 91 R2
  b. 93 R1
  c. 92 R2
  d. 94 R4

18. 1,347 ÷ 7
  a. 192 R3
  b. 193 R2
  c. 190 R4
  d. 191 R5

Find the quotient. Check by multiplying.

19. $3\overline{)339}$ 20. $7\overline{)21{,}430}$ 21. $9\overline{)1{,}314}$ 22. $5\overline{)29{,}347}$

23. Show three different ways to write division problems. Label each part as "dividend," "divisor," or "quotient."

24. Trinity's family visited relatives for a week. They drove 639 mi in two days. About how many miles did they drive each day?

25. Trinity's cousin had to drive 963 mi to visit. If he drove an equal number of miles in each of the three days, how many miles did he drive in one day?

Chapter 5
2-Digit Divisors

The heavens declare the glory of God; the skies proclaim the work of His hands.
Psalm 19:1

Key Ideas:

Division: dividing whole numbers by two-digit divisors

Patterns: identifying sequences

Division: dividing five-digit numbers by two-digit divisors

Division: estimating quotients for problems that have two-digit divisors

5.1 Division Patterns

Construct Meaning

Travis and his friends planned a pizza lunch for the World Impact Mission Conference. The pizzas were cut into a total of 240 slices. Each person was given a plate with an equal number of slices. If 80 people were fed, how many slices of pizza did each person receive?

240 ÷ 80

1. Think of the basic multiplication facts. Observe the pattern.

8 × 3 = 24
80 × 3 = 240
800 × 3 = 2,400

2. Remember that division is the inverse operation. Use basic division facts to find larger quotients.

24 ÷ 8 = 3
240 ÷ 80 = 3
2,400 ÷ 80 = 30

Each person received 3 slices of pizza.

Here are some examples of division patterns.

54 ÷ 9 = 6	49 ÷ 7 = 7	400 ÷ 50 = 8	240 ÷ 60 = 4
540 ÷ 90 = 6	490 ÷ 70 = 7	4,000 ÷ 50 = 80	2,400 ÷ 60 = 40
5,400 ÷ 90 = 60	4,900 ÷ 70 = 70	40,000 ÷ 50 = 800	24,000 ÷ 60 = 400

Check Understanding

Copy and complete each division pattern.

a. 16 ÷ 4 = 4
160 ÷ 40 = ____
1,600 ÷ 40 = ____

b. 32 ÷ 8 = ____
320 ÷ 80 = ____
3,200 ÷ ____ = 40

c. 360 ÷ 60 = ____
____ ÷ 60 = 60
36,000 ÷ ____ = 600

Use mental math to find the quotient.

d. 450 ÷ 50 **e.** 8,100 ÷ 90 **f.** 3,500 ÷ 70 **g.** 18,000 ÷ 60

Practice

Copy the chart. Write the missing numbers to complete the division pattern.

Example: 420 ÷ 70 = 42 tens ÷ 7 tens = →
1. 4,200 ÷ 70 = 42 hundreds ÷ 7 tens = ____ →
2. 42,000 ÷ 70 = 42 thousands ÷ 7 tens = ____ →
3. 420,000 ÷ 70 = 42 ten thousands ÷ 7 tens = ____ →

thousands,	hundreds	tens	ones
			6

Find the quotient.

Example:

$$20\overline{)600}$$ = 30

4. $40\overline{)800}$
5. $30\overline{)900}$
6. $70\overline{)140}$
7. $20\overline{)160}$
8. $50\overline{)200}$
9. $90\overline{)360}$
10. $60\overline{)420}$
11. $80\overline{)560}$

Example:

$$30\overline{)1,200}$$ = 40

12. $40\overline{)2,400}$
13. $90\overline{)5,400}$
14. $70\overline{)2,800}$
15. $50\overline{)4,500}$
16. $30\overline{)2,100}$
17. $20\overline{)4,000}$

Example:

$$50\overline{)40,000}$$ = 800

18. $30\overline{)15,000}$
19. $70\overline{)35,000}$
20. $60\overline{)12,000}$
21. $40\overline{)32,000}$
22. $50\overline{)20,000}$
23. $80\overline{)48,000}$

24. 63,000 ÷ 70
25. 40,000 ÷ 80
26. 45,000 ÷ 90
27. 24,000 ÷ 60
28. 21,000 ÷ 70
29. 30,000 ÷ 50

Challenge

Complete the sequence.

30. 8,500,000,000; 85,000,000; 850,000; ____; ____

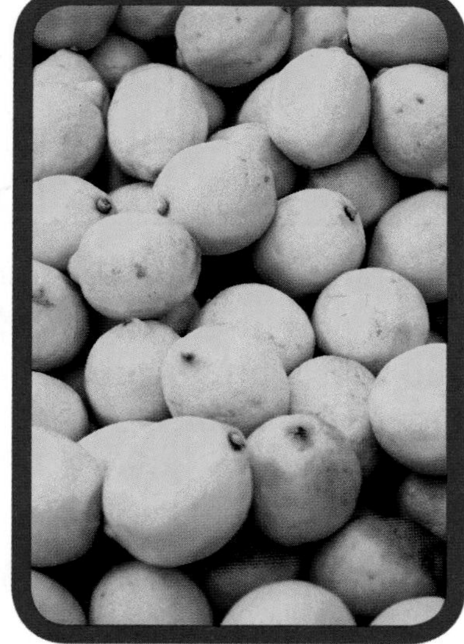

Apply

31. Over a 30-day period, 60,000 people attended the fair. If an equal number of people attended the fair each day, how many attended in one day?

32. During the 70 days of the fair, 14,000 cups of lemonade were sold. What was the average number of cups sold each day?

Review

Multiply.

33. 27×3
34. 482×24
35. 971×87
36. $4,050 \times 9$

Solve.

37. $8.6 + 9.4$
38. $5.33 - 4.63$
39. $84.12 + 9.39$
40. $3.6 - 2.72$

5.2 Estimate Quotients

Construct Meaning

Since bananas are a favorite fruit of many people, the fifth-grade classes decided to conduct a survey to find out how many pounds of bananas their friends and family members ate in one year. If 60 people ate 1,980 pounds of bananas, about how many pounds were eaten by each person?

1,980 pounds ÷ 60 people

Estimate the quotient to find the approximate number of pounds of bananas that one person ate.

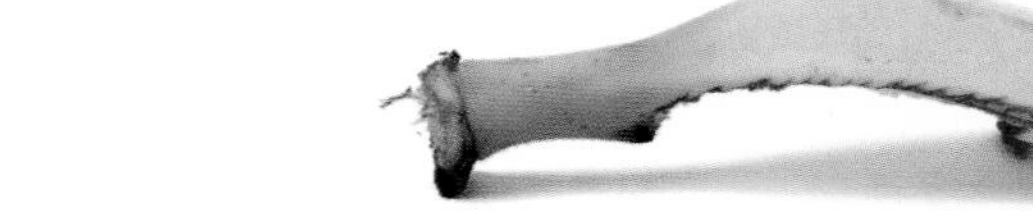

Find compatible numbers.

$$1{,}980 \div 60 \;\rightarrow\; 1{,}800 \div 60$$

Consider the multiplication pattern to help find the quotient.

$60 \times 3 = 180$

$60 \times 30 = 1{,}800$

$60 \times 300 = 18{,}000$

Divide.

$$\begin{array}{r} 30 \\ 60\overline{)1{,}800} \\ -1\,80 \\ \hline 00 \\ -0 \\ \hline 0 \end{array}$$

Check the estimate.

$$\begin{array}{r} 60 \\ \times\,30 \\ \hline 1{,}800 \end{array}$$

Each person ate about 30 pounds of bananas.

Estimate 3,490 ÷ 48 by finding compatible numbers.

Use the front-end digit of the divisor and substitute the dividend with a compatible number.

$3{,}490 \div 48 \rightarrow 3{,}600 \div 40 = 90$

OR

Round the divisor and substitute the dividend with a compatible number.

$3{,}490 \div 48 \rightarrow 3{,}500 \div 50 = 70$

Which estimate is closer to the actual answer?

Rounding the divisor led to a closer estimate of 70.

Check Understanding

Copy and complete each problem. Use compatible numbers to find the estimated quotient.

a. 2,377 ÷ 65
   2,400 ÷ ____ = 40

b. 5,540 ÷ 92
   ____ ÷ 90 = 60

c. 1,023 ÷ 35
   1,200 ÷ 30 = ____

d. 71,900 ÷ 94
   72,000 ÷ 90 = ____

e. 62,566 ÷ 71
   ____ ÷ 70 = 900

f. 44,023 ÷ 53
   45,000 ÷ ____ = 900

Practice

Write the letter of the best estimate.

1. 1,650 ÷ 43
   a. 1,600 ÷ 40 = 40
   b. 2,000 ÷ 40 = 50
   c. 1,800 ÷ 30 = 60

2. 2,170 ÷ 33
   a. 2,000 ÷ 40 = 50
   b. 2,500 ÷ 50 = 50
   c. 2,100 ÷ 30 = 70

3. 55,000 ÷ 71
   a. 60,000 ÷ 60 = 1,000
   b. 56,000 ÷ 70 = 800
   c. 54,000 ÷ 90 = 600

Use compatible numbers to find the estimated quotient.

4. $41\overline{)2{,}750}$
5. $23\overline{)1{,}890}$
6. $72\overline{)2{,}300}$
7. $92\overline{)8{,}120}$
8. $50\overline{)3{,}600}$
9. $30\overline{)1{,}908}$
10. $62\overline{)3{,}100}$
11. $91\overline{)5{,}320}$
12. $74\overline{)1{,}502}$
13. $47\overline{)1{,}300}$
14. $92\overline{)89{,}200}$
15. $64\overline{)26{,}010}$
16. 6,401 ÷ 82
17. 2,319 ÷ 34
18. 1,260 ÷ 23
19. 56,201 ÷ 84
20. 23,050 ÷ 84

Apply

21. Julieta's Bakery made 2,455 loaves of banana bread in 63 days. About how many loaves did they bake each day?

22. Customers at the bakery ordered 1,390 muffins in 71 days. About how many muffins did they order per day?

23. The bakery sold 1,670 cups of cocoa in 45 days. About how many cups of cocoa did they sell each day?

Review

24. 40×5

25. 132×6

26. 430×30

27. 235×45

28. $5{,}741 \times 70$

29. $2{,}400 \times 40$

30. $3{,}266 \times 55$

31. $4{,}100 \times 10$

5.3 1-Digit Quotients

Construct Meaning

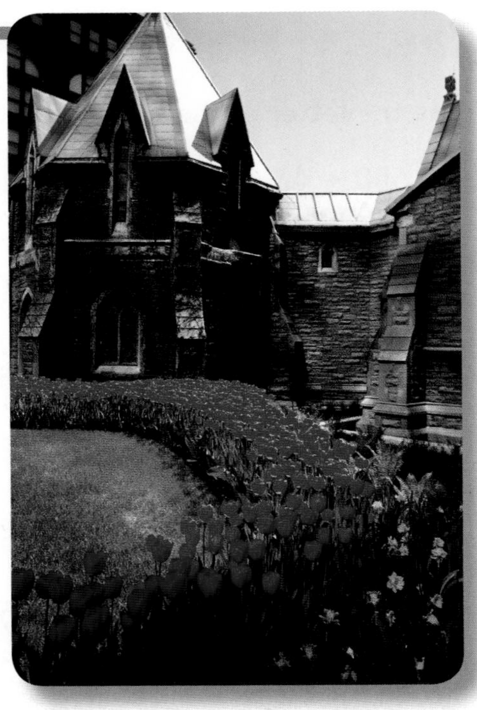

In the fall, Aimee's family helped plant bulbs in the front yard of their church. Thirty-two people planted 288 bulbs. If each person planted an equal number of bulbs, how many did one person plant?

288 bulbs ÷ 32 people

Use front-end digits and compatible numbers to estimate the quotient.

$30 \times 8 = 240$ (too low)
$30 \times 9 = 270$ (close)
$30 \times 10 = 300$ (too high)

Since 270 is close to 288, use 9 as the estimated quotient.

Divide. $32\overline{)288}$ = 9; -288; 0

Check. $32 \times 9 = 288$

Each person planted 9 bulbs.

What if the 32 people had planted 224 bulbs? If each person planted an equal number of bulbs, how many would one person have planted?

224 bulbs ÷ 32 people

Find the estimated quotient. $210 \div 30 = 7$ $240 \div 30 = 8$

Because 240 > 224, 8 is an overestimate. Instead of using 8 as the quotient, try the next lower number, 7.

Divide. $32\overline{)224}$ = 7; -224; 0

Check. $32 \times 7 = 224$

Each person planted 7 bulbs.

Check Understanding

Write the correct quotient.

a. $18\overline{)144}$
- 9
- 8
- 7 R9

b. $62\overline{)558}$
- 7
- 8 R3
- 9

c. $38\overline{)345}$
- 9 R3
- 6 R2
- 5

d. $55\overline{)228}$
- 5 R6
- 6
- 4 R8

Practice

Estimate.

1. $24\overline{)68}$
2. $46\overline{)79}$
3. $21\overline{)82}$
4. $33\overline{)89}$
5. $44\overline{)92}$
6. $12\overline{)39}$
7. $55\overline{)308}$
8. $65\overline{)223}$

Write your estimate. Then, find the quotient.

9. $78\overline{)457}$
10. $68\overline{)273}$
11. $32\overline{)81}$
12. $559 \div 93$
13. $255 \div 83$
14. $394 \div 78$

Divide. Multiply to check your answer.

15. $515 \div 73$
16. $419 \div 78$
17. $39\overline{)166}$
18. $18\overline{)169}$

Divide.

19. $53\overline{)449}$
20. $47\overline{)326}$
21. $27\overline{)240}$
22. $91\overline{)811}$
23. $33\overline{)200}$
24. $64\overline{)498}$
25. $75\overline{)250}$
26. $83\overline{)125}$

Apply

27. Kazuo brought 135 balloons for the school celebration. If 45 balloons were in each package, how many packages did he bring?

28. Lindsey folded brightly colored napkins for the celebration. If she folded 130 napkins in 26 minutes, how many napkins did she fold per minute?

29. Isaac and his friends baked 196 mini-cookies for the celebration. If 98 people each received the same number of cookies, how many would one person have?

Review

Write a multiplication sentence for each product. Do not use 0 or 1 as factors.

30. 88
31. 99
32. 153
33. 576
34. 378

5.4 2-Digit Quotients

Construct Meaning

A comet is a small, celestial body of rock and ice. Most comets follow an elliptical path around the sun. When a comet nears the sun, some of the ice turns into gas. Solar wind blows the gas and dust away, forming a long, luminous tail.

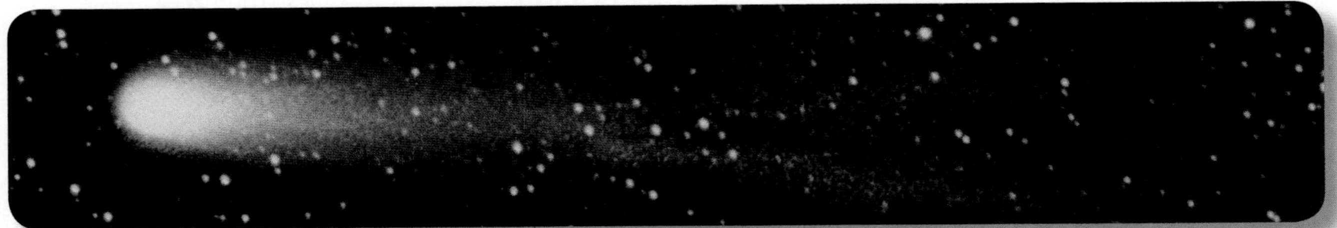

The comet named for astronomer Edmund Halley is visible from the earth every 76 years. How many times would it be seen in 1,748 years?

1,748 ÷ 76 years

First, estimate the quotient. Use compatible numbers.

$1{,}748 \div 76 \rightarrow 1{,}400 \div 70 = 20$

Decide where to place the first digit in the quotient. Since 76 > 17, but 76 < 174, place the 2 in the tens place.

```
      2
 76)1,748
   -1 52
      22
```

Divide.
Multiply.
Subtract.
Compare. 22 < 76

Bring down. Estimate the quotient in the ones place. Use basic facts to help.

$228 \div 76 \rightarrow 210 \div 70 = 3$

Use 3 for the second digit in the quotient.

```
      23
 76)1,748
   -1 52↓
      228
     -228
        0
```

Divide.
Multiply.
Subtract.
Compare. 0 < 76

Check. 76 × 23 = 1,748

Halley's Comet can be seen from Earth 23 times in 1,748 years.

Check Understanding

Write the correct quotient.

a. 23)483

21
21 R5
20

b. 46)1,381

30
30 R1
33 R5

c. 67)4,157

62 R3
60 R4
66

Practice

Copy and complete each problem.

1. $31\overline{)2,759}$ with quotient 8▢; $-2\,48$; 279

3. $25\overline{)1,225}$ with quotient 4▢; $-1\,00$; 225

5. $42\overline{)2,646}$ with quotient ▢3; $-2\,52$; 126

2. $63\overline{)3,529}$ with quotient 5▢ R▢

4. $34\overline{)2,138}$ with quotient ▢2 R▢

6. $74\overline{)7,252}$ with quotient 9▢

Find the quotient. Remember to estimate first.

7. $27\overline{)1,242}$
8. $17\overline{)515}$
9. $41\overline{)867}$
10. $72\overline{)1,730}$
11. $58\overline{)3,659}$
12. $26\overline{)2,419}$
13. 4,929 ÷ 53
14. 1,908 ÷ 36
15. 3,570 ÷ 42
16. 2,527 ÷ 72
17. 3,528 ÷ 86
18. 1,518 ÷ 52

Apply

19. The fifth-grade class was boxing the cans of food that they collected for a local food bank. They had 325 cans of food. If they could fit 25 cans in a box, how many boxes did they need?

20. During the summer, Kayla's older brother mowed lawns to make extra money. He mowed a total of 132 lawns. If he spent 11 weeks mowing lawns, how many lawns did he mow each week?

21. There were 391 children that signed up for swimming lessons. If 17 children attended each swim session, how many swim sessions were there?

Review

22. $3\overline{)218}$
23. $4\overline{)179}$
24. $6\overline{)378}$
25. $9\overline{)136}$
26. $8\overline{)2,356}$
27. $5\overline{)4,505}$

5.5 Adjust Estimated Quotients

Construct Meaning

Asteroids are small, rocky objects that are irregular in shape. All asteroids orbit the sun. Most are found in the asteroid belt, which is a region between Mars and Jupiter. Asteroids are also called minor planets because they are too small to be classified as true planets.

The largest known asteroid, 1 Ceres, has a diameter of nearly 600 miles. If 1 Ceres rotates 46 times in 414 hours, how many hours does it take to complete one rotation on its axis?

414 hours ÷ 46 rotations

Round the divisor and use compatible numbers to estimate the quotient.

$$414 \div 46 \rightarrow 400 \div 50 = 8$$

The estimated quotient is 8 hours.

Divide. Try 8 as the quotient.

$$46\overline{)414}$$ quotient 8; -368 Multiply. Subtract. 46 Compare. $46 = 46$

Because the remainder 46 is equal to the divisor, raise the digit in the quotient to the next higher number, 9.

$$46\overline{)414}$$ quotient 9; -414 Multiply. Subtract. 0 Compare. $0 < 46$

1 Ceres completes one rotation in 9 hours.

If an asteroid rotates 54 times in 378 hours, how long does it take to complete one rotation?

Use compatible numbers to find the estimated quotient.

$$378 \div 54 \rightarrow 400 \div 50 = 8$$

Try 8 as the quotient.

$$54\overline{)378}$$ quotient 8; -432 Multiply. Compare. $432 > 378$

Because the estimate was too large, try the next lower number, 7.

$$54\overline{)378}$$ quotient 7; -378; 0

It takes 7 hours for this asteroid to complete one rotation.

Check Understanding

If the estimated quotient is the same as the exact quotient, write "correct." If the estimated quotient needs to be adjusted, write "adjust up" or "adjust down."

a. $31\overline{)240}$ with estimated quotient 8 **b.** $51\overline{)458}$ with estimated quotient 9 **c.** $45\overline{)123}$ with estimated quotient 2 **d.** $47\overline{)332}$ with estimated quotient 6 **e.** $21\overline{)128}$ with estimated quotient 6

Practice

Find the quotient.

1. $19\overline{)855}$ **4.** $24\overline{)846}$ **7.** $42\overline{)672}$ **10.** $63\overline{)820}$

2. $27\overline{)974}$ **5.** $56\overline{)674}$ **8.** $72\overline{)864}$ **11.** $32\overline{)576}$

3. $38\overline{)646}$ **6.** $15\overline{)347}$ **9.** $28\overline{)759}$ **12.** $13\overline{)679}$

13. $928 \div 58$ **14.** $769 \div 24$ **15.** $963 \div 72$ **16.** $532 \div 19$

Divide. Check by multiplying.

17. $14\overline{)588}$ **18.** $41\overline{)422}$ **19.** $38\overline{)363}$ **20.** $25\overline{)226}$

Apply

21. There were 126 students that met at the school football field to look at stars. They shared 14 telescopes. If an equal number of students shared each telescope, how many students used one telescope?

22. Some students went home shortly after arriving. Only 84 students stayed to watch the stars. How many of these students shared each telescope?

5.6 3-Digit Quotients

Construct Meaning

Heidi organized a food drive at her school. Students from each grade donated food. Each class donated the same amount. If 2,214 lb of food were donated by 18 classes, how many pounds did each class collect?

2,214 lb ÷ 18 classes

First, estimate the quotient by using compatible numbers.

2,214 ÷ 18
↓ ↓
2,000 ÷ 20 = 100

Use 100 as the estimated quotient.

To find the exact quotient, divide 2,214 by 18.

Decide where to place the first digit of the quotient.

$18\overline{)2{,}214}$

There are not enough thousands. The first digit will be in the hundreds place because 22 can be divided by 18.

Try the first digit of the estimated quotient. (1 × 18 = 18)

$$\begin{array}{r} 1 \\ 18\overline{)2{,}214} \\ -1\,8 \\ \hline 4 \end{array}$$

Multiply. Subtract.
Compare. 4 < 18

Bring down. Divide 41 by 18. (2 × 18 = 36)

$$\begin{array}{r} 12 \\ 18\overline{)2{,}214} \\ -1\,8 \\ \hline 41 \\ -36 \\ \hline 5 \end{array}$$

Multiply. Subtract.
Compare. 5 < 18

Bring down. Divide 54 by 18. (3 × 18 = 54)

$$\begin{array}{r} 123 \\ 18\overline{)2{,}214} \\ -1\,8 \\ \hline 41 \\ -36 \\ \hline 54 \\ -54 \\ \hline 0 \end{array}$$

Multiply. Subtract.
Compare. 0 < 18

Check.

$$\begin{array}{r} 123 \\ \times\ \ 18 \\ \hline 984 \\ +1\ 230 \\ \hline 2{,}214 \end{array}$$

Each class donated 123 pounds of food.

Check Understanding

Choose the correct answer.

a. $23\overline{)5{,}428}$ 246 236 231

b. $45\overline{)6{,}615}$ 157 146 147

Practice

Divide. Check by multiplying.

1. 27)83   2. 48)95   3. 17)93   4. 28)78   5. 54)166

Copy and complete each problem.

6.
```
     5   R2
13)7,399
```

7.
```
          R
41)5,826
  -4 1
```

8.
```
      37
53)19,822
  -15 9
    3 92
   -3 71
     212
```

9.
```
       2
47)12,173
   - 9 4
     2 77
```

Divide.

10. 22)279
11. 41)1,460
12. 60)485
13. 82)1,073
14. 70)536
15. 87)12,356
16. 46)21,988
17. 22)19,119
18. 17)14,369

Apply

19. Greenville Gymnastics has 144 students. There are 18 students in each class. How many classes are held at Greenville Gymnastics?

20. Bible covers woven in Guatemala sell for $28 each. How many Bible covers would be in a shipment valued at $3,472?

Review

Write >, <, or =.

21. 57,630 ◯ 57,603
22. 69,992 ◯ 69,998
23. 14.79 ◯ 14.790
24. 360.028 ◯ 360.030
25. 23.25 ◯ 25.23

5.7 Zero in the Quotient

Construct Meaning

Beautiful fireworks are displayed during Fourth of July celebrations in the United States. One fireworks display launched 4,725 fireworks in 45 minutes. If an equal number were displayed each minute, how many fireworks were displayed in one minute?

4,725 fireworks ÷ 45 minutes

Estimate the quotient by finding compatible numbers.

$$4{,}725 \div 45$$
$$\downarrow \quad \downarrow$$
$$5{,}000 \div 50 = 100$$

The estimated quotient is 100 fireworks per minute.

Decide where to place the first digit.
Divide the hundreds. Think: 45 × 1 = 45.

$$\begin{array}{r} 1 \\ 45\overline{)4{,}725} \\ -4\,5 \\ \hline 2 \end{array}$$

Multiply.
Subtract.
Compare. 2 < 45

Bring down.
Divide the tens.
There are not enough tens.
Think: 45 × 0 = 0.

$$\begin{array}{r} 10 \\ 45\overline{)4{,}725} \\ -4\,5\downarrow \\ \hline 22 \\ -0 \\ \hline 22 \end{array}$$

45 > 22. Show that there are not enough tens by writing a zero in the tens place.

Bring down.
Divide the ones.
Think: 45 × 5 = 225.

$$\begin{array}{r} 105 \\ 45\overline{)4{,}725} \\ -4\,5 \\ \hline 22 \\ -0\downarrow \\ \hline 225 \\ -225 \\ \hline 0 \end{array}$$

Multiply.
Subtract.
Compare. 0 < 45

Check.

$$\begin{array}{r} 105 \\ \times\ \ 45 \\ \hline 525 \\ +4\,200 \\ \hline 4{,}725 \end{array}$$

105 fireworks were displayed each minute.

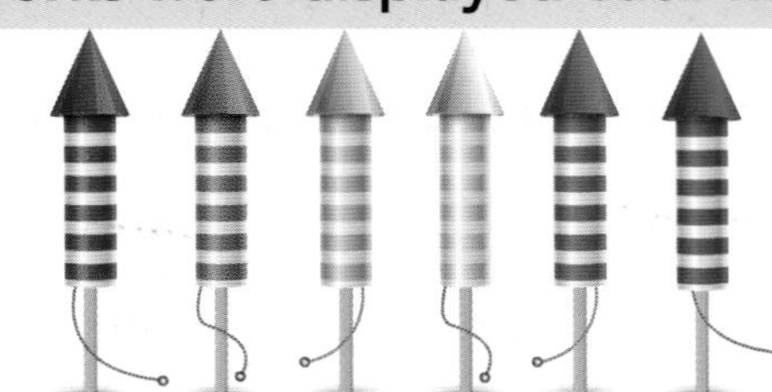

Check Understanding

Choose the correct quotient.

a. $23\overline{)7,061}$	b. $21\overline{)14,868}$	c. $36\overline{)18,036}$	d. $32\overline{)13,059}$
307	70	51	408 R3
37	780	501	480 R3
370	708	510	48 R3

Practice

Find the quotient. Check by multiplying.

1. $45\overline{)27,135}$
2. $62\overline{)6,386}$
3. $58\overline{)12,122}$
4. $37\overline{)18,574}$
5. $22\overline{)13,288}$
6. $41\overline{)12,548}$
7. $85\overline{)8,673}$
8. $72\overline{)21,748}$
9. $12\overline{)9,615}$
10. $25\overline{)10,225}$
11. $56\overline{)11,424}$
12. $81\overline{)8,427}$

Divide.

13. $10,764 \div 52$
14. $13,222 \div 22$
15. $7,635 \div 15$
16. $4,983 \div 47$
17. $19,572 \div 95$
18. $11,594 \div 23$
19. $36\overline{)21,746}$
20. $58\overline{)11,778}$
21. $23\overline{)16,146}$

Use a calculator to find the quotient.

Example:

22. $86\overline{)43,516}$
23. $55\overline{)44,495}$
24. $67\overline{)60,769}$
25. $89\overline{)63,012}$

Review

How would you solve the problem? Write "divide," "multiply," "subtract," or "add."

26. Mona wanted to figure how many more cookies she baked than Anita.
27. Mark wanted to know the total number of tickets sold by his class.
28. Machau wanted to find out how many pencils were lost per day.

5.8 Problem Solving: 2-Digit Divisors

Construct Meaning

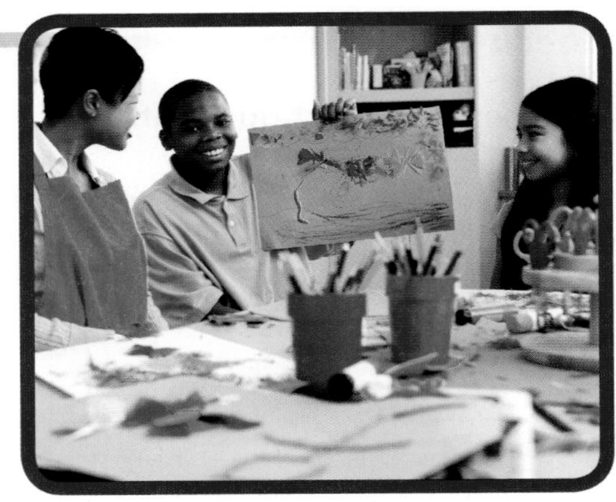

A local paint-supply store donated 1,522 paintbrushes to Ridgeview Christian School. The students are going to use the paintbrushes to paint art murals in their classrooms. If the paintbrushes are equally divided among 13 classes, how many will each class receive?

Understand the question.

- Find the number of paintbrushes per class.

Analyze the data.

- List the necessary information.
  1,522 paintbrushes and 13 classes
- Ignore the distracters.
  The paintbrushes will be used for art murals.
  This is not necessary information.

Plan the strategy.

- Divide the total number of paintbrushes by the number of classes.
  1,522 paintbrushes ÷ 13 classes
- Estimate the quotient.
  Use compatible numbers to estimate. 1,500 ÷ 10 = 150 paintbrushes per class

Solve the problem.

- 1,522 ÷ 13 = 117 R1
- Drop the remainder.

Each class will receive 117 paintbrushes.

Evaluate the result.

- Compare the answer to the estimate.
  The answer of 117 paintbrushes is close to the estimate of 150 paintbrushes.
  The answer seems reasonable.

Check Understanding

a. If 26 classes shared the 1,522 paintbrushes, how many paintbrushes would each class receive?

b. What would you do with the remainder?

Practice

Solve.

1. Nadia's parents own a paint store. They donated 50 cans of paint to Ridgeview Christian School for Mission Week. If the paint cans are divided equally, how many cans will each of the 16 classes receive?

2. Mrs. Zhang, Ling's mom, was in charge of gathering enough sunscreen to help protect students during outdoor Mission Week activities. Mrs. Zhang collected 132 tubes of sunscreen for 13 classes. How much sunscreen will Ling give each class?

3. Rasheed brought 108 water bottles to school to give to students in his class for the week. If there are 15 students in his class, how many water bottles will each student receive for the week?

4. Lupe's class brought a box of 60 granola bars to share with her class of 24 during Mission Week. Are there enough granola bars for each child to have two?

5. Mr. Weiss is responsible for coordinating church bus transportation for a field trip with 202 students during mission week. Each bus can hold 14 students. How many buses will he need to reserve?

6. Samuel collected 58 buckets for 13 classes to use during Mission Week. The extra buckets will be used by parent volunteers. How many buckets will each class receive for the painting project? How many buckets will the parent volunteers receive?

Review

Write >, <, or =.

7. 0.09 ◯ 0.009
8. 52.6 ◯ 0.526
9. 0.13 ◯ 1.3
10. 7.80 ◯ 7.8

Solve.

11. $\begin{array}{r} 506 \\ \times \quad 6 \\ \hline \end{array}$

12. $\begin{array}{r} 55 \\ \times 22 \\ \hline \end{array}$

13. $\begin{array}{r} 6{,}789 \\ \times \quad 4 \\ \hline \end{array}$

14. $\begin{array}{r} 3{,}723 \\ \times \quad 21 \\ \hline \end{array}$

5.9 Chapter 5 Review

Estimate the quotient by using compatible numbers.

1. 329 ÷ 33
2. 374 ÷ 12
3. 2,111 ÷ 30
4. 5,603 ÷ 52
5. 31,210 ÷ 80
6. 15,489 ÷ 32

Copy and complete each problem.

7. $\begin{array}{r} \underline{\quad}\text{ R}\underline{\quad} \\ 40\overline{)1,624} \end{array}$

8. $\begin{array}{r} \underline{\quad} \\ 17\overline{)10,340} \end{array}$

Write the letter of the correct quotient.

9. 736 ÷ 61
10. 989 ÷ 43
11. 2,688 ÷ 28
12. 42,390 ÷ 54
13. 35,464 ÷ 36

Answer Bank

a. 23
b. 96
c. 12 R4
d. 785
e. 985 R4

Find the quotient. Check by multiplying.

14. $48\overline{)624}$
15. $69\overline{)1,725}$
16. $52\overline{)3,278}$
17. $74\overline{)2,889}$

Divide.

18. 1,932 ÷ 84
19. 5,952 ÷ 62
20. 9,225 ÷ 25
21. 35,786 ÷ 42
22. 26,526 ÷ 38

If the estimated quotient is the same as the exact quotient, write "correct." If the estimated quotient needs to be adjusted, write "adjust up" or "adjust down."

23. $\begin{array}{r} 5 \\ 20\overline{)89} \end{array}$

24. $\begin{array}{r} 2 \\ 35\overline{)107} \end{array}$

Complete the following sequence.

25. 2,900,000,000; 29,000,000; 290,000; ____; ____

Catalina's family owns an ice cream shop. The graph shows their sales for five months. Use the graph to answer the questions.

26. Which month did they sell the most ice cream? How much did they sell that month?

27. Which month did they sell the least ice cream? How much did they sell that month?

28. If Catalina's family had the ice cream shop open for 5 days in September, what were their total sales per day?

29. If the ice cream shop was open for 28 days in July and only 10 days in May, in which month did they sell the most ice cream per day?

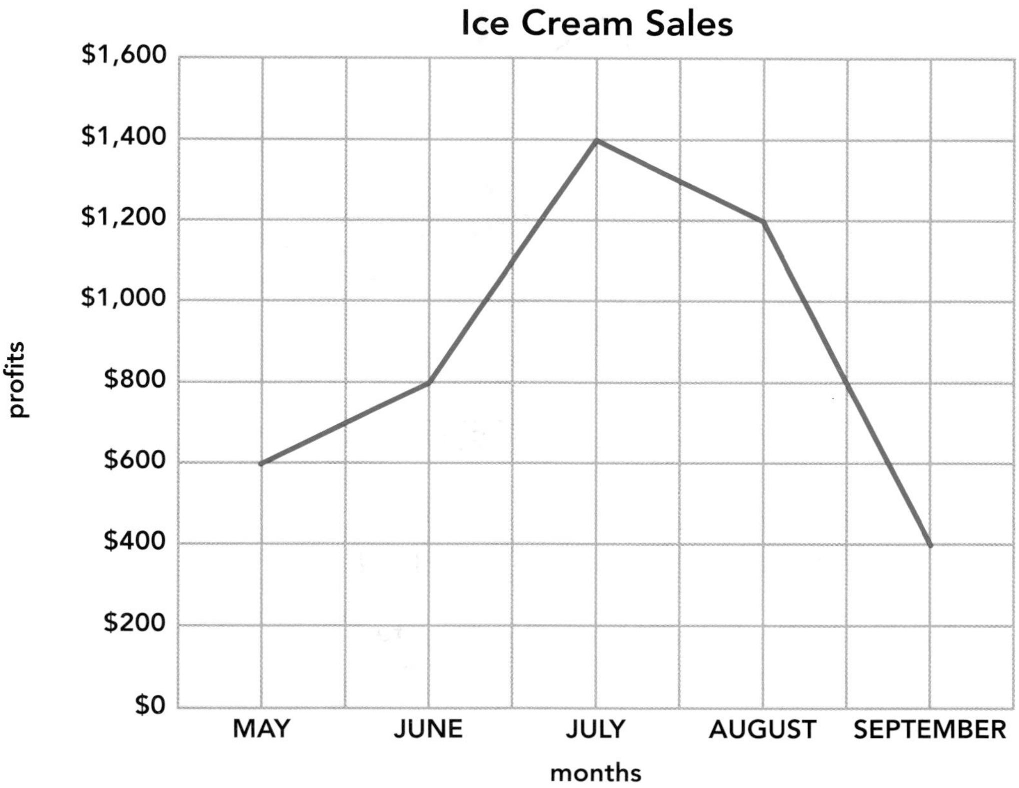

Ice Cream Sales

profits

$1,600
$1,400
$1,200
$1,000
$800
$600
$400
$200
$0

MAY JUNE JULY AUGUST SEPTEMBER

months

5.10 Chapters 3–5 Review

1. Which set of numbers contains only multiples of 8?

   a. 48, 16, 23, 59, 60 b. 24, 72, 40, 56, 64 c. 27, 36, 48, 64, 80

2. Silas baked 36 muffins. Tammie baked 24. The baking pans they used held the number of muffins that is the greatest common factor (GCF) of 36 and 24. How many muffins could be baked in each pan?

3. Mitzi packed 9 pairs of socks for a camping trip. Dave packed 7. What is the least common multiple (LCM) of 9 and 7?

4. Zoe counted the geese along the way to school. She counted a total of 105 geese in five days. If she counted an equal number of geese each day, how many did she count in one day?

5. What is the best estimated quotient for 490 ÷ 52?

   a. 10 b. 100 c. 5

Find the product.

6. $\begin{array}{r} 29 \\ \times 16 \\ \hline \end{array}$

7. $\begin{array}{r} 4{,}281 \\ \times \quad 65 \\ \hline \end{array}$

Write a multiplication sentence for the product given. Do not use 0 or 1 as a factor.

8. 300 ____________________

9. 122 ____________________

10. 592 ____________________

Divide.

11. $32\overline{)226}$

12. $63\overline{)514}$

13. $68\overline{)476}$

14. $42\overline{)128}$

Find the quotient.

15. $37\overline{)9{,}472}$ with quotient 2 _ 6; $-7\,4$; $2\,07$

16. $64\overline{)23{,}488}$ with quotient 3 _; $-19\,2$; $4\,28$

17. $73\overline{)26{,}939}$ with quotient ___ R _

18. $32\overline{)19{,}872}$

Choose the correct quotient.

19. $50\overline{)10{,}050}$

a. 210
b. 201
c. 21

20. $17\overline{)18{,}067}$

a. 1,162 R13
b. 162 R13
c. 1,062 R13

21. $80\overline{)87{,}769}$

a. 197 R9
b. 1,097 R9
c. 1,297 R9

Use lattice multiplication to find the product.

22. 42 × 53

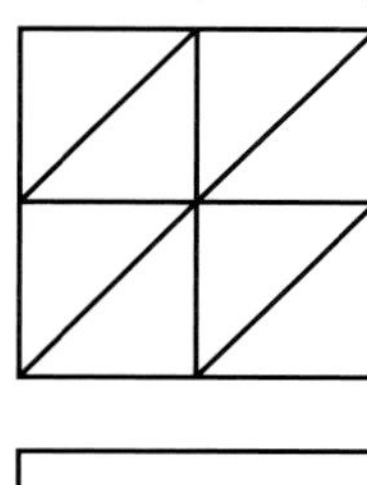

23. 22 ×11

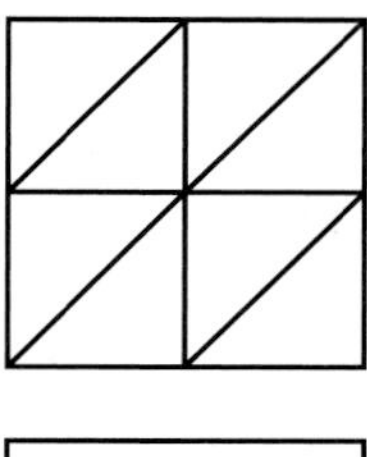

Divide.

24. $21\overline{)7{,}254}$

25. $17\overline{)651}$

26. 1,687 ÷ 22

27. 1,151÷ 12

28. 9,875 ÷ 15

Complete the sequence.

29. 450,000; 45,000; ____; ____; ____

30. If a total of 5,313 ft of cotton thread was needed to weave 21 panels of Guatemalan textiles, how many feet would be used for each piece?

31. On Monday, Abby swam the length of the pool 17 times. On Tuesday and Thursday, she swam the length of the pool 23 times. On Wednesday, Abby had a dentist appointment so she swam only 14 lengths. On Friday, she completed 28 lengths. How many lengths did Abby swim altogether? What was the average number of lengths she swam each day? What information was not needed?

Chapter 6
Multiply and Divide Decimals

You alone are the Lord. You made the heavens, even the highest heavens, and all their starry host, the earth and all that is on it, the seas and all that is in them.
Nehemiah 9:6a

Key Ideas:

Multiplication: multiplying decimals

Division: dividing decimals

Money: multiplying and dividing

Algebra: understanding order of operations

6.1 Estimate Decimal Products

Construct Meaning

The science club spent 3.5 days at the planetarium. They spent 2.4 hours each day focused on the planet Mercury. The science club learned that Mercury is the closest planet to the sun and that it travels around the sun faster than any other planet.

The club members gathered information about Mercury's temperature. They learned that the average temperature of the side facing the sun is 806°F and the side away from the sun is −261°F.

About how much time did the club members spend focused on Mercury?

Estimate decimal products two ways.

 Round both factors to the greatest place value and multiply.

$$\begin{array}{r} 3.5 \\ \times 2.4 \\ \hline \end{array} \begin{array}{c} \longrightarrow \\ \longrightarrow \\ \end{array} \begin{array}{r} 4 \\ \times 2 \\ \hline 8 \end{array}$$

The science club members spent about 8 hours focused on Mercury.

One way to say "about" in symbol form when estimating is by using the symbol ≈. 3.5 × 2.4 ≈ 8. Read, "3.5 times 2.4 is about 8."

 Round a factor to a multiple of five so that computing mentally is easy.

$$\begin{array}{r} 33.5 \\ \times \ 4.6 \\ \hline \end{array} \begin{array}{c} \longrightarrow \\ \longrightarrow \\ \end{array} \begin{array}{r} 30 \\ \times \ 5 \\ \hline 150 \end{array} \quad \text{or} \quad \begin{array}{r} 35 \\ \times \ 5 \\ \hline 175 \end{array}$$

The exact answer of 154.10 is in the estimated range.
150 < 154.10 < 175

Decimal products and whole-number products can be estimated the same way.

Check Understanding

Estimate the product by rounding to the greatest place value.

a. $\begin{array}{r} 4.6 \\ \times 1.3 \\ \hline \end{array}$ b. $\begin{array}{r} 8.2 \\ \times 4.7 \\ \hline \end{array}$ c. $\begin{array}{r} 5.4 \\ \times 7.3 \\ \hline \end{array}$ d. $\begin{array}{r} 26.5 \\ \times \ 8.1 \\ \hline \end{array}$ e. $\begin{array}{r} 32.3 \\ \times \ 6.4 \\ \hline \end{array}$

f. 2.4 × 42 ≈ __ g. 3.5 × 11 ≈ __ h. 18 × 4.6 ≈ __ i. 27 × 3.4 ≈ __

Estimate. Write >, <, or =.

j. 2.6 × 4.7 ◯ 8
k. 3.2 × 7.3 ◯ 25
l. 4.4 × 24.31 ◯ 76
m. 7.25 × 26.5 ◯ 175
n. 5.3 × $42.95 ◯ $270
o. 200.4 × 6.3 ◯ 1,100

Practice

Estimate.

1. $\begin{array}{r} 7.2 \\ \times 3.4 \\ \hline \end{array}$

2. $\begin{array}{r} 28.3 \\ \times \ 1.6 \\ \hline \end{array}$

3. $\begin{array}{r} 4.3 \\ \times 4.5 \\ \hline \end{array}$

4. $\begin{array}{r} 37.1 \\ \times 49.4 \\ \hline \end{array}$

5. $\begin{array}{r} 7.8 \\ \times 6.1 \\ \hline \end{array}$

6. 42 × 1.6
7. 56 × 2.3
8. 8.7 × 19
9. 2.6 × 279

Choose the best estimate. Write a, b, or c.

10. $31.2 \times 6.81 = y$
    - a. 210
    - b. 280
    - c. 310

11. $27.6 \times 4.54 = y$
    - a. 100
    - b. 150
    - c. 200

12. $19.8 \times 7.66 = y$
    - a. 160
    - b. 190
    - c. 260

13. $8.4 \times 52.1 = y$
    - a. 300
    - b. 200
    - c. 400

Apply

14. Club dues are $28.75 per person per year. There are 10 members in the club. Using the two closest multiples of five to round the money amount, what is the range of the estimated amount paid in dues each year? Which estimate is closer to the exact amount of $287.50?

15. Ella rode her bike 6.5 mi to the planetarium. Chang rode his bike 2.4 times that distance. About how many miles did Chang ride his bike?

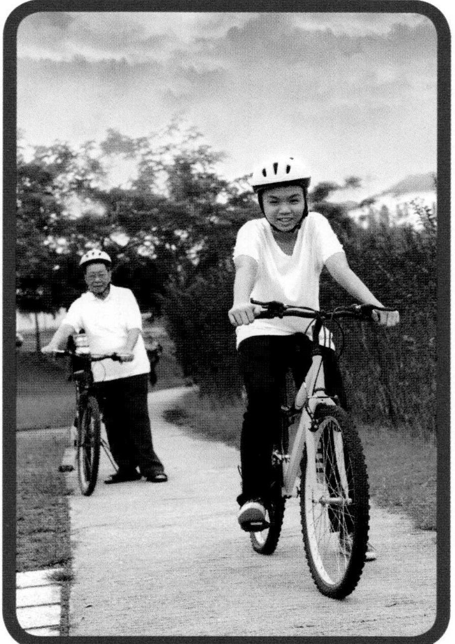

Review

Round each addend to the greatest place value and add.

16. 826 + 1,104 + 102
17. 83 + 204 + 12 + 46
18. 36,406 + 23,653 + 42,856

Multiply.

19. $\begin{array}{r} 24 \\ \times \ 6 \\ \hline \end{array}$

20. $\begin{array}{r} 314 \\ \times \ \ 9 \\ \hline \end{array}$

21. $\begin{array}{r} 5{,}782 \\ \times \ \ \ \ 7 \\ \hline \end{array}$

22. $\begin{array}{r} 46 \\ \times 39 \\ \hline \end{array}$

23. $\begin{array}{r} 287 \\ \times 145 \\ \hline \end{array}$

Solve each problem. Check by multiplying.

24. $2\overline{)68}$
25. $9\overline{)657}$
26. $16\overline{)704}$
27. $27\overline{)6{,}431}$
28. $9\overline{)568}$

Write "yes" if the first number is evenly divisible by the second number. Write "no" if it is not.

29. 36 9
30. 44 7
31. 83 9
32. 56 8

6.2 Multiply by Whole Numbers

Construct Meaning

The science club researched the planet Venus before their planetarium visit. Here are some facts they learned.

- Venus is the closest planet to Earth when it is directly in line with the sun and Earth.
- Venus has the brightest appearance from Earth.
- The temperature on Venus is higher than that of any other planet.
- The surface consists of flat ground, mountains, canyons, and valleys.
- The *US Mariner 2* first observed Venus in 1962.
- In 1970, the Soviet spacecraft *Venera 7* landed on Venus.

Encyclopedias, magazines, books, and the Internet were sources the club members used. Each of the four websites provided 0.15 of the data researched.

Look at the hundred flat below. The entire flat equals one whole and the small units represent 0.01 of a whole. Was the whole project researched from the websites? If not, what part came from the websites? Use graph paper divided into hundredths to find $4 \times 0.15 = x$.

$$\begin{array}{r} 0.15 \\ \times \quad 4 \\ \hline \end{array}$$

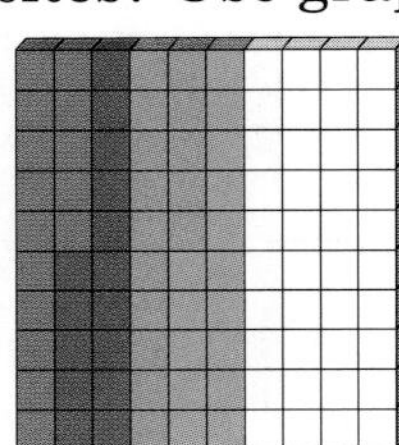

Sixty hundredths is part of the research data that came from the websites.

$$\begin{array}{r} {}^{2} \\ 0.15 \\ \times \quad 4 \\ \hline 0.60 \end{array}$$

Multiply the hundredths. Regroup 20 as 2 tenths and 0 hundredths.
Multiply the tenths and then the ones.
Total the number of decimal places in both factors. 2
Show the product with the same number of decimal places. 2

More Examples

$$\begin{array}{rl} {}^{4\,2} & \\ 2.74 & \text{2 decimal places} \\ \times \quad 6 & +\text{0 decimal places} \\ \hline 16.44 & \text{2 decimal places} \end{array}$$

$$\begin{array}{rl} {}^{1} & \\ 4.132 & \text{3 decimal places} \\ \times \quad 4 & +\text{0 decimal places} \\ \hline 16.528 & \text{3 decimal places} \end{array}$$

$$\begin{array}{rl} {}^{1\,1} & \\ 5.069 & \text{3 decimal places} \\ \times \quad 12 & +\text{0 decimal places} \\ \hline 10\,138 & \\ +50\,690 & \\ \hline 60.828 & \text{3 decimal places} \end{array}$$

Check Understanding

Write the equation that matches the graph model. A flat equals one whole and a small unit represents 0.01 of a whole.

a.

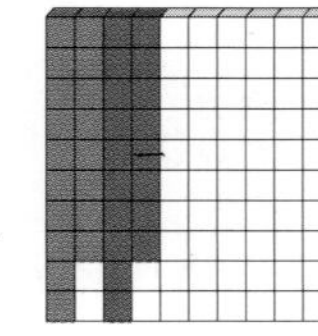

$2 \times 18 = 36$

$2 \times 0.18 = 0.36$

b.

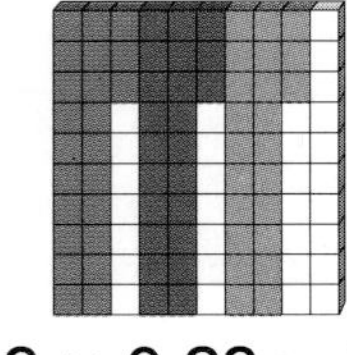

$3 \times 0.23 = 0.69$

$3 \times 23 = 69$

c.

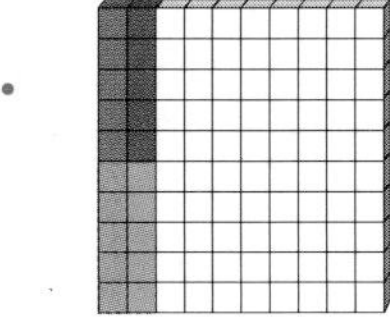

$4 \times 0.05 = 0.20$

$4 \times 5 = 20$

d.

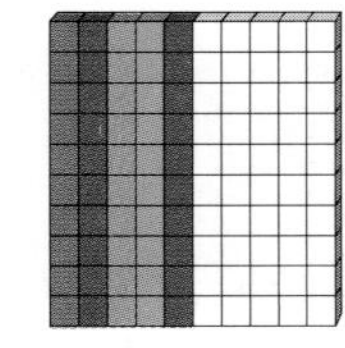

$5 \times 10 = 50$

$5 \times 0.10 = 0.50$

Practice

Multiply.

1. $3 \times 0.12 = z$
2. $2 \times 0.31 = z$
3. $4 \times 0.10 = z$
4. $6 \times 0.06 = z$

Write the number of decimal places in each product.

5. $9 \times 0.4 = n$
6. $35 \times 0.86 = n$
7. $6 \times 0.905 = n$
8. $17 \times 1.84 = n$

Find the product.

9. 0.4×5
10. 1.8×9
11. 3.072×8
12. 7.62×24
13. 2.64×17

The gravitational pull of Venus is 0.91 times that of the earth.
Find how much the object would weigh on Venus.
If the product is a decimal, round it to the nearest whole number.

Weight on Earth	× 0.91 =	Weight on Venus
14. 100 lb boat		____
15. 35 lb swordfish		____
16. 300 lb football player		____
17. 11 lb watermelon		____

Multiply using pencil and paper. Then, multiply using a calculator. Compare your product with the one displayed. Do you see any similarities or differences? Explain.

18. Your Work: 25×8 — Calculator Display: 25×8

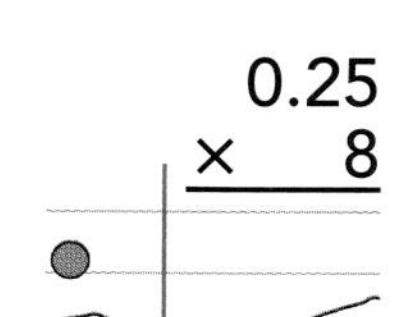

19. Your Work: 0.25×8 — Calculator Display: 0.25×8

Review

Write the least common multiple of each pair.

20. 6 and 4
21. 2 and 8
22. 3 and 5
23. 5 and 4

Multiply.

24. 305×4
25. 74×6
26. 59×3
27. 45×8
28. 269×4

Divide.

29. $6\overline{)456}$
30. $8\overline{)749}$
31. $9\overline{)847}$
32. $7\overline{)658}$
33. $5\overline{)870}$

6.3 Multiply Decimals

Construct Meaning

The science club spent time stargazing with a telescope. Club members wanted to find the celestial poles—points on the celestial sphere above the north and south poles. The members used paper, pencil, and a map to record the brightest stars. Two hours later, they recorded changes. Some stars had moved and some appeared motionless near the locations of the celestial poles. The location of one pole is found between the northern hemisphere Big Dipper and Cassiopeia. The other pole is in the southern hemisphere between the Southern Cross and the Small Magellanic Cloud.

The club spent 0.3 of an hour looking at the sky and 0.7 of that time taking notes. What part of the hour was spent taking notes?

Solve $0.7 \times 0.3 = h$.

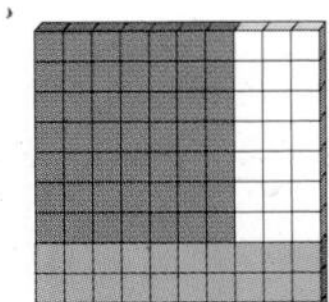

$$\begin{array}{r} \overset{2}{0.7} \\ \times\, 0.3 \\ \hline 0.21 \end{array}$$

Multiply the tenths. Regroup the 21.
Multiply the ones.
Count the decimal places in both factors. 2
Show the product with 2 decimal places.

0.21 of the hour was spent taking notes.

Compare 0.7×0.3 with 7×3.

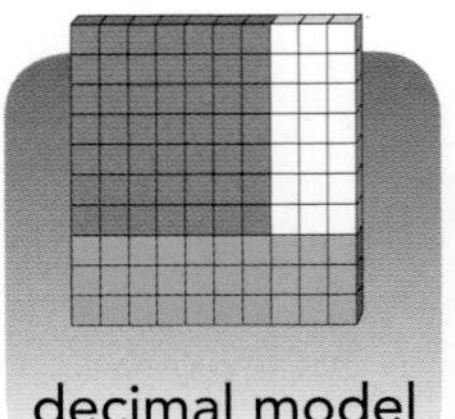

decimal model

whole-number model

Which model shows less than one whole?
In 0.7×0.3, the product 0.21 is less than 1.

Which model shows more than one whole?
In 7×3, the product 21 is more than 1.

More Examples

$$\begin{array}{r l} 0.24 & \text{2 decimal places} \\ \times\ \ 0.3 & +\,\text{1 decimal place} \\ \hline 0.072 & \text{3 decimal places} \end{array}$$

$$\begin{array}{r l} 34.781 & \text{3 decimal places} \\ \times\ \ .03 & +\,\text{2 decimal places} \\ \hline 1.04343 & \text{5 decimal places} \end{array}$$

$$\begin{array}{r l} 1.62 & \text{2 decimal places} \\ \times\, 3.24 & +\,\text{2 decimal places} \\ \hline 6\,48 & \\ 32\,40 & \\ +\,486\,00 & \\ \hline 5.24\,88 & \text{4 decimal places} \end{array}$$

Check Understanding

Write the equation that matches the model.

a. 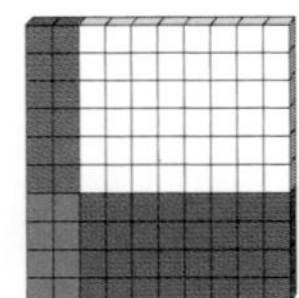

b. 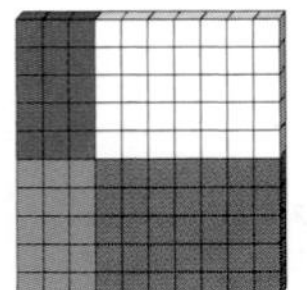

c. 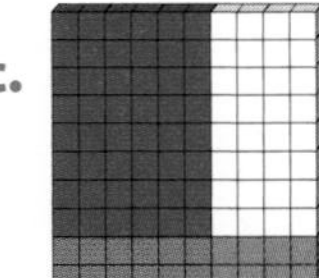

$0.6 \times 0.2 = 0.12$

$0.2 \times 0.4 = 0.08$

$0.3 \times 0.5 = 0.15$

Practice

Rewrite the product with the decimal in the correct place.

1. $\begin{array}{r} 7.1 \\ \times\ 4.9 \\ \hline 3479 \end{array}$

2. $\begin{array}{r} 25.8 \\ \times\ 0.7 \\ \hline 1806 \end{array}$

3. $\begin{array}{r} 18.32 \\ \times\ 0.7 \\ \hline 12824 \end{array}$

4. $\begin{array}{r} 126 \\ \times\ 0.2 \\ \hline 252 \end{array}$

Multiply.

5. 0.8×0.3
6. 241×1.3
7. 4.3×0.6
8. 0.01×10
9. 0.6×0.5
10. 2.2×8.6
11. 8.52×0.9
12. 11.1×20.42

13. $\begin{array}{r} 9.7 \\ \times 0.3 \\ \hline \end{array}$

14. $\begin{array}{r} 24 \\ \times 0.16 \\ \hline \end{array}$

15. $\begin{array}{r} 3.562 \\ \times\ 0.14 \\ \hline \end{array}$

16. $\begin{array}{r} 5.90 \\ \times 0.02 \\ \hline \end{array}$

17. $\begin{array}{r} 10.6 \\ \times\ 0.9 \\ \hline \end{array}$

18. $\begin{array}{r} 82.37 \\ \times\ 0.5 \\ \hline \end{array}$

19. $\begin{array}{r} 0.46 \\ \times\ 0.6 \\ \hline \end{array}$

Apply

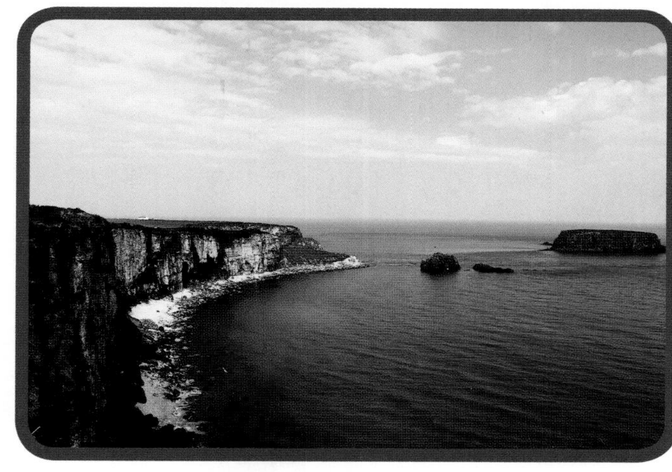

20. The gravitational pull of the sun is 27.8 times greater than that of Earth. If a man who weighed 116.5 lb on Earth could stand on the sun, how much would he weigh? Round the product to the nearest whole number.

21. Land covers about 0.3 of the surface of planet Earth. The oceans cover 2.33 times more surface than the land. How much of Earth is covered by oceans? Round the product to the nearest tenth.

Review

Add.

22. $6.5 + 3.6$
23. $8.3 + 4.8$
24. $13.936 + 6.881$

Subtract.

25. $5.7 - 4.05$
26. $92.4 - 21.9$
27. $16.82 - 12.096$

Estimate the product.

28. $\begin{array}{r} 4.8 \\ \times 1.9 \\ \hline \end{array}$

29. $\begin{array}{r} 6.3 \\ \times 3.7 \\ \hline \end{array}$

30. $\begin{array}{r} 5.3 \\ \times 2.9 \\ \hline \end{array}$

6.4 Zero in the Product

Construct Meaning

The earth, traveling through space around the sun, is only a small part of the universe. People, plants, and animals thrive on Earth because it is the right distance from the sun. When the northern hemisphere tilts away from the sun and the days get shorter, the leaves of deciduous trees change colors and fall from the trees.

Camilla's neighborhood is full of trees, and the neighbors will pay her to rake and bag the leaves. Camilla charges $0.75 per bag. How much would Camilla make if she raked 10 bags of leaves? How much would she make if she raked 100 bags of leaves?

1 bag × $0.75 each = $0.75
10 bags × $0.75 each = $7.50
100 bags × $0.75 each = $75.00

Camilla would make $7.50 for raking 10 bags of leaves and $75.00 for 100 bags of leaves.

The number of zeros in 10, 100, and 1,000 tells how many places to move the decimal to the right.

Use mental math. Observe how the number becomes larger as the decimal point moves to the right.

1 × 1.75 = 1.75
10 × 1.75 = 17.5
100 × 1.75 = 175
1,000 × 1.75 = 1,750

1 × 14.03 = 14.03
10 × 14.03 = 140.3
100 × 14.03 = 1,403
1,000 × 14.03 = 14,030

Write a zero so there are 3 places to move the decimal.

Multiply. Write extra zeros in the product if needed.

Find 0.03 × 0.069.

0.069	3 decimal places
× 0.03	+ 2 decimal places
0.00207	5 decimal places

Write an extra zero and place the decimal because there are only 4 places.

Find $4.25 × 0.50.

$4.25
× 0.50
$2.1250 rounded to the nearest cent is $2.13.

Check Understanding

Multiply. Observe the pattern.

a. 1 × $0.79
10 × $0.79
100 × $0.79

b. 1 × 2.04
10 × 2.04
100 × 2.04
1,000 × 2.04

c. 1 × 52.98
10 × 52.98
100 × 52.98
1,000 × 52.98

Find the product. Write extra zeros if needed.

d. 10 × 0.9
e. 1,000 × 0.069
f. 100 × 0.32
g. 0.04 × 0.03
h. 1.6 × 0.007
i. 0.09 × 0.007

Practice

Use mental math to multiply. Observe the pattern.

1. 1×1.37
   10×1.37
   100×1.37
   $1{,}000 \times 1.37$

2. 1×20.68
   10×20.68
   100×20.68
   $1{,}000 \times 20.68$

3. $1 \times \$4.59$
   $10 \times \$4.59$
   $100 \times \$4.59$
   $1{,}000 \times \$4.59$

Multiply. Write extra zeros if needed.

4. 0.03×0.6
5. 0.13×0.5
6. 0.081×0.09
7. 0.01×0.05
8. 36×0.005
9. 1.7×0.62
10. 37.01×0.003
11. 44×0.2
12. 84×0.07
13. 0.008×65
14. 0.4×0.4
15. 100×63.2

Multiply the number by 10, 100, and 1,000.

16. 84.013
17. 34.9
18. 1.6
19. 2.82
20. 0.798

Apply

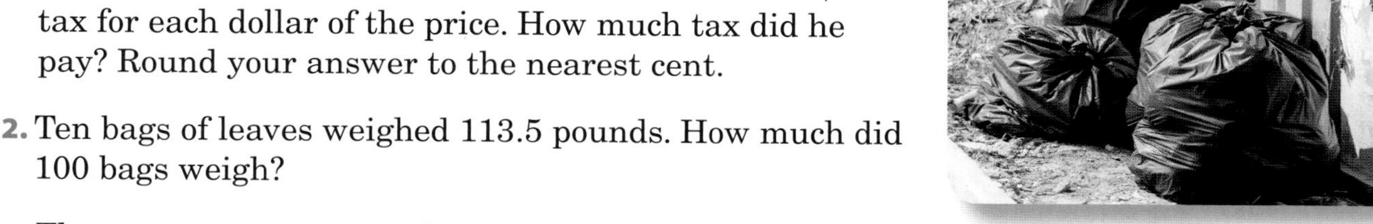

21. Jordan bought four packages of plastic lawn and garden bags that cost a total of \$10.98. The cashier added \$0.07 tax for each dollar of the price. How much tax did he pay? Round your answer to the nearest cent.

22. Ten bags of leaves weighed 113.5 pounds. How much did 100 bags weigh?

23. The waste management department picked up the bags on 10 different occasions. The cost of each trip was \$0.75. How much did the department charge Jordan to pick up the bags?

24. Use the chart to find how much Jordan earned after he had bagged 30, 50, and 80 bags of leaves.

×	30	50	80
\$0.75			

Challenge

25. If you multiply $100{,}000 \times 35.8$, how many zeros will you need to add to the product?

Review

Write the decimal for each word form.

26. two and thirty-four hundredths
27. thirteen and five tenths
28. three hundred sixty-three and eight thousandths
29. one and one thousandth

Multiply.

30. 153×416
31. 531×382
32. 718×395
33. 274×947
34. $8{,}343 \times 535$

6.5 Problem Solving: Multiply

Construct Meaning

Earth is the third planet in order from the sun. The earth's interior is iron and nickel surrounded by a mantle of minerals and a rocky crust. As a geologist, Tommy's dad gave him a valuable rock collection, which inspired Tommy to collect rocks too.

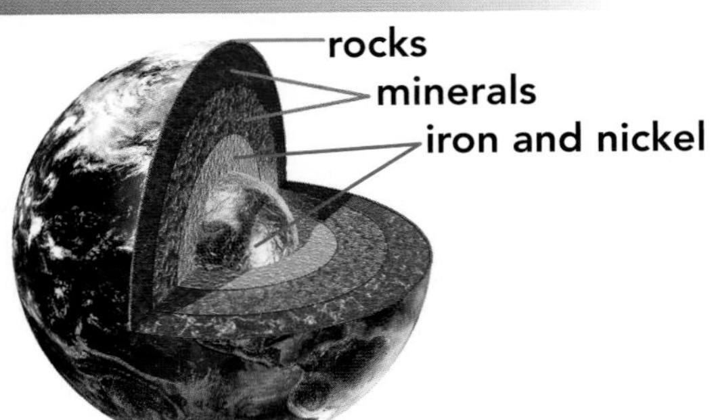

Data—information, facts, figures, statistics—are used to solve equations. Check the following paragraph to determine whether the information is
sufficient—just enough,
insufficient—not enough, or
extra—unnecessary.

Southgate Christian School ordered a rock collection that cost \$24.99 for each of the four fifth-grade classrooms. Each collection contained 18 samples of igneous, sedimentary, and metamorphic rocks. How much money did the school invest in the rock collections?

Understand the question.
How much money did the school spend on the four rock collections?

Analyze the data.
Each rock collection cost \$24.99. The school bought four. All other data are extra and can be ignored.

Plan the strategy.
Because the problem asks how much, multiply the price of one rock collection by four. Round \$24.99 to \$25 to estimate the answer. $4 \times \$25 = \$100$

Solve the problem.
$4 \times \$24.99 = \$99.96$ spent on the rock collections

Evaluate the result.
Yes, it is reasonable that the school spent \$99.96 on four rock collections because the predicted amount was \$100.

Practice

Label each problem as having sufficient, insufficient, or extra information. If the problem contains insufficient information, write what is needed. Write the first and last words of any sentence containing extra information. Solve the problems.

1. Eduardo priced a geologist's hammer at $7.59 and a hand lens for $6.89. He bought two of each of the tools. He found a nearby quarry that would allow him to use the tools to break off rock specimens for $10.00 an hour. How much did Eduardo spend on the tools?

2. Connor's father, a gemologist, cut and polished five emeralds for a jewelry show. He charged $75.00 per emerald. How much money did he make?

3. High-school rings often contain gemstones. A jeweler displayed various rings at an assembly. Five students bought the same style ring with a blue sapphire stone. How much money did the company receive from the sale of those five rings?

4. For Valentine's Day, Mr. Han bought a 3-piece set of ruby jewelry for his wife. Each piece cost $52.50. For Christmas, he bought a 4-piece pearl set. Each piece cost $27.50. Which set of jewelry cost more? How much more?

5. The weight of Nina's tanzanite ring is 1.5 carats. A tanzanite carat is worth $300.00. How much is her ring worth?

6. A gem cutter repaired some jewelry for Mrs. Burgess. He charged $8.75 per piece. How much did Mrs. Burgess pay for the repairs?

7. Mrs. Cruz paid $0.06 sales tax on every dollar when she purchased a topaz necklace that cost $113.00. The matching earrings were on sale for $49.00. What was the final amount she paid for the necklace?

Find the price of each gemstone. Round the final cost to the nearest dollar.

8.

	gemstone	number of carats	price per carat	final cost
a.	Specimen A	37.87	$0.66	____
b.	Specimen B	141.50	$0.53	____
c.	Specimen C	94.33	$5.30	____
d.	Specimen D	164.55	$3.95	____

9. In the parable of the pearl of great price, Jesus relates the kingdom of heaven to a merchant seeking beautiful pearls. Read **Matthew 13:45–46** to find out what the merchant did when he found a pearl of great price. What is the takeaway from the parable?

6.6 Divide by Whole Numbers

Construct Meaning

Did you know that space-shuttle astronauts took radar images of much of Earth's surface to make a three-dimensional map of the planet? The map helps experts deal with issues such as climate change and beach erosion.

When a hurricane hits an area, beach erosion and property destruction can occur. Ryker spent a total of 4.38 hours on two different days taking safety measures prior to the forecasted hurricane. How many hours did he average per day?

Solve $4.38 \div 2 = x$

Use flats, rods, and units to show dividing decimals by a whole number.

4 flats (4 ones) | 3 rods (3 tenths) | 8 units (8 hundredths)

Divide the 4 ones (flats) into 2 equal groups

Share the 3 tenths (rods) between each group.

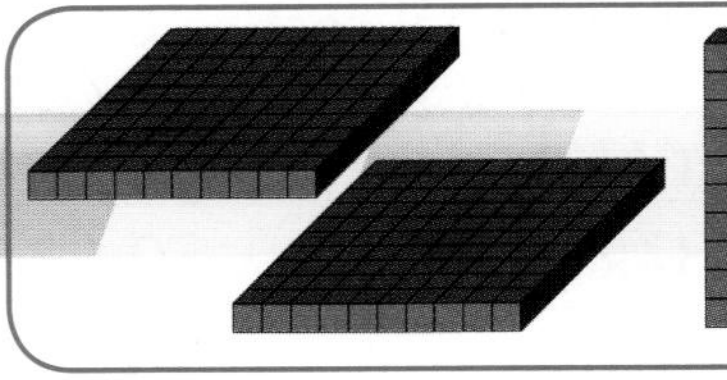

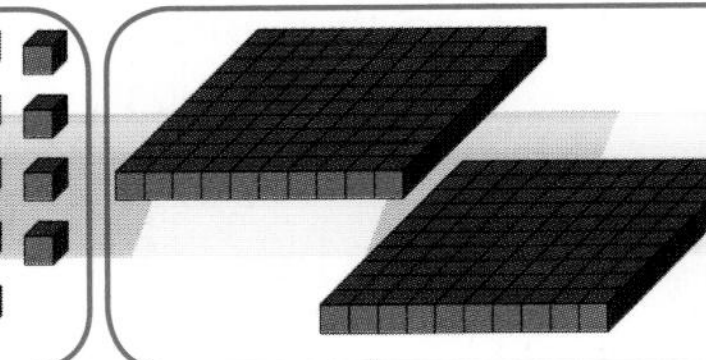

left over

Regroup the one tenth (rod) left over as 10 hundredths (units). Share the 18 hundredths between each group.

2 flats in each group
1 rod in each group
9 units in each group

$$
\begin{array}{r}
2.19 \\
2\overline{)4.38} \\
-4 \\
\hline
0\,3 \\
-2 \\
\hline
18 \\
-18 \\
\hline
0
\end{array}
$$

Place the decimal in the quotient.
Divide the whole number. $4 \div 2$
Divide the tenths. $3 \div 2$
Divide the hundredths. $18 \div 2$

Ron spent 2 and 19 hundredths hours each day taking safety measures.

Divide as with whole numbers. Remember to place the decimal first.

$$6\overline{)1.8} = 0.3 \quad 2\overline{)4.8} = 2.4 \quad 4\overline{)25.2} = 6.3 \quad 7\overline{)39.69} = 5.67 \quad 12\overline{)1.584} = 0.132$$

0.3	2.4	6.3	5.67	0.132
6)1.8	2)4.8	4)25.2	7)39.69	12)1.584
−	−4	−	−35	−1 2
0	0 8	1 2	4 6	
	− 8	−1 2	−	−36
		0	49	24
			−49	−
			0	0

Check Understanding

Write the decimal division sentence shown by the model.

a. 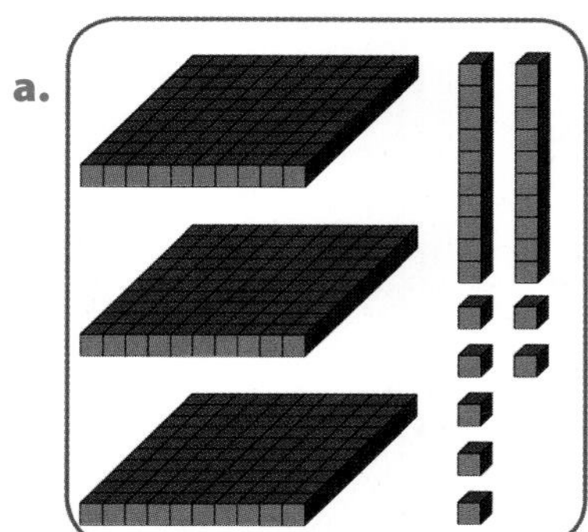 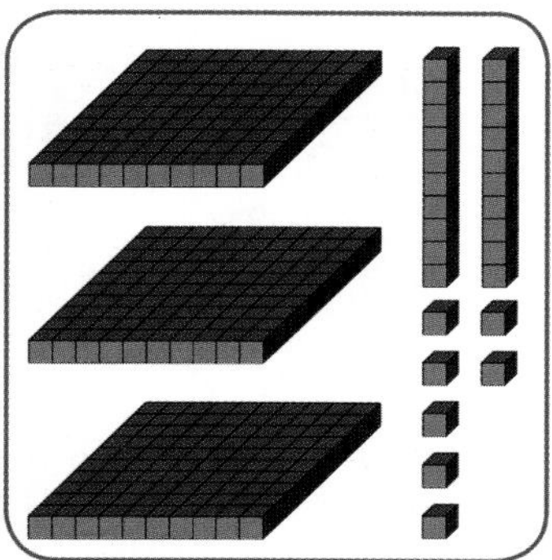 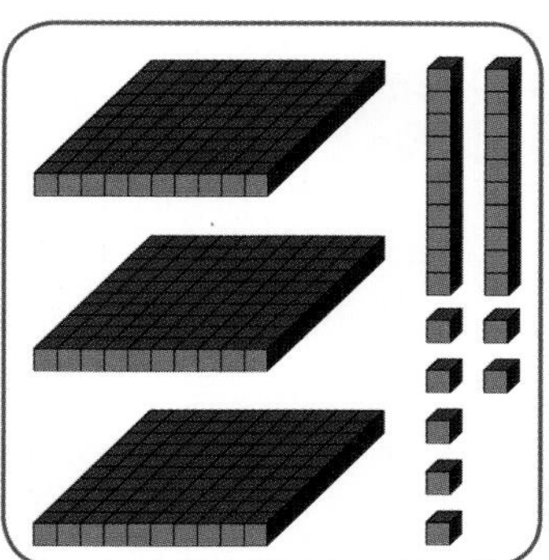

Practice

Divide.

1. 2)6.54	4. 3)9.33	7. 5)25.75	10. 3)14.853	13. 26)54.6
2. 6)3.6	5. 5)4.5	8. 9)85.5	11. 17)3.978	14. 35)423.5
3. 4)2.8	6. 8)67.12	9. 7)14.994	12. 42)8.82	15. 18)2.16

Apply

16. Destiny and her two roommates share a phone. If they equally divide the January bill of $59.55, what is the amount each must pay?

17. After the hurricane, 235.4 mi of beachfront property contained debris. It took 11 days to clean up the entire area. What was the average number of miles cleaned each day?

18. The Kimura family drove 8 hours and covered 412.8 mi while the sun was shining. The weather changed to snow, so they stopped to spend the night. Did they average more or less than 50 mph?

Review

Find the product.

19. 0.15 × 0.2

20. 0.04 × 1.3

Find the quotient.

21. 912 ÷ 24

22. 2,652 ÷ 17

6.7 Zeros in Division

Construct Meaning

The equator, an imaginary circle on the earth, is found at 0° latitude on a globe or map. The prime meridian is located at 0° longitude. Other circles, spaced specific distances apart, help locate places in relation to the equator and the prime meridian. On a globe or a map, zero has significance.

Zero also has significance in dividing decimals.

- A zero holds a place value in the quotient of a decimal problem just as it does in the quotient of a whole-number problem.

```
   4.01   Place the decimal.
3)12.03   Divide 12 by 3.
 -12      Divide the tenths.
          Write 0.
   0 03   Divide the hundredths.
  -   3
      0
```

```
    401   Divide 12 by 3.
3)1,203   Divide the tens.
 -1 2     Write 0.
          Divide the ones.
    003
  -   3
      0
```

More Examples of Zero in the Quotient

```
  0.003   There are 0 ones, tenths, and
3)0.009   hundredths. Place a 0 in those places
 -    9   in the quotient.
      0   Continue to divide.
```

```
  0.513   2 cannot be divided by 4, so place a 0 in
4)2.052   the ones place in the quotient. Continue
 -2 0     to divide.
    05
  -  4
     12
    -12
      0
```

```
   50.8   4 cannot be divided by 6, so place a
6)304.8   0 in the quotient.
 -30      Continue to divide.
   04 8
   -4 8
      0
```

- A zero placed at the end of the dividend can sometimes help complete a decimal problem so there is no remainder.

```
    3.47
25)86.85
  -75
   11 8
  -10 0
    1 85
   -1 75
      10 ←— Continue to divide to
            eliminate any remainder.
```

```
    3.474
25)86.850
  -75
   11 8
  -10 0
    1 85
   -1 75
      100
     -100
        0
```

Check by using the inverse operation.

```
   3.474
 ×    25
  17 370
+ 69 480
  86.850 ✓
```

Check Understanding

Place the decimal and divide.

a. $2\overline{)0.008}$ b. $7\overline{)49.70}$ c. $8\overline{)209.6}$ d. $15\overline{)65.19}$

Practice

Find the quotient.

1. $3\overline{)1.08}$
2. $6\overline{)0.024}$
3. $7\overline{)205.1}$
4. $35\overline{)40.6}$
5. $24\overline{)5.40}$
6. $9\overline{)0.234}$
7. $14\overline{)19.04}$
8. $4\overline{)0.06}$
9. $11\overline{)0.242}$
10. $25\overline{)4.075}$

Divide and check.

11. $5\overline{)1.705}$
12. $8\overline{)83.04}$
13. $18\overline{)38.052}$
14. $2\overline{)4.9}$
15. $7\overline{)0.014}$

Apply

16. The five-member Welch family spent $2,046.50 on their summer vacation in 2015. One of their daughters got married and did not go on the family vacation in 2016 when the family spent $1,804.00 on their vacation. In which year did the Welch family spend more per person?

17. Eva and Chloe went shopping for the Sunday school department. They bought packages of items and divided them among several classes. Help the girls find the price per item.

item	number per package	price per package	price per item
pencils	8	$2.08	a.
pens	10	$2.00	b.
erasers	15	$0.75	c.
glue sticks	2	$2.40	d.
colored pencils	12	$2.28	e.
sticker sheets	2	$2.80	f.
glitter pens	6	$4.26	g.

Review

Multiply.

18. 401×18
19. $2,456 \times 8$
20. $1,608 \times 23$
21. 53.46×1.9
22. 25.62×32

Divide. Round to 3 decimal places.

23. $7\overline{)846}$
24. $46\overline{)1,450}$
25. $23\overline{)7,694}$
26. $10\overline{)1,480}$
27. $5\overline{)49,723}$

6.8 Divide by 10, 100, and 1,000

Construct Meaning

Mars is the fourth planet from the sun. Known as the Red Planet, it looks fiery red in the sky at night. Phobos and Deimos are its two moons. The core is believed to be mostly made of iron. Olympus Mons, located on Mars, is the tallest volcano in the solar system. It is three times as high as Earth's Mount Everest. Robotic rovers have explored Mars' surface and have transmitted exciting information about the planet.

MARS

If a rover analyzed 10 rock samples that weighed a total of 86.5 lb, what would the average sample weigh?

Find 86.5 ÷ 10.

USE MENTAL MATH OR LONG DIVISION.

When you divide by 10, all the digits change to a lower place value. 86.5 becomes 8.65 when the decimal point moves one place to the left.

```
     8.65
10)86.50
  -80
    6 5
   -6 0
     50
    -50
      0
```

The average sample weight would be 8.65 lb.

Dividing decimals by 10, 100, and 1,000 can be done mentally. The number of zeros tells how many places to move the decimal point to the left.

10	86.5 ÷ 10	= 8.65	
100	86.5 ÷ 100	= 0.865	Write a zero so there are
1,000	86.5 ÷ 1,000	= 0.0865	3 places to move the decimal.

Look for a pattern. Observe how the number becomes smaller as the decimal point moves to the left.

17.6 ÷ 10 = 1.76		239.74 ÷ 10 = 23.974	
17.6 ÷ 100 = 0.176		239.74 ÷ 100 = 2.3974	
17.6 ÷ 1,000 = 0.0176		239.74 ÷ 1,000 = 0.23974	

Divide decimals by 10, 100, and 1,000 using long division.

```
     1.76         0.176            0.0176
10)17.60    100)17.600    1,000)17.6000
  -10          -10 0           -10 00
    7 6          7 60            7 600
   -7 0         -7 00           -7 000
     60           600             6000
    -60          -600            -6000
      0             0                0
```

Dividing decimals by 10, 100, and 1,000 is easier using mental math than long division.

Check Understanding

Use mental math to divide.

a. $25.9 \div 10$
$25.9 \div 100$
$25.9 \div 1{,}000$

b. $4.76 \div 10$
$4.76 \div 100$
$4.76 \div 1{,}000$

c. $591.7 \div 1{,}000$

d. $873 \div 100$

e. $7.4 \div 10$

Practice

Use mental math to divide. Observe the pattern.

1. $16.2 \div 10$
$16.2 \div 100$
$16.2 \div 1{,}000$

2. $25.38 \div 10$
$25.38 \div 100$
$25.38 \div 1{,}000$

3. $748.9 \div 10$
$748.9 \div 100$
$748.9 \div 1{,}000$

Use mental math to divide.

4. $4.3 \div 100$
5. $39.1 \div 10$
6. $46.23 \div 1{,}000$
7. $843.7 \div 100$
8. $0.05 \div 10$
9. $0.18 \div 1{,}000$
10. $5.7 \div 100$
11. $91.23 \div 10$
12. $487.32 \div 100$
13. $116.4 \div 1{,}000$
14. $1.1 \div 10$
15. $61.1 \div 100$

Compare the quotient with the dividend. Count how many places each decimal moved. Write whether the divisor is 10, 100, or 1,000.

16. $39.4 \div x = 0.394$
17. $125.6 \div x = 12.56$
18. $8.9 \div x = 0.0089$
19. $2.1 \div x = 0.021$

20. Copy and complete the chart.

÷	10	100	1,000
6.2			
18.5			
243.7			

Apply

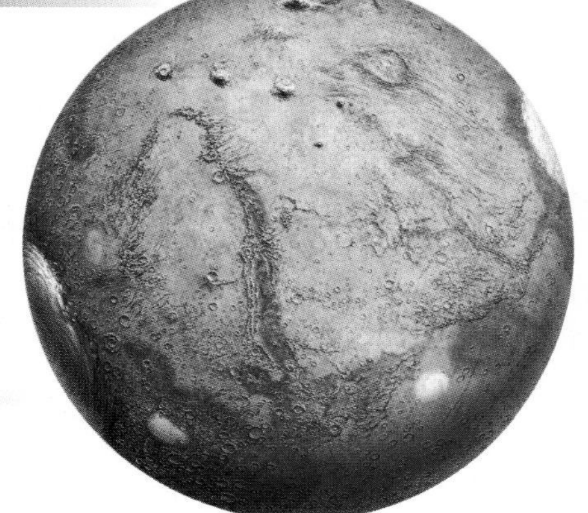

21. If Minne worked on a Mars project for 10 weeks and earned $1,250, how much did she earn each week?

22. The corporation paid student scientists $9,750 for 1,000 hours of research on the project. Was the hourly rate more or less than $10 per hour?

Review

Multiply.

23. 0.08×13.7

24. 12.8×0.06

25. 8.9×4.7

26. 0.09×14

27. 35.5×0.24

Divide.

28. $14\overline{)73.92}$

29. $26\overline{)598.78}$

30. $56.304 \div 9$

31. $16.64 \div 8$

32. $10.010 \div 10$

6.9 Order of Operations

Construct Meaning

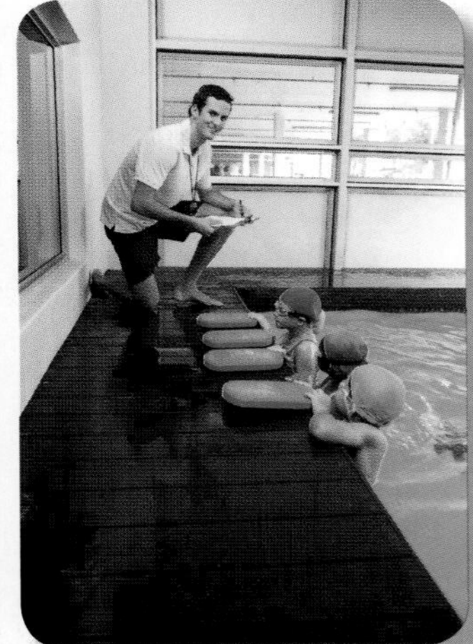

Raphael and Renee began working as swim instructors at the Fast Fins Swim School. When they started, they were told that they would receive a $5 bonus at the end of every week that they worked in addition to their pay rate of $9 per hour. They are both scheduled to work 15 hours per week. They did the math to find out how much they will make per week. Raphael figured that they will make $140 per week and Renee figured that they will make $210 per week. Who is right? Their weekly pay equals p.

Raphael figured his answer with the following equation:

$$15 \text{ hours} \times \$9 + \$5 = p$$
$$\$135 + \$5 = p$$
$$\$140 = p$$

Renee figured her answer with the following equation:

$$15 \text{ hours} \times \$9 + \$5 = p$$
$$15 \text{ hours} \times \$14 = p$$
$$\$210 = p$$

The order in which Raphael and Renee performed the operations affected their answers. Raphael figured the hourly pay first and then added the bonus. Renee added the bonus to the hourly wage and then multiplied this by the number of hours worked. Renee did not perform the operations in the correct order.

Raphael was correct. They will make $140 per week.

In math, there is a set of rules with a specific sequence for solving an equation that has more than one operation. These rules are the order of operations. To solve a problem that has more than one operation, follow the order of PEMDAS:

1. **P** parentheses
2. **E** exponents
3. **M** multiplication and
   D division (from left to right)
4. **A** addition and
   S subtraction (from left to right)

Solve the equation for *n*.

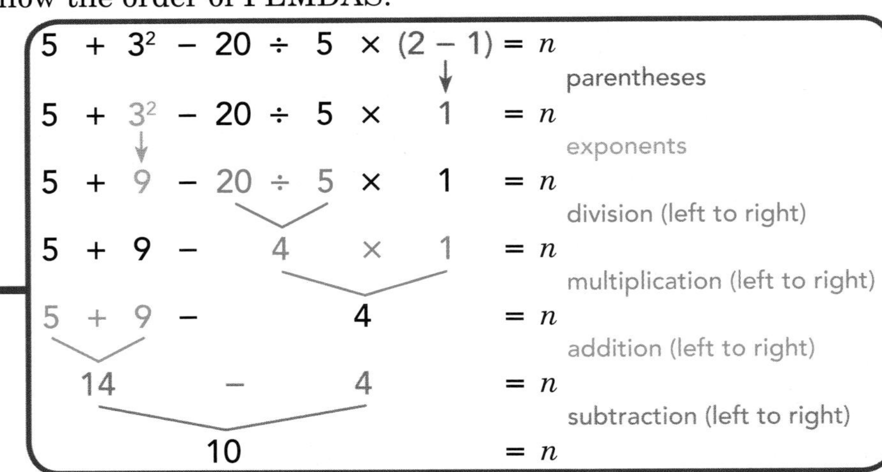

Check Understanding

Solve.

a. $5 \times (4 + 6)$

b. $12 + 9 \div 3^2$

c. $(5 \times 10) - 13$

d. $20 + 3 \times 4 \div 3$

Practice

Write the letter of the operation that should be done first.

1. $36 + 2 \times 2 + (16 \div 4) + 2$
   a. $(16 \div 4)$
   b. 2×2
   c. $36 + 2$

2. $45 \div 5 \times 4 + 1$
   a. 5×4
   b. $45 \div 5$
   c. $4 + 1$

Solve.

3. $4 \times 4 + 2 + 13$
4. $3 \times (26 - 16) \div 10$
5. $3 \times (16 \div 4) + 2$
6. $(1 + 8) \times (3 - 1)$

Solve for the variable.

7. $26 + 30 \div 5 = n$
8. $2^2 + (12 \div 4) \times 8 = r$
9. $18 \div (12 \div 2) - 2 = s$
10. $(5 + 13) \times (16 - 6) = y$

Challenge

Solve.

11. $3^3 - 72 \div (6 + 3) \times 3$

12. Carlos has $350 to spend on his week-long class trip to Ireland. He spends $110 for his train tickets to visit some of the castles in Ireland. Then, he divides the remaining money into two parts, one part for souvenirs and one part for food. He receives an additional $30 from his teacher for food. Write an expression using the order of operations to find how much money Carlos has to spend on food.

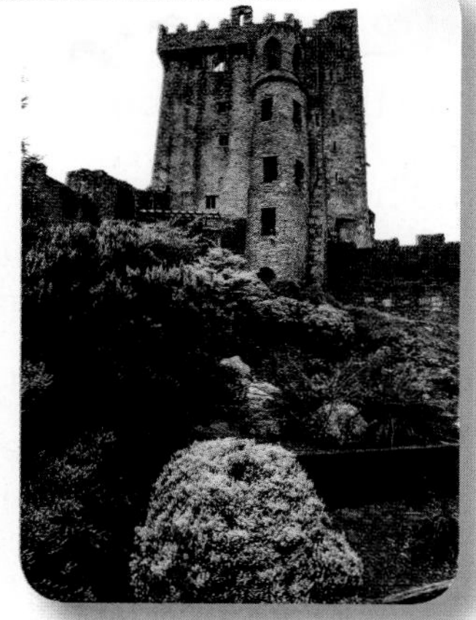

Apply

13. Adeline and Elsie worked together to solve $160 - 100 \div 10$ from their math homework. Adeline thinks the answer is 6 and Elsie thinks the answer is 150. Who performed the order of operations correctly to get the right answer?

14. Ki received this grade on his math test: $200 - 121 \div 11 \times 10$. Jacob received this grade on his math test: $40 + 80 \div 20 \times 10$. Who received the higher grade? What were their grades?

Review

Solve.

15. 0.9×7
16. 6.3×0.4
17. $6\overline{)3.63}$
18. $33\overline{)\$103.95}$
19. $3.9 \times 1{,}000$
20. $52.4 \div 100$

6.10 Problem Solving: Divide

Check Understanding

The fifth-grade students at Pinecreek Christian School are making plans to raise money for Teacher Appreciation Day. They would like to give their teacher a classroom gift and a gift certificate to spend at the mall. They plan to raise money by setting up booths that contain fun things to do. They will invite other classes and parents to participate.

Complete the chart to find out the amount each person raised.

activity	number of students working	amount raised	amount raised per student
dart game	4	$40.56	a.
skit	4	$52.72	b.
cupcake decorating	4	$23.72	c.
shell necklace	4	$68.96	d.
volleyball game	4	$47.52	e.
computer game	4	$66.52	f.

Use the chart above to solve these word problems.

g. The total amount of $300 will be evenly divided between a classroom gift and a personal gift. How much money will go toward each gift?

h. The dart and volleyball games together made $88.08. If all 8 students worked at the game booths, what would be the amount raised per student?

i. Three shell necklaces are made from one package of shells. One package of shells costs $4.95. What is the cost of one necklace?

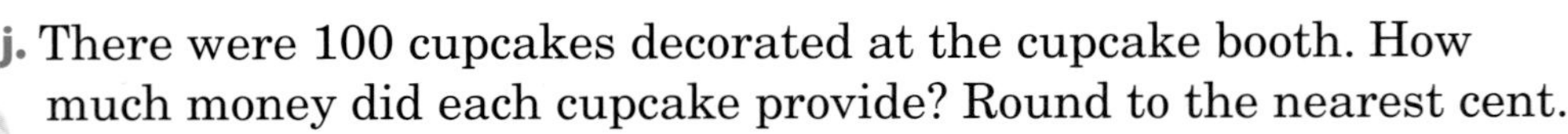

j. There were 100 cupcakes decorated at the cupcake booth. How much money did each cupcake provide? Round to the nearest cent.

k. There were five different computer games available to play at the computer game booth. If each game was played an equal number of times, how much did each computer game make? Round to the nearest dollar.

l. A planet mobile was purchased as the classroom gift. The mobile cost $150. If there are 24 students in the class, what is the average amount each student raised for the mobile?

Practice

Solve.

1. The fishermen caught 167.5 lb of seafood. If a bushel basket holds 25 lb of seafood, how many bushels of seafood do the fishermen have?

2. Cal drove an average of 58 mph on his trip from Florida to South Carolina. He started driving at night and drove for 12.5 hours. How many miles did he travel?

3. Mother made a refreshing pitcher of iced tea. She used one large tea bag for eight cups of water. How many cups of water would she use for three large tea bags?

4. Four mail trucks ran their regular deliveries. The total mileage report for those four trucks on Monday was 678.8 mi. What was the average number of miles each truck traveled?

5. Grandmother's prescription costs $12.57 per month. How much does she pay for a yearly prescription?

6. Tonia bought 2.5 dozen doughnuts to be shared among her 15-member Sunday school class. How many doughnuts could each member receive?

7. Jayden and three friends folded letters for a local business. The job paid a total of $250. How much did each person get paid for the job?

8. Michelle's father invited his fellow employees over for a cookout. He bought 9 lb of steak for a total of $56.61. What was the cost per pound?

Creekview Rainfall per Month

month	total rainfall in inches
March	3.6
April	3.5
May	5.7
June	7.2
July	8.9
August	7.7

Use the chart above to answer the following questions.

9. What was the total rainfall in Creekview for the six months shown?

10. What was the average rainfall per month?

11. If it rained seven days in April, what was the average rainfall for each day it rained in April?

6.11 Chapter 6 Review

Estimate the product by rounding to the greatest place value.

1. 5.2×1.6
2. 8.1×5.7
3. 3.8×2.5
4. $\$22.50 \times 5.1$
5. 317.2×45.6

Estimate. Write >, <, or =.

6. $24.6 \times 3.4 \bigcirc 55$
7. $5.64 \times 8.17 \bigcirc 58$
8. $\$14.98 \times 7.2 \bigcirc \$68$

Choose the equation that matches the model.

9. 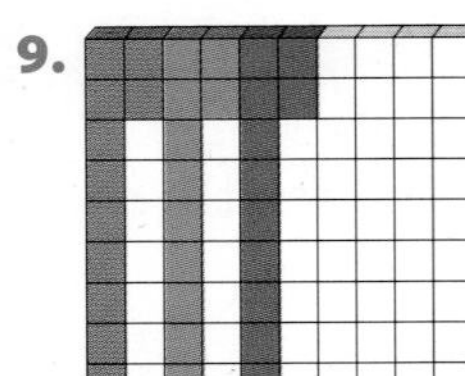

a. $3 \times 12 = 36$
b. $3 \times 0.12 = 0.36$
c. $0.3 \times 0.12 = 0.36$

10. 

a. $0.4 \times 0.8 = 0.32$
b. $4 \times 8 = 32$
c. $0.4 \times 8 = 32$

11. 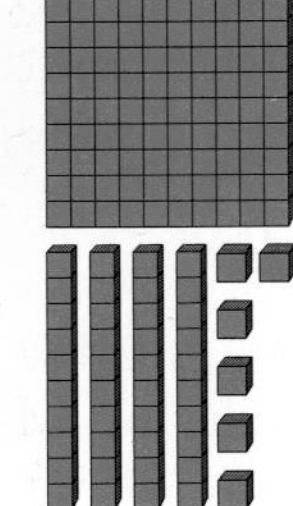

a. $2.92 \div 2 = 1.46$
b. $1.46 \div 2 = 0.73$

Find the product.

12. 0.5×6
13. 2.7×8
14. 4.093×7
15. 6.74×32
16. 4.72×16

17. 0.7×0.4
18. 351×1.4
19. 6.2×0.4
20. 12.3×30.41

Use a calculator to find the product.

21. 0.04×0.7
22. 24.01×0.003
23. 45×0.3
24. 0.006×44

Complete the pattern.

$1 \times 2.56 = 2.56$
25. $10 \times 2.56 =$ ____
26. $100 \times 2.56 =$ ____
$1{,}000 \times 2.56 = 2{,}560$

$1 \times 38.4 = 38.4$
27. $10 \times 38.4 =$ ____
$100 \times 38.4 = 3{,}840$
28. $1{,}000 \times 38.4 =$ ____

$1 \times \$0.25 = \$0.25$
$10 \times \$0.25 = \$2.50$
29. $100 \times \$0.25 =$ ____
30. $1{,}000 \times \$0.25 =$ ____

Divide.

31. $3\overline{)9.78}$ 32. $6\overline{)12.882}$ 33. $24\overline{)55.2}$ 34. $12\overline{)4.788}$ 35. $8\overline{)\$65.84}$

Use a calculator to find the quotient.

36. $6.8 \div 100$ 37. $286.2 \div 1{,}000$ 38. $13.8 \div 10$ 39. $0.18 \div 100$

Choose the equation that is a match for the given answer.

40. Answer: 0.143

a. $14.3 \div 10 = n$
b. $14.3 \div 100 = n$
c. $14.3 \div 1{,}000 = n$

41. Answer: 2.435

a. $24.35 \div 10 = n$
b. $24.35 \div 100 = n$
c. $24.35 \div 1{,}000 = n$

42. Answer: 0.5638

a. $563.8 \div 10 = n$
b. $563.8 \div 100 = n$
c. $563.8 \div 1{,}000 = n$

Solve.

43. Mr. Richardson, his wife, and two children attended a baseball series that lasted five days. They drove 64.8 miles round trip each day. How many miles did traveling to this event add to the odometer on their car?

44. The Richardson family spent $127.95 on refreshments and memorabilia while at the games. What was the average amount spent per day?

45. Multiply to complete the chart to find the weight on various surfaces. Then, answer the questions below the chart.

	gravitational factor	Mercury 0.28	Venus 0.91	Earth's Moon 0.17	Mars 0.38
weight on Earth	75 lb	a.	b.	c.	d.

46. On which planet would a 75-pound person weight the most?
47. On which two planets would a 75-pound person weigh close to the same amount?

Use order of operations to solve.

48. $6 \times 6 + 2 + 13 = y$ 49. $(13 + 6) \times (6 - 2) = c$ 50. $5^2 + (6 \div 3) \times 4 = r$

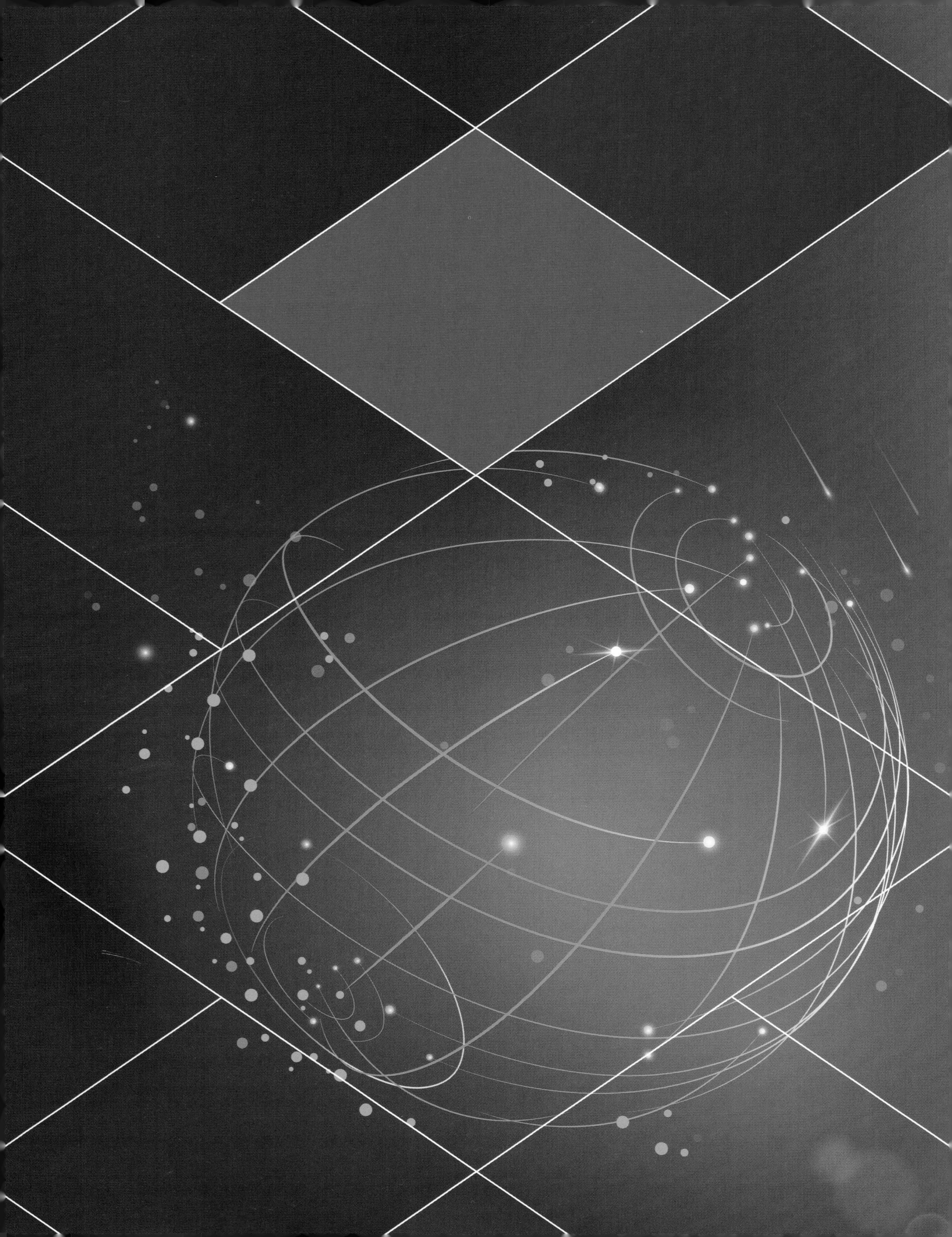

Chapter 7
Geometry

Therefore since we are God's offspring, we should not think that the divine being is like gold or silver or stone—an image made by human design and skill.
Acts 17:29

Key Ideas:

Patterns: identifying patterns in geometric shapes

Geometry: identifying points, lines, rays, angles, triangles, polygons, quadrilaterals, and circles

Geometry: identifying solid figures

Geometry: congruence and symmetry

7.1 Line Relationships

Construct Meaning

The term *geometry* comes from two Greek words: "geo," meaning "earth," and "metria," meaning "measure." It is important to know geometric terms in order to study the many lines, shapes, and figures that are part of God's creation.

Geometric Terms

Term	Definition	Figure	Notation
point	a fixed location in space	A	point *A*
line	a straight path that continues without end in both directions	B C	line *BC* or line *CB* $\overleftrightarrow{BC}$ or $\overleftrightarrow{CB}$
line segment	a part of a line that has two distinct endpoints	D E	segment *DE* or segment *ED* $\overline{DE}$ or $\overline{ED}$
ray	a part of a line that has one endpoint and continues without end in one direction	F G	ray *FG* or $\overrightarrow{FG}$
intersecting lines	lines that cross each other at a common point	H J L K I	$\overleftrightarrow{HI}$ intersects $\overleftrightarrow{JK}$
perpendicular lines	lines that intersect to form a right angle	N L M O	$\overleftrightarrow{LM}$ is perpendicular to $\overleftrightarrow{NO}$ $\overleftrightarrow{ML} \perp \overleftrightarrow{ON}$
parallel lines	lines in the same plane that do not intersect	P Q R S	$\overleftrightarrow{PQ}$ is parallel to $\overleftrightarrow{RS}$ $\overleftrightarrow{QP} \parallel \overleftrightarrow{SR}$
plane	a flat surface that extends without end in all directions	$\mathscr{R}$	plane $\mathscr{R}$

Check Understanding

Name the figure.

a. V W

b. Z

c. X Y

d. R S

e. 

Describe the relationships. Write "intersecting," "perpendicular," or "parallel."

f. A B C D

g. E G H F

h. 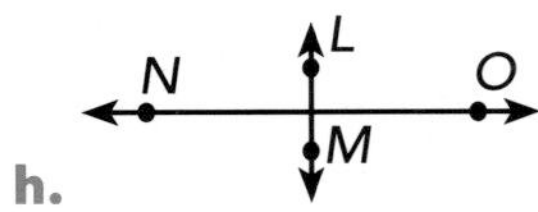

Practice

Draw each figure.

1. point G
2. line segment AB
3. line RS
4. ray XY
5. line FG parallel to line HI
6. lines JK and LM intersecting at point P
7. line CD perpendicular to line EF
8. point Y on line PQ
9. plane C

Apply

Use the drawing of *Pioneer 11*, an early unmanned space probe, to choose the best word(s) to complete each sentence.

10. The red line segment showing the electric cable appears to _____ the yellow line segment above it.
    a. intersect **b.** be parallel to **c.** be perpendicular to

11. The green rays near the Geiger counter appear to be _____.
    a. perpendicular **b.** parallel line segments **c.** neither choice applies

12. The purple rays that meet near the RTGs _____.
    a. are parallel **b.** intersect **c.** are perpendicular

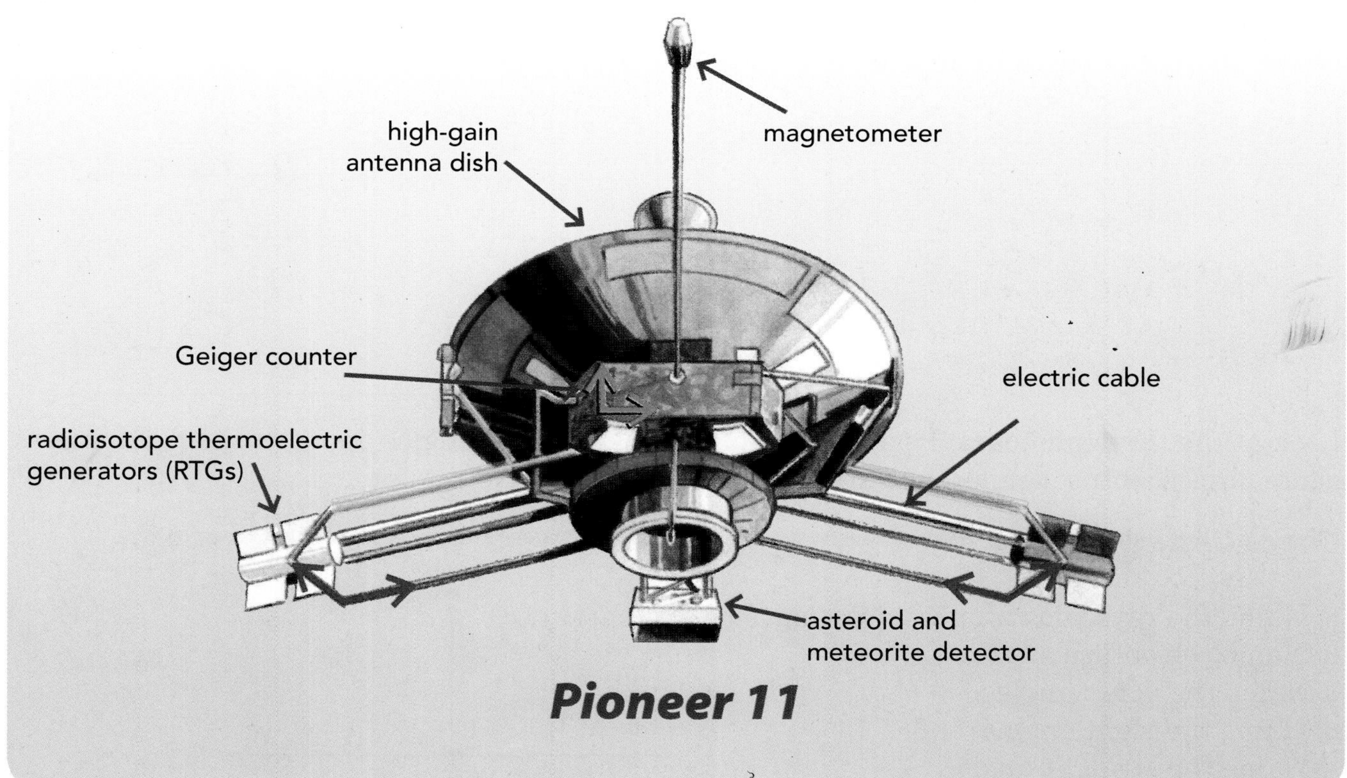

Pioneer 11

7.2 Name Rays and Angles

Construct Meaning

An angle is formed by two rays that have the same endpoint. The endpoint at which the rays intersect is called the vertex. Notice the angles formed at the corners of the level, by the scissor blades, and by the hands of the clock.

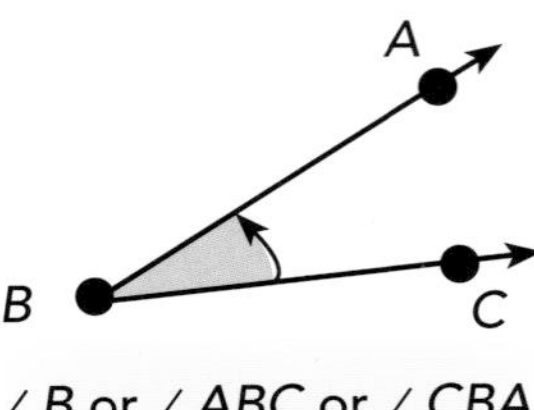

$\angle B$ or $\angle ABC$ or $\angle CBA$

In this drawing of an angle, point B is the vertex of the angle. The letter of the vertex may name the angle or the angle may be named with three letters, with the letter of the vertex in the middle. This is angle B or angle ABC or angle CBA. The symbol used to name an angle is $\angle$. The unit used to measure an angle is the degree, shown by the symbol °.

Types of Angles

When two rays meet to form an angle of 90°, a right angle is formed.

$\angle DEF = 90°$

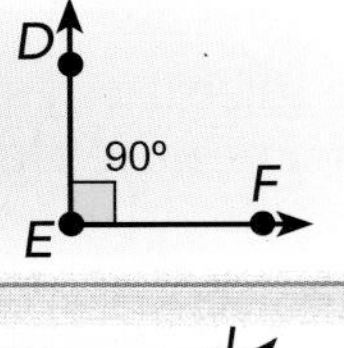

An angle measuring less than 90° is an acute angle.

$\angle JKL = 45°$

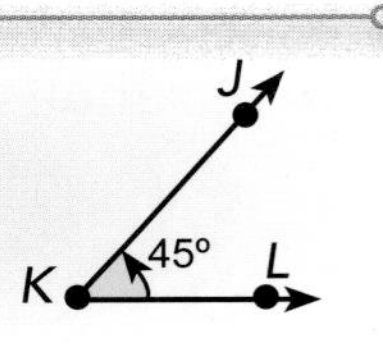

An angle of 180° is a straight angle.

$\angle GHI = 180°$

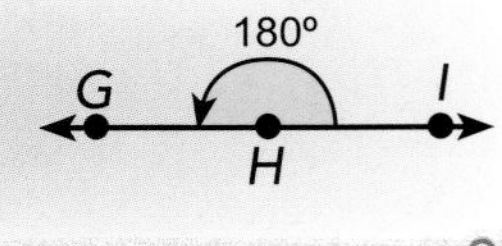

An angle greater than 90° but less than 180° is an obtuse angle.

$\angle MNO = 140°$

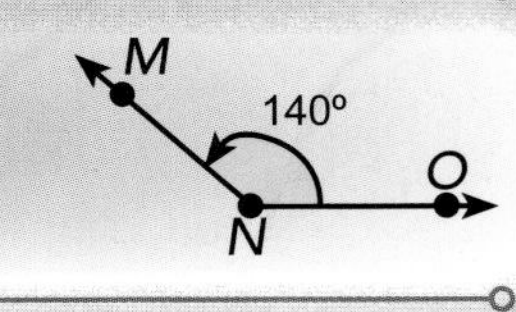

Look at the three photographs at the top of the page. Which angles appear to be right angles, acute angles, obtuse angles, and straight angles?

Check Understanding

a. Name the rays shown in the drawing.
b. Name the obtuse angles.
c. Name the acute angles.
d. Name the right angles.
e. Name the straight angle.

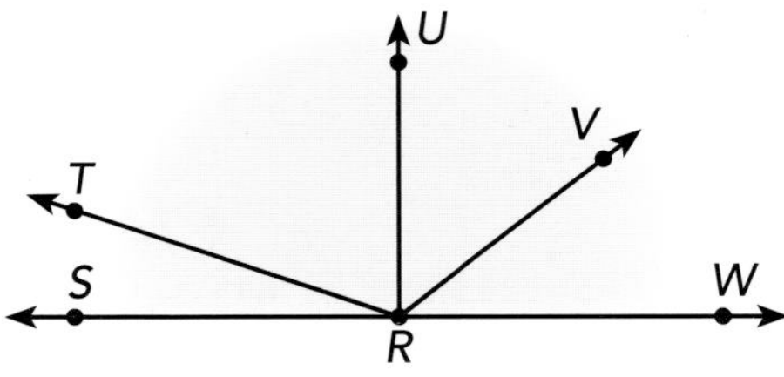

Practice

Name the type of angle shown.

1. 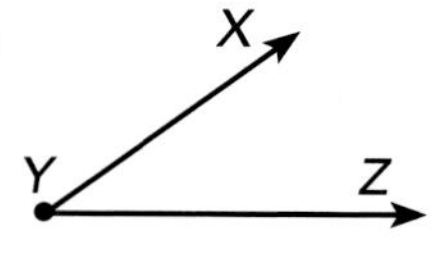

2. 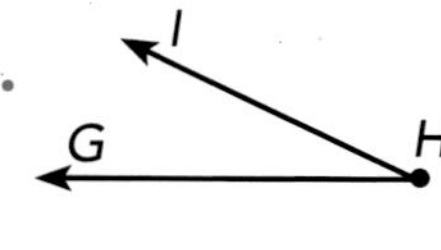

3. R S T

4. 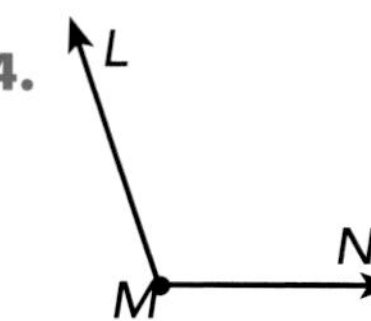

5. 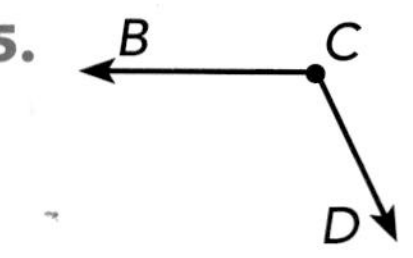

6. 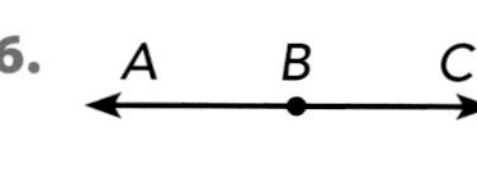

7. 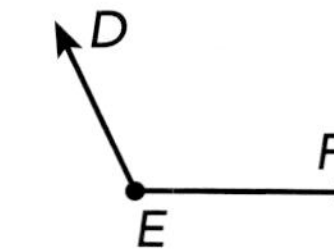

8. 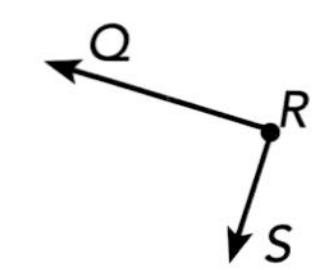

Draw the hands on a clock to show each time. Identify the type of angle the hands display.

9. 9:10
10. 11:00
11. 9:00
12. 8:00
13. 6:00
14. 3:00

Apply

15. What is the name of the plane in this drawing?
16. Name a line segment that is parallel to $\overline{NO}$.
17. Name a line that is perpendicular to $\overleftrightarrow{VX}$.
18. Point W is within which angle?
19. Which angle has fewer degrees, $\angle OST$ or $\angle QSO$?
20. Which is a right angle, $\angle STN$ or $\angle SVT$?
21. Name the angle closest to point M.
22. Name two angles that have $\overline{TS}$ as a side.
23. Name all the points on $\overleftrightarrow{KQ}$.
24. What is the vertex of $\angle LTV$?
25. Name the point where $\overleftrightarrow{QK}$ and $\overleftrightarrow{VX}$ intersect.

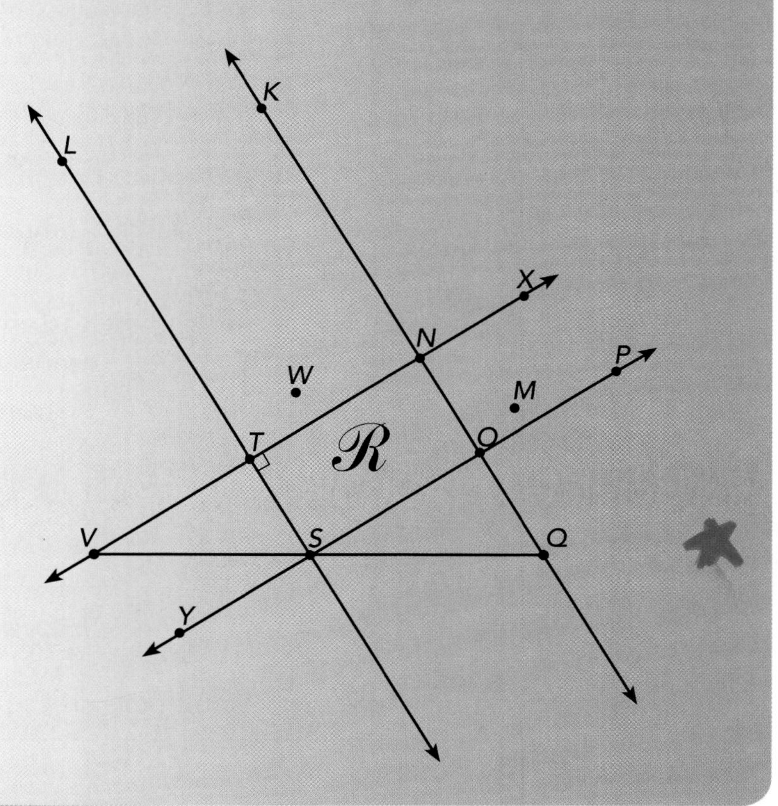

Review

26. $\begin{array}{r} 42.81 \\ \times \quad 66 \\ \hline \end{array}$

27. $\begin{array}{r} 0.733 \\ \times \ 0.25 \\ \hline \end{array}$

28. $\begin{array}{r} 589 \\ \times 0.75 \\ \hline \end{array}$

29. $\begin{array}{r} 321 \\ \times 0.07 \\ \hline \end{array}$

30. $\begin{array}{r} 0.92 \\ \times 0.33 \\ \hline \end{array}$

7.3 Use a Protractor

Construct Meaning

A kite maker must measure the angles of the kite frame carefully so the kite will be able to fly. An instrument that is used for constructing and measuring angles is called a protractor.

A protractor is used to measure the angles of two-dimensional shapes. It has two scales marked from 0° to 180° that allow you to measure from right to left or from left to right. A point at the center near the bottom of the protractor should be placed on the vertex of the angle you are measuring. The zero line across the bottom of the protractor is placed on one of the rays of the angle.

To measure $\angle CDE$, place the protractor as shown below.

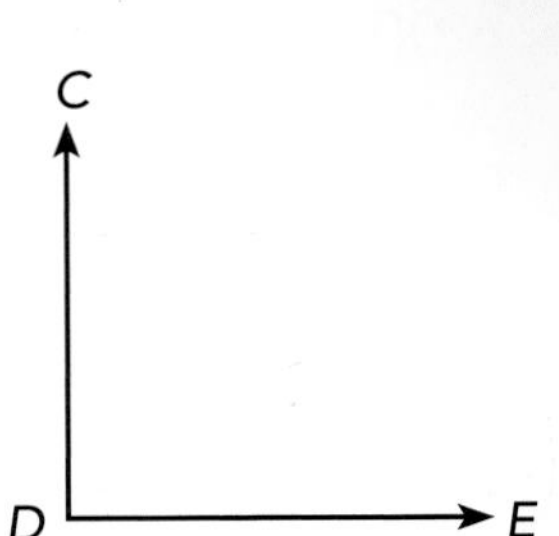

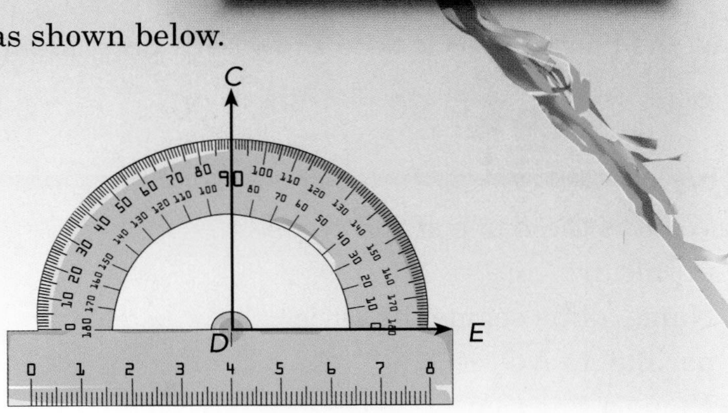

Read the number of degrees where $\overrightarrow{DC}$ crosses the protractor.
$\angle CDE = 90°$, a right angle.

$\angle FGH$ is an acute angle. It measures 50°.

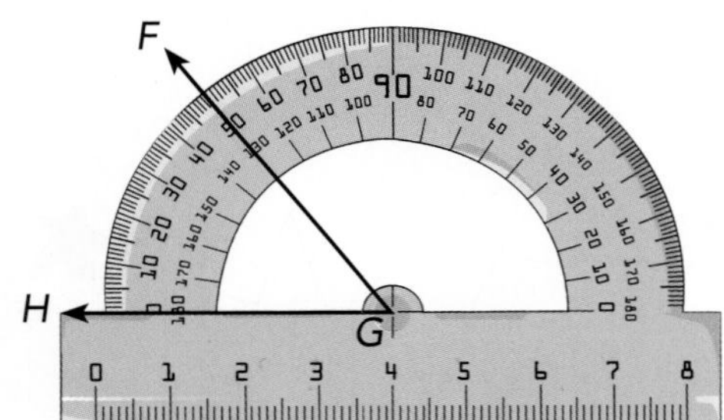

$\angle JKL$ is an obtuse angle. It measures 130°.

Why are there two opposite scales of numbers on the protractor?

To construct $\angle RST$, a 70° angle, use your protractor.

1. Make point S, the vertex.
2. Draw $\overrightarrow{ST}$.
3. Place the point of the protractor on point S, lining up $\overrightarrow{ST}$ with the zero line.
4. Make a mark below the line where you see 70° on the protractor.
5. Draw $\overrightarrow{SR}$ from point S to the mark you made.

Check Understanding

a. Use a protractor to measure $\angle LMN$, using these steps.

Step 1: Place the appropriate point on the protractor over the vertex of the rays.

Step 2: Line up the zero line of the protractor with $\overrightarrow{MN}$.

Step 3: Read the degrees from the zero line up to the point where $\overrightarrow{ML}$ crosses.

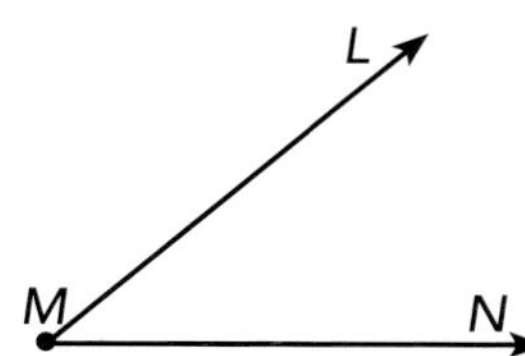

$\angle LMN = 40°$

If your answer is different, reposition your protractor, using the steps above to guide you.

b. Why is the measure of $\angle LMN$ equal to 40° rather than 140°?

Practice

Measure each angle.

1.

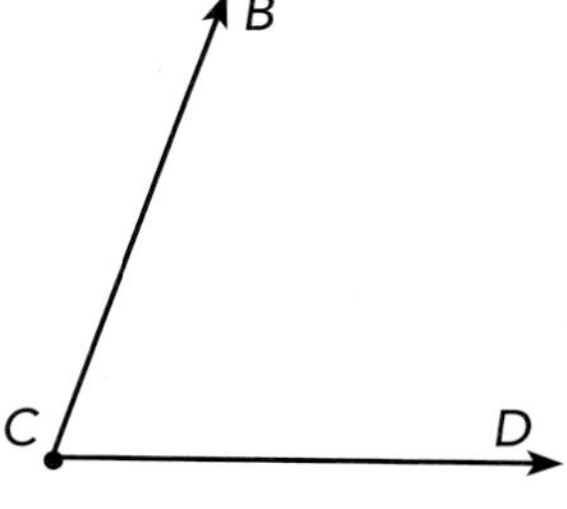

2.

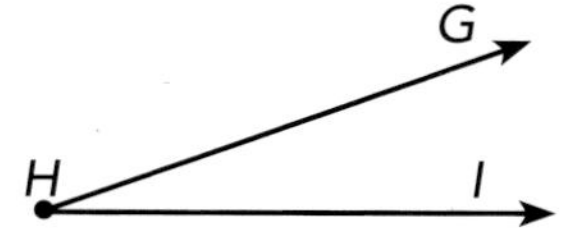

3.

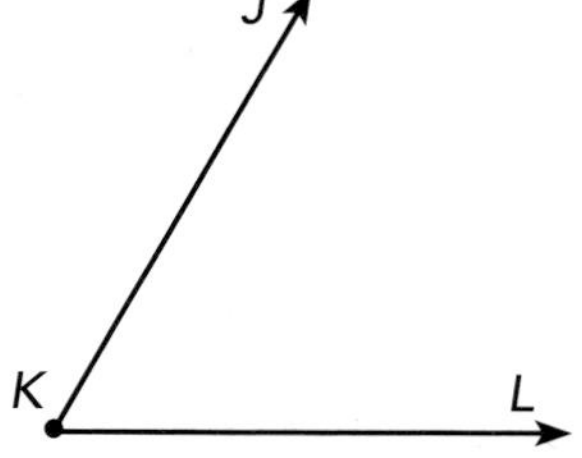

4.

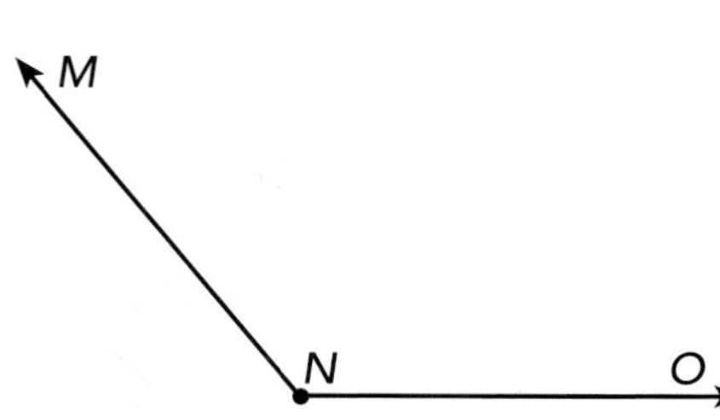

5.

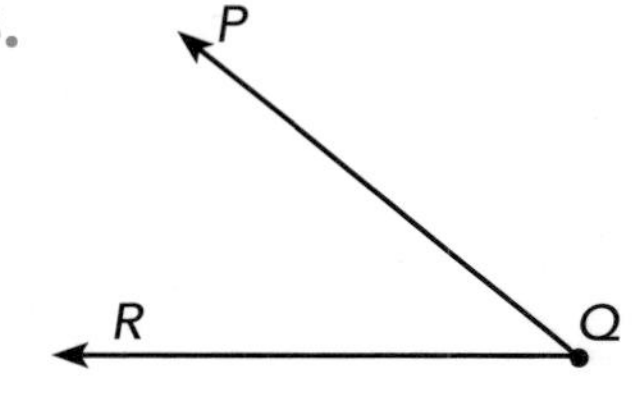

Use a protractor to draw each angle.

6. $\angle KLM$, a right angle
7. $\angle RST$, a straight angle
8. $\angle EFG = 45°$
9. $\angle HIJ = 30°$
10. $\angle UVW = 150°$

Apply

11. Could the sum of the degrees in two acute angles be greater than 180°? Explain your answer.

12. What type of angle do the hands on the clock show when your school day begins? What type of angle do you see when the final bell rings?

7.4 Classify Triangles

Construct Meaning

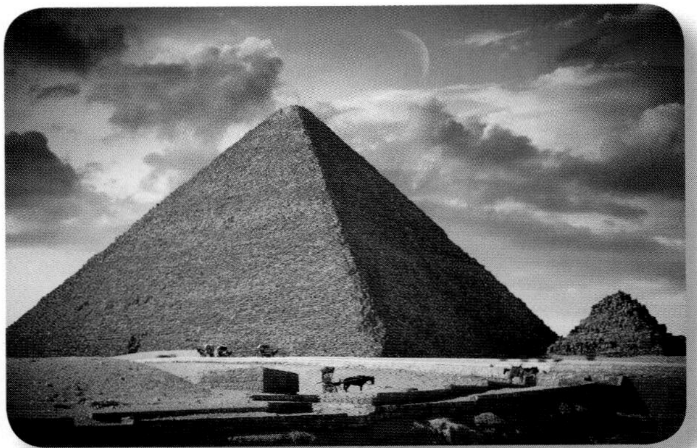

The Great Pyramid, which still stands near Cairo, Egypt, is the only survivor of the original Seven Wonders of the Ancient World. It was built approximately 2,600 years before the birth of Christ and is an amazing architectural feat. It has a square base and each visible face is a triangle that measures 230 m at the base.

A triangle is a plane figure that has three sides, three vertices, and three angles. A triangle is classified by the relative length of its sides or by the types of angles it contains.

Triangles Classified by Relative Length of the Sides

Term	Definition
equilateral triangle	a triangle that has three equal sides
isosceles triangle	a triangle that has at least two equal sides
scalene triangle	a triangle that has three unequal sides

Triangles Classified by Angles

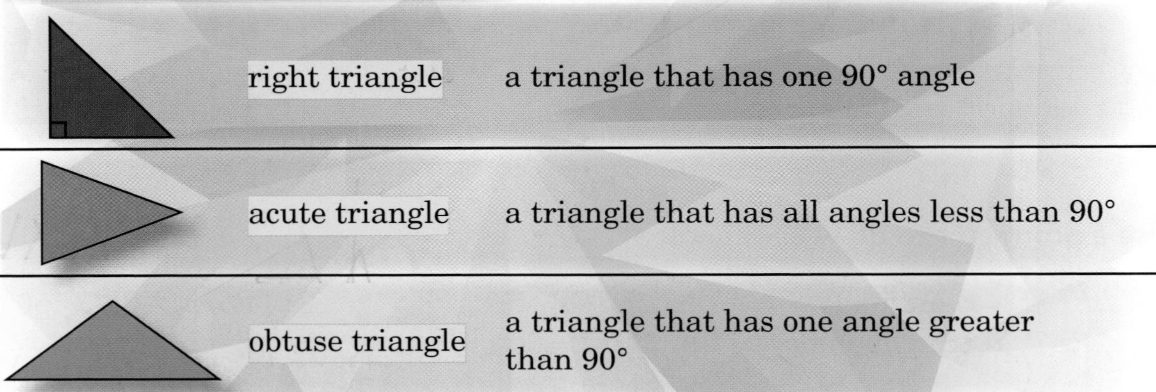

Term	Definition
right triangle	a triangle that has one 90° angle
acute triangle	a triangle that has all angles less than 90°
obtuse triangle	a triangle that has one angle greater than 90°

What is the sum of the angles in a triangle?

Trace and cut out the triangle shown. Cut off each corner. Place the corners back together on a straight angle to find the sum of the degrees of the three angles. Draw another triangle and try again.

Check Understanding

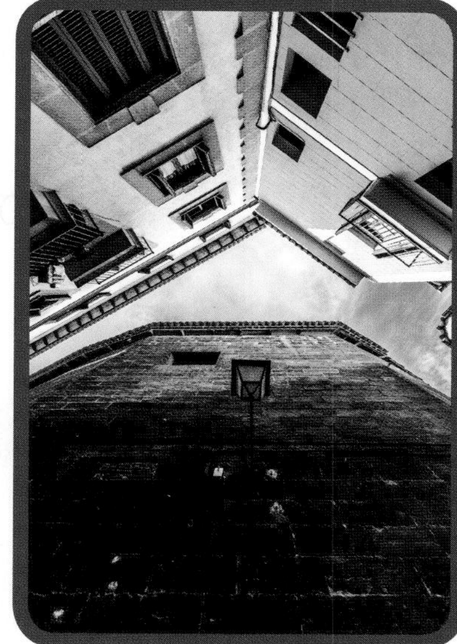

Classify each triangle by its sides.

a. 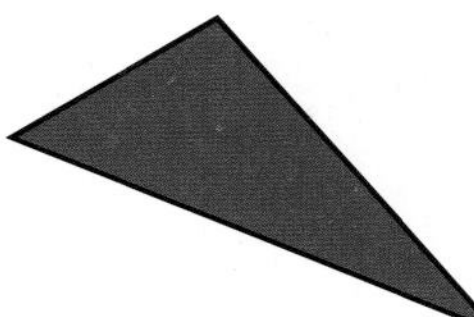

b. 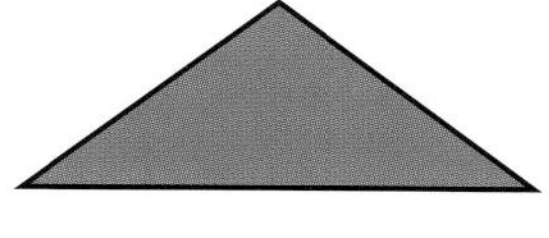

c. 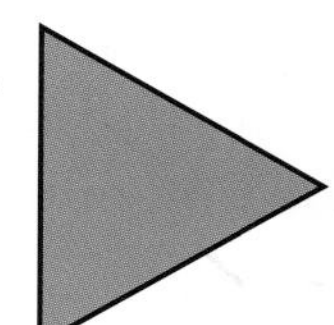

Classify each triangle by its angles.

d. 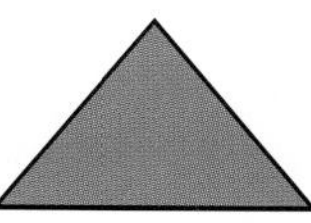

e. 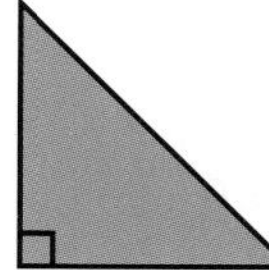

f. 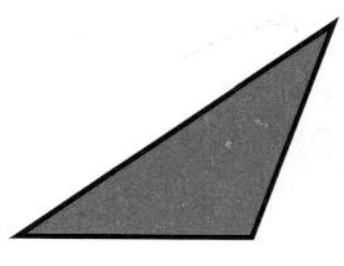

g. If ΔABC has two 60° angles, how many degrees does the third angle contain?

Practice

Label each triangle "equilateral," "isosceles," or "scalene."

1. 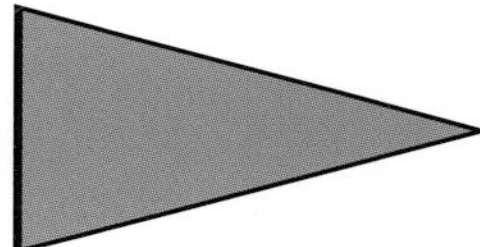

2. 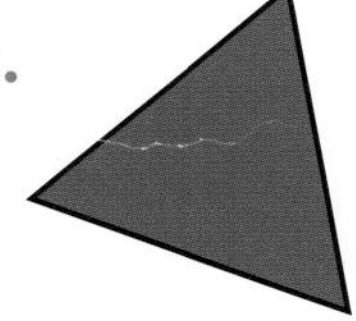

3. 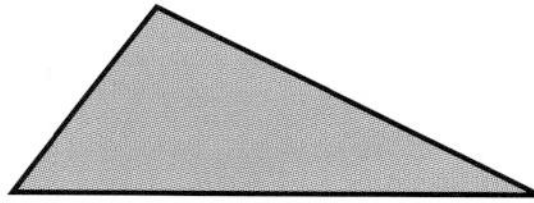

4. 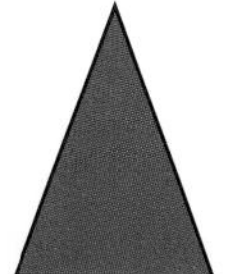

5. 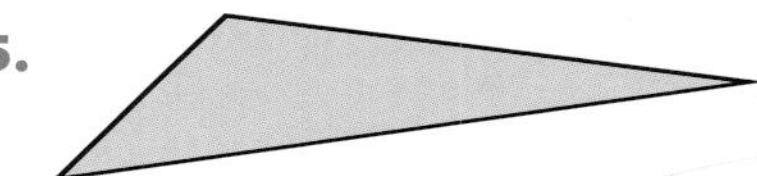

6. 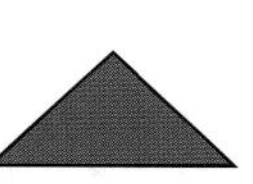

Label each triangle "right," "acute," or "obtuse." State the number of degrees in the third angle for each triangle.

7. 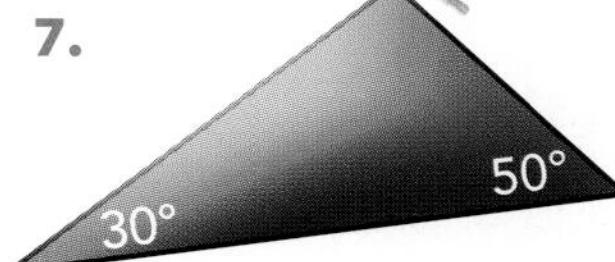

8. 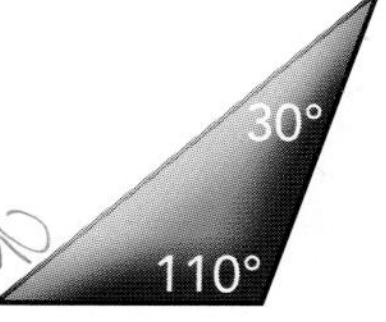

9. 

10. 80° 80°

Apply

11. Use a ruler and a protractor to construct a right triangle. Label each vertex and name the triangle. Use the protractor to measure each angle and write the number of degrees in it. Use the ruler to measure each side and write the length of each side in inches. Is your triangle an equilateral, isosceles, or scalene triangle?

12. Draw a two-inch square. Use one diagonal line to divide the square into triangles. What type of triangles result? Try the same with three-, four-, and five-inch squares. Is the result the same?

7.5 Polygons

Construct Meaning

Habitat for Humanity is an organization dedicated to building housing for people who are unable to purchase a home. In a short period of time, Habitat's many volunteers do all the necessary work to make a home for a family in need.

As you observe the picture of a house shown above, notice the many polygons that can be seen. A polygon is a closed plane figure formed by three or more straight sides. How many polygons do you count in the house silhouette?

Polygon	Sides	Vertices	Angles
Triangle	3	3	3
Quadrilateral	4	4	4
Pentagon	5	5	5
Hexagon	6	6	6
Octagon	8	8	8
Decagon	10	10	10

A regular polygon has sides that are equal in length and angles that are equal in size. These are called congruent sides and angles. An equilateral triangle is a regular polygon that has congruent sides and angles. Scalene and isosceles triangles are not regular polygons. Identify the regular polygons in the drawing of the house.

Compare the pentagons shown. Identify the regular pentagon that has congruent sides and angles.

Check Understanding

Write "true" or "false." Give a reason.

a. A scalene triangle is a regular polygon.
b. An equilateral triangle and a square are regular polygons.
c. Cubes are sometimes polygons.
d. Pentagons, hexagons, and octagons are often, but not always, regular polygons.
e. A right triangle may be a regular polygon.

Practice

Name each polygon. Decide whether it is a regular polygon. Write "yes" or "no."

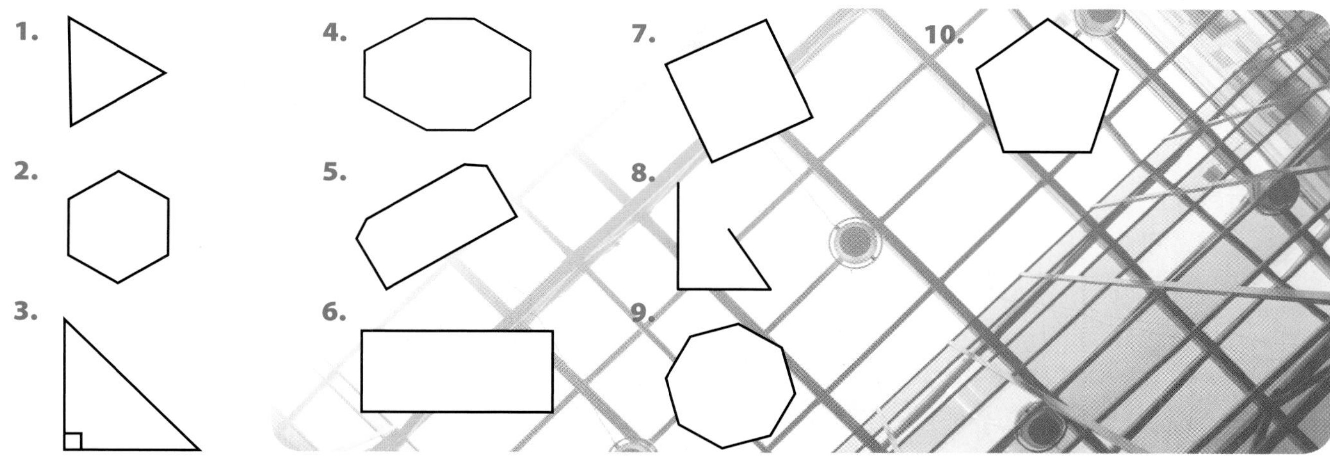

Complete each analogy.

11. Triangle is to quadrilateral as pentagon is to ____.
12. Scalene triangle is to polygon as equilateral triangle is to ____ ____.
13. Quadrilateral is to octagon as pentagon is to ____.

Apply

14. Mrs. Robinson wants her students to consider the attributes of various polygons. As she describes a polygon, her students must identify and draw it. For each description below, write which polygon her students should draw.
    - **a.** This polygon has three angles. The angles are 90°, 45°, and 45°.
    - **b.** This polygon has three pairs of parallel line segments and six angles.
    - **c.** This polygon has two pairs of parallel line segments. One pair is greater in length than the other pair. There are four right angles.
    - **d.** This regular polygon has four pairs of parallel line segments and eight angles.

15. Select an object in the classroom that is a polygon. Write a complete description of the polygon, including the number of sides and vertices, the types of angles, and properties of the line segments. Is it a regular polygon? Why or why not?

7.6 Quadrilaterals

Construct Meaning

Students planning the school fair developed a layout for 10 booths. They wanted to use a quadrilateral shape for each booth. The plan they drew is shown here. Is every booth a quadrilateral?

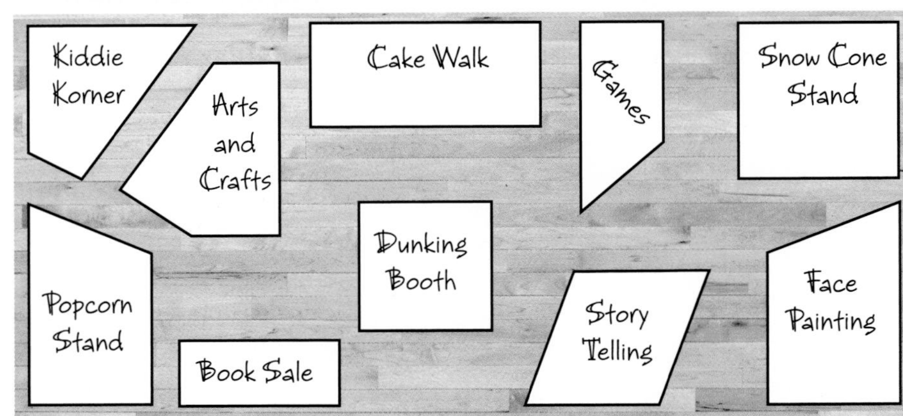

A quadrilateral is a polygon that has four sides. The most common quadrilaterals in geometry are the parallelogram, rectangle, rhombus, square, and trapezoid.

parallelogram
a quadrilateral that has two sets of parallel sides and opposite sides that are congruent

rectangle
a parallelogram that has four right angles and two pairs of sides that are congruent

rhombus
a parallelogram that has sides that are all congruent

square
a rectangle that has four congruent sides

trapezoid
a quadrilateral that has one set of parallel sides (called bases)

Check Understanding

a. Which quadrilateral above is not a parallelogram?

b. Name the quadrilaterals given above that appear in the drawing of the layout of booths.

c. What is the total number of degrees in a rectangle? Will the total be the same for the square? Explain.

d. Which of the quadrilaterals are regular polygons?

Practice

Identify the figure that does not belong.

1. quadrilateral **a.** **b.** **c.** **d.**
2. parallelogram **a.** **b.** **c.** **d.**
3. rectangle **a.** **b.** **c.** **d.**
4. rhombus **a.** **b.** **c.** **d.**
5. trapezoid **a.** **b.** **c.** **d.**

Using the words from the Answer Bank, write three correct statements about quadrilaterals.

6. Every _____ is a _____.
7. Every _____ is a _____.
8. Every _____ is a _____.

Answer Bank

rhombus, square, rectangle, trapezoid, parallelogram

Write the letters of all the figures that match the polygon name.

9. rhombus
10. parallelogram
11. quadrilateral
12. rectangle

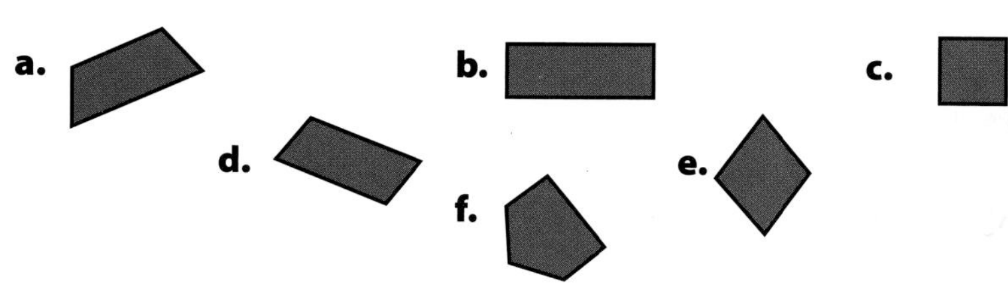

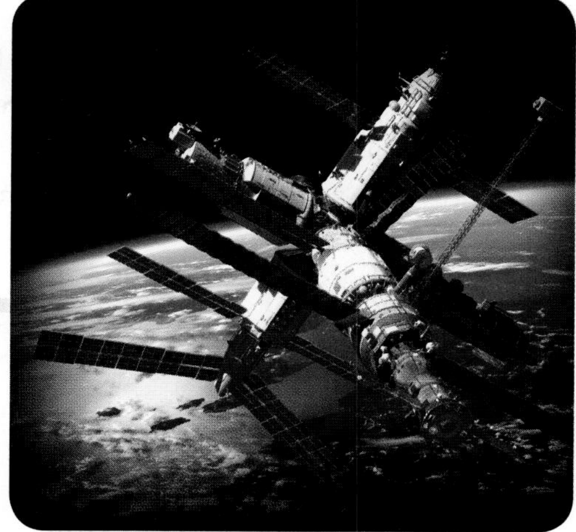

Apply

Complete.

13. Write "true" or "false." All rectangles are quadrilaterals but not all quadrilaterals are rectangles.
14. What types of parallelograms have four right angles?
15. Which parallelograms have four sides of equal length?
16. Explain how the drawings illustrate the total number of degrees in a quadrilateral.

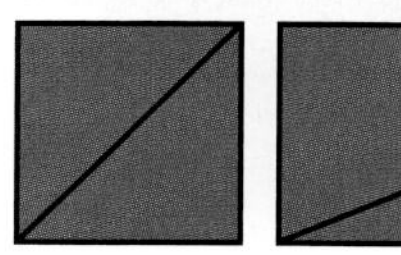

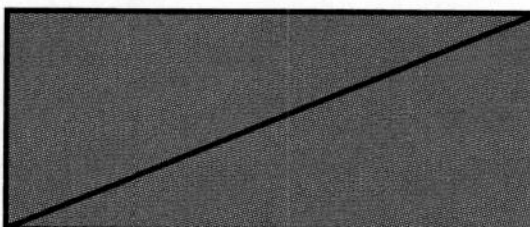

7.7 Solids

Construct Meaning

When Mrs. Larson asked her fifth graders to compare a plane figure with a solid, Tyler drew a rectangle and compared his drawing to his math book. He said, “The rectangle I drew is a plane figure, but the book is a solid.”

A solid has length, width, and height.

Students in Mrs. Larson’s class charted and categorized familiar solids.

solids with curved surfaces
sphere
cylinder
cone

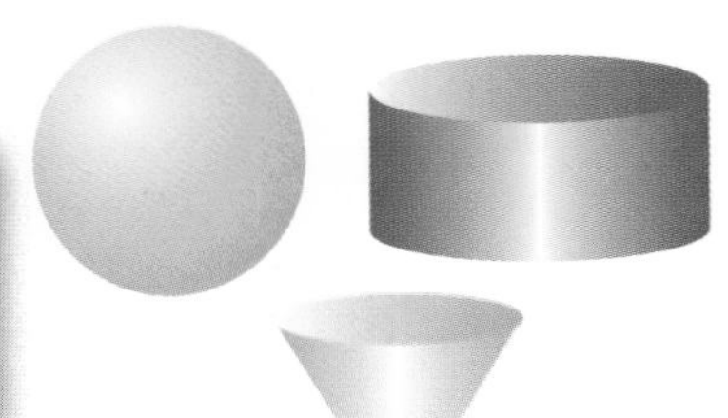

solids with flat surfaces	
Prisms	**Pyramids**
triangular prism	triangular prism
cube	square pyramid
rectangular prism	rectangular pyramid

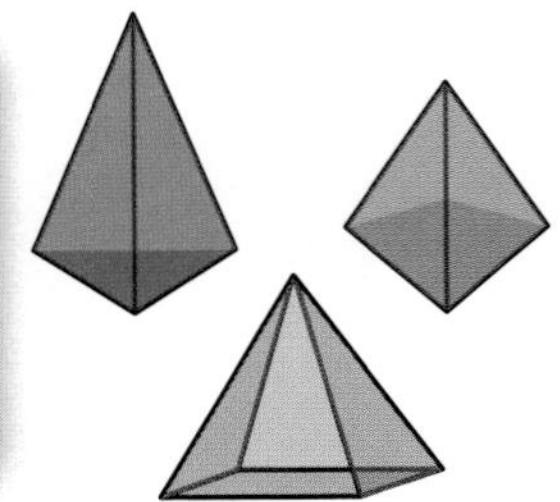

Any solid having only flat surfaces is called a polyhedron. Polyhedrons have faces, vertices, and edges.

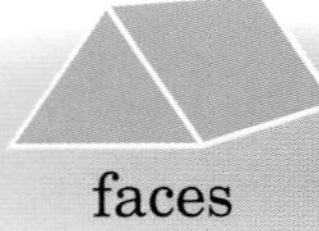

faces

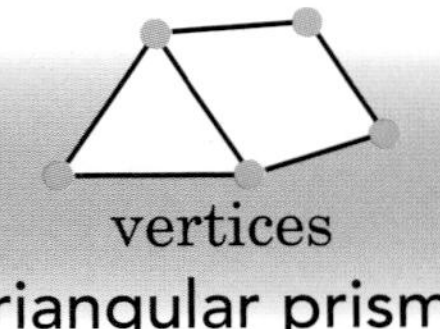

vertices

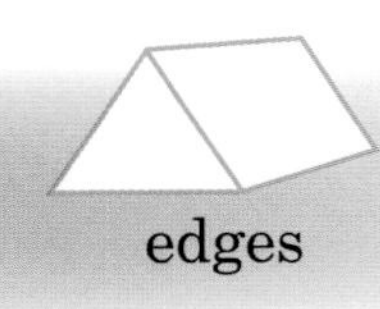

edges

triangular prisms

A prism is a polyhedron that has two congruent bases and rectangular sides. Count the faces, vertices, and edges on the triangular prisms shown.

Each student in Mrs. Larson’s class constructed a pyramid, which is a polyhedron that has a polygon base and triangles for faces. The table shows the polygons needed to construct each type of pyramid.

type of pyramid	polygon faces
triangular pyramid	1 triangle base + 3 triangles
square pyramid	1 square base + 4 triangles
rectangular pyramid	1 rectangle base + 4 triangles

Check Understanding

a. How many faces, edges, and vertices are on the triangular pyramid?
b. Are cones and cylinders polyhedrons? Explain your answer.

Complete the following chart by listing the number and shape of each polygon face.

type of prism	polygon faces
cube	c.
triangular prism	d.
rectangular prism	e.

Practice

1. Write the letter of each figure that is a polyhedron.

a. 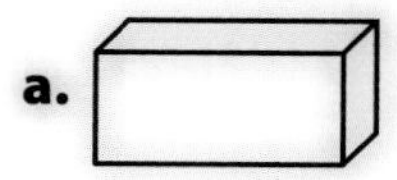
c. 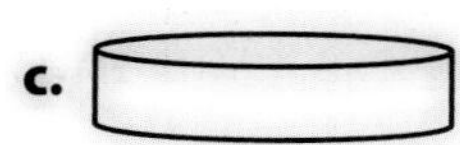
e. 
g. 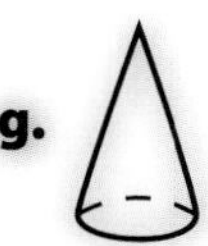

b. 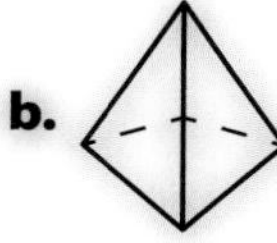
d. 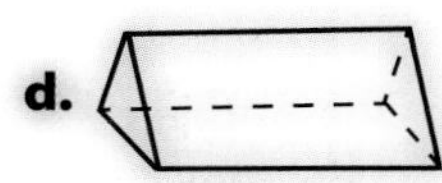
f. 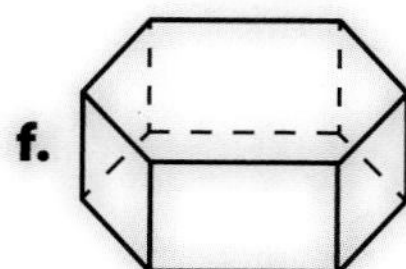
h. 

Write the geometric meaning for each of the following terms. Refer to the Glossary or a dictionary if necessary.

2. face
3. edge
4. vertex
5. polyhedron
6. polygon

Challenge

7. Choose three polyhedrons to construct.

Review

8. If two angles of a triangle are 30° and 40°, what is the third angle?

Write "acute," "right," or "obtuse" to describe the angle.

9. 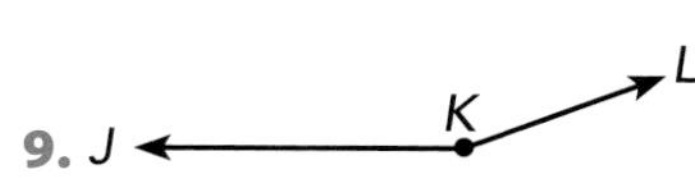

10. 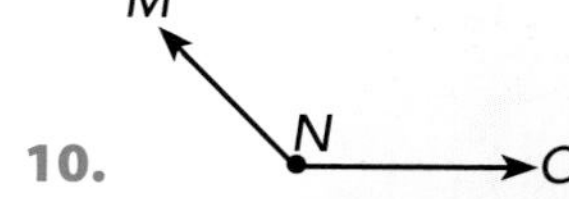

11. 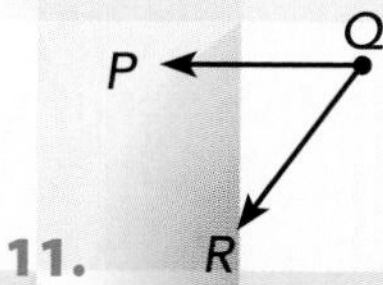

Complete the analogy.

12. Square is to rhombus as rectangle is to ____.

7.8 Practice: Polygons and Solids

Construct Meaning

It is important to know many problem-solving strategies in mathematics. You may use these strategies alone or in combination with each other to solve problems every day.

WRITE AN EQUATION	USE A KNOWN EQUATION
USE DATA FROM A TABLE	USE LOGICAL REASONING

Only part of Polygon A is showing. Visualize what may be hidden by the box using logical reasoning. Name each polygon.

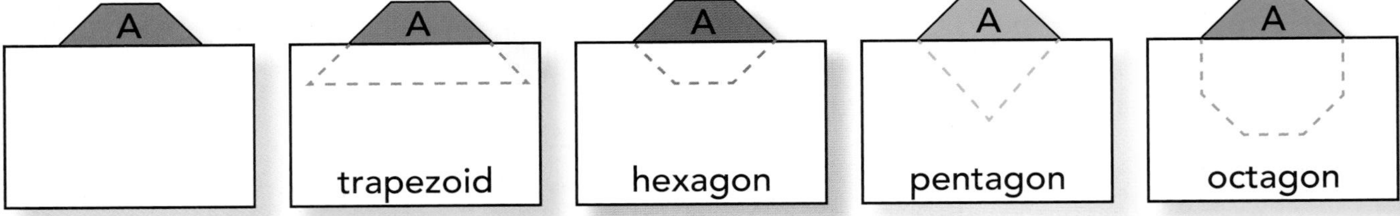

Practice

Use Table 1 to solve the following.

Table 1

polygon	degrees
triangle	180°
quadrilateral	360°
pentagon	540°
hexagon	720°
octagon	1,080°

1. The angles in a parallelogram are 60°, 120°, and 60°. What is the measure of the fourth angle?

2. If a stop sign is a regular octagon, what is the measure of each of its angles?

3. A triangle has angles that measure 20° and 85°. What is the measure of the third angle?

4. The length of each of the five outer walls of the Pentagon building in Washington, D.C. is 921 ft. What is the angle where two walls of the Pentagon meet?

5. What is the measure of each angle in a regular hexagon?

6. Can a triangle have two right angles? Why or why not?

Write the names of some of the polygons which may be hidden by each box.

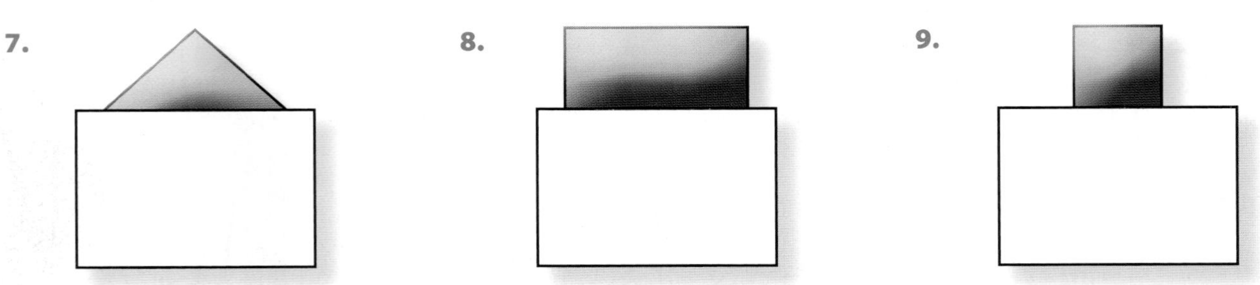

In 1752, a mathematician named Leonhard Euler made a discovery that is true for solid figures. He wrote his findings in an equation:

faces + vertices - edges = 2

Use the information about a cube to try Euler's equation. Then, solve the following problems using the information from Table 2. Write an equation to show your work.

10. How many edges are on a triangular pyramid?

11. What is the total number of vertices on a triangular prism?

12. How many vertices are found on a square pyramid?

Table 2

solids	faces	vertices	edges
cube	6	8	12
triangular pyramid	4	4	
square pyramid	5		8
triangular prism	5		9
rectangular prism	6	8	

13. The number of edges on a rectangular prism is _____.

14. Mitch and his parents are planning to construct a frame for a flowerbed using concrete pavers. The frame will be a 6-foot by 4-foot rectangle. The pavers may be purchased as 1-foot squares for $3 each or 1-foot by 2-foot rectangles for $5 each. Mitch drew a picture to determine the cost of using the square pavers. What will be the cost of the frame using the square pavers? The rectangular pavers?

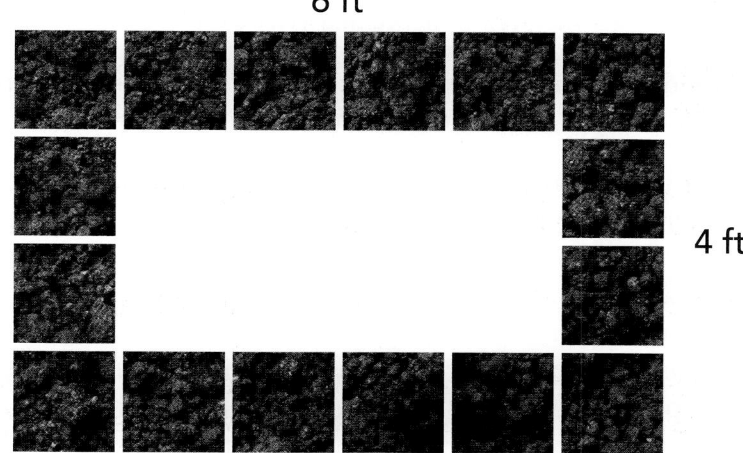

15. Robin said, "I can draw a parallelogram, rhombus, rectangle, square, and trapezoid by drawing only two polygons." Is that possible? If so, use a ruler to draw the two polygons.

7.9 Circles

Construct Meaning

The rose window of the Chartres Cathedral in France is made of many geometric shapes. The largest is the circle. A circle is a closed plane figure that has all points an equal distance from the center.

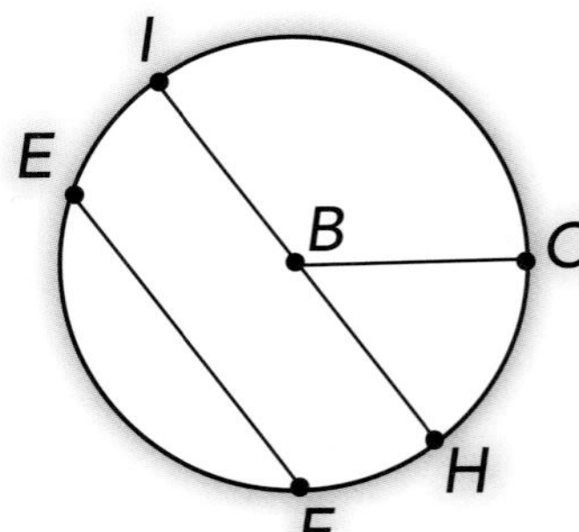

A circle is named by its center point. This is circle B.

A circle contains a radius, which is a line segment that goes from the center to any point on the circle. $\overline{BC}$ is a radius of this circle. A circle can have more than one radius, or radii.

The diameter is a line segment that connects any two points on a circle and passes through the center of the circle. $\overline{IH}$ is a diameter of this circle. A circle can also have more than one diameter. A chord is a line segment drawn between any two points on a circle. $\overline{EF}$ is one chord of this circle. A chord can also be a diameter if it passes through the center of the circle.

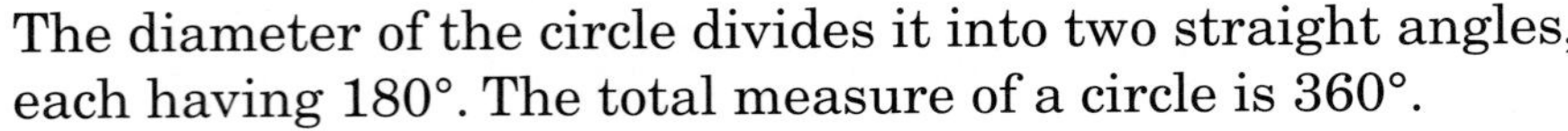

The diameter of the circle divides it into two straight angles, each having 180°. The total measure of a circle is 360°.

Because the diameter of a circle is a straight angle, which measures 180°, the two halves of a circle equal 360°.

Use a compass and a ruler to draw a circle.

1. Use a ruler to draw a line segment for the radius.
2. Place the compass point at one end of the radius.
3. Open the compass to the length of the radius.
4. Turn the pencil around the center to make a circle.

If you open a compass 3 inches, what diameter results?

Check Understanding

Construct a circle that has a 2-inch diameter. Cut out the circle. Follow these directions.

a. Mark a point at the center and label it point A.
b. Fold the circle in half to make a semicircle. Open it and trace across the fold line. This fold is the diameter. Label the endpoints of the diameter B and C.
c. Fold the semicircle in half. Open it and trace the vertical fold line from point A to the top of the circle. This line segment shows a radius of the circle. Label the endpoint D.
d. Join the endpoint of this radius with each endpoint of the diameter to make two chords. Label the chords $\overline{BD}$ and $\overline{CD}$.

Practice

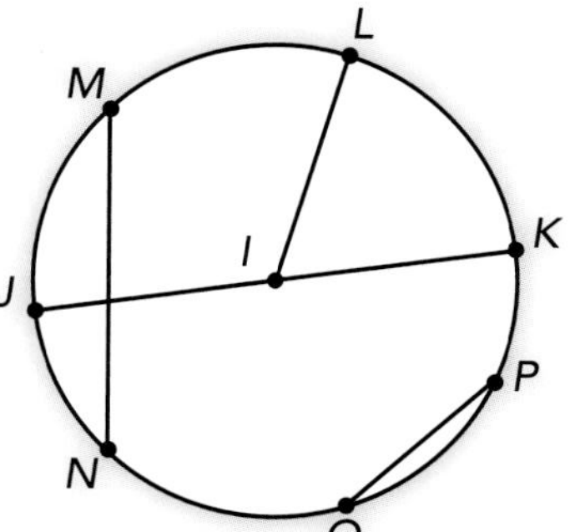

1. What is the name of the circle?
2. Name the diameter.
3. Name the three radii.
4. Name the chords that are not diameters.
5. Measure $\angle LIK$ and $\angle JIL$, recording each angle. What is the sum of the two angles?

Apply

6. A circle has 360°. If it is divided into four equal parts, what is the measure of each angle? Draw a model.
7. If the radius of circle S is 4.5 in., what is the diameter?
8. How many degrees are in a semicircle?
9. To make an octagon within a circle, should you draw chords or radii for the edges of the octagon? How many?

Write "true" or "false" for each statement.

10. Every point on a circle is an equal distance from the center.
11. A chord has the center of the circle as one endpoint.
12. A circle may have more than one diameter.
13. A circle may have more than one radius.
14. A circle divided into eight equal parts has 40° in each part.
15. The diameter of a circle may be three times as long as the radius.

Review

16. $3 \times 12 =$ ____ $\times 4$
17. $15 \times 4 = 3 \times$ ____
18. ____ $\times 2.5 = 5 \times 3$
19. $8.5 \times$ ____ $= 5 \times 17$
20. $9 \times 12 = 6 \times$ ____
21. ____ $\times 11 = 6 \times 22$
22. $5 \times 8 = 2 \times$ ____
23. $12 \times 2 =$ ____ $\times 4$
24. $35 \times 2 =$ ____ $\times 5$
25. $16 \times 3 = 6 \times$ ____
26. ____ $\times 21 = 28 \times 3$
27. $7 \times 8 =$ ____ $\times 3.5$

7.10 Line Symmetry

Construct Meaning

Line symmetry exists when at least one line of symmetry can be drawn in a figure. A line of symmetry makes the two parts appear as mirror images. There are many examples of symmetry in the things created by God as well as in objects built by humans.

These research aircraft from NASA's Neil A. Armstrong Flight Research Center in California show examples of both symmetry and asymmetry, or lack of symmetry. Discuss your parallel observations of the *X-36* tailless fighter and the *Gossamer Albatross*.

X-36

Gossamer Albatross

Imagine folding a figure on the line of symmetry. If the parts are an exact match, the figure is symmetrical.

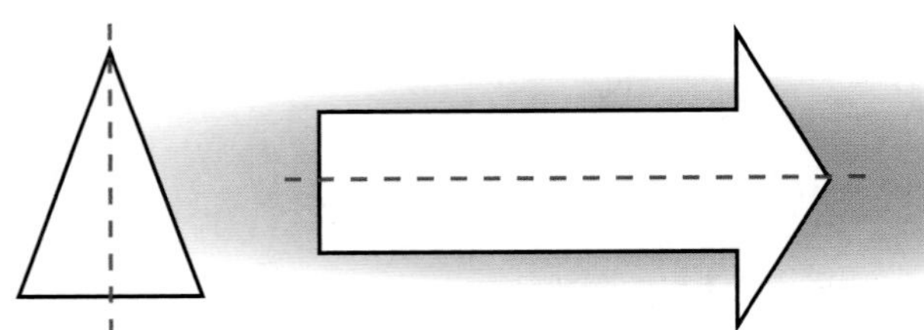

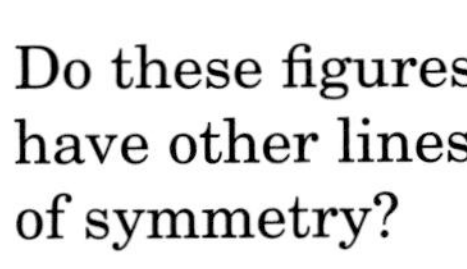

Do these figures have other lines of symmetry?

Look closely to determine how many lines of symmetry exist in each of the following designs.

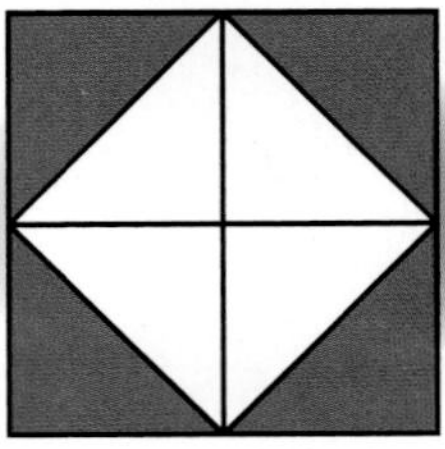

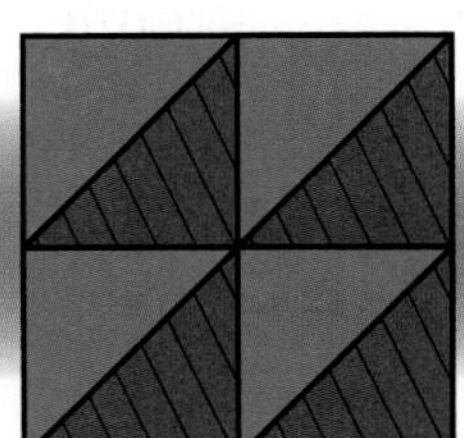

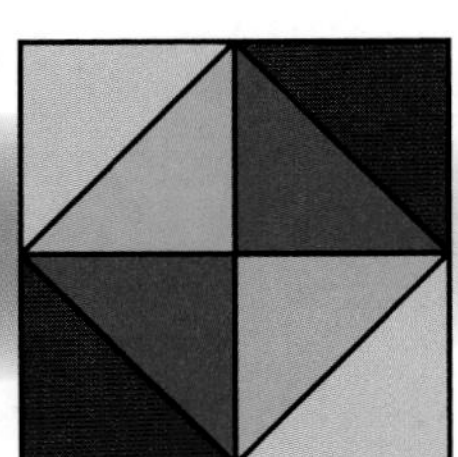

Check Understanding

Copy each figure. Draw the line(s) of symmetry.

a. 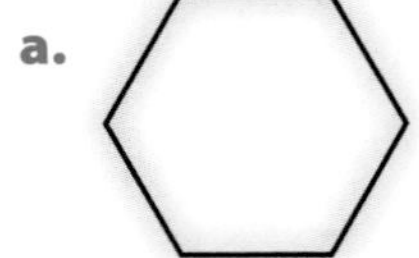

b.

c. 

d. 

e. 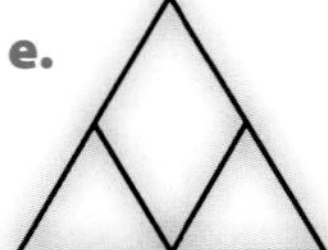

Practice

Copy each figure. Draw all the lines of symmetry. Write "none" if there are none.

1. 
2. 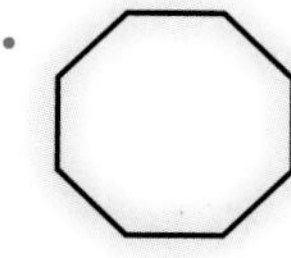
3. 
4. 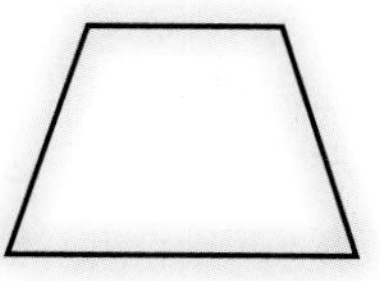
5. 
6. 

7. 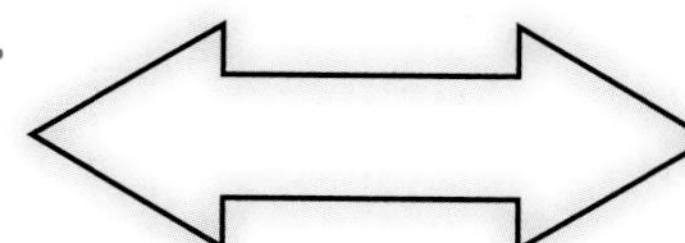
8. 

Copy and complete each figure. Use the red dotted line as the line of symmetry.

9. 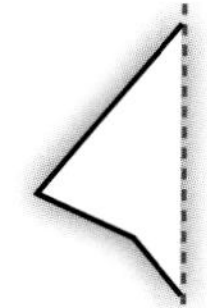
10. 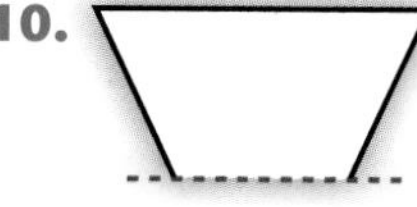
11. 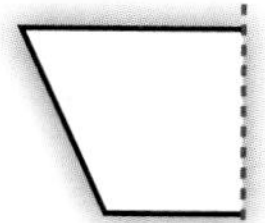
12. 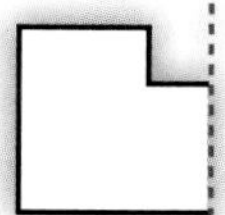
13. 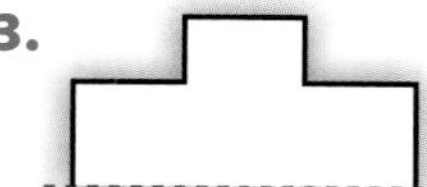

Apply

Observe each border pattern. Write how many lines of symmetry you find for each picture.

14. 
15. 
16. 

17. How many lines of symmetry are in a circle?

18. On May 5, 1961, the first manned space flight of the US Space Program took place. Astronaut Alan Shepard, Jr., flew a sub-orbital mission in a space capsule called *Freedom 7*. Write the name of the space capsule in uppercase letters. Which letters show horizontal symmetry? Which show vertical symmetry?

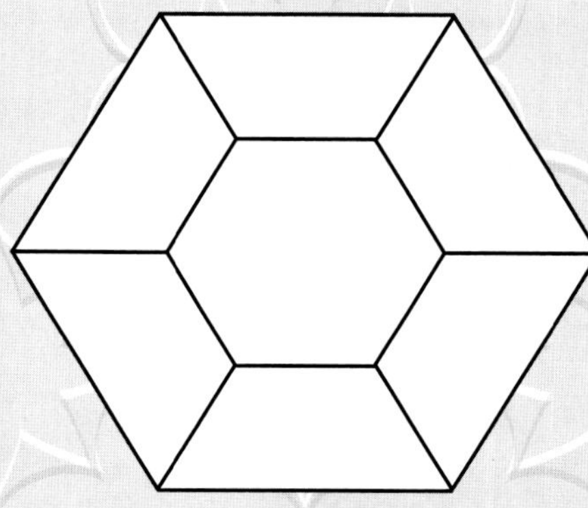

19. Consider the two hexagon designs. How many lines of symmetry can you count in the design at the left?

20. If you consider the colors shown on the right, how many line of symmetry are there? (Pretend you are folding and yellow must touch yellow and blue must touch blue.)

7.11 Motion in Geometry

Construct Meaning

There are many examples of real-life geometric transformations. Which transformation is illustrated in the picture above of Mount Fujiyama in Japan? Geometric transformations change the location or position of the figure but not its size or shape.

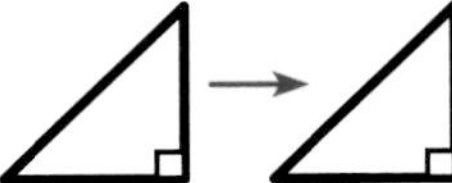

A translation requires moving the figure in a straight line. The figure changes its location but not its position.

A reflection is a move that turns the figure over on a line of symmetry.

A rotation moves the figure around a fixed point.

Use a ruler to construct a scalene triangle that has sides of 1 inch, $1\frac{1}{2}$ inches, and 2 inches. Cut it out carefully and follow the directions below. Make a chart.

1. Title your chart "Transformations."
2. List the name of each type of transformation in the left column of the chart.
3. Next to each term, trace your triangle and then use it to perform the transformation, tracing it in the new location or position to show your work.

Transformations		
type	figure 1	figure 2
translation		
reflection		
rotation		

Check Understanding

A pattern of right triangles may be made by using transformations.

Example:

start → translation → reflection → translation → reflection

Name the transformations for each pattern below.

a. 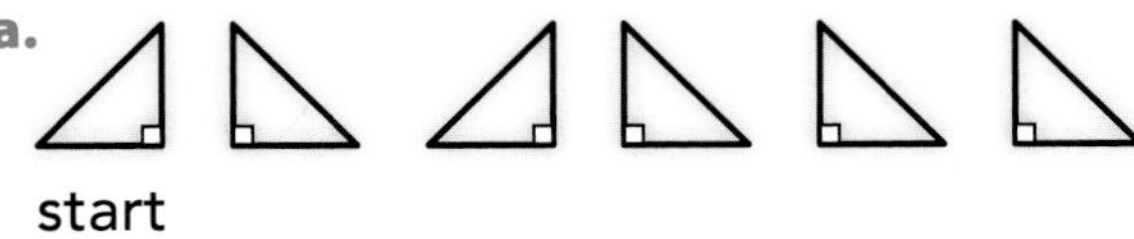

b. 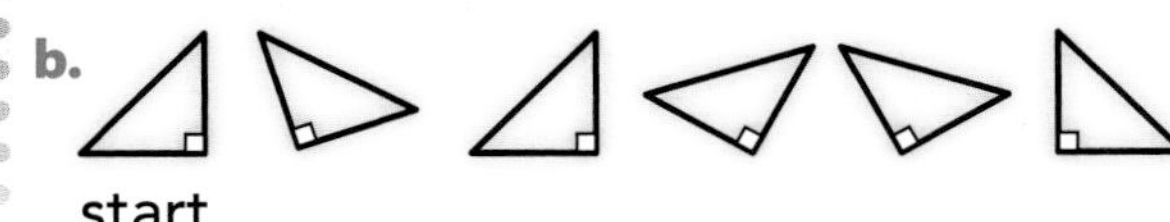

Practice

Identify each transformation. Write "translation," "reflection," or "rotation."

1. 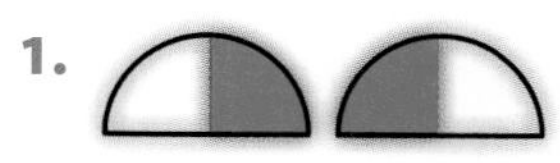
2. 
3. 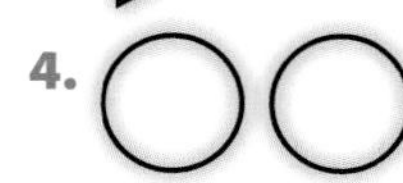
4.
5. 
6.
7. 
8.

Write the possible series of transformations that were used.

9. 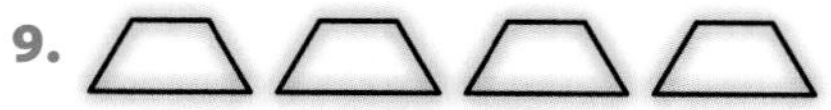
10. 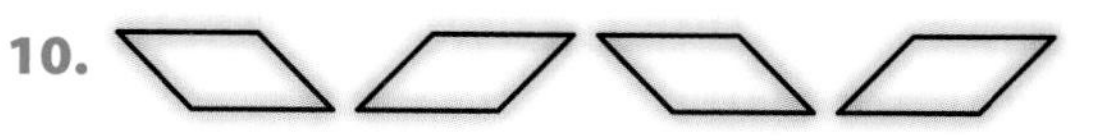
11. 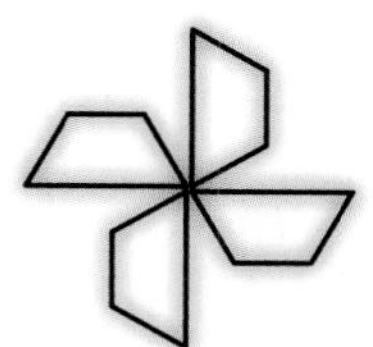

Apply

12. Below are the first three steps for making an origami paper cup. Which step shows a reflection on a line of symmetry?

13. After you complete Step 2, what type of transformation would you do to reposition the paper for Step 3?

Step 1:

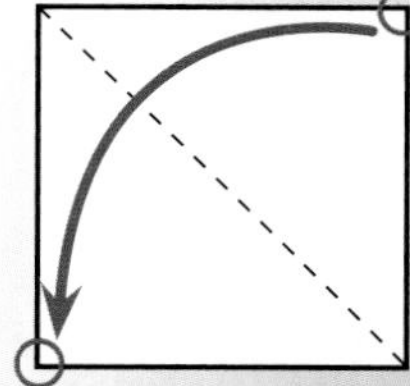

Fold the top corner to the opposite corner.

Step 2:

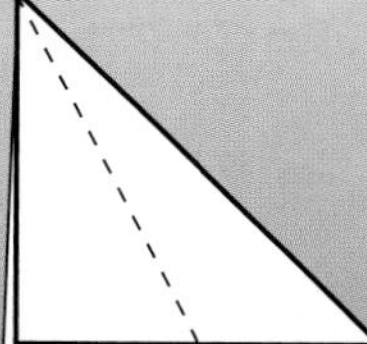

Fold the top layer only, dividing the upper angle in half. Return to the position above.

Step 3:

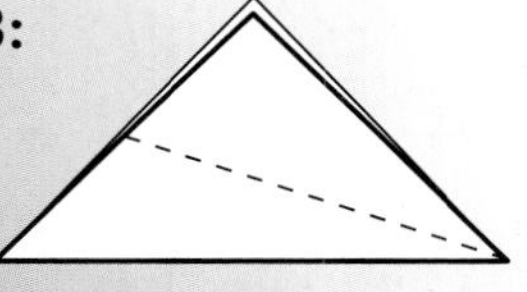

Hold it like this.

14. Cut an 8-inch square of dot paper and follow Steps 1–6 to make an origami cup.

Step 4:

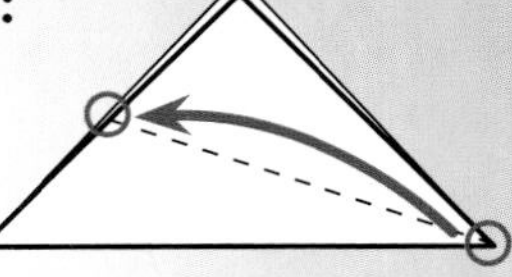

Fold the lower corner to the opposite edge.

Step 5:

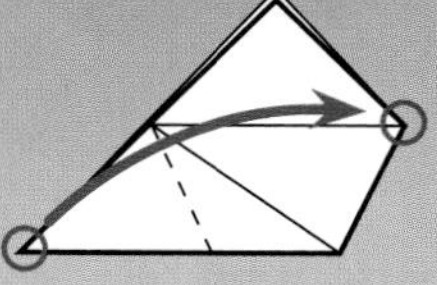

Fold the opposite side in a similar manner.

Step 6:

Separate the top flaps and bring them down to finish.

15. Look at the shape of your cup. Is it symmetrical? Does the drawing in Step 6 show a symmetrical figure?

7.12 Congruence and Similarity

Construct Meaning

Samantha printed a picture of *Skylab* to use on the cover of her report on space exploration. She needed to show more details of the satellite. She enlarged the photograph and printed it again.

The photographs on the left show congruent figures that are the same shape and the same size.

Compare *Skylab* in the enlarged photograph with the photograph on the left. Figures that are the same shape but are different sizes are called similar figures.

Rules of Congruence

The symbol that means "congruent to" is ≅.

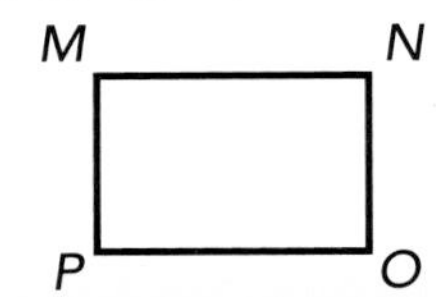

ABCD is congruent to *MNOP*.

$ABCD \cong MNOP$

The corresponding parts of the congruent figures are congruent.

$\overline{AB} \cong \overline{MN}$ $\angle BAD \cong \angle NMP$

Name the other congruent line segments and angles.

The triangles below are congruent. They remain congruent when transformations are applied.

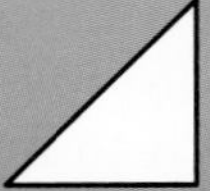

Congruent solids are the same shape and size. They have the same number of faces, edges, and vertices.

Rules of Similarity

Similar polygons must have the same shape.

The trapezoids above are similar. The trapezoids below are not.

Rectangles and squares are not similar. Why?

These are similar triangles.

equilateral
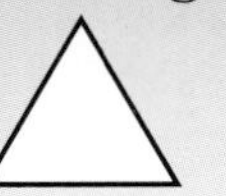

isosceles
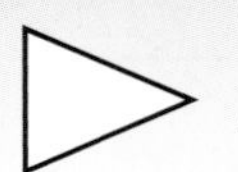

scalene

Solids are similar if they are the same shape.

Check Understanding

a. *MNOPQ* and *RSTUV* are both pentagons. Name the congruent line segments and angles.

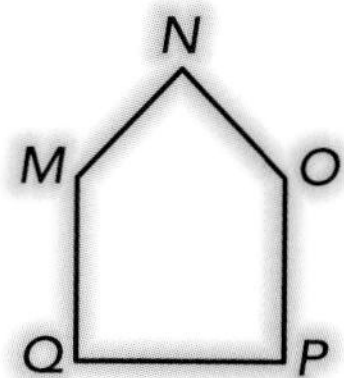

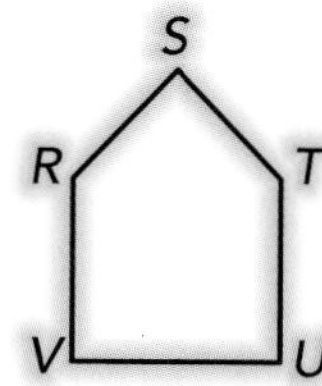

b. Are the two pentagons shown below congruent or similar? Why?

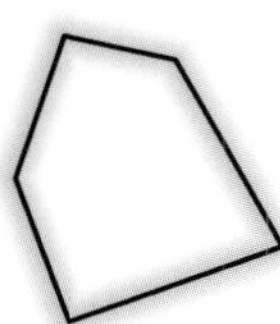

Practice

Use a ruler to draw a congruent figure for each of the following. Each figure should face a different direction.

1. 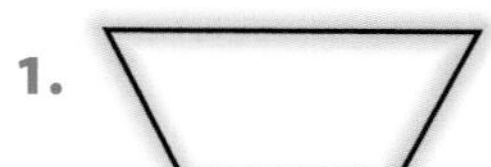

2. 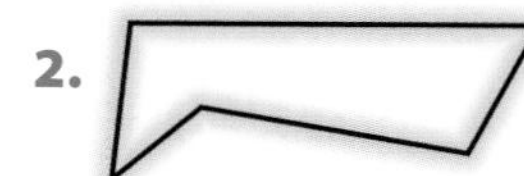

3. 

4. 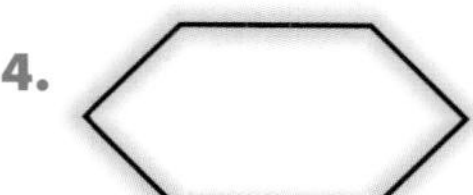

Draw a similar figure for each of the following.

5.

6. 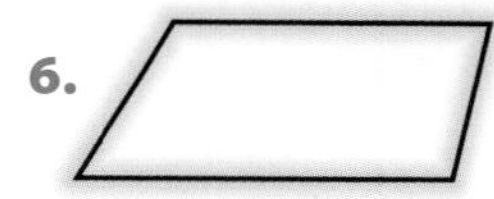

7. 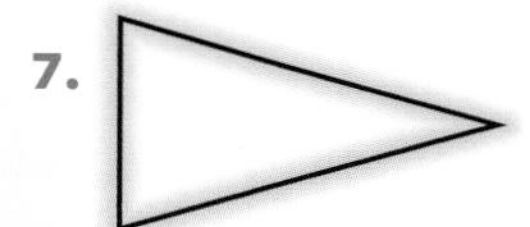

8. 

Apply

9. Landon built a miniature that was an exact replica of the *Vanguard 1* satellite launched by the United States in 1958. Was Landon's model congruent or similar to *Vanguard 1*?

10. Samir and Nichole had two identical sets of pattern blocks. Nichole blocked Samir's view of her workspace. She asked him to listen and try to copy her design as he heard her explain which blocks she used and where she placed them. When they finished, Samir's design was a mirror image of hers. Were the designs similar or congruent? Why?

Review

Write the letter of the correct description for each term.

11. obtuse angles	**a.** do not intersect
12. line segments	**b.** connect two points on a circle
13. lines of symmetry	**c.** sum of the angles is 360°
14. parallel lines	**d.** greater than 90°, less than 180°
15. perpendicular lines	**e.** intersect at right angles
16. acute angles	**f.** have one endpoint and continue in the other direction
17. triangles	**g.** divide figures into mirror images
18. quadrilaterals	**h.** sum of the angles is 180°
19. chords	**i.** have two endpoints
20. rays	**j.** less than 90°

7.13 Problem Solving: Geometry

Construct Meaning

Students in Mr. Warner's class discovered that many letters of the alphabet display interesting geometric patterns. They created a guessing game called Geometry Letters. When it was Maria's turn to give a riddle, she said, "I am thinking of three uppercase letters that form a word that is something we all like to do." Here are the clues she gave to solve the riddle:

One of the letters looks like a triangle at the top and has no parallel or perpendicular lines.

One letter is formed by two perpendicular line segments and has two right angles at the top.

Another letter begins with a straight angle that has three shorter lines perpendicular to it.

Can you write and unscramble the letters to form a word?

Drawing pictures and diagrams can be helpful problem-solving strategies for some geometry problems. Your drawing can help you see how to solve the problem. Other problems require you to use what you know about geometry concepts to solve them.

Practice

Use a drawing or a diagram to help you solve.

1. Lizzie asked her classmates to guess her cousin's initials. She said that her cousin's first initial consists of two vertical parallel lines with a perpendicular line segment at their center. The last initial is a right angle. What are his initials?

2. Your class is making a quilt. You need to cover a 4-inch by 4-inch square with colored 1-inch by 2-inch rectangles. How many rectangles will you need to cover your square?

Use your knowledge of geometry concepts to solve.

3. In art class, Walter decided to create a snowman with four circles instead of three. He used a compass to make the circles, and then he cut them out of construction paper. The top circle had a 1.5 cm radius.
   a. What was the diameter of the top circle?
   b. Walter decided to double the diameter of the previous circle for each circle that followed. What are the diameters of the remaining three circles?
   c. Did Walter make congruent or similar circles?

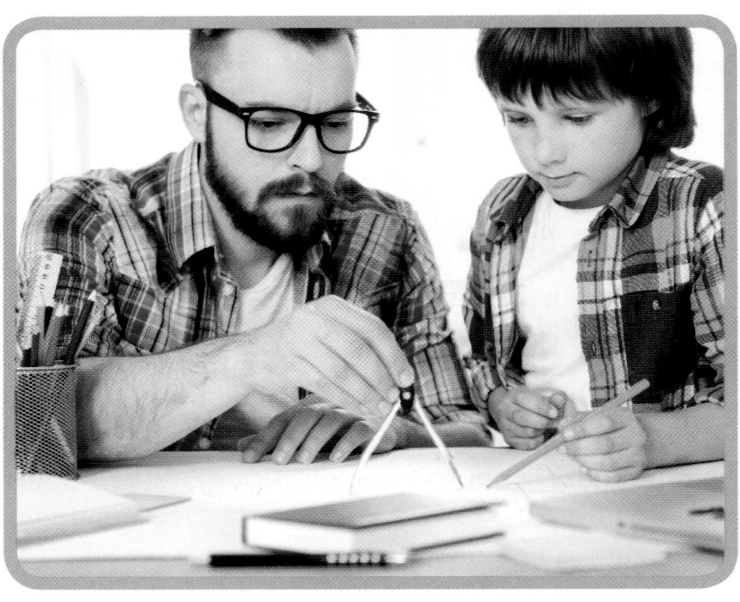

4. Wyatt wanted to draw an obtuse triangle. After drawing it, he measured and found that one angle was 40° and another was 60°. Does he need to measure the third angle? Has he made an obtuse triangle?

5. The fifth-grade class played a geometry review game. Their teacher gave them the following clues. Use the clues to name the geometric solids.
   a. It is a solid but not a polyhedron. It has zero faces, vertices, or edges. It can be found at many sports games.
   b. It is a polyhedron that has faces all the same size. A frozen object is named for this shape.
   c. It is a polyhedron that has one square base and four triangular faces. You may find one in Egypt.
   d. It is a solid that has two circular bases and zero faces. The grocery store has many of these solid shapes.

Challenge

Solve. Draw a diagram if needed.

6. Shelly's family is visiting a newly opened wilderness area. Draw the trail map Shelly and her parents will make as they follow the directions.

Begin at the wooden sign at the trailhead. The path goes north for about 2 mi. Come to a trail that runs perpendicular to this one and turn right. This trail is parallel to a large meadow of wildflowers that you will see on the left. After about 3 mi, a trail on the right that makes a 90° turn to the south emerges. There is a pond 2 mi down the trail. At the pond, there are two trails. The first trail takes a 45° turn to the left and the second trail takes a 90° turn to the right. Choose the second trail, and you will return to the point where you started.

What polygon did your trail map make? How many pairs of parallel lines and congruent sides are in this polygon?

7. Rusty lives by a park that is shaped like a square. A path that goes around the perimeter of the park is 8 mi long. A diagonal path goes across the park, dividing it into two triangles that are the same size. Rusty's brother, Zach, says the diagonal path is also 2 mi long. Rusty disagrees. Who is correct? Why?

7.14 Chapter 7 Review

Identify each term.

1. a fixed location in space
2. an angle greater than 90° but less than 180°
3. a polygon that has all sides equal in length and all angles equal in measure
4. a polygon that has four sides
5. a straight path that continues without end in both directions
6. the endpoint where two rays intersect
7. a closed plane figure that has 3 or more straight sides
8. a tool used in the construction of angles
9. a solid figure that has flat faces
10. a closed plane figure that has all points an equal distance from the center

Identify each triangle as acute, obtuse, or right. Give the measure of the third angle.

11. 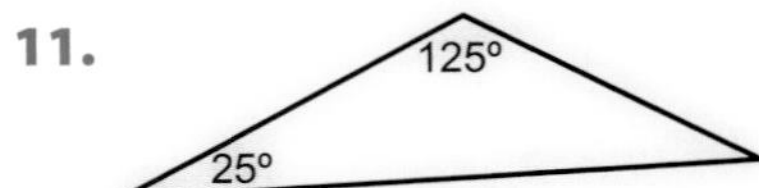

12. 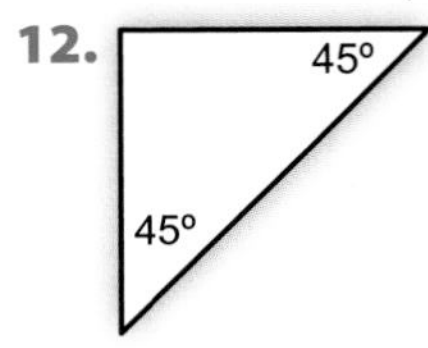

13. 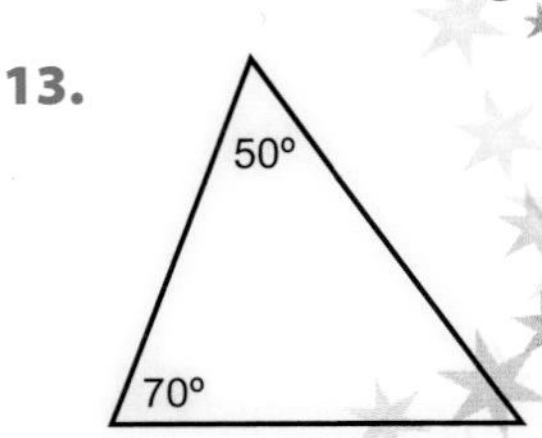

Write the letter of the best answer.

14. a quadrilateral that has two sets of parallel lines that are all the same length
    - **a.** parallelogram
    - **b.** square
    - **c.** rhombus
    - **d.** both square and rhombus

15. a triangle that has three sides of unequal length
    - **a.** isosceles triangle
    - **b.** right triangle
    - **c.** scalene triangle
    - **d.** obtuse triangle

16. a polygon that has eight congruent angles and eight congruent sides
    - **a.** pyramid
    - **b.** hexagon
    - **c.** octagon
    - **d.** regular octagon

17. a polygon that has only one set of perpendicular lines
    - **a.** regular hexagon
    - **b.** right triangle
    - **c.** parallelogram
    - **d.** rhombus

18. a term describing many types of motion in geometry
    - **a.** transformation
    - **b.** translation
    - **c.** rotation
    - **d.** reflection

19. a polyhedron that has only triangular faces
    - **a.** prism
    - **b.** pyramid
    - **c.** triangular pyramid
    - **d.** cylinder

Use the circle to answer the following:

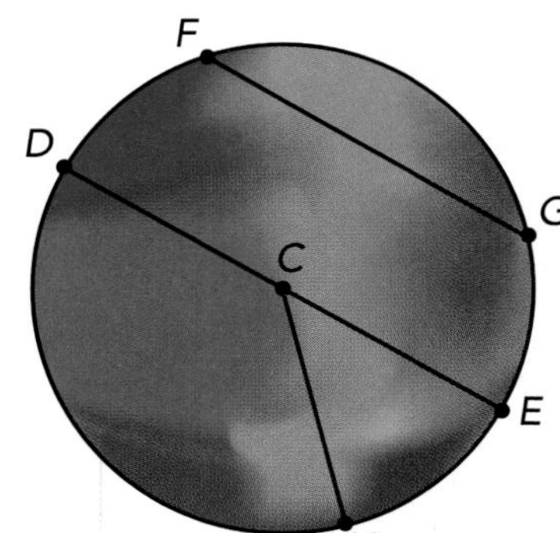

20. Name the circle.
21. Name the diameter shown.
22. $\overline{FG}$ is a _____.
23. $\overline{CD}$ and $\overline{CE}$ are _____.
24. _____ is another radius of the circle.
25. $\angle HCE$ is a(n) _____ angle.
26. $\angle DCH$ is a(n) _____ angle.
27. $\angle ECD$ is a(n) _____ angle.

Write "true" or "false."

28. All intersecting lines are perpendicular.
29. An isosceles triangle and a scalene triangle could be similar.
30. When a symmetrical design is folded on a line of symmetry, the parts will match exactly.
31. A baseball and a soccer ball are congruent solids.

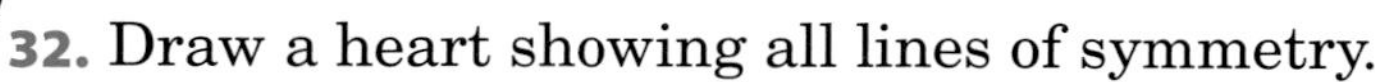

32. Draw a heart showing all lines of symmetry.

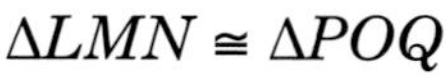

$\Delta LMN \cong \Delta POQ$

33. Name the congruent angles.
34. Name the congruent sides.

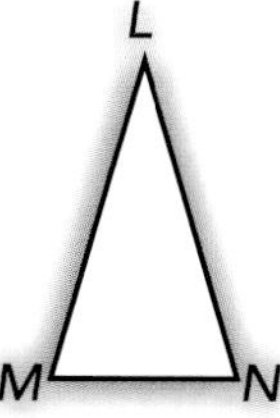

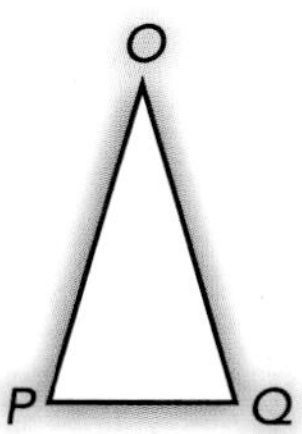

Name the transformation illustrated by each pair of figures.

35. 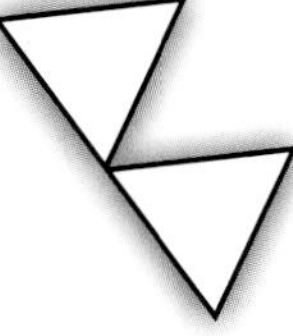

36. 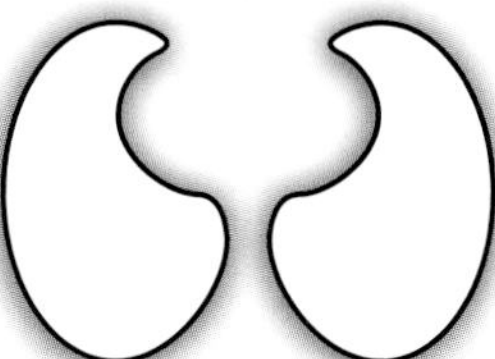

37. 

38. 

39. Molly wants to use paper polygons to make polyhedrons. Name three polyhedrons she can make if she has seven squares and eight triangles.

40. Design a border that shows symmetry. Identify the line(s) of symmetry.

7.15 Chapters 6–7 Review

Estimate the product by rounding to the greatest place value.

1. $\begin{array}{r} 9.3 \\ \times 2.5 \\ \hline \end{array}$

2. $\begin{array}{r} 322.6 \\ \times\ 37.8 \\ \hline \end{array}$

3. $\begin{array}{r} \$14.60 \\ \times\ \ \ 3.9 \\ \hline \end{array}$

Find the product.

4. $\begin{array}{r} 0.8 \\ \times\ \ 5 \\ \hline \end{array}$

5. $\begin{array}{r} 6.042 \\ \times\ \ \ \ 9 \\ \hline \end{array}$

6. $\begin{array}{r} 5.82 \\ \times\ 23 \\ \hline \end{array}$

7. 0.3×0.6

8. 34.02×0.005

9. 13.2×40.91

Complete the pattern.

$1 \times 45.22 = 45.22$

10. $10 \times 45.22 =$ ____

11. $100 \times 45.22 =$ ____

$1{,}000 \times 45.22 = 45{,}220$

$456.7 \div 1 = 456.7$

$456.7 \div 10 = 45.67$

12. $456.7 \div 100 =$ ____

13. $456.7 \div 1{,}000 =$ ____

Divide.

14. $3\overline{)8.67}$

15. $6\overline{)18.66}$

16. $15\overline{)5.088}$

Use order of operations to solve.

17. $6^2 + (10 \div 2) \times 8 = y$

18. $(18 \div 6) \times (12 - 2) = h$

Solve.

19. The four Woodgate brothers ran a lemonade stand to raise money for summer camp. They made $191.32 in lemonade sales and were given a $20 donation toward camp. Between the sales and the donation, how much did each brother make?

Write the letter of the correct term from the Answer Bank.

20. a part of a line that has one endpoint and continues without end in one direction
21. a flat surface that extends without end in all directions
22. a part of line that has two distinct endpoints
23. the unit used to measure an angle
24. a polygon that has four sides
25. a quadrilateral that has two sets of parallel sides and opposite sides that are congruent
26. a solid figure made of flat surfaces called faces
27. a line segment from the center to a point on a circle

Answer Bank

a. degree
b. line segment
c. parallelogram
d. plane
e. polyhedron
f. quadrilateral
g. radius
h. ray

Identify each triangle as acute, obtuse, or right.

28. 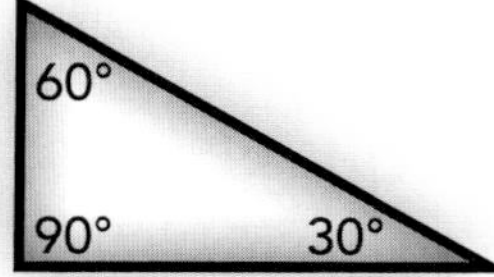

29. 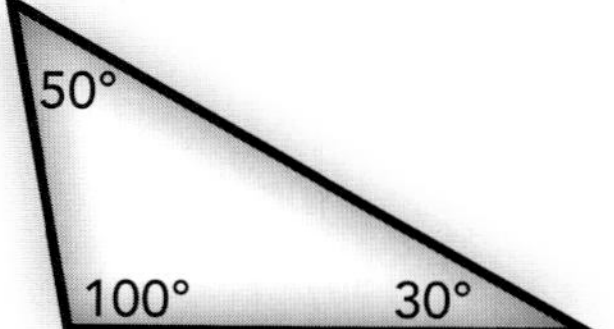

30. 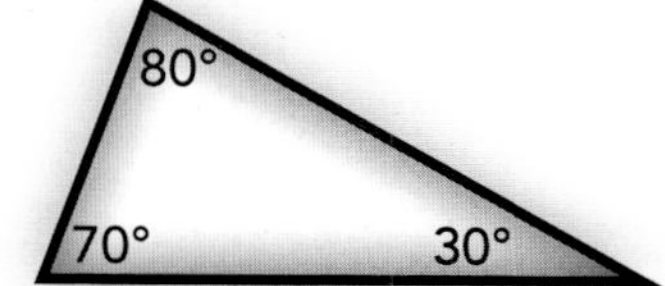

Name the transformation illustrated by each pair of figures.

31. 

32. 

33. 

Use the circle shown to complete the exercises.

34. Name the circle.
35. Name the chord that is not a diameter.
36. Name the diameter.

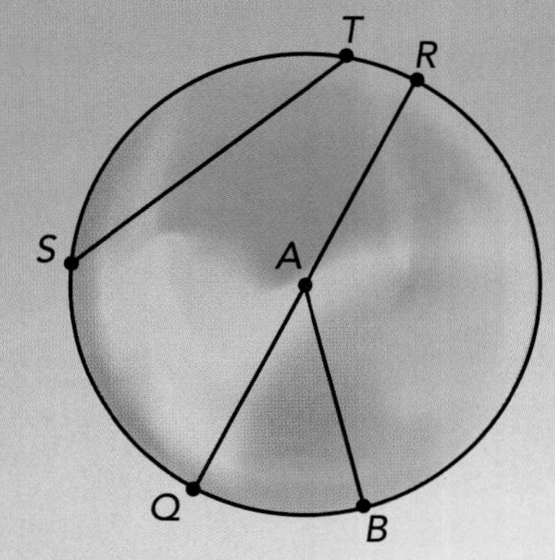

Chapter 8
Integers and Fractions

Praise the Lord. Praise the Lord from the heavens; praise Him in the heights above. Praise Him, all His angels; praise Him, all His heavenly hosts.
Psalm 148:1–2

Key Ideas:

Patterns: prime and composite numbers

Number Theory: reading, writing, and problem solving with integers, rational numbers, and real numbers

Fractions and Decimals: greatest common factor

Fractions and Decimals: comparing and ordering fractions and mixed numbers

8.1 Integers

Construct Meaning

During a board game, a player often moves ahead two spaces but then draws a card that instructs him to move back several spaces. The distance of moving two spaces forward and three spaces back may be expressed using positive numbers and negative numbers.

- The two steps forward can be written +2 and read, "positive two." Three steps backward would be −3, which is read, "negative three." The numbers +2 and −3 are called integers.

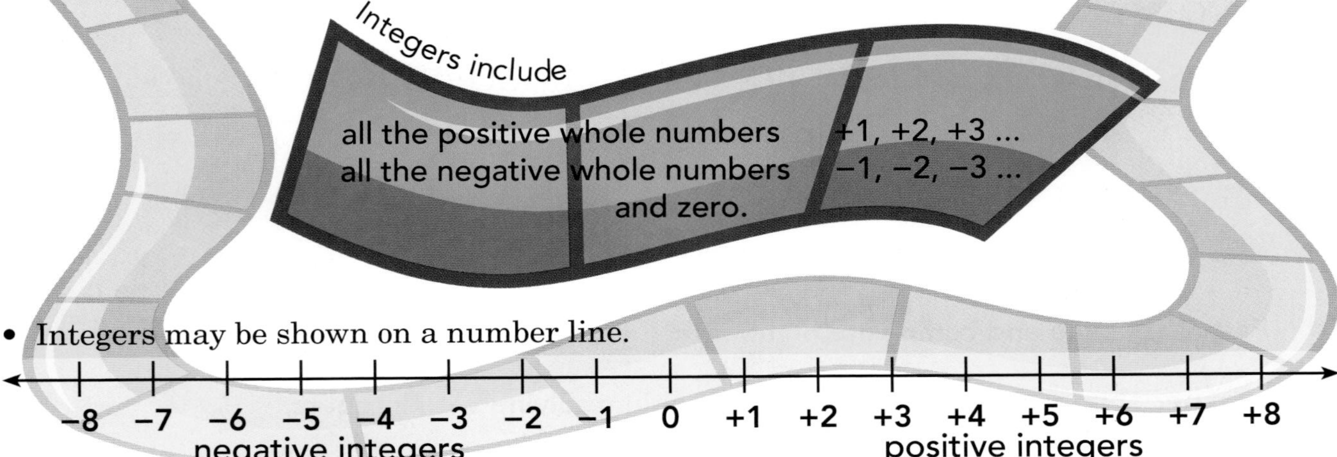

- Integers may be shown on a number line.

−8 −7 −6 −5 −4 −3 −2 −1 0 +1 +2 +3 +4 +5 +6 +7 +8

negative integers — positive integers

Zero is considered neither positive nor negative.

Four units to the left of 0 is −4. Four units to the right of 0 is 4. Because they are on opposite sides of zero but are the same distance from zero, −4 and +4 are opposite numbers.

A thermometer has a scale showing positive and negative integers. Ten degrees above zero may be expressed as +10°F or 10°F. Ten degrees below zero may be expressed as −10°F.

Check Understanding

Write the integer and its opposite.

a. a profit of $6
b. a 10-point penalty
c. an 8-point loss
d. a debt of $15.00
e. the freezing point of water on a Fahrenheit thermometer

Practice

Complete each sentence.

1. _____ include all the positive and negative whole numbers and zero.
2. _____ is neither positive nor negative.
3. −9 is nine units to the _____ of zero on a number line.
4. +8 and −8 are _____ integers.

Write the opposite in words using the opposite integer.

Example:

3 feet upward is +3.
3 feet downward is −3.

5. 15 miles north is +15.
6. 9 steps backward is −9.
7. A $20 loss is −20 dollars.
8. A 10-foot fall is −10.
9. 3 hours after rocket launch is +3.

Apply

10. The summit of Mount Everest rises to 29,028 ft above sea level. The shoreline of the Dead Sea is the lowest place on Earth and is 1,312 ft below sea level. If sea level sits at zero, how can you express the highest and lowest points on Earth as integers?
11. Name the two integers that are 100 units from zero.
12. Identify the least positive integer and the greatest negative integer.
13. Explain why you agree with this statement: The integer that indicates freezing on a Celsius thermometer is neither positive or negative.
14. How many degrees separate −2°F from the freezing point of water shown on a Fahrenheit thermometer?
15. Naomi and Ken were playing a game on a number line marked with positive and negative integers. Ken placed his game piece on −3. Naomi's game piece was 9 units to the right of Ken's. Where was Naomi's game piece?

8.2 Compare Integers

Construct Meaning

On a January morning, it may be 10°F in Gunnison, Colorado, 5° below zero in Fairbanks, Alaska, and 2° below zero in Yellowstone Park.

Use a number line to compare the integers. Which of the three temperatures is a positive integer? Identify the two temperatures that are negative integers. State the warmest and coldest temperatures of the three.

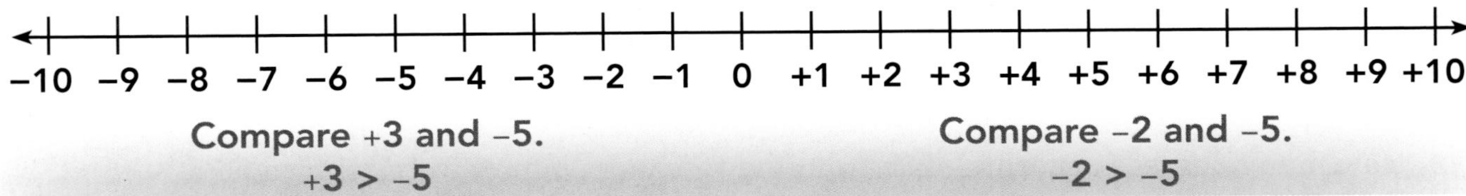

Compare +3 and −5.
+3 > −5

Compare −2 and −5.
−2 > −5

The integers become greater toward the right on the number line.

Compare +1 and −7.
−7 < +1

Compare −1 and −7.
−7 < −1

−7 is to the left of +1 and −1, so it is less than both of those integers.

To order a set of integers:
- Compare them two at a time.
- Remember that the greater integer is farther to the right on the number line.

Order +4, −4, −3, and +6 from greatest to least.
+6 > +4 +4 > −3
−3 > −4
The order is +6, +4, −3, −4.

Identify the missing integers on the number line. Name them in order from least to greatest. Then, name them from greatest to least.

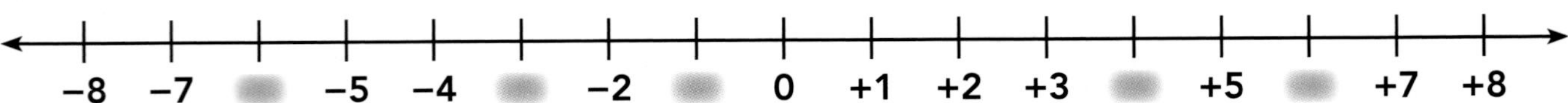

Check Understanding

Write > or <.

a. +3 ◯ +7 b. +5 ◯ −1 c. −7 ◯ −2 d. −4 ◯ 0

Write in order from greatest to least.

e. +2, −8, −6, 0 f. +4, +1, +2, −1

Practice

Write "true" or "false" for each statement.

1. Of two negative integers, the greater one is located closer to zero on a number line.
2. The integers on a number line become greater as you move to the right.
3. Of two positive integers, the greater one is located closer to zero on a number line.

Write > or <.

4. +2 ◯ +10
5. +5 ◯ −5
6. −1 ◯ 0
7. +3 ◯ −4
8. −9 ◯ −10
9. −5 ◯ −2
10. +6 ◯ −12
11. −3 ◯ +3
12. 0 ◯ −6
13. −8 ◯ −6
14. +5 ◯ −7
15. −2 ◯ −1

Identify the missing numbers from each pattern. Write "greatest to least" or "least to greatest" to tell the order of the integers.

16. +2 +1 0 ____ −2 ____
17. −3 −4 ____ −6 −8
18. −15 −10 ____ 0 +5 ____
19. +16 +8 ____ −8 ____ −24

Death Valley, California, United States

20. Which location is closer to sea level, China's Turfan Depression at 505 ft below sea level, or the United States' Death Valley, which is 282 ft below sea level?

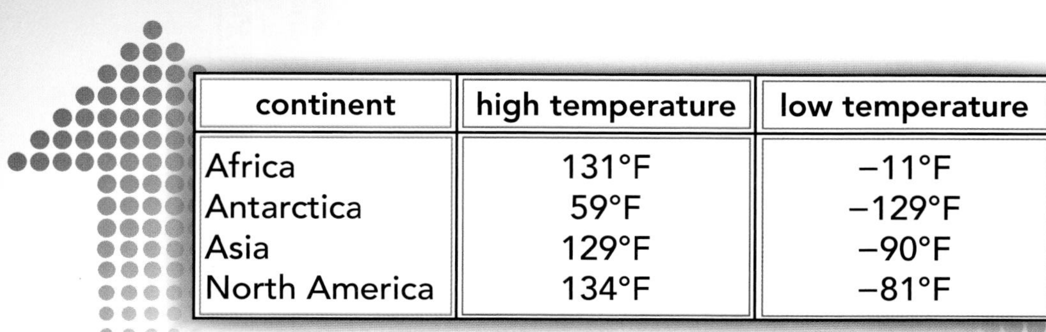

continent	high temperature	low temperature
Africa	131°F	−11°F
Antarctica	59°F	−129°F
Asia	129°F	−90°F
North America	134°F	−81°F

21. The chart shows extreme temperatures (rounded to whole numbers) that have been recorded on four of the world's seven continents. Order all eight temperatures from least to greatest.

8.3 Relate Fractions to Integers

Construct Meaning

Dora and Elon played a game that involved the gain and loss of points. They used positive and negative integers to keep track of their individual scores.

Dora's Scorecard

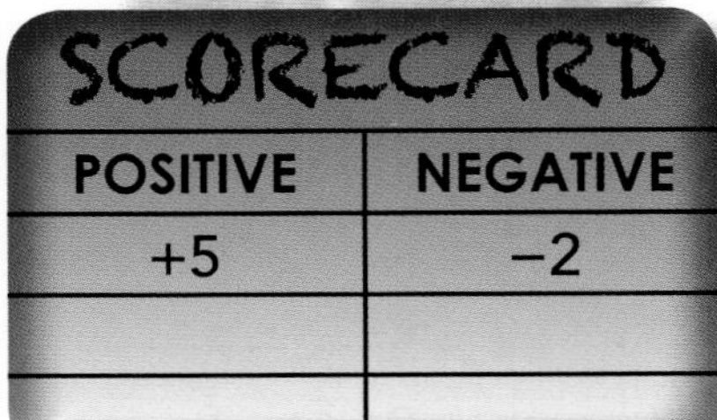

SCORECARD

POSITIVE	NEGATIVE
+5	−2

Dora made five points on her first turn but lost two points in the next round.

Begin at +5 on the number line.
Move back two numbers.
Her score is +3.

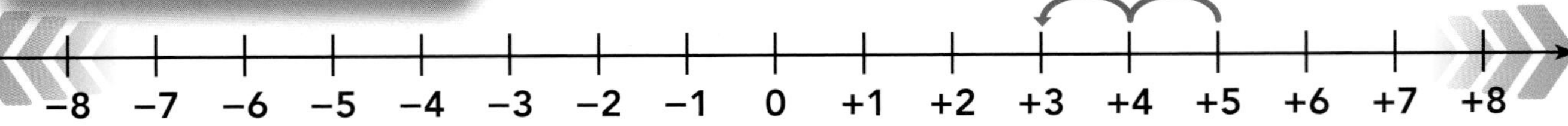

Elon's Scorecard

SCORECARD

POSITIVE	NEGATIVE
	−3
	−5

The scorecard shows that Elon lost points on his first two turns. What is his score?

Begin at −3 on the number line.
Move back five numbers.
His score is −8.

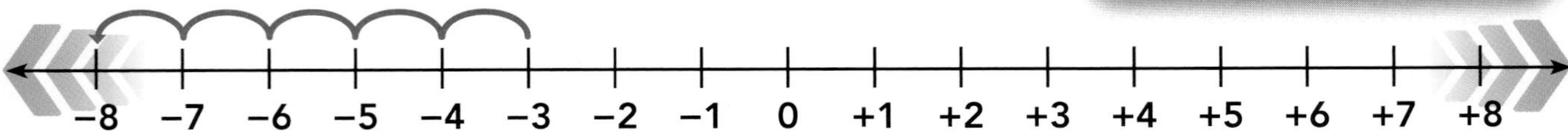

How much greater is Dora's score? Use a number line to compare.
Count forward from Elon's score to Dora's score.

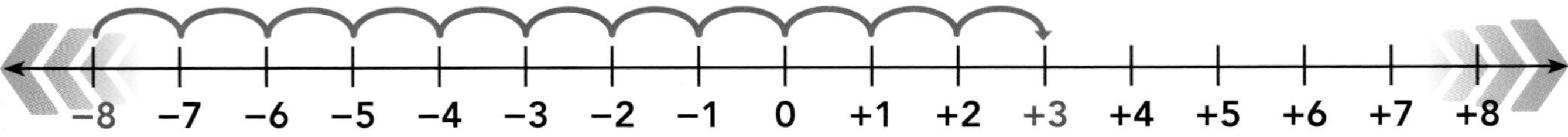

Dora is ahead by 11 points.

Dora earned a one-half point bonus. How many points is she ahead now?

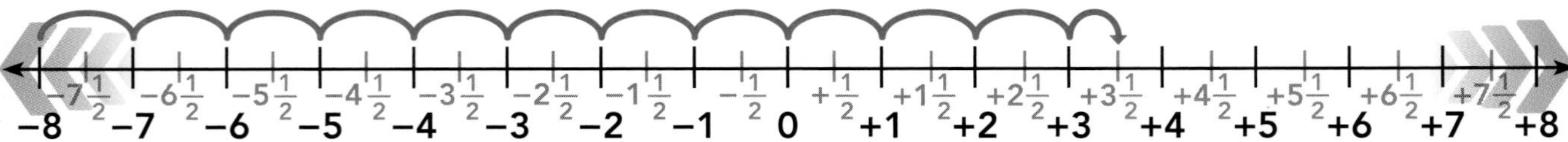

Dora is ahead by $11\frac{1}{2}$ points.

Remember, integers include positive and negative numbers as well as zero. Fractions and mixed numbers can be found on a number line but are not integers.

Check Understanding

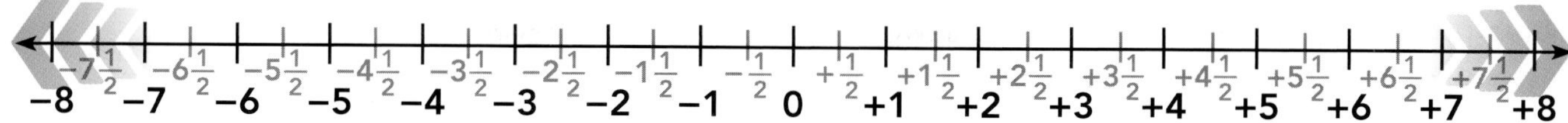

a. If Elon's score is −8, how many points does he need to have a total score that is a positive integer?

b. If Dora's score for her third turn is −3, will her total score be a positive or negative number?

c. Dora gained a point on her fourth turn and then lost one-half point. What is her score now?

Apply

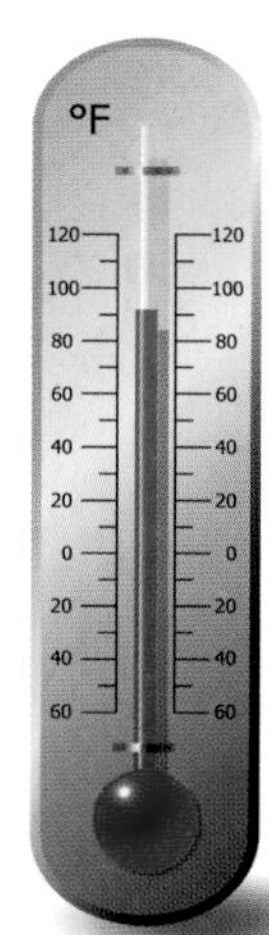

1. Kalini is playing a game on a number line. The game uses the numbers from two cubes, one marked with positive integers and one with negative, to move along the line. If she begins at 0 and rolls −4 and +6, where will she land?

2. On her next turn, Kalini's numbers were +5 and −5. Where will she place her game piece?

3. Kalini earned a one-half point bonus. What is her score now?

4. If it was −2°F at 6:00 PM, and the temperature dropped 14° in the next six hours, what was the temperature at midnight?

5. When Katie went to the movies with Jada, it was 96°F. When they left the theater, it was 92.5°F. What is the temperature difference in degrees?

Justin traveled to Israel with his church. The surface of the Dead Sea is about 1,300 ft below sea level. The elevation of a location tells how far it is above or below sea level.

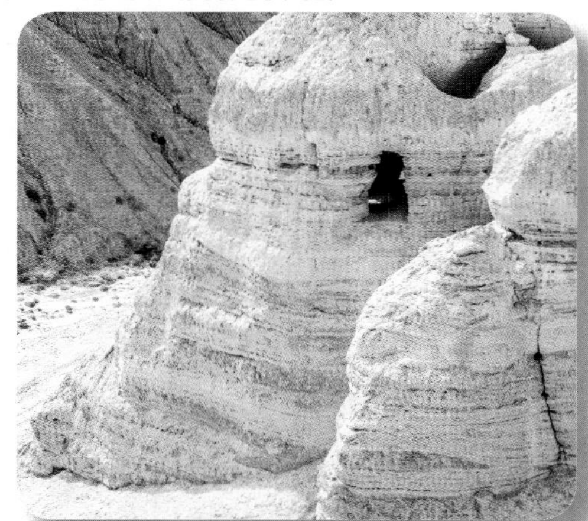

6. Justin visited the caves where the Dead Sea Scrolls were found. He traveled to Qumran, which is about 100 ft above the Dead Sea. What is the approximate elevation of Qumran?

7. Justin went to the Judean Hills to visit Bethlehem, which has an elevation of 2,500 ft above sea level. Bethlehem, the birthplace of Christ, was also the birthplace of David, who took care of his father's sheep on the nearby hills. What is the difference between the elevation of the Dead Sea and the city of Bethlehem?

8. Justin traveled from Jerusalem to the Dead Sea. When Justin left, it was 68.5°F, and it was 85°F when he finished his day at the Dead Sea. What was the temperature difference?

8.4 Fraction Review

Construct Meaning

Solar panels generate electrical power to energize satellites in space. Specialized types of equipment, such as satellites, are important to communication systems on Earth.

Fractions are used to describe parts of a whole.

A whole:

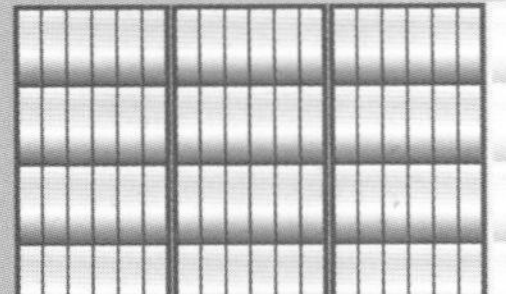

3 of the 4 sections are colored.

number of parts colored ⟶ 3 numerator
total number of equal parts ⟶ 4 denominator

Write $\frac{3}{4}$. Say, "three-fourths."

Fractions are used to describe the parts of a set.

A set:

2 of the 5 satellites are colored.

number of parts colored ⟶ 2 numerator
total number of equal parts ⟶ 5 denominator

Write $\frac{2}{5}$. Say, "two-fifths."

Fractions can be counted on a number line.

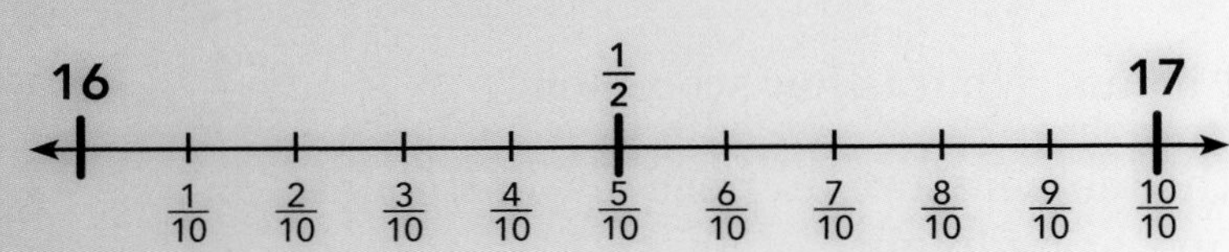

Each section is $\frac{1}{10}$.
$\frac{10}{10}$ is called one whole.

A fraction names part of a whole or part of a set.
A numerator represents the number of equal parts being considered.
A denominator represents the total number of equal parts of a whole.

Check Understanding

Write the fraction for the colored part.

a.

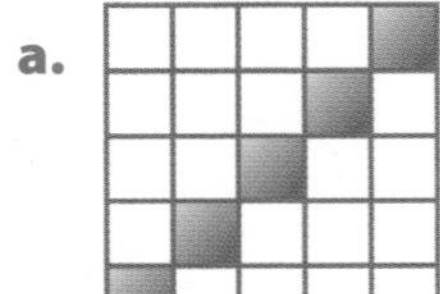

b.

c.

d.

e. Write the missing eighths as you count from 29 to 30.

29 — $\frac{1}{8}$, $\frac{2}{8}$, __, $\frac{4}{8}$ ($\frac{1}{2}$), $\frac{5}{8}$, __, $\frac{7}{8}$, $\frac{8}{8}$ — 30

Write whether the picture is a whole or a set. Write a fraction for the colored part. Label the numerator and the denominator.

1. 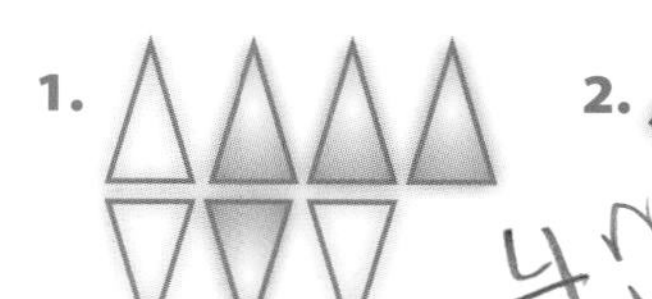 2. 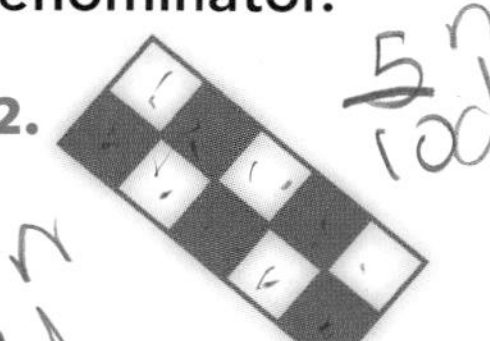 3.  4.  5. 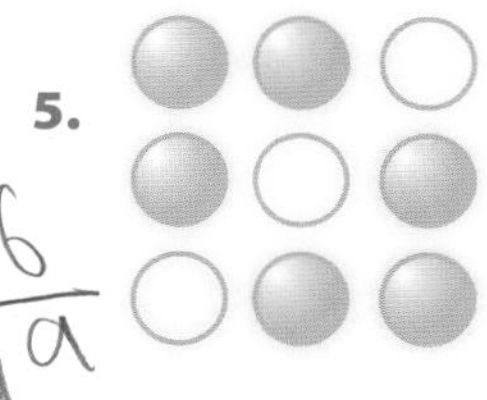

Draw a picture of a whole and another of a set to show each fraction.

6. $\frac{3}{8}$ 7. $\frac{2}{9}$  8. $\frac{3}{4}$ 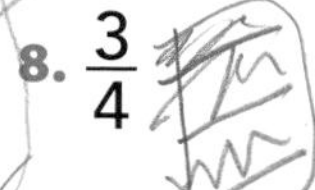 9. $\frac{4}{5}$ 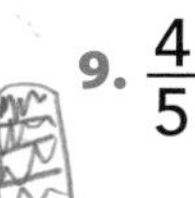 10. $\frac{5}{6}$ 

Write each fraction.

11. five-eighths 12. two-thirds 13. seven-twelfths 14. one-fifth

15. What fraction of the week are Tuesday and Wednesday?
16. What part of a dozen are three eggs?
17. What fraction of the year is January through June?
18. What part of the year is the week of Christmas?

Apply

19. The Defense Support Program had 9 satellites orbiting Earth. Two of the satellites had their solar panels extended. What fraction of the satellites had their solar panels spread out?

20. One solar panel has 22 sections, but 15 are damaged. What fraction of this solar panel needs repair?

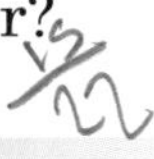

Review

Write the letter of the figure that does not belong.

21. quadrilateral

a.  b.  c.  d. 

22. parallelogram

a.  b.  c.  d. 

Solve.

23. 42×7 24. 56.2×0.19 25. 53×23 26. $61\overline{)38{,}552}$ 27. $8\overline{)6.904}$

8.5 Equivalent Fractions

Construct Meaning

Christians around the world observe the birth of Christ in the month of December. Some families celebrate by preparing a birthday cake for Jesus.

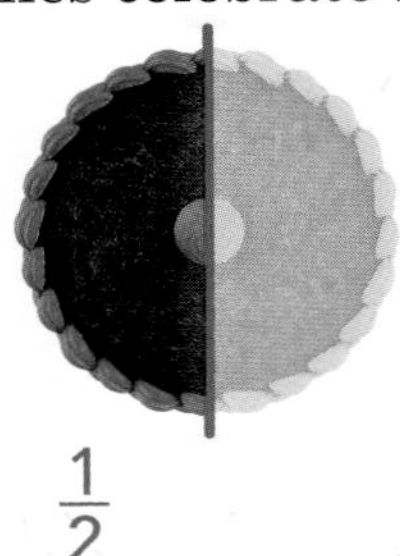

$\frac{1}{2}$

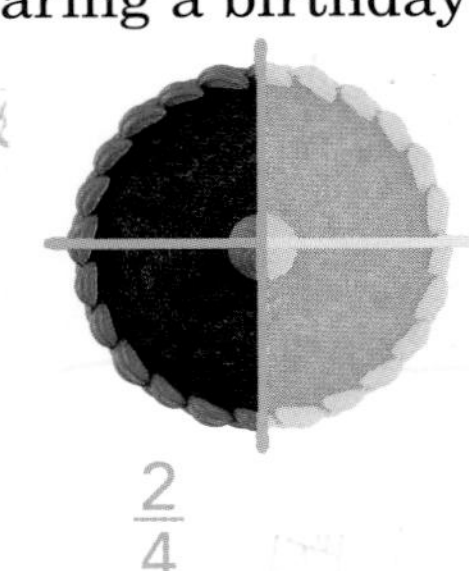

$\frac{2}{4}$

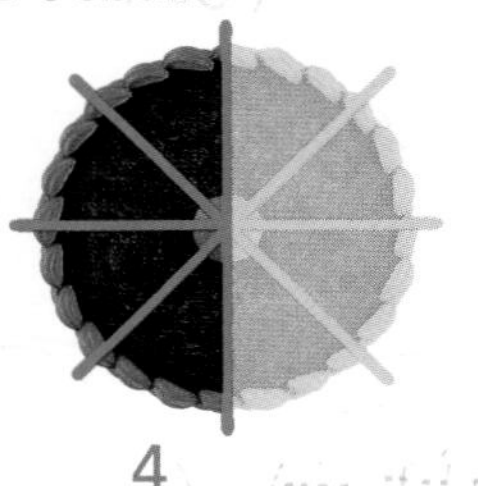

$\frac{4}{8}$

$\frac{8}{16}$

Equivalent fractions name the same amount or number. One-half, two-fourths, four-eighths, and eight-sixteenths are equivalent fractions.

- Multiplying the numerator and the denominator by the same number is one way to find equivalent fractions.

$$\frac{1 \times 2}{3 \times 2} = \frac{2}{6}$$

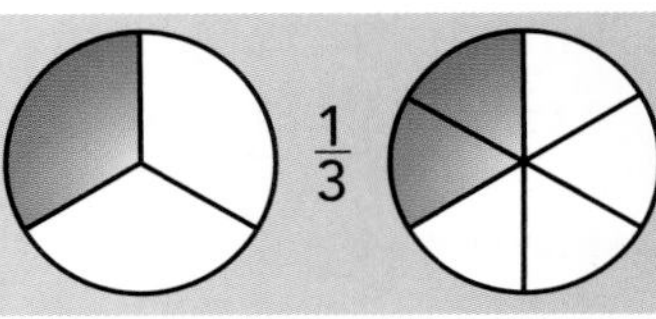

One-third and two-sixths are equivalent fractions.

- Another way to find equivalent fractions is by dividing the numerator and the denominator by the same number.

$$\frac{4 \div 4}{12 \div 4} = \frac{1}{3}$$

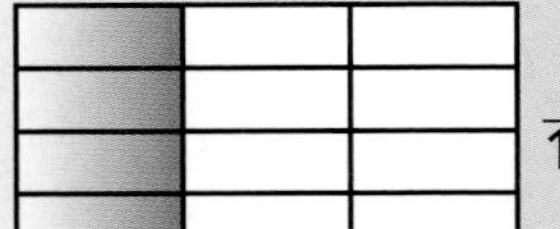

$\frac{4}{12}$

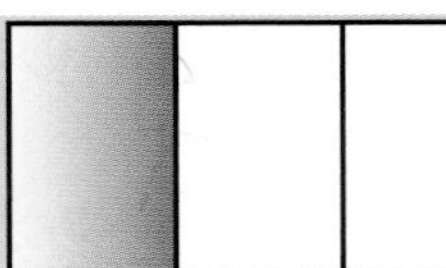

$\frac{1}{3}$

Four-twelfths and one-third are equivalent fractions.

- To find a missing numerator of an equivalent fraction, find the number the denominator was multiplied or divided by. Perform the same operation on the numerator.
- Use the same strategy to find a missing denominator.

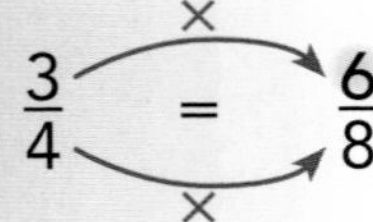

Think: $4 \times 2 = 8$
$3 \times 2 = 6$

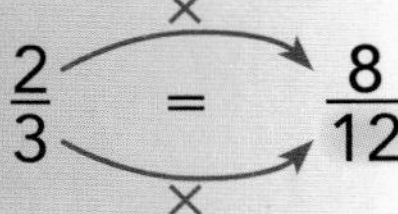

Think: $2 \times 4 = 8$
$3 \times 4 = 12$

Use a number line to list equivalent fractions.

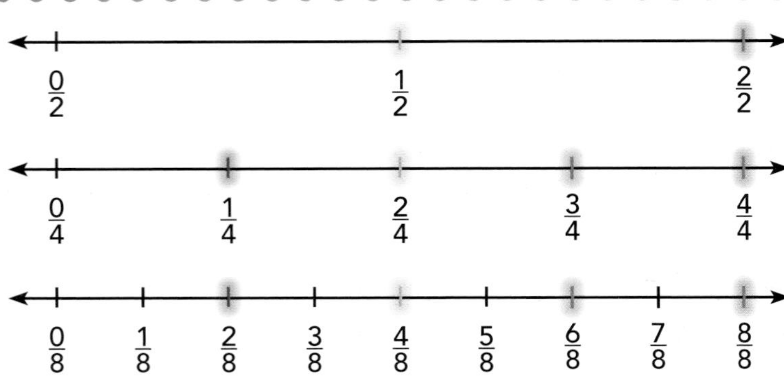

$\frac{1}{4} = \frac{2}{8}$　　$\frac{1}{2} = \frac{\_}{\_} = \frac{\_}{\_}$

$\frac{3}{4} = \frac{\_}{\_}$　　$\frac{2}{2} = \frac{\_}{\_} = \frac{\_}{\_}$

Check Understanding

Draw two pictures to show equivalent fractions.

Example:

$\frac{3 \times 2}{5 \times 2} = \frac{6}{10}$

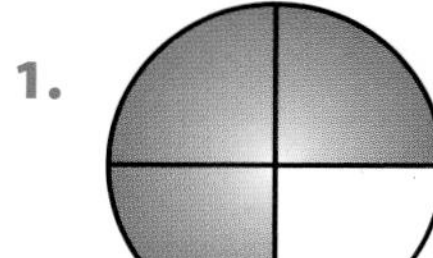

a. $\frac{2 \div 2}{12 \div 2} = \frac{}{}$ b. $\frac{3}{8}$ c. $\frac{4}{16}$

Practice

Write equivalent fractions for the models.

1. 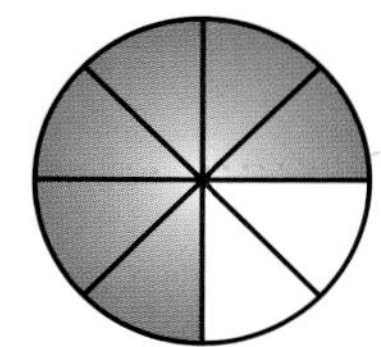

2.  

Write an equivalent fraction.

3. $\frac{2}{5}$ 4. $\frac{2}{3}$ 5. $\frac{4}{6}$ 6. $\frac{5}{25}$ 7. $\frac{8}{32}$

Use the models to find the missing number.

8. 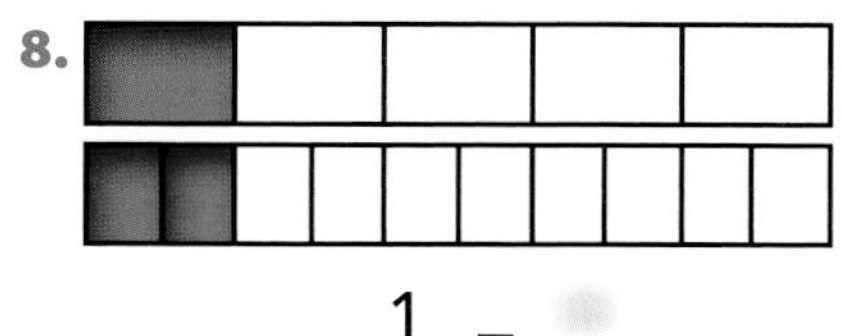

$\frac{1}{5} = \frac{}{10}$

9.  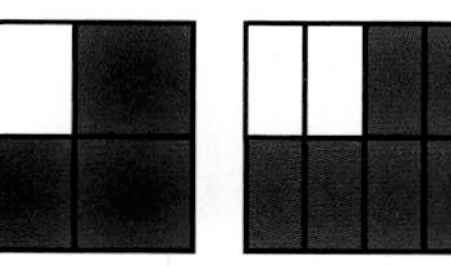

$\frac{3}{4} = \frac{}{8}$

10. 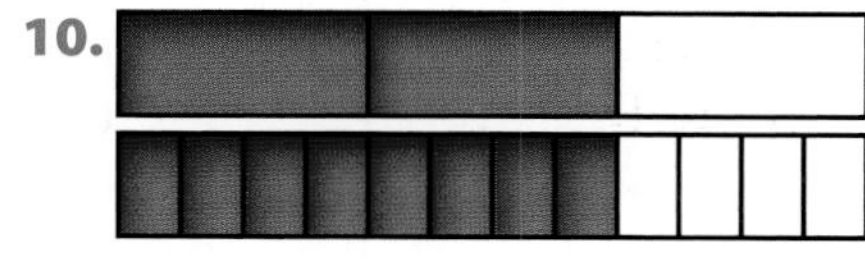

$\frac{2}{3} = \frac{8}{}$

Write the missing number.

11. $\frac{2}{4} = \frac{}{16}$ 13. $\frac{1}{7} = \frac{}{28}$ 15. $\frac{10}{50} = \frac{20}{}$ 17. $\frac{7}{8} = \frac{}{40}$

12. $\frac{4}{5} = \frac{16}{}$ 14. $\frac{5}{9} = \frac{15}{}$ 16. $\frac{9}{10} = \frac{}{30}$ 18. $\frac{2}{7} = \frac{12}{}$

Write the next three equivalent fractions.

19. $\frac{1}{3}, \frac{2}{6}, \frac{3}{9}, \frac{4}{12}$ 20. $\frac{2}{7}, \frac{4}{14}, \frac{6}{21}, \frac{8}{28}$ 21. $\frac{4}{5}, \frac{8}{10}, \frac{12}{15}, \frac{16}{20}$

Apply

22. The Christmas tree was beautifully decorated. Two-fourths of the glass ornaments were red and four-eighths were green. Was the number of red ornaments more, less, or equal to the number of green ornaments?

23. Judy's sugar-cookie recipe calls for one-fourth dozen eggs. Sue's recipe calls for four eggs. Whose recipe uses fewer eggs?

8.6 Fractions and Decimals

Construct Meaning

Jupiter has a rocky, metallic, gaseous core and a diameter about 11 times that of Earth. The dark bands around Jupiter are called belts and the light bands are called zones. Jupiter's most distinctive feature is the Great Red Spot, which is a storm system. The color comes from chemicals in Jupiter's clouds. Nine-tenths of Jupiter's atmosphere is hydrogen.

- Fractions and decimals can name numbers less than one.

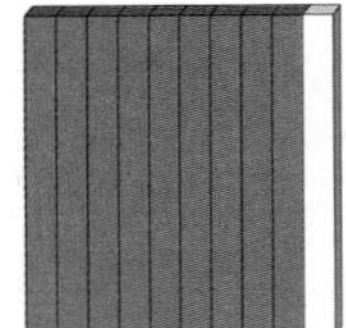

word form: nine-tenths

fraction: $\frac{9}{10}$

decimal: 0.9

ones .	tenths	hundredths	thousandths
0 .	9	0	0

$\frac{1}{4}$ of Jupiter's moons are significantly larger than the others.

Change $\frac{1}{4}$ to a decimal by multiplying the numerator and the denominator by the same number to make a fraction with a denominator of 10, 100, or 1,000. Write a decimal.

$$\frac{1}{4} \underset{\times 25}{\overset{\times 25}{=}} \frac{25}{100} = 0.25$$

OR

Change $\frac{1}{4}$ to a decimal by dividing the numerator by the denominator. Use long division.

$$\begin{array}{r} 0.25 \\ 4\overline{)1.00} \\ -\ \ 8 \\ \hline 20 \\ -20 \\ \hline 0 \end{array}$$

Use a calculator to check your division.

1 ÷ 4 = 0.25

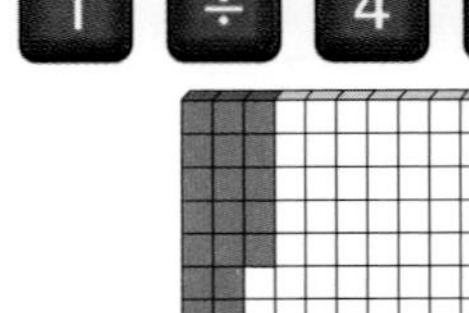

word form: twenty-five hundredths

fraction: $\frac{25}{100}$

decimal: 0.25

ones .	tenths	hundredths	thousandths
0 .	2	5	0

- Fractions and decimals can name numbers greater than one.

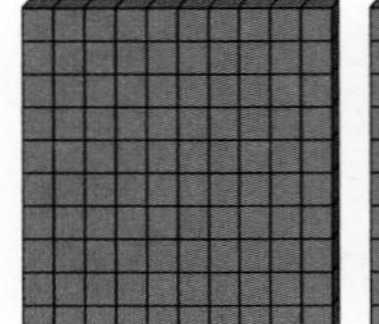
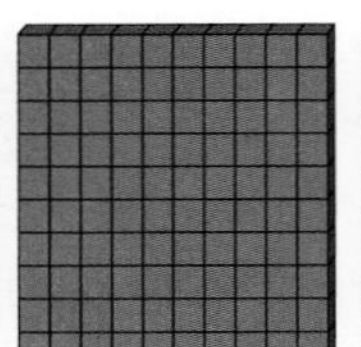
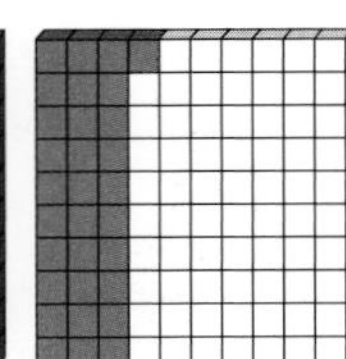

word form: two and thirty-one hundredths

fraction: $2\frac{31}{100}$

decimal: 2.31

ones .	tenths	hundredths	thousandths
2 .	3	1	0

Check Understanding

Write the number from the Answer Bank that matches the picture.

a. 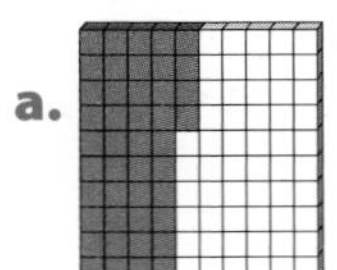

b. 

c.

ones .	tenths	hundredths	thousandths
0 .	5	3	0

Answer Bank

$\frac{1}{10}$

0.01

fifty-three hundredths

0.44

d. Use the denominator of 1,000 to rename the fraction and write it as a decimal on the place value chart.

$\frac{31}{200} = \frac{}{}$

ones	. tenths	hundredths	thousandths
	.		

e. Divide the numerator by the denominator to find the decimal equivalent of $\frac{5}{8}$.

Practice

Write the word form, a fraction, and a decimal for each model.

1. 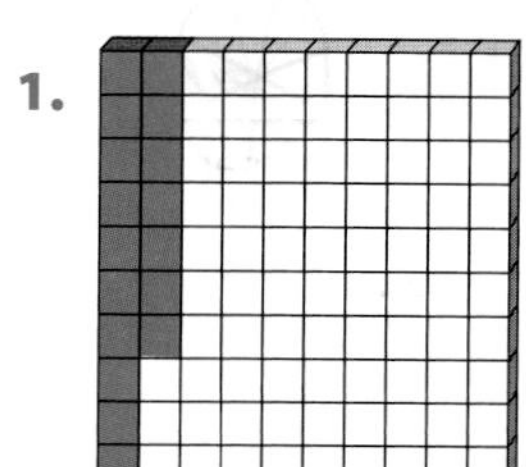

2. 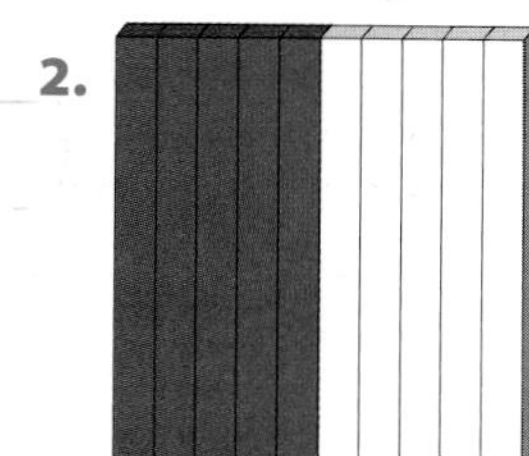

3. 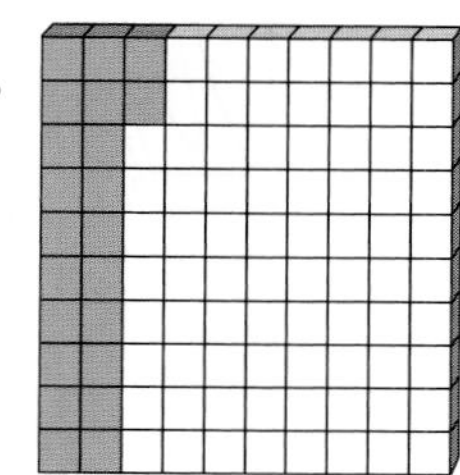

Write an equivalent fraction using the given denominator. Then, write it as a decimal.

4. $\frac{1}{2} = \frac{}{10}$

5.

6. $\frac{7}{20} = \frac{}{100}$

7. $\frac{8}{25} = \frac{}{100}$

8. $\frac{32}{125} = \frac{}{1{,}000}$

9. $\frac{11}{250} = \frac{}{1{,}000}$

Divide the numerator by the denominator to find the decimal equivalent.

10. $\frac{3}{4}$ **11.** $\frac{4}{5}$ **12.** $\frac{1}{8}$ **13.** $\frac{5}{10}$ **14.** $\frac{3}{20}$

Write each decimal as a fraction.

15. 0.29 **16.** 0.2 **17.** 0.32 **18.** 0.07 **19.** 0.327

Apply

20. The moon named Io orbits Jupiter in one and seventy-seven hundredths days. Write the orbital period as a decimal.

21. Two other moons complete their orbits faster than Io. Adrastea orbits Jupiter in about 0.3 of a day. Thebe's orbital period is 0.67 of a day. Which moon orbits in less time than Amalthea, whose orbit time is 0.5 of a day? Which moon has a longer orbit than Amalthea?

Review

22. $4.07 + 3.294$

23. $89.5 - 76.784$

24. 0.54×0.7

25. $18\overline{)96.912}$

26. $60.04 - 13.15$

8.7 Prime and Composite Numbers

Construct Meaning

Jim's fifth-grade class painted two large Christmas cards on 4' × 8' sheets of plywood to be displayed in the schoolyard during the holiday season. The first was a picture of an angel and the second was one of the star over Bethlehem. The class discussed arranging the cards horizontally or vertically.

When a number has exactly two factors, 1 and itself, it is called a prime number. The number 2 is a prime number because it can be divided by 1 and itself.

1 × 2

2 × 1

The class showed the Christmas story using six cards as part of an outreach to the city. Showing the possible ways to arrange the cards helped students find the factors of the number 6.

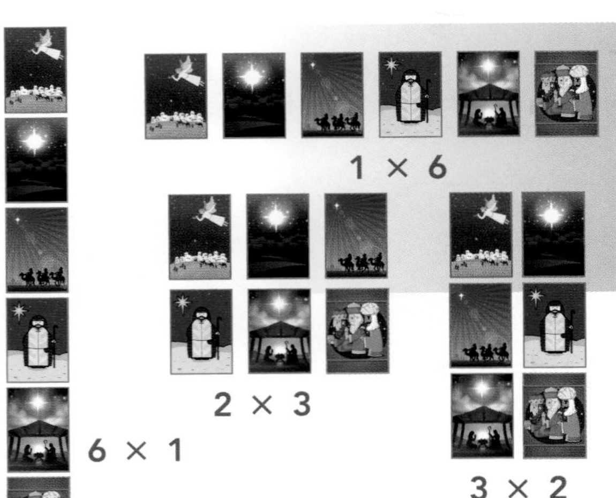

The different factors used to make these arrangements are 1, 2, 3, and 6.

When a number has more than two factors, it is called a composite number. The number 6 is a composite number.

The number 1 has only one factor—itself. It is neither prime nor composite.

A factor tree is another way to find how many factors are in a number. Factoring a number until all the numbers are prime is called prime factorization.

Think of two factors whose product is 24. List them.

The number 3 is a prime number.

Find two factors whose product is 8. List them.

Find two factors of 4. List them.

24
prime → 3 × 8 ← composite
prime 3 × 2 × 4 ← composite
3 × 2 × 2 × 2 ← prime

or

24
4 × 6
2 × 2 × 2 × 3

Since 24 has more than two factors (1, 2, 3, 4, 6, 8, 12, and 24), it is a composite number. The prime factors of 24 at the bottom of each tree are 3 × 2 × 2 × 2. The order of the factors on the second tree does not affect the product.

Check Understanding

Copy and complete each factor tree.

a. 12
3 × ___
3 × ___ × ___

b. 32
___ × 8
___ × ___ × ___ × ___
___ × ___ × ___ × ___ × ___

c. 48
8 × ___
___ × ___ × ___ × ___
___ × ___ × ___ × ___ × ___

Practice

List all the factors of each number. Write "prime," "composite," or "neither."

1. 6 2. 30 3. 43 4. 10 5. 9 6. 5 7. 1

Copy and complete each factor tree.

8. 4
___ × ___

9. 15
___ × ___

10. 16
4 × ___
___ × ___ × ___ × ___

11. 40
2 × 20
2 × ___ × ___
___ × ___ × ___ × ___

List the prime factors.

12. 4 13. 15 14. 16 15. 40

Draw a factor tree for each number.

16. 24 17. 72 18. 6 19. 125 20. 248 21. 390

Use your calculator to multiply the prime numbers to check the accuracy of the factorization. Write "yes" or "no." If no, correct the mistake.

22. 418
2 × 209
2 × 19 × 11

23. 168
4 × 42
2 × 2 × 6 × 7
2 × 2 × 2 × 2 × 7

24. 210
6 × 35
2 × 3 × 5 × 7

25. What are the two prime numbers whose product is 141?

Review

26. Two angles of a triangle are 40° and 50°. What is the third angle?

27. Which angle is obtuse?

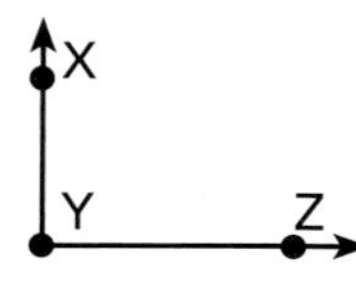

A
B
C

8.8 Greatest Common Factor

Construct Meaning

During the open house at Covenant Christian Academy, students displayed several exhibits they had designed. One of the exhibits consisted of a drawing of the planet Saturn with its rings. Saturn is the sixth planet from the sun, and its rings are made up of dust, rock, and ice that orbit the planet.

John's exhibit included models of the planet Saturn that students could complete by using attachable rings. John challenged his friends to make identical models with 12 black and 18 yellow rings. What is the greatest number of identical models they can make?

1. List the multiplication facts for each number.

12: 1 × 12, 2 × 6, 3 × 4

18: 1 × 18, 2 × 9, 3 × 6

2. List the factors of each number in numerical order.

12: 1, 2, 3, 4, 6, 12
18: 1, 2, 3, 6, 9, 18

Factors of a number divide a number evenly with no remainder.

3. Compare the factors of 12 and 18.

The factors that appear for both products are 1, 2, 3, and 6. These factors are called common factors because they are factors of both products. The largest common factor is known as the greatest common factor (GCF). The GCF of 12 and 18 is 6.

There are 6 models of Saturn, each using 2 black and 3 yellow rings.

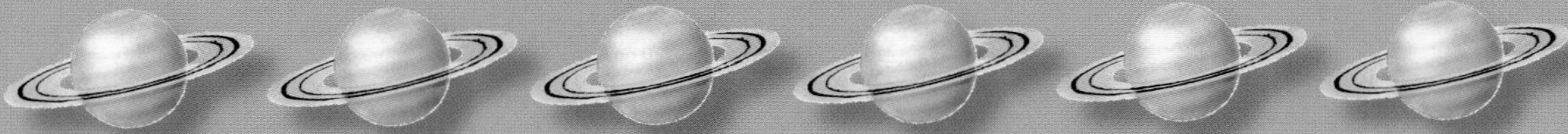

Check Understanding

List the factors of each number.

a. 30 b. 12 c. 9 d. 1 e. 21

List the common factors of each number. Circle the GCF.

f. 4 and 8 g. 6 and 15 h. 14 and 36 i. 9 and 24 j. 6, 18, and 27

k. List all the products that have a factor of 12.

24 36 40 48 60 69 72 81 84

Practice

List the factors of each number.

1. 12
2. 20
3. 11
4. 32

List the common factors for each set of numbers. Circle the GCF.

5. 14 and 28
6. 24 and 32
7. 25 and 35
8. 55 and 66
9. 18 and 27
10. 3 and 5
11. 18 and 81
12. 18 and 36

Write the letter of the numbers that match each GCF.

13. 4
 a. 8 and 12
 b. 9 and 12
 c. 6 and 12

14. 6
 a. 8 and 10
 b. 12 and 18
 c. 6 and 9

15. 9
 a. 14 and 16
 b. 36 and 54
 c. 27 and 45

16. 10
 a. 65 and 75
 b. 70 and 80
 c. 35 and 40

Apply

17. Kimberly's class sold school supplies at the open house. Pens and pencils were packaged separately, but each package contained the same number of items. If there were 18 pencils and 14 pens, what was the greatest number of items in one package?

18. Thirty lollipops, 42 pens, 48 stickers, and 18 note cards were divided evenly to make gift baskets for the exhibit winners.
 a. What is the greatest number of identical gift baskets you can make using all the items?
 b. How many of each item will be in each basket?
 c. If you make 3 identical gift baskets using stickers and notecards, what is the maximum number of each that you could use?

Review

Add.

19. 36,795 + 67,038

20. 2,456 + 891 + 3,657

21. 1,356 + 4,768 + 2,347 + 6,902

22. 376 + 894 + 25 + 762

Subtract.

23. 84,762 − 56,184

24. 6,000 − 2,597

25. 501 − 105

26. $98.79 − 96.97

Solve.

27. 7,324 × 16

28. 0.724 × 0.03

29. $7\overline{)0.049}$

30. $23\overline{)9{,}223}$

8.9 Fractions in Simplest Form

Construct Meaning

Alice's teacher permitted students to choose where they went on their field trip—the zoo, the war memorial, or the space museum. 24 of the 32 students decided to go to the space museum where they could learn more about the planet Uranus, which lies on its side, unlike the other planets.

The class vote of 24 out of 32 can be expressed as a fraction.

$\frac{24}{32}$ numerator / denominator

A fraction is in simplest form when the GCF of the numerator and denominator is 1. Write $\frac{24}{32}$ in simplest form.

List the factors of 24 and 32 to find the greatest common factor (GCF).

24: 1, 2, 3, 4, 6, 8, 12, 24

32: 1, 2, 4, 8, 16, 32

The GCF of 24 and 32 is **8**.

The GCF is the largest number that will evenly divide the numerator and the denominator.

Divide the numerator and denominator by the GCF, 8.

$\frac{24 \div 8}{32 \div 8} = \frac{3}{4}$ $\frac{24}{32}$ in the simplest form is $\frac{3}{4}$.

Write $\frac{24}{32}$ in simplest form using another method.

Divide the numerator and denominator by any common factor until the GCF is 1.

$\frac{24 \div 4}{32 \div 4} = \frac{6}{8} \longrightarrow \frac{6 \div 2}{8 \div 2} = \frac{3}{4}$

3 and 4 have no common factor greater than 1.

$\frac{3}{4}$ is in simplest form.

Look at the fraction drawing above. The fraction $\frac{24}{32} = \frac{3}{4}$ because both the numerator and denominator can be divided by 8.

Check Understanding

List the factors of the numerator and denominator of $\frac{6}{18}$ to find the GCF.

a. 6: ___, ___, ___, ___ b. 18: ___, ___, ___, ___, ___, ___ c. The GCF of 6 and 18 is ___.

Divide the numerator and denominator by the GCF to find the simplest form.

d. 6 ÷ ___ = ___ e. 18 ÷ ___ = ___ f. $\frac{6}{18}$ = — in simplest form.

g. $\frac{6 \div 2}{18 \div 2} = \frac{3}{9} \longrightarrow \frac{3 \div 3}{9 \div 3} = \frac{1}{3}$ The numerator and denominator were divided by ___ and then ___ until the GCF was 1.

Practice

List the factors of the numerator and the denominator. Use the GCF to divide. Write the fraction in simplest form.

1. $\frac{16}{24}$ 2. $\frac{15}{35}$ 3. $\frac{9}{12}$ 4. $\frac{3}{15}$ 5. $\frac{8}{24}$

Write each fraction in simplest form.

6. $\frac{8}{20}$ 9. $\frac{9}{15}$ 12. $\frac{5}{25}$ 15. $\frac{5}{100}$ 18. $\frac{200}{400}$

7. $\frac{10}{15}$ 10. $\frac{4}{28}$ 13. $\frac{16}{48}$ 16. $\frac{63}{75}$ 19. $\frac{170}{198}$

8. $\frac{28}{42}$ 11. $\frac{3}{27}$ 14. $\frac{22}{44}$ 17. $\frac{168}{224}$ 20. $\frac{102}{408}$

Is the fraction in simplest form? Write "yes" or "no." If no, divide and simplify.

21. $\frac{6}{13}$ 22. $\frac{7}{11}$ 23. $\frac{6}{8}$ 24. $\frac{9}{18}$ 25. $\frac{3}{5}$

Apply

Write the fractions in simplest form.

26. Nine out of the 11 rings of Uranus are less than 6 mi wide. What fraction are more than 6 mi wide?

27. Uranus has 5 moons that are named Miranda, Ariel, Umbriel, Titania, and Oberon. Ten more small moons were discovered by the *Voyager* spacecraft. What fraction of Uranus' moons have been named?

Solve.

Scientists believe the atmosphere of Uranus consists of 85 parts hydrogen, 12 parts helium, and 3 parts methane. What fraction of the atmosphere is each of the following?

28. hydrogen
   a. $\frac{12}{100} = \frac{3}{25}$
   b. $\frac{85}{100} = \frac{17}{20}$
   c. $\frac{3}{100}$

29. helium
   a. $\frac{12}{100} = \frac{3}{25}$
   b. $\frac{3}{100}$
   c. $\frac{22}{25}$

30. hydrogen and methane
   a. $\frac{88}{100} = \frac{22}{25}$
   b. $\frac{85}{100} = \frac{17}{20}$
   c. $\frac{12}{100} = \frac{3}{25}$

31. helium and methane
   a. $\frac{85}{100} = \frac{17}{20}$
   b. $\frac{3}{100}$
   c. $\frac{15}{100} = \frac{3}{20}$

Review

Write four equivalent fractions for each given fraction.

32. $\frac{1}{3}$ 33. $\frac{1}{4}$ 34. $\frac{1}{2}$ 35. $\frac{1}{5}$ 36. $\frac{1}{6}$

8.10 Least Common Multiple

Construct Meaning

Mrs. King invited her students to decorate the classroom. They chose a space theme. There were planets, stars, moons, rings, pictures of astronauts, spacecraft, and interstellar material. Stars came in packages of 4 and moons came in packages of 6. If an equal number of stars and moons were used, what was the least number of stars and moons used?

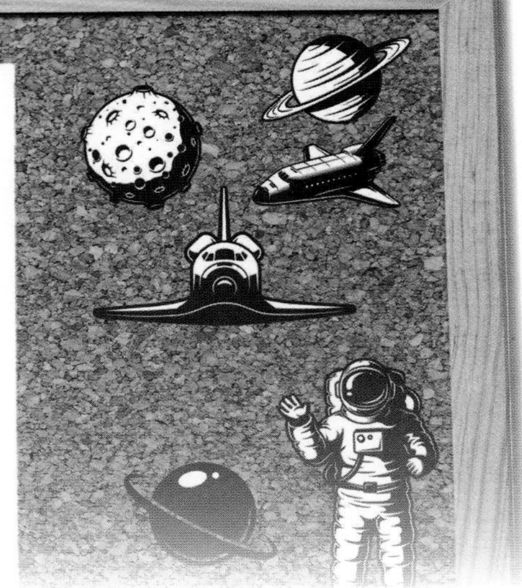

The multiples of a number are found by multiplying that number by 1, 2, 3, and so on.

List the multiples of 4 and 6.

4:	4, 8, 12, 16, 20, 24, 28, 32, 36, 40
6:	6, 12, 18, 24, 30, 36, 42, 48, 54, 60

The multiples that are the same for two or more numbers are called common multiples. The common multiples of 4 and 6 are 12, 24, and 36.

The smallest multiple that is common to two or more numbers is the least common multiple (LCM). The LCM of 4 and 6 is 12.

12 moons and 12 stars were used.

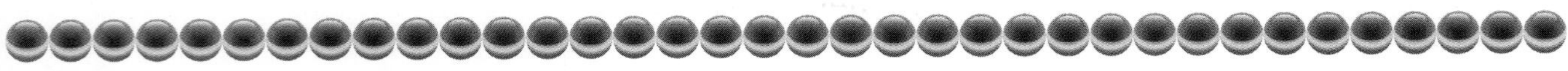

Find the least common multiple of 2, 3, and 4.

2:	2, 4, 6, 8, 10, 12, 14, 16, 18, 20
3:	3, 6, 9, 12, 15, 18, 21, 24, 27, 30
4:	4, 8, 12, 16, 20, 24, 28, 32, 36, 40

The LCM of 2, 3, and 4 is 12.

Check Understanding

List six multiples of each number.

a. 5 b. 7 c. 8 d. 9 e. 10

List at least five multiples of each number.

f. 3 and 6 g. 5 and 3 h. 8 and 10 i. 4 and 5 j. 4 and 12

Find the least common multiple for each set of numbers.

k. 5 and 6 l. 2 and 5 m. 9 and 12 n. 3 and 8 o. 2, 4, and 6

Practice

List four multiples of each number.

1. 6
2. 4
3. 12
4. 3
5. 11

List at least six multiples of each number.

6. 4 and 8
7. 5 and 10
8. 6 and 12
9. 4 and 6
10. 9 and 11

Find the least common multiple for each set of numbers.

11. 6 and 9
12. 3 and 7
13. 2 and 4
14. 7 and 9
15. 3, 6, and 9

Apply

16. Mrs. King divided her class into two groups. Group 1 was scheduled to go to the library to do research three times a week. Group 2 was scheduled four times a week. Monday was the first day they all began. When both groups had gone the same number of times, how many weeks had passed for Group 1? How many weeks had passed for Group 2? How many times had each group gone?

Group 1	Week 1	Week 2	Week 3	Week 4	___ times
Group 2	Week 1	Week 2	Week 3		___ times

17. One group went for 15-minute sessions. Another group went for 20-minute sessions. How many minutes had each group spent when all students had spent an equal amount of time?

18. Use a calculator to find the multiples of larger numbers. Find the LCM of 36 and 42.

Review

Copy the set of fractions if they are equivalent. If they are not, write "not equivalent."

19. $\frac{1}{2} = \frac{13}{26}$
20. $\frac{3}{7} = \frac{22}{49}$
21. $\frac{2}{5} = \frac{12}{30}$
22. $\frac{4}{6} = \frac{12}{24}$
23. $\frac{2}{3} = \frac{14}{21}$

Name each figure.

24. A B (ray)
25. F (point)
26. J K (segment)
27. O P (line)
28. 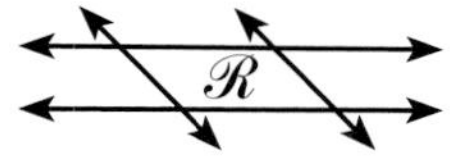

8.11 Compare Fractions

Construct Meaning

Two fifth-grade classes were asked whether they would rather have an astronaut or an astronomer visit them at the end of the unit on planets. In Mrs. Cook's room, $\frac{1}{2}$ of students voted to have an astronaut visit the classroom. In Mr. Farmer's room, $\frac{3}{8}$ of students voted for the astronaut. Use the two fractions to find out which classroom had more students vote for the astronaut.

- Use fraction bars to compare fractions.

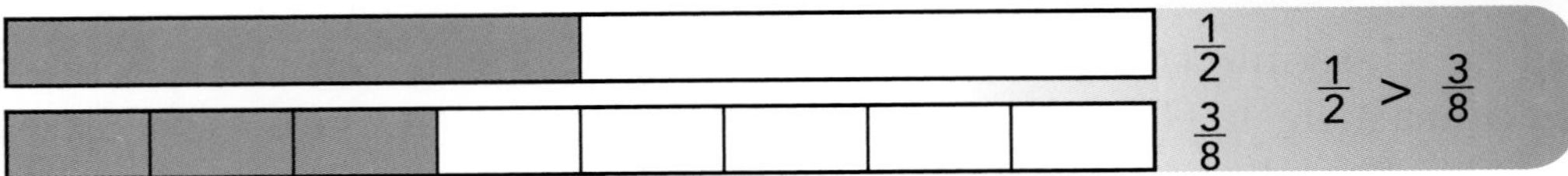

$\frac{1}{2} > \frac{3}{8}$

- Use a number line to compare fractions.

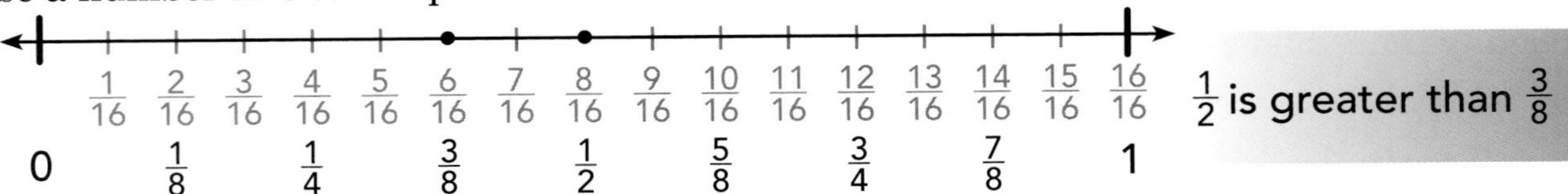

$\frac{1}{2}$ is greater than $\frac{3}{8}$

- Use equivalent fractions that have a common denominator. The least common multiple can be used to find the least common denominator (LCD) for fractions.

Check the denominators of $\frac{1}{2}$ and $\frac{3}{8}$.

Since they are different, find a common denominator to write equivalent fractions.

The least common multiple of 2 and 8 is 8. Use the LCM as the denominator to rewrite the fractions. $\frac{1}{2} = \frac{4}{8}$ $\frac{3}{8} = \frac{3}{8}$

Compare the numerators. Since $\frac{4}{8} > \frac{3}{8}$, then $\frac{1}{2} > \frac{3}{8}$.

REMEMBER:
If the denominators are the same, just compare the numerators. $\frac{2}{5} < \frac{4}{5}$

Mrs. Cook's class had more students vote for the astronaut.

Check Understanding

Follow the steps to compare $\frac{2}{3}$, $\frac{3}{4}$, and $\frac{1}{6}$.

Write the missing multiple for each denominator.

a. 3: 3, 6, 9, ____, 15
b. 4: 4, 8, ____, 16
c. 6: 6, ____, 18
d. The LCM is ____.

Write an equivalent fraction using the LCM as the LCD.

e. $\frac{2}{3} = \frac{}{}$ f. $\frac{3}{4} = \frac{}{}$ g. $\frac{1}{6} = \frac{}{}$

h. Compare the numerators to order the fractions above from greatest to least.

Practice

Compare. Write $>$, $<$, or $=$.

1. $\frac{1}{3} \bigcirc \frac{1}{4}$
2. $\frac{1}{5} \bigcirc \frac{1}{2}$
3. $\frac{3}{6} \bigcirc \frac{5}{6}$
4. $\frac{2}{3} \bigcirc \frac{1}{2}$
5. $\frac{6}{8} \bigcirc \frac{3}{4}$
6. $\frac{7}{9} \bigcirc \frac{5}{9}$
7. $\frac{5}{8} \bigcirc \frac{9}{10}$
8. $\frac{5}{20} \bigcirc \frac{1}{4}$
9. $\frac{5}{12} \bigcirc \frac{1}{4}$
10. $\frac{5}{7} \bigcirc \frac{6}{7}$

Write a fraction sentence that contains the symbol shown.

11. $>$
12. $<$
13. $=$

Draw and shade the models. Compare them by writing $>$, $<$ or $=$.

14. 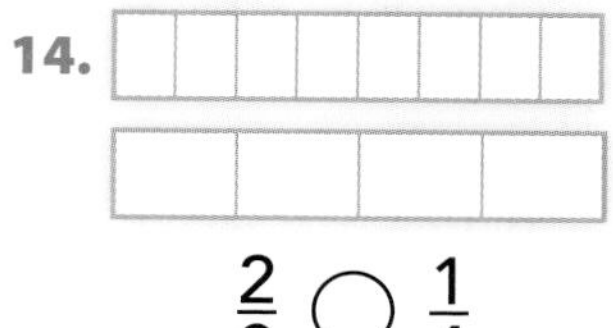

$\frac{2}{8} \bigcirc \frac{1}{4}$

15. $\frac{1}{6} \bigcirc \frac{1}{3}$

16. 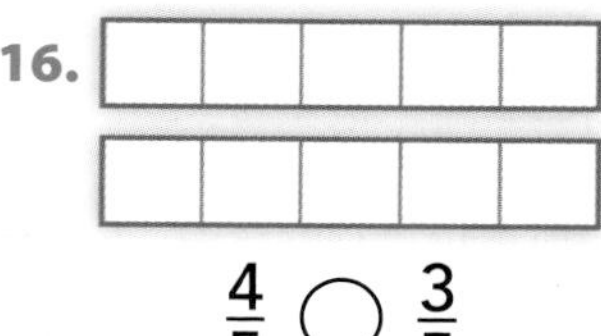

$\frac{4}{5} \bigcirc \frac{3}{5}$

17. 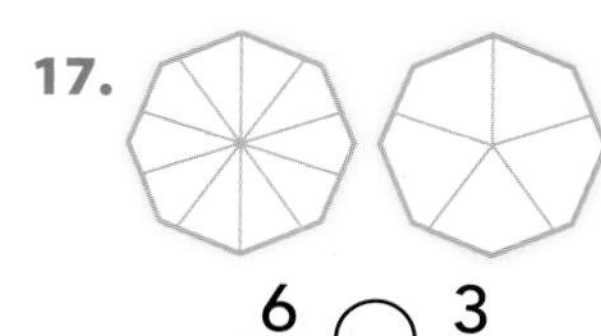

$\frac{6}{10} \bigcirc \frac{3}{5}$

Write in order from least to greatest.

18. $\frac{1}{2}, \frac{1}{3}, \frac{1}{4}$
19. $\frac{2}{5}, \frac{3}{4}, \frac{1}{10}$
20. $\frac{3}{6}, \frac{1}{6}, \frac{3}{9}$
21. $\frac{4}{6}, \frac{1}{3}, \frac{3}{8}$

Apply

22. The astronaut brought some delicious freeze-dried snacks for a group of 20 students to sample. About $\frac{1}{2}$ the students chose the Berry Blast, $\frac{1}{5}$ chose the Double Chocolate Saucer, and $\frac{3}{10}$ chose the Ice Cream Sandwich.
    a. Which dessert was sampled by the most students?

    b. Order the desserts from the most popular to the least popular.
    c. Which would you have sampled?

Review

Find the GCF.

23. 24 and 32
24. 28, 42, and 35

Find the LCM.

25. 3 and 7
26. 3, 6, and 9

Solve.

27. 472×0.8
28. $94{,}763 + 8{,}507$
29. $17\overline{)39.695}$
30. $572.9 - 48.376$
31. $1{,}207 \times 36$

8.12 Improper Fractions

Construct Meaning

The guest astronaut displayed two air tanks and discussed their features. He invited students to lift the tanks. Charles announced that one was heavier than the other. The gauge on one tank showed one full tank. The other tank was $\frac{3}{4}$ full.

The amount of air contained in both tanks is $\frac{7}{4}$ or $1\frac{3}{4}$ tanks.

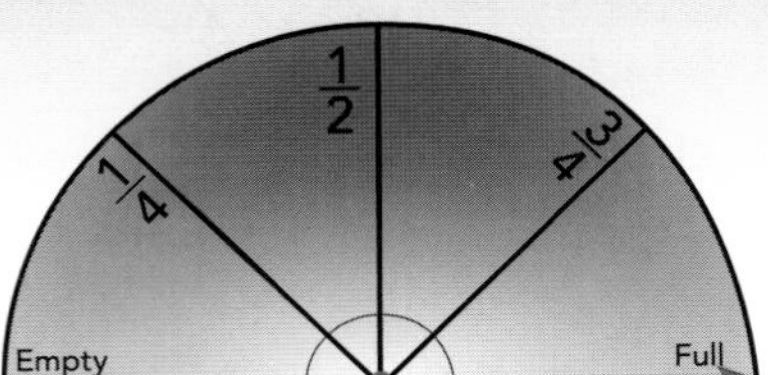

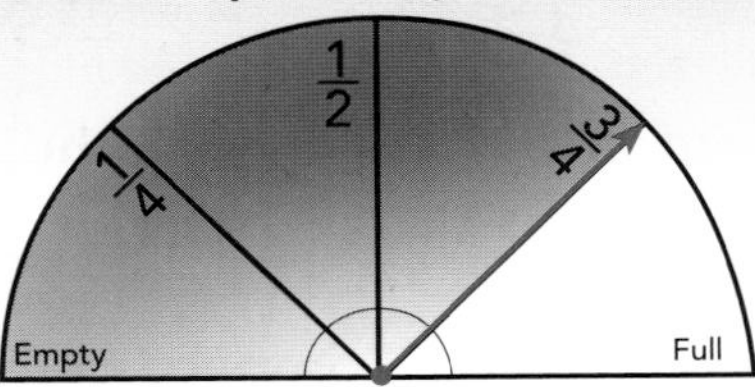

A mixed number consists of a whole number and a fraction. One example of a mixed number is $1\frac{3}{4}$.

A proper fraction is less than one, such as $\frac{2}{3}$. The fraction $\frac{7}{4}$ is an improper fraction. An improper fraction has a numerator greater than or equal to the denominator.

Rename the improper fraction $\frac{8}{5}$ as a mixed number.

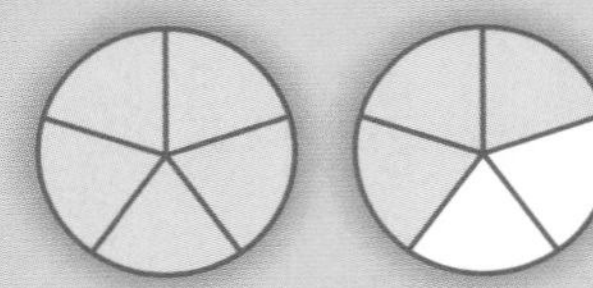

$$5\overline{)8} = 1\tfrac{3}{5}, \quad 8 - 5 = 3$$

Divide the numerator by the denominator.

Write the remainder over the divisor in fractional form in the quotient.

$\frac{8}{5} = 1\frac{3}{5}$ mixed number

Rename the mixed number $2\frac{2}{3}$ as an improper fraction.

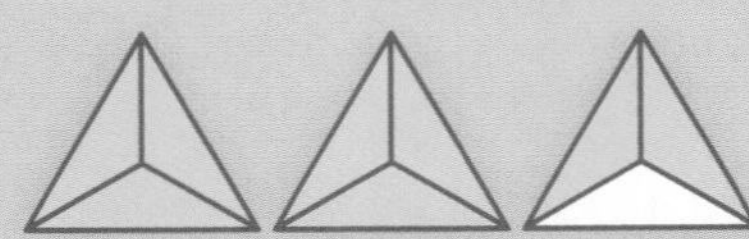

$3 \times 2 = 6$

$6 + 2$

$\frac{8}{3}$

Multiply the denominator by the whole number.
Add the numerator.
Write the sum over the denominator.

$2\frac{2}{3} = \frac{8}{3}$ improper fraction

Sometimes an improper fraction can be renamed as a whole number. $\frac{6}{3} \rightarrow 3\overline{)6}$ = 2

A whole number can be renamed as an improper fraction. $9 \rightarrow \frac{9}{1}$

Check Understanding

Write a fraction and a mixed number for each picture.

a. 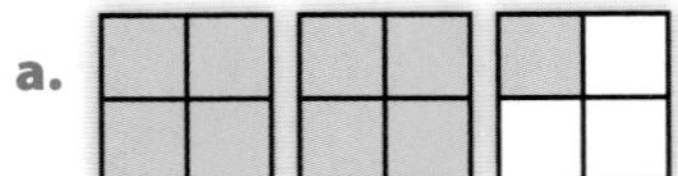

b. 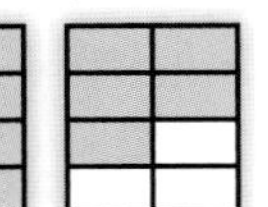

c. 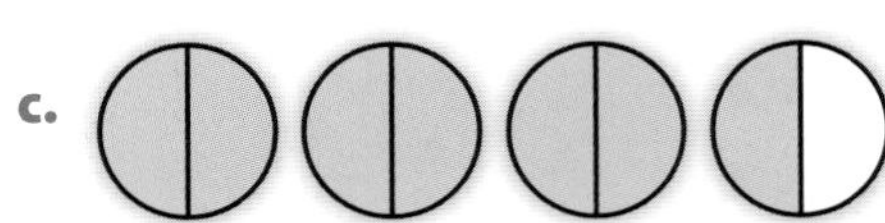

Use the Answer Bank to identify each number.

d. $\frac{9}{5}$ **e.** $\frac{4}{7}$ **f.** $1\frac{2}{3}$ **g.** 8

Answer Bank
- mixed number
- improper fraction
- proper fraction
- whole number

Practice

Draw and color a model for each number.

1. $1\frac{1}{3}$ 2. $2\frac{3}{4}$ 3. $\frac{4}{2}$ 4. $3\frac{1}{5}$ 5. 4

Rename as mixed numbers or whole numbers. Write in simplest form.

6. $\frac{7}{4}$ 8. $\frac{14}{2}$ 10. $\frac{12}{9}$ 12. $\frac{10}{5}$ 14. $\frac{24}{7}$

7. $\frac{6}{5}$ 9. $\frac{9}{7}$ 11. $\frac{8}{3}$ 13. $\frac{11}{5}$ 15. $\frac{50}{6}$

Rename as improper fractions.

16. $4\frac{2}{3}$ 18. 6 20. $9\frac{1}{4}$ 22. $3\frac{4}{9}$ 24. $8\frac{2}{5}$

17. $1\frac{1}{2}$ 19. $7\frac{5}{8}$ 21. $2\frac{1}{6}$ 23. $5\frac{3}{7}$ 25. 2

Apply

26. The class enjoyed the astronaut's visit. After he left, a parent brought pizza for everyone. Each student was given 1 slice of pizza at snack time. The pizzas were cut into 8 slices each. There were 23 students in the class. Write an improper fraction and rename it as a mixed number to show how much pizza was eaten.

27. If the parent brought in 3 whole pizzas, was there a slice left for the teacher?

28. The parent also brought string licorice. She gave each student a piece $\frac{1}{2}$ foot long. Write an improper fraction and rename it as a mixed number to show how many feet of licorice she gave to the class.

Review

Write in order from least to greatest.

29. $\frac{1}{2}, \frac{1}{8}, \frac{1}{4}, \frac{3}{8}$ 30. $\frac{3}{4}, \frac{5}{8}, \frac{1}{2}, \frac{1}{3}$ 31. $\frac{2}{5}, \frac{6}{10}, \frac{4}{5}, \frac{5}{10}$

Solve.

32. $4\overline{)90.72}$

33. $\begin{array}{r} 596 \\ \times\ 34 \\ \hline \end{array}$

34. $\begin{array}{r} 87{,}002 \\ -\ 30{,}863 \\ \hline \end{array}$

35. $17\overline{)16{,}779}$

36. 0.247 + 1.8

8.13 Problem Solving: Fractions

Check Understanding

The class wanted to show their appreciation to the visiting astronaut by making some cookies. Mrs. Cook assigned different ingredients to be measured by students. Who measured the larger amount of each ingredient?

a. Kiko measured $\frac{3}{4}$ c of flour and Joel measured $\frac{2}{3}$ c.
b. Jessica measured $\frac{1}{4}$ c of butter and Ira measured $\frac{1}{3}$ c.
c. Caleb measured $\frac{1}{8}$ tsp of salt and Anka measured $\frac{1}{4}$ tsp.
d. Gabriel measured $\frac{1}{2}$ c of sugar and Harper measured $\frac{1}{3}$ c.

Practice

Write the fraction in simplest form.

1. Mrs. Harp uses a recipe that calls for nine ingredients. She has five of the ingredients. What fraction of the ingredients does Mrs. Harp need to purchase?

2. Charlotte made a birthday cake for her friend. If it took 0.4 of an hour to bake, what fraction of an hour did it take?

3. A salad requires two-fourths of a cup of green peppers. The recipe book records that amount in fractional form. How would it appear in the recipe book?

The school had a banquet at the end of the year. Many students received awards. Out of 100 students, 35 received athletic awards, 42 received academic awards, and 23 received music awards. Write the letter of the fraction of the awards for each category.

4. athletic
   a. $\frac{42}{100} = \frac{21}{50}$
   b. $\frac{35}{100} = \frac{7}{20}$
   c. $\frac{23}{100}$

5. academic
   a. $\frac{35}{100} = \frac{7}{20}$
   b. $\frac{58}{100} = \frac{29}{50}$
   c. $\frac{42}{100} = \frac{21}{50}$

6. music
   a. $\frac{23}{100}$
   b. $\frac{35}{100} = \frac{7}{20}$
   c. $\frac{42}{100} = \frac{21}{50}$

7. athletic and music
   a. $\frac{42}{100} = \frac{2}{50}$
   b. $\frac{23}{100}$
   c. $\frac{58}{100} = \frac{29}{50}$

Use the chart to find which color(s) of fabric each person should buy.

Color	Length
red	$\frac{3}{6}$ yard
blue	$\frac{2}{3}$ yard
green	$\frac{3}{4}$ yard
yellow	$\frac{1}{4}$ yard
pink	$\frac{4}{8}$ yard

8. Ayana calculates she can use $\frac{6}{9}$ yd of this color to make a scarf.
9. Clara needs a little more than $\frac{2}{3}$ yd to decorate a table.
10. Henry needs $\frac{1}{2}$ yd of two different colors.
11. Ben needs $\frac{3}{8}$ yd for his project. Is there enough yellow fabric?

Problem-Solving Guide

Understand the question.

Analyze the data.

Plan the strategy.

Solve the problem.

Evaluate the result.

12. Carter's grandfather planted a small garden last spring. He planted 20 rows of vegetables. Three of the rows were corn. What fraction of the garden was planted in corn?

13. During a typical February, the United States celebrates the birthdays of George Washington and Abraham Lincoln, two great American presidents. What fraction of the month do these two days represent?

14. Axel and his brother drank $2\frac{1}{3}$ glasses of milk while enjoying some of their mother's chocolate-chip cookies. The glasses show thirds. Copy the drawing and shade sections to show how much milk they drank. Write that amount as an improper fraction.

15. Caroline has three brothers. Their ages are 24, 32, and 18. What is the greatest common factor of the ages of the brothers?

16. Mr. Kat used a board $16\frac{1}{2}$ feet long to replace a rotten board in the fence. The other boards in the fence were $\frac{33}{2}$ feet long. Was the replacement board too long, too short, or just the right length?

17. Make each fraction equivalent to $\frac{1}{2}$. Make each fraction equivalent to $\frac{1}{3}$.

a. $\frac{\quad}{12}$ b. $\frac{\quad}{16}$ c. $\frac{\quad}{56}$ d. $\frac{\quad}{9}$ e. $\frac{\quad}{24}$ f. $\frac{\quad}{30}$

18. What is the greatest number of identical Valentine bags that could be made if 20 stickers, 40 heart candies, and 30 Valentine cards were divided evenly?

8.14 Chapter 8 Review

Write the letter of the definition that matches the term.

____ 1. equivalent fractions
____ 2. composite number
____ 3. LCD
____ 4. integer
____ 5. improper fraction
____ 6. prime number

a. a number that only has two factors, itself and 1
b. a fraction with a numerator greater than or equal to the denominator
c. a number that has more than two factors
d. fractions that name the same amount
e. positive and negative whole numbers and zero
f. the least common multiple of two or more denominators

Write a fraction for the shaded part.

7. 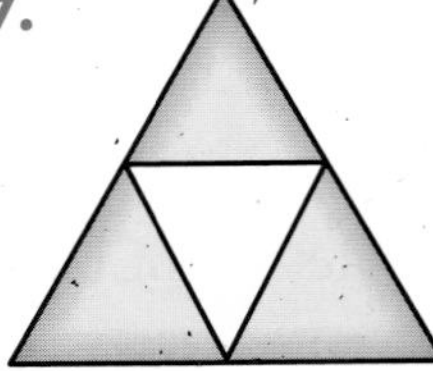

8. 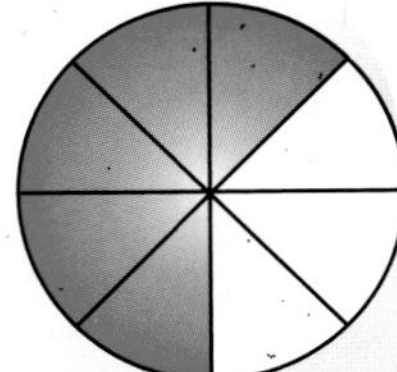

Write the fraction.

9. three-sevenths **10.** four-eighths **11.** nine-seventeenths

Write the word form, the fraction, and the decimal for each picture.

12. 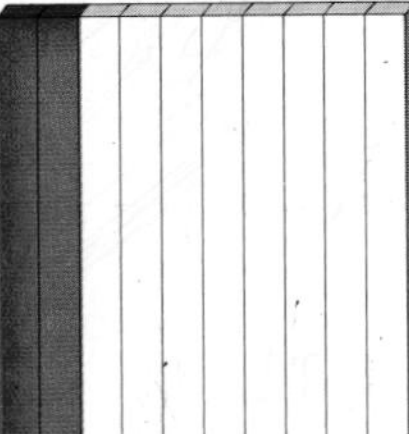

13. 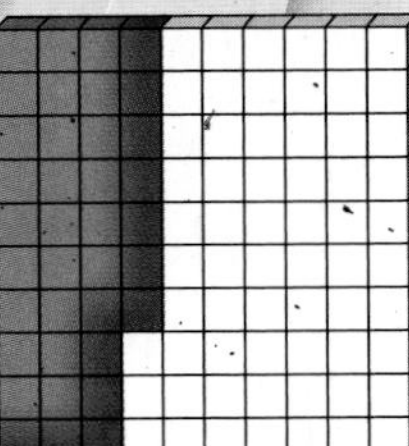

Rename the fraction using the given denominator.

14. $\frac{2}{5} = \frac{}{10}$ **15.** $\frac{1}{2} = \frac{}{100}$ **16.** $\frac{13}{250} = \frac{}{1,000}$

Write the decimal.

17. four and thirty-six hundredths **18.** two and thirteen-thousandths

Find the missing number of the equivalent fraction.

19. $\frac{2}{3} = \frac{}{12}$ **20.** $\frac{4}{7} = \frac{}{35}$

List all the factors of each number. Write "prime" or "composite."

21. 20 **22.** 17

Draw a factor tree for each number.

23. 72

24. 25

List the common factors. Circle the GCF.

25. 9 and 12

26. 4 and 16

Write each fraction in simplest form.

27. $\frac{18}{21}$

28. $\frac{10}{45}$

29. $\frac{12}{24}$

Find the least common multiple for each set of numbers.

30. 3 and 4

31. 7 and 9

Compare. Write >, <, or =.

32. $\frac{2}{3}$ ◯ $\frac{6}{9}$

33. $\frac{3}{6}$ ◯ $\frac{4}{6}$

Write in order from least to greatest.

34. $\frac{1}{2}, \frac{1}{3}, \frac{1}{4}$

35. $\frac{3}{4}, \frac{2}{3}, \frac{4}{5}$

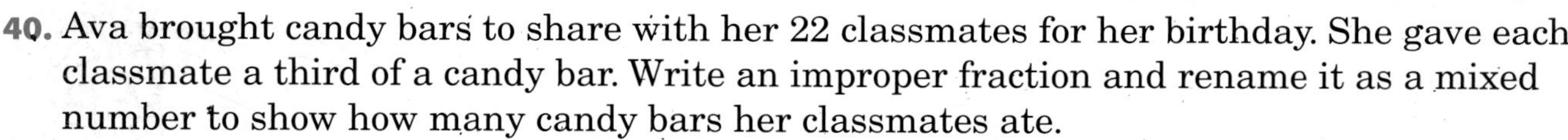

Rename as a mixed number.

36. $\frac{8}{3}$

37. $\frac{35}{6}$

Rename as a fraction.

38. $3\frac{2}{5}$

39. $6\frac{1}{8}$

Solve.

40. Ava brought candy bars to share with her 22 classmates for her birthday. She gave each classmate a third of a candy bar. Write an improper fraction and rename it as a mixed number to show how many candy bars her classmates ate.

Chapter 9
Add and Subtract Fractions

Lift up your eyes to the heavens,
look at the earth beneath.
Isaiah 51:6a

Key Ideas:

Addition: adding fractions and mixed numbers that have like denominators

Addition: adding fractions and mixed numbers that have unlike denominators

Subtraction: subtracting fractions and mixed numbers that have like denominators

Subtraction: subtracting fractions and mixed numbers that have unlike denominators

9.1 Like Denominators

Construct Meaning

Laney and her mother made trail mix for a family camping trip. They put $\frac{2}{3}$ c of sunflower seeds into the mixture. Laney's friend Monica brought $\frac{1}{3}$ c of sunflower seeds for the trail mix when she came to help with the food preparation. What was the total amount of sunflower seeds?

$$\frac{2}{3} \text{ cup} + \frac{1}{3} \text{ cup} = \frac{3}{3} \text{ cup} = 1 \text{ cup}$$

At the campground, Laney and Monica found a one-mile fitness course marked with signs showing tenths of a mile. Monica completed $\frac{9}{10}$ of the course, and Laney finished at the sign that said $\frac{6}{10}$ mile. What is the difference between the distances the girls covered?

$$\frac{9}{10} \text{ mile} - \frac{6}{10} \text{ mile} = \frac{3}{10} \text{ mile}$$

When fractions have like denominators, add or subtract the numerators. The denominator stays the same.

Monica asked Laney's mother to tell her the proportions, or parts, of the trail mix. The proportions may be stated as fractions.

$\frac{1}{6}$ nuts $\frac{2}{6}$ sunflower seeds The rest of the trail mix was raisins.

What proportion of the trail mix was raisins?

Add $\frac{1}{6} + \frac{2}{6} = \frac{}{}$ Subtract $\frac{6}{6} - \frac{}{} = \frac{}{}$

Express the proportion of raisins in simplest form.

Make a model to show the fractional parts of the trail mix. Use your circle divided into six equal parts. To show the proportions of trail mix, label the appropriate fractional parts as "nuts," "sunflower seeds," or "raisins."

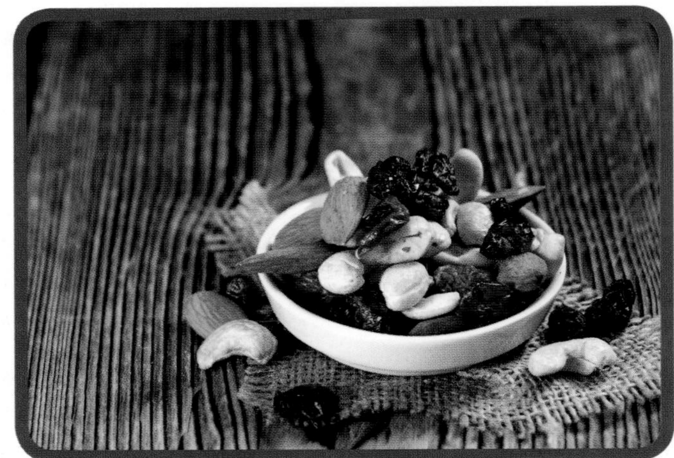

Check Understanding

Write the correct answer in simplest form.

a. $\frac{8}{12} + \frac{3}{12}$ b. $\frac{3}{8} + \frac{1}{8}$ c. $1 - \frac{5}{10}$ d. $\frac{7}{8} - = \frac{3}{8}$

Practice

Find the sum. Write the answer in simplest form.

1. $\frac{2}{4} + \frac{1}{4}$
2. $\frac{3}{8} + \frac{3}{8}$
3. $\frac{5}{7} + \frac{1}{7}$
4. $\frac{2}{6} + \frac{3}{6}$
5. $\frac{2}{5} + \frac{2}{5}$

Find the missing addend.

6. $\frac{1}{2} + \square = 1$
7. $\frac{1}{3} + \square = \frac{2}{3}$
8. $\frac{6}{11} + \square = \frac{10}{11}$
9. $\square + \frac{3}{8} = \frac{7}{8}$
10. $\frac{2}{9} + \square = 1$

Subtract. Write the answer in simplest form.

11. $\frac{11}{12} - \frac{9}{12}$
12. $\frac{5}{6} - \frac{3}{6}$
13. $\frac{8}{11} - \frac{2}{11}$
14. $\frac{5}{9} - \frac{3}{9}$
15. $\frac{9}{17} - \frac{4}{17}$

Complete each equation.

16. $\frac{11}{15} - \square = \frac{8}{15}$
17. $\frac{3}{4} - \square = \frac{1}{4}$
18. $\frac{5}{8} - \square = \frac{3}{8}$
19. $\frac{7}{9} - \square = \frac{5}{9}$
20. $\frac{5}{12} - \square = \frac{1}{12}$

Use the drawing to write the equation.

21. 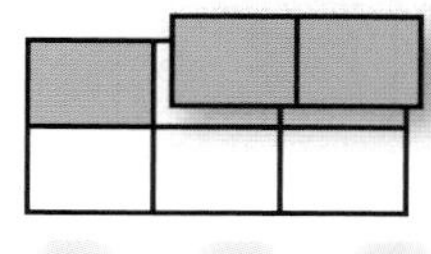

$\square - \square = \square$

22. 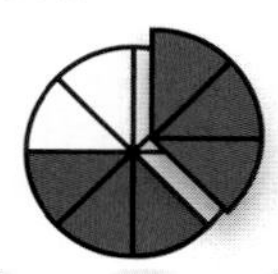

$\square - \square = \square$

23. $\square + \square = \square$

Apply

24. A recipe for salt dough is 1 part flour and 3 parts salt. Express the amount of salt in the recipe as a fraction. If you double the recipe to make the dough for crafts, using 2 cups of flour, how much salt will you need?

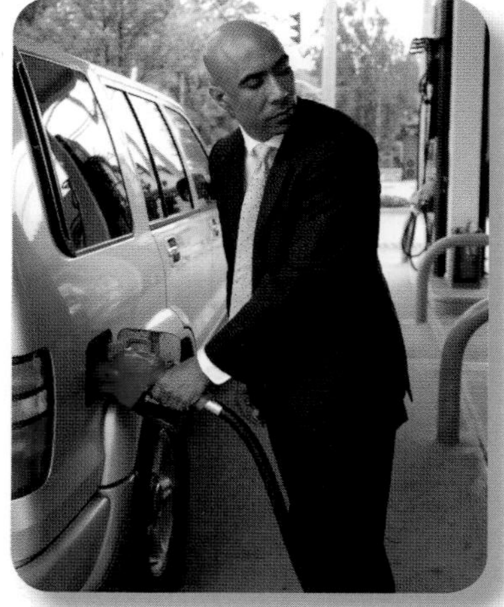

25. Lucas had a chocolate bar that was divided into 8 equal segments. He gave 3 friends 2 segments each. Express as a fraction the amount each friend received. How much does Lucas have left?

26. Mr. Murray drives 20 mi to work each weekday. He fills the tank of his car with gasoline on Monday morning and calculates that he uses $\frac{1}{6}$ of a tank each day. Use a fraction to tell how much gasoline is in the tank on Thursday morning.

Review

Find the least common multiple.

27. 2, 3, 4
28. 2, 5, 6
29. 3, 6, 12
30. 6, 9, 12
31. 2, 5, 8

9.2 Mixed Numbers

Construct Meaning

Captain Dominic L. Gorie, United States Navy, became an astronaut in 1995. He was the pilot of the *Discovery* Space Shuttle for a mission that orbited and docked with the Russian space station *Mir*. On his second trip into space, Captain Gorie and his crew were part of the Shuttle Radar Topography Mission that mapped more than 47 million square miles of the earth's land surface.

In space, astronauts use prepackaged food. If two packages of drink mix weighing $1\frac{1}{4}$ ounces each are combined, what is the total weight?

To add mixed numbers

$1\frac{1}{4}$ ounces	Add the fractions.
$+ 1\frac{1}{4}$ ounces	Add the whole numbers.
$2\frac{2}{4} = 2\frac{1}{2}$ ounces	Write the answer in simplest form.

The total weight of the drink mix is $2\frac{1}{2}$ ounces.

A larger container of juice contained $48\frac{6}{10}$ ounces. If $16\frac{1}{10}$ ounces of it are poured into a pitcher, how many ounces are left in the container?

To subtract mixed numbers

$48\frac{6}{10}$ ounces	Subtract the fractions.
$- 16\frac{1}{10}$ ounces	Subtract the whole numbers.
$32\frac{5}{10} = 32\frac{1}{2}$ ounces	Write the answer in simplest form.

There are $32\frac{1}{2}$ ounces left in the container.

Check Understanding

a. A student worked on homework for $1\frac{1}{4}$ hours, $\frac{3}{4}$ hour, 1 hour, and $1\frac{3}{4}$ hours. Was the total time period greater than or less than five hours? Express the difference between five hours and the total time spent doing homework as a fraction and as minutes.

b. Write the steps needed to add or subtract mixed numbers.

Practice

Add or subtract the mixed numbers. Write the answer in simplest form.

1. $21\frac{1}{2} + 19\frac{1}{2}$

3. $18\frac{4}{5} - 7\frac{2}{5}$

5. $33\frac{6}{8} - 29\frac{1}{8}$

7. $14\frac{11}{12} - 9$

9. $15\frac{1}{3} + 15\frac{1}{3}$

11. $19\frac{5}{16} - 6\frac{1}{16}$

2. $15\frac{2}{8} + 2\frac{3}{8}$

4. $6\frac{7}{10} + 5\frac{1}{10}$

6. $9\frac{2}{3} - 8\frac{1}{3}$

8. $50\frac{1}{4} - 25\frac{1}{4}$

10. $37\frac{8}{9} - 4\frac{5}{9}$

12. $31\frac{5}{12} - 2\frac{3}{12}$

13. $8\frac{1}{10} + 18\frac{6}{10} + 13$

14. $2\frac{5}{12} + 23\frac{1}{12} + 16\frac{4}{12}$

15. $17 + 9\frac{2}{9} + 6\frac{5}{9}$

Apply

16. A 10-kilometer race is $6\frac{2}{10}$ miles in length and a 5-kilometer race is $3\frac{1}{10}$ miles long. What is the mileage a runner covers in a 15-kilometer race?

17. An astronaut involved in a medical study recorded his liquid intake. On Monday, he drank $40\frac{5}{8}$ oz of juice. On Tuesday, he drank $38\frac{5}{8}$ oz of juice and $8\frac{2}{8}$ oz of milk. What was his total liquid intake on Tuesday? What was the difference between his intake on Monday and Tuesday?

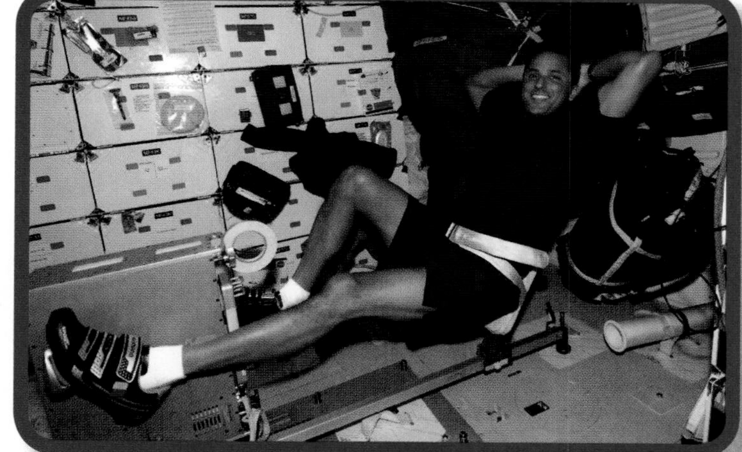

18. Astronauts are required to exercise daily while orbiting the earth. If an astronaut exercised $\frac{3}{4}$ of an hour on Monday, Wednesday, and Friday, and $\frac{1}{4}$ hour on Tuesday and Thursday, what is the total exercise time for the five days?

Review

Compare. Write >, <, or =.

19. $\frac{5}{6} \bigcirc \frac{2}{3}$

21. $\frac{8}{16} \bigcirc \frac{12}{24}$

23. $\frac{7}{21} \bigcirc \frac{1}{3}$

25. $\frac{7}{8} \bigcirc \frac{1}{2}$

27. $\frac{5}{8} \bigcirc \frac{3}{4}$

20. $\frac{3}{8} \bigcirc \frac{3}{4}$

22. $\frac{4}{5} \bigcirc \frac{7}{10}$

24. $\frac{2}{3} \bigcirc \frac{3}{4}$

26. $\frac{1}{3} \bigcirc \frac{4}{12}$

28. $\frac{1}{4} \bigcirc \frac{1}{12}$

9.3 Add and Rename

Construct Meaning

The fifth-grade classes at Ocean View Academy earned a pizza party for their help with a community project. After school, the pizza remaining from three classes was served at the Bible Club meeting. Determine the amount of pizza given to the Bible Club.

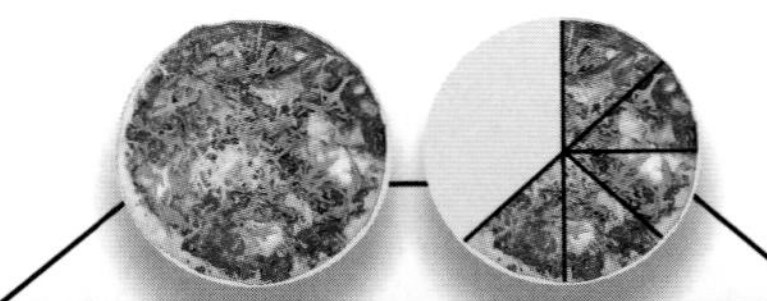

Mrs. Babbitt's Class	Mr. Gordon's Class	Mrs. Burdick's Class
$1\frac{1}{8}$ pizzas	$1\frac{5}{8}$ pizzas	$1\frac{6}{8}$ pizzas

Add the mixed numbers.

$$\begin{array}{r} 1\frac{1}{8} \\ 1\frac{5}{8} \\ +\ 1\frac{6}{8} \\ \hline 3\frac{12}{8} \end{array}$$

Add the fractions.
Add the whole numbers.

Rename the sum.

$3\frac{12}{8} = 3 + 1\frac{4}{8}$ Change the improper fraction to a mixed number.

$= 4\frac{4}{8}$ Add.

$= 4\frac{1}{2}$ Write the answer in simplest form.

The Bible Club was given $4\frac{1}{2}$ pizzas.

Use mental math when possible.

Suppose the remaining pizza had been $1\frac{1}{8}$, $1\frac{5}{8}$, and $1\frac{7}{8}$.

Find the mixed numbers with fractions that have a sum of 1.

$1\frac{1}{8} + 1\frac{5}{8} + 1\frac{7}{8}$

$1\frac{1}{8} + 1\frac{7}{8} = 2\frac{8}{8} = 2 + 1 = 3$

Add the whole number to the remaining mixed number. $3 + 1\frac{5}{8} = 4\frac{5}{8}$

Check Understanding

Choose the correct sum.

a. $2\frac{4}{5} + 3\frac{2}{5}$ — $5\frac{1}{5}$ $6\frac{1}{5}$ $5\frac{4}{5}$

b. $6\frac{3}{10} + 7\frac{9}{10}$ — $14\frac{3}{10}$ $13\frac{9}{10}$ $14\frac{1}{5}$

c. $15\frac{7}{8} + 12\frac{7}{8}$ — $27\frac{6}{8}$ $28\frac{3}{4}$ $28\frac{5}{8}$

d. $1\frac{2}{7} + 2\frac{5}{7} + 4\frac{2}{7}$ — $8\frac{3}{7}$ $7\frac{2}{7}$ $8\frac{2}{7}$

e. Use mental math to find the sum of $21\frac{3}{4} + 10 + 5\frac{1}{4}$.

Practice

Add the mixed numbers and rename the sum. Write the answer in simplest form.

1. $5\frac{6}{10} + 3\frac{5}{10}$
2. $2\frac{5}{6} + 4\frac{5}{6}$
3. $6\frac{2}{5} + 7\frac{4}{5}$
4. $3\frac{1}{7} + 7\frac{6}{7}$
5. $2\frac{7}{8} + 3\frac{3}{8}$
6. $17\frac{2}{5} + 3\frac{3}{5}$
7. $4\frac{3}{8} + 3\frac{6}{8}$
8. $9\frac{5}{9} + 5\frac{6}{9}$
9. $8\frac{3}{4} + 2\frac{3}{4}$
10. $10\frac{4}{6} + 11\frac{3}{6}$
11. $13\frac{9}{8} + \frac{9}{8}$
12. $8\frac{2}{3} + 4\frac{2}{3}$
13. $5\frac{3}{10} + 11\frac{8}{10}$
14. $20\frac{5}{9} + 32\frac{4}{9}$
15. $15\frac{5}{12} + 14\frac{7}{12}$
16. $1\frac{6}{8} + 4\frac{3}{8} + 7\frac{7}{8}$
17. $8 + 32\frac{2}{3} + 24\frac{2}{3}$
18. $7\frac{4}{5} + 9\frac{2}{5} + 8\frac{3}{5}$

Use mental math to find and rename the sum.

19. $2\frac{1}{7} + 10 + 3\frac{6}{7}$
20. $3\frac{2}{3} + 5\frac{1}{3} + 6\frac{1}{3}$
21. $3\frac{3}{4} + 4 + 6\frac{1}{4}$
22. $5\frac{6}{8} + 2\frac{2}{8} + 9$

Apply

23. Astronauts spend many hours to complete training in all aspects of spaceflight. If an astronaut trains for $7\frac{2}{4}$ hours on Monday, $6\frac{3}{4}$ hours on Tuesday, and $7\frac{3}{4}$ on Wednesday, what is the total training time in a week?

24. On a space mission, an astronaut may tell time according to how long it has been since liftoff. Suppose an astronaut ate a meal $5\frac{1}{4}$ hours after liftoff and slept $8\frac{3}{4}$ hours after starting the meal. At the time she went to sleep, how many hours had passed since liftoff?

25. Compute the total weekly mileage of an exercise program for astronauts if they ran the following distances during one week: $3\frac{1}{10}$ miles, $4\frac{5}{10}$ miles, $5\frac{6}{10}$ miles, and $6\frac{2}{10}$ miles.

9.4 Subtract from Whole Numbers

Construct Meaning

A student at New Life Christian Academy donated 4 yards of fabric to his teacher. The class used two-thirds of a yard for an art project. How much fabric was left after the project was completed?

The models show two ways to think of the 4 yards of fabric.

4 yards or 3 yards + $\frac{3}{3}$ yards

To subtract a fraction from a whole number, rename the whole number using fractional parts that match the number being subtracted.

$$\begin{array}{r} 4 \\ -\ \frac{2}{3} \\ \hline \end{array}$$

Rename the whole number to match the fraction. →

$$\begin{array}{r} 3\frac{3}{3} \\ -\ \frac{2}{3} \\ \hline 3\frac{1}{3} \end{array}$$

Subtract the fractions.

Subtract the whole numbers.

$3\frac{1}{3}$ yards remaining

There were $3\frac{1}{3}$ yards of fabric remaining.

Suppose the class had used $2\frac{1}{4}$ yards of fabric for the art project.

$$\begin{array}{r} 4 \\ -\ 2\frac{1}{4} \\ \hline \end{array}$$

Rename the whole number. →

$$\begin{array}{r} 3\frac{4}{4} \\ -\ 2\frac{1}{4} \\ \hline 1\frac{3}{4} \end{array}$$

Subtract the fractions.

Subtract the whole numbers.

$1\frac{3}{4}$ yards remaining

Nora bought 1 yard of fabric. If she used $\frac{3}{8}$ yard to make book covers, how much fabric would she have left?

1 yard $- \frac{3}{8}$ yards = ____

A fraction may be subtracted from the number 1 by changing the 1 to a fraction with the same denominator.

$1 - \frac{3}{8} = \frac{8}{8} - \frac{3}{8} = \frac{5}{8}$ yards **Nora would have $\frac{5}{8}$ yard of fabric remaining.**

Check Understanding

Rename and subtract.

a. $5 - 2\frac{3}{5}$

b. $1 - \frac{7}{16}$

c. $6 - \frac{3}{10}$

d. A student wrote the following during math practice.

$4 - 2\frac{3}{8} = 2\frac{5}{8}$ $\quad$ $12 - 9\frac{1}{6} = 3\frac{5}{6}$

What error did the student make when he renamed the whole numbers?

Practice

Write the missing number to rename each whole number.

1. $2 = 1\frac{\ }{10}$
2. $12 = 11\frac{\ }{3}$
3. $1 = \frac{\ }{20}$
4. $7 = 6\frac{\ }{5}$
5. $14 = 13\frac{\ }{6}$

Subtract. Write the answer in simplest form.

6. $9 - 3\frac{1}{3}$
7. $1 - \frac{5}{6}$
8. $15 - 5\frac{1}{2}$
9. $6 - 3\frac{3}{8}$
10. $4 - \frac{1}{4}$
11. $7 - 3\frac{2}{6}$
12. $10 - \frac{6}{10}$
13. $7 - 3\frac{3}{5}$
14. $8 - \frac{3}{8}$
15. $20 - \frac{2}{5}$
16. $43 - 12\frac{5}{9}$
17. $14 - 13\frac{2}{3}$
18. $62 - 40\frac{5}{8}$
19. $38 - 17\frac{1}{7}$
20. $50 - 10\frac{3}{12}$

Apply

21. Lawrence practiced playing the guitar for three-fourths of an hour on Monday and played the same amount of time on Tuesday. If his goal was to practice for three hours before his lesson on Wednesday, how much more time will he need to practice before the lesson?

22. Mrs. Portillo filled the 18-gallon gasoline tank of her car. She used 3 gallons of gasoline on her weekend trip. What fraction of the gasoline was left in the tank?

Review

Solve. Write the answer in simplest form.

23. $\frac{9}{10} - \frac{5}{10}$
24. $\frac{3}{4} + \frac{2}{4}$
25. $1\frac{2}{3} + \frac{2}{3}$
26. $3\frac{5}{6} + 2\frac{3}{6}$
27. $5\frac{3}{5} - 1\frac{2}{5}$
28. $\frac{7}{8} - \frac{3}{8}$
29. $20\frac{1}{2} + 14\frac{1}{2}$
30. $18\frac{4}{5} - 11\frac{2}{5}$
31. $10\frac{6}{7} - \frac{2}{7}$
32. $4\frac{2}{10} + 7\frac{9}{10}$
33. $\frac{8}{15} + \frac{7}{15}$
34. $6\frac{5}{9} + \frac{7}{9}$

9.5 Rename and Subtract

Construct Meaning

Sergio and his sister Marta need $2\frac{1}{3}$ c of flour for a birthday cake they are making for their mother. They found $\frac{2}{3}$ c of flour in the pantry. How much more flour do they need for the cake?

Subtract to find the difference between $2\frac{1}{3}$ and $\frac{2}{3}$. Rename the mixed number to increase the numerator of its fraction.

Rename $2\frac{1}{3}$ in order to subtract $\frac{2}{3}$.

$$2\frac{1}{3} - \frac{2}{3}$$

1 1 $\frac{1}{3}$

$$2\frac{1}{3} = 2 + \frac{1}{3} = 1 + 1 + \frac{1}{3} = 1 + \frac{3}{3} + \frac{1}{3} = 1 + \frac{4}{3} = 1\frac{4}{3}$$

1 $\frac{3}{3}$ $\frac{1}{3}$

Use the renamed number.

$$1\frac{4}{3} - \frac{2}{3} = 1\frac{2}{3}$$

Subtract the fractions.

Subtract the whole numbers.

$1\frac{2}{3}$ **cups of flour needed**

Solve $8\frac{3}{8} - 2\frac{7}{8}$. Rename $8\frac{3}{8}$ and use the renamed number to subtract.

$$8\frac{3}{8} = 7 + 1 + \frac{3}{8} = 7 + \frac{8}{8} + \frac{3}{8} = 7 + \frac{11}{8} = 7\frac{11}{8}$$

$$7\frac{11}{8} - 2\frac{7}{8} = 5\frac{4}{8} = 5\frac{1}{2}$$

Subtract the fractions.

Subtract the whole numbers.

Write in simplest form.

Check Understanding

Rename each mixed number as a whole number with an improper fraction.

a. $7\frac{3}{8}$ **b.** $12\frac{1}{10}$ **c.** $3\frac{1}{4}$

d. Select the problem that requires renaming. Explain your reasoning. Solve.

$3\frac{5}{8} - 2\frac{3}{8}$ $11\frac{5}{7} - 9\frac{6}{7}$ $20\frac{7}{9} - 15\frac{5}{9}$

Practice

Rename and subtract. Write the answer in simplest form.

1. $9\frac{1}{4} - 4\frac{3}{4}$
2. $3\frac{2}{5} - 2\frac{3}{5}$
3. $6\frac{5}{8} - 3\frac{6}{8}$
4. $10\frac{3}{5} - 3\frac{4}{5}$
5. $12\frac{2}{6} - 6\frac{5}{6}$
6. $15\frac{2}{9} - 9\frac{7}{9}$
7. $16\frac{3}{11} - 4\frac{9}{11}$
8. $24\frac{2}{7} - 12\frac{6}{7}$
9. $20\frac{5}{13} - 18\frac{9}{13}$
10. $5\frac{1}{3} - 2\frac{2}{3}$

Subtract. Rename if needed. Write the answer in simplest form.

11. $10\frac{4}{5} - 7\frac{2}{5}$
12. $4\frac{1}{4} - \frac{3}{4}$
13. $13 - 3\frac{5}{9}$
14. $21\frac{6}{8} - 4\frac{3}{8}$
15. $9\frac{1}{7} - \frac{5}{7}$
16. $7\frac{1}{7} - 3$

Apply

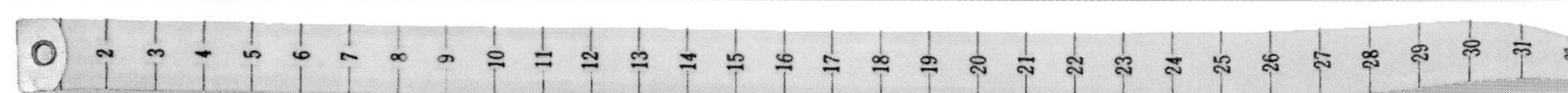

17. Mrs. Lirley wanted her students to help her paint a mural on one of her walls. She measured the wall that the mural would go on and found the height of the mural section to be $3\frac{7}{8}$ ft and the width to be $5\frac{5}{8}$ ft. What is the difference between the height and the width of the mural?

18. The border that the students made for the longer side of the mural extended to $6\frac{1}{8}$ ft. How much of the border must be trimmed to make it fit the mural section?

Review

Write each improper fraction as a mixed number. Write the answer in simplest form.

19. $\frac{12}{10}$
20. $\frac{15}{2}$
21. $\frac{26}{3}$
22. $\frac{30}{7}$
23. $\frac{21}{4}$

Subtract. Write the answer in simplest form.

24. $7 - \frac{2}{3}$
25. $16 - \frac{3}{8}$
26. $9 - 1\frac{3}{4}$
27. $12 - \frac{7}{8}$
28. $15 - 3\frac{3}{10}$

9.6 Estimate with Fractions

Construct Meaning

The owner of Fabulous Fabrics donated partial spools of ribbon to a group of students planning a mission trip to an orphanage in Turkey. The group sorted the ribbon by the length written on each spool. In one box, they placed ribbon that had less than $\frac{1}{2}$ yard remaining. In the second box, they stored spools with $\frac{1}{2}$ yard or more. The group used the guidelines below to help them sort the ribbon as they read the fraction on each spool.

3 ways to tell that a fraction is $< \frac{1}{2}$

- The numerator is 1 and the denominator is greater than 2.

  $\frac{1}{3} < \frac{1}{2}$ $\quad$ $\frac{1}{4} < \frac{1}{2}$

- The numerator is less than half of the denominator.

  $\frac{5}{12} < \frac{1}{2}$ $\quad$ $\frac{4}{16} < \frac{1}{2}$

- Find an equivalent fraction that is less than $\frac{1}{2}$.

  $\frac{3}{7} = \frac{6}{14}$ $\quad$ Think: $\frac{7}{14} = \frac{1}{2}$ $\quad$ $\frac{3}{7} < \frac{1}{2}$

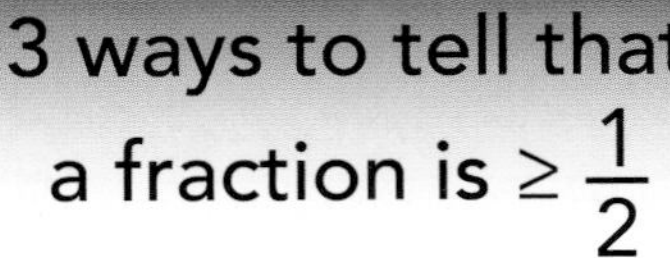

- The fraction may be written in simplest form as $\frac{1}{2}$.

  $\frac{4}{8} = \frac{1}{2}$ $\quad$ $\frac{8}{16} = \frac{1}{2}$

- The numerator is almost equal to the denominator.

  $\frac{7}{8} > \frac{1}{2}$ $\quad$ $\frac{6}{7} > \frac{1}{2}$

- Find an equivalent fraction that is greater than $\frac{1}{2}$.

  $\frac{5}{9} = \frac{10}{18}$ $\quad$ Think: $\frac{9}{18} = \frac{1}{2}$ $\quad$ $\frac{5}{9} > \frac{1}{2}$

Box 1 $< \frac{1}{2}$ yard

Box 2 $\geq \frac{1}{2}$ yard

The students had boxes weighing $2\frac{3}{8}$ lb, $5\frac{1}{6}$ lb, $4\frac{1}{2}$ lb, and $3\frac{5}{8}$ lb to combine into one large package. Estimate the total weight.

To estimate a sum (or difference) round each fraction to the nearest whole number.

Round down (whole number stays the same) if the fraction is less than $\frac{1}{2}$. Round up if the fraction is equal to or greater than $\frac{1}{2}$. Then, add (or subtract).

$$2\frac{3}{8} + 5\frac{1}{6} + 4\frac{1}{2} + 3\frac{5}{8}$$
$$2 + 5 + 5 + 4 = 16 \text{ pounds}$$

or

For a more precise estimate, round to the nearest half.

Round to the nearest half. Add (or subtract) the fractions and the whole numbers.

$$2\frac{3}{8} + 5\frac{1}{6} + 4\frac{1}{2} + 3\frac{5}{8}$$
$$2\frac{1}{2} + 5 + 4\frac{1}{2} + 3\frac{1}{2} = 15\frac{1}{2} \text{ pounds}$$

Check Understanding

Identify the correct box for each spool of ribbon. Write "Box 1" or "Box 2."

a. $\frac{4}{5}$ yd　　**b.** $\frac{3}{8}$ yd　　**c.** $\frac{5}{10}$ yd

d. Estimate the difference between $8\frac{9}{10}$ and $4\frac{1}{2}$. Use both methods.

Practice

Write each fraction. Use >, <, or = to compare it with $\frac{1}{2}$.

Example: $\frac{2}{3} > \frac{1}{2}$

1. $\frac{3}{4}$　**3.** $\frac{7}{8}$　**5.** $\frac{4}{5}$　**7.** $\frac{5}{6}$　**9.** $\frac{4}{9}$　**11.** $\frac{6}{10}$

2. $\frac{3}{8}$　**4.** $\frac{1}{3}$　**6.** $\frac{4}{16}$　**8.** $\frac{2}{7}$　**10.** $\frac{7}{12}$

Estimate the sum or difference by rounding to whole numbers.

12. $7\frac{5}{9} - 3\frac{2}{18}$

13. $10\frac{3}{10} + 12\frac{4}{5}$

14. $3\frac{3}{4} + 2\frac{2}{3}$

15. $8\frac{1}{8} + 5\frac{3}{5}$

16. $12\frac{6}{9} - 6\frac{5}{10}$

Estimate the sum or difference by rounding to the nearest half.

17. $5\frac{1}{6} + 6\frac{7}{8} + 9\frac{1}{2}$　**18.** $22 + 3\frac{4}{8} + 10\frac{6}{7}$　**19.** $33\frac{1}{3} - 8\frac{5}{6}$

Apply

20. Maisie eats $2\frac{1}{2}$ cups of dog food in the morning and $1\frac{7}{8}$ cups at night. Estimate how many cups she eats daily by using both methods below.

a. rounding to the nearest half　　**b.** rounding to whole numbers

21. What is the difference between each estimate and the actual amount needed? Which estimate would be better to use for planning the amount of dog food to take on a one-week vacation if space is limited? Explain your reasoning.

Review

Subtract. Rename if needed. Write the answer in simplest form.

22. $3\frac{1}{4} - 2\frac{3}{4}$　**24.** $12\frac{5}{6} - 3\frac{1}{6}$　**26.** $31\frac{9}{10} - 27\frac{3}{10}$　**28.** $4\frac{1}{8} - 2\frac{3}{8}$

23. $8 - \frac{7}{8}$　**25.** $50 - 25\frac{1}{4}$　**27.** $7 - 3\frac{2}{3}$　**29.** $3\frac{3}{5} - 2$

9.7 Least Common Denominator

Construct Meaning

While shopping at a fruit and vegetable stand, Nita and her mother found pineapples that cost $3 each. Nita selected one pineapple that weighed $\frac{3}{4}$ lb and another that was $\frac{5}{8}$ lb. She thought the pineapple that weighed $\frac{3}{4}$ lb was a better buy. Was she correct?

Fractions with unlike denominators may require renaming only one fraction. For example, is $\frac{3}{4}$ >, <, or = to $\frac{5}{8}$? Find the least common denominator (LCD).

Find the least common multiple (LCM) of the denominators.	The LCM of 4 and 8 is the LCD for fourths and eighths.	Rename $\frac{3}{4}$ using the LCD.	Compare the fractions using the LCD.
4: 4, 8, 12, 16 8: 8, 16, 24		$\frac{3 \times 2}{4 \times 2} = \frac{6}{8}$	$\frac{6}{8} > \frac{5}{8}$, so $\frac{3}{4} > \frac{5}{8}$

The pineapple that weighs $\frac{3}{4}$ lb is the better buy.

Why was only one fraction renamed to compare $\frac{3}{4}$ and $\frac{5}{8}$?

When you work with fractions that have unlike denominators, more than one fraction may require renaming. Compare $\frac{2}{3}$ and $\frac{3}{5}$. Find the least common denominator.

Multiples of 3: 3, 6, 9, 12, <u>15</u>
Multiples of 5: 5, 10, <u>15</u>

The LCM of 3 and 5 = 15.
15 is the least common denominator.

Rename both fractions, using 15 as the LCD.

$\frac{2}{3} = \frac{\square}{15}$ $\quad \frac{2 \times 5}{3 \times 5} = \frac{10}{15}$

$\frac{3}{5} = \frac{\square}{15}$ $\quad \frac{3 \times 3}{5 \times 3} = \frac{9}{15}$

Compare the renamed fractions.

$\frac{10}{15} > \frac{9}{15}$, so $\frac{2}{3} > \frac{3}{5}$

Check Understanding

Is it necessary to rename both fractions with the LCD? Write "yes" or "no."

a. $\frac{1}{2}$ and $\frac{3}{4}$ **b.** $\frac{1}{3}$ and $\frac{3}{7}$ **c.** $\frac{1}{2}$ and $\frac{1}{9}$ **d.** $\frac{1}{3}$ and $\frac{5}{6}$

e. Rename $1\frac{3}{4}$ and $2\frac{5}{12}$ with the least common denominator.

Practice

Rename the fractions by using the least common denominator.

1. $\frac{1}{2}$ and $\frac{1}{3}$
2. $\frac{2}{5}$ and $\frac{3}{10}$
3. $\frac{2}{3}$ and $\frac{3}{4}$
4. $\frac{3}{5}$ and $\frac{5}{8}$
5. $\frac{1}{2}$ and $\frac{1}{9}$
6. $\frac{2}{3}$ and $\frac{1}{8}$
7. $\frac{1}{4}$ and $\frac{3}{5}$
8. $\frac{1}{6}$ and $\frac{5}{9}$

Rename the mixed numbers by using the least common denominator.

9. $4\frac{1}{2}$ $1\frac{2}{3}$
10. $10\frac{3}{4}$ $5\frac{5}{8}$
11. $2\frac{2}{3}$ $6\frac{5}{6}$
12. $1\frac{2}{5}$ $2\frac{1}{6}$

Write the fraction pair that requires renaming both fractions with the least common denominator.

13. $\frac{1}{4}$ and $\frac{1}{12}$ or $\frac{1}{4}$ and $\frac{1}{9}$
14. $\frac{1}{16}$ and $\frac{1}{3}$ or $\frac{1}{5}$ and $\frac{1}{15}$

Apply

15. Nava lives $\frac{5}{6}$ mile from school, and Ralph's house is $\frac{7}{8}$ mile from the school. Who lives closer to school? How much closer?
16. Palmer's father wanted to purchase a backpack for a long, difficult hiking trip. He saw a pack that weighed $5\frac{3}{5}$ lb and another that weighed $5\frac{7}{10}$ lb. If he purchased the lighter backpack, which one did he buy?
17. On the backpack trip, the hikers needed $2\frac{3}{4}$ cups of water to cook the rice for dinner. One of the men put 2 cups of water in the pot and another gave $\frac{5}{8}$ cup from his water supply. Did they have enough water to prepare the rice? Compare the amount of water they had for the rice with the amount they needed.
18. Do $\frac{3}{4}$ and $\frac{2}{3}$ have more than one common denominator? Why is it important to use the least common denominator for fractions?

9.8 Related Denominators

Construct Meaning

Martin was making a snack mix to take to school. He put $\frac{3}{4}$ cup of pretzels in the bowl of mix before going to answer the telephone. His sister wanted to help so she added an additional $\frac{3}{8}$ cup of pretzels to the bowl. What is the total amount of pretzels in the bowl of snack mix?

To add fractions that have unlike denominators, find the least common denominator.

$$\begin{array}{r} \frac{3}{4} \text{ cup} \\ + \frac{3}{8} \text{ cup} \\ \hline \end{array}$$

What is the LCD of $\frac{3}{4}$ and $\frac{3}{8}$?
8 is a multiple of 4. The LCD is 8.

Only the fraction $\frac{3}{4}$ needs to be renamed. $\frac{3}{4} = \frac{}{8}$ $\frac{3 \times 2}{4 \times 2} = \frac{6}{8}$

Add the fractions that now have a common denominator.

$$\begin{array}{r} \frac{6}{8} \text{ cup} \\ + \frac{3}{8} \text{ cup} \\ \hline \frac{9}{8} \text{ cup} \end{array} = 1\frac{1}{8} \textbf{ cups of pretzels}$$

Remember: If one denominator is a multiple of the other denominator, only one fraction must be renamed.

To subtract fractions that have unlike denominators, find the least common denominator.

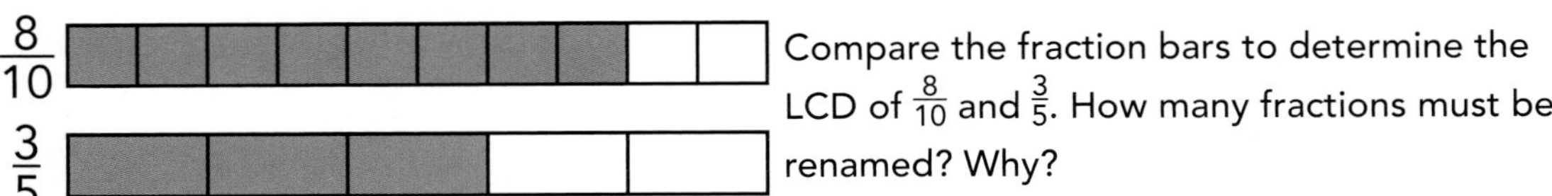

$\frac{8}{10}$ / $\frac{3}{5}$

Compare the fraction bars to determine the LCD of $\frac{8}{10}$ and $\frac{3}{5}$. How many fractions must be renamed? Why?

Rename $\frac{3}{5}$ with the LCD.

$\frac{3}{5} = \frac{}{10}$ $\frac{3 \times 2}{5 \times 2} = \frac{6}{10}$

Subtract using the renamed fraction.

$\frac{8}{10} - \frac{6}{10} = \frac{2}{10} = \frac{1}{5}$

Check Understanding

Write the LCD for each pair of numbers.

a. $\frac{1}{4}$ $\frac{3}{8}$ **b.** $\frac{5}{24}$ $\frac{3}{8}$ **c.** $\frac{5}{6}$ $\frac{5}{12}$

Rename the fractions using the LCD and solve. Write the answer in simplest form.

d. $\frac{11}{12} - \frac{3}{4}$ **e.** $\frac{1}{6} + \frac{11}{18}$ **f.** $\frac{8}{9} - \frac{2}{3}$

Practice

Rename the fractions using the LCD. Add or subtract. Write the answer in simplest form.

1. $\frac{3}{5} - \frac{1}{10}$
2. $\frac{1}{2} + \frac{1}{6}$
3. $\frac{1}{6} + \frac{3}{12}$
4. $\frac{5}{8} - \frac{1}{4}$
5. $\frac{4}{9} + \frac{1}{18}$
6. $\frac{5}{6} - \frac{2}{3}$
7. $\frac{14}{15} - \frac{1}{5}$
8. $\frac{3}{7} + \frac{2}{21}$
9. $\frac{3}{4} - \frac{5}{12}$
10. $\frac{9}{20} - \frac{2}{5}$
11. $\frac{5}{8} + \frac{3}{24}$
12. $\frac{5}{16} - \frac{1}{8}$
13. $\frac{2}{3} + \frac{1}{12}$
14. $\frac{7}{10} - \frac{1}{5}$
15. $\frac{8}{18} + \frac{5}{6}$
16. $\frac{2}{3} + \frac{5}{9}$

Apply

Melody's favorite brand

cashews $\frac{3}{8}$
peanuts $\frac{1}{4}$
almonds $\frac{1}{8}$
walnuts $\frac{1}{4}$

Slade's favorite brand

Melody and Slade each brought a can of their favorite brand of mixed nuts to class. Both cans were the same price and each held 1 cup of nuts, but they found that the brands differed in the amount of each type of nut in the package.

Solve.

17. What is the total amount of cashews and peanuts in Melody's brand?
18. Add the amount of cashews to the amount of peanuts in Slade's brand. Is that figure greater than, less than, or equal to the amount in Melody's brand?
19. Find the difference between the amounts of walnuts in the two brands.
20. If cashews and walnuts are the most expensive types of nut, whose brand is the better buy?
21. If your personal favorites are cashews and almonds, whose brand should you buy?

Review

Solve. Write each answer in simplest form.

22. $6\frac{7}{8} - 4\frac{5}{8}$
23. $15\frac{9}{10} - 2\frac{3}{10}$
24. $8 - 3\frac{1}{3}$
25. $25 - 10\frac{1}{4}$
26. $20\frac{1}{4} + 35\frac{2}{4}$
27. $19\frac{5}{12} + 10\frac{7}{12}$
28. $7\frac{3}{4} - 5$
29. $15\frac{5}{8} + 4\frac{3}{8}$

9.9 Add: Unlike Denominators

Construct Meaning

Seth and his family visited Space Adventure Camp. They toured the camp for a day to determine if Seth's attendance there would help him pursue his goal of becoming an astronaut.

Seth's family walked from the entrance to the Information Center. They walked on to the Lecture Hall, where they heard a short talk by a retired astronaut. How far had they walked from the entrance?

To add $\frac{1}{4}$ mile and $\frac{2}{3}$ mile, find the least common denominator.

multiples of 4:	4,	8,	(12)	16
multiples of 3:	3,	6,	9,	(12)

The LCD is 12.
Rename both fractions to add.

$\frac{1}{4} = \frac{\square}{12}$ $\quad \frac{1 \times 3}{4 \times 3} = \frac{3}{12}$ $\qquad \frac{2}{3} = \frac{\square}{12}$ $\quad \frac{2 \times 4}{3 \times 4} = \frac{8}{12}$

Add the renamed fractions. $\frac{3}{12} + \frac{8}{12} = \frac{11}{12}$

Seth and his family walked $\frac{11}{12}$ mile.

Check Understanding

a. Seth and his parents left the Lecture Hall to go to lunch at the Dining Hall. Then, they walked to Student Housing. What is the distance they traveled from the Lecture Hall?

b. List the necessary steps for adding fractions that have unlike denominators when neither denominator is a multiple of the other.

Practice

Add the fractions using the LCD. Write the answers in simplest form.

1. $\frac{1}{6} + \frac{3}{5}$
2. $\frac{2}{4} + \frac{7}{8}$
3. $\frac{2}{3} + \frac{2}{5}$
4. $\frac{1}{2} + \frac{1}{3}$
5. $\frac{1}{4} + \frac{3}{5}$
6. $\frac{2}{3} + \frac{1}{8}$
7. $\frac{5}{6} + \frac{1}{5}$
8. $\frac{2}{9} + \frac{1}{6}$
9. $\frac{1}{3} + \frac{4}{9}$
10. $\frac{3}{7} + \frac{2}{3}$
11. $\frac{1}{6} + \frac{3}{8}$
12. $\frac{3}{10} + \frac{6}{15}$
13. $\frac{5}{8} + \frac{4}{5}$
14. $\frac{3}{4} + \frac{2}{9}$
15. $\frac{5}{6} + \frac{1}{4}$
16. $\frac{7}{20} + \frac{9}{10}$

Apply

Use the map of Space Adventure Camp to solve.

17. If Seth took the Tourist Trolley from the station to the Launch Pad and went on to the Rocket Garden, what distance would he travel?

18. Seth can easily jog a half mile in five minutes. Could he make it from the Rocket Garden to the Space Theater in five minutes?

19. A group of students got up early every morning and jogged from Student Housing to the Lecture Hall and back to change before breakfast. Another group jogged every evening, making a round trip from Student Housing to the Flight Simulator. Which group ran a longer distance each day?

20. How much greater is the distance between the Launch Pad and the Rocket Garden than the distance between the Rocket Garden and the Flight Simulator?

21. Think of equivalent fractions to determine whether a trip from the Tourist Trolley Station to the Rocket Garden is greater or less than half a mile. Explain your reasoning.

22. If a student at Space Adventure Camp made three daily round-trips from Student Housing to the Dining Hall, how many miles would he or she walk in one day?

9.10 Subtract: Unlike Denominators

Construct Meaning

When Mrs. Sommer was previewing books for her reading students, she found two books of adventure stories. One was $\frac{3}{4}$ full of nonfiction selections, while the other was $\frac{1}{3}$ nonfiction adventures. What is the difference in the amount of nonfiction the books contain?

To find the difference, rename the fractions that have unlike denominators and subtract.

Find the LCD.

$$\frac{3}{4} - \frac{1}{3}$$

multiples of 4: 4, 8, **12**, 16
multiples of 3: 3, 6, 9, **12**

Rename the fractions and subtract.

$$\frac{3}{4} = \frac{3 \times 3}{4 \times 3} = \frac{9}{12}$$

$$-\ \frac{1}{3} = \frac{1 \times 4}{3 \times 4} = \frac{4}{12}$$

$$\frac{5}{12}$$

The difference in the amount of nonfiction is $\frac{5}{12}$.

The fraction bars show renaming with the least common denominator and subtracting.

$$\frac{3}{4} = \frac{9}{12} \qquad \frac{1}{3} = \frac{4}{12}$$

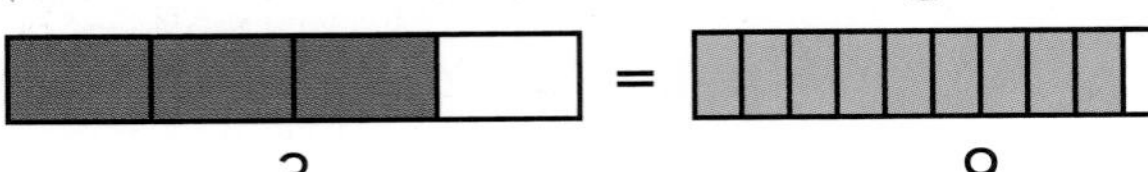

$$\frac{9}{12} - \frac{4}{12} = \frac{5}{12}$$

Solve $\frac{5}{6} - \frac{7}{10}$.

Find the LCD.

$$\frac{5}{6} - \frac{7}{10}$$

Multiples of 6: 6, 12, 18, 24, **30**
Multiples of 10: 10, 20, **30**

Rename and subtract.

$$\frac{5}{6} = \frac{}{30}$$

$$-\ \frac{7}{10} = \frac{}{30}$$

$$ = $$

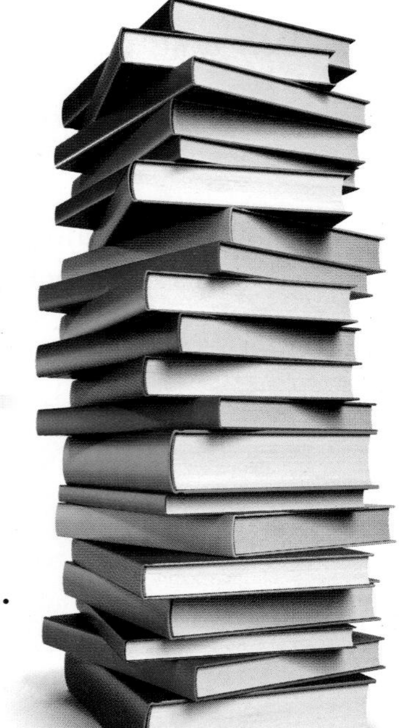

Check Understanding

a. Draw fraction models with circles to show renaming with the LCD and subtracting $\frac{1}{4}$ from $\frac{5}{8}$.

Rename with the LCD and subtract. Write the answers in simplest form.

b. $\frac{2}{3} - \frac{1}{6}$

c. $\frac{3}{5} - \frac{1}{3}$

d. $\frac{3}{4} - \frac{2}{5}$

Practice

Rename with the LCD and subtract. Write the answers in simplest form.

1. $\frac{1}{2} - \frac{2}{5}$
2. $\frac{7}{8} - \frac{2}{3}$
3. $\frac{9}{10} - \frac{1}{5}$
4. $\frac{3}{4} - \frac{1}{8}$
5. $\frac{2}{3} - \frac{1}{4}$

6. $\frac{5}{6} - \frac{1}{7}$
8. $\frac{7}{8} - \frac{3}{4}$
10. $\frac{7}{10} - \frac{1}{8}$
12. $\frac{5}{9} - \frac{1}{3}$
14. $\frac{3}{5} - \frac{4}{10}$

7. $\frac{4}{5} - \frac{2}{3}$
9. $\frac{5}{6} - \frac{1}{4}$
11. $\frac{11}{12} - \frac{3}{5}$
13. $\frac{1}{4} - \frac{1}{5}$
15. $\frac{1}{3} - \frac{3}{12}$

Apply

16. A bag of flower bulbs contained $\frac{1}{5}$ daffodil bulbs and $\frac{1}{3}$ lily bulbs. The remainder of the bag contained tulip bulbs. What portion of the bag was tulip bulbs?

17. After planting the flower bulbs, Sheila and her mother walked $\frac{3}{5}$ mi from their home to a convenience store. Sheila suggested walking on to the park, but Mother said that would require walking about another half mile. It is $\frac{9}{10}$ mi from their home to the park. What is the exact distance from the convenience store to the park?

18. Tori and her brother Tyrese each had a Nutty Chocolate Bar. Tori divided her candy bar equally with one friend. Tyrese divided his candy equally among two friends and himself. How much more Nutty Chocolate Bar did Tori and her friend each eat than Tyrese and his friends?

Review

Write each fraction. Compare with $\frac{1}{2}$ by writing >, <, or =.

19. $\frac{9}{10}$
20. $\frac{3}{4}$
21. $\frac{2}{3}$
22. $\frac{5}{12}$
23. $\frac{4}{7}$
24. $\frac{8}{16}$
25. $\frac{9}{20}$

Estimate the sum or difference by rounding to whole numbers.

26. $2\frac{3}{5} + 5\frac{1}{3}$
27. $15\frac{3}{4} - 6\frac{1}{2}$
28. $19\frac{7}{8} - 9\frac{7}{9}$
29. $3\frac{1}{3} + 2\frac{1}{4}$
30. $6\frac{2}{10} + 10\frac{1}{2}$

9.11 Add: Mixed Numbers

Construct Meaning

Valentina Tereshkova (Russia) was the first woman to travel into space.

Changes in gravitational pull affect the body of an astronaut in space. An astronaut may grow $\frac{7}{8}$ inch to $1\frac{1}{4}$ inches in height because her spine lengthens after an extended time in a weightless environment.

Suppose a female astronaut is 5 feet $5\frac{1}{2}$ inches tall on Earth. She gains $\frac{7}{8}$ inch in height while living aboard the International Space Station. What is her height while in space?

To add mixed numbers and fractions that have unlike denominators, find the least common denominator.

$$\begin{array}{r} 5 \text{ feet } 5\frac{1}{2} \text{ inches} \\ + \quad \frac{7}{8} \text{ inch} \\ \hline \end{array}$$

What is the LCD of $\frac{1}{2}$ and $\frac{1}{8}$?
8 is a multiple of 2.
The LCD is 8.

Only the fraction $\frac{1}{2}$ is renamed. $\frac{1}{2} = \frac{}{8}$ $\quad \frac{1 \times 4}{2 \times 4} = \frac{4}{8}$

Add the fractions with the LCD, and then add the whole numbers.

$$\begin{array}{r} 5 \text{ feet } 5\frac{4}{8} \text{ inches} \\ + \quad \frac{7}{8} \text{ inch} \\ \hline 5 \text{ feet } 5\frac{11}{8} \text{ inches} \end{array} = 5 \text{ feet } 6\frac{3}{8} \text{ inches}$$

Her height in space is 5 feet $6\frac{3}{8}$ inches.

Solve $9\frac{2}{9} + 5\frac{1}{6}$. Rename the mixed numbers with the LCD.

$9\frac{2}{9} = 9\frac{}{18}$ $\qquad 5\frac{1}{6} = 5\frac{}{18}$

Think: $\frac{2}{9} = \frac{2 \times 2}{9 \times 2} = \frac{}{18}$ $\qquad$ Think: $\frac{1}{6} = \frac{1 \times 3}{6 \times 3} = \frac{}{18}$

$9\frac{2}{9} = 9\frac{}{18}$ $\qquad 5\frac{1}{6} = 5\frac{}{18}$

Add the renamed mixed numbers, writing the answers in simplest form.

$$\begin{array}{r} 9\frac{}{18} \\ + \; 5\frac{}{18} \\ \hline 14\frac{}{18} \end{array}$$

Add the fractions.

Add the whole numbers.

Check Understanding

Add the mixed numbers, renaming when necessary. Write the answer in simplest form.

a. $3\frac{2}{3} + 10\frac{1}{3}$ **b.** $18\frac{1}{4} + 22\frac{1}{5}$ **c.** $5\frac{3}{4} + \frac{1}{2}$ **d.** $2\frac{1}{4} + \frac{3}{8} + \frac{1}{2}$

Practice

Add. Write the sum in simplest form.

1. $9\frac{1}{8} + 7\frac{4}{5}$
2. $21\frac{6}{10} + 13\frac{2}{20}$
3. $52 + 3\frac{7}{8}$
4. $65\frac{2}{3} + 30\frac{4}{9}$
5. $33\frac{1}{3} + 25\frac{1}{4}$
6. $1\frac{5}{6} + 43\frac{2}{10}$
7. $12\frac{1}{2} + 5\frac{3}{7}$
8. $50\frac{1}{12} + 16\frac{2}{3}$
9. $71\frac{6}{15} + \frac{1}{2}$
10. $85 + 10\frac{5}{9}$
11. $4\frac{1}{3} + 6\frac{1}{4} + 8\frac{1}{2}$
12. $10\frac{1}{10} + 9\frac{1}{5} + 4\frac{3}{5}$

Apply

Coach Schwartz requires the cross-country runners to do short sprints called intervals as part of their training. He set a goal of $1\frac{1}{2}$ miles of interval training over a period of three days. Zayden recorded his interval training in his running log.

13. What was the total distance of Zayden's interval training for the three-day period?
14. How much greater or less than the coach's goal was Zayden's total mileage for interval training?
15. In addition to the interval training, Zayden ran a total of $9\frac{3}{4}$ miles on a cross-country course during the same three-day period. What was the total amount of interval training and cross-country running for the three days?

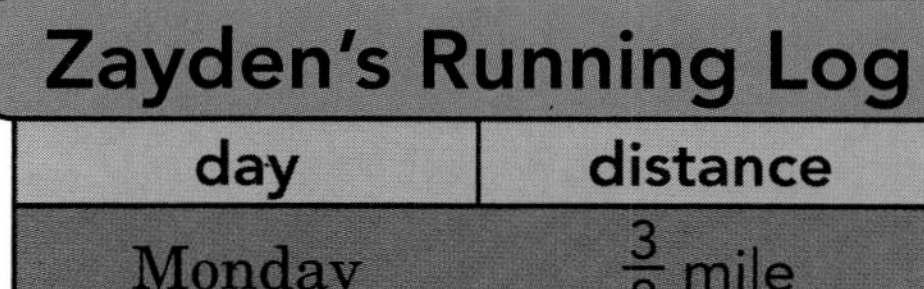

Zayden's Running Log

day	distance
Monday	$\frac{3}{8}$ mile
Tuesday	$\frac{3}{4}$ mile
Wednesday	$\frac{1}{2}$ mile

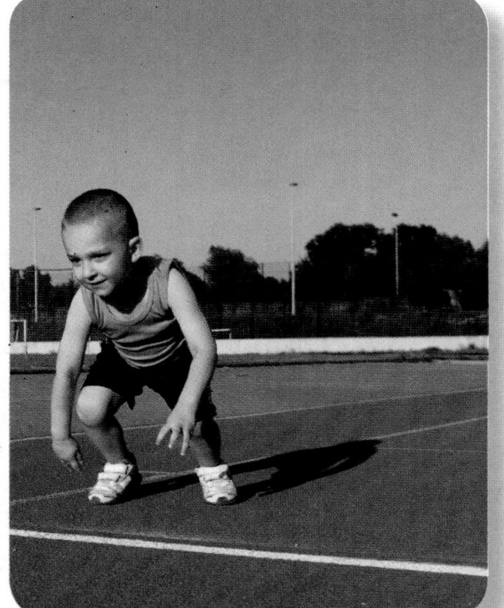

16. At the cross-country meet, Zayden ran the first half of the course in $8\frac{1}{2}$ minutes and the second half in $9\frac{1}{4}$ minutes. What was his time for the race?
17. Zayden's younger brother, Trey, likes to run on the track while Zayden trains. One trip around the track equals $\frac{1}{4}$ mile. Trey ran completely around the track twice on Thursday, three times on Friday, and five times on Saturday. What was his total mileage?

1 2 3 4 5 6 7

9.12 Subtract: Mixed Numbers

Construct Meaning

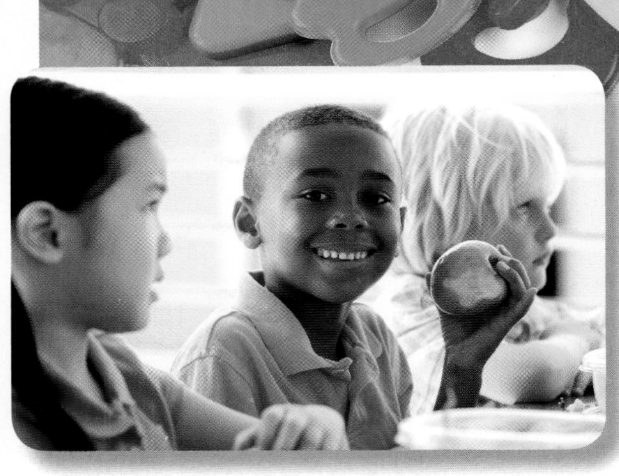

At Fairview Christian School, the fifth graders worked with kindergarten buddies. They invited the younger children to an event they called Tasting Fruits and Vegetables from A to Z. Each child chose a letter of the alphabet and brought a fruit or vegetable beginning with that letter.

Pam and her buddy brought $3\frac{2}{3}$ lb of grapes. Only $2\frac{1}{2}$ lb were eaten. How many pounds were left?

$3\frac{2}{3} - 2\frac{1}{2}$ pounds = ▢

ABCDEFGHIJKLMNOPQRSTUVWXYZ ABCDEFGHIJKLMNOPQRSTUVWXYZ ABCDEFGHIJKLMNOPQRSTUVWXYZ

To subtract mixed numbers with unlike denominators, rename the fractions with the LCD.

$3\frac{2}{3} = 3\frac{4}{6}$

and

$2\frac{1}{2} = 2\frac{3}{6}$

Use the renamed mixed numbers to subtract.

$$\begin{array}{r} 3\frac{4}{6} \\ -\ 2\frac{3}{6} \\ \hline 1\frac{1}{6} \end{array}$$

Subtract the fractions.
Subtract the whole numbers.

There were $1\frac{1}{6}$ lb of grapes left.

The total amount of fruits and vegetables for the tasting event was $68\frac{1}{4}$ lb. If $33\frac{2}{3}$ lb were vegetables, what was the amount of fruit?

- Rename with the LCD.

$68\frac{1}{4} = 68\frac{3}{12}$ $33\frac{2}{3} = 33\frac{8}{12}$

- Rename $68\frac{3}{12}$ to increase the numerator.

$68\frac{3}{12} = 67 + 1 + \frac{3}{12} = 67 + \frac{12}{12} + \frac{3}{12} = 67\frac{15}{12}$

$$\begin{array}{r} 68\frac{1}{4} = 68\frac{3}{12} = 67\frac{15}{12} \\ -\ 33\frac{2}{3} = 33\frac{8}{12} = 33\frac{8}{12} \\ \hline 34\frac{7}{12} \end{array}$$

There were $34\frac{7}{12}$ lb of fruit.

Check Understanding

a. Write all the steps required to subtract mixed numbers that have unlike denominators.

Subtract. Write the answer in simplest form.

b. $\begin{array}{r} 7\frac{7}{9} \\ -\ 5\frac{1}{3} \\ \hline \end{array}$

c. $\begin{array}{r} 25\frac{1}{4} \\ -\ 15\frac{7}{8} \\ \hline \end{array}$

d. $\begin{array}{r} 30 \\ -\ 4\frac{3}{4} \\ \hline \end{array}$

Practice

Subtract, renaming if necessary. Write the answers in simplest form.

1. $2\frac{5}{8} - 1\frac{1}{2}$
2. $25\frac{2}{10} - 9\frac{3}{5}$
3. $8\frac{4}{9} - 3\frac{2}{6}$
4. $3\frac{2}{3} - 2\frac{1}{6}$
5. $16\frac{4}{5} - 5\frac{3}{4}$
6. $7\frac{1}{4} - 5\frac{3}{8}$
7. $12\frac{5}{6} - 10\frac{2}{3}$
8. $18\frac{1}{3} - 4\frac{1}{2}$
9. $6\frac{2}{9} - 1\frac{2}{3}$
10. $16\frac{4}{5} - 8\frac{5}{6}$
11. $9\frac{6}{16} - 5\frac{1}{4}$
12. $5\frac{7}{10} - 3\frac{3}{20}$

Identify the value of *y* in each equation.

13. $3\frac{1}{3} - 2\frac{y}{2} = \frac{5}{6}$
14. $10\frac{3}{4} - 5\frac{y}{3} = 5\frac{1}{12}$
15. $16\frac{1}{10} - 8\frac{y}{5} = 7\frac{1}{2}$

Write the next two numbers in the subtraction pattern.

16. $12, 10\frac{1}{2}, 9, 7\frac{1}{2}$
17. $18\frac{1}{2}, 16\frac{1}{4}, 14, 11\frac{3}{4}$
18. $20, 18\frac{2}{3}, 17\frac{1}{3}, 16$

Apply

19. Paxton contributed $3\frac{7}{10}$ lb of zucchini to the tasting event. He sliced $1\frac{1}{2}$ lb and set it out for the students. When that was eaten, he sliced and served another $1\frac{1}{4}$ pounds. What amount of zucchini was left?

20. Macy brought $\frac{3}{4}$ lb of bananas, Ting brought $1\frac{3}{8}$ lb, and Marcie brought $1\frac{1}{2}$ lb of bananas. What was the total weight of the bananas?

21. There were plenty of fruits and vegetables for the letter T at the tasting event. $1\frac{3}{4}$ lb of tomatoes were served and $\frac{5}{8}$ lb was eaten. Of the $2\frac{1}{4}$ lb of tangerines, $\frac{3}{4}$ lb was eaten. Was there a greater amount of tomatoes or tangerines left? Compare the remaining amounts using >, <, or =.

Review

Write the fractions in order from least to greatest.

22. $\frac{1}{3}$ $\frac{1}{4}$ $\frac{1}{2}$
23. $\frac{2}{3}$ $\frac{3}{4}$ $\frac{1}{2}$
24. $\frac{5}{6}$ $\frac{7}{12}$ $\frac{3}{4}$
25. $\frac{2}{5}$ $\frac{3}{10}$ $\frac{5}{8}$

26. In Miss Roper's class, $\frac{5}{8}$ of the students said they like citrus fruit. In Mr. Walter's class, $\frac{3}{5}$ of the students enjoy citrus fruit. Which class has the greater fraction of students that do not like citrus fruit?

9.13 Problem Solving: Use a Map

Construct Meaning

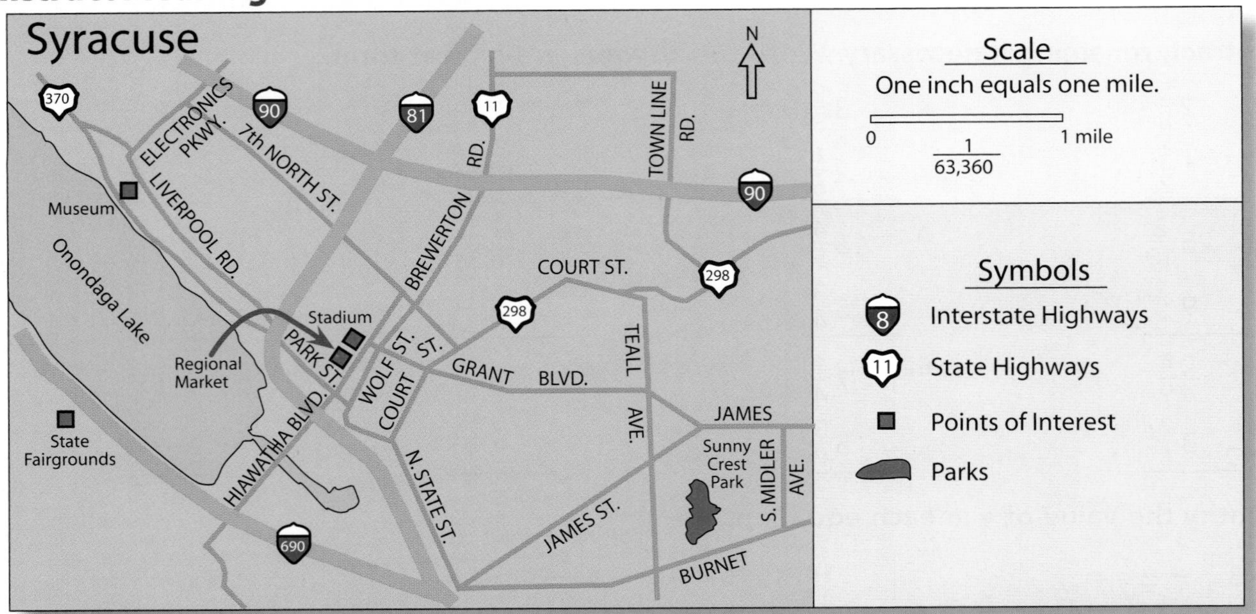

Laila and her family are planning a trip to Syracuse, New York. They looked at an online map that shows part of the city. A map is an abstract representation of reality. The symbols on a map describe streets, locations, and other features. The scale shows the relationship between a unit of distance on the map and a unit of distance on the ground.

There are three types of map scales.

verbal scale: The scale is expressed with words.

visual scale: The unit of measurement is shown and labeled. 0 ——— 1 mile

representative fraction: $\frac{\text{map distance}}{\text{ground distance}}$

Check Understanding

a. Name the three types of scales on the map of Syracuse.

b. Explain why the representative fraction for a scale of one inch equals one mile is $\frac{1}{63,360}$.

c. Use the map symbols to name the interstate highways, state highways, parks, and points of interest.

Practice

Use the map and a ruler to solve Exercises 1–5.

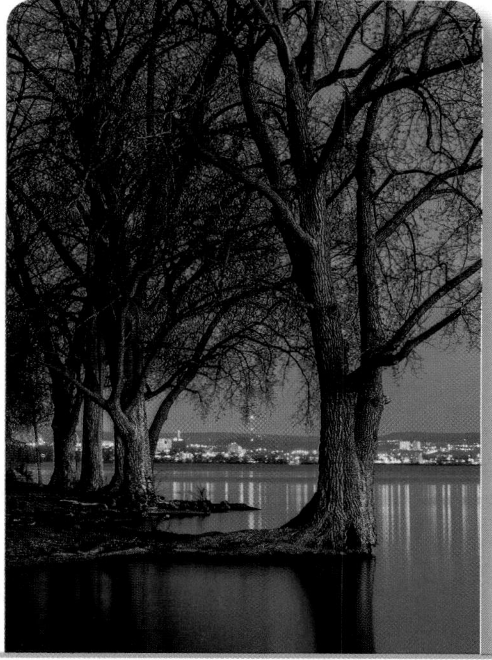

Onondaga Lake, Syracuse, New York, USA

1. How many miles would you travel on I-90 from Town Line Road to Brewerton Road?

2. Suppose you are in front of the Stadium at Hiawatha Boulevard and Grant Boulevard. What is the shortest street route from there to the point where 7th North Street intersects I-81? What is a reasonable whole-number estimate of the distance?

3. To travel from the point where I-90 and Electronics Parkway meet to the Regional Market, you would travel $\frac{1}{4}$ mi on Electronics Parkway, $1\frac{9}{16}$ mi on 7th North Street, and $\frac{1}{2}$ mi on Hiawatha Boulevard. What is the total distance?

4. What is the length of South Midler Avenue to the nearest quarter mile?

5. What is the length of James Street between North State Street and Teall Avenue to the nearest quarter mile?

6. If a map has a scale of one-half inch equals one mile, what is the ground distance between two points that are $3\frac{1}{2}$ inches apart on the map?

Challenge

7. A state map has a representative fraction of $\frac{1}{500,000}$. About how many miles are represented by one inch on that map? (Remember: $\frac{1}{63,360}$ means one inch equals one mile.)

8. Use a ruler to draw the visual scale for a map with a representative fraction of $\frac{1}{316,800}$.

9.14 Chapter 9 Review

Write the equation shown by the fraction models. Write the answer in simplest form.

1.
2.
3.

Complete each equation.

4. $\frac{4}{15} + \square = \frac{7}{15}$

5. $\square - \frac{1}{4} = \frac{1}{2}$

6. $1\frac{2}{3} + \square = 2\frac{1}{3}$

7. $5 - \square = 3\frac{5}{6}$

Find the least common denominator for each pair of fractions. Write the equivalent fractions using the LCD.

8. $\frac{1}{10}$ and $\frac{3}{5}$

9. $\frac{3}{4}$ and $\frac{1}{12}$

10. $\frac{5}{8}$ and $\frac{3}{5}$

Write each fraction or mixed number in simplest form.

11. $\frac{3}{21}$

12. $\frac{7}{8}$

13. $12\frac{4}{12}$

14. $10\frac{2}{5}$

15. $\frac{15}{30}$

16. $\frac{12}{36}$

17. $\frac{25}{100}$

Add or subtract the fractions using the LCD. Write the answer in simplest form.

18. $\frac{3}{5} + \frac{1}{5}$

19. $\frac{13}{14} - \frac{3}{7}$

20. $\frac{5}{6} + \frac{7}{12}$

21. $\frac{7}{8} - \frac{1}{4}$

22. $\frac{1}{6} + \frac{4}{9}$

Identify the value of y by renaming each whole number.

23. $12 = 11\frac{y}{3}$

24. $7 = 6\frac{y}{5}$

Rename the mixed numbers using the LCD.

25. $19\frac{1}{3}$ and $3\frac{4}{5}$

26. $5\frac{7}{8}$ and $16\frac{1}{4}$

Estimate the sum or difference by rounding to whole numbers.

27. $18\frac{5}{8} + 3\frac{1}{3}$

28. $50\frac{7}{8} - 13\frac{2}{3}$

29. $7\frac{3}{4} + 5\frac{1}{3}$

30. $39\frac{2}{5} - 21\frac{4}{5}$

Estimate the sum or difference by rounding to the nearest half.

31. $10\frac{9}{10} + 3\frac{1}{2} + 16 + 8$

32. $9\frac{7}{8} - 6\frac{5}{10}$

Add or subtract, renaming as needed. Write the answer in simplest form.

33. $5\frac{9}{10} + 4\frac{2}{3}$

34. $6\frac{1}{5} - 2\frac{1}{4}$

35. $17\frac{1}{2} + 19\frac{5}{6}$

36. $9\frac{7}{12} - 3\frac{3}{4}$

Use mental math to add.

37. $16 + 1\frac{6}{8} + 2\frac{2}{8}$

38. $9\frac{1}{5} + 14 + 10\frac{4}{5}$

Solve.

39. Nick's parents budget their household income carefully. They give $\frac{1}{10}$ to the church, $\frac{2}{5}$ is used for their house payment, and $\frac{1}{4}$ is budgeted for groceries. What fraction of the total remains after they have paid their tithe, house payment, and grocery bill?

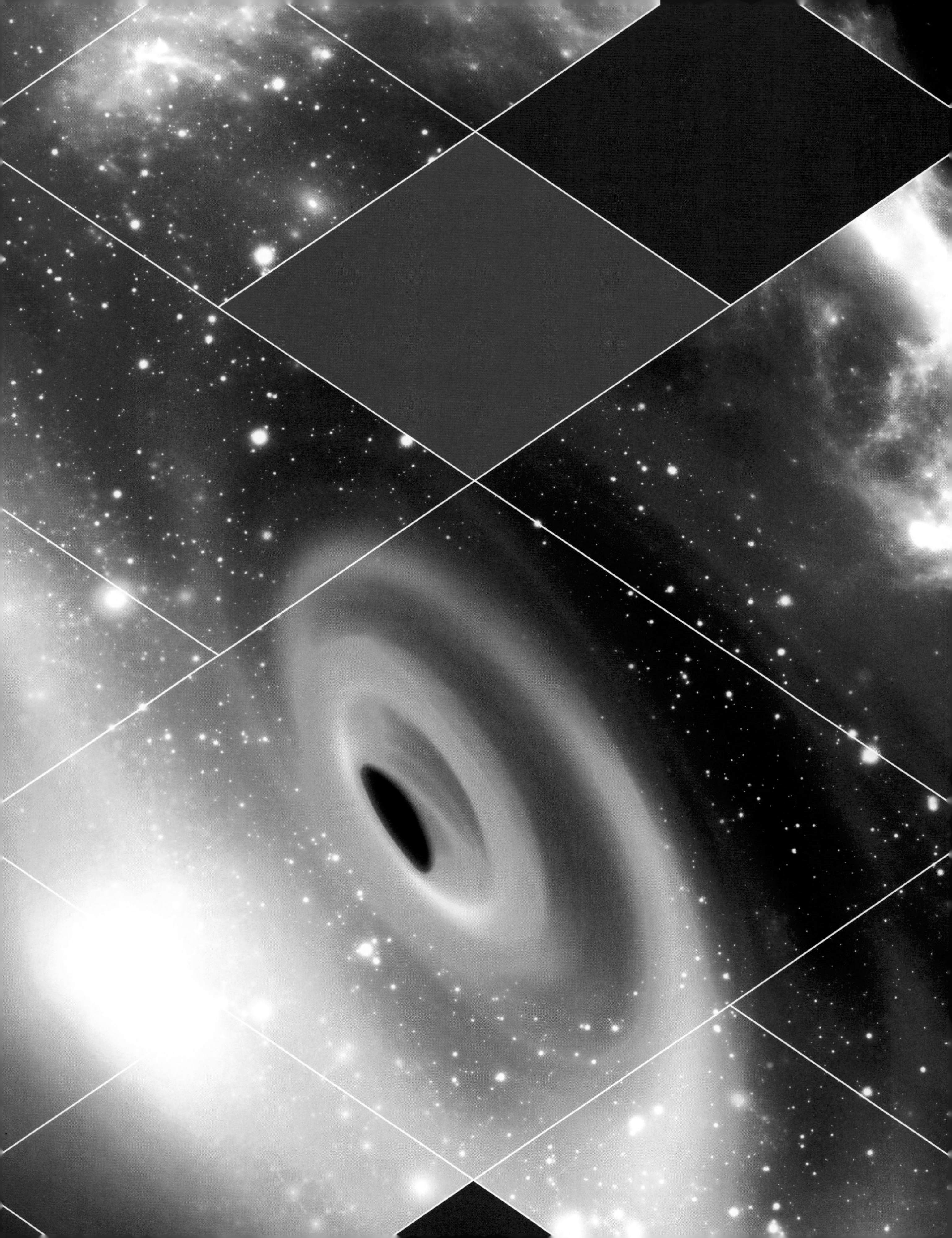

Chapter 10
Multiply and Divide Fractions

Commit to the Lord whatever you do,
and He will establish your plans.
Proverbs 16:3

Key Ideas:

Multiplication: multiplying fractions

Multiplication: multiplying mixed numbers

Division: dividing fractions

Division: dividing mixed numbers

Patterns: repeating and terminating decimals

10.1 *Multiply Fractions: Models*

Construct Meaning

NASA stands for the National Aeronautics and Space Administration. NASA's vision is to reach for new heights and reveal the unknown for the benefit of humankind.

NASA sent the Hubble Space Telescope into orbit on April 24, 1990. The telescope is about the size of a school bus. It is 43.5 ft (13.3 m) long and 7 ft, 10.5 in. (2.4 m) wide. It weighs about 27,000 lb. The telescope was named for astronomer Edwin Powell Hubble (1889–1953). It can point to a specific place in space for days at a time while moving at 17,000 mph!

If about $\frac{3}{4}$ of a picture Hubble took was visible, and about $\frac{1}{3}$ of the visible area was blurry, how much of the total picture was blurry?

A model can help show $\frac{1}{3}$ of $\frac{3}{4}$.

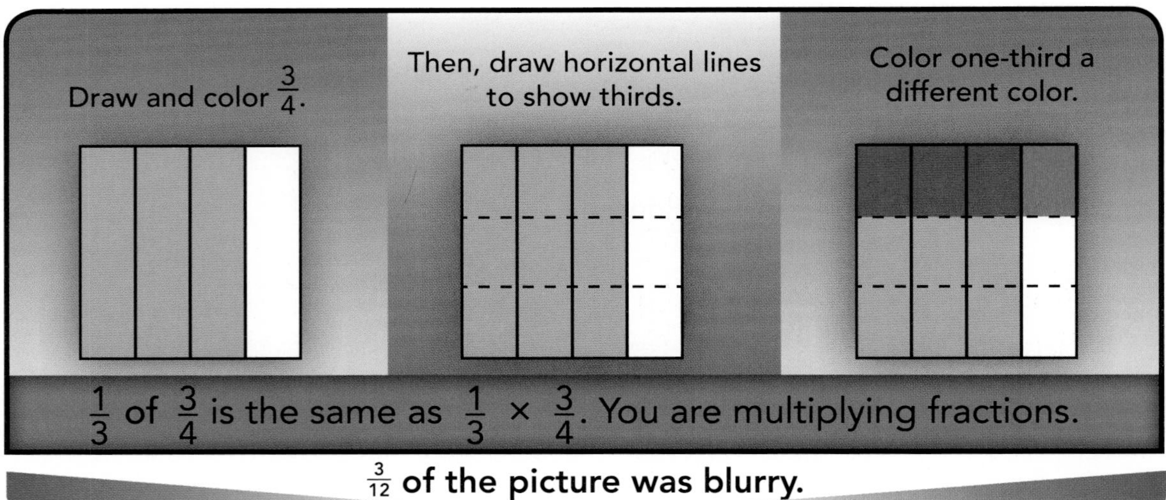

Would the answer be the same if the order of the fractions changed? Draw a model to explain the answer. Is the answer greater than or less than one?

Check Understanding

Use the model to determine which fractions to multiply. Use "of" and "×" to write each equation two ways. Solve.

a. 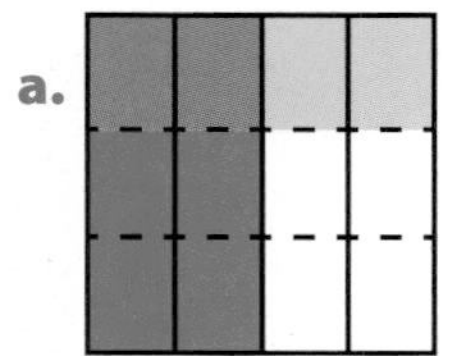

b.  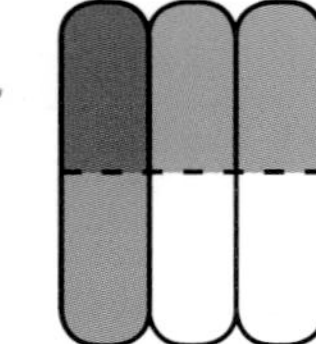

c. 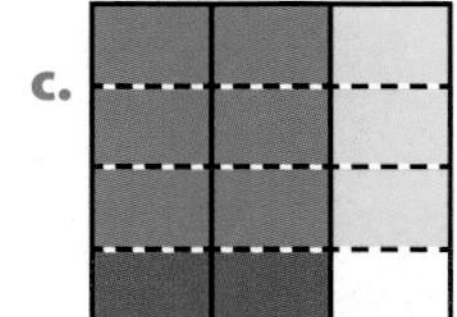

d. 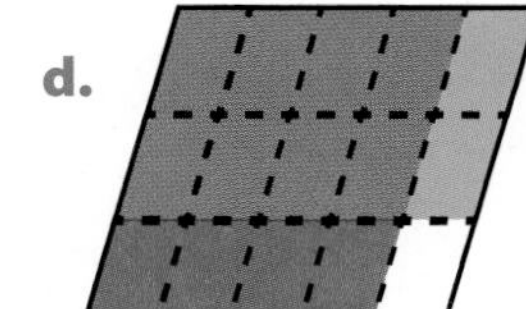

e. 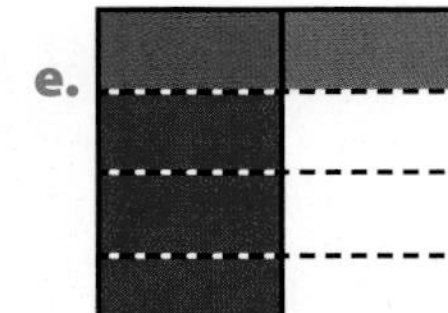

Practice

Draw a model that shows the fractions being multiplied.

1. $\frac{1}{2} \times \frac{1}{4}$
2. $\frac{1}{3} \times \frac{3}{4}$
3. $\frac{1}{5} \times \frac{2}{4}$
4. $\frac{1}{4} \times \frac{1}{3}$
5. $\frac{2}{3} \times \frac{1}{6}$

Write an equation for each model.

6. 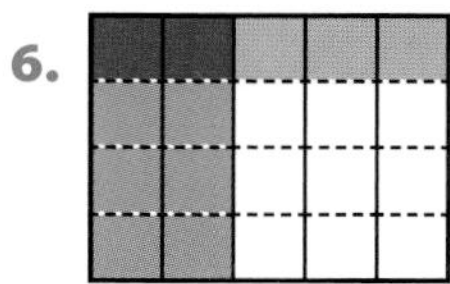

7. 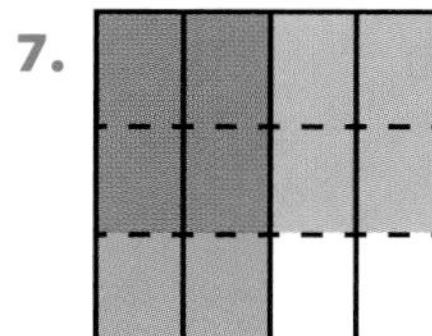

8. 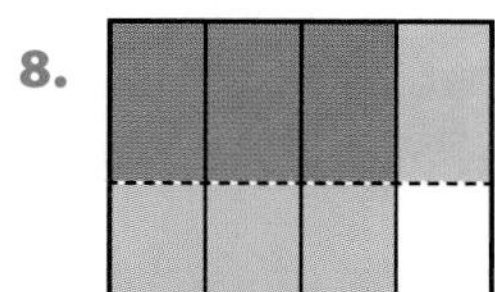

9. 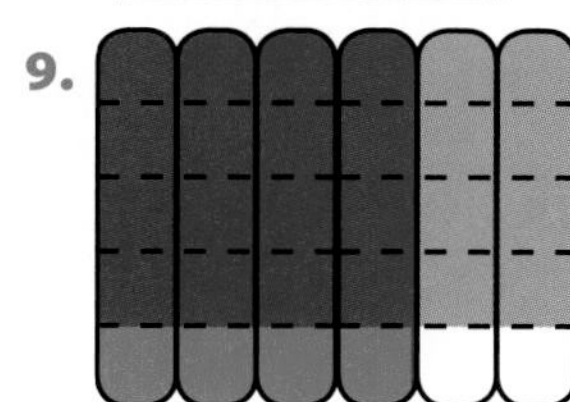

10. 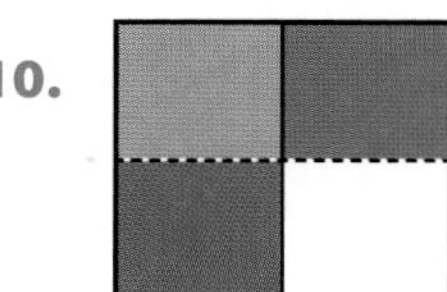

11. 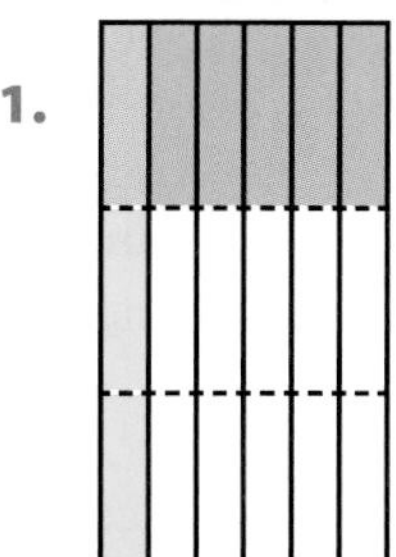

12. 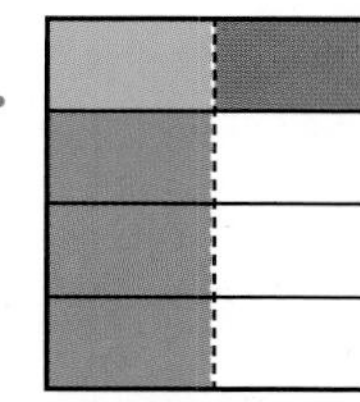

13. 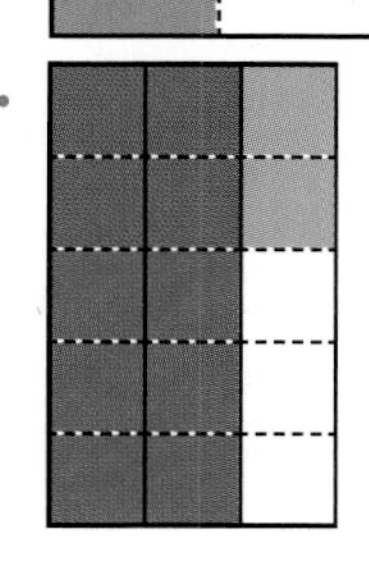

Apply

14. Avery spent $\frac{1}{4}$ of an hour drawing a picture of the Hubble Telescope in her math journal. She spent $\frac{1}{3}$ of that time adding color to her picture. What part of an hour did she spend coloring the telescope?

15. Mr. Kirby read $\frac{1}{2}$ of a magazine article about the Hubble Space Telescope and saw that $\frac{2}{3}$ of each page was planet images. What fraction represents $\frac{2}{3}$ of $\frac{1}{2}$?

16. To prepare for the race, Aaron needed to run 5 mi. On Monday, he ran $1\frac{3}{4}$ mi and $1\frac{1}{2}$ mi on Wednesday. He ran $1\frac{1}{3}$ mi Friday. Did he meet the goal? Why or why not?

Review

Identify the greatest common factor.

17. 6 and 8
18. 24 and 36
19. 20 and 30
20. 15 and 45
21. 4 and 12
22. 7 and 21
23. 8 and 16
24. 18 and 24

10.2 Multiply by Fractions

Construct Meaning

What happens to the data collected by the Hubble Telescope? It goes to the Goddard Space Flight Center in Greenbelt, Maryland. The center is named after Dr. Robert Hutchins Goddard, who built and tested the first rocket that used liquid fuel. He advanced space exploration in the same way that the Wright brothers influenced aviation.

Angela, a scientist at Goddard, was given a project on Monday and had to finish $\frac{1}{2}$ of it by Friday. Her goal was to finish $\frac{1}{5}$ of that amount each day. What part would she complete each day?

Because Angela would complete $\frac{1}{5}$ "of" half of the project each day, multiply to solve the problem. Draw a model to multiply fractions.

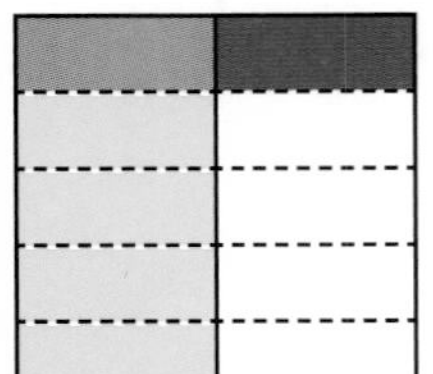

$\frac{1}{5}$ of $\frac{1}{2}$ is $\frac{1}{10}$

Is the product greater than or less than the whole number 1?

The product is less than 1.

How do you multiply fractions?

$\frac{1 \times 1}{5 \times 2} = \frac{1}{10}$ Multiply the numerators.
Multiply the denominators.
Write the product in simplest form.

Angela will complete $\frac{1}{10}$ of the project each day.

You can multiply either the numerators or denominators first. The order does not change the answer.

When you multiply fractions, the denominators can be different.

$\frac{2}{4} \times \frac{1}{3} = \frac{2}{12} = \frac{1}{6}$ $\quad \frac{3}{4} \times \frac{5}{7} = \frac{15}{28}$ $\quad \frac{1}{2} \times \frac{9}{4} = \frac{9}{8} = 1\frac{1}{8}$

Check Understanding

Write a multiplication equation for each model.

a. 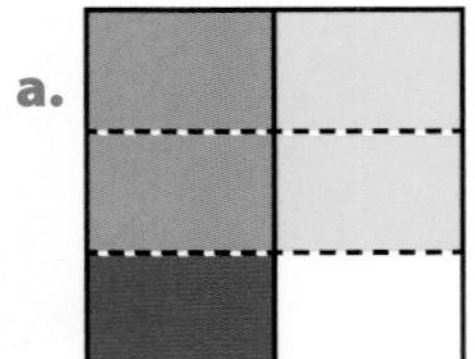

b. 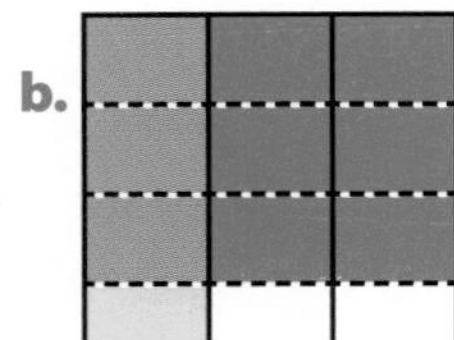

c. 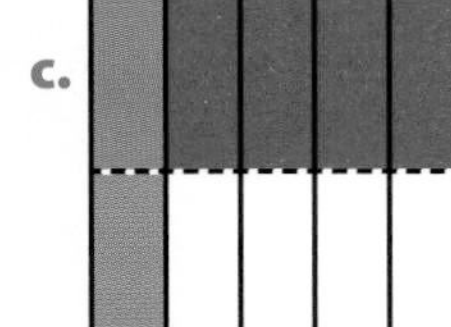

d. 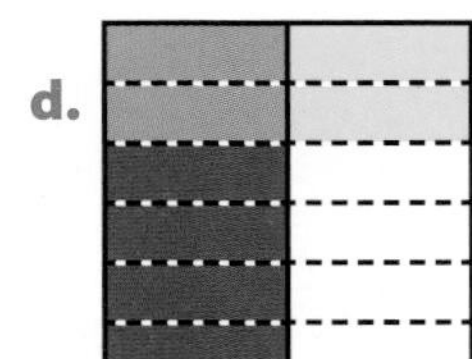

e. 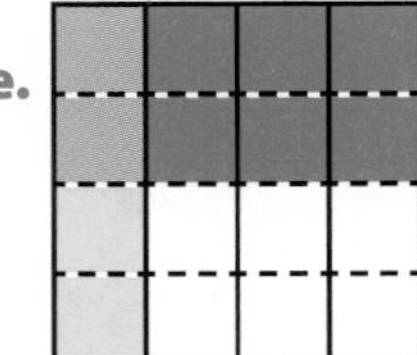

Copy and complete.

f. $\frac{3}{4} \times \frac{1}{2} = \frac{\square \times \square}{\square \times \square} = \frac{\square}{\square}$

g. $\frac{2}{3} \times \frac{9}{10} = \frac{\square \times \square}{\square \times \square} = \frac{\square}{\square} = \frac{\square}{\square}$

Practice

Multiply. Write the product in simplest form.

1. $\frac{2}{5} \times \frac{2}{4}$
2. $\frac{8}{10} \times \frac{2}{3}$
3. $\frac{6}{7} \times \frac{1}{6}$
4. $\frac{10}{11} \times \frac{4}{5}$
5. $\frac{5}{8} \times \frac{3}{4}$
6. $\frac{1}{3} \times \frac{7}{8}$
7. $\frac{1}{2} \times \frac{2}{3}$
8. $\frac{8}{2} \times \frac{1}{3}$
9. $\frac{1}{2} \times \frac{15}{17}$
10. $\frac{5}{4} \times \frac{9}{2}$
11. $\frac{3}{10} \times \frac{4}{10}$
12. $\frac{1}{4} \times \frac{2}{3}$

Write >, <, or =.

13. $\frac{1}{2} \times \frac{1}{3}$ ◯ $\frac{2}{6}$
14. $\frac{2}{3} \times \frac{4}{5}$ ◯ $\frac{6}{15}$
15. $\frac{3}{4} \times \frac{2}{7}$ ◯ $\frac{3}{28}$
16. $\frac{3}{6} \times \frac{2}{4}$ ◯ 1

Apply

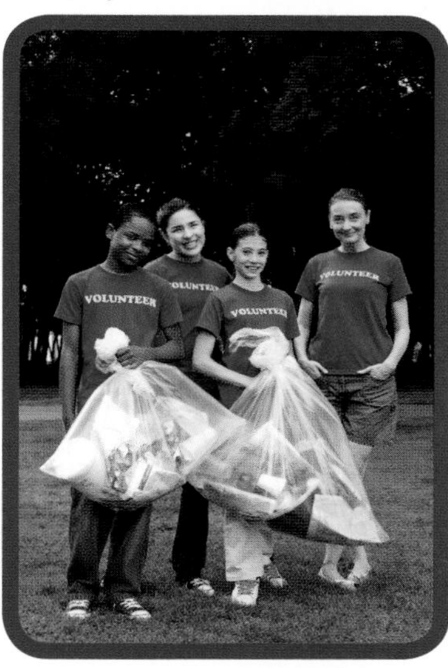

17. Emiyo's fifth-grade class is assigned to clean the schoolyard. They are responsible for the playground area, which is $\frac{1}{3}$ of the schoolyard. Emiyo's group is assigned to clean $\frac{1}{2}$ of the playground area. What part of the schoolyard did Emiyo's group clean?
18. Waste cans of equal size are placed in different locations. The can in the playground area was five-eighths full. The can in the parking area was one-fourth full. Tom emptied the can from the parking area into the can from the playground area. How full is the can from the playground area now?
19. The playground area is $\frac{3}{4}$ of an acre. The parking area is $\frac{2}{3}$ of an acre. Which area is larger? How much larger?
20. The scientist at Goddard finished $\frac{1}{2}$ of a project the first week. She finished $\frac{1}{3}$ of the project the second week. What part of the project was completed by the end of the second week?

Review

Solve. Write the answer in simplest form.

21. $25\frac{1}{3} + 17\frac{2}{3}$
22. $72\frac{2}{5} - 65\frac{3}{10}$
23. $46\frac{1}{2} - 18\frac{5}{8}$
24. $38\frac{3}{7} + 49\frac{9}{14}$
25. $50\frac{1}{8} - 24\frac{1}{3}$

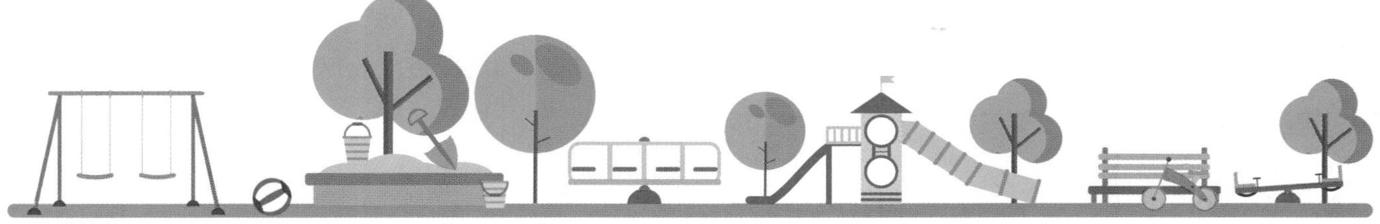

10.3 Multiply by Whole Numbers

Construct Meaning

Man-made satellites come in different shapes and sizes and have many different uses. They orbit the earth, collecting data and helping people communicate. All satellites have a frame that holds the parts together in space. They have a computer and radio. A control system keeps them facing the right direction. Weather satellites track changes in the weather and help meteorologists create weather forecasts.

About 15 weather forecasters are calling for snow. About $\frac{3}{5}$ of them think a blizzard will happen. How many think a blizzard will happen?

- Find a fraction of a whole number by drawing a picture.

$\frac{3}{5}$ of 15 or $\frac{3}{5} \times 15$ 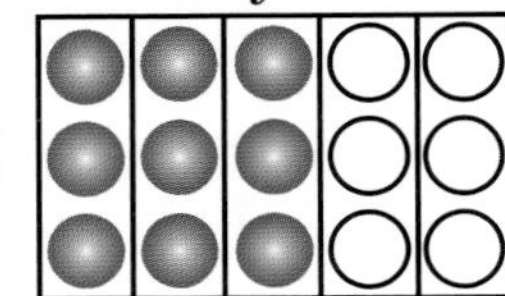 3 out of 5 equal groups = 9

- Find a fraction of a whole number by multiplying.

$\frac{3}{5} \times \frac{15}{1}$ — Write a 1 under the whole number. The whole number may be listed first. $15 \times \frac{3}{5}$ is the same as $\frac{15}{1} \times \frac{3}{5}$

$\frac{3 \times 15}{5 \times 1} = \frac{45}{5}$ — Multiply the numerators. Multiply the denominators.

$5\overline{)45}$ = 9 — Write the product in simplest form. Change the improper fraction to a whole or mixed number by dividing the numerator by the denominator.

The line in a fraction is a division bar.
A whole becomes a fraction by putting a 1 under it.

whole number 6 → fraction $\frac{6}{1}$ → $1\overline{)6}$ = 6

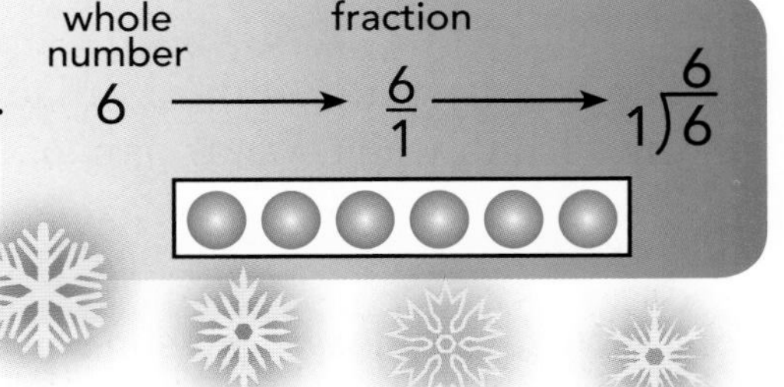

Check Understanding

Write a multiplication sentence for each picture.

a. 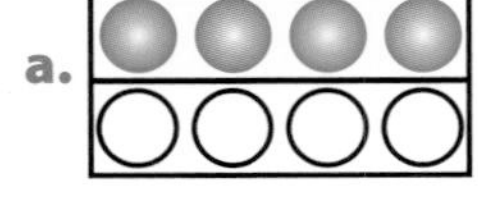
b. 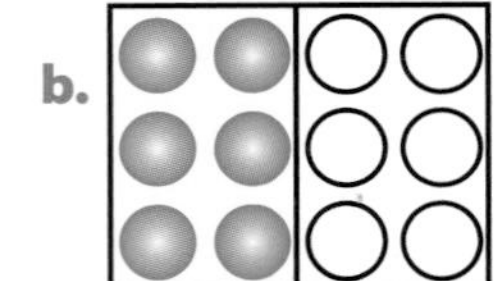
c. 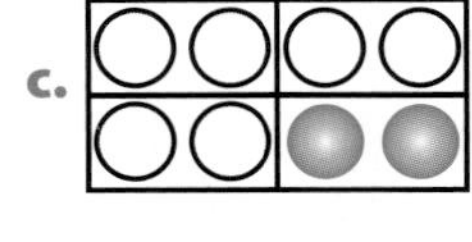
d. 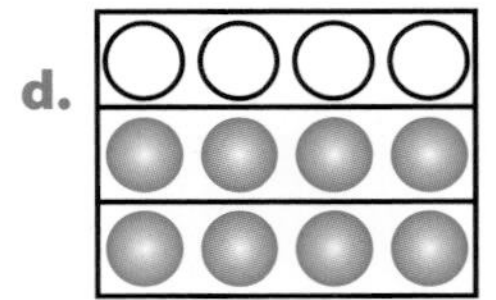
e. 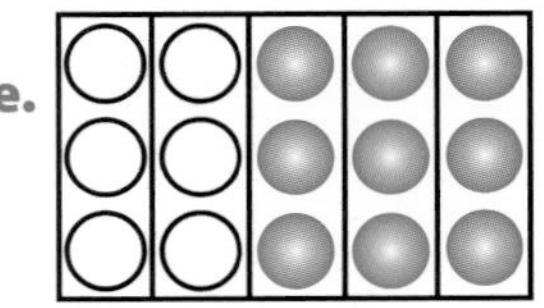

Multiply. Write the product in simplest form.

f. $\frac{1}{2} \times 20$ g. $42 \times \frac{2}{3}$ h. $\frac{1}{6} \times 38$ i. $81 \times \frac{2}{9}$ j. $\frac{3}{7} \times 53$

Practice

Multiply. Write the product in simplest form.

1. $\frac{3}{5} \times 10$
2. $\frac{7}{8} \times 4$
3. $5 \times \frac{2}{7}$
4. $\frac{5}{6} \times 8$
5. $3 \times \frac{5}{9}$
6. $\frac{1}{4} \times 48$
7. $\frac{2}{3} \times 24$
8. $40 \times \frac{4}{5}$
9. $19 \times \frac{3}{6}$
10. $\frac{1}{2} \times 6$
11. $6 \times \frac{1}{7}$
12. $\frac{2}{12} \times 10$
13. $\frac{4}{8} \times 15$
14. $2 \times \frac{2}{9}$
15. $9 \times \frac{3}{10}$
16. $\frac{4}{11} \times 2$
17. $1 \times \frac{9}{10}$
18. $\frac{1}{2} \times 76$
19. $64 \times \frac{3}{4}$
20. $\frac{1}{13} \times 4$

Apply

21. Dr. Willis Carrier designed the first modern air-conditioning system. Out of 100 new homes built, only 80 installed an air-conditioning system. About $\frac{1}{4}$ of the homes with an air-conditioning system had fewer windows. How many homes had fewer windows?

22. The classroom is set for 78°F. There are 28 students in the classroom. About $\frac{2}{7}$ of students are comfortable. How many students are uncomfortable?

23. For 3 hours, Dae researched the effects of pollutants such as smoke and fumes on the quality of the air. Ciro spent $1\frac{3}{4}$ hours and Ballard spent $\frac{2}{3}$ hour researching. How much time did the three boys research?

24. Because of a storm, $\frac{1}{2}$ of the 200 homes on the south side of town lost power. $\frac{1}{4}$ of the 100 homes on the north side of town had no power. $\frac{2}{5}$ of the 300 homes on the east side, and $\frac{7}{10}$ of the 100 homes on the west side experienced the same outage. Which side of town had the greatest number of homes affected by the storm?

25. If $\frac{2}{10}$ of an area with a population of 4,000 people felt the effects of a flood, how many people were affected?

Review

Write >, <, or =.

26. $\frac{5}{6}$ ◯ $\frac{24}{30}$
27. $\frac{3}{4}$ ◯ $\frac{8}{9}$
28. $\frac{10}{30}$ ◯ $\frac{2}{5}$
29. $\frac{27}{42}$ ◯ $\frac{4}{7}$
30. $\frac{2}{3}$ ◯ $\frac{7}{21}$

10.4 Multiply by Mixed Numbers

Construct Meaning

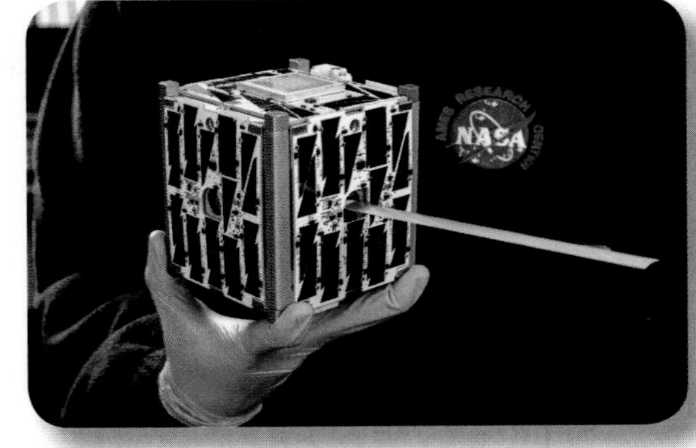

Satellites relay data from one place to another. The information might be phone conversations or technical data. A satellite has a radio called a transponder that receives at one frequency and sends back to Earth at a different frequency. NASA controls some satellites with phones that are shaped like cubes.

Anika wrote a paper on satellite phones. She needed more information on PhoneSat 2.4, a cube-shaped phone that controls satellites from Earth. Her friend Cooper sent an e-mail with pictures that filled $1\frac{1}{2}$ sheets of paper. Andrea sent a scanned document about phones that was $3\frac{1}{3}$ times longer than the e-mail from Cooper. Anika must figure out how many sheets of paper to load in the printer. She wants to be a good steward of God's resources.

Multiply mixed numbers.

$3\frac{1}{3} \times 1\frac{1}{2} = n$	Rename both mixed numbers as improper fractions.
$\frac{10}{3} \times \frac{3}{2} = \frac{30}{6}$	Multiply the fractions.
$\frac{30}{6} = 5$	Write the product in simplest form.

The e-mail from Andrea took 5 sheets of paper.

Multiply a mixed number by a fraction.

$2\frac{1}{4} \times \frac{2}{5} = n$	Rename the mixed number as an improper fraction.
$\frac{9}{4} \times \frac{2}{5} = \frac{18}{20}$	Multiply the fractions.
$\frac{18}{20} = \frac{9}{10}$	Write the product in simplest form.

Multiply a mixed number by a whole number.

$4\frac{1}{2} \times 5 = n$	Rename the mixed number as an improper fraction. Rename the whole number as a fraction by putting 1 under it.
$\frac{9}{2} \times \frac{5}{1} = \frac{45}{2}$	Multiply the fractions.
$\frac{45}{2} = 22\frac{1}{2}$	Write the product in simplest form.

Check Understanding

Copy and complete.

a. $2\frac{1}{3} \times 4\frac{2}{4} = \frac{\square}{3} \times \frac{18}{\square} = \frac{\square}{\square} = \square = \square$

b. $6\frac{3}{5} \times \frac{4}{7} = \frac{33}{\square} \times \frac{\square}{7} = \frac{\square}{\square} = \square$

c. $8\frac{1}{2} \times 4 = \frac{\square}{\square} \times \frac{\square}{\square} = \frac{\square}{\square} = \square$

Practice

Multiply. Write the letter of the answer in simplest form.

1. $1\frac{1}{3} \times 2\frac{1}{2}$ **a.** 4 **b.** $3\frac{1}{3}$ **c.** $5\frac{1}{2}$ **d.** 7
2. $3\frac{5}{6} \times \frac{6}{7}$ **a.** $3\frac{2}{7}$ **b.** $3\frac{1}{7}$ **c.** $2\frac{2}{7}$ **d.** $3\frac{3}{7}$
3. $4\frac{3}{4} \times 6$ **a.** $27\frac{1}{2}$ **b.** $28\frac{2}{3}$ **c.** $28\frac{1}{2}$ **d.** $29\frac{1}{2}$
4. $\frac{5}{8} \times 1\frac{1}{6}$ **a.** $\frac{36}{49}$ **b.** $1\frac{13}{48}$ **c.** $\frac{34}{49}$ **d.** $\frac{35}{48}$

Multiply. Write the product in simplest form.

5. $2\frac{1}{3} \times 5\frac{1}{3}$
8. $10\frac{2}{3} \times 4$
11. $2\frac{1}{5} \times 1\frac{3}{7}$
14. $1\frac{4}{5} \times 9\frac{1}{2}$
17. $\frac{1}{4} \times 12$
6. $4\frac{1}{8} \times 2\frac{2}{3}$
9. $12\frac{1}{2} \times 6\frac{1}{2}$
12. $3\frac{1}{2} \times 9\frac{5}{6}$
15. $8\frac{3}{4} \times 3\frac{1}{3}$
18. $11\frac{1}{4} \times 7$
7. $6\frac{2}{5} \times 5$
10. $1\frac{1}{6} \times \frac{3}{8}$
13. $3\frac{3}{5} \times 5$
16. $8\frac{5}{6} \times \frac{2}{7}$
19. $2\frac{4}{7} \times \frac{1}{2}$

Apply

20. For a history assignment, Cam watched the news on television $1\frac{1}{2}$ hours each day for four days. How many hours did Cam spend on the assignment?

21. Aidan invited 11 friends over to watch the basketball game and the reviews. If $\frac{3}{4}$ of the group, including Aidan, agreed with the reviews, how many friends disagreed?

22. Alessandra's mother was in the kitchen making a dip recipe. It required $1\frac{1}{2}$ c of sour cream. She made it $2\frac{1}{2}$ times. How many cups of sour cream did she use?

23. At a party, $\frac{2}{3}$ bag of corn chips, $\frac{3}{4}$ bag of barbecue chips, and $\frac{1}{2}$ bag of ruffled potato chips were served. How many bags of chips were served?

24. A bag contained $3\frac{1}{3}$ dozen cookies. The boys ate $2\frac{1}{2}$ dozen. How many dozen cookies were left over?

Review

Write "prime" or "composite."

25. 15
26. 7
27. 24
28. 19
29. 99

Solve.

30. $\begin{array}{r} 58{,}403 \\ -\ 19{,}084 \\ \hline \end{array}$

31. $\begin{array}{r} 479 \\ 58 \\ 102 \\ +\ 13 \\ \hline \end{array}$

32. $\begin{array}{r} 43.7 \\ -\ 2.801 \\ \hline \end{array}$

33. $13\overline{)5.278}$

34. $\begin{array}{r} 3.7 \\ \times\ 0.65 \\ \hline \end{array}$

10.5 Problem Solving: Multiply

Check Understanding

The fifth-grade students at North Beach Christian School sell organic salads and produce from the school garden. The profit goes toward a field trip.

Mrs. Covel wrote a salad recipe on the board and told students to triple the amount of all ingredients. To triple a recipe means to use exactly three times of each ingredient.

Multiply by three to find each amount.

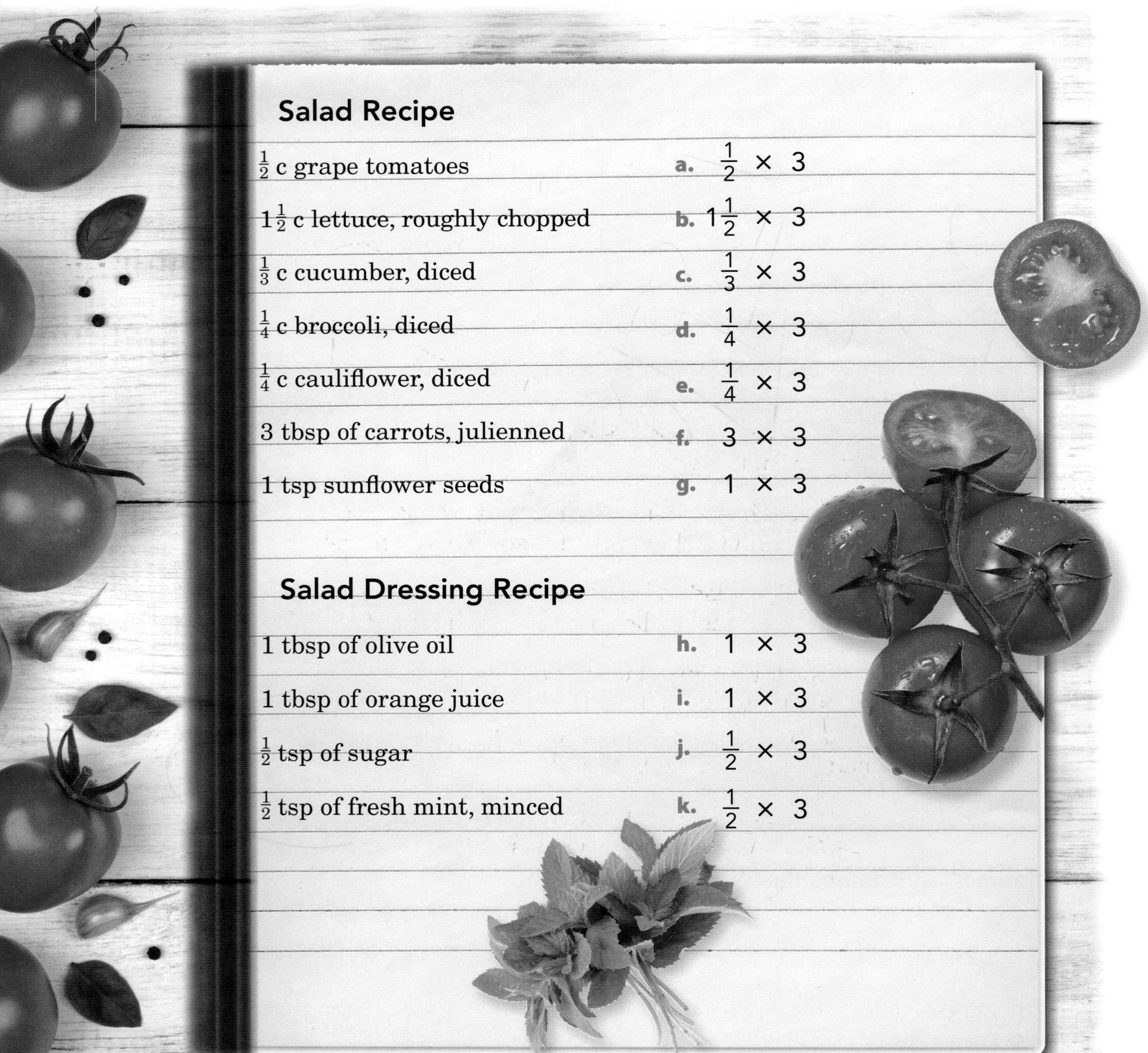

Salad Recipe

Ingredient	
$\frac{1}{2}$ c grape tomatoes	**a.** $\frac{1}{2} \times 3$
$1\frac{1}{2}$ c lettuce, roughly chopped	**b.** $1\frac{1}{2} \times 3$
$\frac{1}{3}$ c cucumber, diced	**c.** $\frac{1}{3} \times 3$
$\frac{1}{4}$ c broccoli, diced	**d.** $\frac{1}{4} \times 3$
$\frac{1}{4}$ c cauliflower, diced	**e.** $\frac{1}{4} \times 3$
3 tbsp of carrots, julienned	**f.** 3×3
1 tsp sunflower seeds	**g.** 1×3

Salad Dressing Recipe

Ingredient	
1 tbsp of olive oil	**h.** 1×3
1 tbsp of orange juice	**i.** 1×3
$\frac{1}{2}$ tsp of sugar	**j.** $\frac{1}{2} \times 3$
$\frac{1}{2}$ tsp of fresh mint, minced	**k.** $\frac{1}{2} \times 3$

The sale was a success, and the fifth graders were excited to attend the trip!

Practice

1. Josiah surveyed 45 fifth graders. If $\frac{1}{5}$ said they preferred strawberry ice cream, how many preferred a different flavor?

2. Jing's brother began first grade with 20 teeth. During the year he lost $\frac{1}{4}$ of them. How many permanent teeth will replace the missing ones?

3. If $\frac{2}{3}$ of the 15 runners in the race slowed down as it got hotter, how many were affected by the heat?

4. Addy, Hua, and Kade ordered a pizza with 12 slices. Addy ate $\frac{1}{6}$ of the pizza, Hua ate $\frac{1}{3}$, and Kade ate the remaining slices. What part of the pizza did Kade eat?

5. Dakota finished $\frac{3}{4}$ of a test, which had 20 questions. How many questions were left?

6. Mr. Haskell owns $9\frac{1}{2}$ acres of farmland. If $\frac{1}{6}$ of the land is used for dairy cows, and $\frac{2}{3}$ of the land is used for growing wheat and corn, how many acres remain for his home and yard?

7. Karah is 28 years old. Janya's age is $\frac{3}{4}$ the age of Karah. Alexis is $1\frac{1}{3}$ times as old as Janya. How old is Alexis?

8. If the ingredients of the salad recipe are multiplied by four, how many cups of lettuce are needed? How many cups of tomatoes are needed?

9. A ball drops 50 ft from a window of a building. When it hits the ground, it bounces $\frac{2}{5}$ of the height it dropped. Calculate the total distance the ball traveled after it dropped.

10. The fisherman caught $17\frac{1}{2}$ pounds of seafood. The next day he caught $3\frac{1}{5}$ times as much as the first day. How many pounds did he catch the second day?

11. To prepare for the basketball tournament, Kyle shot baskets for $\frac{1}{3}$ hour. Jeremiah shot baskets $1\frac{1}{2}$ times as long as Kyle. Jayce shot baskets $1\frac{1}{4}$ times as long as Jeremiah. What is the total number of hours the boys shot baskets?

12. About 486 tourists visited the US Olympic Training Center in Colorado Springs, Colorado. If $\frac{2}{3}$ of the tourists visited the US Olympic Spirit Store, how many were there?

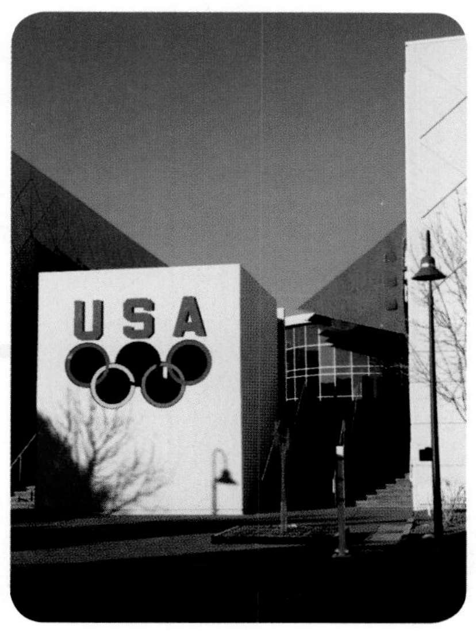

Challenge

13. Three numbers have a sum of 30. Their product is 100. What are the three numbers?

10.6 Estimate Products

Construct Meaning

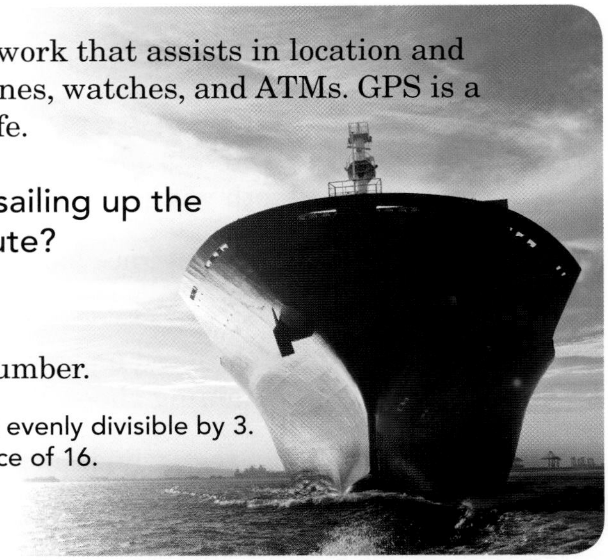

GPS, or global positioning system, is a satellite network that assists in location and navigation. It is used all over the world for cell phones, watches, and ATMs. GPS is a technology that has become common to everyday life.

About $\frac{1}{3}$ of 16 ships took the same route for sailing up the coast. How many took the same route?

Estimate products using fractions.

- Substitute a compatible number for the whole number.

$\frac{1}{3} \times 16$ 16 is not evenly divisible by 3. 15 is evenly divisible by 3. $15 \div 3 = 5$. Substitute 15 in the place of 16.

$\frac{1}{3}$ of 15 is 5, so $\frac{1}{3}$ of 16 is about 5.

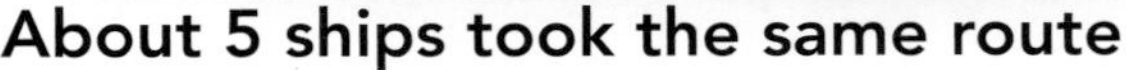

About 5 ships took the same route.

$\frac{1}{4} \times 21$ 21 is not evenly divisible by 4. 20 is evenly divisible by 4. $20 \div 4 = 5$. Substitute 20 in the place of 21. $\frac{1}{4}$ of 20 is 5, so $\frac{1}{4}$ of 21 is about 5.

- Round each number to the nearest whole number.

$4\frac{3}{4} \times 3\frac{1}{3}$ Round, and then multiply. $5 \times 3 = 15$.
Solve. $4\frac{3}{4} \times 3\frac{1}{3} = \frac{19}{4} \times \frac{10}{3} = \frac{190}{12} = 15\frac{5}{6}$

A reasonable estimate for $4\frac{3}{4} \times 3\frac{1}{3}$ is 15.

- When you multiply a proper fraction by a proper fraction, the product will be less than 1. This is true because you begin with a number less than 1, and the other factor is also less than 1.

$\frac{2}{3} \times \frac{5}{6}$ $\frac{2}{3} \times \frac{5}{6} = \frac{10}{18} = \frac{5}{9}$

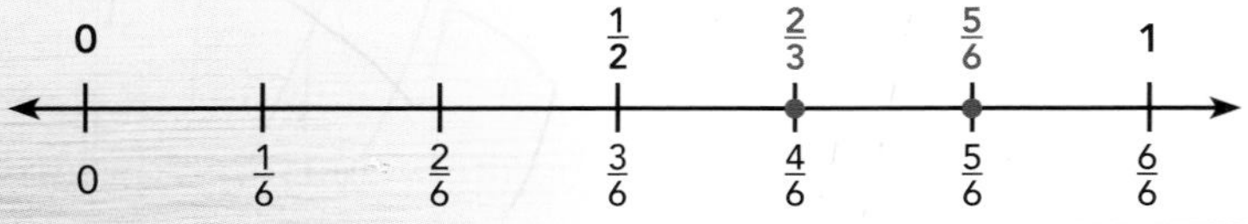

Check Understanding

Use compatible numbers to complete the estimate.

a. $\frac{1}{7} \times 58$ ⟶ $56 \div 7 =$ ____, so $\frac{1}{7}$ of 58 is about ____.

b. $\frac{1}{8} \times 39$ ⟶ $40 \div 8 =$ ____, so $\frac{1}{8}$ of 39 is about ____.

Use rounding to the nearest whole number to estimate.

c. $12\frac{2}{3} \times 12\frac{1}{8}$ ⟶ $13 \times 12 =$ ____, so $12\frac{2}{3} \times 12\frac{1}{8}$ is about ____.

d. $5\frac{1}{3} \times 7\frac{1}{2}$ ⟶ ____ $\times$ ____ $=$ ____, so $5\frac{1}{3} \times 7\frac{1}{6}$ is about ____.

e. What do you know about the product of two proper fractions?

Practice

Substitute compatible numbers to complete the estimate.

1. $\frac{1}{4} \times 25$
2. $\frac{1}{5} \times 36$
3. $\frac{1}{3} \times 29$
4. $\frac{1}{2} \times 55$
5. $\frac{1}{5} \times 14$
6. $\frac{1}{3} \times 34$
7. $\frac{1}{3} \times 41$
8. $\frac{1}{4} \times 11$
9. $\frac{1}{7} \times 65$
10. $\frac{1}{10} \times 43$
11. $\frac{1}{25} \times 27$
12. $\frac{1}{7} \times 15$
13. $\frac{1}{9} \times 16$
14. $\frac{1}{8} \times 21$
15. $\frac{1}{2} \times 51$

Estimate by rounding each number to the nearest whole number.

16. $7\frac{1}{2} \times 9\frac{1}{3}$
17. $14\frac{2}{3} \times 15\frac{1}{8}$
18. $20\frac{2}{5} \times 6\frac{7}{9}$
19. $4\frac{1}{2} \times 5\frac{3}{8}$
20. $8\frac{2}{3} \times 1\frac{2}{3}$

Apply

21. There are 43 new yachts in the harbor. About $\frac{1}{6}$ of them take evening cruises. How many cruise in the evenings?

22. The airplane flew $4\frac{3}{4}$ hours and signaled help for $1\frac{1}{3}$ hours of that time because they lost contact with the radar system. About how much time did the airplane fly with the radar connection intact?

23. The rancher chose an area of land for his cattle that was $\frac{1}{3}$ of a mile long and $\frac{5}{6}$ of a mile wide. Estimate the product to find the approximate number of square miles in this section of land.

Review

Write each fraction as a decimal.

24. $\frac{2}{10}$
25. $\frac{25}{100}$
26. $\frac{7}{10}$
27. $\frac{250}{1,000}$
28. $\frac{9}{100}$

Write each decimal as a fraction in simplest form or as a mixed number.

29. 2.95
30. 0.01
31. 56.349
32. 1.17
33. 0.4

10.7 Divide Fractions: Models

Construct Meaning

Technology designed for space has led to new products on Earth. The insulation used by the space shuttle to resist extreme temperatures is used to insulate homes. It is also used in NASCAR cockpits to protect drivers from engine heat during a race. New materials to make artificial limbs and a new cancer therapy have come from space technology. Freeze-dried foods created for astronauts are now used for outdoor sports such as backpacking, fishing, and hunting.

During their hike, Atticus and Cela ate two packs of freeze-dried ice cream.

Each package was split into four parts. How many fourths were in the two packages? Use a model to help divide a whole number by a fraction.

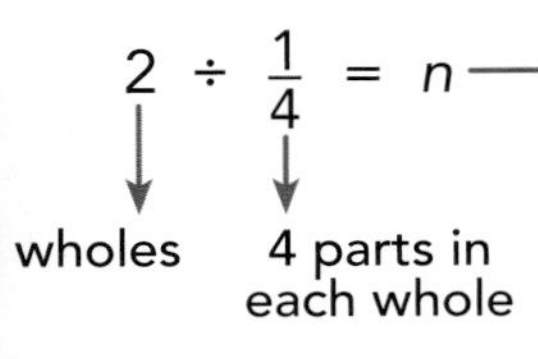

There are 8 fourths in two whole packages.

How many geoboards are shown?

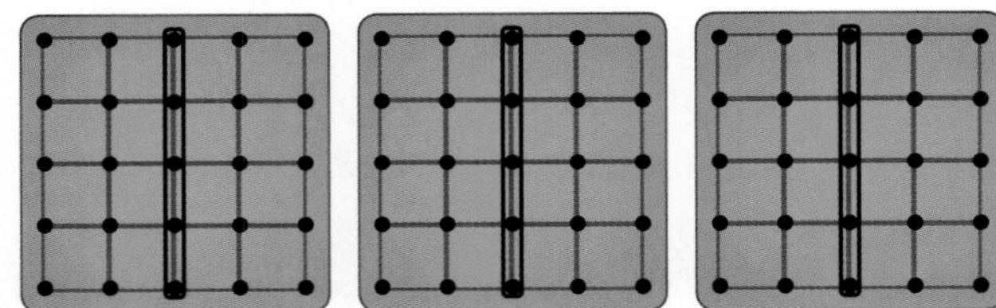

What part of a whole board is each section?

$3 \div \frac{1}{2} = n$

There are 6 halves in three geoboards.

$n = 6$

How many cups are shown?

What part of a cup is each section?

$4 \div \frac{1}{3} = n$

There are 12 thirds in four cups.

$n = 12$

How many fraction bars are shown?

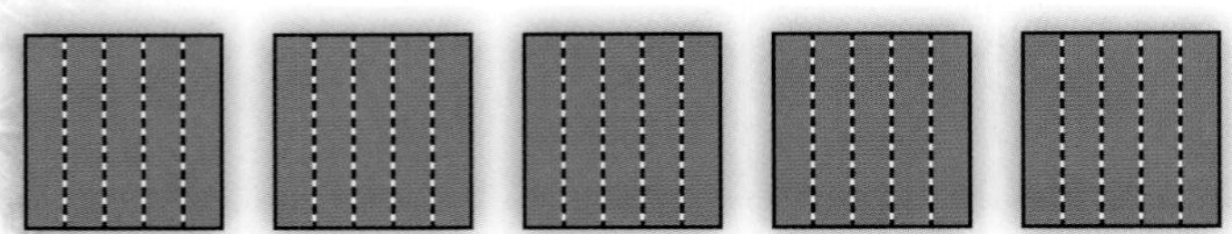

What part of a bar is each section?

$5 \div \frac{1}{5} = n$

There are 25 fifths in five bars.

$n = 25$

How many circles are shown?

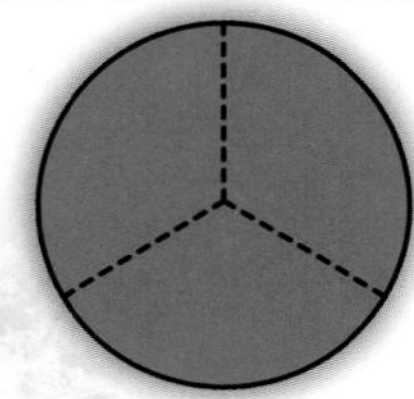

What part of the circle is each section?

$1 \div \frac{1}{3} = n$

There are 3 thirds in the circle.

$n = 3$

Models can help you divide a fraction by a fraction. A whole pie was divided into eighths. How many eighths are in half the pie?

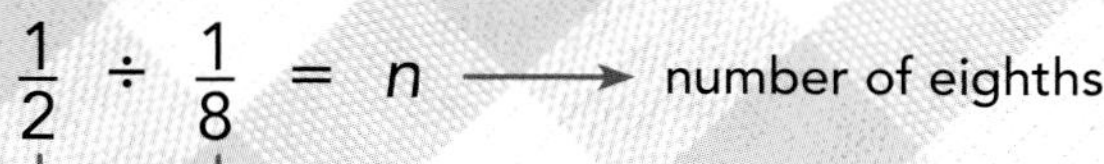

$$\frac{1}{2} \div \frac{1}{8} = n \longrightarrow \text{number of eighths}$$

Consider one half of the whole. 8 parts in the whole

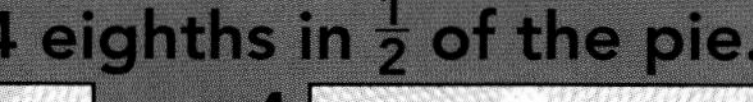

There are 4 eighths in $\frac{1}{2}$ of the pie.
$n = 4$

This box has been divided into fourths. How many fourths are in half of the box?

$$\frac{1}{2} \div \frac{1}{4} = n$$

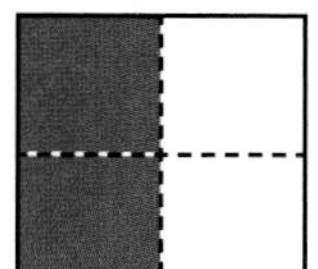

There are 2 fourths in $\frac{1}{2}$.
$n = 2$

This egg carton has 12 sections. Each section is $\frac{1}{12}$. How many eggs are in $\frac{1}{3}$ of the carton?

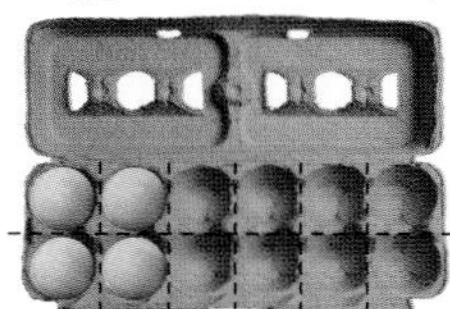

$$\frac{1}{3} \div \frac{1}{12} = n$$

There are 4 eggs in $\frac{1}{3}$ of the carton.
$n = 4$

This muffin pan has six sections. How many muffins are in $\frac{5}{6}$ of the pan?

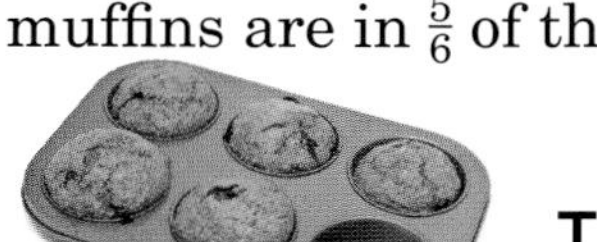

$$\frac{5}{6} \div \frac{1}{6} = n$$

There are 5 muffins in $\frac{5}{6}$ of the pan.
$n = 5$

Check Understanding

Write the number sentence that matches the model.

a.  

b. 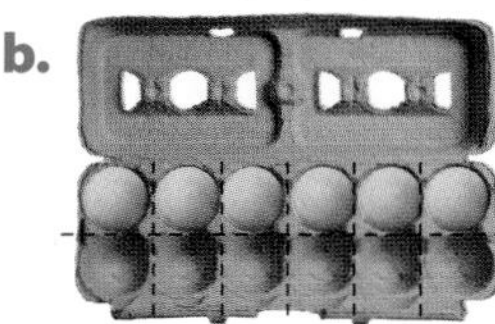

c.  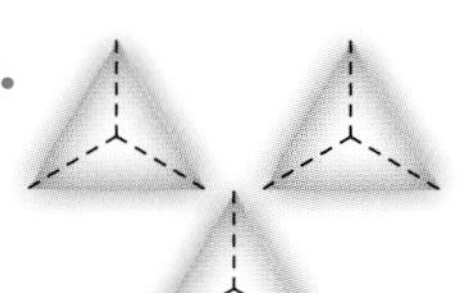

d. 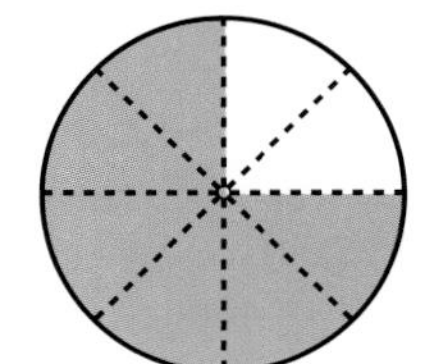

$\frac{1}{2} \div \frac{1}{12} = 6$

$2 \div \frac{1}{3} = 6$

$\frac{3}{4} \div \frac{1}{8} = 6$

$3 \div \frac{1}{3} = 9$

Practice

Write the letter of the number sentence that matches the model.

1. 

a. $3 \div \frac{1}{3} = 9$

b. $3 \div \frac{1}{4} = 12$

c. $3 \div \frac{1}{3} = 12$

2. 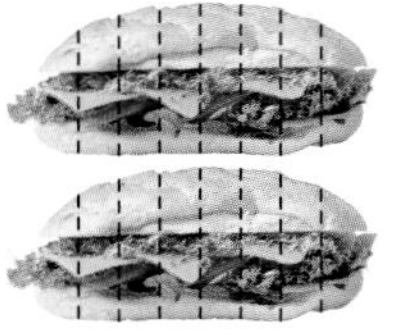

a. $2 \div \frac{1}{8} = 16$

b. $2 \div \frac{1}{7} = 14$

c. $2 \div \frac{1}{8} = 14$

3. 

a. $6 \div \frac{1}{6} = 36$

b. $\frac{1}{2} \div \frac{1}{6} = 3$

c. $1 \div \frac{1}{3} = 6$

4. 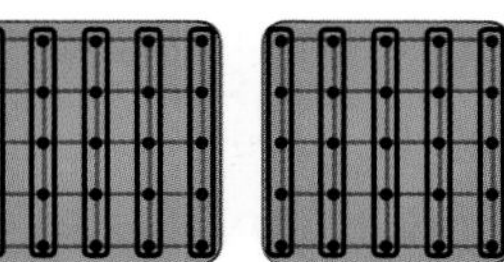

a. $4 \div \frac{1}{5} = 20$

b. $2 \div \frac{1}{5} = 10$

c. $2 \div \frac{1}{4} = 8$

Draw a model for each number sentence. Copy and solve the equation.

5. $\frac{1}{3} \div \frac{1}{9} = n$ **6.** $2 \div \frac{1}{5} = n$ **7.** $1 \div \frac{1}{7} = n$ **8.** $\frac{1}{4} \div \frac{1}{12} = n$

10.8 Divide by Fractions

Construct Meaning

The Fisher Space Pen's special ink is used on manned space flights in the United States. It works in weightless and underwater environments. The pens can write even in extreme temperatures of −30°F to +250°F.

Dev's father uses one of the pens in his outdoor work in Alaska. He carefully labels soil samples to send to two labs in Anchorage. One-half of each of three samples is sent to each lab for testing. How many fractional halves are in three whole-number samples?

When dividing a whole number by a fraction, you are asking how many of this fraction are in this whole number.

Site 1 Site 2 Site 3

There are 6 halves in 3 samples.
A division equation illustrates the picture.

$$3 \div \frac{1}{2} = 6$$

3 → wholes; $\frac{1}{2}$ → fraction; 6 → parts in 3 wholes

Cameron's lunch bag contained a sushi roll cut into thirds. Cameron cut each third in half so that he had 6 pieces. How many sixths are in $\frac{1}{3}$?

There are 2 sixths in $\frac{1}{3}$.
This is the division equation that illustrates the picture.

$$\frac{1}{3} \div \frac{1}{6} = 2$$

$\frac{1}{3}$ → each of the 3 parts of the whole; $\frac{1}{6}$ → 6 total parts; 2 → parts in each $\frac{1}{3}$

How many sixths are in $\frac{2}{3}$? Write a division equation.

Check Understanding

Decide whether the model shows division of a whole number or division of a fraction. Write "whole number" or "fraction."

a. 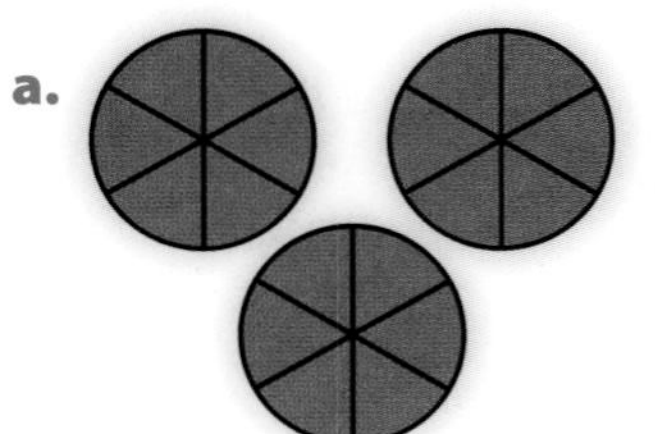

b. 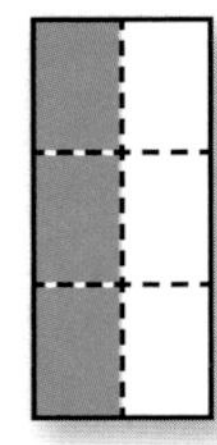

c. 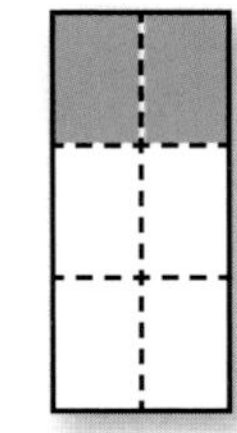

d.

Practice

Use the model to write a division equation.

1. 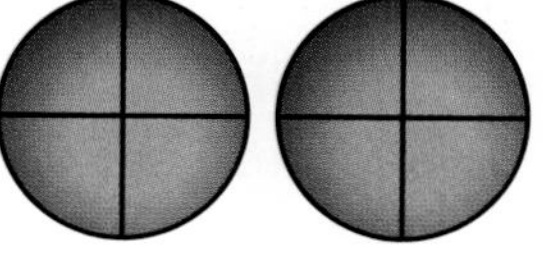

2. 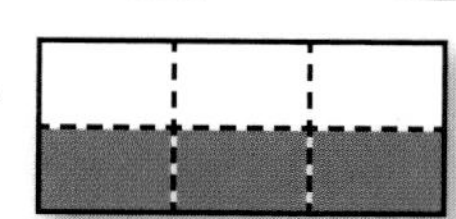

3. 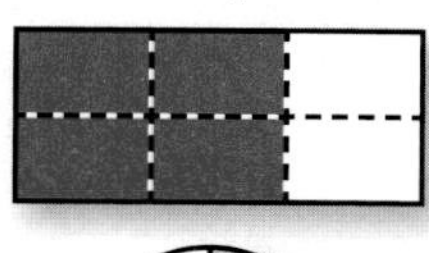

4. 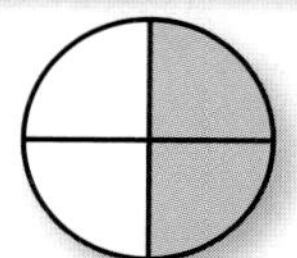

5.

6.

7.

8. 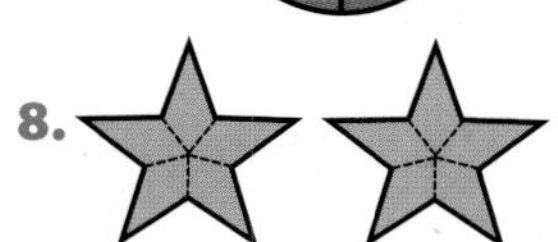

Use models, if needed, to find the quotient.

9. $3 \div \frac{1}{3} = x$

Think: How many thirds are in 3 whole models?

10. $5 \div \frac{1}{4} = x$

Think: How many fourths are in 5 whole models?

11. $\frac{1}{2} \div \frac{1}{4} = x$

Think: How many fourths are in $\frac{1}{2}$ of a model?

12. $\frac{1}{3} \div \frac{1}{9} = x$

Think: How many ninths are in $\frac{1}{3}$ of a model?

Apply

Write a division sentence to solve.

13. A piece of fabric is $\frac{12}{18}$ yd. Mrs. Brown cuts the fabric into pieces that are $\frac{6}{18}$ yd long.

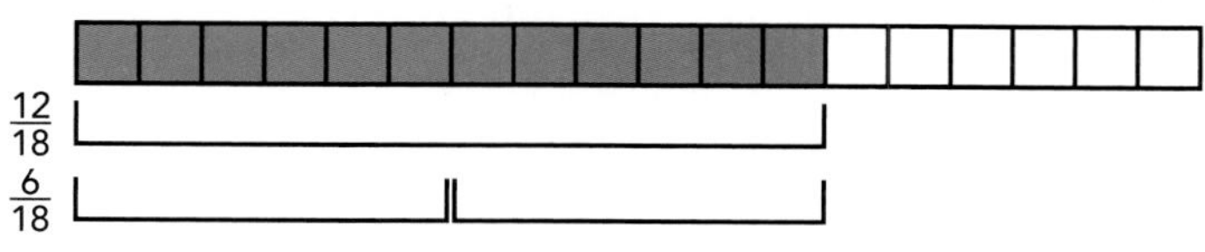

a. How many pieces will Mrs. Brown have? (How many sets of $\frac{6}{18}$ are in $\frac{12}{18}$?)

b. If she cuts the fabric into pieces that are $\frac{4}{18}$ of a yd long, how many pieces will she have? (How many sets of $\frac{4}{18}$ are in $\frac{12}{18}$?)

c. If she cuts the fabric into pieces that are $\frac{3}{18}$ yd each, how many pieces will she have? (How many sets of $\frac{3}{18}$ are in $\frac{12}{18}$?)

14. Ana Sofía cut a round cake into 11 slices. If each person eats $\frac{2}{11}$ of the cake, how many people can be served? Will the whole cake be eaten? Explain.

Review

Solve.

15. $1\frac{2}{3} + 5\frac{2}{3}$

16. $9\frac{3}{4} - 6\frac{2}{5}$

17. 2.4×7.9

18. $8\overline{)26.064}$

19. 47.9×0.62

10.9 Problem Solving: Patterns

Construct Meaning

The Expedition One crew launched on October 31, 2000, and arrived safely at the International Space Station. The first resident crew members were Bill Shepherd, Yuri Gidzenko, and Sergei Krikalev. They were sent to start systems, do experiments, work on construction, and welcome new crew members.

Avi, Botan, and Facundo are watching videos of life in space. They are finding facts for a project. The teacher asked them to write about a day at the ISS. Avi found three facts per session. Botan found two facts. Facundo found four. How many facts will Botan and Facundo have when Avi has 15? Make a table to find a pattern.

There is a pattern in the way each person's number of facts increases. Avi's facts increase by three each session, so the next number is 15. Botan adds two facts. The next number is 10. Facundo adds four facts. The next number is 20.

Avi	3	6	9	12	___
Botan	2	4	6	8	___
Facundo	4	8	12	16	___

When Avi has 15 facts, Botan will have 10, and Facundo will have 20.

Patterns can also be seen in decimals. All fractions can be written as decimals. Decimal numerals can take two forms. A terminating decimal has a fixed number of digits. If you were to divide 3 by 10, you would get 0.3, which is a terminating decimal.

The fractions "terminate." The decimal equivalents may or may not. What happens if you divide 1 by 9? The decimal equivalent of $\frac{1}{9}$ is an example of a repeating decimal. A repeating decimal has one or more digits that repeat continuously. In repeating decimals, a bar is placed over the digits that repeat.

Use a calculator to find the decimal equivalent of $\frac{1}{9}$.

The quotient is written as $0.\overline{1}$.

Check Understanding

Copy and complete the table. Solve by finding the pattern.

a. About 32 fifth graders are waiting for their turn on a space simulator. Each ride lasts for 8 minutes. Four people ride each time. How long will it take 32 students ride?

Time	8	16	24	32	40	48	56	___
People	4	8	12	16	20	24	28	32

b. Brielle was saving her babysitting money for spring break. She earned $15.00 the first week. She earned $8.00 for each of the following weeks. If the pattern continues, how much money will she have saved after the fifth week?

Week	1	2	3	4	5
Money Saved	$15	$23	$31	$39	____

Practice

Solve by finding a pattern. Make a table if necessary.

1. About 720 people cast a vote every two minutes. How long will it take to cast 5,040 votes?

2. Students held a car wash to help pay for a trip. If they washed four cars each hour, how many cars did they wash by the end of the sixth hour? If they made $30.00 profit per hour, how much money did they raise?

3. Jamaar delivers newspapers daily. For every 30 papers he sells, he makes $2.50. How many newspapers will he need to sell to make $20?

4. Space technology has led to cell phones. Over an 8-hour period, a company sold 3 phones during each of the first 4 hours. They sold 4 phones during each of the last 4 hours. What was the total number of sales during the 8-hour period? If the number of sales increased at the same rate, how many phones would sell during each of the next 4 hours?

5. Mr. Clark enjoys putting puzzles together. During his first sitting, he put 25 pieces together. The next time, he put 30 pieces together. The third time, he put 35 pieces together. If the pattern continues, how many sittings will it take Mr. Clark to put a 225-piece puzzle together?

6. The lawn mower cuts a width of $1\frac{1}{2}$ ft. How many widths will it take to mow a strip of grass that is $16\frac{1}{2}$ ft wide?

7. During the state volleyball tournament, 6 student tickets were sold for every 2 adult tickets. At this rate, how many adult tickets had been sold when 96 student tickets were sold?

8. The fifth graders at Community Christian School decided to raise money to support a fifth-grade student's tuition to Alliance Academy in Quito, Ecuador. If $25.00 was pledged weekly, how many weeks will it take to raise $1,148.75?

9. For each of the following fractions divide the numerator by the denominator to determine whether the decimal answer is a repeating decimal or a terminating decimal.

   a. $\frac{1}{8}$ **b.** $\frac{4}{6}$ **c.** $\frac{4}{36}$ **d.** $\frac{2}{5}$

10.10 Chapter 10 Review

Write T for true and F for false.

1. When multiplying fractions, numerators must be multiplied first.
2. When multiplying fractions, the denominators must be the same.
3. When multiplying $\frac{1}{3} \times \frac{3}{4}$, the product is less than the whole number 1.
4. The line in a fraction represents division.

Copy and complete the multiplication sentence for each model. Write the product in simplest form.

5.  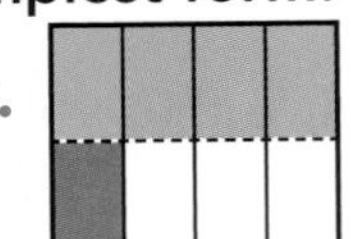 $\frac{1}{2} \times \frac{1}{4} = \frac{\square}{\square}$

6. 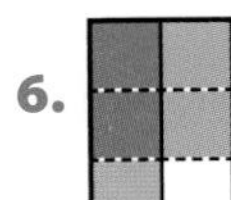 $\frac{2}{3} \times \frac{\square}{\square} = \frac{\square}{\square} = \frac{\square}{\square}$

7. 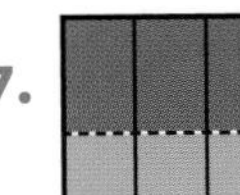 $\frac{1}{2} \times \frac{\square}{\square} = \frac{\square}{\square}$

Multiply. Write the product in simplest form.

8. $\frac{2}{3} \times \frac{1}{4}$
9. $\frac{3}{4} \times \frac{4}{7}$
10. $\frac{5}{2} \times \frac{3}{9}$
11. $\frac{3}{5} \times \frac{7}{2}$
12. $\frac{1}{4} \times 24$
13. $45 \times \frac{3}{5}$

Use >, <, or = to complete the number sentence.

14. $\frac{1}{4} \times \frac{2}{3} \bigcirc \frac{2}{6}$
15. $\frac{4}{5} \times \frac{1}{2} \bigcirc \frac{2}{10}$
16. $\frac{7}{14} \times \frac{5}{10} \bigcirc 1$
17. $\frac{1}{3} \times \frac{3}{7} \bigcirc \frac{1}{8}$
18. $\frac{1}{2} \times \frac{3}{7} \bigcirc \frac{7}{14}$
19. $\frac{2}{5} \times \frac{5}{6} \bigcirc \frac{1}{2}$

Write the letter that shows the answer in simplest form.

20. $2\frac{1}{3} \times 3\frac{1}{2}$ **a.** $7\frac{1}{2}$ **b.** $8\frac{1}{6}$ **c.** $8\frac{2}{3}$ **d.** $8\frac{1}{5}$

21. $4\frac{5}{6} \times \frac{4}{5}$ **a.** $3\frac{14}{15}$ **b.** $3\frac{2}{3}$ **c.** $2\frac{13}{15}$ **d.** $3\frac{13}{15}$

22. $5\frac{3}{4} \times 7$ **a.** $40\frac{1}{2}$ **b.** $40\frac{1}{3}$ **c.** $39\frac{3}{4}$ **d.** $40\frac{1}{4}$

23. $3 \div \frac{1}{2}$ **a.** $1\frac{1}{2}$ **b.** $\frac{2}{3}$ **c.** 6 **d.** $\frac{1}{3}$

Estimate the product by substituting a compatible number.

24. $\frac{1}{5} \times 29$
25. $\frac{1}{7} \times 58$

Round each number to the nearest whole number to estimate the product.

26. $15\frac{1}{6} \times 2\frac{7}{8}$

27. $6\frac{1}{2} \times 7\frac{3}{8}$

28. $10\frac{1}{2} \times 4\frac{1}{2}$

29. $8\frac{1}{3} \times 4\frac{3}{4}$

Choose the letter of the number sentence that matches the model.

30. 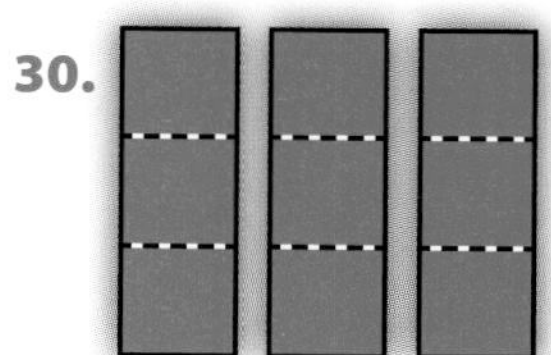

a. $3 \div \frac{1}{3} = 9$

b. $3 \div \frac{1}{9} = 27$

c. $3 \div \frac{1}{6} = 18$

31.

a. $\frac{1}{4} \div \frac{1}{8} = \frac{1}{32}$

b. $\frac{1}{4} \div \frac{1}{8} = 2$

c. $\frac{1}{5} \div \frac{1}{4} = \frac{1}{12}$

32. 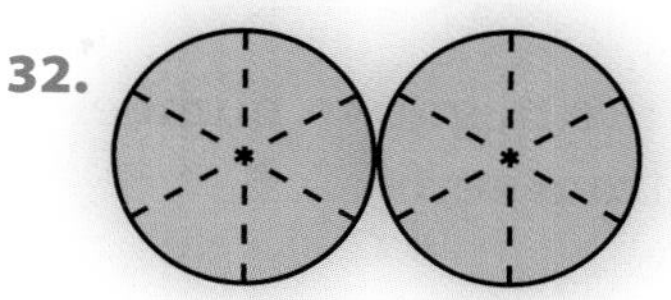

a. $2 \div \frac{1}{5} = 10$

b. $2 \div \frac{1}{7} = 14$

c. $2 \div \frac{1}{6} = 12$

33. 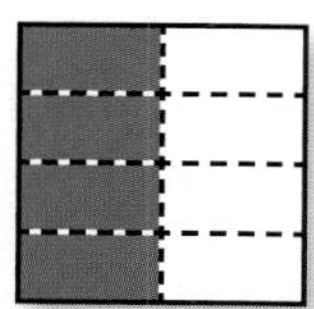

a. $\frac{1}{2} \div \frac{1}{8} = 4$

b. $\frac{1}{2} \div \frac{1}{4} = \frac{1}{8}$

c. $\frac{1}{2} \div \frac{1}{8} = \frac{1}{16}$

Cell phones have GPS that allows people to use online maps. Some people navigate the wilderness using GPS services. If GPS sales continue in the same pattern, what is the number of sales for week seven?

week	1	2	3	4	5	6	7
hikers	7	14	21	28	35	42	34. ____
anglers	3	6	9	12	15	18	35. ____
hunters	3	7	12	18	25	33	36. ____

37. The Penguin Water Company uses a filtration module designed for the International Space Station. About $\frac{1}{5}$ of the 60 local companies use bottled water with this system. How many companies will be helped by this technology?

38. Bailey shares 13 candy apples. She cuts each one in half. How many people can be served if each person gets one-half?

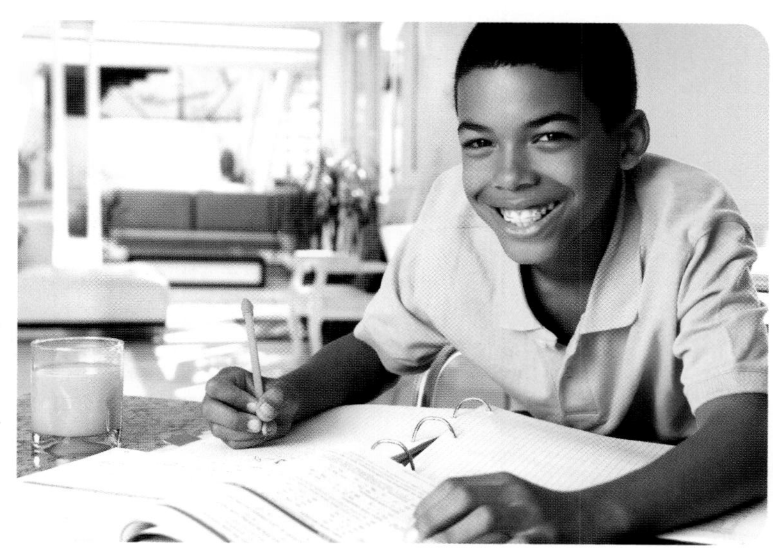

39. Cannon studied $1\frac{3}{4}$ hours of math on Monday. He studied $2\frac{1}{3}$ hours on Tuesday for a math test. How many hours did he study?

40. For each of the following fractions, divide the numerator by the denominator to determine what type of fraction results. Write "repeating" or "terminating."

a. $\frac{2}{12}$

b. $\frac{2}{25}$

10.11 Chapters 8–10 Review

Read the statement. Write T for true and F for false.

1. Positive and negative integers, fractions, and mixed numbers can be shown on a number line. ____
2. Opposite numbers are negative numbers the same distance from zero. ____
3. The numerator is found on the bottom of the fraction. ____
4. A prime number is a whole number that has exactly two factors. ____

Find the GCF.

5. 14, 21, 35, 42
6. 10, 15, 30

Find the LCM.

7. 2 and 6

Find the LCD.

8. $\frac{1}{2}$ and $\frac{1}{9}$

Solve. Write the answer in simplest form.

9. $\frac{3}{4} + \frac{1}{4}$
10. $\frac{10}{12} - \frac{7}{12}$
11. $16 + 9\frac{1}{9} + 7\frac{1}{9}$
12. $22\frac{1}{2} - 19\frac{1}{2}$
13. $\frac{1}{4} + \frac{1}{12}$
14. $\frac{2}{5} - \frac{1}{10}$

Multiply. Write the product in simplest form.

15. $\frac{1}{2}$ of $\frac{1}{4}$
16. $\frac{6}{7} \times \frac{1}{9}$
17. $3\frac{1}{3} \times 2\frac{1}{2}$
18. $\frac{1}{3} \times 12$

Estimate by rounding each number to the nearest whole number.

19. $5\frac{3}{4} \times 2\frac{2}{3}$

20. $2\frac{1}{4} \times 13$

Estimate the product by substituting a compatible number.

21. $\frac{1}{5} \times 31$

22. $\frac{1}{9} \times 82$

Use models, if needed, to find the quotient.

23. $2 \div \frac{1}{2}$

24. $6 \div \frac{1}{4}$

25. $\frac{1}{3} \div \frac{1}{12}$

26. $\frac{1}{5} \div \frac{1}{15}$

Solve.

27. A half marathon is $21\frac{1}{10}$ km in length. Running two half marathons equals a marathon. How many kilometers are in a marathon?

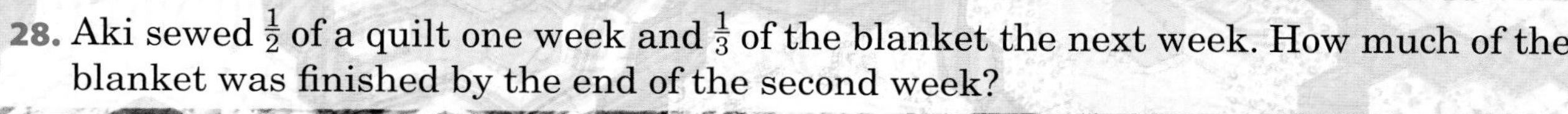

28. Aki sewed $\frac{1}{2}$ of a quilt one week and $\frac{1}{3}$ of the blanket the next week. How much of the blanket was finished by the end of the second week?

29. Gael cut a round cake into 15 slices. Each person ate $\frac{2}{15}$ of the cake. How many people were served?

30. Mrs. Hess coaches a running club after school. During the first practice, students ran for 15 minutes. They ran 20 minutes at the second practice. Finally, they ran 25 minutes at the third practice. If the pattern continues, how many minutes will students run during the fourth practice?

Chapter 11
Ratio, Proportion, and Percent

For the Lord God is a sun and shield; the Lord bestows favor and honor; no good thing does He withhold from those whose walk is blameless.
Psalm 84:11

Key Ideas:

Algebra: writing equations with and without variables

Fractions and Decimals: finding ratios and proportions

Fractions and Decimals: finding percent

11.1 Explore Ratios

Construct Meaning

The Hartman family wants to buy more organic fruits and vegetables. Washing produce is very important, but the Hartman family does not want soap on their food. Mrs. Hartman made a recipe to clean the food. It has a 3:1 ratio of water to vinegar. The 3:1 means Mrs. Hartman must use three parts water to one part vinegar.

A ratio compares two quantities. The quantities compared are called terms.

In this group of apples, the ratio of green apples to red apples is 3 to 4.

3 to 4

number of green apples — number of red apples

A ratio can be written in three ways.

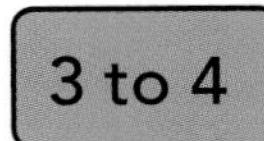

3 to 4 | 3:4 | $\frac{3}{4}$

This ratio compares one part to another part, or green apples to red apples. The ratio for red apples to green apples would be 4 to 3, 4:3, or $\frac{4}{3}$.

The order in which you write a ratio is important.

$$\frac{\text{green apples}}{\text{red apples}} \quad \frac{3}{4} \quad \text{is different from} \quad \frac{\text{red apples}}{\text{green apples}} \quad \frac{4}{3}$$

A ratio can also compare one part to the whole.

$$\frac{\text{green apples}}{\text{total apples}} \quad \frac{3}{7} \quad \text{and} \quad \frac{\text{red apples}}{\text{total apples}} \quad \frac{4}{7}$$

Check Understanding

Write a ratio that shows each of the following.

a. minivans to motor homes

b. trolleys to trains

c. moons to suns

Practice

Use the table. Write each ratio in three ways.

Votes for Class Trip	
Brock Canyon	卌 卌
Hamilton Park	卌
Latimer Zoo	卌 III

1. Brock Canyon to Hamilton Park
2. Hamilton Park to Brock Canyon
3. Brock Canyon to total votes
4. Hamilton Park to Latimer Zoo
5. Latimer Zoo to Hamilton Park
6. Hamilton Park to total votes
7. Latimer Zoo to Brock Canyon
8. Latimer Zoo to total votes
9. Write the numbers of the exercises that show part-to-part ratios.
10. Write the numbers of the exercises that show part-to-whole ratios.
11. On the table, what is being compared by the ratio of $\frac{10}{8}$?

Apply

12. A poll shows that 11 out of 24 students picked the sun as their favorite celestial body. Write a ratio that compares the number of students who did not pick the sun to the total number of students.

13. There are two pilots on the flight. There are also three other airline workers and 72 travelers. What is the ratio of all employees to travelers?

Review

Solve each fraction problem. Pay attention to the operation signs.

14. $2\frac{2}{3} + 3\frac{2}{3}$
15. $\frac{1}{4} \times \frac{5}{9}$
16. $11 - 6\frac{7}{8}$
17. $\frac{3}{4} \times \frac{1}{2}$
18. $\frac{3}{5} - \frac{1}{3}$
19. $\frac{6}{7} \times \frac{2}{3}$
20. $5\frac{1}{12} + 7\frac{5}{6}$
21. $\frac{9}{14} \times \frac{3}{5}$
22. $20\frac{1}{8} - 16\frac{3}{4}$
23. $12 + 4\frac{1}{8}$

11.2 Find Equal Ratios

Construct Meaning

Brandon loves to watch car racing. During a recent race, Brandon's favorite driver averaged three miles per minute. At this rate, how long would it take the driver to travel 18 miles? Use equal ratios to find the number of minutes it will take to travel 18 miles.

Two ratios are equal if they can be written as equivalent fractions.
Finding an equal ratio is like finding an equivalent fraction.

miles → / minutes → $= \frac{3}{1}$ Find an equal ratio. Think: $\frac{3}{1} = \frac{18}{n}$ (× 6) ← miles / ← minutes

The equal ratio would be $\frac{18}{6}$. Since $n = 6$, the car will travel 18 miles in 6 minutes.

A ratio table can show a series of equal ratios.

miles	3	6	9	12	15	18
minutes	1	2	3	4	5	6

The ratios 3:1, 6:2, 9:3, 12:4, 15:5, and 18:6 are equal ratios.

Pit crews are important to a driver's position on the track. When the driver pulls in for service, the fueling, tire changes, and minor adjustments must be completed in seconds. If a driver pits four times in a race for a total of 76 seconds, what is the average number of seconds required for two pits?

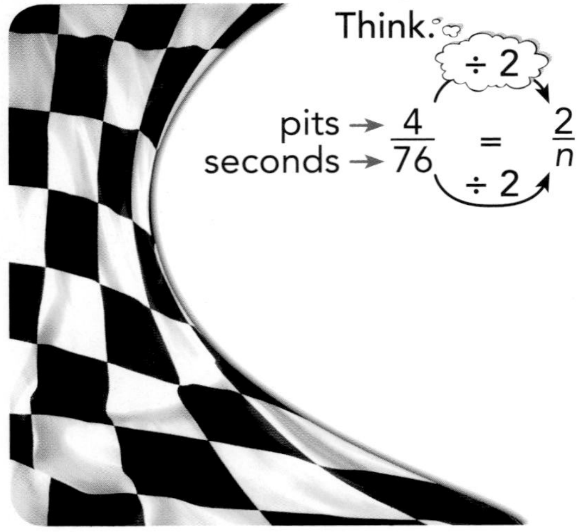

pits → / seconds → Think: $\frac{4}{76} = \frac{2}{n}$ (÷ 2)

The equal ratio would be $\frac{2}{38}$.
The average number of seconds required for two pits is 38 seconds.

number of pits	1	2	3	4
number of seconds	19	38	57	76

The ratios $\frac{1}{19}$, $\frac{2}{38}$, $\frac{3}{57}$, and $\frac{4}{76}$ are equal ratios. They are named by equivalent fractions.

Check Understanding

Copy and complete each ratio table.

a. To make two omelets, you need five eggs.

omelets	2	4	6	8
eggs	5			

b. To make one pie, you need six apples.

pies	1	2		4	
apples	6		18		30

Practice

Refer to the pictures. Write what is being compared. Write each ratio as a fraction.

1. 5 to 3
2. 8 to 5
3. 3 to 8
4. 3 to 5

Write two ratios that are equal to the given ratio.

5. $\frac{3}{4}$
6. $\frac{2}{3}$
7. $\frac{3}{5}$
8. $\frac{6}{7}$
9. $\frac{4}{9}$

Find the missing number. Write the answer as $n =$ ___.

10. $\frac{3}{8} = \frac{15}{n}$
11. $\frac{4}{n} = \frac{16}{44}$
12. $\frac{9}{12} = \frac{n}{36}$
13. $\frac{n}{15} = \frac{8}{60}$
14. $\frac{16}{48} = \frac{n}{6}$

Write = or ≠ for each pair of ratios.

15. $\frac{3}{4}$ ◯ $\frac{9}{10}$
16. $\frac{9}{18}$ ◯ $\frac{27}{54}$
17. $\frac{18}{27}$ ◯ $\frac{6}{9}$
18. $\frac{8}{6}$ ◯ $\frac{32}{48}$
19. $\frac{12}{21}$ ◯ $\frac{4}{7}$

Apply

Make a ratio table with the data given.

20. A pint of wild rice provides 11.5 mg of calcium. Show the number of milligrams of calcium in 1, 2, 3, 4, and 5 pints.

21. It costs $4.00 to make three subs. How many sub sandwiches can be made for $8.00, $12.00, and $16.00?

22. The ratio of race-car drivers to pit-crew members is 1:7. Show the number of pit-crew members required by 1, 2, 3, 4, and 5 drivers.

Review

Write the word or number that will complete each sentence.

23. A triangle that has sides with different lengths on each side is a _____ triangle.
24. A _____ is a line segment that connects the center to a point on the circle.
25. Lines that intersect at right angles are called _____ lines.
26. The sum of the three angles of a triangle is _____ degrees.

11.3 Explore Proportions

Construct Meaning

Are these two rugs proportional?

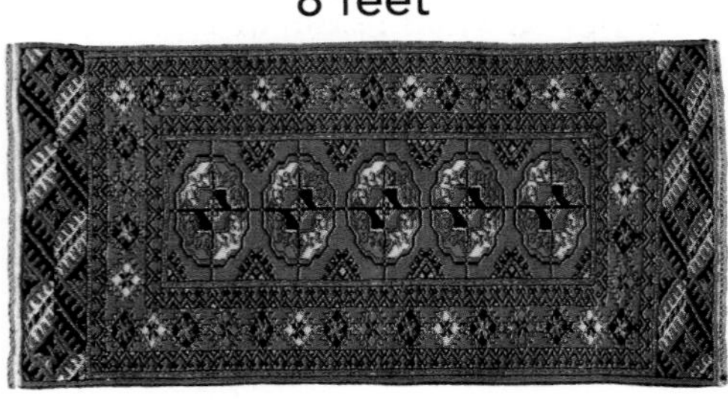

Each ratio compares the width of the rug to its length.

$\frac{\text{3 feet}}{\text{6 feet}} \longleftarrow \frac{\text{width}}{\text{length}} \longrightarrow \frac{\text{4 feet}}{\text{8 feet}}$ The numerator of each ratio represents width in feet. Both denominators show length in feet.

An equation that shows that the two ratios are equal is called a proportion. $\frac{3}{6} = \frac{4}{8}$

In a proportion, the cross products are equal. To find cross products of two ratios, multiply each numerator by the denominator of the other ratio.

$\frac{3}{6} = \frac{4}{8}$ $3 \times 8 = 4 \times 6$
$24 = 24$

Because the cross products are equal, the rugs are proportional.

Amaira and Caden are making bags of trail mix for a camping trip. If one recipe serves 12, how many cups of mix do they need for 32 students?

Trail Mix

Makes 6 cups. Serves 12.

- **2 cups toasted rice-squares cereal**
- **$1\frac{3}{5}$ cups cinnamon-squares cereal**
- **$\frac{2}{5}$ cup candy-coated chocolate pieces**
- **$1\frac{1}{4}$ cups roasted peanuts**
- **$\frac{1}{4}$ cup of raisins**
- **$\frac{2}{5}$ cup of dried cranberries**

To find the answer, write a proportion showing two equal ratios. Use cross products to solve for n.

$\frac{\text{number of servings}}{\text{cups of mix}} \longrightarrow \frac{12}{6} = \frac{32}{n}$ In the proportion $\frac{12}{6} = \frac{32}{n}$, n is the unknown term.

Find the cross products. $12 \times n = 32 \times 6$
$12 \times n = 192$

Divide to find *n*. $n = 192 \div 12$
$n = 16$

They need 16 cups for 32 students.

Check Understanding

Write the cross products. Solve for the missing number.

a. $\frac{2}{7} = \frac{r}{28}$

b. $\frac{4}{5} = \frac{32}{n}$

c. $\frac{8}{3} = \frac{a}{21}$

d. $\frac{7}{3} = \frac{y}{9}$

Practice

Write the cross products. Write = or ≠.

1. $\frac{3}{4} \bigcirc \frac{6}{8}$
2. $\frac{4}{9} \bigcirc \frac{6}{18}$
3. $\frac{6}{7} \bigcirc \frac{2}{5}$
4. $\frac{17}{20} \bigcirc \frac{34}{40}$
5. $\frac{9}{12} \bigcirc \frac{7}{9}$
6. $\frac{6}{4} \bigcirc \frac{18}{12}$
7. $\frac{12}{48} \bigcirc \frac{3}{8}$
8. $\frac{6}{9} \bigcirc \frac{2}{3}$

Find the value of the unknown term.

9. $\frac{x}{6} = \frac{2}{3}$
10. $\frac{8}{10} = \frac{4}{n}$
11. $\frac{20}{y} = \frac{4}{5}$
12. $\frac{6}{8} = \frac{n}{24}$
13. $\frac{32}{36} = \frac{8}{x}$
14. $\frac{4}{5} = \frac{x}{35}$
15. $\frac{n}{25} = \frac{6}{5}$
16. $\frac{2}{3} = \frac{x}{9}$

Apply

Write a proportion. Solve for the unknown term.

17. A drink mix uses 3 tablespoons of mix to 8 cups of water. How many tablespoons are needed for 32 cups of water?

18. A formula for paint uses 12 drops of yellow color to 1 gallon of green paint. How much yellow is needed for 3 gallons of green paint?

19. For every three drops of red color, Cailida used four drops of yellow to make a shade of orange. If she used 21 drops of red, how many drops of yellow did she use?

Review

Solve. Draw a model if needed.

20. $7 \div \frac{1}{3}$
21. $12 \div \frac{1}{2}$
22. $\frac{1}{2} \div \frac{1}{4}$
23. $\frac{1}{3} \div \frac{1}{9}$

11.4 Solve Proportions

Construct Meaning

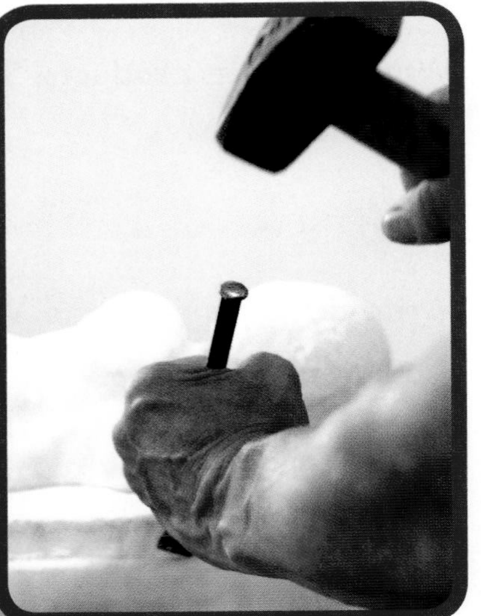

Artists have worked with proportions for centuries. Greek sculptors used an 8 to 1 ratio for total body height to head height. Suppose you plan to make a clay sculpture of a person and the head will be 2 inches high. Using an 8 to 1 ratio, what would be the total height of the sculpture?

To find the height, you can write a proportion.

$$\frac{\text{human body height}}{\text{human head height}} \quad \frac{8}{1} = \frac{h}{2} \quad \frac{\text{sculpture's body height}}{\text{sculpture's head height}}$$

A proportion is an equation that states that two ratios are equal.

Remember:

There are two ways to find x.

1. **You can use equal ratios. Multiply or divide both the numerator and the denominator of the fraction by the same number.**

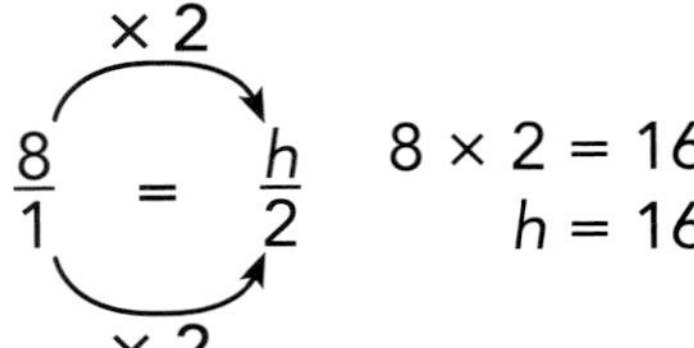

$\frac{8}{1} = \frac{h}{2}$ (× 2, × 2)

$8 \times 2 = 16$

$h = 16$

2. **You can find the cross products of the two fractions. Multiply each numerator by the denominator of the other fraction.**

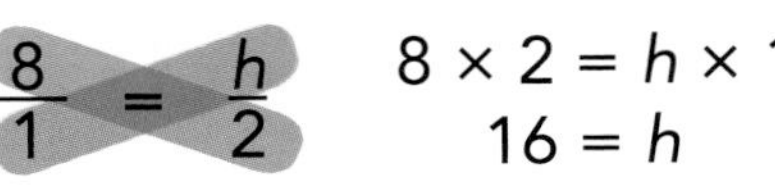

$\frac{8}{1} = \frac{h}{2}$

$8 \times 2 = h \times 1$

$16 = h$

To be proportional, the total height of the sculpture must be 16 inches.

Check Understanding

a. If an artist is using the 8 to 1 ratio to sculpt a statue of a human, and the head height is 3 in., what is the total body height?

b. If a sculpture of a man has a total height of 72 in., what would the head height be?

c. It takes an artist seven hours to cast three small copies of a sculpture. How many hours would it take to make 96 copies? Use cross products.

Practice

Use equivalent fractions or cross products to solve.

1. $\frac{4}{7} = \frac{n}{21}$
2. $\frac{5}{10} = \frac{50}{x}$
3. $\frac{4}{5} = \frac{48}{y}$
4. $\frac{n}{10} = \frac{12}{15}$

Copy and complete the ratio table to solve the problem.

5. Adrian can walk two miles in 15 minutes. How far can he walk in 60 minutes?

miles	2	4	6	
minutes	15			

6. A punch recipe uses two quarts of cranberry juice for each gallon of punch. How much cranberry juice is needed for seven gallons?

quarts of cranberry juice	2			8			
gallons of punch	1		3			6	

Apply

7. Harrison, who is on a weight-loss program, has lost 3 lb in 5 weeks. At the same rate, how long will it take him to lose 27 lb?
8. A brick wall 24 ft long contains 1,040 bricks. Use the same pattern to find how many bricks it will take to build a wall 48 ft long.
9. Twenty-four jars can be packed in six boxes. How many jars can be packed in 15 boxes of the same size?
10. A dose of a medication is 2 oz for every 50 lb of body weight. How many ounces are required for a 150-pound man?
11. Huan uses 2 lb of fertilizer per 100 square feet of lawn. How much fertilizer is needed for a lawn that measures 2,500 square feet?

Review

Order each set of fractions from greatest to least.

12. $\frac{7}{10}, \frac{3}{5}, \frac{4}{15}, \frac{15}{30}$
13. $\frac{2}{3}, \frac{4}{12}, \frac{3}{4}, \frac{14}{24}$
14. $\frac{1}{2}, \frac{6}{8}, \frac{4}{10}, \frac{8}{80}$
15. $\frac{7}{9}, \frac{18}{81}, \frac{2}{18}, \frac{27}{36}$
16. $\frac{3}{7}, \frac{2}{14}, \frac{25}{35}, \frac{16}{28}$
17. $\frac{1}{3}, \frac{2}{12}, \frac{21}{36}, \frac{5}{6}$

11.5 Problem Solving: Scale Drawings

Construct Meaning

A scale drawing represents an area or an object in a smaller or larger size. Maps, blueprints, landscape plans, and diagrams are examples of scale drawings.

The scale of this map shows that 2 cm represents a distance of 5 km. This can be shown as the ratio 2 cm:5 km. If the map distance of the road between Badger Pass and Glacier Point is 7 cm, what is the actual driving distance?

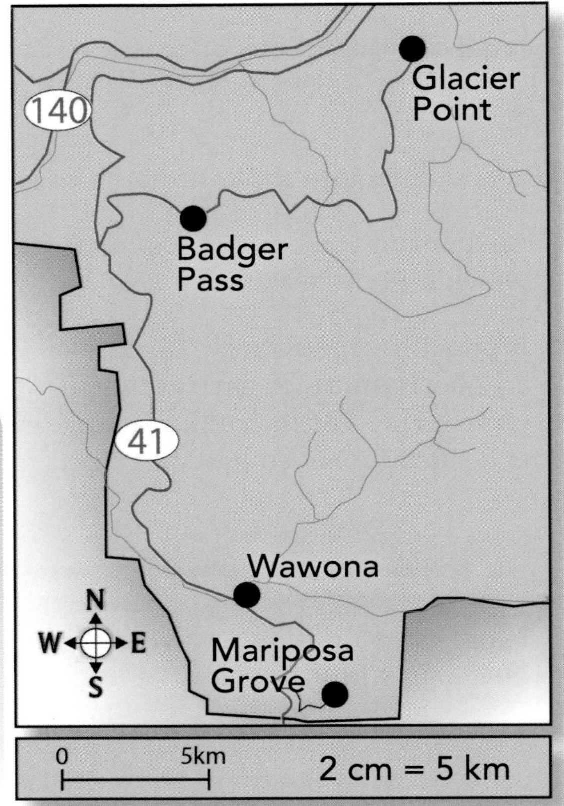

$$\frac{\text{map distance}}{\text{actual distance}} = \frac{2 \text{ cm}}{5 \text{ km}} = \frac{7 \text{ cm}}{y}$$

Use cross products.

$$2 \text{ cm} \times y = 7 \text{ cm} \times 5 \text{ km}$$
$$2 \times y = 35$$
$$y = 35 \div 2$$
$$y = 17.5$$

The actual driving distance is 17.5 km.

Check Understanding

Use a ruler to measure the diagram. Write and solve a proportion for each exercise.

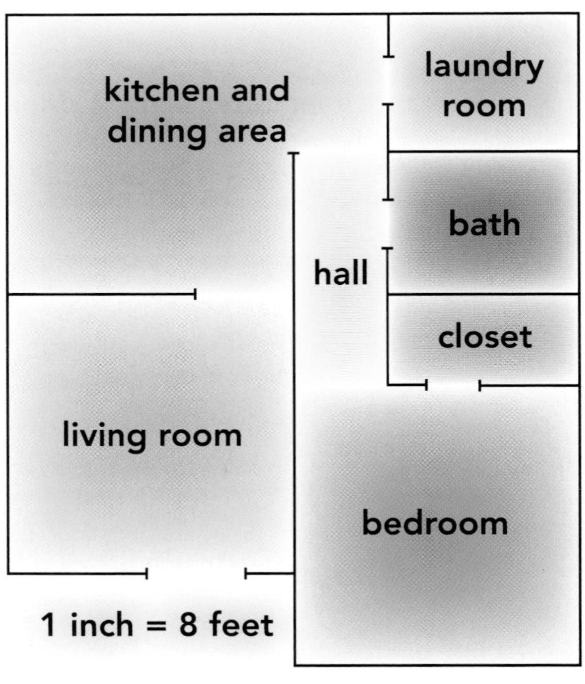

a. What is the length of the apartment on its longest wall?

b. What is the length of the apartment from the front door to the back wall?

c. Will a rug that measures 12 ft by 10 ft fit into the living room?

d. What is the length of the wall that separates the dining area from the living room?

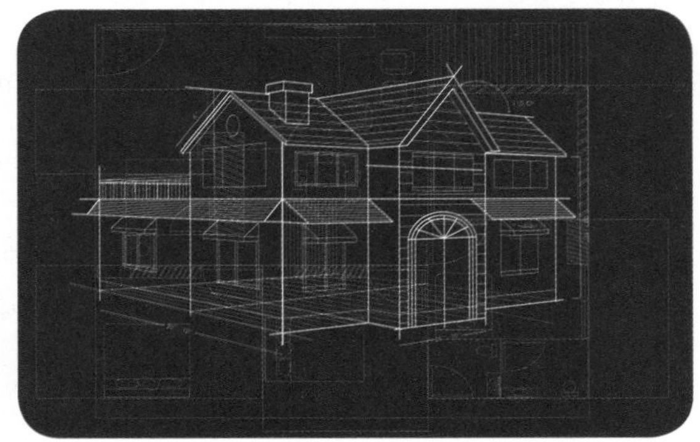

Practice

On a scale drawing of a portion of the moon, 2 cm represents 15 km. Write an equation. Solve to find the actual distance for each map measurement.

1. a crater that is 4 cm long
2. two mountains on the moon that are located 8 cm apart
3. a lunar mountain that is 1 cm wide
4. a rill, or crack, on the surface of the moon that is 3.2 cm long
5. a mare, or lava-filled crater, that is 5 cm long

A scale drawing can be smaller than, larger than, or the same size as the object it represents. For each object, write whether the scale is reasonable or not reasonable.

6. 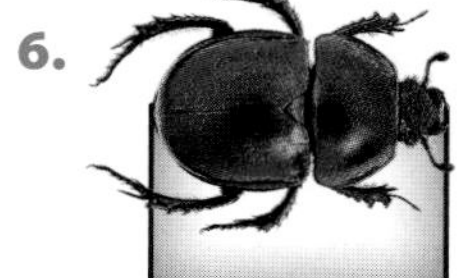

2 cm:10 cm

7. 

2 cm:40 cm

8. 

1 in.:8 ft

9. 

1 in.:1 in.

Write an equation to solve each problem.

10. The model car is 4 in. long. The scale is 1 in.:4 ft. What is the length of the actual car?
11. The scale model of the house is 12 in. long. The length of the actual house is 48 ft. Which scale was used: 1 in. = 4 ft or 1 in. = 8 ft?
12. The *Spirit of Saint Louis*, flown by Charles Lindbergh in 1927, had a wingspan of 46 ft. How long would the wingspan be in a scale drawing if the scale was 1 in.:2 ft?
13. An 8 in. by 10 in. photograph must be reduced to 4 in. by 5 in. to fit on a Christmas card. Are the two sizes proportional?
14. A map scale is 1 in. equals 20 mi. How far apart are two towns if the map distance measures 3 in.?

11.6 Explore Percent

Construct Meaning

Mrs. Daubach's fifth-grade students conducted a poll of 100 fifth and sixth graders. The students were asked to pick their favorite sport from a list of five choices. The chart shows the results.

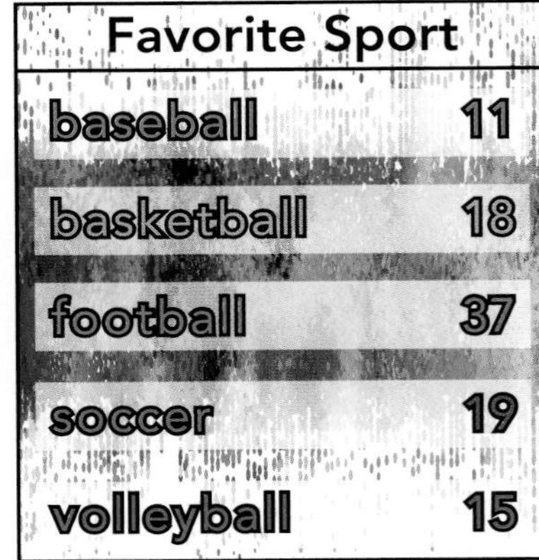

Favorite Sport	
baseball	11
basketball	18
football	37
soccer	19
volleyball	15

Mrs. Daubach asked her students to show the results on a 10 by 10 grid, using five different colors. Then, they wrote a ratio comparing the number of students who chose each sport to the total number of students polled. The students wrote: 11:100, 18:100, 37:100, 19:100, and 15:100.

When you compare a number to 100, you are using a special ratio called a percentage. Percent means per one hundred. The symbol for percent is %.

What percentage of the grid is colored?

100% of the grid is colored.

The same number can be expressed in several ways.

problem	ratio	fraction	decimal	percent
Show 89 out of 100	89:100	$\frac{89}{100}$	0.89	89%
Show 43¢ out of $1.00	43:100	$\frac{43}{100}$	0.43	43%

Check Understanding

Write a ratio, fraction, decimal, and percentage to show the part shaded.

a. 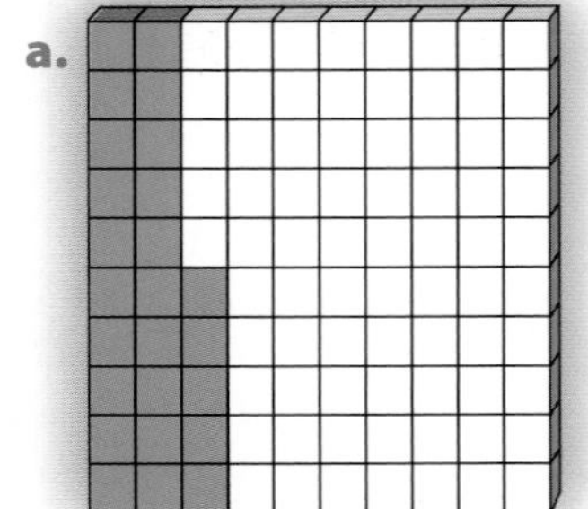

b. 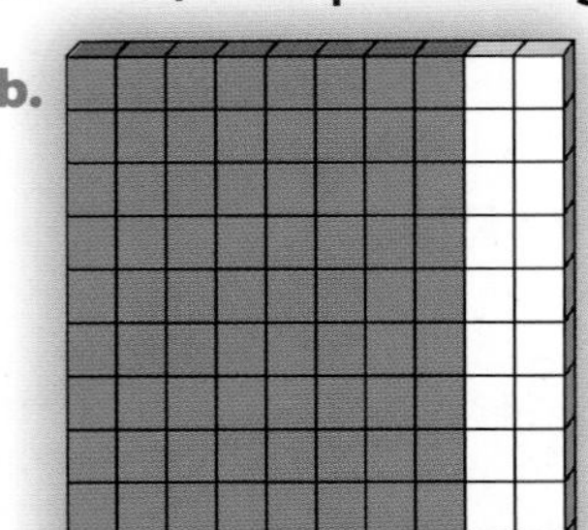

c. 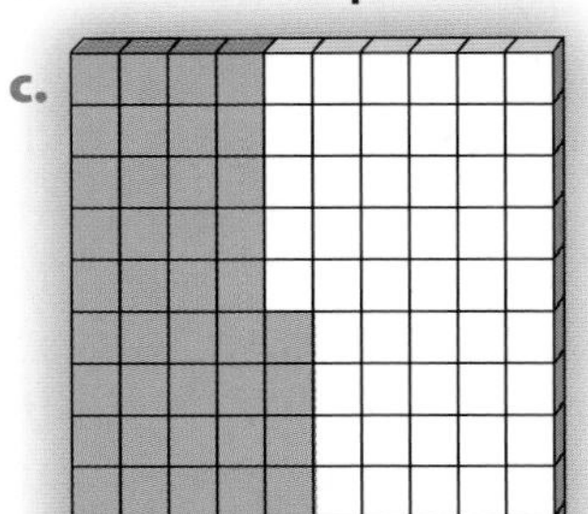

d. 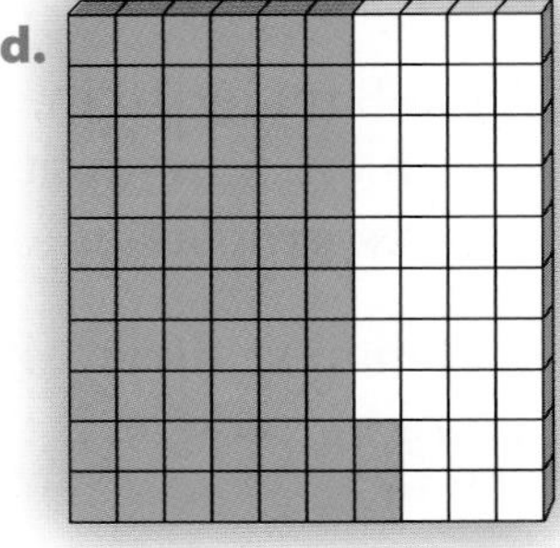

Practice

The grid shows the number of each type of book by color.

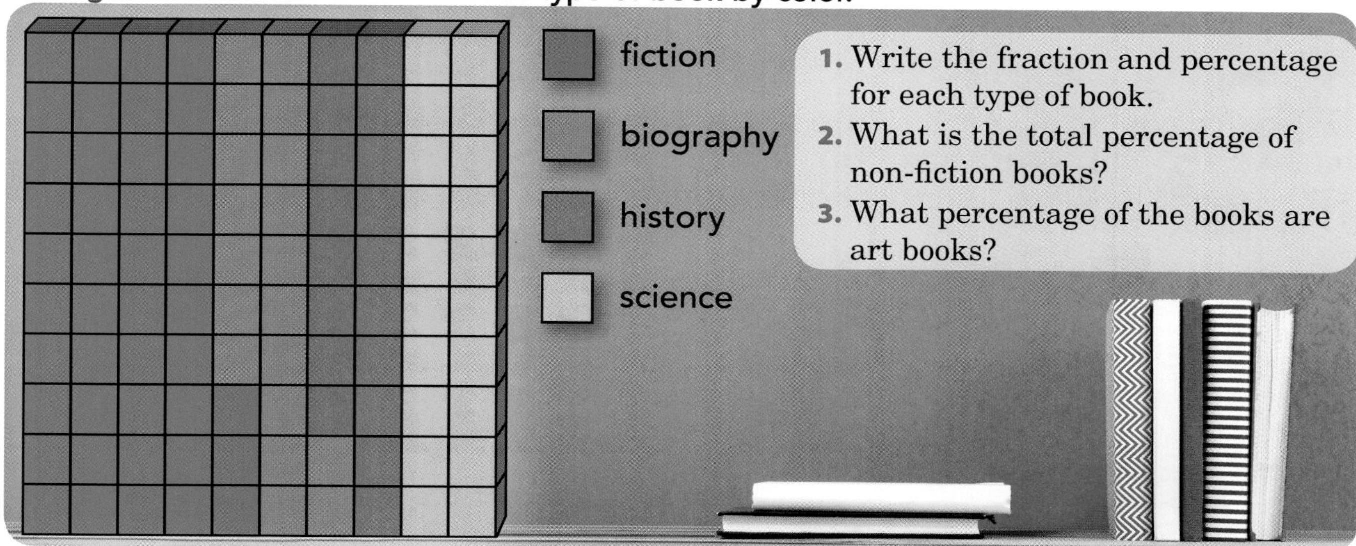

1. Write the fraction and percentage for each type of book.
2. What is the total percentage of non-fiction books?
3. What percentage of the books are art books?

Write each ratio as a percent.

4. $\frac{57}{100}$
5. 1 to 100
6. 55:100
7. $\frac{79}{100}$
8. 23 to 100
9. 10:100
10. 61 to 100
11. 75:100
12. $\frac{100}{100}$
13. 5 to 100

Write each percentage as a fraction that has a denominator of 100.

14. 16%
15. 98%
16. 3%
17. 25%
18. 47%
19. 9%
20. 50%
21. 88%
22. 33%
23. 65%

Apply

24. Mrs. Hammond has driven 33 of 100 miles. What percent of the drive remains?

25. Isamu answered 83 out of 100 problems correctly. Write his grade as a percentage.

26. Six percent of the students picked planets as a topic. What percentage did not pick planets?

Review

Solve. Write the answer in simplest form.

27. $9\frac{6}{8} - 6\frac{2}{3}$
28. $10\frac{5}{6} - 4\frac{1}{2}$
29. $16\frac{4}{9} - 3\frac{3}{4}$
30. $13\frac{3}{6} - 2$
31. $21\frac{1}{2} - 5\frac{1}{3}$
32. $31 - 11\frac{3}{22}$
33. $7 - 5\frac{1}{2}$

11.7 Ratio and Percent

Construct Meaning

Mrs. Kirkland asked two fifth-grade classes which pet they preferred, cats or dogs. She found that $\frac{17}{50}$ preferred cats.

What percent of the students preferred cats?

Percent means per one hundred. If a ratio has a denominator of 100, it is easy to express it as a percentage.

1. **Write the ratio as a fraction.** $\frac{17}{50}$ ← number that preferred cats / ← total students surveyed
2. **Write a proportion in which one ratio has a denominator of 100.** $\frac{17}{50} = \frac{t}{100}$
3. **Solve the proportion by using multiplication or cross products.** $\frac{17}{50} = \frac{t}{100}$ (× 2, × 2) $t = 34$
4. **Rewrite the fraction as a percentage.** $\frac{34}{100} = 34\%$

34% of the students preferred cats.

Check Understanding

Copy and complete the chart.

	ratio	proportion	solution	percent
a.	$\frac{9}{25}$	$\frac{9}{25} = \frac{n}{100}$	$\frac{9}{25} = \frac{\ }{100}$ (× , ×)	___%
b.	$\frac{7}{20}$	$\frac{7}{20} = \frac{x}{100}$	$\frac{7}{20} = \frac{\ }{100}$ (× , ×)	___%
c.	$\frac{3}{5}$	$\frac{3}{5} = \frac{a}{\ }$	$\frac{3}{5} = \frac{\ }{\ }$ (× , ×)	___%

Practice

Write a percentage to tell how much of each set is made up of dark gray cats.

1. 

2. 

Write each ratio as a percent.

3. 8 to 100

4. 6:10

5. $\frac{1}{5}$

6. $\frac{3}{4}$

7. $\frac{11}{25}$

8. 19:20

9. $\frac{55}{100}$

10. $\frac{24}{25}$

11. $\frac{7}{10}$

12. $\frac{1}{4}$

Apply

13. Mrs. Kirkland surveyed a fourth-grade class to see which animal they liked better, cats or dogs. She found that 12 of the 25 students liked dogs better. What percentage of the fourth-grade class liked dogs?

14. Kiptyn opened a package of cookies for a party. By the end of the party, the guests had eaten $\frac{2}{5}$ of the cookies. What percent of the cookies were eaten?

15. A mosaic includes the colors silver, black, red, and white. If 69% of the mosaic is silver, what percentage is not silver?

Review

Write each fraction in simplest form.

16. $\frac{28}{35}$

17. $\frac{18}{36}$

18. $\frac{10}{25}$

19. $\frac{49}{63}$

20. $\frac{48}{54}$

21. $\frac{9}{60}$

22. $\frac{24}{32}$

23. $\frac{27}{81}$

24. $\frac{40}{72}$

25. $\frac{60}{100}$

11.8 Fractions and Percent

Construct Meaning

Akio's class recently voted for class president. Two-fourths of the class voted for Akio and two-fifths voted for one of his opponents. Which candidate received the larger percentage of the votes?

You can write a fraction as a percent.

Percent means per one hundred. For each ratio, find an equal fraction with a denominator of 100.

$$\frac{2}{4} \xrightarrow{\times 25} = \frac{50}{100} = 50\% \qquad \frac{2}{5} \xrightarrow{\times 20} = \frac{40}{100} = 40\%$$

$$50\% > 40\%$$

Akio received the larger percent of votes.

You can write a percentage as a fraction that has a denominator of 100. Then, write the fraction in simplest form.

On a test of 20 spelling words, Asha received a 90% and Carissa had 18 correct answers. Which student had the higher score?

Asha	Carissa
$90\% = \frac{90}{100} = \frac{9}{10}$	$\frac{18}{20} = \frac{9}{10} = \frac{90}{100} = 90\%$
percent → fraction	fraction → percent

Both students had $\frac{9}{10}$ of the problems correct. Both had scores of 90%.

Check Understanding

Write a percent and a fraction in simplest form for each model.

a. 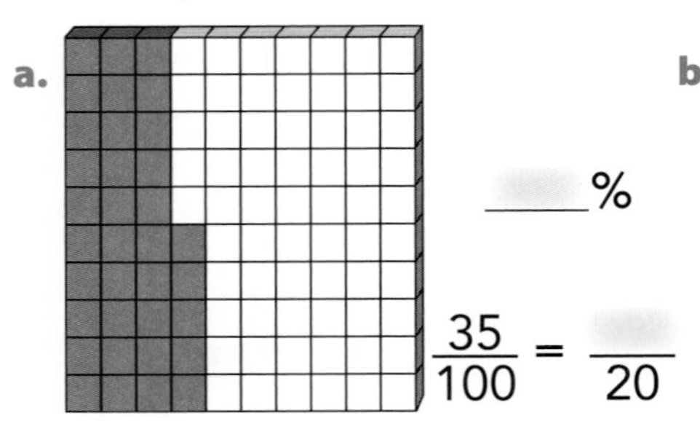

____%

$\frac{35}{100} = \frac{\_\_\_}{20}$

b. 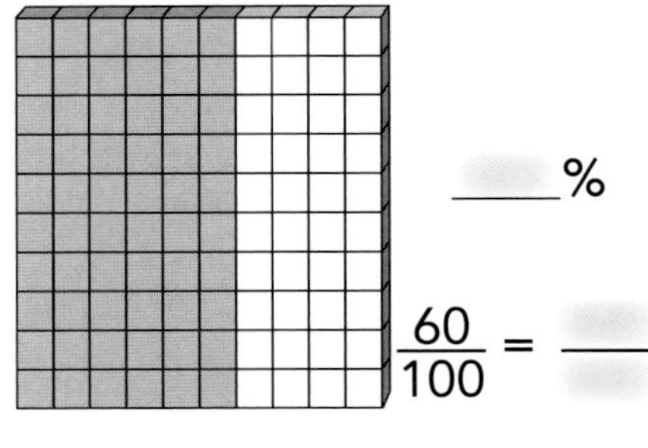

____%

$\frac{60}{100} = \frac{\_\_\_}{\_\_\_}$

c. 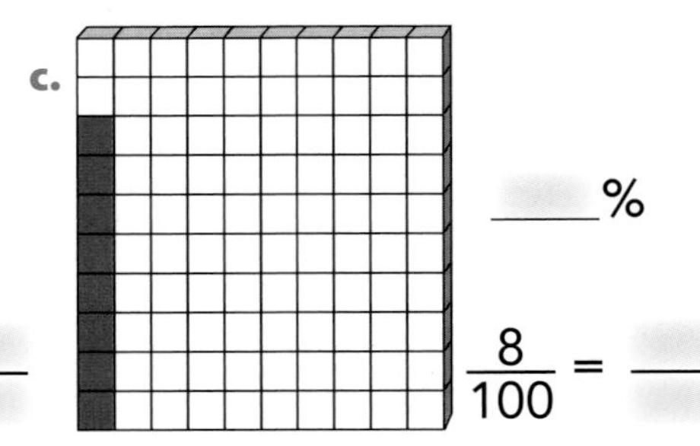

____%

$\frac{8}{100} = \frac{\_\_\_}{\_\_\_}$

d. Write $\frac{2}{8}$ as a percentage. Hint: Write the fraction in simplest form first.

e. Write 16% as a fraction in simplest form.

Practice

Write each fraction as a percent. If needed, first write the fraction in simplest form.

1. $\frac{1}{4}$
2. $\frac{1}{2}$
3. $\frac{2}{5}$
4. $\frac{4}{4}$
5. $\frac{7}{10}$
6. $\frac{4}{5}$
7. $\frac{3}{4}$
8. $\frac{9}{100}$
9. $\frac{17}{20}$
10. $\frac{30}{50}$
11. $\frac{16}{25}$
12. $\frac{24}{30}$
13. $\frac{8}{25}$
14. $\frac{11}{50}$
15. $\frac{18}{90}$

Write each percentage as a fraction in simplest form.

16. 40%
17. 85%
18. 16%
19. 4%
20. 25%
21. 75%
22. 30%
23. 50%
24. 60%
25. 42%
26. 12%
27. 58%
28. 20%
29. 5%
30. 15%

Apply

31. A new cell-phone cover comes in six colors. If 20% of the order from the store was for the green color, what part of the order was for the other colors? Show the answer as a fraction in simplest form.

32. Red was the most popular color. If nine of the 12 covers bought were red, what percent of the covers sold were red?

33. Fujita completed $\frac{1}{3}$ of a project before dinner and $\frac{1}{4}$ after dinner. Is he closer to having the assignment half done or totally finished?

Review

Change each fraction to a mixed number. Then, write it in simplest form.

34. $\frac{160}{50}$
35. $\frac{24}{11}$
36. $\frac{14}{6}$
37. $\frac{62}{30}$
38. $\frac{175}{100}$
39. $\frac{80}{50}$
40. $\frac{65}{25}$

11.9 Decimals and Percent

Construct Meaning

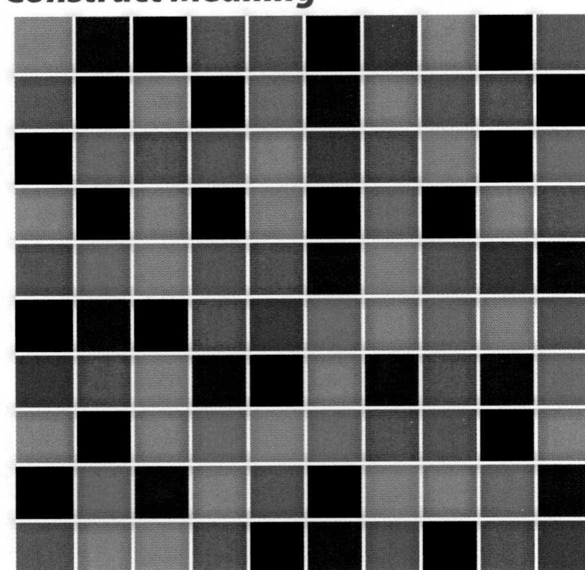

Look at the grid of 100 squares. What percent of the large square is blue? Count the squares. There are six blue squares. Write this as a fraction, as a decimal, and as a percentage.

$$6 \text{ out of } 100 = \frac{6}{100}$$

Remember that a fraction bar represents division. Divide the numerator by the denominator to express a fraction as a decimal.

$$\begin{array}{r} 0.06 \\ 100\overline{)6.00} \\ -6\,00 \\ \hline 0 \end{array}$$

How do you write six-hundredths as a percent? Use the model to read the decimal as a percent.

$$\frac{6}{100} = 0.06 = \mathbf{6\%}$$

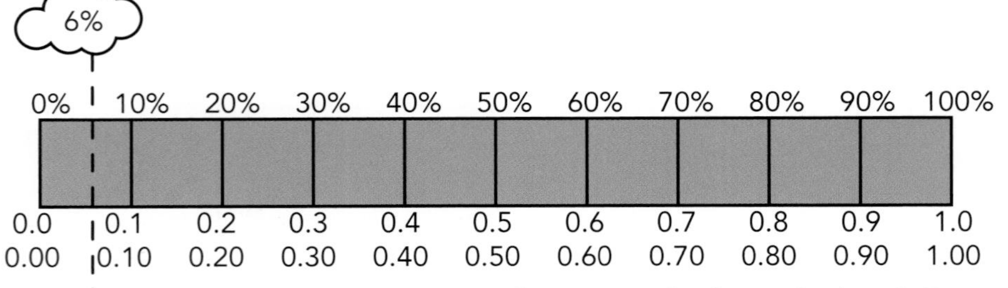

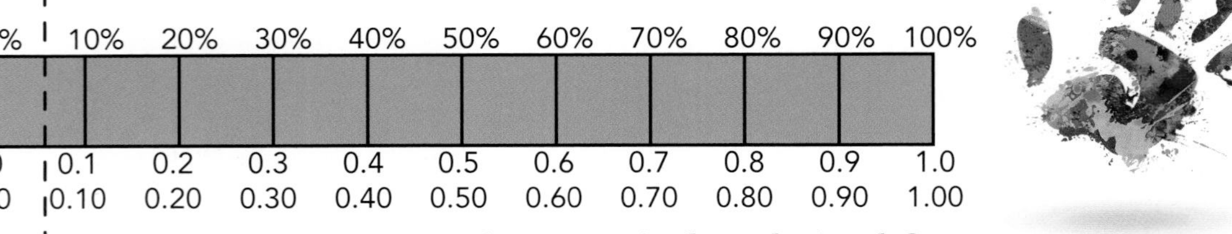

Why are 0.2 and 0.20 equivalent decimals?

The decimals 0.2 and 0.20 are equivalent decimals because they represent the same percentage.

How would you write 120% as a decimal?

120% = 1.2

Check Understanding

Copy and complete each chart.

	fraction	decimal	percent
a.	$\frac{15}{100}$		
b.	$\frac{7}{10}$		
c.		0.34	
d.			3%

	fraction	decimal	percent
e.		0.90	
f.	$\frac{2}{100}$		
g.		0.08	
h.		1.00	

Practice

Write the percent of one dollar (100 cents) represented by the coins.

1. 3 dimes, 4 nickels
2. 1 quarter, 1 dime
3. 3 nickels, 4 pennies
4. 3 quarters
5. 5 dimes, 3 nickels
6. 1 quarter, 2 pennies

Write each decimal as a percentage.

7. 0.30
8. 0.04
9. 0.4
10. 0.64
11. 0.1
12. 0.01
13. 0.18
14. 0.53
15. 0.8
16. 0.25

Write each percent as a decimal.

17. 15%
18. 76%
19. 2%
20. 93%
21. 60%
22. 26%
23. 10%
24. 88%
25. 6%
26. 33%

Apply

Choose the most reasonable answer.

27. Asmita has written _____ of her research paper.

30% 110% $\frac{4}{3}$

28. Bryson's department store is having a sale. Everything is marked at _____ off.

100% 25% 1%

29. During a certain lunar phase, about 0.20 or _____ of the moon's surface can be seen.

2% 20% 200%

Challenge

30. Breathable air has four main parts. Find the sum of the following portions: 78% nitrogen, 21% oxygen, 0.9% argon, and 0.03% carbon dioxide. Then, subtract it from 100% to find the amount of water vapor and other elements in small amounts that are part of the air. Write your answer as a percent. _____

Review

Divide.

31. $7\overline{)2.457}$
32. $6\overline{)0.042}$
33. $5\overline{)1.505}$
34. $4\overline{)3.564}$
35. $3\overline{)2.79}$
36. $9\overline{)0.8172}$

11.10 Mental Math: Estimate Percent

Construct Meaning

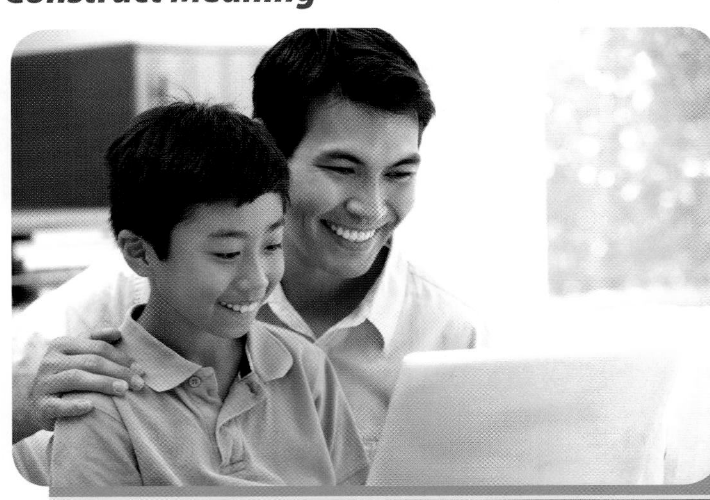

Kiaan's dad said about 9% of his salary is taken from his pay each month for taxes. His dad earns $4,245 each month. What is the estimated amount he takes home after taxes?

To estimate, round dollars and percentages to the greatest place value.

Think:
$4,245 is about $4,000.
9% is about 10%.

Remember that 10% can be written as $\frac{10}{100}$, which is $\frac{1}{10}$ when written in simplest form.

Think

$$10\% \text{ of } \$4,000 = \frac{1}{10} \times 4,000 = \frac{1}{10} \times \frac{4,000}{1} = \frac{4,000}{10} = \$400$$

Subtract.

$$\begin{array}{r} \$4,000 \\ -\quad 400 \\ \hline \$3,600 \end{array}$$

Kiaan's father takes home about $3,600 per month.

Compare your answer to the model drawn below.

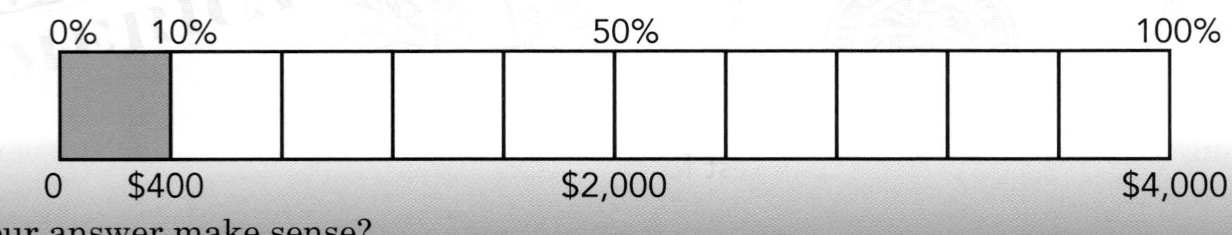

Does your answer make sense?

If you know 10% of a number, you can mentally calculate a percentage that is a multiple of 10.

Find 50% of 150.

$$10\% \text{ of } 150 = \frac{1}{10} \times \frac{150}{1} = \frac{150}{10} = 15$$

$$50\% \text{ of } 150 = 5 \times 15 = 75$$

Find 20% of 80.

$$10\% \text{ of } 80 = \frac{1}{10} \times \frac{80}{1} = \frac{80}{10} = \_\_\_\_$$

$$20\% \text{ of } 80 = 2 \times \_\_\_\_ = \_\_\_\_$$

What is 100% of 5,600?

Remember that 100% is equal to one!

5,600

Check Understanding

Use mental math to find each percent of 500.

a. 10% b. 50% c. 20% d. 70% e. 40%

Practice

Use mental math to find each answer.

1. 10% of 40
2. 50% of 30
3. 20% of 350
4. 80% of 50
5. 10% of 1,000
6. 50% of 250
7. 40% of 700
8. 100% of 210

Estimate each answer by rounding to the highest place value.

9. 80% of 97
10. 30% of 61
11. 39% of 89
12. 51% of 203

Apply

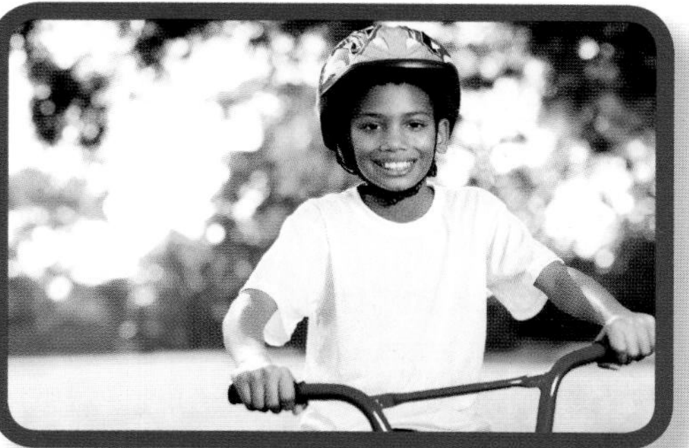

13. Iker wants to buy a bike helmet that costs $29.95. The store has a 30% off sale. How much would he save on the helmet during the sale?
14. For Khaleesi's birthday meal, the bill was $61.53. The restaurant suggested a 20% tip. How much is the tip?
15. In Belle Valley, 10% of the days in September had some rain. Was this more or less than five days?
16. Jia has $60. The bicycle he wants to buy costs 70% of the original price of $90. Does he have enough money?

Review

Subtract. Write the difference in simplest form.

17. $\frac{3}{5} - \frac{2}{10}$
18. $\frac{6}{8} - \frac{1}{3}$
19. $\frac{2}{5} - \frac{3}{15}$
20. $\frac{3}{4} - \frac{8}{16}$
21. $\frac{2}{3} - \frac{3}{9}$
22. $\frac{5}{6} - \frac{6}{24}$
23. $5\frac{2}{3} - 2\frac{2}{5}$
24. $16\frac{3}{4} - 7\frac{5}{9}$

11.11 Find Percent

Construct Meaning

An airline decided to change the paint on its planes. It repainted about 15% of its 80 planes during the first year. What was the number of planes that were repainted?

Find 15% × 80.

Three Methods

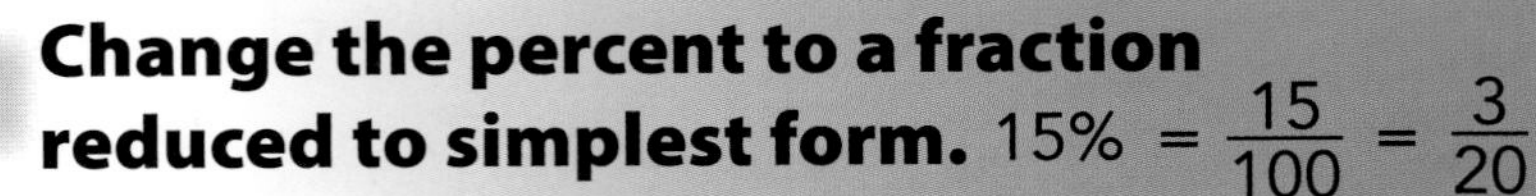

1 Change the percent to a fraction reduced to simplest form. $15\% = \frac{15}{100} = \frac{3}{20}$

Multiply. $\frac{3}{20} \times \frac{80}{1} = \frac{240}{20} =$ **12 planes**

2 Change the percent to a decimal.

$15\% = \frac{15}{100} = 0.15$

$$\begin{array}{r} 80 \\ \times\, 0.15 \\ \hline 400 \\ 800 \\ \hline 12.00 \end{array}$$

Multiply.

Remember to place the decimal.

12 planes

3 Use a calculator.

8 0 × 1 5 % = 12.

12 planes

By each method, the answer is 12 planes.

Find 25% of 540.
First, solve by using a fraction. $25\% = \frac{25}{100} = \frac{1}{4}$ $\quad \frac{1}{4} \times \frac{540}{1} = \frac{540}{4} = 135$

Next, solve by using a decimal.
Check with a calculator. $25\% = \frac{25}{100} = 0.25$ $\quad 0.25 \times 540 = 135$

When finding a percentage, it is often easier to write the percent as a fraction. For example, 25% is $\frac{1}{4}$ and 75% is $\frac{3}{4}$. At other times, it is easier to convert the percentage to a decimal. Use multiplication to solve for both.

Check Understanding

Choose the correct solution.

a. 60% of 1,200	72	720	7.2
b. 5% of 300	150	1.5	15
c. 25% of 900	225	2.25	22.5
d. 40% of 70	2.8	28	280
e. 50% of 3,500	175	17.5	1,750

Practice

Find the percentage of each number.

1. 1% of 100
2. 10% of 100
3. 40% of 340
4. 20% of 60
5. 30% of 210
6. 25% of 600
7. 50% of 62
8. 35% of 80
9. 100% of 19
10. 2% of 2,600
11. 30% of 40
12. 75% of 84
13. 60% of 365
14. 75% of 52
15. 19% of 500
16. 80% of 225
17. 75% of 12
18. 80% of 40
19. 34% of 700
20. 20% of 85

Compare. Write >, <, or =.

21. 15% of 120 ◯ 5% of 300
22. 12% of 400 ◯ 35% of 160
23. 25% of 84 ◯ 30% of 80
24. 60% of 120 ◯ 40% of 180

Apply

Find the sale price for each item.

25. camera: originally \$75, on sale at 28% off the regular price
26. luggage: originally \$80, now at 15% discount
27. computer: original price, \$980, on sale at 20% off

Review

Estimate the product by rounding each factor to the greatest place value. Multiply.

28. 5.6 × 2.3
29. 4.67 × 4.4
30. 8.34 × 5.44

11.12 Problem Solving: Percent

Practice

Calculating sales tax is one use of percent. Amari is helping his parents pick a birthday gift for his brother, Dhia. Sales tax where Amari lives is 6%.

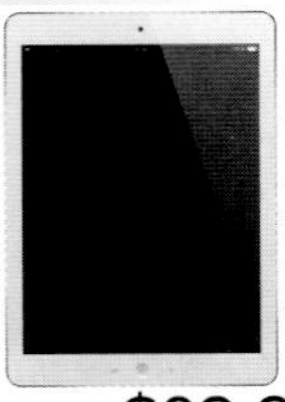

What will each item below cost after adding sales tax? Round each sales tax amount to the nearest cent.

1. art set
2. trading card case
3. tablet
4. digital music player

5. If the tablet is on sale at 20% off, what will be the total cost at the discounted price?

Another use of percent is a tip given for service.
Find the total paid for the service, including tip. Round to the nearest cent.

6. haircut: $14.95, 15% tip
7. soup, salad, and drink: $7.30, 13% tip
8. pizza delivery: $11.95, 10% tip
9. hotel parking: $9.00, 15% tip

Salespeople often earn a commission, or a percentage, of each sale.
Find the commission on each sale.

10. house: sold for $149,000, 7% commission
11. car: sold for $22,775, 4% commission
12. office building: sold for $565,000, 5% commission
13. truck: sold for $19,400, 3% commission

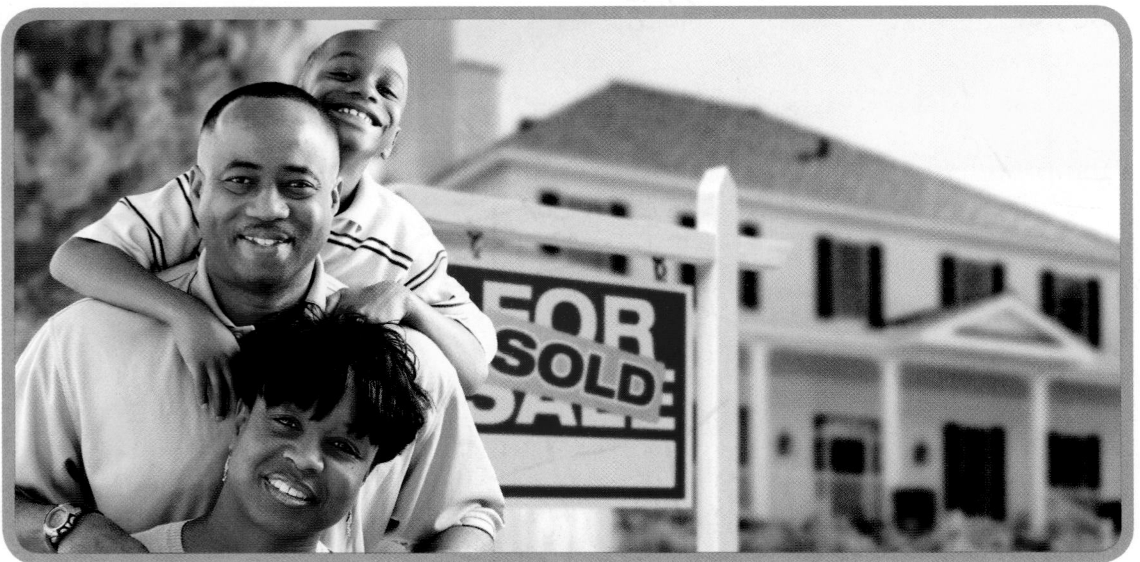

Percentage is used to find interest. People who borrow money pay extra money called interest. For example, Mr. Christman borrowed $1,500 at 12% interest. Find the interest owed for one year.

Money borrowed (principal) $1,500
Rate of interest ⟶ 12% annually

1,500 × 0.12 = $180 interest for 1 year
Total amount owed: $1,500 + $180 = $1,680

14. $1,000 at 13%
15. $2,500 at 9%
16. $4,000 at 18%
17. $7,500 at 15%
18. $875 at 12%
19. $10,000 at 8%

Interest is added to the amount of money to be repaid.

For Exercises 20 through 25, add the interest to the principal in Exercises 14 through 19. Find the total amount owed at the end of one year.

20. $1,000 at 13%
21. $2,500 at 9%
22. $4,000 at 18%
23. $7,500 at 15%
24. $875 at 12%
25. $10,000 at 8%

When a person saves money, he earns interest, which is added to the amount saved.

Find the interest earned for one year.

26. $750 at 4%
27. $1,200 at 5%
28. $5,550 at 7%
29. $925 at 6%

Use the amounts from above and find the total amount saved at the end of one year.

30. $750 at 4%
31. $1,200 at 5%
32. $5,550 at 7%
33. $925 at 6%

Review

Complete the proportion.

34. $\frac{1}{3} = \frac{}{36}$
35. $\frac{5}{10} = \frac{}{100}$
36. $\frac{2}{8} = \frac{}{88}$
37. $\frac{2}{3} = \frac{}{60}$
38. $\frac{4}{6} = \frac{}{90}$

11.13 Chapter 11 Review

Write each ratio two different ways.

1. 3:4
2. 6 to 8
3. 13 out of 21
4. $\frac{5}{6}$

Write the next two equal ratios.

5. $\frac{9}{11}$
6. $\frac{3}{2}$
7. $\frac{4}{5}$
8. $\frac{8}{6}$
9. $\frac{4}{7}$

Are the ratios proportional? Write = or ≠.

10. $\frac{2}{6} \bigcirc \frac{6}{18}$
11. $\frac{4}{17} \bigcirc \frac{8}{35}$
12. $\frac{8}{11} \bigcirc \frac{14}{22}$
13. $\frac{16}{3} \bigcirc \frac{48}{9}$

Find the missing number in each proportion.

14. $\frac{12}{45} = \frac{n}{15}$
15. $\frac{3}{8} = \frac{9}{n}$
16. $\frac{9}{n} = \frac{1}{3}$
17. $\frac{n}{6} = \frac{6}{12}$
18. $\frac{1}{3} = \frac{n}{30}$
19. $\frac{7}{n} = \frac{28}{16}$
20. $\frac{n}{5} = \frac{15}{25}$
21. $\frac{3}{4} = \frac{36}{n}$

Write each ratio as a percent.

22. 48:100
23. $\frac{24}{100}$
24. 35:100
25. $\frac{6}{100}$

Write each percentage as a decimal.

26. 88%
27. 54%
28. 7%
29. 1%

Write each percentage as a fraction in simplest form.

30. 30%
31. 50%
32. 75%
33. 62%

Solve.

34. A standing mirror costs $24.95. Sales tax is 6%. What is the total cost? Round the sales tax to the nearest cent.

35. It takes about 7% of a year for the moon to orbit Earth. How many days does it take to orbit Earth? Round to the nearest day.

now hiring

36. The sales manager reported that when the sale began, there were 250 pairs of shoes on the clearance racks. About 30% have been sold. How many pairs are left?

37. About 700 new employees will be hired by the Topcomp Company. Of the jobs, about 25% will be in customer service. How many will be customer service employees?

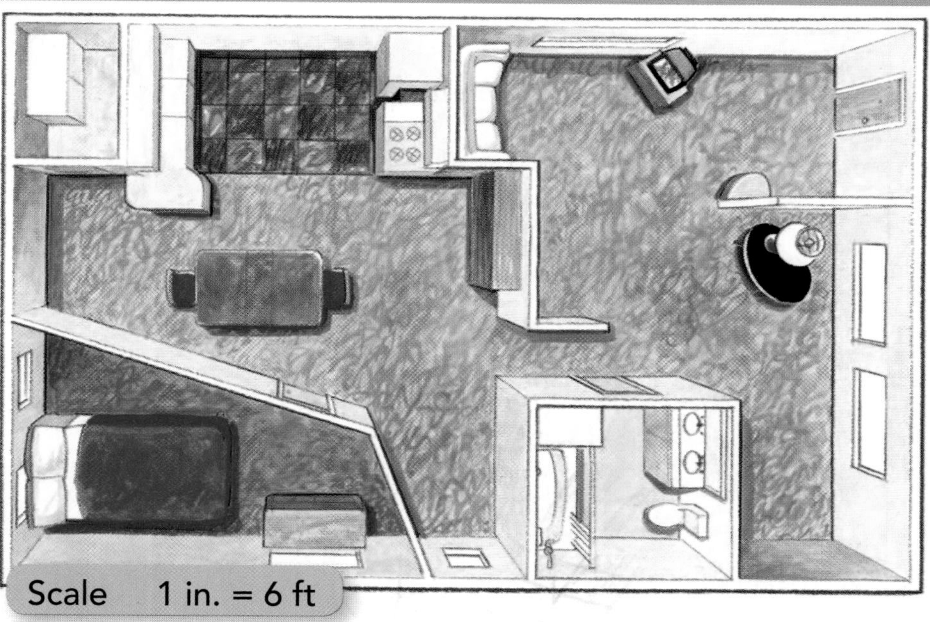

38. Each inch in this floor plan represents 6 ft in the actual apartment. About how long is the actual bed?

39. Write a proportion and solve to find the approximate length of the actual floor from wall to wall.

40. Will a rug that is 5 ft wide and 8 ft long fit on the floor of the kitchen?

C
F
50
40
30
20
10
0
10
20
120
100
80
60
40
20
0

Chapter 12
Measurement

Do you not know? Have you not heard? The Lord
is the everlasting God, the Creator of the ends of
the earth. He will not grow tired or weary, and
His understanding no one can fathom.
Isaiah 40:28

Key Ideas:

Measurement: US customary and metric length, capacity, weight, and temperature

Time: telling time to the nearest minute

Time: understanding timetables, schedules, and time zones

Time: elapsed time

12.1 Customary Units of Length

Construct Meaning

Lottie's class took a trip to the Hoh Rain Forest in Olympic National Park, Washington. The guide explained that a meteorologist (a scientist who studies weather) measures the amount of rain that falls in the forest. Each year Hoh Rain Forest receives about 150 inches of rain. Lottie's teacher asked the class to determine how many feet of rainfall that was.

When you know the number of inches, you can determine the number of feet. To change a smaller unit such as inches to a larger unit such as feet, consider the relationship between the two units.

Customary Units of Length
12 inches (in. or ") = 1 foot (ft or ')
3 feet = 1 yard (yd)
36 inches = 1 yard
5,280 feet = 1 mile (mi)
1,760 yards = 1 mile

12 inches = 1 foot

Divide the total number of inches by 12.

Divide.

$$\begin{array}{r} 12\text{R}\,6 \\ 12\overline{)150} \\ -12 \\ \hline 30 \\ -24 \\ \hline 6 \end{array}$$

6 ← extra inches

Check.

$$\begin{array}{r} 12 \\ \times 12 \\ \hline 144 \\ +\ \ 6 \\ \hline 150 \end{array}$$

About 12 feet 6 inches of rain fall in Hoh Rain Forest each year.

Another rain forest receives 14 feet 3 inches of rain annually. How many inches of rain is that? Consider the relationship between the two units.

Step 1 Since one foot is equal to 12 inches, multiply the number of feet by 12.

14 ← number of feet
×12 ← number of inches in 1 foot
168 ← number of inches in 14 feet

Step 2 Add the number of inches in 14 feet to the number of inches in the original measurement.

168 ← inches in 14 feet
+ 3 ← inches from original measurement
171 ← total inches in 14 feet 3 inches

The rain forest receives 171 inches of rain annually.

Check Understanding

Multiply or divide to complete each equation.

a. 81 in. = ____ ft ____ in.
b. 46 in. = ____ ft ____ in.
c. 16 ft = ____ in.
d. 13 ft 4 in. = ____ in.
e. 7 ft 2 in. = ____ in.
f. 144 in. = ____ ft

Practice

Complete.

Example:

2 yd 1 ft = 7 ft

Multiply.
2 yards
×3 feet in one yard
6 feet in 2 yards

Add.
6 feet in 2 yards
+1 foot from the measurement
7 feet total

1. 5 yd = ____ ft
2. 7 yd 2 ft = ____ ft
3. 4 yd = ____ in.
4. 2 yd 1 ft = ____ in.
5. 39 in. = ____ yd ____ in.
6. 5 ft = ____ yd ____ ft
7. 4 mi = ____ yd
8. 3 mi = ____ ft
9. 112 in. = ____ ft ____ in.
10. 8 ft = ____ in.

This leaf is 6 inches long to the nearest inch. It is 6 inches to the nearest $\frac{1}{2}$ inch. It is $5\frac{3}{4}$ to the nearest $\frac{1}{4}$ inch. It is $5\frac{7}{8}$ to the nearest $\frac{1}{8}$ inch and $5\frac{13}{16}$ inches to the nearest $\frac{1}{16}$ inch.

Use your ruler to draw each line.

11. $1\frac{3}{4}$ in.
12. $4\frac{1}{16}$ in.
13. $\frac{1}{4}$ in.
14. $8\frac{1}{2}$ in.
15. $9\frac{1}{8}$ in.

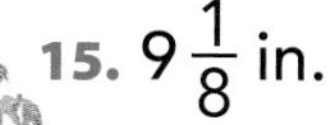

Apply

16. Lisa's curtain pattern calls for 6 yards 2 feet of fabric. She only has a 12-inch ruler to measure with. What is the total number of feet Lisa should cut?

17. Robert measured two saplings in his yard. One stood $7\frac{1}{2}$ inches tall. The other was $7\frac{3}{8}$ inches. Which sapling was taller?

12.2 Customary Units of Capacity

Construct Meaning

Water is extremely important for all of life. Did you know that 71% of the earth is covered by water? Most of that water is found in the oceans. Each day there are about 3 quadrillion gallons of water in the clouds of the atmosphere. About 4 trillion gallons of this water fall on the United States as precipitation each day. Consider the marvelous ingenuity of God, who created a way to suspend that amount and weight of water in the air and cause it to rain down in drops rather than all at once!

Nancy bought a fish tank that has a capacity of 40 gallons. Use the table below to find the number of quarts in 40 gallons.

To change larger units (gallons) to smaller units (quarts), multiply.

1 gallon = 4 quarts

Multiply the number of gallons by 4.

$40 \times 4 = 160$ qt

Customary Units of Capacity
3 teaspoons (tsp) = 1 tablespoon (tbsp)
8 fluid ounces (fl oz) = 1 cup (c)
2 cups = 1 pint (pt)
2 pints = 1 quart (qt)
4 quarts = 1 gallon (gal)

There are 160 quarts in 40 gallons.

Nash has 6 pints of juice. How many quart jars can he fill?
To change smaller units (pints) to larger units (quarts), divide.
Since 2 pints equal 1 quart, divide the number of pints by 2.

$6 \div 2 = 3$ qt 6 pints = 3 quarts

Nash can fill 3 quart jars.

If you have 8 cups of juice and your friend has 3 pints, who has the greater amount of juice?

Check Understanding

Complete.

a. 16 fluid ounces = _____ cups b. 10 tablespoons = _____ teaspoons

Write >, < or =.

c. 6 pints _____ 12 cups d. 30 quarts _____ 8 gallons

Practice

Complete the equation.

1. 48 fl oz = _____ c
2. 6 qt = _____ pt
3. 24 qt = _____ gal
4. 15 tbsp = _____ tsp
5. 4 gal = _____ qt
6. 12 pt = _____ c
7. 8 c = _____ pt
8. 16 pt = _____ qt
9. 3 c = _____ fl oz

Example:

Sometimes changing the units takes more than one step.

Change 16 pints to gallons.

- First, change 16 pints to quarts. $16 \div 2 = 8$ 16 pt = 8 qt
- Next, change 8 quarts to gallons. $8 \div 4 = 2$ 8 qt = 2 gal
- Write the equivalent measurement. **16 pints = 2 gallons**

Change 6 gallons to cups.

- First, change 6 gallons to quarts. $6 \times 4 = 24$ 6 gal = 24 qt
- Next, change 24 quarts to pints. $24 \times 2 = 48$ 24 qt = 48 pt
- Then, change 48 pints to cups. $48 \times 2 = 96$ 48 pt = 96 c
- Write the equivalent measurement. **16 gallons = 96 cups**

Use the examples above and the table of customary units of capacity to complete each equivalent measurement.

10. 24 pt = _____ gal
11. 8 qt = _____ c
12. 48 c = _____ gal
13. 56 c = _____ qt
14. 4 gal = _____ pt
15. 8 gal = _____ c

Apply

16. Paige's math class was planning a celebration. She signed up to bring enough juice for everyone in her class. Paige determined she would need two gallons of juice. How many cups of juice was that?

17. Paige's friend Zhu brought 40 cups of snack mix for the celebration. How many quarts of snack mix was that?

12.3 Customary Units of Weight

Construct Meaning

Precipitation comes in many forms. One type of precipitation is hail. When rain falls from the clouds and is held in the atmosphere by wind, it freezes because of the cold temperatures in the sky. More cold water freezes onto these tiny pieces of ice, and hail is formed. Hail can fall to the earth in various sizes.

After a big hailstorm, Misty decided to collect and weigh 16 hailstones that were all about the same size. Each hailstone weighed about 5 ounces. What was the total weight of the hail in pounds?

Customary Units of Weight
16 ounces (oz) = 1 pound (lb)
2,000 pounds = 1 ton (T)

Look at the customary units of weight table. First, multiply the number of hailstones by the weight of one hailstone.

16 × 5 ounces = 80 ounces

Next, divide the total ounces by the number of ounces in 1 pound.

$$\begin{array}{r} 5 \\ 16\overline{)80} \\ -80 \\ \hline 0 \end{array}$$

5 ← pounds in 80 ounces

ounces in one pound → 16

80 ← total ounces

16 hailstones weigh about 5 pounds.

To change larger units (pounds) to smaller units (ounces), multiply.
To change smaller units (ounces) to larger units (pounds), divide.

Check Understanding

Choose the equivalent amount from the Answer Bank.

a. 4 lb
b. 144 oz
c. 3 T
d. 10,000 lb
e. 2 lb
f. 96 oz

Answer Bank

9 lb	6,000 lb
32 oz	64 oz
5 T	6 lb

Practice

Complete the equation.

1. 112 oz = ____ lb
2. 15 lb = ____ oz
3. 6 T = ____ lb
4. 32,000 lb = ____ T
5. 560 oz = ____ lb
6. 58 lb = ____ oz
7. 1,072 lb = ____ oz
8. 1,568 oz = ____ lb
9. 14 T = ____ lb

Complete the equation.

Example:

6 lb 8 oz = 104 oz

Multiply to find the number of ounces in 6 pounds.

6 × 16 oz = 96 oz

Add the ounces in 6 pounds (96) to the ounces from the original measurement (8).

96 oz + 8 oz = 104 oz

10. 9 lb 10 oz = ____ oz
11. 12 lb 4 oz = ____ oz
12. 24 lb 6 oz = ____ oz
13. 71 lb 11 oz = ____ oz
14. 127 lb 3 oz = ____ oz
15. 154 lb 9 oz = ____ oz

Write each measurement in pounds.

16. 7 T
17. 1,424 oz
18. 11 T
19. 400 oz
20. 832 oz
21. 688 oz
22. 42 T
23. 2,000 oz

Apply

24. Melitta's little sister weighs 17 lb 12 oz. How many ounces does she weigh?

25. Yeni is helping her grandfather make potato salad. The recipe calls for 48 oz of potatoes. How many pounds of potatoes should they purchase?

Challenge

26. Tate weighs three times more than his sister. He weighs 84 lb. How many pounds does Tate's sister weigh?

27. Five more than six times Liana's weight is 317 pounds. What is Liana's weight?

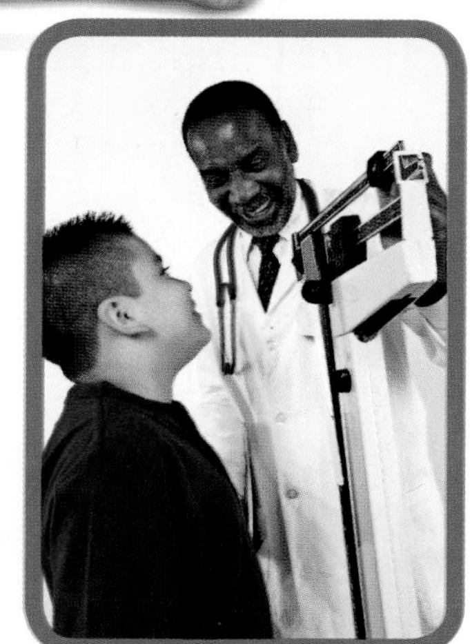

12.4 Metric Units of Length

Construct Meaning

The amount of new snowfall received at ski resorts is important to skiers. Each day, ski resorts report the amount of snow that has fallen within the last 24 hours. Sunlight Mountain Resort reported 22 cm of new snowfall. Change the number of centimeters to millimeters. Use the table of metric units of length to convert the units.

Metric Units of Length
10 millimeters (mm) = 1 centimeter (cm)
10 centimeters = 1 decimeter (dm)
10 decimeters = 1 meter (m)
100 centimeters = 1 meter
1,000 meters = 1 kilometer (km)

Multiply to change larger units to smaller units.
Because there are 10 millimeters in one centimeter, multiply the number of centimeters by 10.

22 × 10 = 220 mm
22 cm = 220 mm

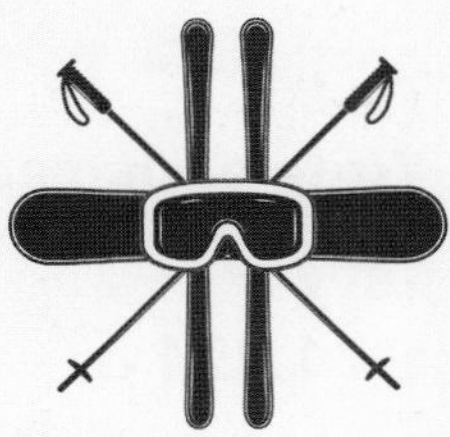

220 mm of snow had fallen.

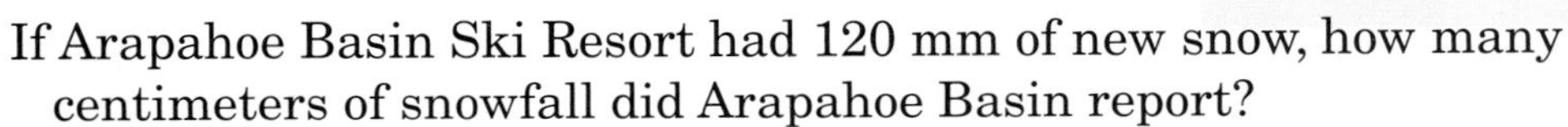

If Arapahoe Basin Ski Resort had 120 mm of new snow, how many centimeters of snowfall did Arapahoe Basin report?

Divide to change smaller units to larger units.
Because there are 10 millimeters in one centimeter, divide the number of millimeters by 10.

120 ÷ 10 = 12 cm
120 mm = 12 cm

12 cm of snow were reported.

Change 326 mm to centimeters. Since there are 10 millimeters in one centimeter, divide 326 millimeters by 10.

$$10\overline{)326.0} = 32.6 \text{ cm}$$

Check Understanding

Complete the equation.

a. 13 cm = _____ mm
b. 145 mm = _____ cm
c. 380 mm = _____ cm
d. 63 cm 5 mm = _____ mm
e. 35.3 cm = _____ mm
f. 178 mm = _____ cm

Practice

Complete the equation.

Example:

5.2 m = 52 dm

Multiply.

$$\begin{array}{r} 5.2 \\ \times\ 10 \\ \hline 00 \\ 52\ \\ \hline 52.0 \end{array}$$

5.2 ← meters
10 ← decimeters in 1 meter
52.0 ← decimeters

1. 3 km = _____ m
2. 15 m = _____ dm
3. 24 cm = _____ mm
4. 6.5 cm = _____ mm
5. 6 m = _____ cm
6. 4,200 m = _____ km
7. 37 dm = _____ m
8. 450 cm = _____ dm
9. 3.4 m = _____ dm
10. 8.9 dm = _____ cm

Use a metric ruler to draw each line.

11. 20 mm
12. 5 cm
13. 5 mm
14. 38 mm

Apply

15. A snowdrift in the mountains was 1.5 m deep. Write the equivalent amount of snow in centimeters.

16. A cross-country skier covered 100 m in one minute. If he maintained that speed, how long would it take him to ski 1 km?

Review

17. $9\overline{)7.2}$
18. $6\overline{)0.54}$
19. $4\overline{)0.084}$
20. $3\overline{)6.33}$
21. $8\overline{)3.20}$
22. $7\overline{)0.0049}$
23. $5\overline{)0.0095}$
24. 5.87 ÷ 10
25. 19.23 ÷ 10
26. 5.6 ÷ 10
27. 564.4 ÷ 100
28. 5.66 ÷ 100

12.5 Metric Units of Capacity

Construct Meaning

When Taylor's baby sister was sick, her mother gave her medicine with a medicine dropper. A medicine dropper holds about one milliliter of liquid. It takes 1,000 milliliters to fill a 1-liter milk carton. How many milliliters are in a 2-liter bottle of soda?

Metric Units of Capacity
1,000 milliliters (mL) = 1 liter (L)

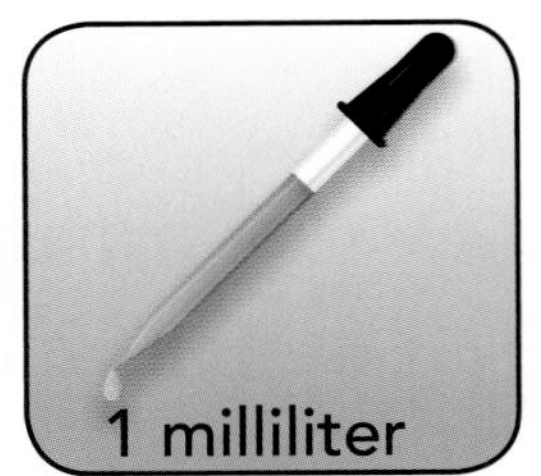

1 milliliter

1 liter

2 liters

Since 1 liter equals 1,000 milliliters, multiply 2 by 1,000.

2 × 1,000 = 2,000 mL **It would take 2,000 milliliters to fill a 2-liter bottle.**

How many liters equal 4,000 milliliters? Because there are 1,000 milliliters in 1 liter, divide 4,000 by 1,000.

4,000 ÷ 1,000 = 4 L **4 liters are equivalent to 4,000 milliliters.**

Sometimes decimals are used when changing units. How would you write 9 milliliters as liters?

9 ÷ 1,000 = 0.009 L **Write 9 milliliters as 0.009 L.**

How many 500 mL bottles could you fill from a 2-liter bottle of sports drink? Explain your reasoning.

Check Understanding

Complete each equation.

a. 56 L = _____ mL b. 9,000 mL = _____ L c. 5 mL = _____ L

Write >, <, or =.

d. 120 mL _____ 0.120 L
e. 20,000 mL _____ 200 L
f. 5.7 L _____ 57,000 mL

Practice

Choose the appropriate unit of measurement. Write "mL" or "L."

1. a sink
2. a teaspoon
3. a pitcher of juice
4. a bottle of vanilla
5. an aquarium
6. a sample of shampoo

Complete.

7. 2 L = ____ mL
8. 5,678 mL = ____ L
9. 87 L = ____ mL
10. 700 mL = ____ L
11. 6 mL = ____ L
12. 0.14 L = ____ mL
13. 3.4 L = ____ mL
14. 134 mL = ____ L
15. 279 L = ____ mL
16. 3,456 mL = ____ L
17. 0.42 L = ____ mL
18. 0.076 L = ____ mL
19. 4.5 L = ____ mL
20. 67 mL = ____ L
21. 5.092 L = ____ mL

Apply

22. Theresa bought a 1-liter bottle of hand lotion for $17.50. Valerie bought the same amount of lotion in 100-mL tubes which sold for $2.00 each. What was the better buy?
23. A 1-cup measure holds about 250 mL of liquid. About how many cups of soda could Spencer pour if he had a 2-liter bottle of soda?

Review

24. $7^2 \times (2 + 3) - 10 + 2$
25. $200 + 4^2 \times 2 - 100$
26. $42 + 3 \times 5 + (16 + 4) \div 2$

12.6 Metric Units of Mass

Construct Meaning

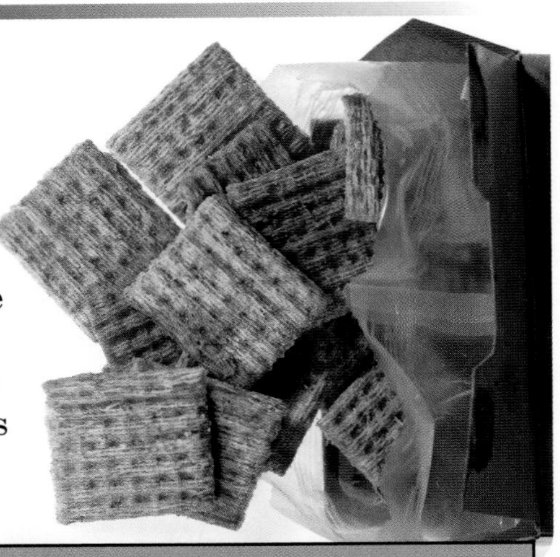

Mass is the measure of the amount of matter in an object. The contents of a box of crackers have a mass of 255 grams (g). One serving of 16 crackers is 29 g. Each cracker has a mass that is a little less than 2 g.

When Viviana read the nutrition facts label on the box, she was alarmed that one serving had 250 milligrams (mg) of sodium. That sounded like a lot. However, she learned that 1,000 mg equal 1 g and that 1 mg has about the same mass as a grain of sand.

There are 3 g of sugar in one serving of crackers. To compare the amount of sugar with the amount of sodium in one serving, change 3 grams to milligrams. To change grams to milligrams, multiply the number of grams by 1,000.

Metric Units of Mass
1,000 milligrams (mg) = 1 gram (g) 1,000 grams = 1 kilogram (kg)

3 × 1,000 = 3,000 mg of sugar

How many times greater is the amount of sugar than the amount of sodium in one serving?

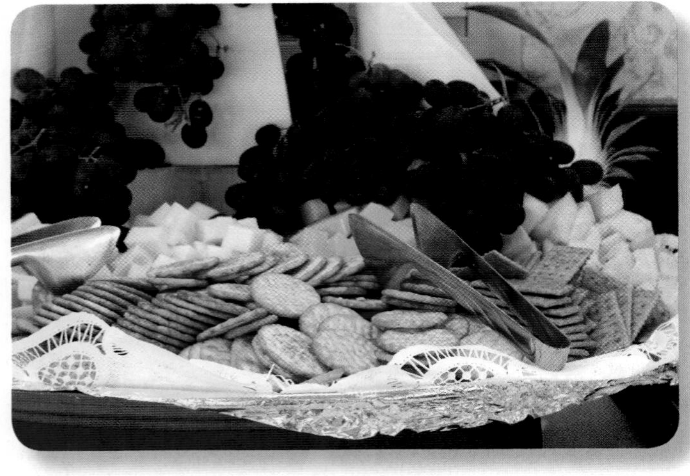

If you need 1 kilogram of crackers for a party, how many boxes should you buy? One kilogram equals 1,000 grams. Divide this amount by the number of grams in one box.

$$\begin{array}{r} 3 \text{ R}235 \\ 255\overline{)1{,}000} \\ -765 \\ \hline 235 \end{array}$$

Should you buy three or four boxes?

A grain of sand is about 1 milligram (mg).

A large paper clip is about 1 gram (g).

A liter of water is about 1 kilogram (kg).

Check Understanding

Complete.

a. 4 kg = ____ g

b. 5 g = ____ mg

c. 2,700 g = ____ kg

d. 450 mg = ____ g

Choose the more reasonable estimate of mass.

e. a balloon
1 mg or 1 kg

f. a dime
4 mg or 4 g

g. an apple
150 g or 150 kg

h. a bicycle
10 g or 10 kg

Practice

Complete.

1. 23 g = ____ mg
2. 46 kg = ____ g
3. 290 mg = ____ g
4. 2 g = ____ mg
5. 3.2 kg = ____ g
6. 765 g = ____ kg
7. 2.3 kg = ____ g
8. 0.964 kg = ____ g
9. 2,300 g = ____ kg
10. 5.23 g = ____ mg
11. 5,600 mg = ____ g
12. 5 kg = ____ g
13. 9 g = ____ mg
14. 4.6 kg = ____ g
15. 0.034 g = ____ mg

Choose the appropriate unit of measurement. Write "mg," "g," or "kg."

16. a snowflake
17. your math book
18. a car
19. a grain of rice
20. a safety pin
21. a pencil

Apply

22. Trina read the nutrition label on her box of cereal. She discovered one serving contained five grams of sugar. How many milligrams of sugar were in one serving?

23. There are 300 milligrams of sodium in one serving of the cereal. Would four servings contain more or less than one gram of sodium?

12.7 Temperature

Construct Meaning

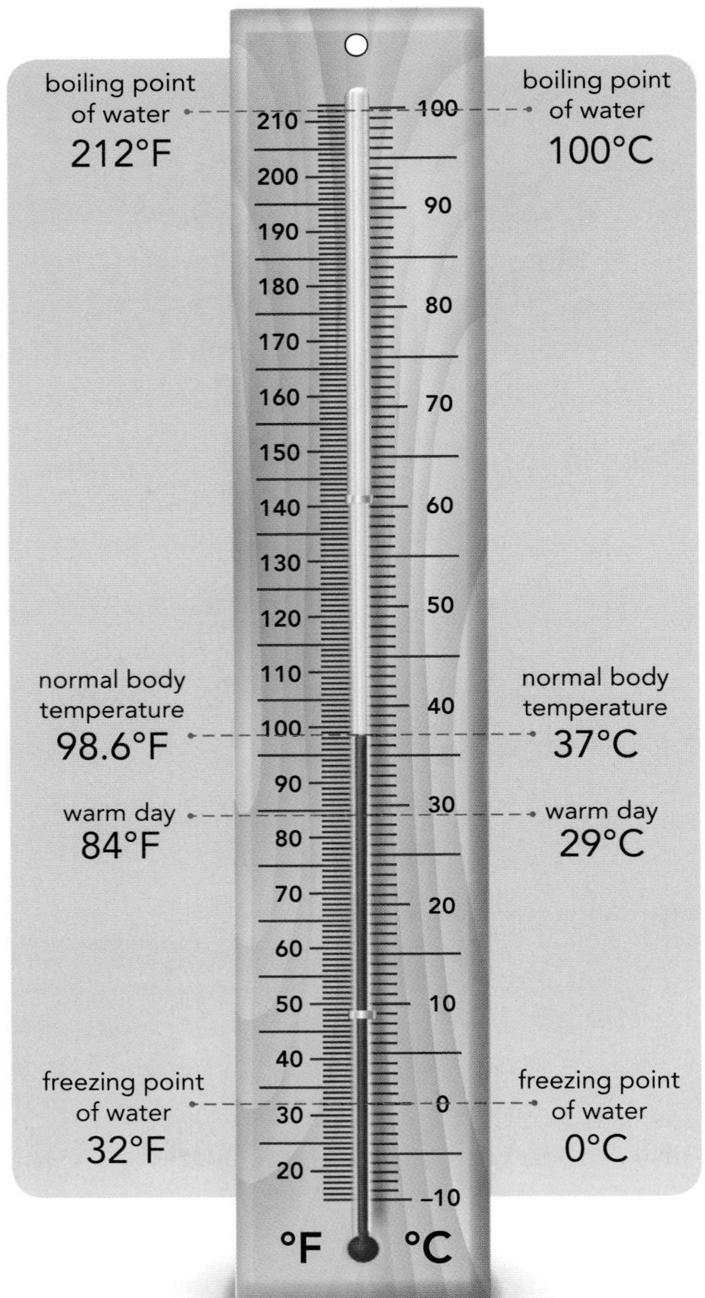

How is the weather today? Does it feel warm, hot, or cold? The way it feels to you is an indication of the temperature. A thermometer is used to measure temperature. The customary unit for temperature is degrees Fahrenheit (°F). The temperature can also be measured in metric units, degrees Celsius (°C). Identify each scale by locating the °F and °C at the bottom of the thermometer.

Locate the freezing point of water on the thermometer. What is the temperature when measured in degrees Fahrenheit? At what temperature does water freeze in degrees Celsius?

Thermometers may be marked in different ways. One may be marked by every degree and another by every two degrees. When a thermometer is marked by every two degrees, skip count by 2s to read the degrees.

Check Understanding

Choose the equivalent temperature.

a. 32°F **b.** 60°C **c.** 190°F **d.** 122°F **e.** 70°C **f.** 28°C

88°C 158°F 0°C 82°F 50°C 140°F

Practice

Write the temperature shown.

1.

2. 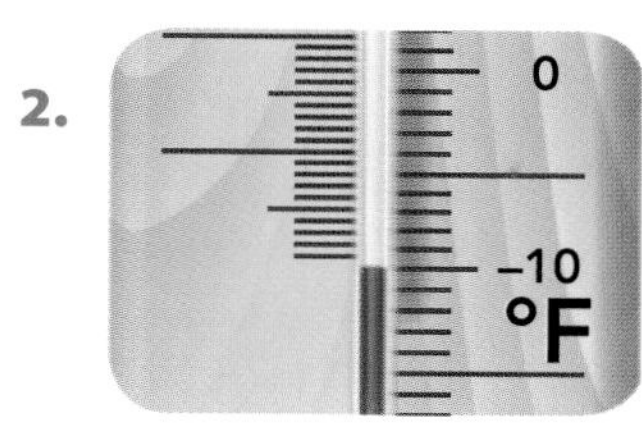

3. 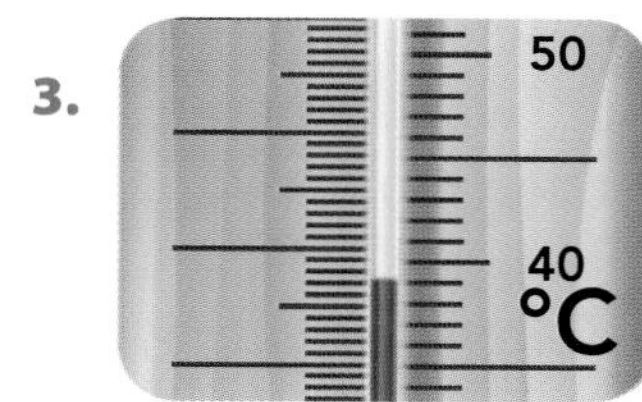

Use the thermometer on the previous page to choose the letter of the closest temperature.

4. 62°F
5. 24°F
6. 41°F
7. 180°F
8. 86°F

a. –4°C	**b.** 30°C	**c.** 82°C	**d.** 17°C	**e.** 5°C

Solve.

9. On the Fahrenheit thermometer, how many degrees are there between the freezing point of water and normal body temperature?

10. On the Celsius thermometer, how many degrees are there between the boiling point of water and normal body temperature?

Apply

11. This morning, Megan read the temperature on her outdoor thermometer. It was 28°F. At noon, Granddad said it was 10°C. How many degrees Fahrenheit warmer was the temperature at noon?

12. Rafael's mom is a meteorologist. She predicted the high temperature for the week to be 68°F. The low temperature was predicted to be 35°F. How many degrees Fahrenheit above freezing are the high and low temperature predictions?

Challenge

13. Find the difference between the freezing point and boiling point of water in degrees Celsius. Then, find the difference in degrees Fahrenheit. Compare the two differences to determine about how many degrees on the Fahrenheit scale are equal to one degree on the Celsius scale.

Review

Find the percent of each number.

14. 23% of 200
15. 16% of 500
17. 56% of 600
18. 75% of 1,000

12.8 Elapsed Time

Construct Meaning

Lilo arrived at school at 8:00 AM on a sunny morning. By the time he went to lunch at 12:20 PM it was snowing. How much time was Lilo in school before lunch?

Find the elapsed time by counting forward from the beginning time.

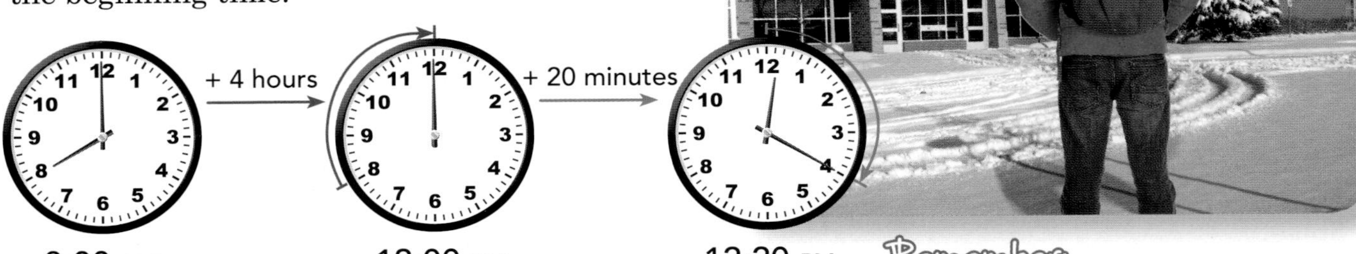

8:00 AM 12:00 PM 12:20 PM

He was in school 4 hours 20 minutes.

Remember:
60 seconds (sec) = 1 minute (min)
60 minutes = 1 hour (hr)
AM begins at 12:00 midnight.
PM begins at 12:00 noon.

If it snowed for 1 hour 30 minutes before lunch, what time did it start to snow?

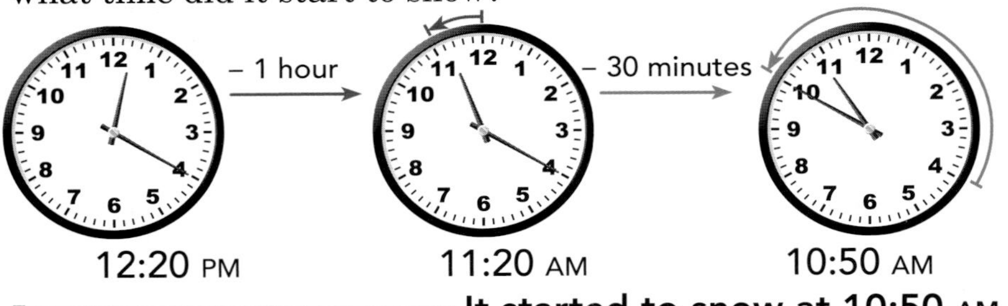

12:20 PM 11:20 AM 10:50 AM

It started to snow at 10:50 AM.

How much time elapsed from when Lilo left for school until he arrived home after soccer practice?

Lilo left for school at:

_____ AM

Lilo arrived at soccer practice at:

_____ PM

Lilo arrived home at:

_____ PM

Orlando, Florida, had 10 hours 20 minutes between sunrise and sunset on December 19. On that same day in Anchorage, Alaska, there were only 5 hours 28 minutes of daylight. What is the difference in the amount of daylight residents in the two locations had that day?

```
  10 hr 20 min  →  (9 + 60 min + 20 min)  →    9 hr 80 min
–  5 hr 28 min          Regroup.             –  5 hr 28 min
                                                4 hr 52 min
```

Orlando had 4 hours and 52 minutes more daylight than Anchorage.

Check Understanding

Find the elapsed time.

a. 6:10 AM to 10:30 AM

b. 4:55 PM to 7:35 PM

c. 11:45 AM to 1:15 PM

Add or subtract.

d.	e.	f.	g.
5 hr 20 min	4 hr 51 min	6 hr 25 min	8 min 10 sec
+ 2 hr 15 min	− 2 hr 40 min	+ 3 hr 35 min	− 3 min 40 sec

Practice

Write the elapsed time.

1. 2:35 PM to 8:10 PM
2. 9:50 AM to 3:14 PM
3. 6:42 PM to 1:45 AM
4. 10:23 AM to 5:55 PM
5. 11:36 AM to 4:19 PM
6. 1:12 PM to 12:00 AM

Write the times shown on the clocks.

7. 

_____ PM

_____ PM

Solve.

Example:

$$\begin{array}{r} 2 \text{ min } 30 \text{ sec} \\ + \ 4 \text{ min } 40 \text{ sec} \\ \hline \end{array}$$

Regroup the seconds. → ^{1}**6 min ~~70~~ sec**

7 min 10 sec

8.	10.	12.	14.
7 min 50 sec	3 hr 45 min	6 hr 13 min	9 hr 51 min
− 5 min 45 sec	+ 6 hr 40 min	− 4 hr 32 min	+ 2 hr 32 min

9.	11.	13.	15.
49 min 30 sec	8 hr 56 min	7 hr 19 min	5 hr
+ 10 min 56 sec	− 5 hr 13 min	+ 2 hr 24 min	− 3 hr 39 min

Apply

16. Mario's family drove to his grandparents' house for a weekend visit. If their trip began at 3:30 PM and ended at 7:48 PM, how much time did it take to travel?

17. If Mario's family took a 30-minute break for dinner, how much time did they actually drive?

Problem Solving: Time Zones

Construct Meaning

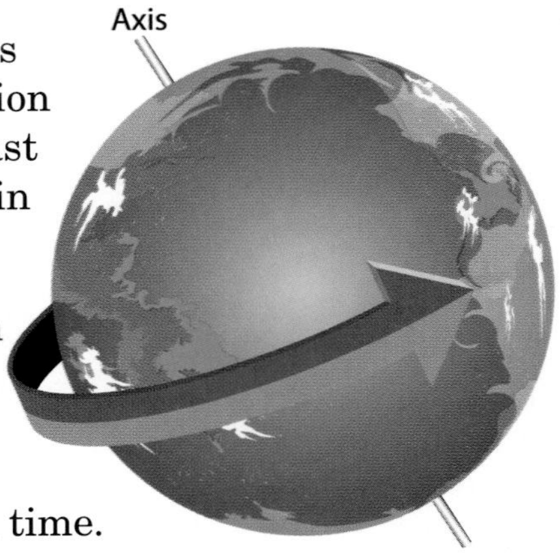

Axis

The world is divided into 24 different time zones. Six time zones divide the United States, each differing by one hour. The direction of the earth's rotation on its axis means that locations to the east will have daylight before your location. When the sun is rising in London, England, it is still dark in Toronto, Canada.

Use the map below to compare the times of various locations in the United States.

- If it is 7:00 AM eastern standard time in Boston, what is the time in Billings?
- A family in Honolulu is sleeping at 4:00 AM Hawaii standard time. What time would it be for their relatives in Omaha?
- Rory's flight left Orlando at 11:00 AM eastern standard time and arrived in Los Angeles at 1:00 PM Pacific standard time. How long was his flight?

What time was it in Los Angeles when Rory's plane left Orlando?

How much time elapsed between the plane's departure from Orlando and its arrival in Los Angeles?

Time-Zone Map

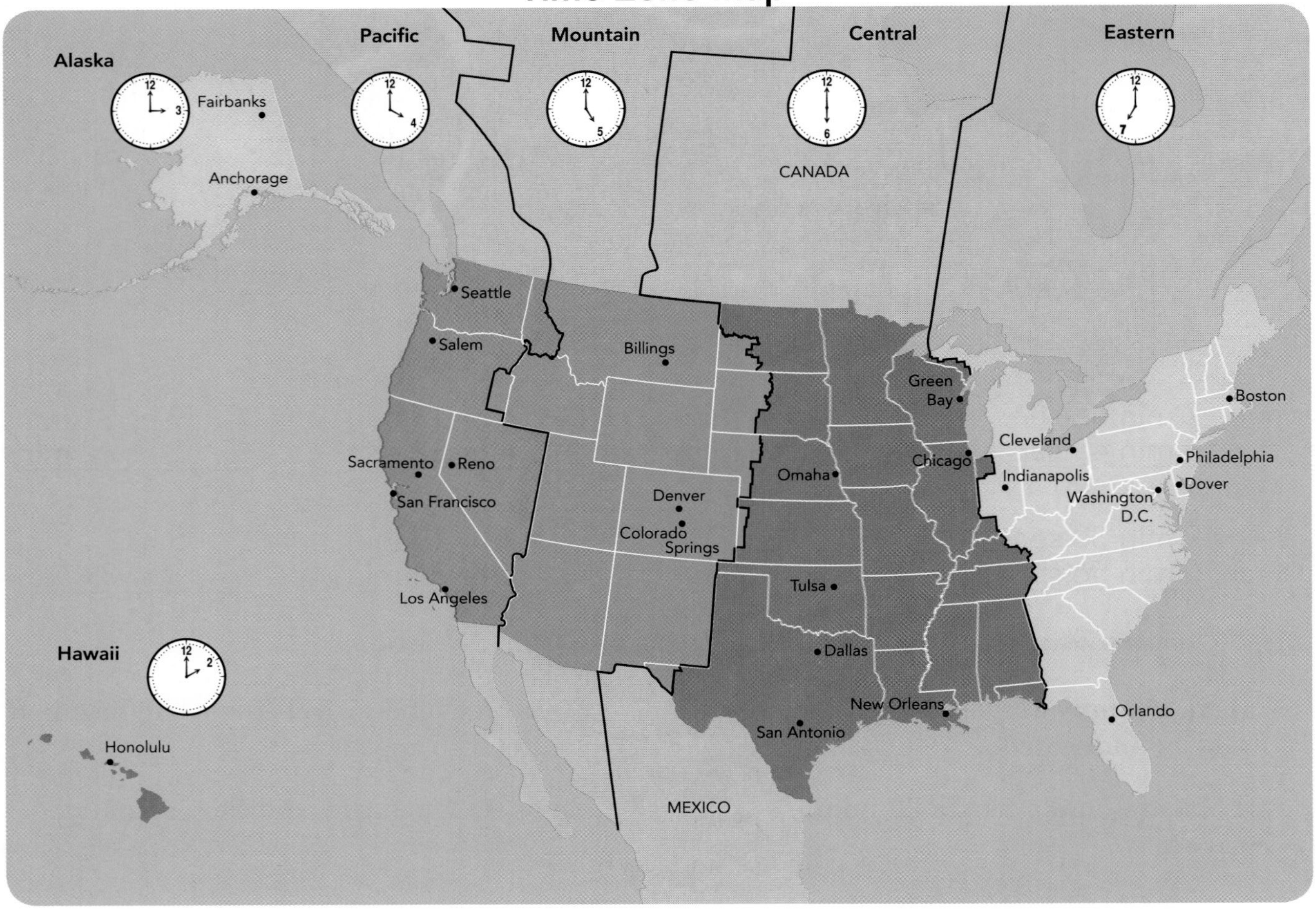

Alaska
Pacific
Mountain
Central
Eastern
Fairbanks
Anchorage
CANADA
Seattle
Salem
Billings
Green Bay
Boston
Cleveland
Sacramento
Reno
Chicago
Philadelphia
Indianapolis
Dover
Omaha
San Francisco
Denver
Washington D.C.
Colorado Springs
Tulsa
Los Angeles
Hawaii
Dallas
New Orleans
Orlando
San Antonio
Honolulu
MEXICO

Check Understanding

Use the map on the previous page to answer each question.

a. If it is 3:00 PM in Cleveland, what is the time in Seattle?
b. It is 12:00 PM in Billings. What time is it in Philadelphia?
c. Name the time zone and a state within that time zone that is two hours ahead of Pacific standard time.

Practice

Use the Problem-Solving Guide and the map to help you find each answer.

Problem-Solving Guide
1. Understand the question.
2. Analyze the data.
3. Plan the strategy.
4. Solve the problem.
5. Evaluate the result.

1. Nyakim lives in Omaha, Nebraska. She called her grandparents who are located in Honolulu, Hawaii. If Nyakim called at 9:00 PM central standard time, what time was it in Honolulu?
2. Lincoln's flight from Denver, Colorado, to New Orleans, Louisiana, took two hours and 30 minutes. If Lincoln's flight departed at 10:00 AM, what time did he arrive in New Orleans?

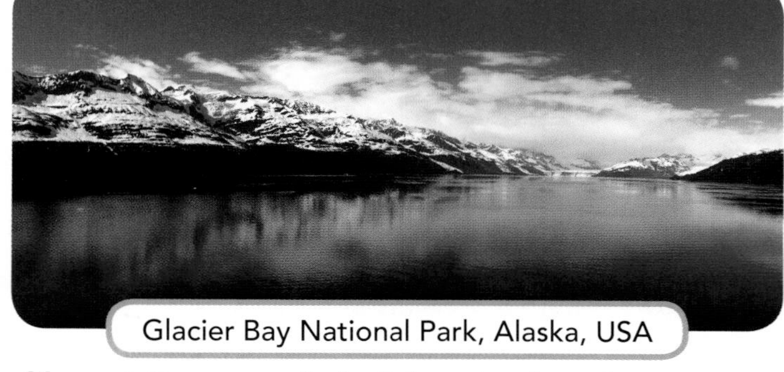
Glacier Bay National Park, Alaska, USA

3. Reese is on an Alaskan cruise. She wants to call home to Orlando, Florida, at 10:00 PM eastern standard time. At what time will Reese make the call?
4. Padma, who lives in Dallas, has a watch that will show the time for two time zones. She set one face to show 12 PM (noon), which was the time in Anchorage where her grandparents live. She set the second clockface to show her own time zone. What time is displayed on the second clockface?

Use the clocks and the map to answer each question.

5. The first clock shows the time in the morning that Maurice and his family left their home in Sterling, Colorado, to travel to his Uncle Niko's house. The second clock shows the time that Maurice and his family arrived in the evening at his Uncle Niko's house in Indianapolis, Indiana, after they made a few stops along the way.
   a. What time did Maurice's family leave Colorado?
   b. What time was it in Indianapolis when they left Colorado?
   c. What time did Maurice and his family arrive in Indianapolis?
   d. What time was it in Colorado when they arrived in Indianapolis?
   e. How much time did it take Maurice and his family to travel to Indianapolis?

12.10 Chapter 12 Review

Answer Bank

yard	kilogram
quart	centimeter
Celsius	ounces
meter	mass
milliliter	

Use the Answer Bank to complete each sentence.

1. The measurement of matter in an object is its ____.
2. The customary unit of length that measures 36 inches or 3 feet is the ____.
3. The metric unit of length that measures 10 decimeters is the ____.
4. The degree ____ is the metric unit of temperature.
5. The ____ is a small metric unit of capacity.
6. A metric unit of mass is the ____.
7. A ____ is equal to 4 c or 2 pt.
8. Ten millimeters equal one ____.
9. Sixteen ____ equal 1 lb.

Choose the appropriate customary unit of capacity. Write "cup," "pint," "quart," or "gallon."

10. 

11. 

12. 

13. 

Complete each equation.

14. 72 fl oz = ____ c
15. 2 gal = ____ qt
16. 6 c = ____ pt
17. 16 qt = ____ pt
18. 12 pt = ____ c
19. 3 yd 2 ft = ____ ft
20. 42 in. = ____ yd ____ in.
21. 7 ft = ____ yd ____ ft
22. 4 mi = ____ ft

Write each measurement in pounds.

23. 5 T 24. 368 oz 25. 80 oz

Write each measurement in ounces.

26. 8 lb 27. 32 lb 28. 21 lb

Compare the measurements. Write >, <, or =.

29. 6 lb ◯ 100 oz 30. 25 c ◯ 1 gal 31. 3 mi ◯ 705 yd

Write the elapsed time.

32. 7:10 AM to 11:30 AM

33. 

Find the time.

34. 9 hr 56 min − 2 hr 39 min

35. 6 min 49 sec + 8 min 50 sec

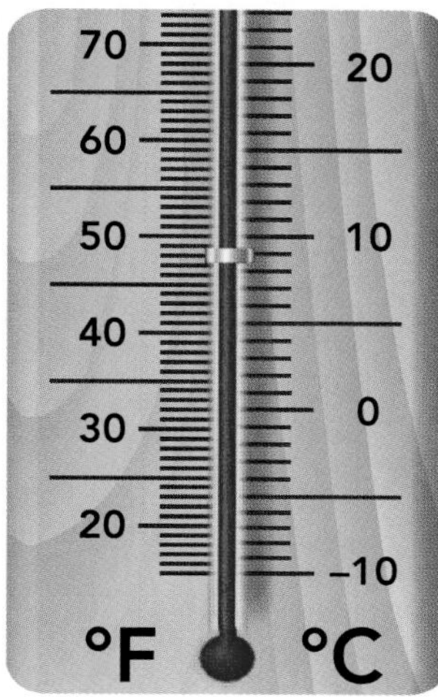

Use the thermometer to complete each equation.

36. 64°F = ____ °C

37. −5°C = ____ °F

38. 0°C = ____ °F

39. 28°F = ____ °C

Complete each equation.

40. 2 dm = ____ cm

41. 15 cm = ____ mm

42. 5 m = ____ cm

43. 5,200 m = ____ km

44. 0.52 L = ____ mL

45. 4,576 mL = ____ L

46. 5.6 kg = ____ g

47. 450 mg = ____ g

Compare the measurements. Write >, <, or =.

48. 5 kg ◯ 5,000 g 49. 200 mL ◯ 5 L 50. 420 cm ◯ 3 m

51. Meili's best friend moved to San Diego, California. Meili still lives in Miami, Florida. She plans to call her friend at 9:00 PM eastern time. What time will it be in California?

52. The basketball tournament at Rohit's school begins at 9:45 AM. Rohit's game begins at 1:25 PM. How much time will Rohit have to wait until his game begins?

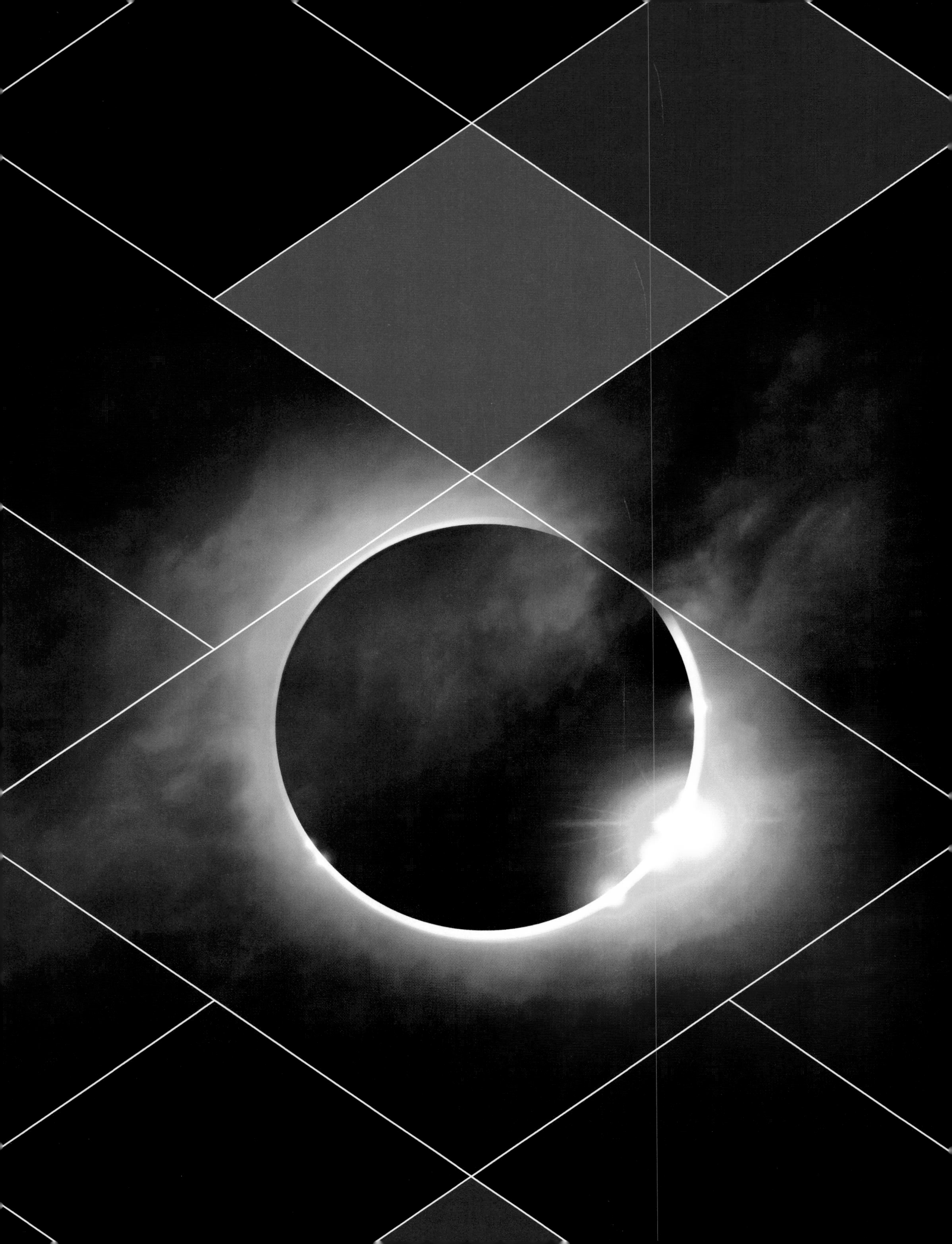

Chapter 13
Area, Perimeter, and Volume

Where were you when I laid the earth's foundation … while the morning stars sang together and all the angels shouted for joy?
Job 38:4a, 7

Key Ideas:

Measurement: finding perimeter and area

Measurement: finding volume

Measurement: finding circumference

13.1 Area: Rectangles

Construct Meaning

The area of a figure is the number of square units that cover the surface. Linear units measure only one dimension, the length. Compare the linear units with the corresponding square units.

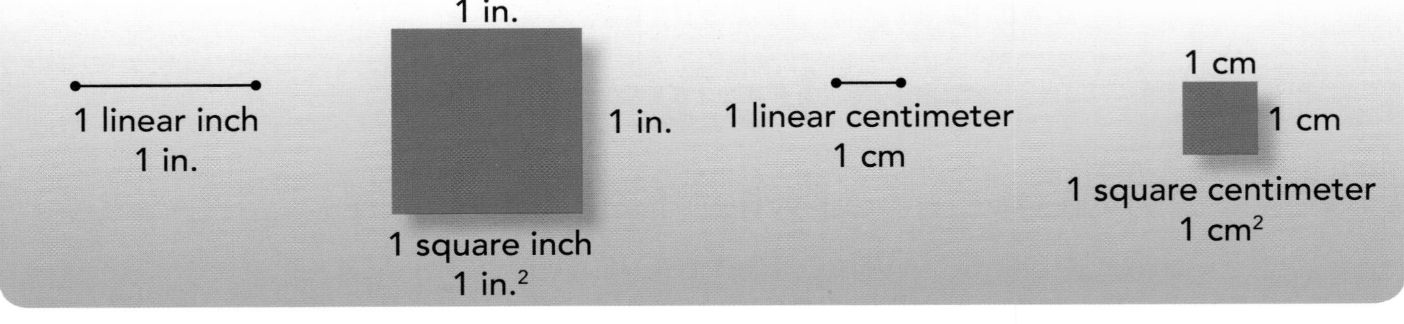

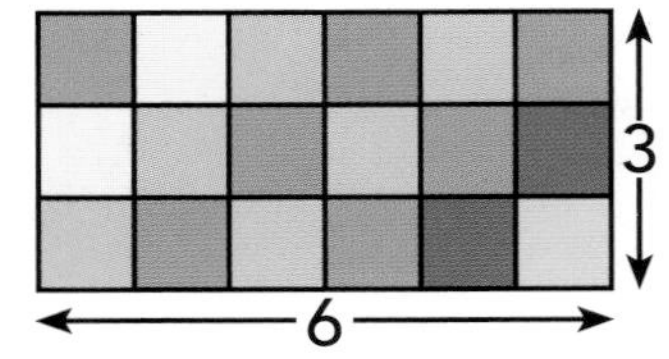

Hina used a square-inch grid to plan a rectangular design of tiles. Each tile measured one square inch. She found the area of her design by counting the total square inches. What is the area of her design?

18 tiles = 18 sq in.

Later, Hina painted a larger design on a piece of paper and framed it. She decided to find the area of the new design. So, she used the formula for finding the area of a rectangle.

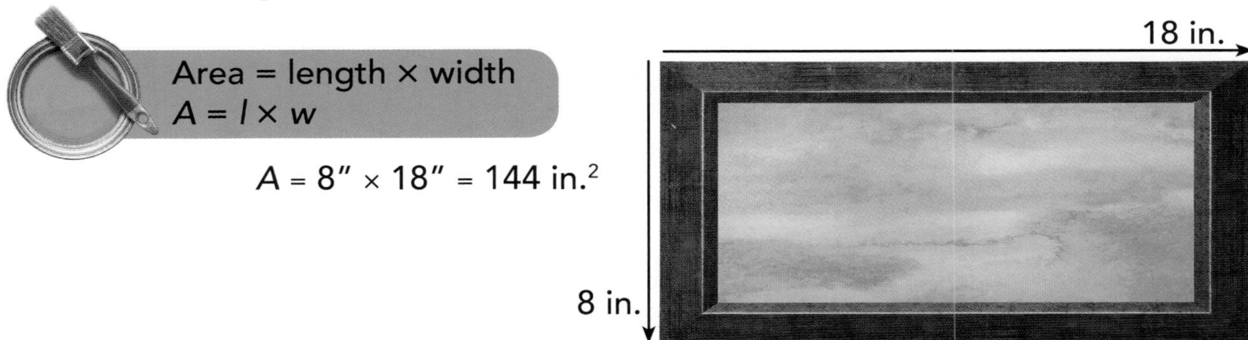

$A = 8'' \times 18'' = 144 \text{ in.}^2$

Check Understanding

Write the area for each figure. Label the answer using square units.

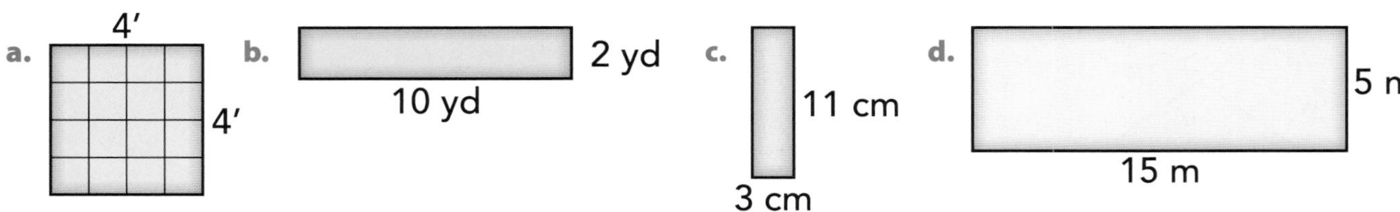

e. Write a formula for finding the area of a square.

f. Copy and complete the table.

rectangle	l	w	A
1	13 cm	6 cm	____
2	2 m	____	24 m²
3	5 yd	____	125 yd²

Practice

Use the formula to find the area.

1. area in square feet of a room that measures 18' × 24'

2. area in square miles of a 12 mi × 6 mi ranch

3. area in square yards of a football field that measures 100 yd × 53.33 yd

Write the missing number.

4. $A = 49$ in.^{2}
   $l = 7''$
   $w =$ ____

5. $A = 311$ sq yd
   $l =$ ____
   $w = 62.2$ yd

6. $A =$ ____
   $l = 59.8$ cm
   $w = 19.9$ cm

7. $A = 608$ square miles
   $l = 19$ mi
   $w =$ ____

Apply

8. A wooden chessboard made in Vermont is a square that has 20" sides. A 2" border surrounds the grid for the game pieces. What is the area of the grid only?

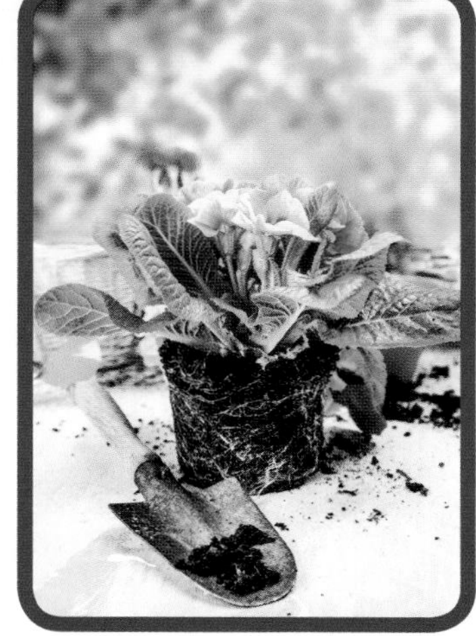

9. A garden has an area of 72 ft^2. Corn is growing in all but $26\frac{1}{2}$ ft^2 of the garden. How many square feet of corn are growing in the garden?

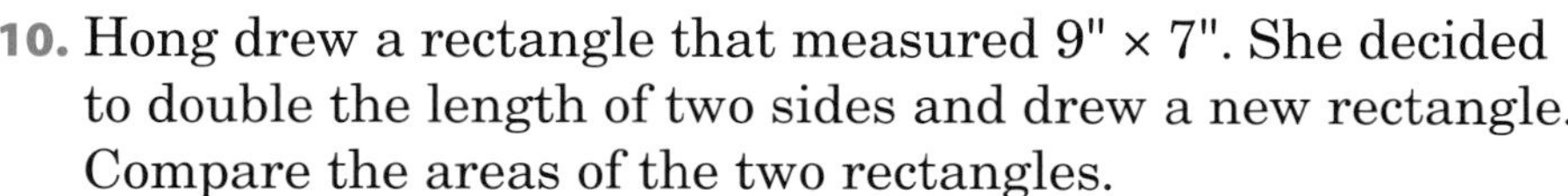

10. Hong drew a rectangle that measured 9" × 7". She decided to double the length of two sides and drew a new rectangle. Compare the areas of the two rectangles.

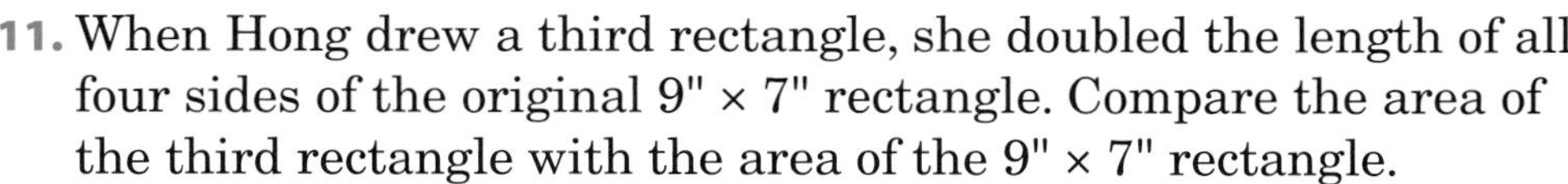

11. When Hong drew a third rectangle, she doubled the length of all four sides of the original 9" × 7" rectangle. Compare the area of the third rectangle with the area of the 9" × 7" rectangle.

12. Mrs. Barnes needs to carpet a room that is 15' × 18'. The carpet she wants is sold for $3.99 per square yard. What will it cost to carpet the room? Hint: 9 sq ft = 1 sq yd.

13. What are three ways you can write the area of a 5 m × 6 m rectangle?

13.2 Perimeter

Construct Meaning

Perimeter is the distance around a figure. A rectangular court has sides that are 94 ft and 50 ft. The perimeter, or distance around the court, is the sum of its four sides.

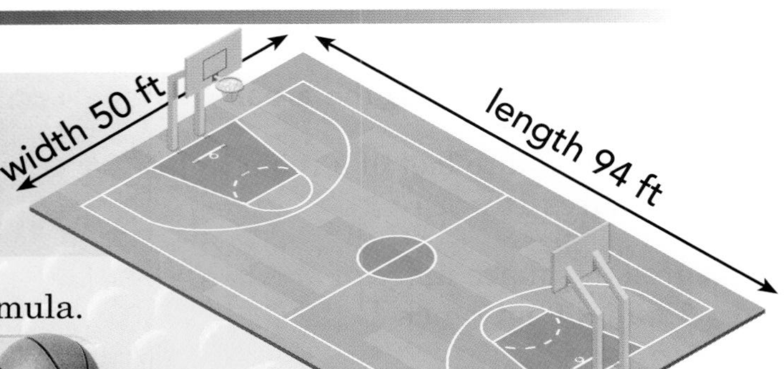

To find the perimeter of a rectangle, use a formula.

Perimeter = (2 × length) + (2 × width)
$P = 2l + 2w$

Use the formula to find the perimeter of the basketball court.

$P = 2l + 2w$
$P = (2 \times 94) + (2 \times 50) = 188 + 100 = 288$
$P = 288'$

To find the perimeter of a square, use a formula.

If s means "side," then $P = s + s + s + s$

If s = 6 cm, what is the perimeter?

$P = 4s$
$P = 4 \times 6$
$P =$ ____ cm

The perimeter of a regular hexagon may be found using the formula $P = 6s$.

$P = 6 \times 5 =$ ____ ″

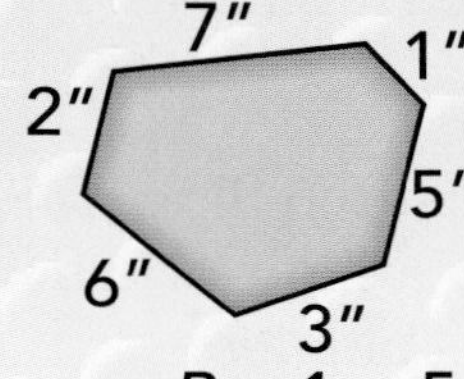

If the hexagon has sides of unequal length, add the length of each side to find the perimeter.

$P = 1 + 5 + 3 + 6 + 2 + 7 =$ ____ ″

Check Understanding

Find the perimeter of each figure.

a.

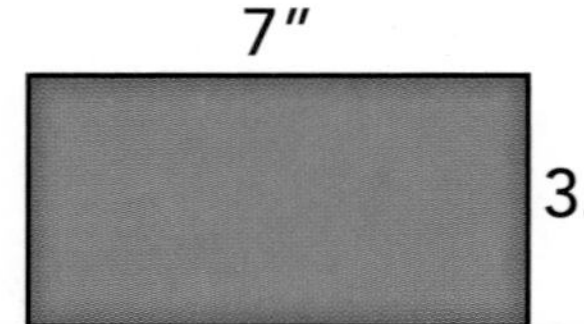

b.

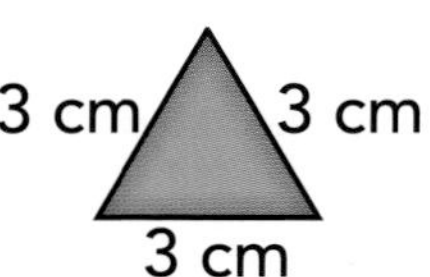

c.

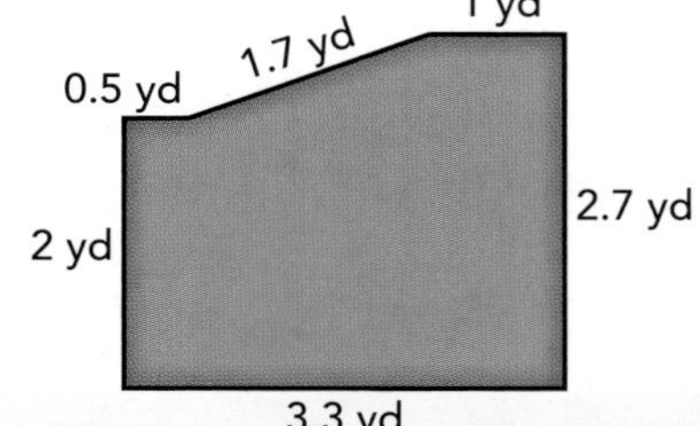

d. Explain why it is easier to find the perimeter of a regular polygon than to find the perimeter of a polygon that has different length sides.

Practice

Find the perimeter for each figure. Label the answers.

1. 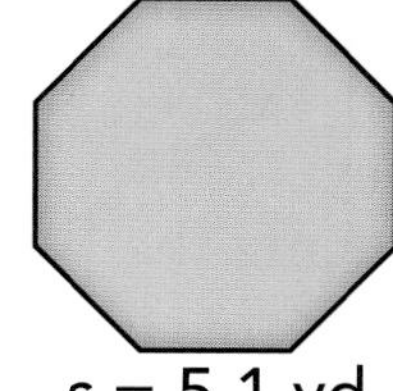

2. 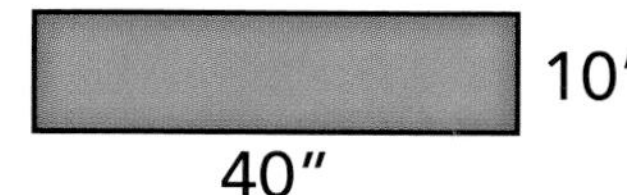

3. 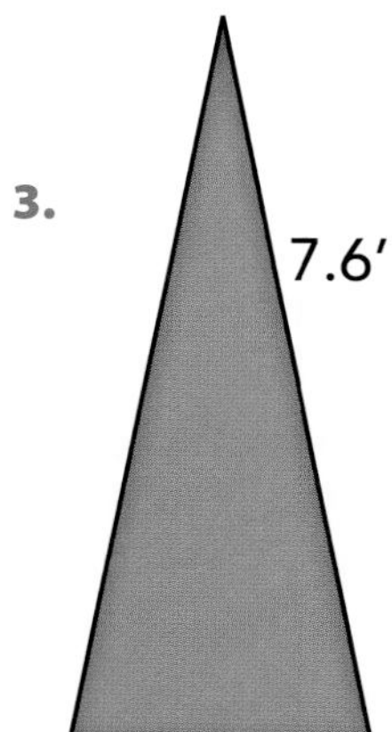

Find the perimeter for each figure.

4. a regular pentagon, if $s = 215$ m

5. a square, if $s = 16.5$ mi

6. a rectangle, if $l = 34$ in. and $w = 22$ in.

7. a scalene triangle, if the sides measure 18.8 yd, 29.9 yd, and 36 yd

8. a rhombus, if $s = 17$ cm

9. Write a formula for calculating the perimeter of each figure.
   a. an equilateral triangle
   b. a rhombus
   c. a regular octagon

Apply

10. The backboard for a basketball hoop is a flat rectangle $3\frac{1}{2}$ ft on each vertical side. If the perimeter of the backboard is 19 ft, how wide is the backboard?

11. Carl, Alicia, Bobby, and Delilah each drew a figure having only 6 in. sides. The figures drawn were a pentagon, a square, an octagon, and a hexagon. Rank the figures in order from largest perimeter to smallest perimeter.

12. Mr. Harper is planning to fence a rectangular play area that is 85 ft long and 48 ft wide. He will leave a 4 ft opening for a gate that he will build later. How much fencing does he need?

13. A swimming pool has a perimeter of 150 m. The pool is twice as long as it is wide. Find the length and width of the pool.

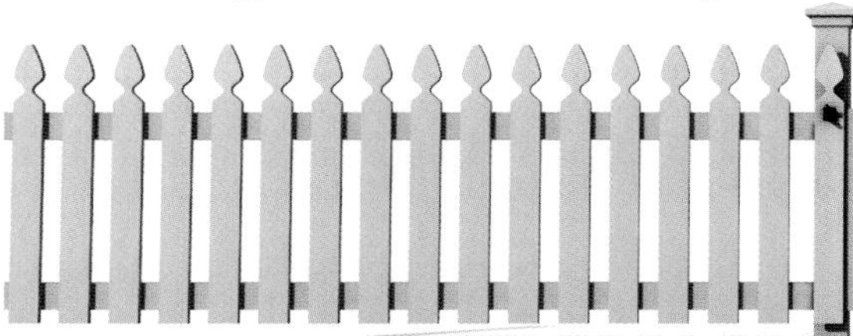

13.3 Circumference

Construct Meaning

The distance around a circle is called the circumference. Mr. Anderson's students found circumference using string as a measuring tool. They wrapped a piece of string around a flashlight. Then, they cut the string to the length of the circumference. They used the same piece of string to measure the diameter of the flashlight, cutting the string to see how many diameters would result. They cut three diameter lengths and had a small amount of string remaining. They tried this on several different objects and the same thing happened each time, no matter the diameter of the object.

The students' findings confirm the ratio of the circumference of a circle to its diameter.

$$\frac{\text{circumference}}{\text{diameter}} = \text{approximately } 3.14 \text{ or } pi\ (\pi) \text{ or } \frac{C}{d} = \pi$$

To find the measure of the circumference of a circle, multiply the diameter by 3.14 (π).

Circumference = π × diameter $C = \pi d$

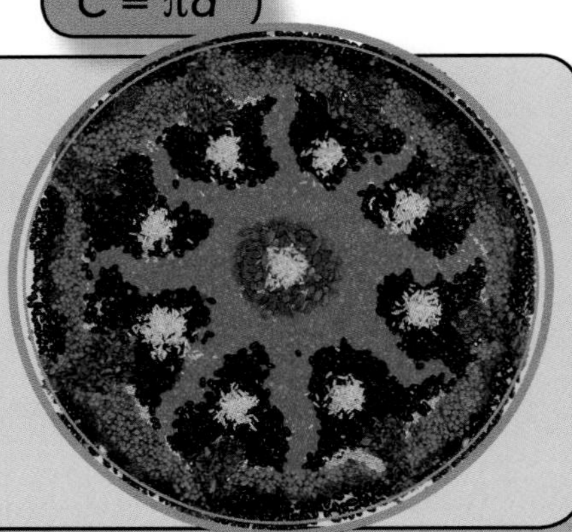

Ariel needs to cut a piece of yarn to fit around the edge of a circular design. The design has a 8 in. diameter. What is the length of yarn she needs? Use the formula for circumference.

$C = \pi d$
$C \approx 3.14 \times 8$
$C \approx 25.12''$

If a piece of yarn is $25\frac{1}{4}$ in. long, will it be long enough?

Yes, the string will be long enough because $25\frac{1}{4}'' = 25.25''$.

Check Understanding

a. Perimeter is to polygon as ____ is to circle.

b. Use a whole number to estimate the circumference of a circle that has a 10 in. diameter.

c. Use π to find the circumference if d = 8.7 cm.

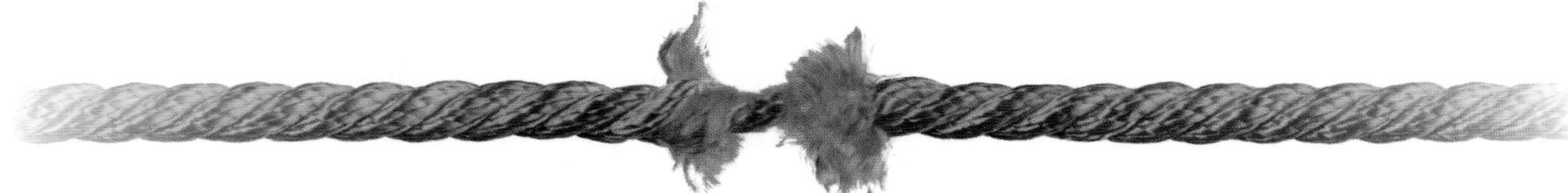

d. How can you find the circumference (C) if you know the length of the radius?

Practice

Find the circumference. Round the answer to the nearest tenth.

1. 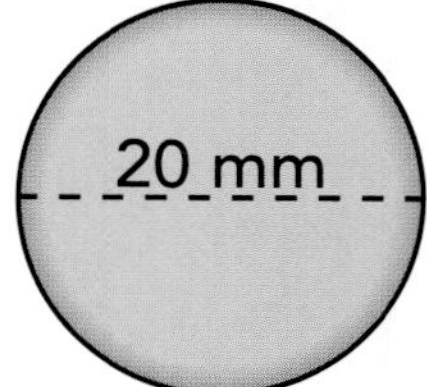

2. 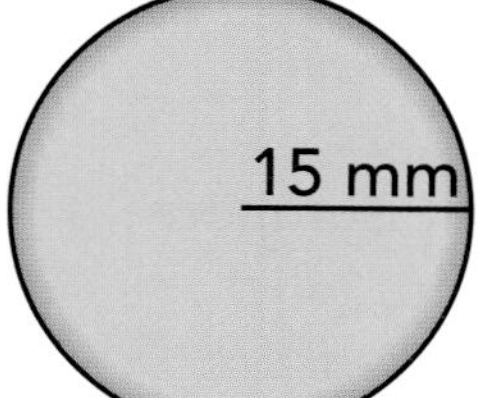

3. 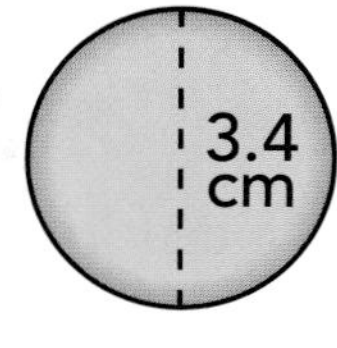

4. 

5. 

$d = 12$ cm

6. 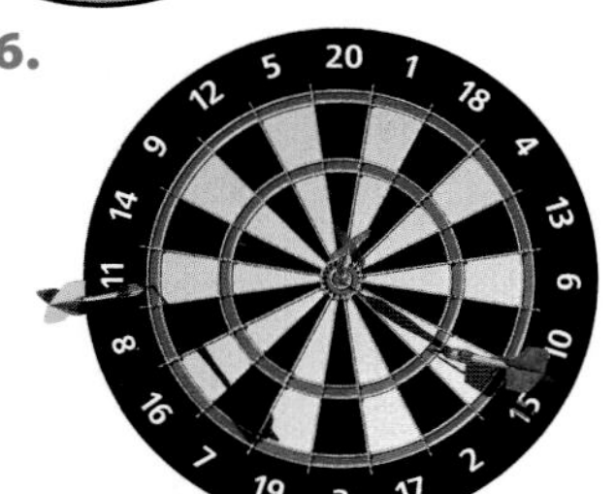

$r = 9$ in.

7. 

$d = 28$ cm

Apply

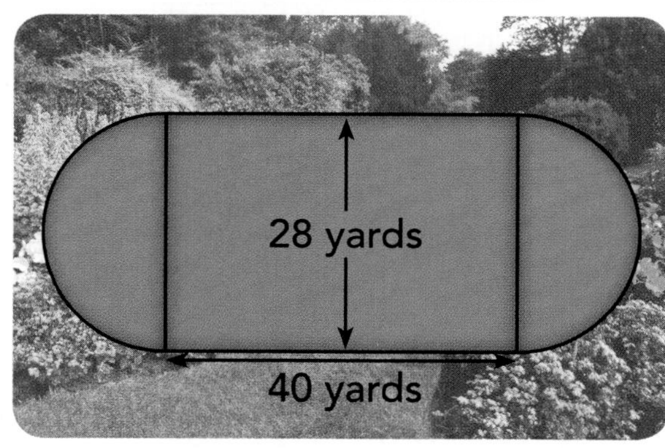

8. A park has roses planted around its perimeter. Each end of the park is a half circle. Use the dimensions on the drawing to find the perimeter. (Round to the nearest tenth and label it.)

9. The front wheel of a bicycle has a 30" diameter. The rear wheel has a diameter about 10" greater. What is the difference in the circumference of the wheels?

10. Mrs. Cowley puts lace around the lids of mason jars after filling them with treats. She has 4' of lace trim. How many lids with a 2.5" diameter can she trim?

11. A tennis ball has a diameter greater than $2\frac{1}{2}$ in. and less than $2\frac{5}{8}$ in. If the diameter of a tennis ball is 2.55 in., what is its circumference? (Round the answer to the nearest hundredth.)

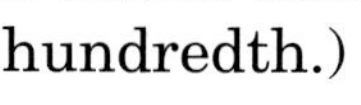

13.4 Coordinate Geometry

Construct Meaning

An archeologist used a coordinate grid similar to the one shown. Points were graphed on the grid to show the location of the objects that had been found.

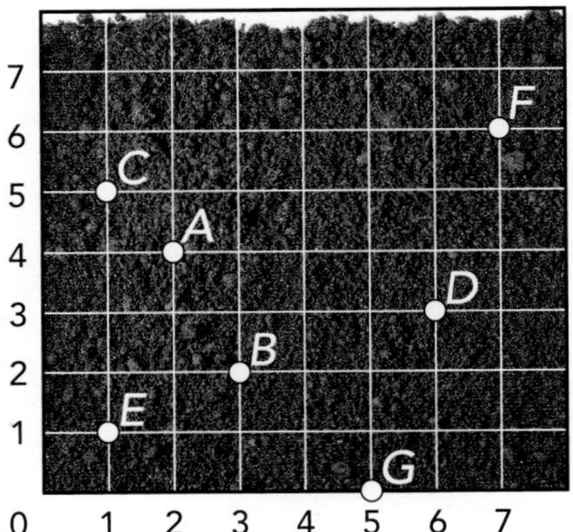

Points on a grid are located using ordered pairs of numbers. The numbers are called the coordinates of the point, such as (2, 4). The first number indicates how far to move from 0 to the right on the horizontal axis. The second number indicates how far to move up. If you place your finger on (0, 0) and move two to the right and up four, you will see that (2, 4) are the coordinates for point *A*.

Follow the steps to locate point *B* on the grid above.

1. Begin at (0, 0). 2. Move three lines to the right. 3. Move up two lines.

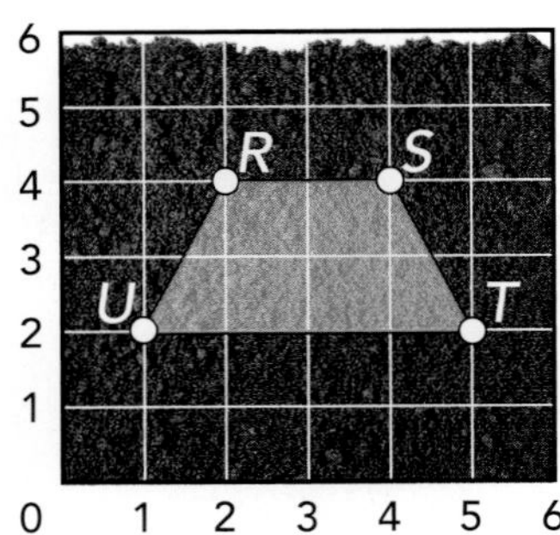

The points on this grid have been connected to form a trapezoid. The ordered pair for point *R* is (2, 4).

Name the ordered pairs for the other vertices of the trapezoid.

Where is the line of symmetry for the trapezoid?

Check Understanding

a. Why are the coordinates of point *T* of the trapezoid called (5, 2) instead of (2, 5)?

b. Identify the only time when changing the order of the numbers in the pair will not change the location of the point.

c. Name the coordinates of points *C* through *G* on the grid at the top of the page.

d. Where is the vertical axis of a coordinate grid?

Practice

Write the point of each ordered pair.

1. (3, 6) 2. (5, 3) 3. (1, 9)

Write the ordered pair for each point.

4. *G* 5. *E* 6. *A* 7. *B*

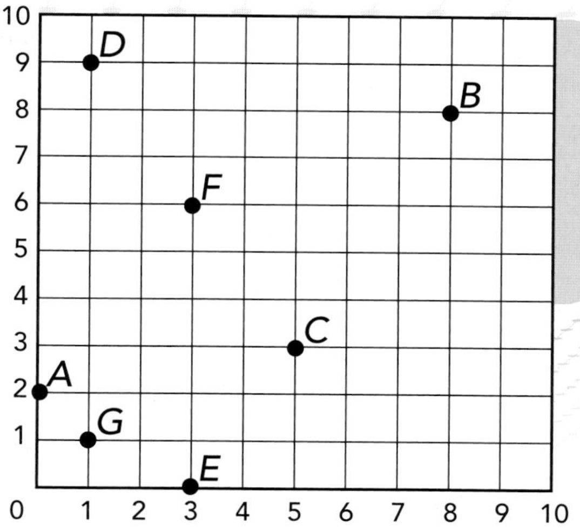

Write the ordered pair for each vertex of the figure. Name the polygon.

8. 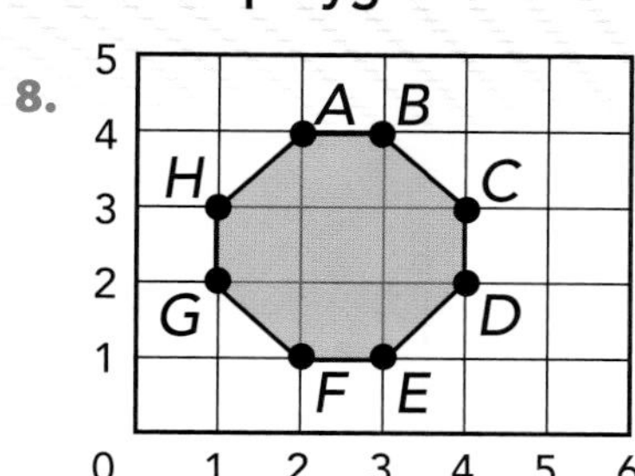

9. 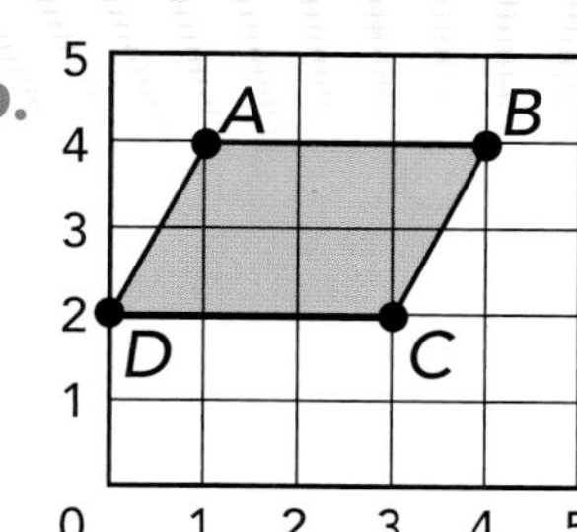

10. Predict what you would see on the graph if you graphed and connected the ordered pairs (0, 0), (1, 1), (2, 2), (3, 3), (4, 4), and (5, 5).

Apply

11. On graph paper, outline and number a 10 × 10 grid. Draw a rectangle on the grid. Assign letter names to each of the vertices of the rectangle. Make a list of the ordered pairs that match each letter name.

12. On the grid from Exercise 11, graph the ordered pairs (2, 1), (9, 7), and (4, 7). Using a different color, connect the points. Name and classify the polygon.

13. When Miss Cash's class played the game Rule Box, she presented a series of ordered pairs. Students pretended that the first number of the pair went into the Rule Box and came out as the second number. They identified the rule performed that led to the second number. For example, the rule "multiply by two" makes the pairs (2, 4), (4, 8), and (8, 16). State the rule for the ordered pairs (3, 6), (4, 7), (5, 8), (6, 9), and (7, 10). Using a third color, graph the points on the grid. What figure was made when you connected the points?

14. Explain the correct process for locating and graphing the ordered pair (8, 5).

13.5 Area: Right Triangles

Construct Meaning

Mrs. Bridges gave graph paper to her students. She asked them to follow these directions.

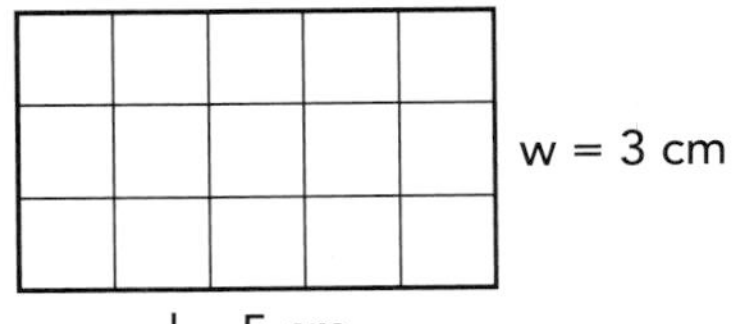

Draw a rectangle that measures 5 cm × 3 cm. Find the area of the rectangle.

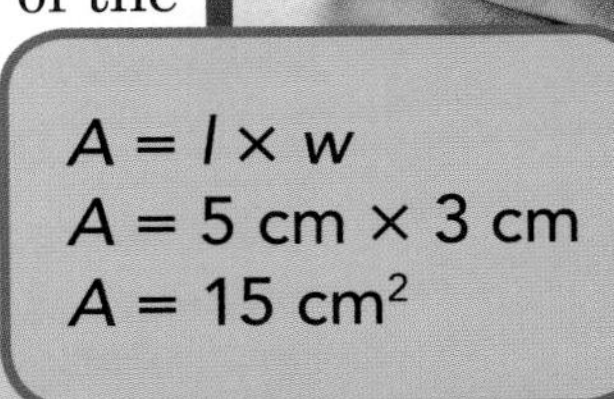

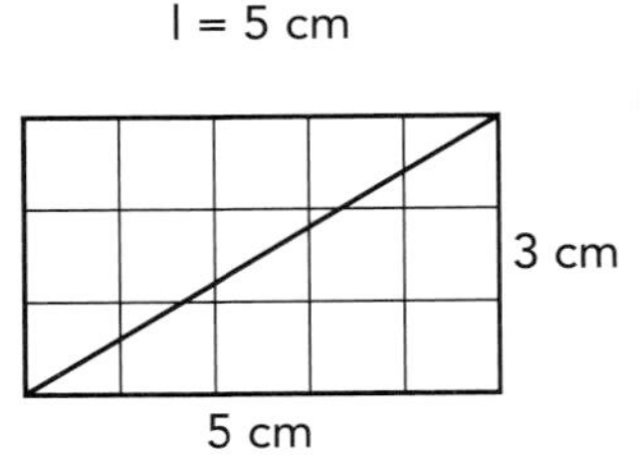

Divide the rectangle with a diagonal line. Cut on the line. What type of triangles result? What fraction of the rectangle does each right triangle represent? How does the area of each right triangle relate to the area of the rectangle?

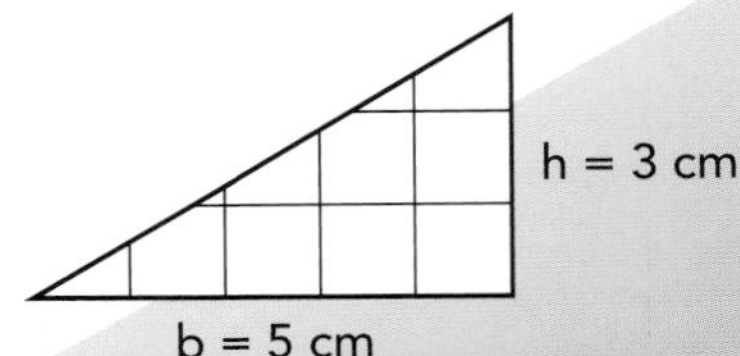

In a right triangle, the base (or length) and height (or width) of the right triangle are the same as the length and width of the rectangle. Therefore, the area of the right triangle is half that of the rectangle.

The formula for finding the area of a right triangle is: Area = $\frac{1}{2}$ × base × height

$$A = \frac{1}{2} \times b \times h$$

Find the area of the triangle.

$$A = \frac{1}{2} \times b \times h$$
$$A = \frac{1}{2} \times 5 \text{ cm} \times 3 \text{ cm}$$
$$A = 7.5 \text{ square centimeters}$$

Draw a rectangle on centimeter grid paper and calculate the area. Divide your rectangle to form two congruent right triangles. Find the area of each triangle.

Check Understanding

a. Find the area of a right triangle that has a height of 12 cm and a base of 29 cm.

b. A rectangular piece of stained glass 15" × 9" was divided into two congruent right triangles. What is the area of each triangle?

c. Name two characteristics of two triangles that when put together form a rectangle.

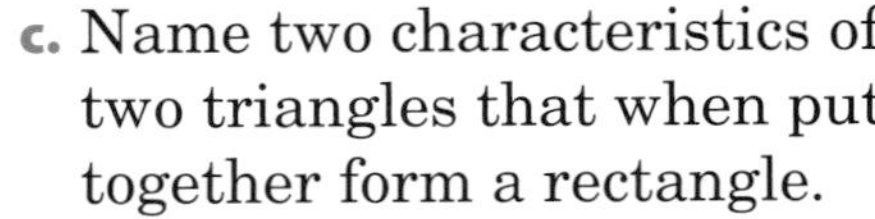

Practice

Example:

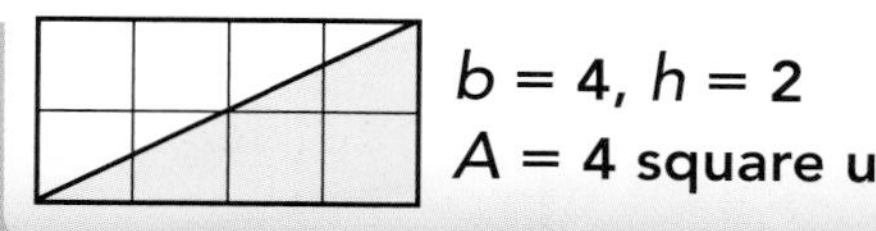

$b = 4$, $h = 2$
$A = 4$ square units

Write the height, base, and area of each right triangle.

 **= 1 square unit**

1. 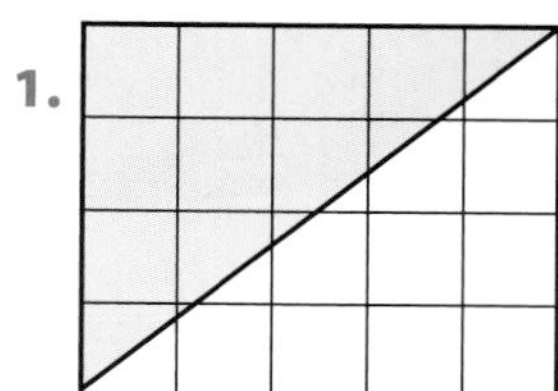

2.

3. 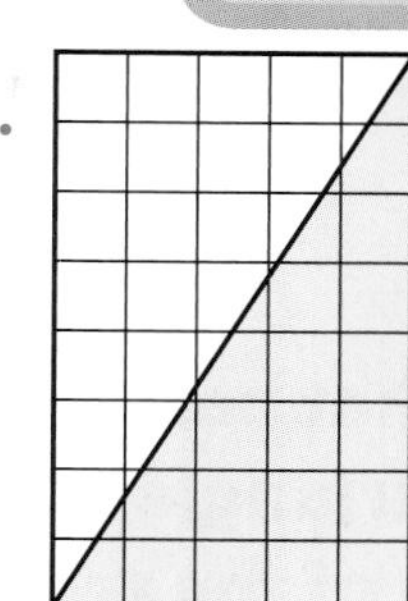

4.

Use the formula to find the area of each right triangle.

5. 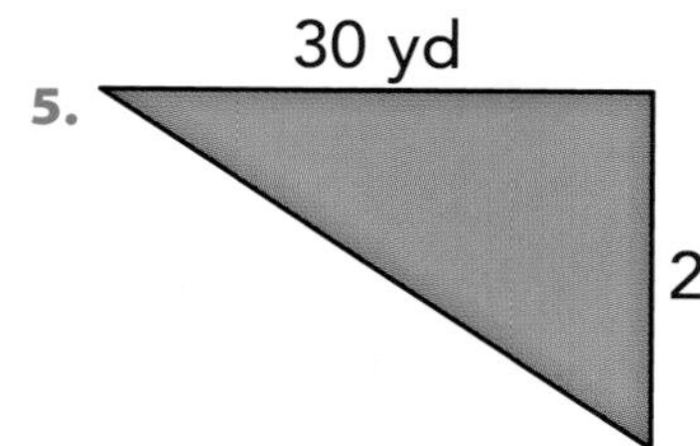

6. 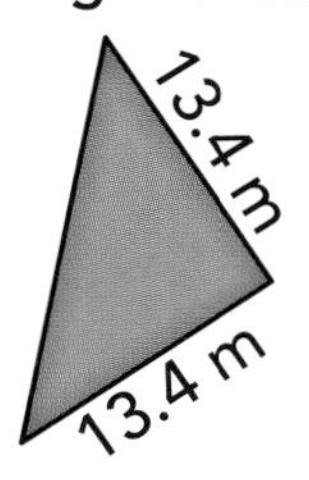

7. 17′
39′

Apply

8. A sailmaker made two sails by dividing an 83 yd × 4 yd piece of cloth into two congruent triangles. What is the area of each sail?

9. A carpenter had a board that measured 12' × 4.5'. She cut it in half diagonally. What is the area of each piece of wood?

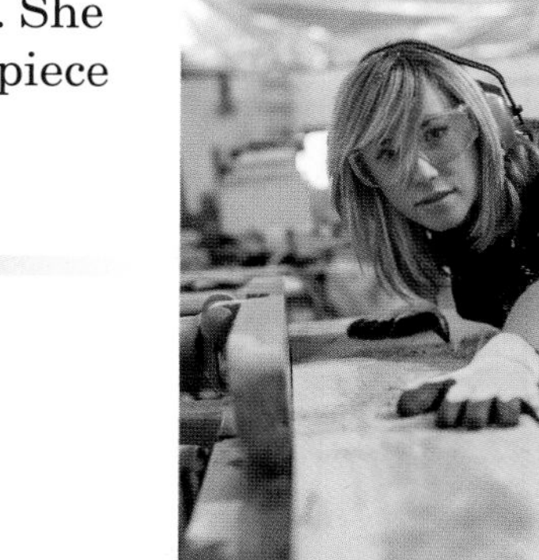

Review

Find the perimeter and area of each figure.

10. 25.5′
25.5′

11. 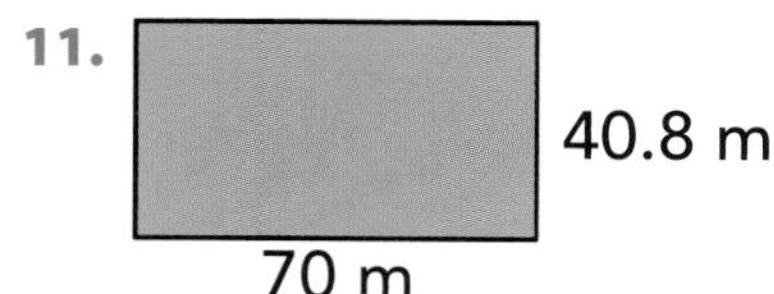

12. 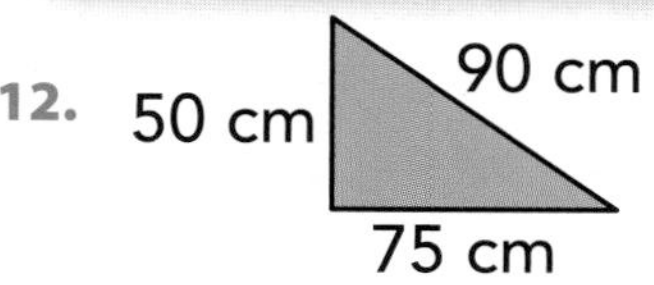

13. 7″
42″

13.6 Area: Triangles

Construct Meaning

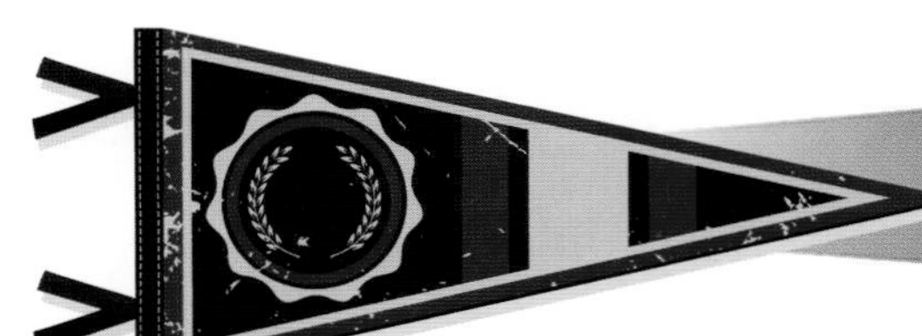

Pennants for schools or teams are made in the shape of triangles. Is the pennant shown a right triangle?

Gwen used a square centimeter grid. She followed these directions.

1. **Draw a rectangle that has a longer length than width. Inside the rectangle, make a triangle with no right angles. Make the base of the triangle the length of the rectangle. Place its opposite vertex on the parallel side.**

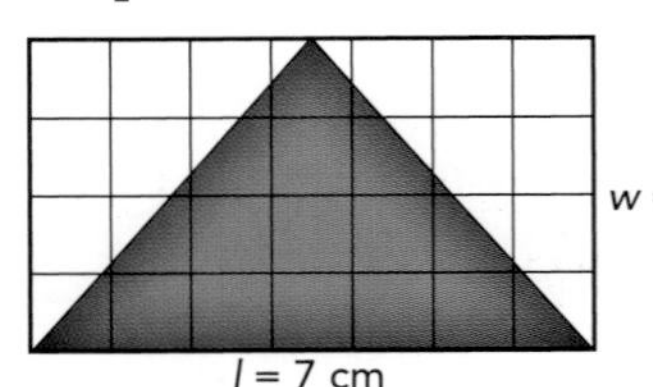

2. **Color the triangle.**
How do the base and height of the triangle relate to the length and width of the rectangle?

3. **Cut the rectangle from the grid. Cut and remove your colored triangle and the two white triangles.**

Will the white triangles fit exactly on the colored triangle? What does that tell you about the relationship between the area of the rectangle and the colored triangle?

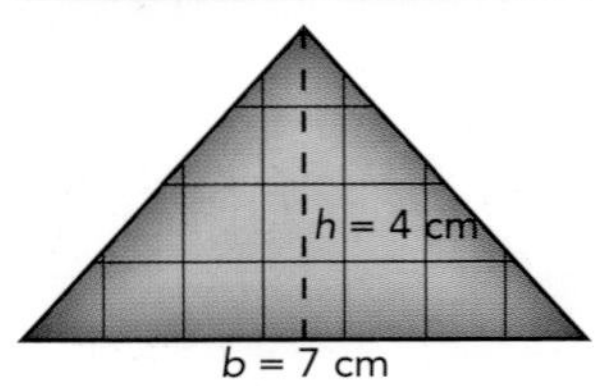

Find the area of any triangle by using the formula:
$A = \frac{1}{2} \times$ base $\times$ height or $A = \frac{1}{2} \times b \times h$

Gwen found the area for her triangle by using the formula.

Using a piece of square centimeter grid paper, draw a rectangle and follow the directions above. Find the area of your colored triangle.

$A = \frac{1}{2} \times b \times h$

$A = \frac{1}{2} \times 7 \text{ cm} \times 4 \text{ cm}$

$A = \frac{1}{2} \times 28 \text{ cm}^2$

$A = 14 \text{ cm}^2$

Check Understanding

Write T for true and F for false for each statement and explain why.

a. A triangle has a base of 24" and a 13" height. It has an area of 312 sq in.

b. Triangles that have the same area are congruent triangles.

c. The formula for finding the area of a right triangle is the same as the formula for finding the area of any triangle.

Practice

Find b, h, and A for each triangle. Each □ = 1 square unit.

1. 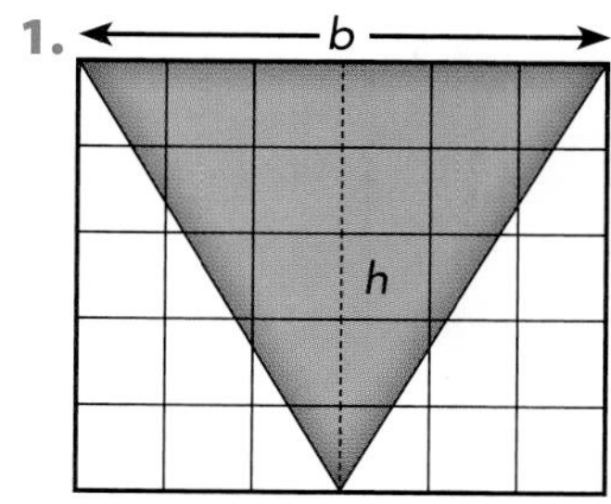

2. 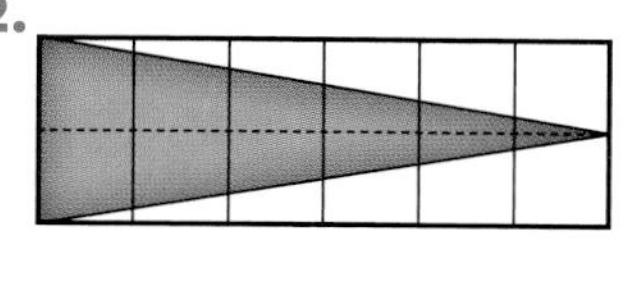

3. 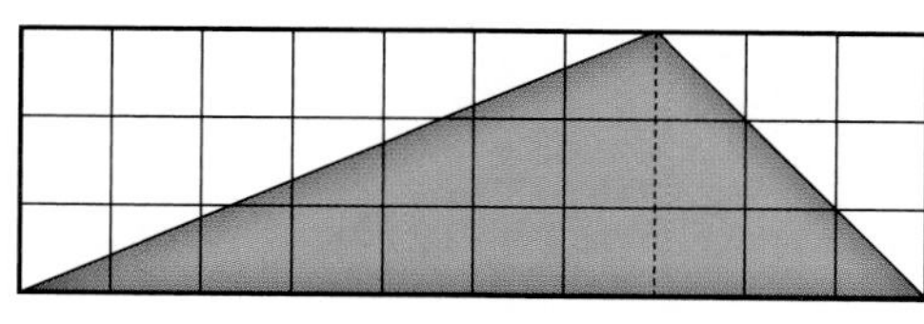

Find the area of the object. Label your answer.

4. 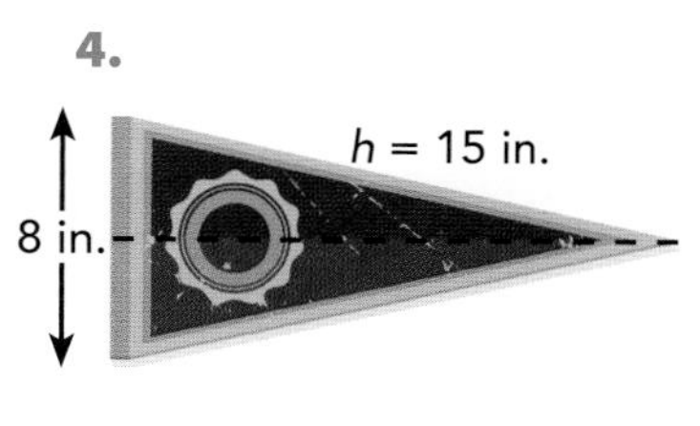

5. 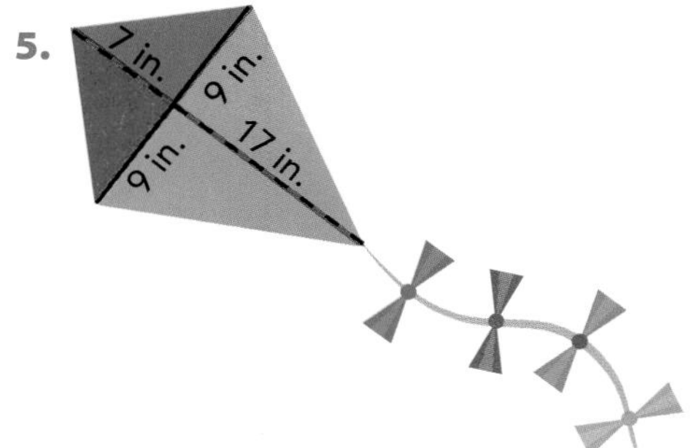

6. 

Apply

7. The triangular face of a model pyramid has an area of 3 in². The base and height measurements are whole numbers greater than an inch. What are the numbers that name the base and height of the triangular face?

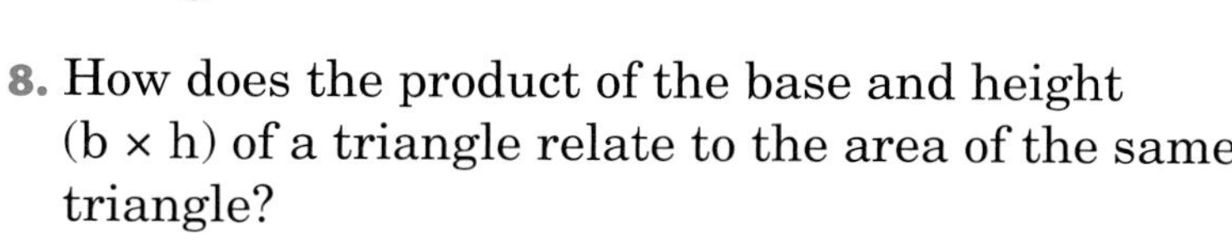

8. How does the product of the base and height ($b \times h$) of a triangle relate to the area of the same triangle?

9. Donald drew three triangles that were not congruent. Each triangle had an area of 12 cm². They all had a base and height that were whole numbers greater than 1. The table shows the base and height of one triangle. Write the numbers needed to complete the information in the table Donald made.

	b	h	A
triangle 1	6 cm	4 cm	12 cm²
triangle 2			12 cm²
triangle 3			12 cm²

Review

10. A rectangle is four times as long as it is wide. If w = 5.2 ft, what is the area of the rectangle?

11. Write the formula for the circumference of a circle.

13.7 Area: Irregular Figures

Construct Meaning

50′ 50′ 25′ 125′

The Garner family is planning to buy sod to cover the backyard with grass. The yard is an irregular shape. How can they find the area of the yard?

Mr. Garner thought of the yard as two rectangles.

50′ 75′ 50′ 25′ 125′

His son, Beck, thought of the yard as two different rectangles.

50′ 25′ 50′ 25′ 125′

Both of them used the formula $A = l \times w$ to find the area of each rectangle. Then, they added the two numbers for the total area.

Mr. Garner's calculations

$50' \times 50' = 2{,}500 \text{ ft}^2$

$75' \times 25' = 1{,}875 \text{ ft}^2$

$2{,}500 \text{ ft}^2 + 1{,}875 \text{ ft}^2 = 4{,}375 \text{ ft}^2$ total area

Beck's calculations

$50' \times 25' =$ ____ square feet

$125' \times 25' =$ ____ square feet

____ ft² + ____ ft² = ____ ft²

Mr. Garner and Beck used the same method for finding the area.

1. **Mentally break the irregular figure into shapes.**
2. **Use a formula to find the area of each shape.**
3. **Find the sum of the areas.**

Find the total area of the yard shown here.

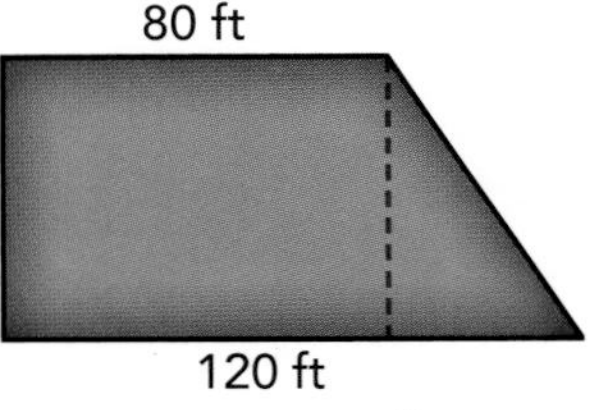

Area of a rectangle $= l \times w$

$A = 80' \times 60' =$ ____ ft²

Area of a triangle $= \frac{1}{2} \times b \times h$

How can you find b for the triangle?

$A = \frac{1}{2} \times 40' \times 60' = \frac{1}{2} \times 2{,}400' =$ ____ ft²

Add the area of the rectangle and the triangle to find the total area of the yard.

Check Understanding

a. List the steps explaining one way to find the area of an irregular figure.

b. Find the total area of the shape.

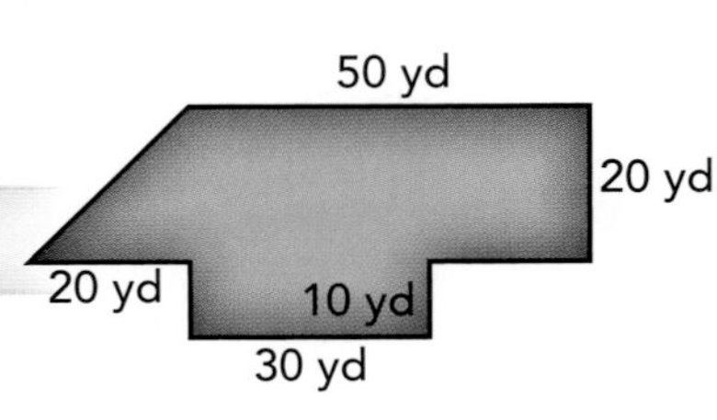

c. In the example above, why did Mr. Garner and his son use different numbers to arrive at the same answer?

Practice

Find the area of each figure.

1. 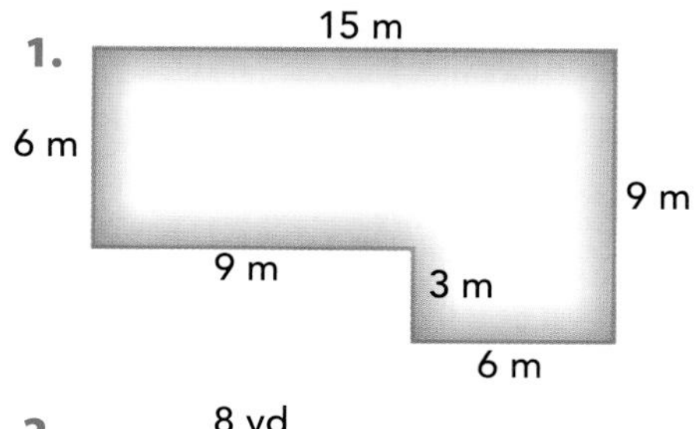

2. 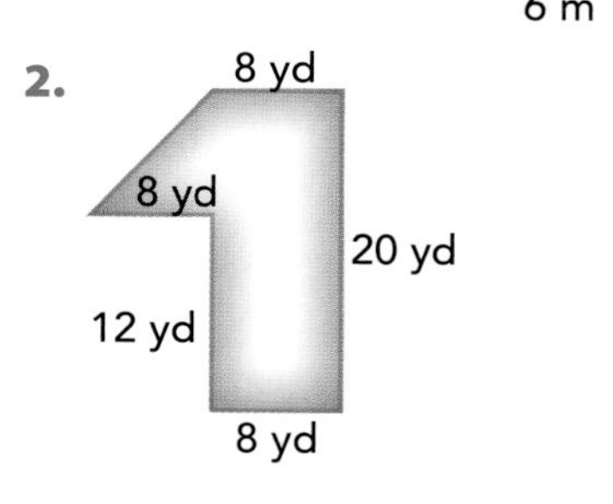

3. 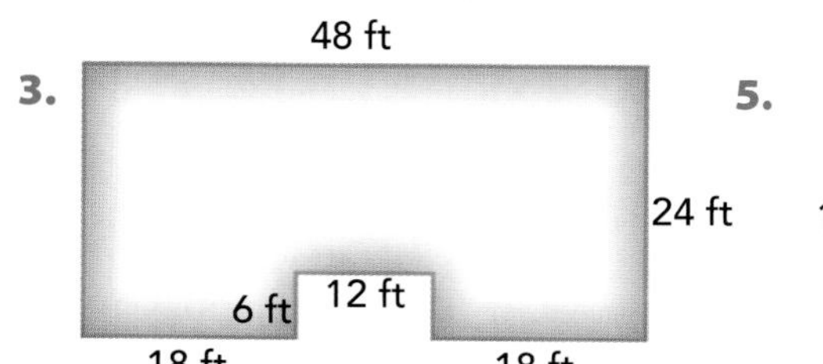

4. 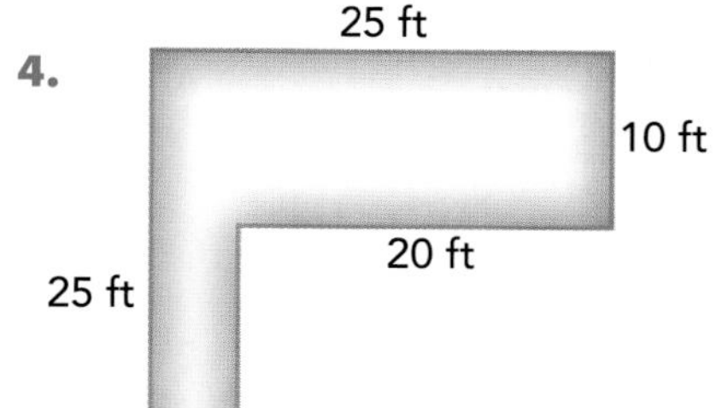

5. 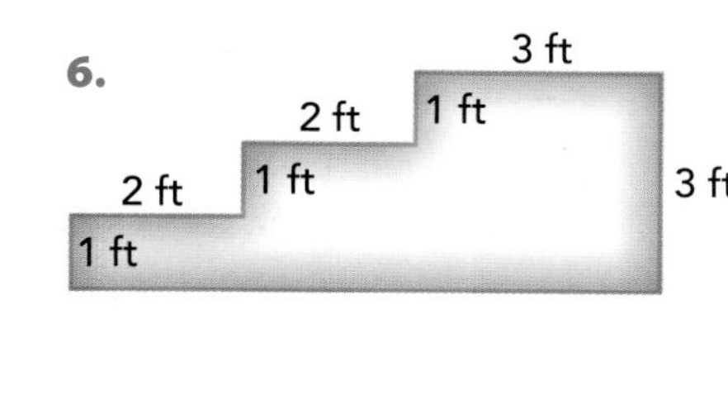

6.

Apply

7. Mrs. Carroll is going to buy wallpaper for one wall in her dining room. The dimensions of the wall are shown, including the window. What is the area that will be covered with wallpaper?

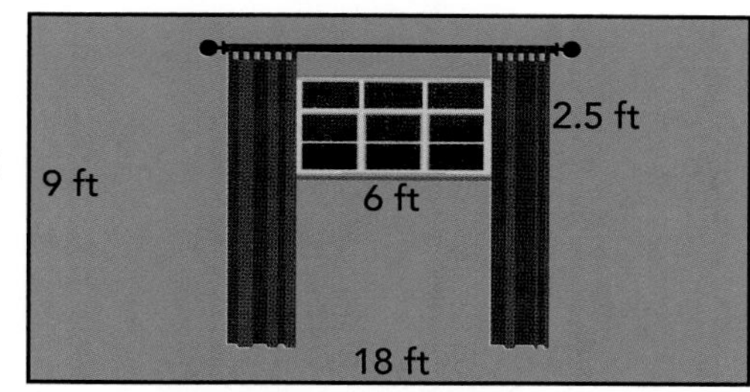

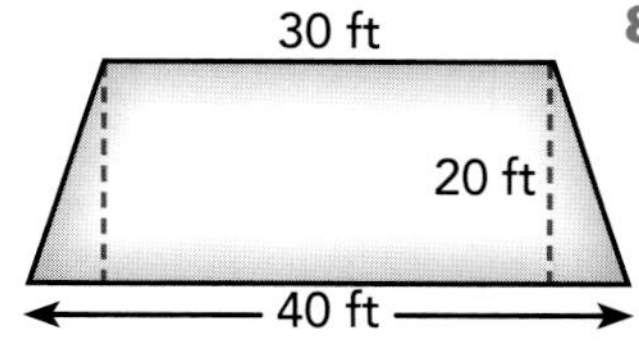

8. Students at Canaan Academy will paint one side of a wall separating two areas of the playground. The wall has the shape and dimensions shown. One gallon of paint covers 300 sq ft. How many gallons of paint should they buy?

Review

9. Name each ordered pair for point A through point H on the grid.

10. List three points that would result in a diagonal line if they were connected.

11. If each square of the grid represents 1 cm^2, find the area and perimeter of the figure that results from connecting points A, B, C, and D.

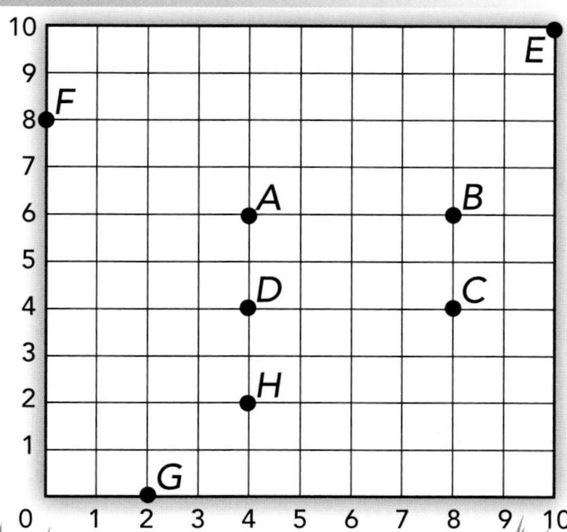

13.8 Surface Area

Construct Meaning

To find the area of a rectangle you must know its length and width. To determine the surface area of a rectangular prism, you must know the length and width of each face. The surface area of a solid figure is the sum of the areas of all the faces.

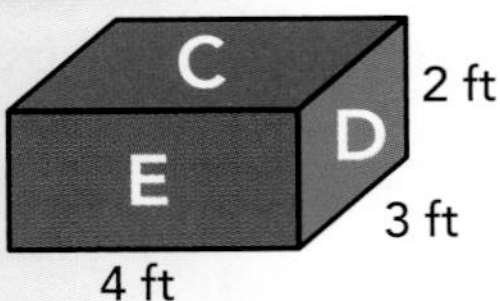

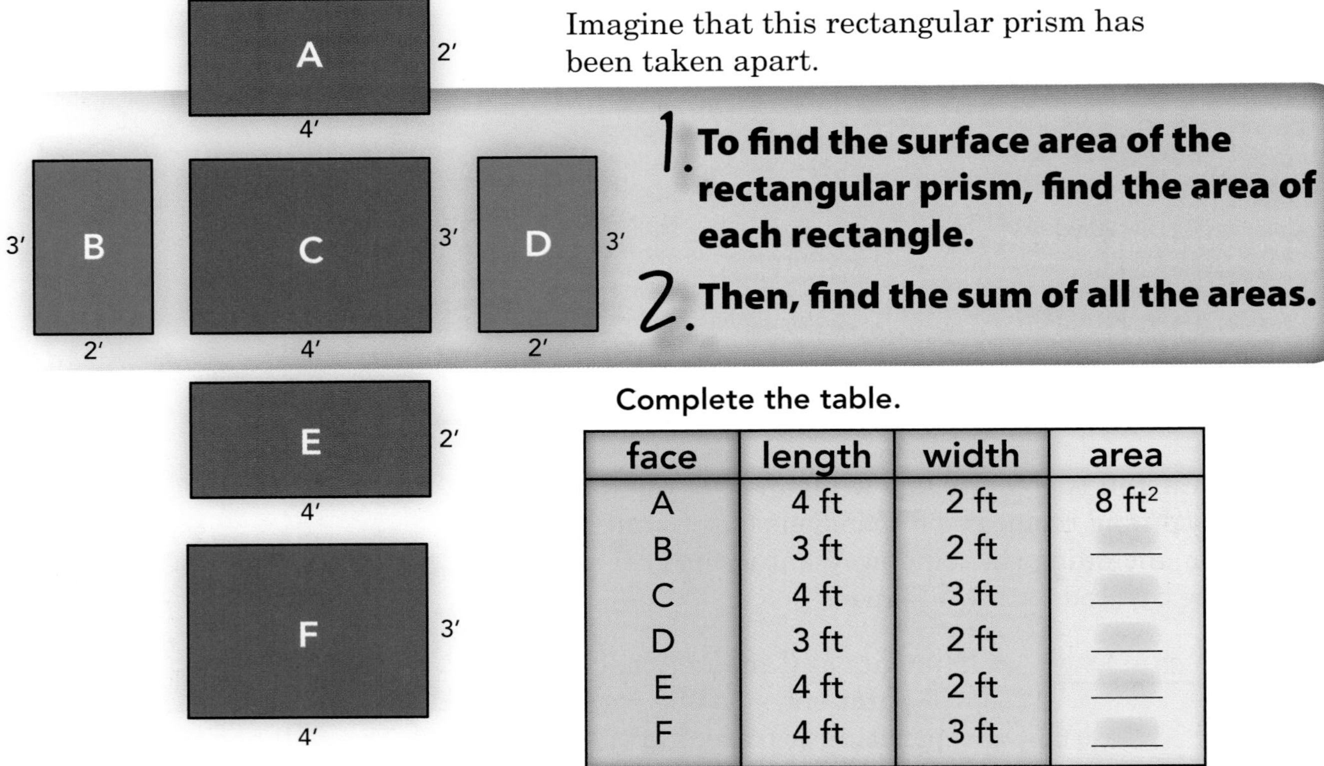

Imagine that this rectangular prism has been taken apart.

1. **To find the surface area of the rectangular prism, find the area of each rectangle.**
2. **Then, find the sum of all the areas.**

Complete the table.

face	length	width	area
A	4 ft	2 ft	8 ft^2
B	3 ft	2 ft	____
C	4 ft	3 ft	____
D	3 ft	2 ft	____
E	4 ft	2 ft	____
F	4 ft	3 ft	____

Add the figures in the last column of the table to find the surface area of the rectangular prism.

Check Understanding

a. What do you notice about the area of opposite faces of a rectangular prism?

b. Is there a more efficient way than the method above to find the surface area of a rectangular prism?

c. Explain the most efficient method of finding the surface area of a cube.

Practice

Find the surface area of each box.

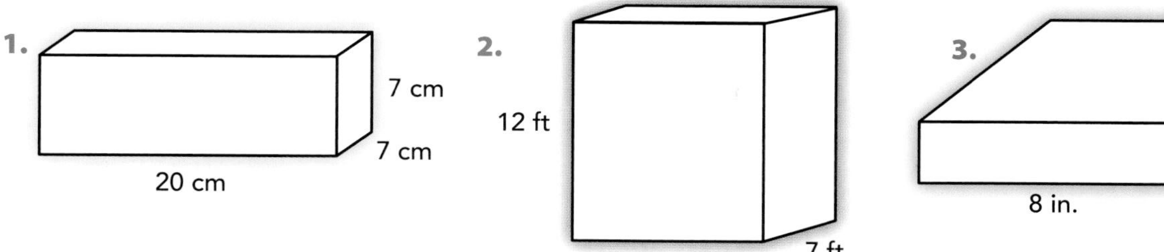

Find the surface area of each object.

Apply

7. Darell is wrapping three boxes like the one shown in Exercise 3 above. What is the total surface area he will cover?

8. The package of wrapping paper Darell bought will cover 5 ft². Does he have enough paper to wrap the three boxes? (144 sq in. = 1 sq ft) Why?

9. Mrs. Henderson used wallpaper to decorate a box shaped like a cube. She did not cover the top of the box because she planned to remove it. The box dimensions were 8" × 8" × 8". What is the total surface area she covered with wallpaper?

Review

Find the perimeter or circumference for each figure.

10. an equilateral triangle, s = 13.9"

11. a circle, d = 2.1 cm

12. a square, s = 8.5 yd

13. a rectangle, l = 5.8 mi, w = 4.6 mi

14. a circle, r = 9 mm

13.9 Understand Volume

Construct Meaning

Volume is the measure of the amount of space within a solid figure or object.

Judah and Holly built a rectangular prism with 1-inch cubes. They found the volume by counting all the cubes that made up the space of the prism.

Each cube of the prism measures 1 inch × 1 inch × 1 inch. It is called 1 cubic inch, 1 cu in., or 1 in^3.

1 in.

1 in. 1 in.

Here is a drawing of the prism students built.

Judah counted the six cubes in the top layer. There were two layers and 6 × 2 = 12 cubes. If each cube measures one cubic inch, the volume is 12 cubic inches. Holly checked the answer by counting all the cubes in their prism.

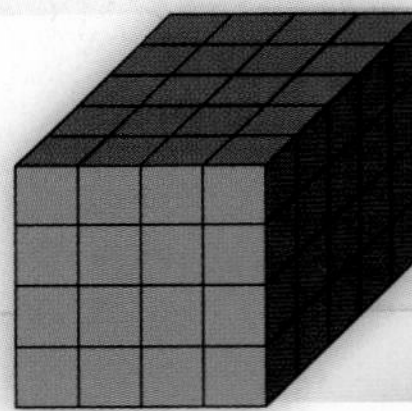

After building a figure like the one shown, Judah realized that they did not have to count every cube in the top layer. He found a faster way to determine the number of cubes in the layer.

What is the faster way?

Find the volume of the new prism.
How many cubes are in one layer?
How many layers are there?
Multiply and express the volume in cubic inches.

If Judah and Holly had used cubes with each edge measuring 1 cm, they would have found the volume in cubic centimeters.

Each cube is 1 cubic centimeter, 1 cu cm, or 1 cm^3.

1 cm

1 cm 1 cm

Check Understanding

a. What is the difference between volume and area?

b. Which is larger, a rectangular prism that has a volume of 31 cm^3 or a cube with a volume of 31 in.^{3}?

Practice

Count the cubes to find the volume. Label your answer. (1 cube = 1 cm^3)

1. 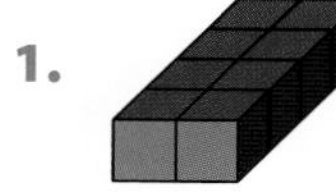

2. 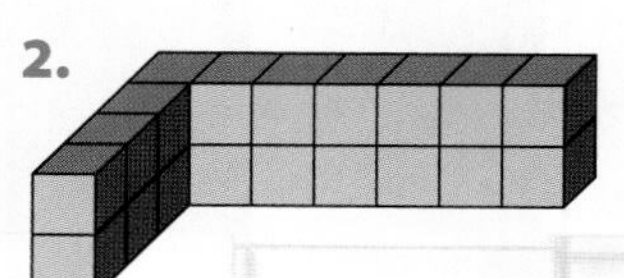

3. 

4. 

5. 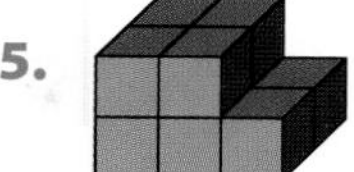

6. 

7. 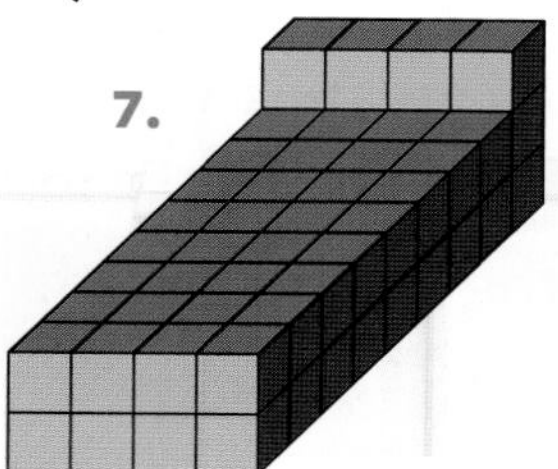

8. 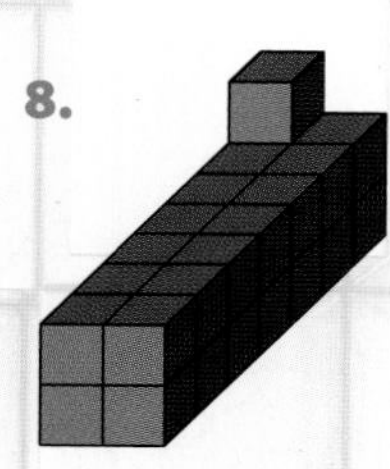

Apply

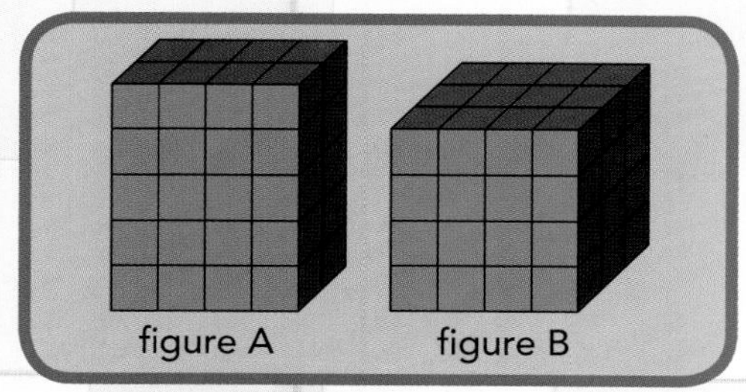

9. Which figure to the right would you guess had the greater volume? Why?

10. Count the cubes. Compare the volume of Figure *A* with the volume of Figure *B*. Use cubic inches as the unit of measure.

11. Kelly used 20 cubes to construct solid figures. He made a figure that was one layer of 20 cubes and another figure that was two layers of 10 cubes. Which figure had the greater volume?

12. Name three different ways you could use cubes in three layers to make a rectangular prism that has a volume of 36 cubic units. Building a model may help.

13. How many centimeter cubes do you need to build a 4 cm × 4 cm × 4 cm cube?

Review

Find the surface area of each figure.

14. 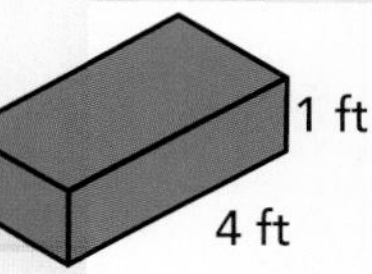

15. 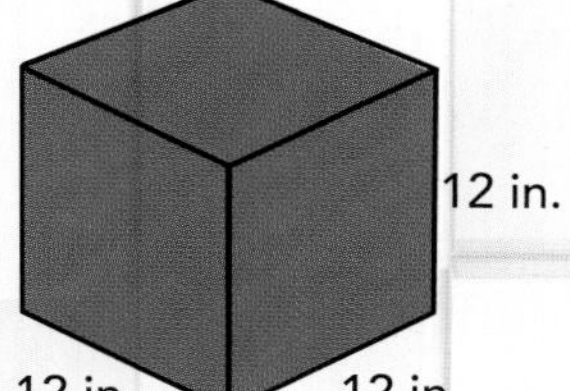

16. 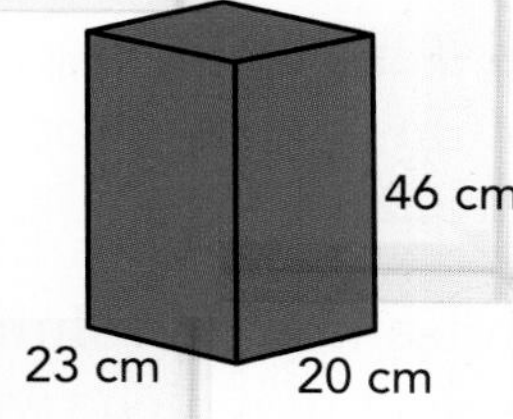

13.10 Find Volume

Construct Meaning

Dale is moving. He will live and work with Christians in Africa. He will leave many of his personal belongings in storage. To choose the box that has the greatest volume for packing, he must find the exact number of cubic units each box will hold.

Use the formula for finding the volume of a rectangular prism.

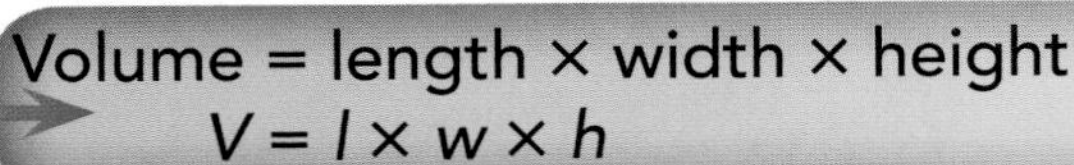

Volume = length × width × height
$V = l \times w \times h$

$V = 20 \text{ in.} \times 8 \text{ in.} \times 8 \text{ in.}$
$V = 20 \text{ in.} \times 64 \text{ in.}^2$
$V =$ _____ in.^3

$V = 18 \text{ in.} \times 13 \text{ in.} \times 10 \text{ in.}$
$V = 18 \text{ in.} \times 130 \text{ in.}^2$
$V =$ _____ in.^3

$V = 19 \text{ in.} \times 8 \text{ in.} \times 10 \text{ in.}$
$V = 19 \text{ in.} \times 80 \text{ in.}^2$
$V =$ _____ cu in.

Which box has the greatest volume?

If you know the length, width, and volume of a rectangular prism, you can find the height.

$V = l \times w \times h$

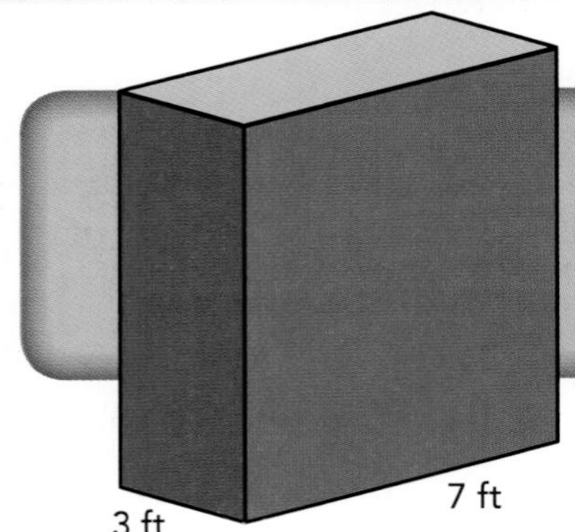

$V = 189$ cu ft

$189 \text{ ft}^3 = 7 \text{ ft} \times 3 \text{ ft} \times h$
$189 \text{ ft}^3 = 21 \text{ ft}^2 \times h$
$189 \text{ ft}^3 \div 21 \text{ ft}^2 = h$
$9 \text{ ft} = h$

The height is 9 ft.

Check Understanding

a. Will the volume change if the length, width, and height are multiplied in a different order? Why or why not?

b. To find h in the example above, you divided the volume by the product of which two measurements?

c. If l is missing, the volume will be divided by the product of which two measurements?

Practice

Find the volume of each object.

1. 

2. 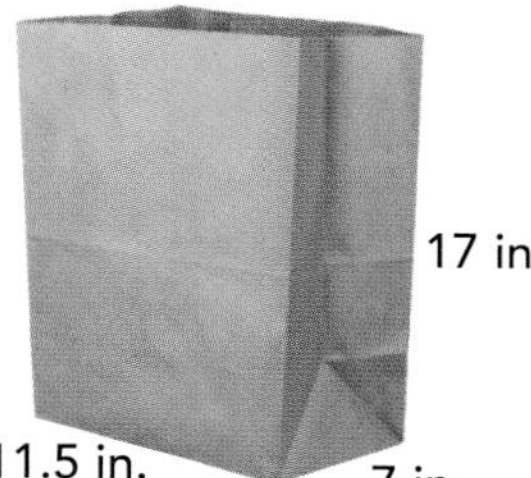

3. 

Using the given dimensions, find the volume of each rectangular prism.

4. 6 yd × 7 yd × 4 yd
5. 13 cm × 10 cm × 8 cm
6. 12' × 24' × 6'
7. 30" × 15" × 9"

Find the missing measurement.

8. l = 11 m
   w = 5 m
   h = 6 m
   V = _____

9. l = 7"
   w = 7"
   h = _____
   V = 343 in.^{3}

10. l = _____
    w = 15 cm
    h = 10 cm
    V = 3,150 cu cm

Apply

11. Blueprints show 8" × 12" × $\frac{1}{2}$" as measurements for a new patio. You have ordered 45 cu ft of concrete. Will there be enough to complete the patio? Why?

12. Select an object nearby that has a volume of about one cubic inch. Pick another that has a volume of about one cubic foot. Find another that has a volume of about one cubic yard. Draw and label the objects below.

13. Corbin wanted to know whether doubling the measure of the length, width, and height of a rectangular prism would double its volume. He worked with many sets of dimensions. He noticed the volume changed when he doubled the measure of length, width, and height. Identify the pattern shown by his samples.

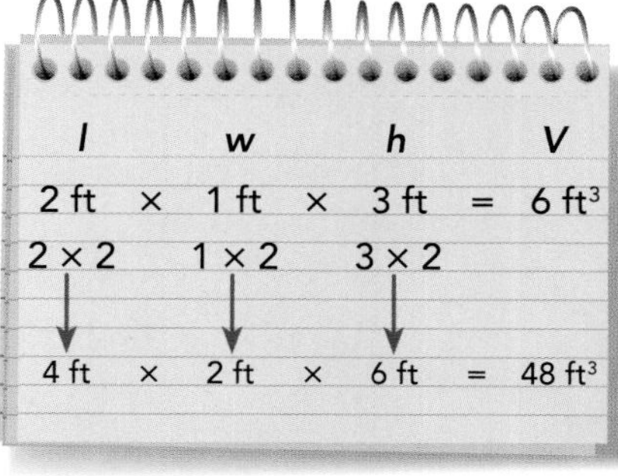

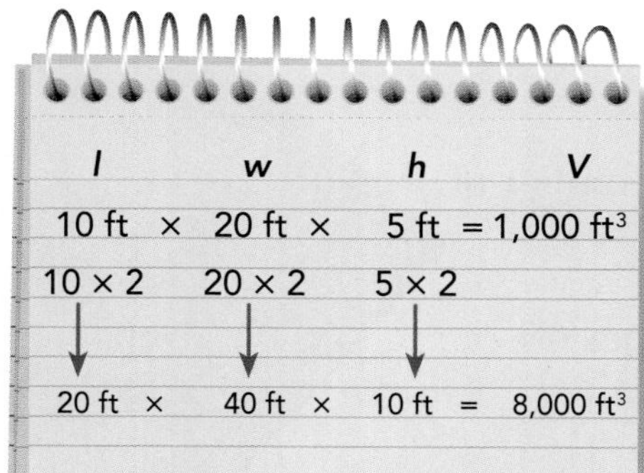

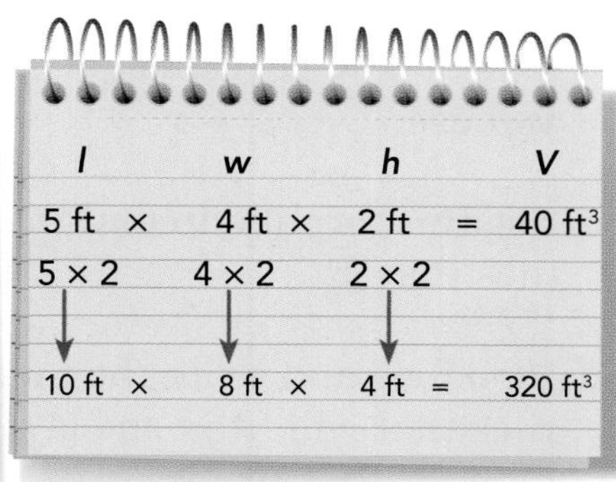

13.11 Problem Solving: Formulas

Construct Meaning

Mr. Bishop planned to update the family room of his home. He will cover the floor with new tile and carpet and put new molding around the perimeter of the room.

He drew a sketch of the floor on graph paper. The side of each square represents three feet. The area to be carpeted was shaded. Mr. Bishop will use formulas to find out how much molding, tile, and carpet to buy.

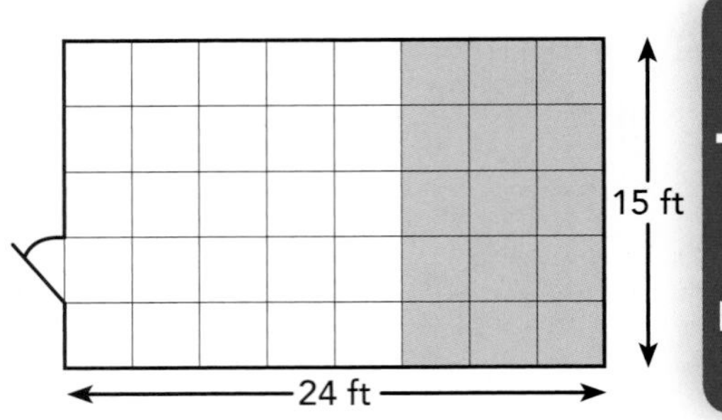

Formulas

Area of a rectangle	$A = l \times w$
Perimeter of a rectangle	$P = 2l + 2w$
Perimeter of a square	$P = 4s$
Circumference of a circle	$C = \pi d$
Area of a triangle	$A = \frac{1}{2} \times b \times h$
Volume of a rectangular prism	$V = l \times w \times h$

Mr. Bishop considered the shape and dimensions of the room before choosing each formula.

He needs to know the area for the tile.

$A = l \times w$
$A = (24 \text{ ft} - 9 \text{ ft}) \times 15 \text{ ft}$
$A = 15 \text{ ft} \times 15 \text{ ft}$
$A = \_\_\_\_ \text{ ft}^2$

He needs to know the perimeter for the molding.

$P = 2l + 2w$
$P = (2 \times 24') + (2 \times 15')$
$P = 48' + 30'$
$P = \_\_\_\_'$

What adjustment should Mr. Bishop make before he purchases molding?

Check Understanding

a. Use the appropriate formula to find the amount of carpet needed for the shaded area on the floor plan.

b. To find how many $8'' \times 8'' \times \frac{1}{4}''$ tiles would fit into a $16'' \times 8'' \times 12''$ carton, which formula should you use?

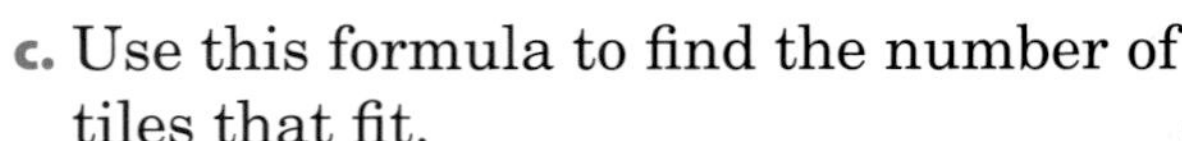

c. Use this formula to find the number of tiles that fit.

d. Visualize and write the number of tiles that will fit in one layer.

e. How many layers of tiles will fit in the carton?

Practice

1. Ellen's youth group decided to make picture puzzles for the younger children at church. Ellen made her puzzle on a piece of 10" × 8" cardboard. She wanted to know the area of the puzzle to determine the size of the picture needed to cover it. What is the area of the puzzle?

2. Colter made a puzzle like the one shown. What is the area of his puzzle?

3. Some of the puzzles were placed into boxes that measured 12" × 9" × 2". The group wrapped these boxes as gifts to be sent to an orphanage. How many wrapped boxes will fit into a mailing carton that measures 2' × 1' × 9"?

20 cm

30 cm

4. A group of parents at Ellen's church are planning to fence the circular play area behind the building. If the diameter of the area is 18', how many feet of fence are needed? Round your answer to the nearest whole number.

5. A porch on a house measures 5' × 10'. If the homeowners double the length and width of the porch, what will be the area of the new porch?

6. How many times greater is the area of the new porch than the area of the old porch?

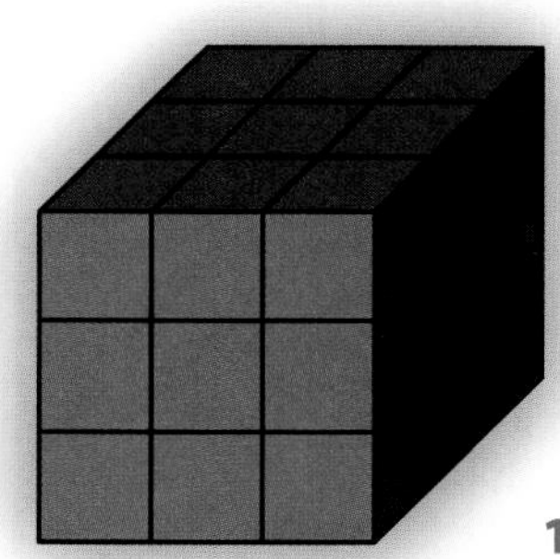

7. Clayton built a cube like the one shown to teach his little sister about surface area and volume. What is the volume of his cube?

8. What is the total surface area of Clayton's cube?

9. What will be the volume if Clayton adds one more layer?

10. Now find the surface area, including the additional layer.

Challenge

11. D'Ette is storing boxes of clothes for the summer in her closet, which has three dimensions: 4' × 3' × 6'. Will she be able to fit the boxes with the following dimensions into the closet? Why?
    - Box 1: 2' × 1' × 1'
    - Box 2: 4' × 3' × 3'
    - Box 3: 2' × 3' × 2'

13.12 Chapter 13 Review

Practice

Find the perimeter of each figure. Label the answer.

1. 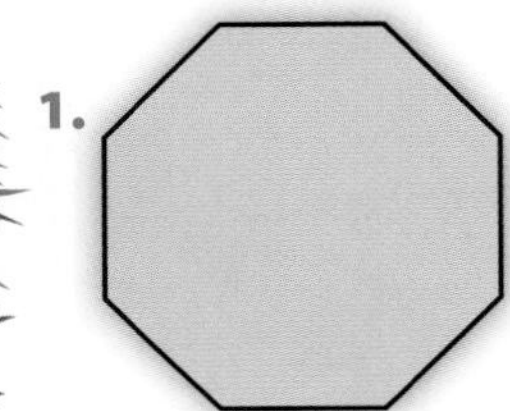

2. 5.4 ft
3.4 ft

3. 3.1 yd
6.2 yd

4. 3.5 cm
3 cm
2.3 cm
3.5 cm
1.5 cm
6.5 cm

Find the circumference of each circle. Round the answer to the nearest tenth.

5. 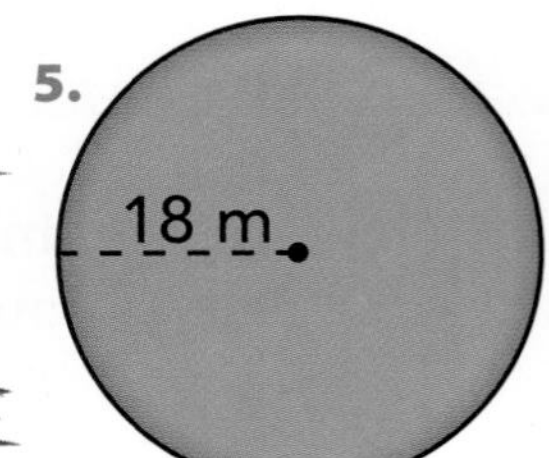

6. 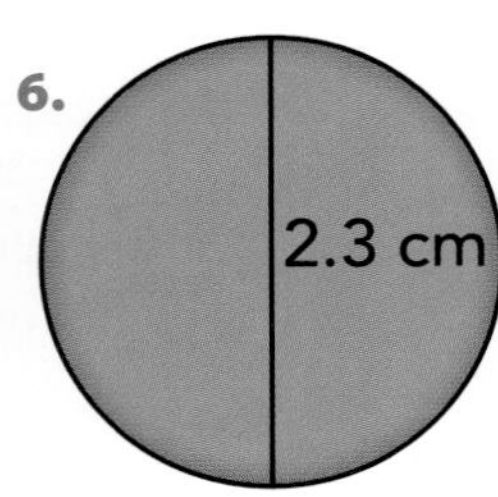

7. 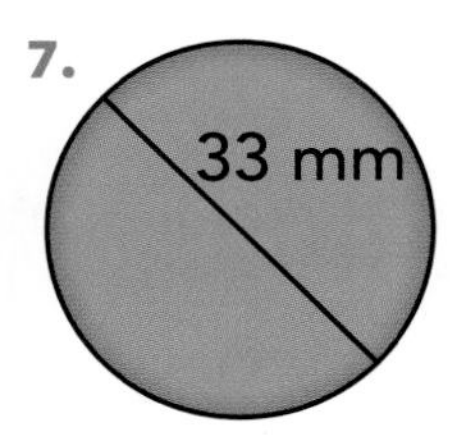

8. 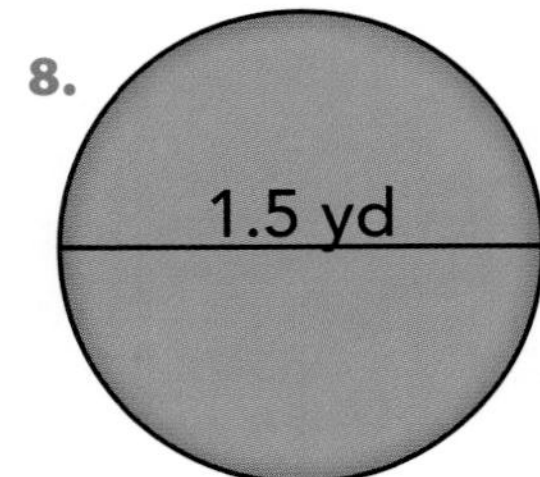

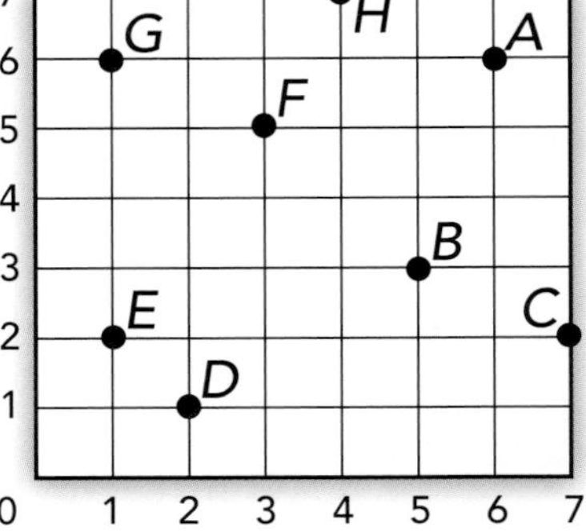

Name the point for each ordered pair.

9. (7, 2) 10. (1, 6) 11. (5, 3) 12. (2, 1)

Name the ordered pair for each point.

13. *E* 14. *F* 15. *A* 16. *H*

Find the area of each outlined figure, using the measurements given.

17. 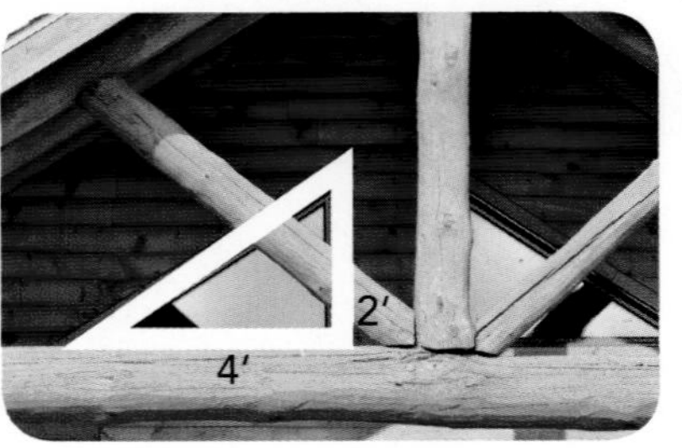

18. 

19. 

Practice

Find the area of each figure.

20. 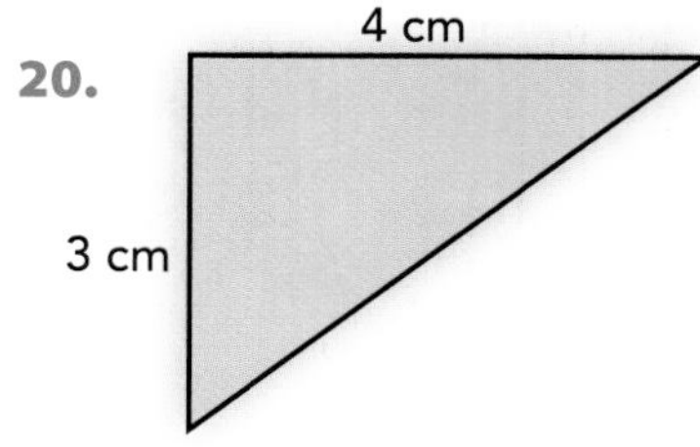

21. 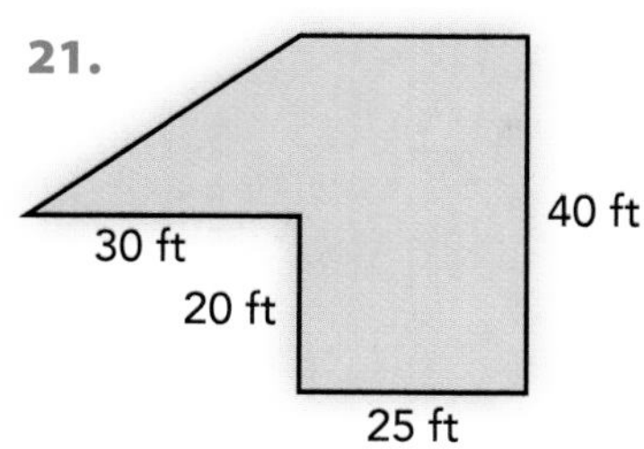

22. 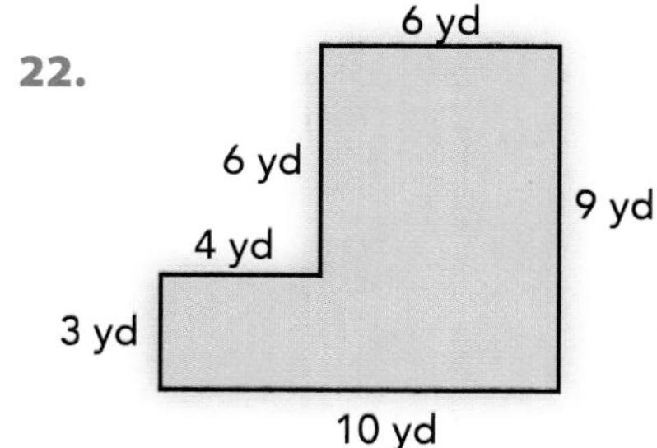

Find the surface area of each rectangular prism.

23. 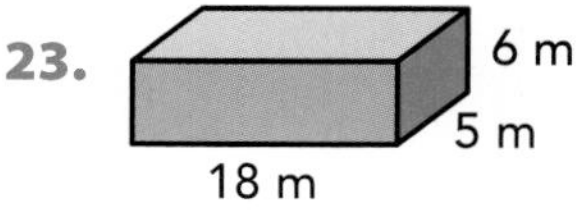

24. 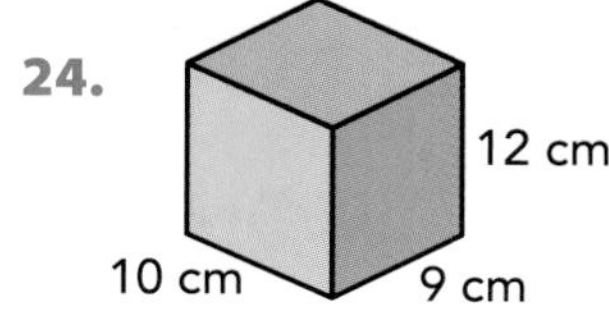

25. 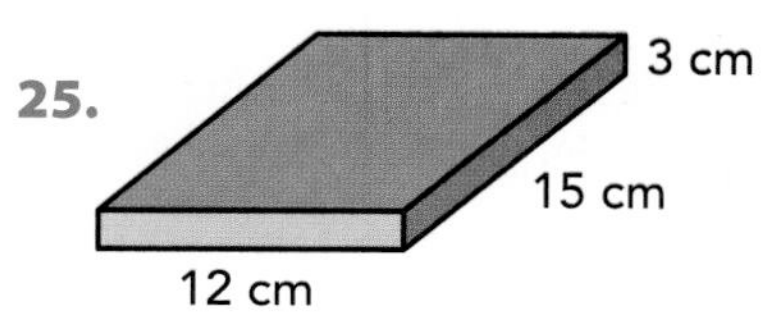

Count the cubes to determine the volume. 1 cube = 1 cm^3

26. 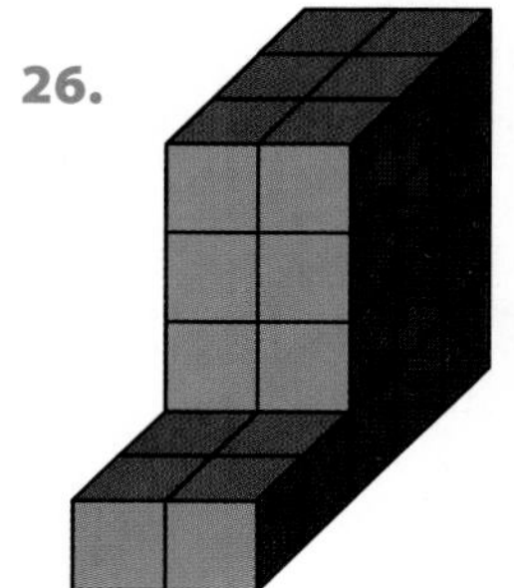

27. 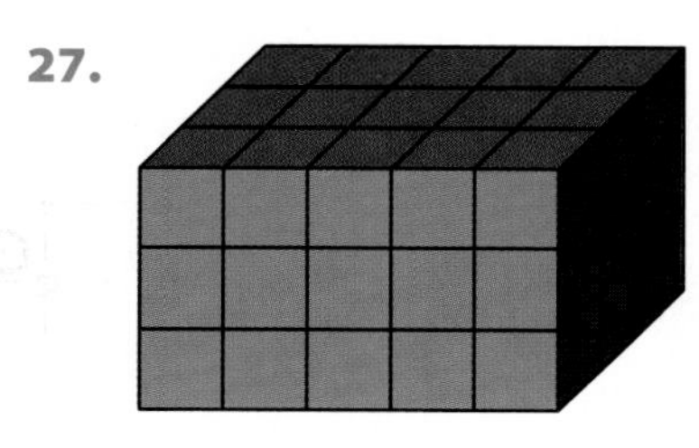

28. 

Find the volume of each object.

29. 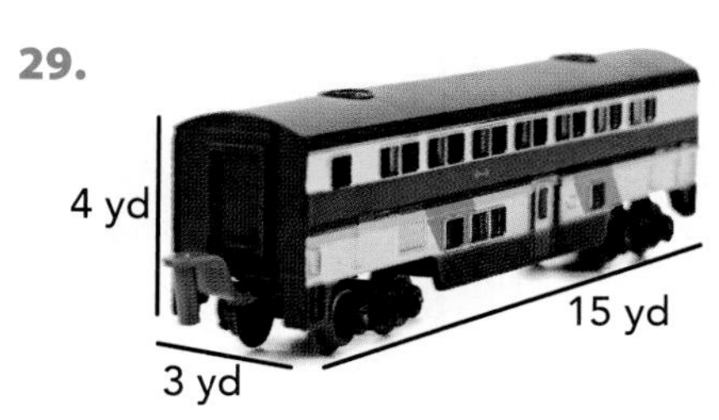

30. 

31. 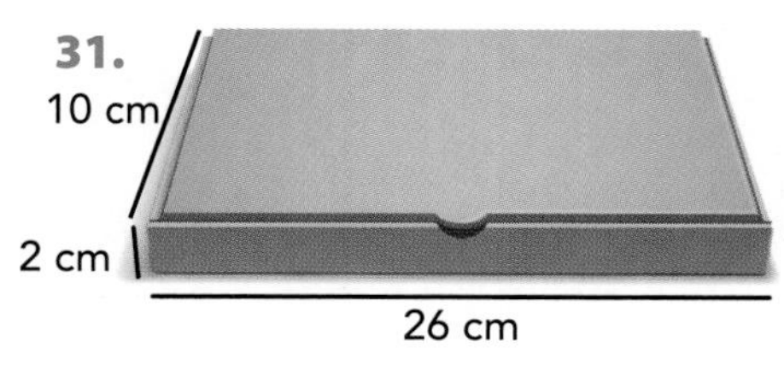

Using the given dimensions, find the volume of each rectangular prism.

32. 10 yd × 11 yd × 8 yd

33. 17 cm × 14 cm × 9 cm

34. 24′ × 36′ × 4′

35. 40″ × 25″ × 7″

36. Deena used 30 cubes to build two solid figures. She built a figure that was two layers with six cubes in each layer. She built another that had one layer of 18 cubes. Which figure had greater volume?

Chapter 14
Graphs, Statistics, and Probability

Ah, Sovereign Lord, You have made the heavens and the earth by Your great power and outstretched arm. Nothing is too hard for You.
Jeremiah 32:17

Key Ideas:

Probability and Statistics: collecting, organizing, and analyzing data

Probability and Statistics: making and interpreting graphs, charts, and tables

Probability and Statistics: understanding mean, median, and mode

Probability and Statistics: interpreting statistics

14.1 Collect and Organize Data

Construct Meaning

Three ways to collect data are surveys, questionnaires, and experiments. Three ways of organizing data are tables, charts, and graphs. Each has a different purpose.

SURVEY

Meryll discovered that calculators, cell-phone chargers, flashlights, and backpacks can be powered by solar energy. She wanted to find out which item her classmates would be most interested in purchasing.

Solar-powered Items Preferred by a Sample of Meryll's Classmates

items	tally	frequency
calculator	||||	4
phone charger	卌 卌 卌 |	16
flashlight	卌 ||	7
backpack	卌 卌	10

Meryll collected data by conducting a survey of a small group, or sample, of students at her school. The results are organized in this table. The table shows the frequency, or the number of times a certain item appears in a set of data.

QUESTIONNAIRE

Nnamdi is from Arusha, Tanzania. He was wondering about solar energy use in his town. He made a questionnaire for residents to complete.

	Yes	No	Maybe
Do you have solar energy?	☐	☑	☐
Do you think solar energy would work in Arusha?	☑	☐	☐
Would you use it to heat water?	☐	☐	☑
Would you use it to run lights?	☑	☐	☐
If it was inexpensive, would you buy it?	☑	☐	☐

EXPERIMENT

After making a prediction about what position would be best for a solar panel on the roof of his house, Nnamdi placed four thermometers on the roof and monitored them during the day. He recorded the temperatures in a chart and made a line graph of thermometer 3.

	Thermometer			
time	1	2	3	4
8:00 AM	61°	54°	72°	60°
10:00 AM	75°	62°	81°	73°
12:00 PM	87°	76°	99°	84°
2:00 PM	98°	82°	110°	96°
4:00 PM	100°	90°	120°	101°
6:00 PM	95°	86°	116°	90°
8:00 PM	89°	80°	109°	84°

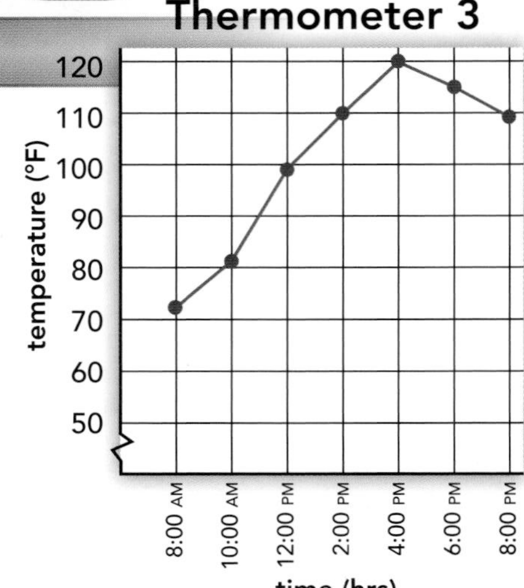

Check Understanding

a. Use the data from Meryll's survey to predict which item would be the most popular in other schools.

b. What would be a good title for Nnamdi's questionnaire?

c. Why should Nnamdi give his questionnaire to a random sample of people?

d. Examine the data from Nnamdi's experiment. Why do you think he chose thermometer 3 to graph?

Practice

1. When collecting data, why would you survey only a sample of the population?

2. Organize the following data in a table: 42 girls chose red, 50 boys chose red, 62 girls chose purple, 30 boys chose purple, 10 girls chose black, 40 boys chose black, 25 girls chose yellow, and 15 boys chose yellow. What is the most popular color for girls? What is the most popular color for boys?

3. Design a survey that determines what type of pets your classmates have. Perform the survey. Make a prediction about a larger population of fifth graders.

4. Pretend you are going to start an after-school club. Develop a five-question questionnaire that you might use.

5. What would be the best way to find answers for each of the following questions? Write "survey," "questionnaire," or "experiment."
   a. What are your classmates' favorite subjects?
   b. What is the most efficient power source?
   c. What type of person makes the best teacher?

6. For each item, explain how you would make sure that a random survey was taken.
   a. favorite food of students in your school
   b. the most important concern for people in your community
   c. favorite place to vacation

Review

Find the perimeter or circumference for each figure.

7. a circle, $d = 6.2$ cm

8. an equilateral triangle, $s = 4.1$ in.

9. a square, $s = 7.9$ yd

14.2 *Pictographs and Bar Graphs*

Construct Meaning

Students in Athletics		
Sport	**Number of Students**	
volleyball	𝍸𝍸𝍸 III	18
basketball	𝍸𝍸𝍸𝍸	20
track	𝍸𝍸𝍸 I	16
wrestling	𝍸𝍸 II	12
football	𝍸𝍸𝍸 I	16
swimming	𝍸 I	6

Yoonie surveyed the students at Heritage Academy to find out how many participated in athletics. She collected the results and recorded them on a frequency table. Then, she used the data to make a pictograph and two bar graphs.

Number of Students in Heritage Academy Athletics	
volleyball	
basketball	
track	
wrestling	
football	
swimming	
Key: = 4 students = 2 students	

A pictograph is a graph that illustrates data by using symbols to represent numbers. The key explains what is represented by the symbols.

A bar graph uses bars to represent and compare numbers for several items.

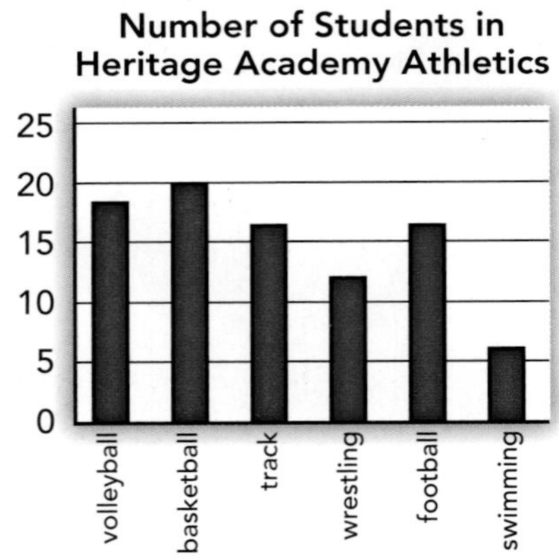

Yoonie surveyed another school and created a double bar graph to compare the two schools. A double bar graph uses sets of two bars to represent and compare numbers for multiple categories at the same time.

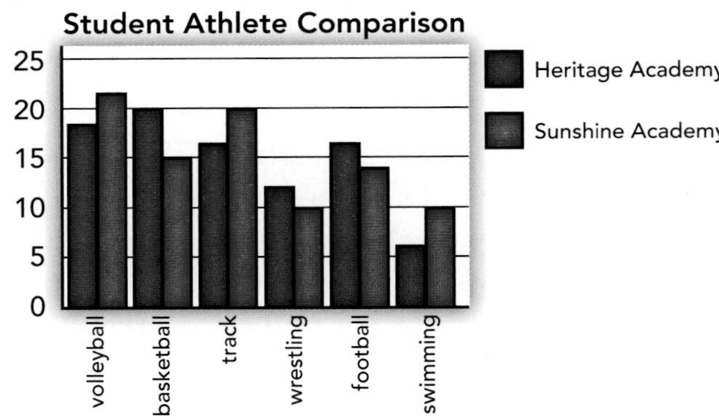

Check Understanding

Use the graphs to answer each question.

a. What is the difference in the number of students who were in basketball and wrestling at Heritage Academy?

b. How could Yoonie show 22 students by using her symbols?

c. List the sports in order of the least to greatest number of students participating at Heritage Academy.

d. List the sports in order of the least to greatest number of students participating at Sunshine Academy.

e. Which school had the most students participating in track?

Practice

Use the double bar graph to answer the questions.

1. What is compared between the cities?
2. Which city receives more total rainfall?
3. Which city receives more rainfall in the month of May?
4. About how many total inches of rainfall does Seattle receive during the four months?

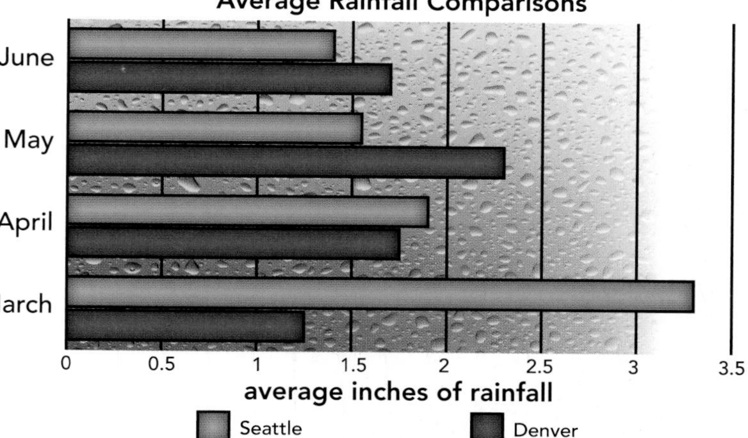

Apply

5. Create a pictograph using the data from this frequency table.

Dogs in the Neighborhood		
street	number of dogs	
Lincoln	𝍸 |||	8
Wallace	𝍸 𝍸 𝍸 |	16
Zena	𝍸 𝍸	10
Edgewater	|||	3
Berry	𝍸 𝍸 ||	12
Fourth	|||	3

6. Design a bar graph using the data from the table.

Favorite Foods of 5th Graders	
foods	number of students
spaghetti	𝍸 ||||
fish sticks	𝍸
pizza	𝍸 𝍸 𝍸
hamburgers	𝍸 𝍸 |
other	𝍸 |

Write "bar graph" or "double bar graph" to indicate how the data would best be displayed.

7.

Sugar Content of One Serving	
apple	16g
cherries	19g
banana	29g
orange	14g

8.

Average Temperature		
month	Minneapolis	Boston
April	48°F	49°F
May	59°F	58°F
June	69°F	68°F
July	74°F	73°F

9.

Spring Valley Orchard Apple Trees	
green	59
yellow	72
red	100
red/yellow	48

14.3 Histograms

Construct Meaning

Energy from water, called hydroelectric power, is an alternate energy source that can be measured in megawatts.

A histogram is a graph that uses bars to represent how many of a particular item are found in a given category or interval. The horizontal axis must show information that can be expressed on a continuous scale such as dollars, hours, or megawatts. The vertical axis shows the number of items. Together they express how many of an item are in a given category.

On this histogram, 2,000 on the horizontal axis represents the interval of 0 to 2,000.

The first bar on the histogram shows that four dams produce between 0 and 2,000 megawatts.

Use the histogram below to answer the following questions.

What is the title?

What is shown on the vertical axis?

What is shown on the horizontal axis?

Which axis expresses a quantity?

Which axis shows a continuous scale?

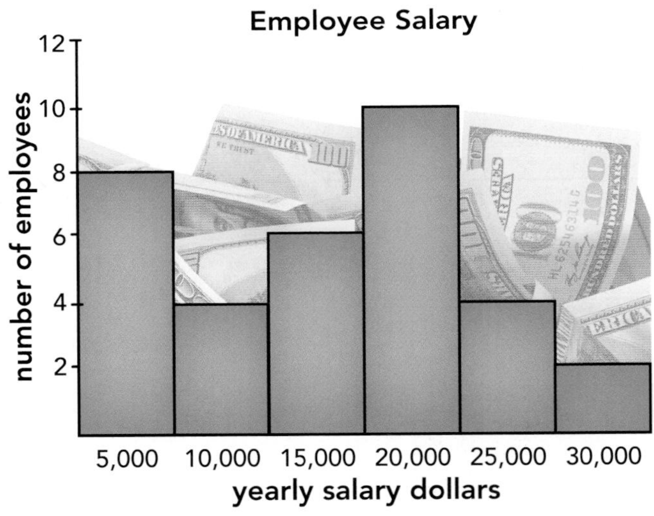

Check Understanding

Use the Employee Salary histogram to answer the following questions.

a. How many employees earn between $15,001 and $20,000?

b. Eight employees are in which salary category?

c. How many employees are in the highest salary category?

d. What are the intervals on the horizontal axis? What are the intervals on the vertical axis?

Practice

1. What type of information is required for the horizontal axis of a histogram?

2. Why is it important to have the intervals, the scale between the numbers on an axis, be equal?

3. Together, what do the horizontal and vertical axes express?

For a class assignment, Larissa was required to research an energy source. She chose hydroelectric power generated by dams. Larissa recorded data about the amount of water released from each turbine of her chosen dam and made the histogram below. Using Larissa's Hydroelectric Production histogram, answer the following questions.

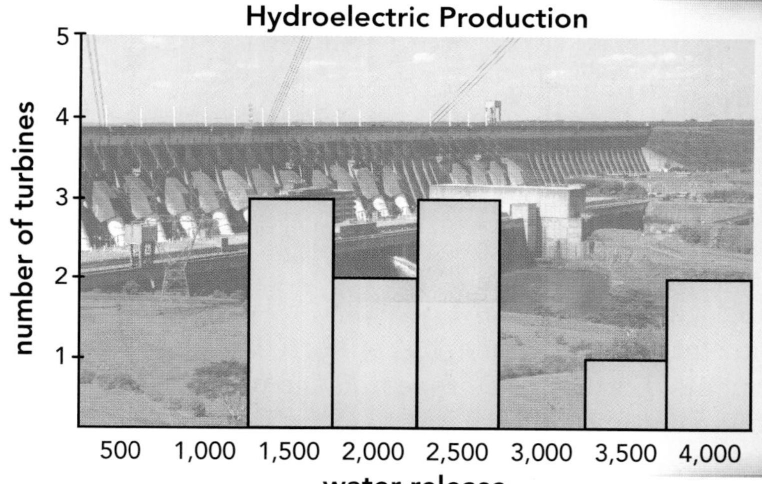

4. What is the histogram telling you?

5. What is the interval on the continuous scale?

6. How many turbines operate between 2,001 and 2,500 cfs?

7. How many turbines operate between 1,001 and 2,500 cfs?

8. Are there five turbines that operate within the same category?

9. Use the data table below to make a histogram. The following statements and questions will help you get started.

The first interval in the continuous scale should start at 0 and end at 2,000. Complete the scale.

What should the vertical axis be called? Remember, it is an amount or a number. (Hint: See the first histogram on the previous page.)

name	power output (megawatts)
A. Itaipu Dam	12,600
B. Grand Coulee Dam	6,480
C. Hoover Dam	2,000
D. LCRA Dams	295

Apply

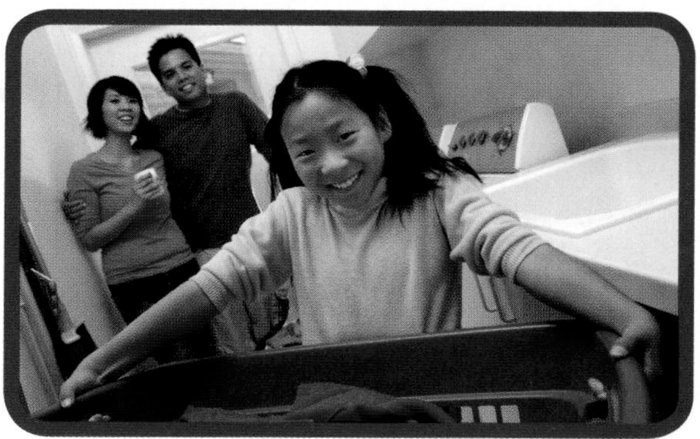

10. Use the data collected by your teacher about the amount of time each student spends doing weekly chores.
    a. Make a data table.
    b. Choose horizontal and vertical axis scales.
    c. Make a histogram from your results.

14.4 Line Graphs

Construct Meaning

Solar heat varies with seasons, years, and days. All life depends on the output of the sun. Genesis 1:14–15 says, "Let there be lights in the vault of the sky to separate the day from the night, and let them serve as signs to mark sacred times, and days and years, and let them be lights in the vault of the sky to give light on the earth...."

A line graph uses lines to represent increases or decreases over a period of time.

Nehemiah wanted to see how much the temperature in his town varied on two days. He used the data to make a line graph. Nehemiah plotted both days' temperatures on the same graph using different colors.

time	Temperature °F day 1	Temperature °F day 2
12:00 AM	35	32
2:00 AM	33	30
4:00 AM	25	29
6:00 AM	29	30
8:00 AM	35	36
10:00 AM	40	39
12:00 PM	48	45
2:00 PM	55	51
4:00 PM	60	60
6:00 PM	54	50
8:00 PM	40	42
10:00 PM	35	38

Here are the steps and questions Nehemiah used to create the line graph:

- He started by drawing the horizontal axis.
- He asked these questions: What is being measured? How is it measured? What is the total interval of time? What would be the best way to draw the intervals in the scale?
- Then, he drew the vertical axis and asked similar questions as above.
- Beginning with the first time on day 1, he plotted each data point for that day. Then, he connected the dots with line segments. For day 2, he repeated the process using a different color and made a key to show the color that represented each day.

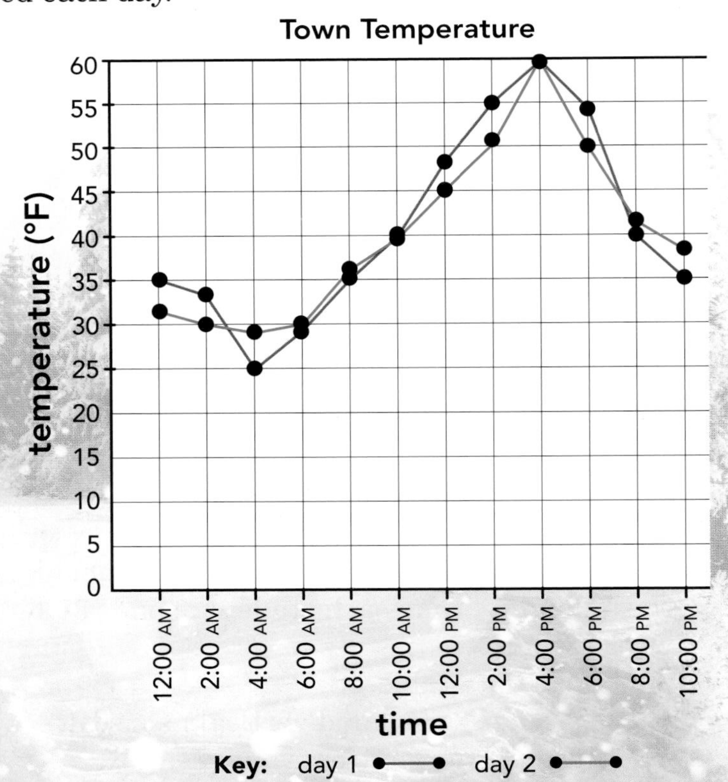

Use the graph at the right to answer the following questions.

 What is the title of the graph?

 Which day had the lowest temperature?

 At 2:00 PM, which day had the higher temperature?

 At 4:00 PM, what was the temperature on day 1? Day 2?

 What is the general trend of the graph?

Remember to ask yourself these questions as you make a graph.

1. What is being measured?
2. What is the interval?
3. What is the best representation of that interval?

Remember to do each step.

1. Label both axes.
2. Connect the points with line segments.
3. Title the graph.

Check Understanding

Use the graph you made to answer each question.

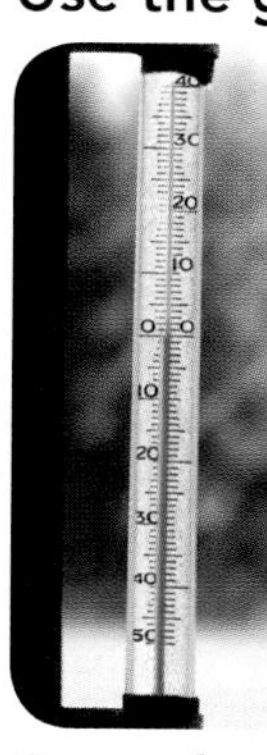

a. When was it 60°F on day 2?

b. What was the greatest increase in temperature during a two-hour period on day 2?

c. What was the temperature at 11:00 AM on day 1?

d. Was one day much warmer than the other?

Practice

Mr. Hausler filled his oil heater with 10 gallons of oil. He started the heater and periodically checked the gauge to see how much oil remained.

elapsed time (hours)	0	4	6	12	14	16
remaining oil (gallons)	10	8	7	4	3	2

1. Make a line graph using Mr. Hausler's data. Label each axis and title the graph.
2. Use the graph to determine how much oil was left after 8 hours.
3. Predict how many hours the heater can run until the oil is gone.

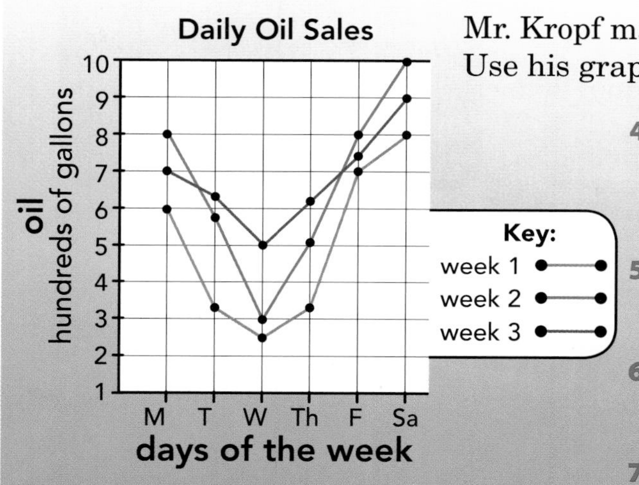

Mr. Kropf made a graph of his daily oil sales for three weeks. Use his graph to answer the questions.

4. How many more gallons of oil were sold on Monday of the second week than on Monday of the first week?
5. On which two days of the week does Mr. Kropf usually sell the most oil?
6. If Mr. Kropf decided to close his shop on one day of the week, what day would probably be best?
7. Which week had the lowest sales?

14.5 Circle Graphs

Construct Meaning

Percentage of Power Types Used

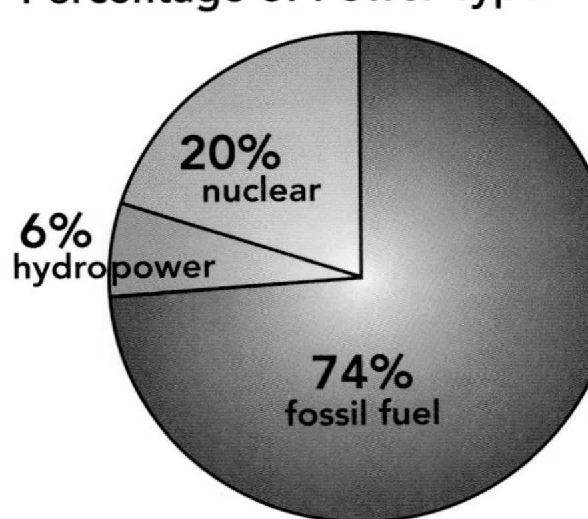

Every time you ride in a car, turn on a light, take a shower, or use the phone, you use power. The circle graph shows the types and amounts of power used in the United States.

A circle graph is a type of graph that compares parts of a whole. The whole circle stands for the total amount of power usage. Each section of the circle shows a percentage of the total power used. Since each section shows a percentage, or fraction, of the whole, the sum of the percentages must be 100%.

Use the circle graph above to answer the following questions.

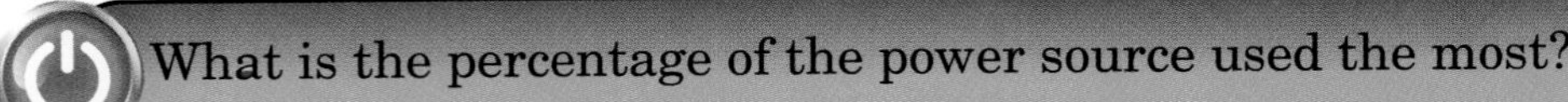
What is the percentage of the power source used the most?

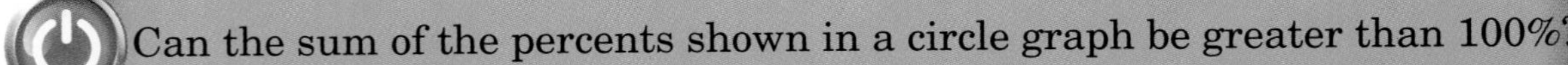
Can the sum of the percents shown in a circle graph be greater than 100%?

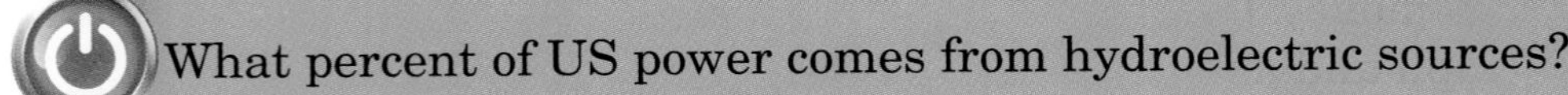
What percent of US power comes from hydroelectric sources?

How much greater is nuclear power usage than hydroelectric power usage?

Check Understanding

a. Use the given information to make a circle graph and label each section of the circle with the percent and name.

b. Do the percents add up to 100%?

c. Which power sources are used the most?

d. Which two power types, when added together, equal 26% of the power used?

US Power Sources

power types	% used
coal	33
natural gas	33
petroleum	1
nuclear	20
hydropower	6
other	7

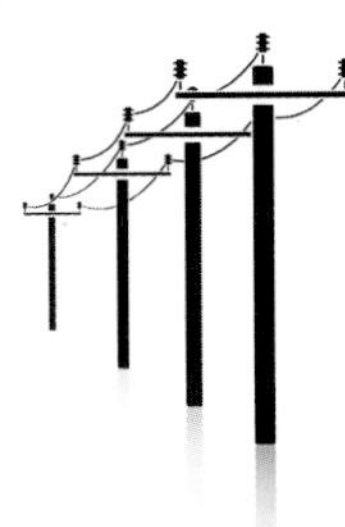

Practice

1. The four countries that were the top megawatt producers of wind energy in 2014 were China, the United States, Germany, and Spain. Of the energy produced by those four countries, China produced 47%, the United States produced 27%, Germany produced 16%, and Spain produced 10%. Use this information to make a circle graph.

Use the graph in Exercise 1.

2. What country produced the greatest amount of wind energy?
3. What two countries together produced almost three-fourths of the total?
4. Which country produced one-tenth of the total wind energy?
5. Use the data at the right to make a circle graph.

Manufacturing Sector Energy Use

sector	% used
paper products	12%
chemical products	25%
petroleum & coal products	30%
primary metal industries	11%
all other manufacturing	22%

6. Mr. Teng's business has $4,000 to spend on solar-powered items. The table describes how he decided to budget his money. Using the data below, make a circle graph and answer the questions.

Solar Budget

item	% of budget
small solar toy cars	14%
one solar panel	25%
solar water heater	38%
portable solar battery	23%

7. How much money will be spent on the solar toy cars?
8. One-fourth of the budget will be spent on which item?

Apply

Energy Consumption

appliance	kilowatt hours
lighting	4
heater	2
clothes dryer	6
power tools	1
oven	10
coffee maker	1
microwave	1

9. During a 24-hour day, Yoshi recorded the energy certain appliances consumed. Use the data given to make a circle graph of the percent of energy used by each appliance.
10. Which appliance was the greatest energy consumer?
11. Which consumed the least amount of energy?

Review

Determine the volume of each rectangular prism with the given dimensions.

12. 13 cm × 10 cm × 6 cm
13. 15 in. × 25 in. × 9 in.

14.6 Problem Solving: Graphs

Construct Meaning

Some day you may get to travel the world. In traveling, you will encounter problems that will require you to use many skills. Using graphs is a good way to compare many types of data. But sometimes graphs can be misleading and confusing. When you solve any problem, make sure you have all the information before you draw a conclusion.

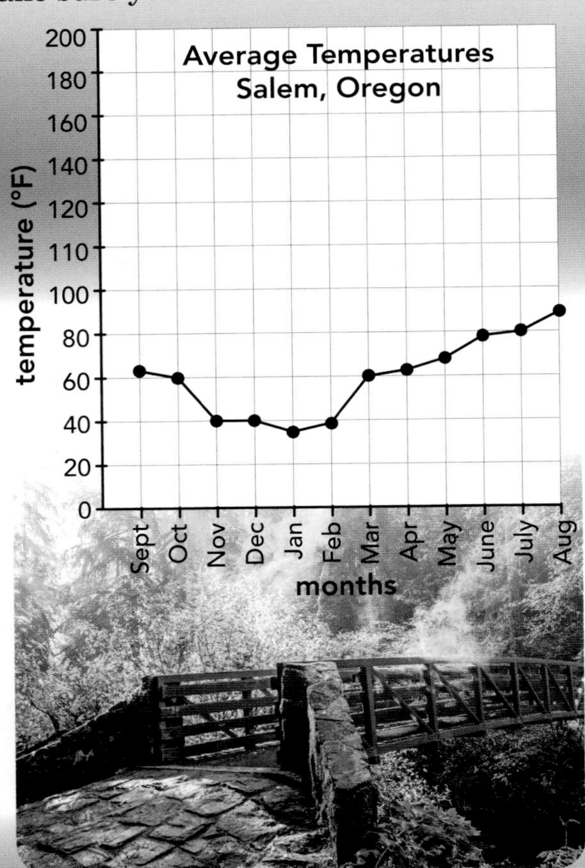

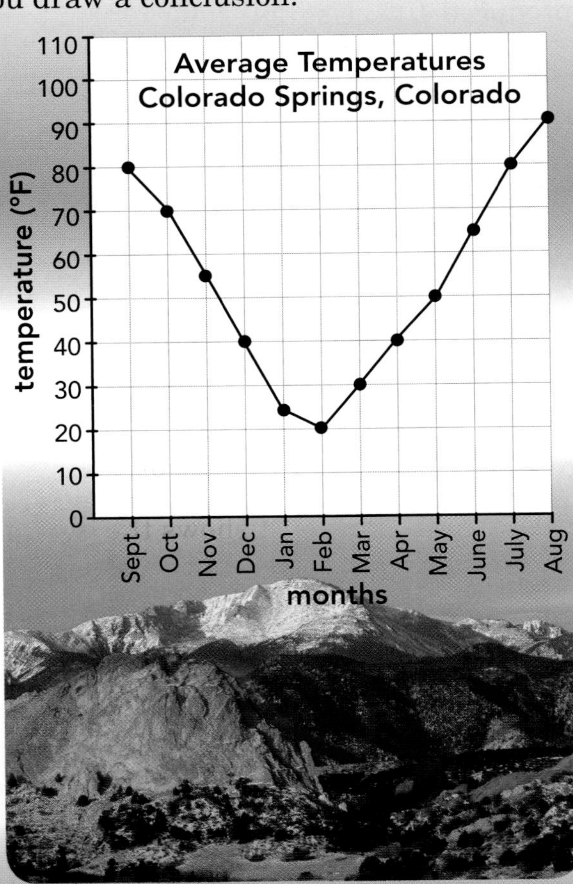

- The titles at the top and the labels at the bottom tell you that both line graphs show average temperature for a one-year period. The graph on the left shows average temperatures for Salem, Oregon. The graph on the right shows average temperatures for Colorado Springs, Colorado.
- The labels at the left side of each graph mark the temperature in degrees Fahrenheit. The intervals are marked in 20°F units on the graph at the left and 10°F units on the graph at the right.
- Critically compare the information in these graphs. Pay special attention to the scales on the vertical axes.

Check Understanding

a. In general, does Salem have lower temperatures than Colorado Springs?

b. In the month of April, what is the average temperature in Colorado Springs?

Practice

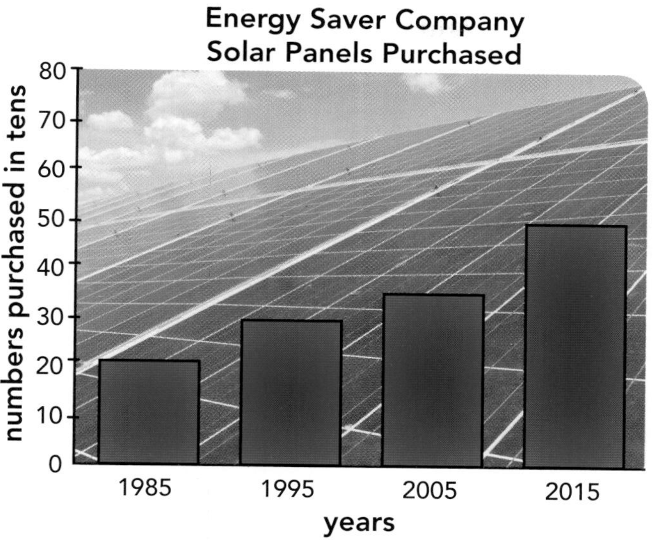

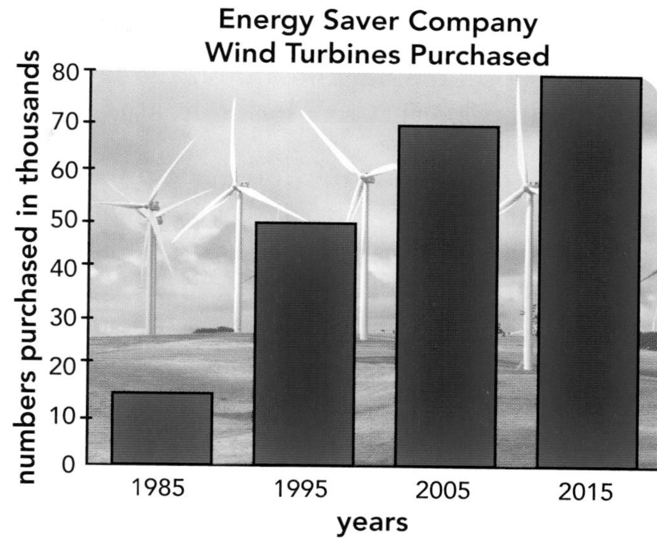

Use the bar graphs above to answer the following questions.

1. In 1985, did Energy Saver Company purchase more solar panels or more wind turbines?
2. Which energy product shows the greatest change between 2005 and 2015?
3. In 2005, how many more wind turbines were purchased than solar panels?
4. Did the number of wind turbines purchased in 1995 equal the number of solar panels purchased in 2015? Explain your answer.
5. In which years did Energy Saver Company purchase more than 40,000 wind turbines?
6. In which years did the company purchase more than 40,000 solar panels?
7. In which years did they purchase more solar panels than wind turbines?
8. Collect a data set of your own. Make a table that will compare the different hair colors in your class and tally how many students fit in each category. Using your data, draw the best type of graph that will fit your data. Explain why you chose that graph type. Do not forget to title and label your graph.

Review

Complete the equations.

9. 4 km = _____ m 10. 7 m = _____ cm 11. 50 cm = _____ dm 12. 7.5 dm = _____ m

14.7 Statistics and Line Plots

Construct Meaning

Statistics is a branch of mathematics that deals with collecting, organizing, and analyzing data. Colored candies are a perfect tool for understanding statistics.

Ten fifth-grade students were each given a bag of candy. Their teacher directed them to each count the total number of purple candies in their bags and to record their answers on a line plot. A line plot is a graph that uses an x to represent a number.

			×					
			×		×			
			×		×			×
			×		×		×	×
0	1	2	3	4	5	6	7	8

This line plot shows the total number of purple candies in each bag. Each × represents one student's total purple candies. There are three ways to analyze the data.

Mode: the number that occurs most often in a set of data
To find the mode, look at the line plot to find the tallest column. The data point (or points) that occurs most often is the mode.

The mode is 3.

Median: the middle number in a set of ordered data
To find the median, put the numbers into numerical order and find the middle number. If there is an even number of data, find the average of the two numbers in the middle.

3, 3, 3, 3, 5, 5, 5, 7, 8, 8

The median is 5.

Mean: the average of a set of data
What is the mean number of purple candies per bag? Add all the numbers in the set of data and divide by 10, because there are 10 bags of candy.

The mean is 5 purple candies per bag.

Check Understanding

a. If a large bag contained 100 candies in 5 different colors, what would be the mean of each color in the bag?

b. What is the median of 50, 75, 100, 101, and 115?

c. Could there ever be more than one mode? Why?

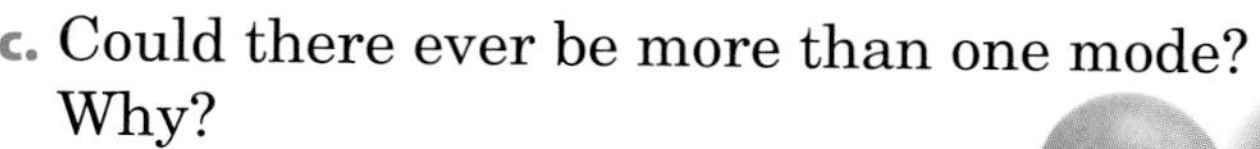

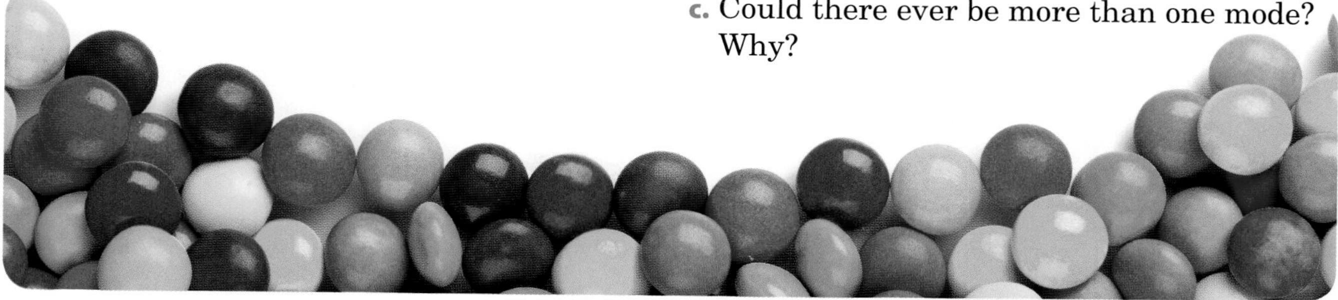

Practice

1. Zaburi recorded the following wind speeds (mph) at hourly intervals during a day.

10, 10, 5, 25, 10, 20, 30, 10, 35, 35, 5, 50

a. Make a line plot with the given information.
b. Calculate the mean wind speed for the day, rounded to the nearest whole number.
c. What is the mode?

USE A CALCULATOR

2. Paula recorded the daily high temperatures (°F) each day of her family vacation as follows:

60, 64, 70, 70, 60, 60, 80, 80, 78, 80, 80, 78, 72

a. Draw a line plot.
b. Find the mode.
c. Find the median.
d. Use a calculator to find the mean. Round to the nearest whole number.

3. What would happen to the mean in Exercise 2 if one of the recorded temperatures was 35°F?

4. Write a definition of each term.
a. mean b. mode c. median

Review

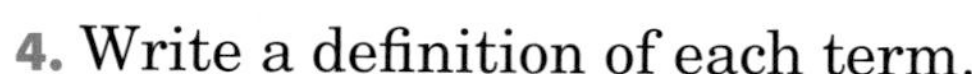

Complete each proportion.

5. $\frac{2}{3} = \frac{}{36}$ 6. $\frac{1}{5} = \frac{}{50}$ 7. $\frac{3}{6} = \frac{}{66}$

14.8 Range, Mean, Median, and Mode

Construct Meaning

Mean, median, and mode are used in statistics to understand data. Range is the difference between the greatest and least numbers in a set of data.

In the southwestern United States, large areas of land are used to raise and herd cattle. These areas are called rangelands. In these areas, it can become very hot.

To find the range, subtract the lowest temperature from the highest temperature.

80°F 95°F 62°F 101°F 95°F

101°F – 62°F = 39°F

If there are two middle numbers, the median is the mean of the two middle numbers. Place the numbers in order and find the median.

84°F 86°F 90°F 95°F 97°F 99°F

(90°F + 95°F) ÷ 2 = 185°F ÷ 2 = 92.5°F

The mode is the number that appears the most often in a set of data. Sometimes, there is not a number that appears more often. If that happens, there is no mode.

120°F 113°F 116°F 118°F 110°F

Check Understanding

a. What is the difference between median and mode?

b. How do the mean and the median differ from each other?

c. Using color tiles, make one stack each of 2, 5, 3, 6, and 9. Arrange the stacks from tallest to shortest and find the range, median, and mode.

d. What would be the best way to use the color tiles to find the mean?

Apply

1. During training, a horse moved at several different speeds. These speeds were recorded in the data set below. Find the range, median, mode, and mean.

   16 mph 21 mph 40 mph 18 mph 32 mph 39 mph 2 mph

2. Logan researched the speed of some fast animals. Find the range, median, mode, and mean. Round to the nearest tenth.

peregrine falcon	200 mph	blue wildebeest	50 mph
frigate bird	95 mph	lion	50 mph
sail fish	68 mph	Thomson's gazelle	50 mph
cheetah	61 mph	brown hare	47 mph
pronghorn antelope	60 mph	elk	45 mph

Bank tellers have different amounts of change during a day. Copy and complete the table below.

	number of quarters	range	median	mode	mean
3.	53 64 100 24 73 89 24				
4.	40 44 41 49 40 40 40				
5.	70 72 70 81 83 70 86				

6. Mr. Ross owns a horse farm where he breeds horses. He needs to know the range, median, mean, and mode of the height of the horses for his records. Use the data below to find the value of each term.

   50 in. 68 in. 35 in. 42 in. 30 in. 50 in.
   62 in. 30 in. 50 in. 50 in. 61 in.

7. To make the range 25, change one number in the data set.

   17 25 5 20 29 7 13

8. Estimate to determine which set of data has the greater mean. Write "a" or "b."

   a. 90 76 45 57 80 81 **b.** 80 92 121 55 43 85

9. To make the mode 15, change one number in the data set.

   10 21 15 31 6 29

Review

Find the missing number.

10. $\frac{5}{8} = \frac{15}{x}$ 11. $\frac{4}{n} = \frac{16}{40}$ 12. $\frac{3}{12} = \frac{n}{36}$

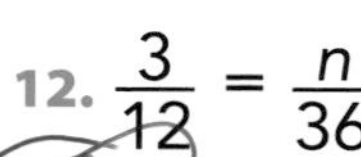

14.9 Practice: Statistics and Graphs

Construct Meaning

Job and his family lived prosperously in the land of Uz. He was a blameless, upright man who feared God and shunned evil. Through several circumstances, he lost his flocks, his children died, and his health failed. Job remained faithful to God in the midst of the hardships. Because of this, the Lord blessed Job later in life more than earlier by giving him children and greater wealth than he had before.

A double bar graph of Job's herds was made using the numbers listed in Job 1:3 and Job 42:12.

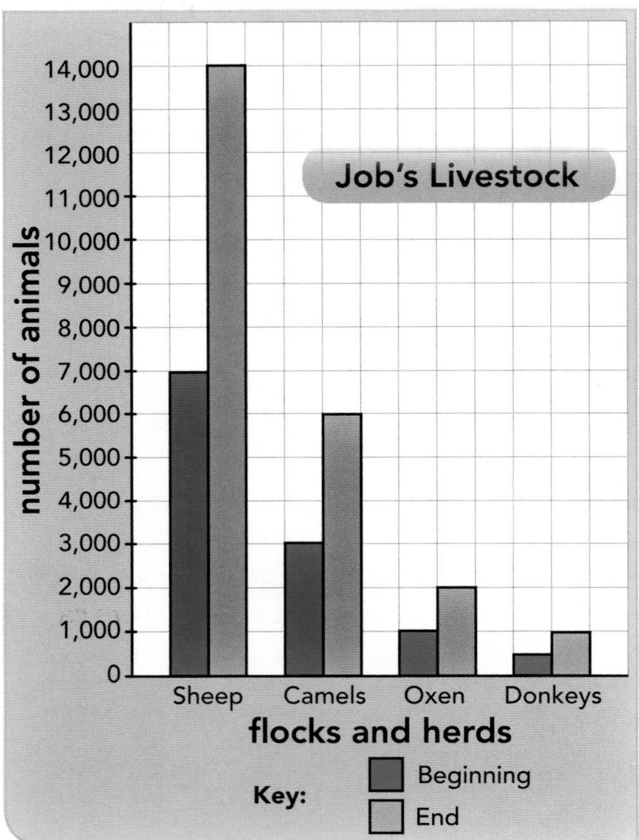

- Why is a key necessary for a double bar graph?
- Job began with the greatest number of which animal?
- How many more camels than donkeys did Job own at the end?
- Did Job have more oxen or donkeys at the beginning?

Check Understanding

Use the double bar graph of Job's livestock to answer the following questions.

a. Find the difference between the beginning numbers and the end numbers for each type of animal.

b. What pattern do you notice when comparing the beginning and end numbers?

Practice

Rancher Teagen has many flocks of sheep. He has listed the numbers in each flock.

100 160 40 240 120 150 240 200 165 90

1. Find the range.
2. Find the mode.
3. Find the mean.
4. Find the median.

Answer Bank:
line graph
circle graph
bar graph
pictograph

5. Bars represent numbers on a ____.
6. Increases or decreases over time are graphed on a ____.
7. Symbols represent numbers on a ____.
8. Parts of a whole are shown on a ____.

9. Patty gives her horse a type of feed that contains 50% alfalfa, 15% barley, 15% oats, 10% corn, 5% molasses, and 5% soybeans. Make a circle graph to show the percentages.

10. Use the table to make a pictograph.

11. Use the table to make a line graph.

Days of Sunshine							
month	January	February	March	April	May	June	July
number of days	2	2	10	12	9	26	22

Apply

Valentina took a survey in her class at school. She asked her classmates what type of transportation they used in order to get to school. Valentina found that seven students came by car, nine came by bus, four came on bicycles, and six walked.

12. Make a frequency table using Valentina's data.
13. Make a line plot using the information from the frequency table.

14.10 Probability of Outcomes

Construct Meaning

If the earth was produced by chance, how many different factors would be involved? The thickness of Earth's crust, the tilt of its axis, and its distance from the sun are all exactly as they must be for life to thrive. God, not chance, designed Earth.

The chance that an event will happen is called probability. Probability is a ratio. It can be shown in three ways: $\frac{1}{100}$, 1:100, and 1 chance in 100. An outcome is a possible result in a probability event.

For example, there are two possible outcomes when a coin is tossed—heads and tails. There is one chance in two of tossing tails. It is equally likely that the coin will show heads (H) as it will show tails (T). The probability can be written as a fraction.

$$P(\text{tails}) = \frac{\text{Number of Favorable Outcomes (tails)}}{\text{Number of Possible Outcomes (tails, heads)}} = \frac{1}{2}$$

Write $P(\text{t}) = \frac{1}{2}$. The variable P represents the probability of a certain outcome (t), tails. The probability of tails as an outcome is one-half or one out of two.

Answer the following questions about the spinner.

Are the sections equivalent?
What are the possible outcomes of spinning the spinner?
How many possible outcomes are there?
What is the probability of the spinner landing on green?

$$P(\text{green}) = \frac{\text{Favorable Outcomes (green)}}{\text{Possible Outcomes (green, purple, yellow, purple)}} = \frac{\quad}{\quad}$$

Check Understanding

Use the spinner from above to answer the questions.

a. On what color will the spinner probably land the most often? Why?

b. $P(\text{purple}) = \frac{\text{Favorable Outcomes (purple, purple)}}{\text{Possible Outcomes (green, purple, yellow, purple)}} = \frac{\quad}{\quad}$

c. $P(\text{yellow}) = \frac{\text{Favorable Outcomes (yellow)}}{\text{Possible Outcomes (green, purple, yellow, purple)}} = \frac{\quad}{\quad}$

d. Use a proportion to make a prediction. If you spin the spinner 16 times, how many times do you calculate it will land on purple? Yellow? Green?

Apply

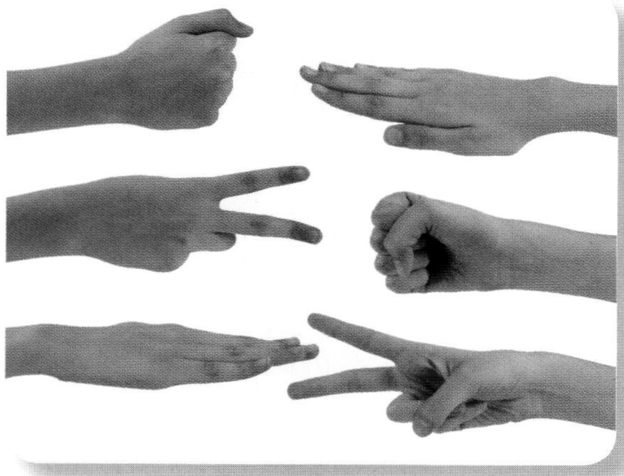

Nat enjoys playing Rock, Paper, Scissors. There are three possible hand signals for the game. Two extended fingers act as scissors, a fist acts as a rock, and a flat hand (fingers extended) acts as paper. Suppose there are never any ties.

1. How many possible outcomes are there?

2. Find each probability.
   a. $P(\text{rock}) =$ _____
   b. $P(\text{paper}) =$ _____
   c. $P(\text{scissors}) =$ _____

Mary and Phil have been married three years. They are expecting their first child. Find the following probabilities.

3. $P(\text{boy}) =$ _____

4. $P(\text{girl}) =$ _____

5. What will be the probability that their third child is a boy?

Lucia has a regular six-sided number cube numbered 1 through 6.

6. What are the possible outcomes when she rolls the cube?

7. How many possible outcomes are there?

8. What is the probability of rolling a 4, $P(4)$?

9. What is the probability of rolling an odd number, $P(\text{odd})$?

10. If she rolled the cube 10 times, what is $P(2)$?

Genetically, Mary and Phil's child is more likely to have brown eyes than blue. This probability is represented on the spinner. Find the probability for each eye color.

11. $P(\text{brown}) =$ _____

12. $P(\text{blue}) =$ _____

14.11 More About Probability

Construct Meaning

In John 6:9–12, a boy brought five loaves and two small fish. Jesus used the boy's small amount of food to provide a meal for a crowd, with basketfuls left over.

If the boy had brought a bag containing the five loaves and two small fish to the disciples, its contents would be unknown. If one item was randomly taken from the bag, what is the probability that it would be a loaf?

$$P(\text{loaf}) = \frac{\text{Favorable Outcomes (loaves)}}{\text{Possible Outcomes (loaf, loaf, loaf, loaf, loaf, fish, fish)}} = \frac{5}{7},\ P(\text{loaf}) = \frac{5}{7}$$

What is the probability that it would be cheese?

$$P(\text{cheese}) = \frac{\text{Favorable Outcomes (cheese)}}{\text{Possible Outcomes}} = \frac{0}{7},\ P(\text{cheese}) = 0$$

When an event is impossible, the probability is zero.

What is the probability that the item is food?

$$P(\text{cheese}) = \frac{\text{Favorable Outcomes (food)}}{\text{Possible Outcomes}} = \frac{7}{7} = 1,\ P(\text{food}) = 1$$

Since all the items are food, it is certain that the item chosen will be food.

When an event is certain, the probability is one.

The closer the probability is to one, the more likely it is the event will happen.

Which probability in each pair represents an event more likely to occur?

$\frac{1}{8}$ or $\frac{1}{2}$

0 or 1

$\frac{5}{16}$ or $\frac{3}{4}$

Check Understanding

If two coins are flipped at the same time, there are four different possibilities for combinations of heads and tails as listed below.

Possible Outcomes

coin 1	coin 2
H	H
H	T
T	H
T	T

a. What is the probability that both coins will be heads?

b. What is the probability that both coins will be tails?

c. What is the probability that the coins will be different?

Practice

A dime, a nickel, and a penny are all flipped at the same time. The possible outcomes are listed below.

Possible Outcomes		
dime	nickel	penny
H	H	H
H	H	T
H	T	H
H	T	T
T	H	H
T	H	T
T	T	H
T	T	T

1. What is the probability that all three coins will show the same side?
2. What is the probability that the dime will be heads?
3. What is the probability that all three coins will show different sides?
4. What is the probability that the dime and the nickel will both be tails?
5. What is the probability that all three coins will be heads?
6. Predict how many times all three coins will be heads for 24 tosses.

Apply

Lin had a world map showing areas where solar energy and wind energy are used. He made a game by cutting the map into 15 pieces and shuffling them.

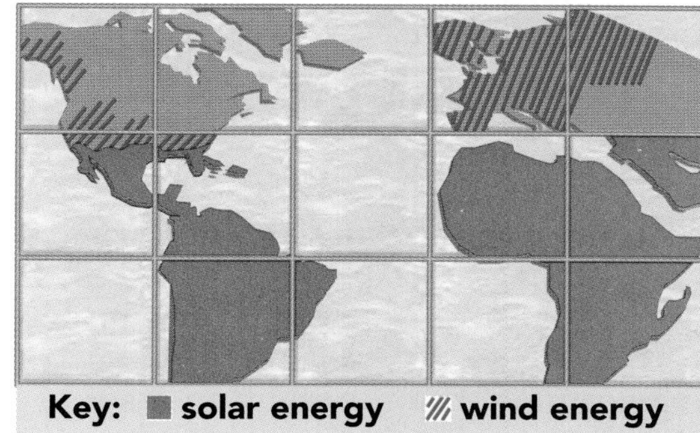

7. If Luna draws one card, what is the probability that her card will be entirely water?
8. What is the probability that she would draw a card that shows wind energy use?
9. What is the probability that she would draw a card that shows solar energy use?

Challenge

10. What would be the probability of choosing a card that shows either wind energy or solar energy?

Review

11. Find the area for a triangle if b = 7 cm and h = 4 cm. _____
12. Find the perimeter of an equilateral triangle that has 4 cm sides. _____
13. Find the circumference of a circle that has an 8 in. diameter. _____
14. Find the area of a square that has a 5 in. side. _____

14.12 Chapter 14 Review

Choose the type of graph that would best represent the given information.

1. Norwegian Energy Council's financial budget
2. classmates' favorite colors of bicycles
3. solar energy output over five years
4. salaries earned by one hundred employees
5. comparing the cost of different types of wind turbines

Graphs

- circle
- histogram
- pictograph
- bar
- line

time	water level
8:30 AM	140 cm
10:30 AM	140 cm
12:30 PM	139 cm
2:30 PM	125 cm
4:30 PM	112 cm
6:30 PM	110 cm
8:30 PM	109 cm
10:30 PM	109 cm
12:30 AM	109 cm

6. A ranch has a holding tank to preserve water in case of drought. Exposure to the hot sun causes the water to evaporate into the air, decreasing the amount of water in the tank. Make a line graph using the given data.
7. What was the total decrease in water level?
8. During which two-hour interval was the water loss the greatest?
9. What could be done to prevent this water loss?
10. Make a prediction about the water level at 2:30 AM.

Complete each sentence.

11. The number that occurs the most often in a set of data is the ____.
12. The middle number in a set of ordered data is the ____.
13. The average of the numbers in a set of data is the ____.
14. The difference between the largest and smallest numbers in a set of data is the ____.

Use the data to find the range, mode, median, and mean.

15. 39 35 16 51 23 16
16. 101 200 243 212 189
17. 10 2 12 4 15 4 16
18. 20 8 32 20 10

Flavor	brand 1	brand 2
vanilla	$2.00	$3.00
chocolate	$4.00	$3.00
strawberry	$4.00	$6.00
peppermint	$1.75	$3.00

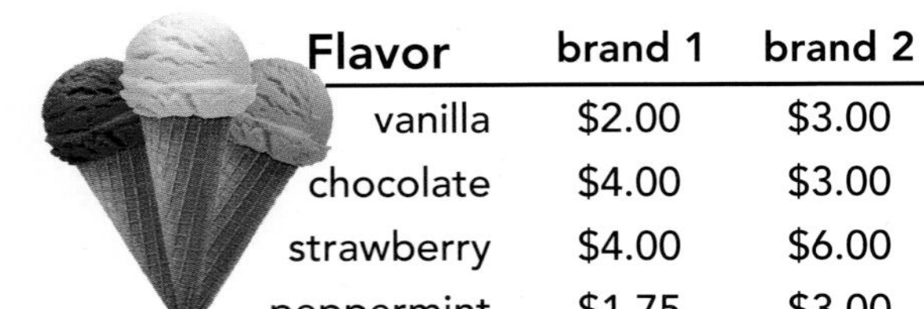

19. Use the table at the left to make a double bar graph.
20. Which brand is usually more expensive?
21. How much does brand 2 strawberry cost?
22. Which is the least expensive brand and flavor?
23. How much more is brand 2 strawberry than brand 1 peppermint?

Mishka and her mother purchased fruit to make fruit baskets for elderly people in their church. Use the circle graph to answer the following questions.

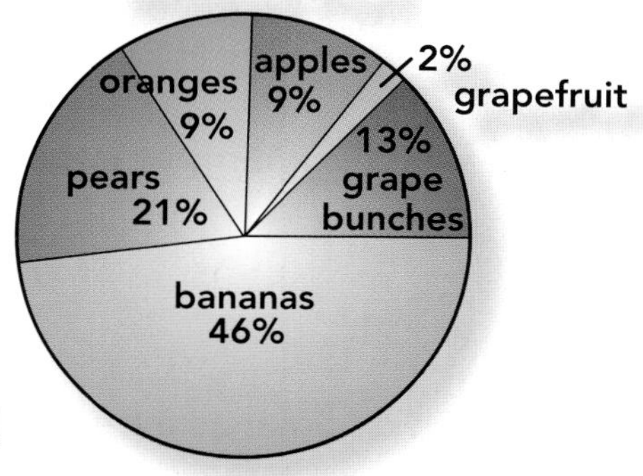

24. Do the percentages add up to 100%?

25. What percentage of the fruit requires peeling before eating?

26. Was the amount of apples and oranges together greater than or less than the amount of pears?

27. Which fruit category represents about one-half of the total fruit?

28. What two fruits have equal amounts?

Use the spinner to complete the exercises.

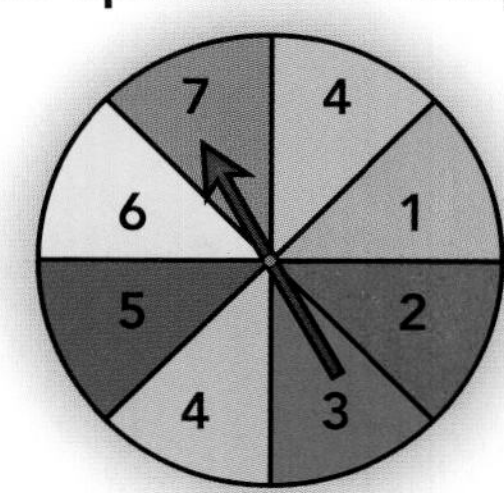

29. How many possible outcomes are there?

30. $P(7) =$ _____

31. $P(4) =$ _____

32. $P(\text{even number}) =$ _____

33. $P(\text{odd number}) =$ _____

These letter tiles are hidden in a bag.

R S A T P A U R R L L O

34. If you draw one tile, how many possible outcomes are there?

35. $P(\text{A}) =$ _____

36. $P(\text{T}) =$ _____

37. $P(\text{R}) =$ _____

38. $P(\text{vowel}) =$ _____

Martha tallied the different candy colors in one bag of her favorite candy. She made a line plot of the results. Use her line plot to answer the following questions.

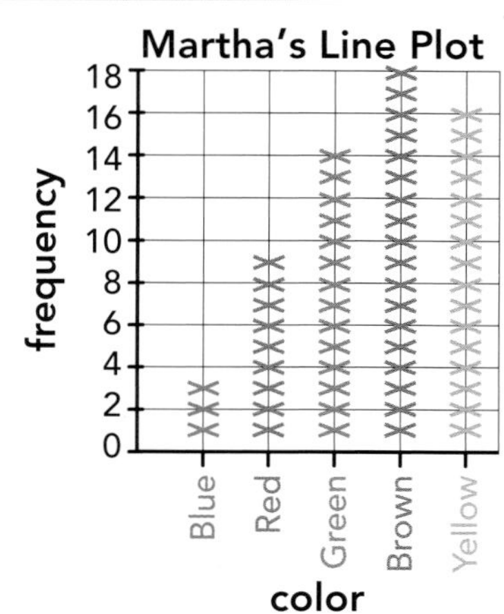

39. What color has the highest frequency?

40. What color occurs the least?

41. How many more yellow candies are there than red?

14.13 Chapters 11–14 Review

Determine whether the following ratios are proportions. Write = or ≠.

1. $\frac{2}{3}$ ◯ $\frac{16}{24}$ 2. $\frac{1}{4}$ ◯ $\frac{20}{100}$ 3. $\frac{15}{3}$ ◯ $\frac{45}{9}$

Find the missing number in each proportion.

4. $\frac{4}{17} = \frac{n}{51}$ 5. $\frac{n}{16} = \frac{2}{4}$ 6. $\frac{3}{4} = \frac{15}{n}$

Write each decimal as a percent.

7. 0.03 8. 0.45 9. 0.77

Write each percent as a fraction in simplest form.

10. 22% 11. 65% 12. 75%

Complete each equation.

13. 64 fl oz = ____ c
14. 45 in. = ____ yd ____ in.
15. 4T = ____ lbs
16. 5 dm = ____ cm
17. 85 mL = ____ L
18. 5 g = ____ mg

Write the elapsed time.

19.

PM

PM

20. 10:39 AM to 1:15 PM

21. Find the circumference of a circle with a diameter of 4.3 cm. Round to the nearest tenth.

22. Find the perimeter of a square that has sides 2.2 m.

23. Find the area of the figure below.

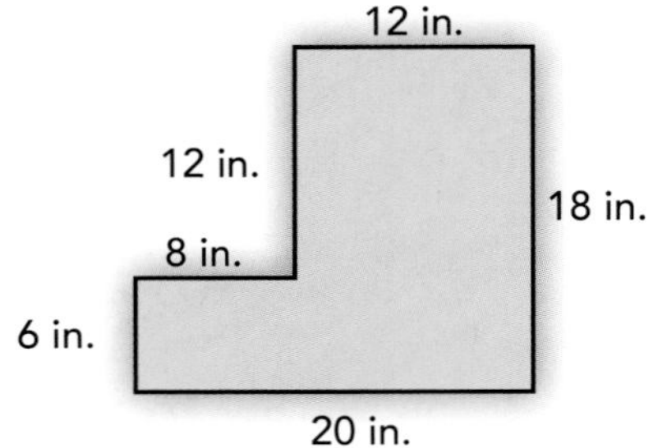

24. Find the surface area of the box below.

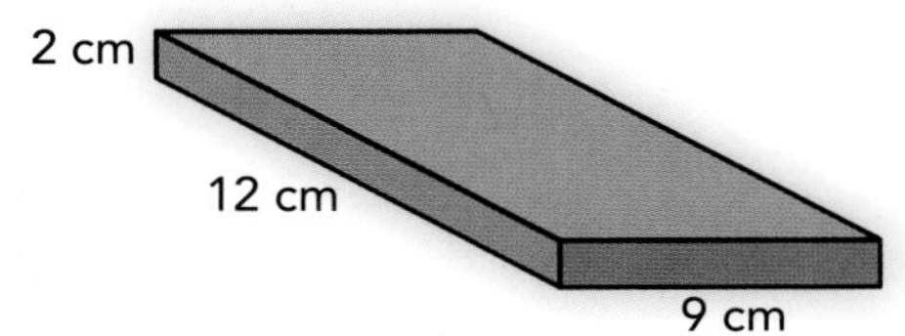

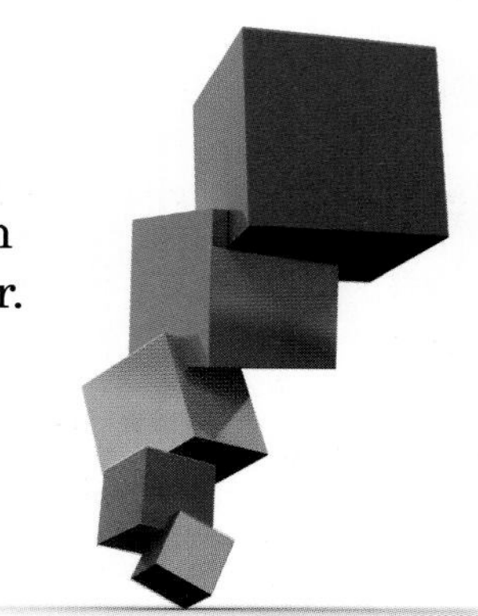

25. Xander used a total of 45 cubes to build two solid figures. He constructed the first figure with three layers of nine cubes in each layer. The second figure was two layers of nine cubes in each layer. Which solid figure had the greater volume?

Name the point for each ordered pair.

26. (7, 4)

28. (1, 2)

27. (5, 3)

29. (3, 5)

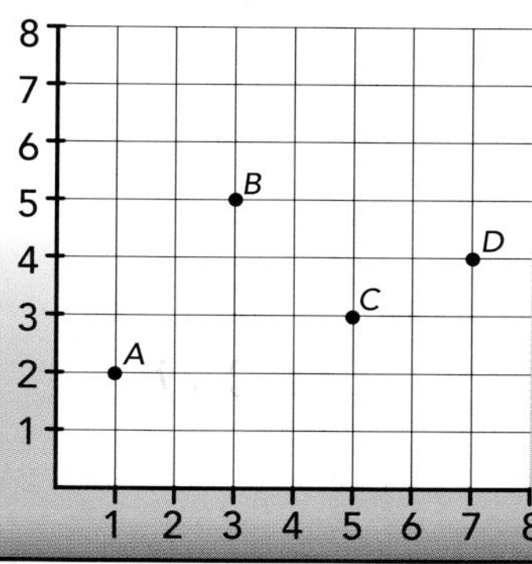

The fifth-grade class held a canned-vegetable drive for a local food shelter. The circle graph below shows the percentages of the total canned vegetables collected.

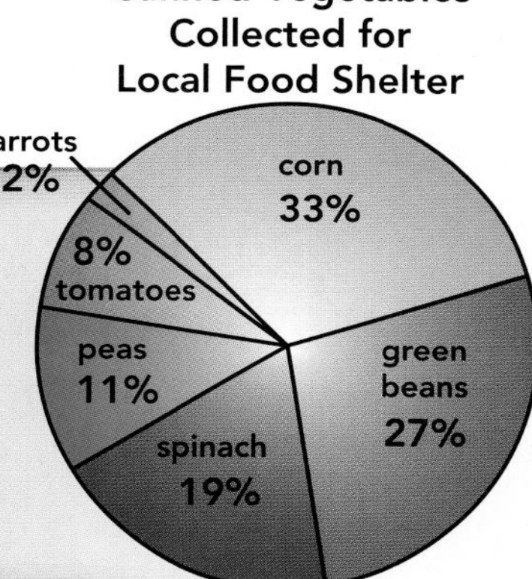

30. Is the amount of corn and peas greater than or less than the amount of green beans and spinach.

31. Which vegetable represents about $\frac{1}{3}$ of the total vegetables?

32. Which two vegetables when added together represent a little over $\frac{1}{2}$ of the total vegetables?

33. Find the range, mode, median, and mean for the set of data below.

15 4 7 12 9 8 8

34. Which graph uses an x to represent numbers?

35. Which graph would be best to show wind-energy output over seven years?

36. If you rolled a number cube labeled 1–6, what is the probability that you would roll an even number?

37. You had 6 blue socks, 8 yellow socks, and 4 red socks in your drawer. If you grabbed a red sock and did not put it back, what is the probability that you would then reach in and pull out a matching sock?

38. Rhys flew on a non-stop flight from San Diego, California, to New York, New York. He departed California at 12:02 PM Pacific time and arrived in New York 7:22 PM eastern time. How long was the flight?

Chapter 15
Cumulative Review

Therefore go and make disciples of all
nations .... And surely I am with you always,
to the very end of the age.
Matthew 28:19a, 20b

Key Ideas:

Review and reinforcement of skills and concepts taught in Grade 5

15.1 *Review: Chapters 1–2*

Name the place value of the underlined digit.

1. $95.\underline{3}92$
2. $0.5\underline{4}6$
3. $845,\underline{7}11$

4. $\underline{4}6,929$

Australia

Round to the nearest place value given.

5. thousandths: 64.0742
6. ten thousands: 12,812
7. thousands: 31,688
8. millions: 727,035,305

Estimate the sum by rounding to the nearest whole number before adding.

9. $\begin{array}{r} 10.5 \\ +30.4 \\ \hline \end{array}$

10. $\begin{array}{r} 61.71 \\ +19.68 \\ \hline \end{array}$

11. $\begin{array}{r} 755.08 \\ +101.39 \\ \hline \end{array}$

12. $\begin{array}{r} 0.60 \\ +52.22 \\ \hline \end{array}$

China

Estimate the difference by rounding to the nearest ten before subtracting.

13. $\begin{array}{r} \$258.52 \\ -\quad 49.99 \\ \hline \end{array}$

14. $\begin{array}{r} 873.618 \\ -122.036 \\ \hline \end{array}$

15. $\begin{array}{r} 95.455 \\ -\quad 9.700 \\ \hline \end{array}$

United States of America

Write in order from least to greatest.

16. 12.632 12.063 12.620 12.263
17. 2,010,000 2,100,000 2,000,100

Write the number in word form.

18. 0.931
19. 22,413
20. 19,988,001

Write the number in expanded form.

21. 608.15 22. 2,826 23. 16,510

Solve.

24. $\begin{array}{r} \$12.43 \\ +\ 76.89 \\ \hline \end{array}$

25. $\begin{array}{r} 64.72 \\ -26.931 \\ \hline \end{array}$

26. 2,848 + 5,620 + 8,012

27. $r + 25 = 172$

28. $a - 33.20 = 70.80$

29. $z - 305 = 66.16$

30. $194 + n = 231$

31. $w - 49 = 685$

32. $781.04 - 59.55 = b$

Write an equivalent decimal for each number.

33. 8.9

34. 13.600

35. 84.10

36. 428.21

Write each number in standard form.

37. fifty-five million, six hundred eighty thousand, three hundred

38. eight hundred forty-two million, four hundred ten thousand, two hundred fifty

39. 900,000 + 80,000 + 2,000 + 200 + 50 + 6

40. 2,000,000 + 500,000 + 60,000 + 9,000 + 800 + 1

15.2 Review: Chapters 3–5

Find the product.

1. 66×4
2. 824×76
3. 307×185
4. $5{,}280 \times 93$
5. 589×30
6. $4{,}762 \times 909$
7. 73×73
8. 175×500

Find the quotient.

9. $6\overline{)366}$
10. $7\overline{)500}$ R
11. $52\overline{)28{,}560}$ R
12. $18\overline{)5{,}400}$
13. $42\overline{)1{,}514}$ R
14. $69\overline{)1{,}725}$
15. $15\overline{)541}$ R
16. $24\overline{)365}$ R

Find the LCM for each pair.

17. 5 and 8
18. 3 and 4
19. 7 and 2
20. 6 and 9

Choose the equivalent equation.

21. $18 \times (51 + 49) =$
   - a. $(18 + 51) \times 49$
   - b. $(18 \times 51) \times (18 \times 49)$
   - c. $(18 \times 51) + (18 \times 49)$

22. $62 \times (225 \times 9) =$
   - a. $(62 + 225) \times 9$
   - b. $(62 \times 225) \times 9$
   - c. $62 \times (225 + 9)$

Find the average for each set of numbers.

23. 22 38 12 42 26
24. 115 120 110 100 125
25. 62 56 40 48 54
26. 1,000 1,500 950 2,050

Estimate the product by rounding both factors to the greatest place value.

27. $\begin{array}{r} 565 \\ \times\ 72 \\ \hline \end{array}$

28. $\begin{array}{r} 1{,}100 \\ \times\ \ \ 39 \\ \hline \end{array}$

29. $\begin{array}{r} 144 \\ \times\ 12 \\ \hline \end{array}$

Find the greatest common factor for each pair.

30. 10 and 20

31. 9 and 21

32. 12 and 16

Select the estimated product using front-end digits.

33. 505 × 41

   a. 20,000
   b. 25,000
   c. 2,000

34. 925 × 12

   a. 9,000
   b. 10,000
   c. 20,000

35. 2,100 × 11

   a. 40,000
   b. 20,000
   c. 30,000

Use mental math to find the product.

36. 900 × 100

37. 5,000 × 80

38. 60 × 300

39. 2,500 × 10

40. Copy the lattice and fill in the missing numbers. Use the lattice to find the product of 486 × 124.

4	8	6	
0/4	0/8	0/6	1
0/8		1/2	2
1/6	3/2	2/4	4

15.3 Review: Chapters 6–7

Write the letter of the best answer.

1. a solid figure made of flat surfaces called faces

   a. angle
   b. polyhedron
   c. polygon
   d. hexagon

2. a polyhedron that has a polygon base and triangles for faces

   a. triangular prism
   b. triangle
   c. prism
   d. pyramid

3. a triangle with all angles less than 90°

   a. right triangle
   b. obtuse triangle
   c. acute triangle
   d. reflex triangle

4. a fixed location in space

   a. point
   b. line segment
   c. plane
   d. level

5. a straight path that continues without end in both directions

   a. line
   b. ray
   c. polygon
   d. figure

6. a line segment that goes from the center to any point on the circle

   a. ray
   b. line
   c. circle
   d. radius

7. a quadrilateral with one set of parallel sides

   a. rectangle
   b. trapezoid
   c. polyhedron
   d. right polygon

pipe organ, Canada

Divide.

8. $4\overline{)6.024}$
9. $3\overline{)12.78}$
10. $25\overline{)75.50}$
11. $8\overline{)0.08}$
12. $15\overline{)42.30}$
13. $12\overline{)13.68}$
14. $8\overline{)\$95.20}$
15. $100\overline{)8.8}$
16. $5\overline{)\$2.50}$
17. $18\overline{)30.96}$

Write the letter of the equation that matches the given number.

18. 0.155

   a. $15.5 \div 10 = n$
   b. $15.5 \div 100 = n$
   c. $15.5 \div 1{,}000 = n$

19. 0.2983

   a. $298.3 \div 10 = n$
   b. $298.3 \div 100 = n$
   c. $298.3 \div 1{,}000 = n$

20. 7.627

   a. $76.27 \div 10 = n$
   b. $76.27 \div 100 = n$
   c. $76.27 \div 1{,}000 = n$

Write "true" or "false."

gongs, Indonesia

21. A rectangular prism is a polygon.

22. A square pyramid may be congruent to a triangular pyramid.

23. A right triangle has only one set of perpendicular lines.

24. A regular hexagon has six congruent sides and six congruent angles.

Use the circle shown to answer 25–31.

Russian balalaika

25. Name the circle.

26. Name the diameter.

27. $\angle XST$ is a(n) _____ angle.

28. $\angle WSX$ is a(n) _____ angle

29. $\angle WST$ is a(n) _____ angle.

30. $\overline{VU}$ is a _____.

31. $\overline{ST}$ is a _____.

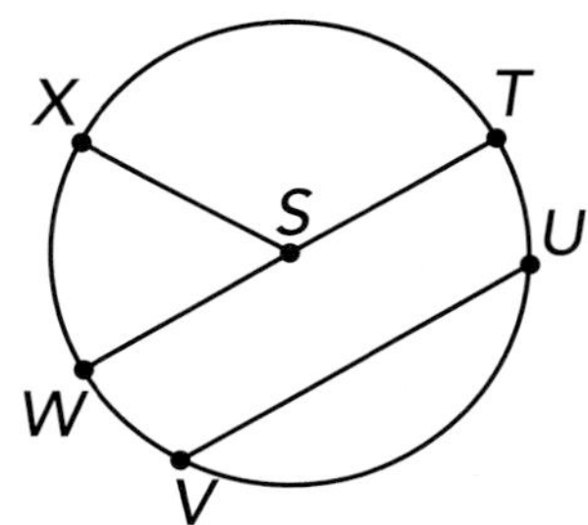

Find the product.

32. $\begin{array}{r} 0.7 \\ \times\ 9 \\ \hline \end{array}$

33. $\begin{array}{r} 5.064 \\ \times\ 8 \\ \hline \end{array}$

34. $\begin{array}{r} 9.21 \\ \times\ 2 \\ \hline \end{array}$

35. $\begin{array}{r} 50.25 \\ \times\ 4 \\ \hline \end{array}$

36. $\begin{array}{r} 2.767 \\ \times\ 0.75 \\ \hline \end{array}$

37. 338 × 5.5

38. 16.08 × 70.41

39. 0.004 × 66

Complete the pattern.

40. 1 × \$0.75 = \$0.75

10 × \$0.75 = \$7.50

100 × \$0.75 = _____

1,000 × \$0.75 = _____

Solve.

41. $4^2 + (16 - 6) \times 3 - 2$

steel drum, Caribbean

15.4 Review: Chapters 8–10

Solve.

Netherlands

1. Tamika and Garth played a game with positive and negative integers. After Tamika's first turn her score was −7. How many points does she need to have a total score that is a positive integer?

2. Garth's score for his first turn was −3, but he also earned a 2-point bonus. Will his score be a positive or negative integer?

3. On Tamika's second turn, she scored $8\frac{1}{2}$ points. What is her score?

4. Garth gained 2 points on his second turn and lost 1 point on his third turn. What is his score now?

5. For the final score, Tamika had a 10. How many points did she gain after her second turn?

Japan

Solve.

6. $\frac{3}{4} = \frac{■}{12}$

7. $\frac{5}{8} = \frac{■}{16}$

8. $\frac{2}{3} = \frac{■}{9}$

9. $\frac{4}{5} = \frac{■}{20}$

Korea

List all the factors of each number. Write "prime" or "composite."

10. 24

11. 19

12. 32

13. 15

List the common factors. Circle the GCF.

14. 6 and 18

15. 9 and 12

16. 7 and 35

17. 18 and 24

Write in order from least to greatest.

18. $\frac{5}{9}$, $\frac{1}{3}$, $\frac{5}{6}$

19. $\frac{1}{2}$, $\frac{2}{3}$, $\frac{1}{4}$

20. $\frac{3}{8}$, $\frac{5}{16}$, $\frac{3}{4}$

21. $\frac{1}{3}$, $\frac{1}{5}$, $\frac{4}{15}$

Rename as a mixed number.

22. $\frac{11}{3}$

23. $\frac{37}{6}$

24. $\frac{23}{5}$

25. $\frac{21}{8}$

Write the equation shown by the fraction models. Write the answer in simplest form.

26. 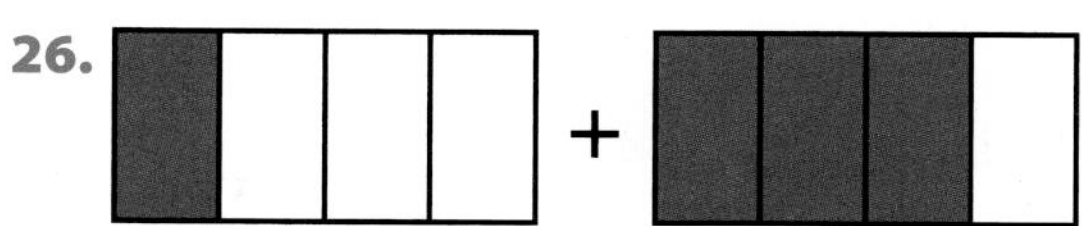

27. 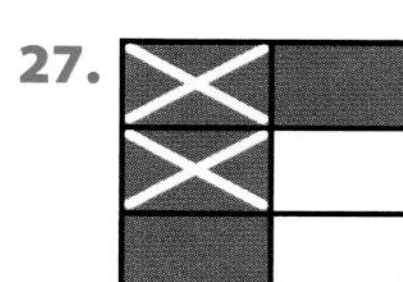

Add or subtract the fractions using the LCD. Write the answer in simplest form.

28. $\frac{1}{2} + \frac{3}{8}$

29. $\frac{11}{14} - \frac{5}{7}$

30. $\frac{12}{15} - \frac{2}{5}$

31. $\frac{2}{3} + \frac{3}{4}$

32. $6\frac{1}{3} + 6\frac{1}{2}$

33. $10\frac{7}{10} - 5\frac{1}{4}$

34. $12\frac{1}{4} - 6\frac{3}{8}$

35. $10\frac{9}{10} + 4\frac{3}{5}$

Multiply. Write the product in simplest form.

36. $\frac{3}{5} \times \frac{1}{2}$

37. $\frac{2}{3} \times \frac{3}{4}$

38. $\frac{4}{9} \times \frac{2}{3}$

39. $\frac{1}{8} \times \frac{4}{10}$

Write the letter of the correct answer.

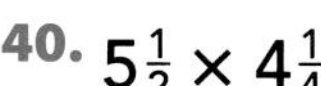

40. $5\frac{1}{2} \times 4\frac{1}{4}$

a. $20\frac{3}{8}$
b. $23\frac{1}{8}$
c. $23\frac{3}{4}$
d. $23\frac{3}{8}$

41. $12\frac{1}{3} \times \frac{1}{5}$

a. $2\frac{9}{15}$
b. $3\frac{1}{15}$
c. $2\frac{1}{2}$
d. $2\frac{7}{15}$

42. $\frac{1}{2} \div \frac{1}{4}$

a. 4
b. $\frac{1}{4}$
c. 2
d. $\frac{1}{2}$

43. $3 \div \frac{1}{6}$

a. 18
b. 12
c. $\frac{1}{2}$
d. 15

Estimate the product by rounding each number to the nearest whole number.

44. $9\frac{1}{3} \times 7\frac{3}{4}$

45. $12\frac{5}{6} \times 10\frac{2}{5}$

15.5 Review: Chapters 11–14

Find the elapsed time.

1. 5:09 AM to 10:29 PM

Write the times shown on the clocks. Write the elapsed time.

2.

_____ AM

_____ AM

3. Find the range, mean, median, and mode for the following numbers: 51, 42, 2, 5, and 15.

Use the graph to answer the following questions.

4. Which baked good was purchased the most?

5. Which baked good was purchased the least?

6. Which two baked goods together were equal to the percentage of cookies purchased?

Percentage of Baked Goods Purchased

pie 12%
brownies 10%
banana bread 33%
cookies 45%

Greece

Find the missing number in each proportion.

7. $\frac{10}{15} = \frac{n}{60}$

8. $\frac{2}{5} = \frac{12}{n}$

Write each ratio two different ways.

9. 2:3

10. 8 to 10

11. $\frac{4}{7}$

Write each ratio as a percentage.

12. 52:100

13. $\frac{23}{100}$

14. 144:100

Write each percentage as a fraction in simplest form.

15. 25%

16. 62%

17. 80%

18. When the shoe sale began, Lynelle's inventory showed 275 pairs of shoes on the clearance racks. 36% have been sold. How many pairs are left?

Complete each equation.

19. 144 fl oz = _____ c

20. 4 gal = _____ qt

21. 6 yd 4 ft = _____ ft

22. 2 mi = _____ ft

23. 4 dm = _____ cm

24. 6,400 m = _____ km

25. 4 g = _____ mg

26. 1,000 mg = _____ g

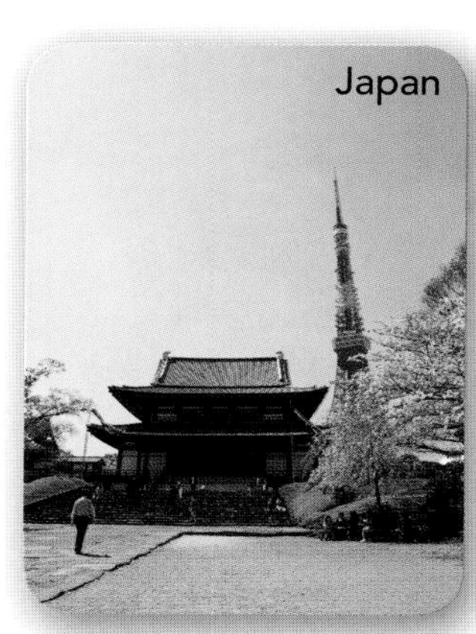

Write each measurement in pounds.

27. 496 oz

28. 48 oz

29. 100 oz

Find the perimeter of each figure. Label the answer.

30.

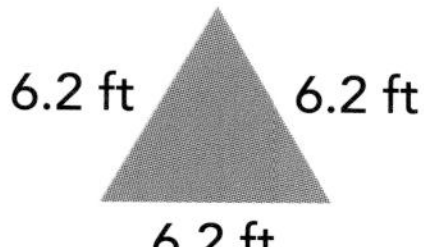

31.

32.

Find the circumference of each circle. Round the answer to the nearest tenth.

33.

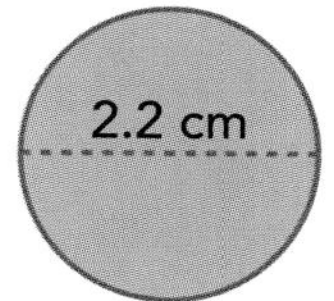

34.

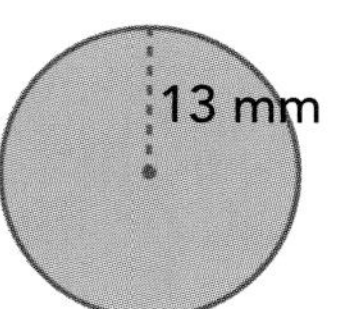

35.

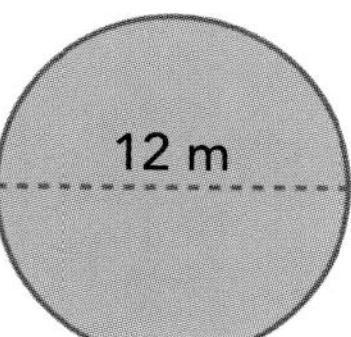

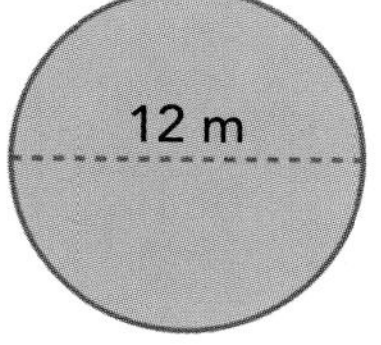

Find the area of each figure.

36.

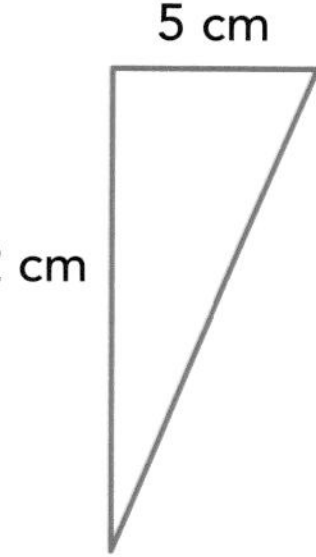

37.

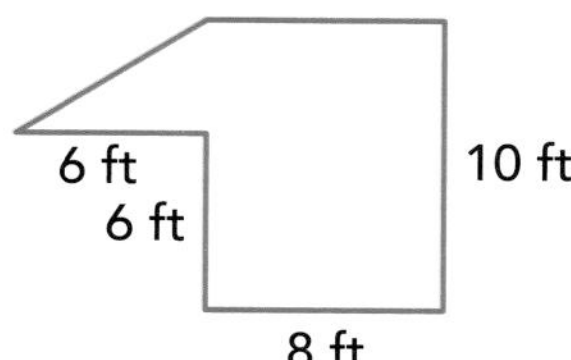

Great Britain

Determine the volume if 1 cube = 1 ft³.

38.

39.

40.

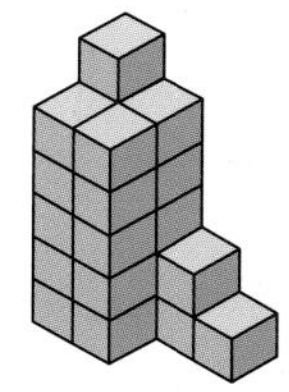

Find the volume of each solid.

41.

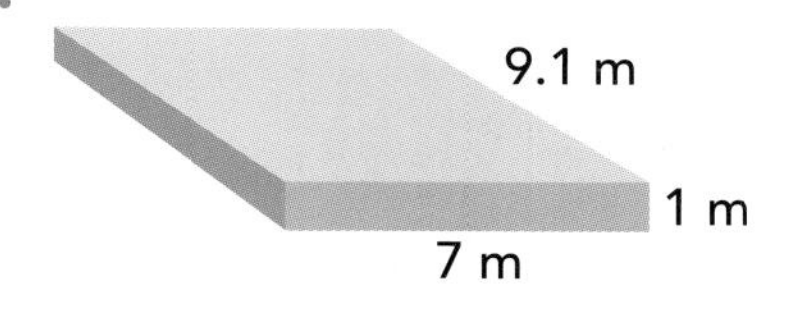

42.

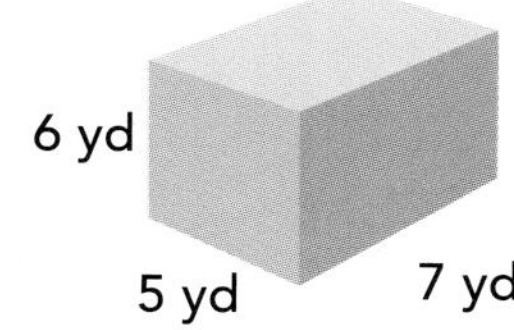

43.

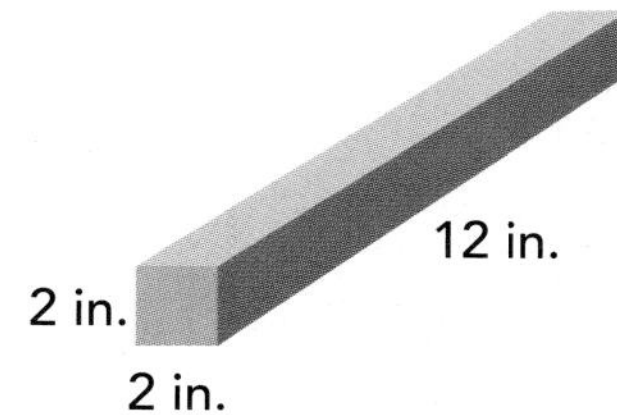

Table of Measures

Customary Units

Length

12 inches (in.) = 1 foot (ft)
3 feet = 1 yard (yd)
36 inches = 1 yard
5,280 feet = 1 mile (mi)
1,760 yards = 1 mile

Capacity

3 teaspoons (tsp) = 1 tablespoon (tbsp)
8 fluid ounces = 1 cup (c)
2 cups = 1 pint (pt)
2 pints = 1 quart (qt)
4 quarts = 1 gallon (gal)

Weight

16 ounces (oz) = 1 pound (lb)
2,000 pounds = 1 ton (T)

Metric Units

Length

10 millimeters (mm) = 1 centimeter (cm)
1,000 millimeters (mm) = 1 meter (m)
10 decimeters = 1 meter (m)
10 centimeters = 1 decimeter (dm)
100 centimeters = 1 meter
1,000 meters = 1 kilometer (km)

Capacity

1,000 milliliters (mL) = 1 liter (L)

Mass (Weight)

1,000 milligrams (mg) = 1 gram (g)
1,000 grams = 1 kilogram (kg)

Temperature

32°Fahrenheit (F)—water freezes
212°F—water boils
98.6°F—normal body temperature
0°Celsius (C)—water freezes
100°C—water boils
37°C—normal body temperature

Units of Time

60 seconds (sec) = 1 minute (min)
60 minutes = 1 hour (hr)
24 hours = 1 day (d)
7 days = 1 week (wk)
about 4 weeks = 1 month (mo)
365 days = 1 year (yr)
52 weeks = 1 year
12 months = 1 year
366 days = 1 leap year
10 years = 1 decade
100 years = 1 century
1,000 years = 1 millennium

Signs and Symbols

Symbol	Meaning	Symbol	Meaning
$<$	is less than	$\overleftrightarrow{AB}$	line *AB*
$>$	is greater than	$\overline{AB}$	line segment *AB*
$=$	is equal to	$\overrightarrow{AB}$	ray *AB*
$\neq$	is not equal to	$\angle ABC$	angle *ABC*
$\approx$	is approximately equal to	ΔABC	triangle *ABC*
$^\circ$	degree	π	*pi* ($\pi = 3.14$)
%	percent	$\parallel$	is parallel to
(2, 3)	ordered pair 2, 3	$\perp$	is perpendicular to
10^4	ten to the fourth power	$\cong$	is congruent to
1:3	ratio of 1 to 3	"	inches
$\frac{3}{4}$	three-fourths	'	feet
•*A*	point *A*		

Properties of Addition

Associative Property: Grouping addends differently does not change the sum.

Commutative Property: Changing the order of the addends does not change the sum

Zero Property: The sum of a number and zero is that number.

Properties of Multiplication

Associative Property: Grouping factors differently does not change the product.

Commutative Property: Changing the order of the factors does not change the product.

Distributive Property: The product remains the same whether a factor is multiplied by the sum of the addends or by each addend.

Identity Property of One: The product of one and any other factor is that factor.

Zero Property: The product of zero and any other factor is zero.

Formulas

Formula	Meaning
$P = 2l + 2w$	Perimeter of a rectangle
$P = 4s$	Perimeter of a square
$C = \pi d$	Circumference of a circle
$A = l \times w$	Area of a rectangle
$A = \frac{1}{2} \times b \times h$	Area of a triangle
$V = l \times w \times h$	Volume of a rectangular prism

Glossary

acute triangle a triangle that has all angles less than 90° (p. 158)

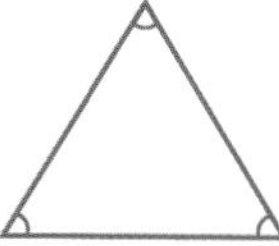

average the sum of a data set divided by the number of items in the set (p. 94)

bar graph a graph that uses bars to represent and compare information (p. 346)

base number the number used as a repeated factor (p. 76)

6^3 ← base number

chord a line segment drawn between any two points on a circle (p. 168)

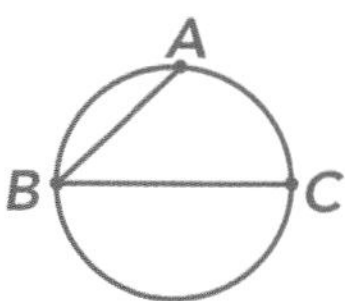

circle graph a round graph that compares parts of a whole (p. 352)

circumference the distance around a circle (p. 322)

common factor a factor shared by two or more numbers (p. 58)

common multiple a multiple shared by two or more numbers (p. 56)

compatible numbers numbers that are easy to compute mentally (p. 90)

composite number a number that has more than two factors (p. 196)

12 is a composite number. Its factors are 1, 2, 3, 4, 6, and 12.

coordinate grid a reference frame used to show the location of ordered pairs (p. 324)

coordinates the numbers of an ordered pair used to locate a point on a grid (p. 324)

cross product the product of the numerator of one ratio and the denominator of another ratio (p. 272)

degree the unit used to measure an angle (p. 154)

denominator the bottom number of a fraction which tells the total number of equal parts in a whole (p. 190)

$\frac{2}{6}$ ← denominator

diameter a line segment that connects any two points on the circle and passes through the center of the circle (p. 168)

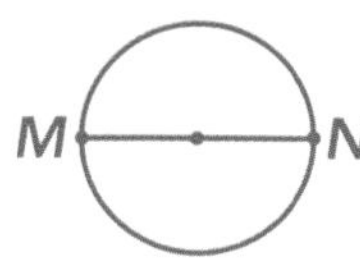

digit any of the numerals 0–9 (p. 2)

dividend the number to be divided (p. 86)

divisible able to be divided evenly with no remainder (p. 84)

divisor the number to divide by (p. 86)

double bar graph a bar graph that uses sets of two bars to represent and compare numbers for multiple categories at the same time (p. 346)

equation a number sentence written with an equals sign (p. 28)

equilateral triangle a triangle that has three equal sides (p. 158)

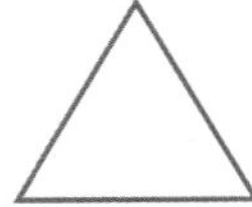

equivalent decimals decimals that represent the same amount (p. 38)

0.2 0.20 0.200

equivalent fractions fractions that name the same amount (p. 192)

$$\frac{1}{2} = \frac{2}{4}$$

exponent the number of times the base number is used as a factor (p. 76)

6^3 ← **exponent**

factor tree a diagram that shows the factors of a number (p. 196)

frequency the number of times a certain item appears in a set of data (p. 344)

front-end estimation a strategy that uses the digit in the greatest place value and replaces the remaining digits with zeros (p. 24)

greatest common factor the largest common factor of two or more numbers (p. 58)

2 is the greatest common factor of 4 and 10.

histogram a graph that uses bars to represent how many of a particular item are found in a given category or interval (p. 348)

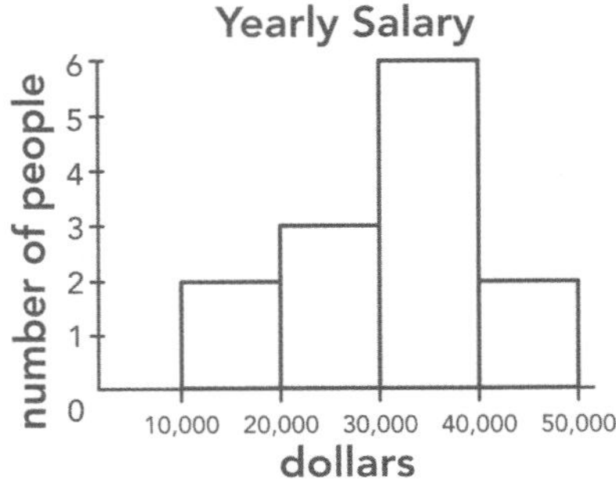

improper fraction a fraction that has a numerator greater than or equal to the denominator (p. 206)

$$\frac{5}{4}$$

integer any positive or negative whole number or zero (p. 184)

intersecting lines lines that cross each other at a common point (p. 152)

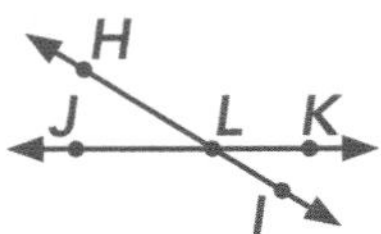

inverse operation the opposite operation (p. 26)

isosceles triangle a triangle that has at least two equal sides (p. 158)

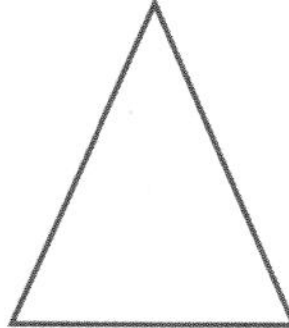

least common denominator (LCD) the least common multiple of two or more denominators (p. 204)

least common multiple the smallest multiple that is common to two or more numbers (p. 56)

line a straight path that continues without end in both directions (p. 152)

B C $\overleftrightarrow{BC}$

line graph a graph that uses lines to represent increases or decreases over a period of time (p. 350)

line plot a graph that uses an *x* to represent a number and show comparisons (p. 356)

1	2	3	4	5
×		×××	××	×

line segment a part of a line that has two distinct endpoints (p. 152)

D E $\overline{DE}$

mass the measure of how much matter is in an object (p. 306)

mean the average of a set of data (p. 356)

median the middle number in a set of ordered data (p. 356)

5, 9, 11, 13, 22
median: 11

mixed number a number consisting of a whole number and a fraction (p. 206)

$2\frac{3}{8}$

mode the number that occurs the most often in a set of data (p. 356)

multiple the product of a given number and another whole number (p. 54)

Multiples of 8 (8 × 1, 8 × 2, 8 × 3, etc.) are 8, 16, 24, etc.

negative number a number less than zero (p. 184)

numerator the top number of a fraction which tells how many parts in a whole are being considered (p. 190)

$\frac{4}{9}$ ← **numerator**

obtuse triangle a triangle that has one angle greater than 90° (p. 158)

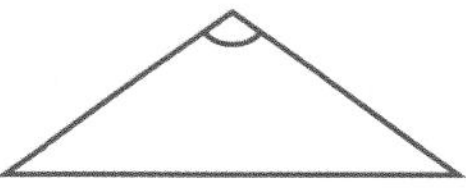

ordered pair a pair of coordinates used to locate a point on a grid (p. 324)

order of operations a set of rules for solving an equation that has more than one operation (p. 144)

outcome a possible result in a probability event (p. 362)

parallel lines lines in the same plane that do not intersect (p. 152)

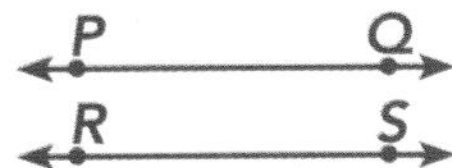

parallelogram a quadrilateral that has two sets of parallel sides and opposite sides that are congruent (p. 162)

percent a number that shows how many out of 100 (p. 278)

perimeter the distance around a figure (p. 320)

period each group of three digits separated by commas in a multidigit number (p. 2)

perpendicular lines lines that intersect to form a right angle (p. 152)

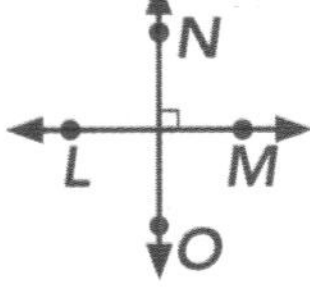

plane a flat surface that extends without end in all directions (p. 152)

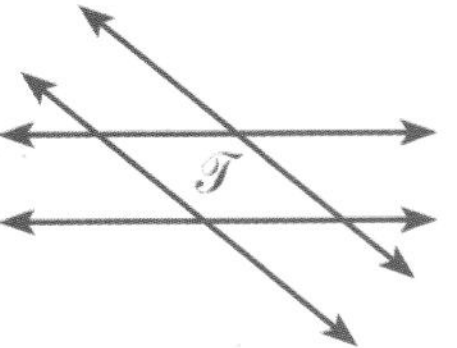

point a fixed location in space (p. 152)

A

polyhedron a solid figure made of flat surfaces called faces (p. 164)

positive number a number greater than zero (p. 184)

prime factorization finding all the factors of a number that are prime (p. 196)

prime number a whole number that only has two factors, itself and 1 (p. 196)

2, 3, 5, 7, and 11 are prime numbers.

prism a polyhedron that has two congruent bases and rectangular sides (p. 164)

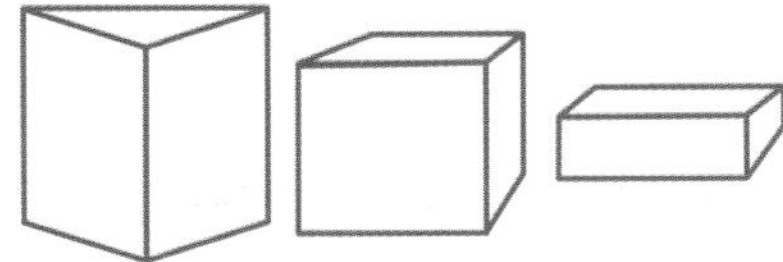

proper fraction a fraction less than one (p. 206)

proportion an equation that shows two equal ratios (p. 272)

pyramid a polyhedron that has a polygon base and triangular faces (p. 164)

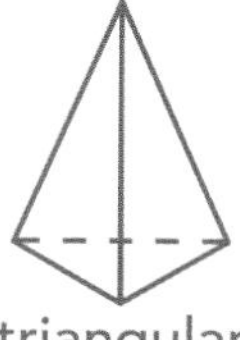

triangular

rectangular

square

quadrilateral a polygon that has four sides (p. 162)

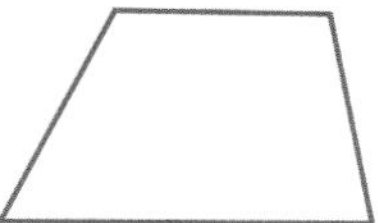

quotient the result of dividing one number by another (p. 86)

radius a line segment from the center to a point on a circle (p. 168)

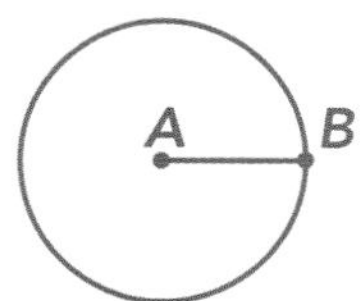

range the difference between the greatest and least numbers in a set of data (p. 94)

ratio a comparison of two quantities (p. 268)

$\frac{10}{100}$ **10 to 100** **10:100**

ratio table a table that shows a series of equal ratios (p. 270)

miles	3	6	9
minutes	1	2	3

ray a part of a line that has one endpoint and continues without end in one direction (p. 152)

F G $\overrightarrow{FG}$

reflection a transformation that turns a figure over on a line of symmetry (p. 172)

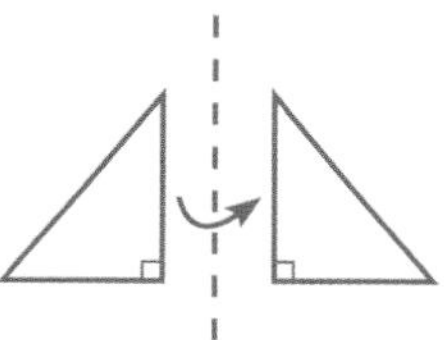

remainder the part of the quotient that is left over after division (p. 88)

repeating decimal a decimal number where one or more of the digits repeat continuously (p. 260)

rhombus a parallelogram that has sides that are all congruent (p. 162)

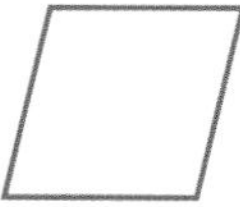

right triangle a triangle that has one 90° angle (p. 158)

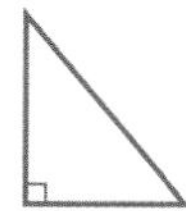

rotation a transformation that moves a figure around a fixed point (p. 172)

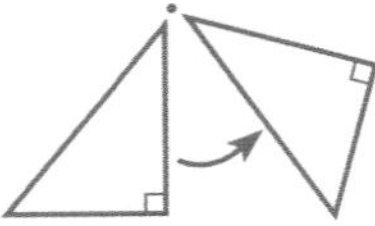

scale the relationship between distance on the ground and distance on a map (p. 238)

scalene triangle a triangle that has three unequal sides (p. 158)

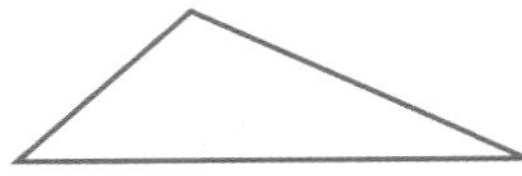

similar figures figures that have the same shape but may not be the same size (p. 174)

statistics a branch of mathematics that deals with collecting, organizing, and analyzing data (p. 356)

straight angle an angle that has a measure of 180 degrees (p. 154)

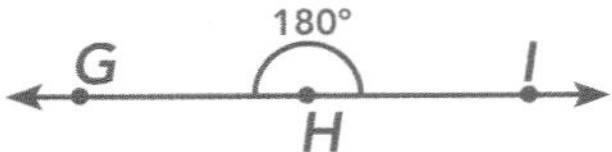

surface area the sum of the areas of all of the faces of a solid figure (p. 332)

terminating decimal a decimal number that has a fixed number of digits (p. 260)

translation a transformation that moves a figure in a straight line, changing location but not position (p. 172)

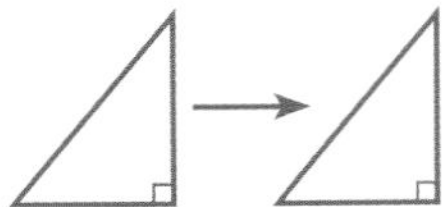

trapezoid a quadrilateral that has one set of parallel sides (p. 162)

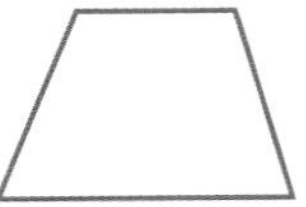

variable a symbol or letter that stands for an unknown number (p. 28)

volume the measure of the space within a solid figure (p. 334)

Index

The index refers to lesson numbers. The boldfaced numbers refer to vocabulary word definitions.

A

acute angle 7.2, 7.3
acute triangle **7.4**
addend 2.6
  missing 2.3
  more than two 2.1, 2.2
addition
  column 2.1, 9.3
  decimals 1.9, 2.4–2.5, 2.8, 2.10–2.11
  estimation in 1.9, 2.1, 2.4, 9.6
  fraction 9.1, 9.8–9.9
  larger numbers 2.2
  mixed numbers 9.2–9.3, 9.11
  money 1.9, 2.4, 2.10
  number sentences 2.3
  patterns 3.12
  properties 2.6
    Associative Property 2.6
    Commutative Property 2.6
    Zero Property 2.6
  regrouping in 2.2, 2.5, 2.8
  related to subtraction 2.2
  repeated 3.1
  sum 2.1, 2.4–2.6, 3.14, 9.3, 9.6, 9.11
  three- or more-digit numbers 2.1–2.3
  whole number 2.1–2.3
  zero 2.1, 2.5–2.6, 2.8, 2.11
algebra readiness
  equation 2.3, 6.2–6.3, 6.6, 10.7–10.8, 11.3–11.5
  exponent 3.13
  factoring 3.4, 8.7
  formula 13.1–13.3, 13.5–13.7, 13.11
  integer 8.1–8.3
  missing addend 2.3, 3.1, 3.10
  missing factor 3.1, 3.10, 6.1
  ordered pair 13.4
  properties 2.6, 3.1
  ratio and proportion 11.3–11.4
  rules of division 4.1–4.2
  scale drawing 11.5
algorithm
  addition 2.1–2.2, 2.5, 2.8, 2.11
  decimal 2.5, 2.7–2.8, 2.11, 6.1–6.3, 6.6–6.7
  division 4.3, 4.5, 4.7–4.8, 5.2, 5.4–5.8, 6.6–6.7
  fraction 9.1–9.5, 9.8–9.12, 10.2–10.4, 10.6
  measurement 12.1
  multiplication 3.5–3.6, 3.8, 3.10, 6.1–6.3
  ratio and percent 11.7
  subtraction 2.1–2.2, 2.7–2.8, 2.11
AM 12.8
angle 7.2–7.3, 7.7, 7.13
approximately-equal-to symbol (≈) 2.1
area
  calculating
    by counting 13.1
    by multiplication 13.1, 13.5–13.7
  irregular figure 13.7
  of a rectangle 13.1
  of a right triangle 13.5
  of a triangle 13.6
  square units
    centimeters 13.1
    inches 13.1
  surface 13.8
array 3.1, 3.4, 10.3–10.4
Astronaut Dominic Gorie 9.2, 9.8
asymmetry 7.10
average **4.6**, 4.7, 6.6, 6.8, 14.9
axes 14.2

B

bar graph **14.2**
base number **3.13**

C

calculator
  addition with 1.10, 2.1–2.2, 2.6–2.11, 4.3
  averaging 4.6
  constant multiplier 3.3
  critical thinking with 1.9
  decimals with 1.5–1.6, 2.6, 2.10–2.11, 6.2–6.3, 6.5, 6.8
  division with 3.11, 4.3, 4.6, 4.8–4.9, 5.6–5.7, 6.8, 8.6, 10.9, 11.9, 14.9
  large numbers with 4.8
  multiplication with 3.3, 3.8, 3.12, 4.3, 6.2–6.3, 6.5, 8.7, 10.6
  percentage 11.11
  problem solving with 1.9–1.10, 2.10, 3.11–3.12, 4.6, 4.9, 5.7, 8.10, 14.9
  statistics with 14.7
  subtraction with 2.1, 2.11, 3.12
calendar 3.3, 11.9
capacity
  customary 12.2
  metric 12.5
Celsius 12.7
centimeters 12.4
checking
  addition 2.2
  division 4.1, 4.3, 4.5, 4.8, 5.2–5.4, 5.6–5.8, 6.7, 12.1
  subtraction 2.2–2.3, 2.9
chord **7.9**
circle 7.9, 13.3
circle graph **14.5**
circumference **13.3**
clocks 12.8, 14.9
column addition 2.1
common denominator 8.10, 9.7–9.10
common factor **3.4**, 8.8–8.9
common multiple **3.3**, 8.10, 9.7, 9.9–9.10
comparing and ordering
  decimals 1.7, 2.5
  fractions 8.11, 8.13, 9.7
  whole numbers 1.3
compass 7.9
compatible numbers **4.4**, 5.2–5.8, 10.6
composite number **8.7**
concrete representations
  decimals 2.9, 6.6
  division 4.1, 6.6
  fractions 8.11
  geometry 7.3, 7.9
  money 1.5
  multiplication 3.2
  place value 1.1
  regrouping 2.9, 6.6
  subtraction 2.9
cone 7.7
congruent figure 7.12

consumer
advertisements 6.4, 6.7
change 2.10, 3.12
commission 11.12
discount 10.6, 11.12
estimating costs 1.9, 3.7, 3.9
finding costs 1.6, 2.10, 3.9, 4.2
hourly wage 3.12, 6.2
interest 11.12
maintaining a budget 3.7, 3.9
mileage chart 3.10–3.11
money 1.9, 2.4, 2.10, 3.7, 4.2, 4.5, 6.2, 6.4
prices 3.12
profit 3.12
raising money 3.11, 6.10, 10.5
sales tax 6.5, 11.12
savings 2.4
tip 11.12
converting customary measures 12.1–12.3
converting metric measures 12.4–12.6
coordinate grid 13.4
coordinates 13.4
critical thinking
analyzing 1.9, 2.3, 3.9, 6.5, 14.9
comparing polygons 7.5
finding, extending, and using patterns 3.2
reasoning with graphs and charts 1.3, 1.6, 1.8–1.10, 3.13, 4.6, 4.9, 6.8, 6.11, 7.5, 7.7–7.8, 7.11, 8.13, 9.8, 14.1–14.7, 14.9
cross product 11.3, 11.4–11.5, 11.7
cube 7.7, 13.9
cubic unit 13.9–13.10
cup 12.2
customary system of measures
area 13.1, 13.5–13.8
capacity 12.2
conversion within the system 12.1–12.3
length 12.1
perimeter 13.2
tables 12.1–12.3, 12.8
temperature 8.1, 12.7
volume 13.9–13.10
weight 12.3
cylinder 7.7

D

data
analyzing 1.9, 2.3, 2.10, 3.9, 14.9, 6.5, 14.2–14.9
collecting and organizing 14.1, 14.2, 14.7
comparing 14.2, 14.6
doing an investigation 14.1–14.2, 14.4–14.7
drawing conclusions from data 1.9, 14.2–14.7
finding mean, median, mode, and range 14.7–14.8
making predictions 14.1
sufficient, insufficient, extra data 6.5
using graphs to display data
bar graph 14.2
circle graph 14.5
histogram 14.3
line graph 14.4
line plot 14.7
pictograph 14.2
dates 3.3
decagon 7.5
decimal
addition 1.9, 2.4–2.5, 2.8, 2.10–2.11
comparing and ordering 1.7
counting decimal places 6.2–6.4, 6.8
division 6.6–6.8, 6.10
equivalent 2.5, 2.8, 2.11
estimation 1.9, 2.4, 2.7, 6.1
fractions 8.6, 8.13, 11.6, 11.9
hundredths 1.5–1.6, 2.4–2.5, 2.7–2.9, 2.11, 6.2, 6.6–6.7, 8.6
models 1.5–1.6, 2.5, 2.8–2.9, 6.2–6.3, 8.6
multiplication 6.1–6.4
number line 1.7–1.8, 2.4
percentage 11.6, 11.9
place value 1.5–1.7, 2.4–2.5, 2.8, 2.11, 6.6–6.8
reading and writing 1.5–1.8, 2.4, 2.8, 2.11, 6.2, 8.6
repeating 10.9
rounding 1.9, 1.8–1.10, 2.4, 2.7, 6.1
subtraction 1.9, 2.7, 2.9–2.11
tenths 1.5–1.6, 1.8, 2.4–2.5, 2.9–2.10, 2.11, 6.2–6.3, 6.6–6.7, 8.6
terminating 10.9
thousandths 1.6, 2.4, 2.8, 2.11, 14.9, 6.7
decimeter 12.4
degree Celsius, 8.1, 12.7
degree Fahrenheit 8.1, 12.7
degree of angles 7.2, 7.3
degree of temperature 8.1, 12.7
denominator 8.4, 8.5–8.6, 8.11–8.12, 10.2–10.3
common 8.11
least common 8.10, 9.7–9.12
estimating 9.6
like 9.1–9.2, 9.4
unlike 9.7–9.12
diameter 7.9
digit 1.1
dividend 4.2, 4.3, 4.5, 5.8
divisible 4.1
division
average 4.6–4.7, 6.6, 6.8, 14.9
basic facts 5.1, 5.4
compatible numbers 4.4, 5.2–5.8
decimals 6.6–6.10
dividend 4.2, 4.3, 4.5, 5.8
divisible 4.1
divisor 4.2, 4.3, 4.5, 5.8
fractions 10.7–10.8
interpret the remainder 4.3, 4.9
inverse operations 2.1, 4.2, 5.1
larger numbers 4.8
money related to 4.2, 4.5
multiples of 10 as divisors 5.1, 6.8
one-digit divisors
estimating quotients 4.4, 4.7–4.8, 5.2
finding averages 4.6–4.7, 14.9
four- and five-digit dividends 4.8
remainders 4.3, 4.8–4.9
three-digit dividends 4.3–4.5, 4.7, 4.9
two-digit dividends 4.1, 4.3–4.5

zero in the quotient 4.3–4.4, 4.7–4.8, 5.2, 6.7
patterns 5.1, 6.8
quotient 4.2–4.5, 4.7–4.9, 5.2–5.8, 6.6–6.7
related to multiplication 4.2, 5.1
rules of 4.1–4.2
two-digit divisors
estimating quotients 5.2–5.5, 5.6–5.8
four- and five-digit dividends 5.2, 5.6–5.8
mental computation 6.8
multiples of 10 5.1
remainder 5.5–5.6
three-digit dividends 5.3–5.6
zero in the quotient 5.7
zero and one in 4.2–4.4, 6.7–6.8
division symbol (÷) 2.1
divisor **4.2**, 4.3, 4.5, 5.8
double bar graph **14.2**

E

edge of solid figure 7.7
elapsed time 12.8, 12.9
endpoint
line segment 7.1–7.2, 7.9
number line 1.4, 1.7–1.8, 2.4, 8.4–8.5, 8.11
equal ratios 11.2–11.4
equation **2.3**, 3.2, 3.4, 4.2, 6.2–6.3, 7.8
equilateral triangle **7.4**
equivalent decimal 2.5, **2.8**, 2.11
equivalent fraction **8.5,** 8.13, 9.6, 11.2, 11.8
estimation
adjusting in 2.4, 5.5
compatible numbers 4.4, 5.2–5.8, 10.6
decimals 2.4, 2.7
fractions and mixed numbers 9.6
front-end 2.1, 2.4, 2.7, 3.7, 5.2–5.3
money 1.9, 2.4, 3.7, 3.12, 6.5
percentage 11.10
problem solving 1.9, 2.1, 2.3, 3.7, 3.9, 6.1
products using fractions 10.6
rounding 1.9, 2.1, 2.3–2.4, 2.7, 3.7, 3.9–3.10, 5.2, 6.1, 9.6, 10.6, 11.10
skills applications 1.6, 1.9, 2.1, 2.4, 2.7, 3.7, 3.10, 6.1, 9.6
whole numbers
addition 2.1
division 4.4, 4.7–4.8, 5.2–5.8
multiplication 3.7, 3.10, 6.1
subtraction 2.1, 2.3
Euler's equation 7.8
expanded form
multiplication 3.6
place value 1.1–1.2, 1.6
experiment 14.1
exponent **3.13**

F

face of a solid figure 7.7
fact families
in addition and subtraction 2.2
in multiplication and division 3.1, 4.2
factor 3.1
common 3.3–3.4, 8.8–8.9
missing 3.1, 6.1
factoring 3.4, 8.7
factorization, prime 8.7
factor tree **8.7**
Fahrenheit 8.1, 12.7
figure
congruent 7.5–7.7
irregular 13.7
plane 7.1, 7.4–7.6, 7.8–7.9
similar 7.12
solid 7.7–7.8
flip 7.11
foot 12.1
formulas 13.1–13.3, 13.5–13.7, 13.10–13.11
four-digit quotient 4.8
fractions 8.4
addition
like denominators 9.1–9.3
unlike denominators 9.8–9.9, 9.11
bars 8.5, 8.11
comparing and ordering 8.11, 9.7
decimals and 8.6, 11.6, 11.9
denominator 8.4–8.6, 8.9, 8.11–8.12, 9.1, 9.6, 10.2–10.3
least common 9.7–9.12
related 9.8
division 10.7–10.8
equal to one 8.4–8.5, 8.12
equivalent 8.5, 8.11, 9.6
estimating 9.6
finding fractional parts 8.4, 9.1, 9.4, 10.2–10.3
greater than one 8.6, 8.12
hundredths 8.6
improper 8.12, 9.3
less than one 8.6, 8.12, 10.2
missing numerator or denominator 8.5
mixed number 8.12, 9.2–9.3, 9.5–9.6, 9.11–9.12, 10.4
multiple 8.10–8.11
least common 9.7, 9.9–9.10
multiplication 10.1, 10.2
estimation 10.6
model 10.1–10.3
numerator 8.4–8.6, 8.9, 8.11–8.12, 9.1, 9.5–9.6, 9.12, 10.2–10.3
on a number line 8.4–8.5, 10.6
part of a set 8.4
part of a whole 8.4
percents and 11.6–11.9
problem solving 8.4–8.6, 8.9, 8.11–8.13, 9.1–9.13, 10.1–10.6, 10.8, 11.8
proper 8.12
ratios 11.1–11.8
reading and writing 8.4, 8.6
renaming 9.7–9.12
rounding 9.6
simplest form 8.9, 9.1–9.3, 9.5–9.6, 9.11, 10.2–10.4
subtraction
like denominators 9.1–9.2, 9.4
unlike denominators 9.8, 9.10, 9.12
whole numbers 9.4, 10.3
tenths 8.6
thousandths 8.6

frequency 14.1
front-end estimation 2.1, 2.4, 2.7, 3.7, 5.2–5.3

G

gallon 12.2
geometry
- angles 7.2, 7.3, 7.4, 7.13
- area
  - rectangle 13.1
  - square 13.1
  - triangle 13.5–13.6
- asymmetry 7.10
- bases 7.6–7.7
- chord 7.9
- circles 7.9, 13.3
- circumference 13.3
- compass 7.9
- cone 7.7
- congruence 7.5–7.7, 7.12
- coordinate 13.4
- cube 7.7
- cylinder 7.7
- decagon 7.5
- degree 7.2–7.3
- diameter 7.9
- edge 7.7
- endpoint 7.1, 7.9
- face 7.7
- hexagon 7.5, 7.8
- irregular figure 13.7
- line 7.1
- line segment 7.1, 7.9
- line symmetry 7.10
- motion in 7.11
- octagon 7.5, 7.8
- parallelogram 7.6
- pentagon 7.5, 7.8
- perimeter 13.2
- plane 7.1
- plane figure 7.4–7.6, 7.8–7.9
- point 7.1, 7.9
- polygon 7.5, 7.8
- polyhedron 7.7
- prism 7.7
  - cube 7.7, 13.9
  - rectangular 7.7, 13.8–13.10
  - triangular 7.7
- protractor 7.3
- pyramid 7.7
- quadrilateral 7.5–7.6
- radius 7.9
- rays 7.1, 7.3, 7.13
- rectangles 7.6, 13.1–13.2
- reflection 7.11
- rhombus 7.6
- rotation 7.11
- semicircle 7.9
- side 13.2
- similar figures 7.12
- solid figure 7.7–7.8
- sphere 7.7
- square 7.6, 13.2
- surface area 13.8
- symmetry 7.10
- three-dimensional figure 7.7–7.8
- transformation 7.11
- translation 7.11
- trapezoid 7.6, 7.8
- triangle 7.4–7.5, 7.8, 13.6
- two-dimensional figure 7.4–7.6, 7.8
- vertex 7.2
- volume 13.9–13.10

gram 12.6
graphic representations
- comparing and ordering 1.3, 1.7
- decimals 1.5–1.8, 2.4–2.5, 2.8, 2.11, 6.2–6.3, 11.9
- fractions 8.4–8.6, 8.9, 8.11–8.12, 9.3–9.5, 9.8, 9.10, 10.1–10.3, 10.7–10.8
- geometry 7.1–7.4, 7.5–7.12, 13.1–13.11
- graphs 14.2–14.7
- ordered pairs 13.4
- percent 11.6, 11.10
- place value 1.1–1.3, 1.5–1.7, 2.4, 2.8, 2.11
- rounding on a number line 1.4, 1.8, 2.4

graphs
- bar 14.2
- circle 14.5
- double bar 14.2
- grid 14.4
- histogram 14.3
- labels on 14.2–14.4, 14.6
- line 14.4, 14.6
- line plots 14.7
- number scales on 14.2–14.4
- ordered pairs of 13.4, 14.4
- percentage on 14.5
- pictographs 14.2
- titles on 14.2–14.4, 14.6

greater-than symbol (>) 1.3–1.4, 1.7–1.8, 2.2, 4.3, 4.5, 4.8, 5.1, 5.3–5.7, 8.2, 9.6–9.7, 11.8, 14.9
greatest common factor (GCF) 3.4, 8.8–8.9, 8.13

H

hexagon 7.5, 7.8
histogram 14.3
hour 12.8–12.9
hundred billions place 1.2–1.3
hundred millions place 1.2–1.3
hundreds place 1.1–1.3, 1.5, 1.7, 3.6, 3.10, 4.3, 4.5, 4.7–4.8, 5.6–5.8
hundred thousands place 1.1–1.3
hundredths 1.5–1.7, 2.4–2.5, 2.8–2.9, 2.11, 6.2, 6.6–6.7, 8.6, 14.9

I

improper fraction 8.12
inch 12.1
inequality 11.2–11.3
integer 8.1–8.3
interpreting remainders 8.5, 8.11
intersecting lines 7.1
interval 14.2, 14.4
inverse operations 2.2, 4.2, 6.7, 13.10
irregular figures 13.7
isosceles triangle 7.4

K

kilogram 12.6
kilometer 12.4

L

least common denominator (LCD) 8.11, 9.7–9.12
least common multiple (LCM) 3.3, 8.10–8.11, 8.13, 9.7

length
customary 12.1
metric 12.4
less-than symbol (<) 1.3–1.4, 1.7– 1.8, 4.2–4.3, 4.5, 4.7–4.8, 5.1, 5.3–5.7, 6.1, 8.2, 9.6–9.7
line 7.1
line graph 14.4, 14.6
line of symmetry 7.10
line plot 14.7
line segment 7.1, 7.9
linear unit 13.1
liter 12.5

M

map 2.10, 9.9, 9.13, 11.5
mass 12.6
customary 12.3
metric 12.6
mean 4.6, **14.7**–14.8
measurement
area 13.1, 13.5–13.8
capacity 12.2, 12.5
circumference 13.3
customary system of 12.1–12.3
length 12.1, 12.4
mass 12.3, 12.6
metric system of 12.4–12.6
perimeter 13.2
temperature 8.1, 12.7
time
elapsed 12.8
telling 12.8
zones 12.9
volume 13.9–13.10
median 14.7–14.8
mental math
addition 2.1, 3.7
division 4.4, 6.8
estimation 2.1, 3.7, 3.12, 6.1, 11.10
fractions 9.3
multiplication 3.1–3.2, 3.6, 6.3–6.4
subtraction 2.7
meter 12.4
metric system of measures
area 13.1, 13.5–13.8
capacity 12.5
circumference 13.3
conversion within the system 12.4–12.6
cubic centimeter 13.9–13.10
length 12.4
mass 12.6
perimeter 13.2
tables 12.4–12.6
temperature 12.7
volume 13.9-13.10
mile 12.1
milligram 12.6
milliliter 12.5
millimeter 12.4
millions place 1.2–1.4
minuend 2.1
minute 12.8
mixed numbers 8.12
addition 9.2–9.3, 9.11
estimating 9.6
improper fraction 8.12, 9.3
renaming 9.5, 9.12, 10.4
subtraction 9.2, 9.5, 9.12
mixed operations 2.10, 3.7, 3.9, 3.12, 6.5, 10.1
mode 14.7–14.8
money
addition 1.9, 2.4, 2.10, 2.12, 3.7
decimals 1.5–1.6, 2.4, 2.10, 6.4–6.6, 6.10
division 4.2, 4.5, 6.6, 6.10
estimation 1.9, 2.4, 2.12, 3.7, 3.9, 3.12, 11.10
hundredths of a dollar 1.5, 2.4
making change 2.10, 3.12
multiplication 3.7, 3.9, 3.12, 6.4–6.5, 6.10
regrouping 4.7, 6.2
rounding 1.8–1.9, 3.7, 3.9, 6.5
skills applications 1.6, 1.9, 2.4, 2.10, 3.7, 3.12, 6.5, 10.9
subtraction 1.9, 2.10, 2.12, 3.7, 3.12
multiple 3.2
chart 3.3, 6.8, 8.10, 9.9
common 3.3–3.4, 8.10, 9.7
least common 3.3, 8.10–8.11, 9.7, 9.9–9.10
of 5 6.1
of 10 3.2, 5.1, 11.10
of 100 3.2
of 1,000 3.2
multiplication
addition 3.1
area model 13.1, 13.5–13.8
array 10.3
basic facts 3.1, 3.6, 5.1
basic fact strategies
finding factors 3.4
finding patterns 3.2, 3.12, 5.2, 6.2, 6.4
skip count 3.2–3.3
estimating 3.7, 3.10, 10.6
expanded form 3.6
factor 3.1–3.2, 3.4, 3.13–3.14, 6.1–6.3, 8.7–8.9
common 8.8–8.9
missing 3.10, 6.1
factoring 3.4, 8.7
fractions
using models 10.1–10.2
whole numbers 10.3
lattice multiplication 3.14
mixed numbers 10.4
models 6.2–6.3, 8.7, 10.1–10.2
multiple 3.2–3.4, 4.4, 6.1
multiples of 10, 100, and 1,000 3.2
no regrouping 3.5, 3.8
four-digit numbers 3.6
money 3.12
multiples of 10, 100, and 1,000 3.2, 3.6, 3.8, 6.4
three-digit numbers 3.5
two-digit numbers 3.5, 3.11
partial product 3.8, 3.10
patterns 3.2, 3.12, 5.2, 6.2, 6.4
place value in 3.5–3.10
product 3.1–3.2, 3.4, 3.6–3.7, 3.10, 3.14, 6.1–6.4, 10.2
properties
Associative Property 3.1
Commutative Property 3.1, 6.1–6.4, 6.10, 13.5, 13.10
Distributive Property 3.1, 3.6
Identity Property of One 3.1
Zero Property 3.1
regrouping 3.5–3.6, 3.8, 3.10, 6.2–6.3
related to division 4.2, 5.1

multiplication, ***continued***
repeated addition 3.1
three-digit multiplier 3.10–3.11
two-digit multiplier
money 3.7, 3.9, 6.4
three-digit numbers 3.8, 3.11
two-digit numbers 3.8–3.9
using the hundred chart 3.3
with 10, 100, 1,000 3.6, 3.10
with large numbers 3.6

N

Napier's bones 3.6
negative number 8.1
temperature 8.1
whole numbers 8.1–8.3
number line
comparing fractions 8.5, 8.11, 10.6
comparing integers 8.1–8.3
decimals 1.7–1.8, 2.4, 2.9
rounding numbers 1.4, 1.8, 2.4
number patterns 5.1, 10.9
numbers
comparing and ordering
decimals 1.7
fractions 8.11, 9.7
whole numbers 1.3
compatible 4.4, 5.2–5.8, 10.6
composite 8.7
cubed 3.13, 13.9–13.10
expanded form 1.1–1.2, 1.6
mixed 8.12, 9.2–9.3, 9.5–9.6, 9.11–9.12, 10.4
place value 1.1–1.3, 1.5–1.7, 2.4–2.5, 2.8, 2.11, 4.1, 4.3, 4.5, 4.7–4.8, 5.4, 5.6, 5.8, 6.2–6.3, 6.6–6.8, 8.6
prime 8.7
Roman numerals 10
rounding 1.4, 1.8–1.9, 2.1, 2.3–2.4, 2.7, 3.9, 3.13, 4.9, 5.2, 5.5, 6.1, 6.5, 9.6, 11.10, 11.12
square 3.13, 13.1, 13.5–13.8
standard form 1.1–1.2, 1.6
word form 1.1, 1.2, 1.7, 2.1, 3.6
number sense
decimal 1.5, 2.8
fraction 8.4
whole number 1.1–1.2
number sentence
addition and subtraction 2.3
multiplication and division 4.2, 5.1
number theory
composite number 8.7
divisibility 4.1–4.2
expanded form 1.1–1.2, 1.6
factor 3.1, 3.4, 8.7–8.9
greatest common factor 8.8–8.9
least common multiple 8.10–8.11
multiple 3.2–3.4, 8.10, 9.7, 9.9–9.10
pattern 3.2, 3.12, 5.1, 6.2
prime factorization 8.7
prime number 8.7
standard form 1.1–1.2, 1.6
numerator 8.4–8.6, 8.9, 8.11–8.12, 9.1, 9.5–9.6, 9.12, 10.2–10.3

O

obtuse angle 7.2, 7.3
obtuse triangle 7.4
octagon 7.5, 7.8
one-digit quotients 4.3, 4.5, 5.1, 5.3, 5.5
one in division 4.2
ones, place value 1.1–1.3, 1.5–1.7, 2.4, 2.8, 2.11, 3.6, 3.8, 4.1, 4.3, 4.5, 4.7–4.8, 5.4, 5.7, 6.2–6.3, 6.6–6.7, 8.6, 14.9
opposite number 8.1
ordered pair 13.4
order of operations 6.9
organizing data 14.1
ounce 12.2-12.3
outcome 14.10–14.11
overestimate 1.9, 4.4, 4.8, 5.3

P

parallel lines 7.1
parallelogram 7.6
partial product 3.8, 3.10
part of a set 8.4
part of a whole 8.4
Pascal's triangle 3.12
patterns
in division 4.4, 5.1, 6.8
in multiplication 3.2, 6.4
in problem solving 10.9
number 3.12, 5.1, 6.2
pentagon 7.5, 7.8
percent 11.6
decimals and 11.9, 11.11
finding 11.11
fractions and 11.8, 11.10–11.11
problem solving 11.12
ratio and 11.7
percent symbol (%) 11.6
perimeter 13.2
period 1.1–1.2
perpendicular lines 7.1
pictograph 14.2
pint 12.2
***pi* symbol (π)** 13.3
place value
billions 1.2–1.3
chart 1.1–1.3, 1.5–1.7
decimals 1.5–1.7, 2.4–2.8, 2.10–2.11, 6.2–6.3, 6.6–6.8, 8.6
digits 1.1–1.4, 1.6–1.8
division 4.1, 4.3, 4.7
hundred billions 1.2–1.3
hundred millions 1.2–1.3
hundreds 1.1–1.3, 1.5, 1.7
hundred thousands 1.1–1.3
hundredths 1.5–1.7, 2.4–2.5, 2.8–2.9, 2.11, 6.2, 6.6–6.7, 8.6, 14.9
millions 1.2–1.4
multiplication and 3.5–3.7, 3.9–3.10
ones 1.1–1.3, 1.5–1.7, 2.4, 2.8, 2.11, 3.6, 3.8, 4.1, 4.3, 4.5, 4.7–4.8, 5.4, 5.7, 6.2–6.3, 6.6–6.7, 8.6, 14.9
periods 1.1–1.3
ten billions 1.2–1.3
ten millions 1.2–1.3
tens 1.1–1.3, 1.5–1.7
ten thousands 1.1–1.3, 3.6, 4.8
tenths 1.5–1.8, 2.4–2.5, 2.7–2.9, 2.11, 6.2–6.3, 6.6–6.7, 8.6, 14.9
thousands 1.1–1.4
thousandths 1.6–1.7, 2.4, 2.8, 2.11, 14.9, 6.7, 8.6
whole numbers 1.1–1.4

plane 7.1
plane figure 7.4, 7.5–7.6, 7.8–7.9
PM 12.8
point 7.1
decimal 1.5–1.6, 2.4–2.8, 2.10–2.11, 6.1–6.10, 8.6
endpoint
line segment 7.1, 7.9
number line 8.4–8.5, 8.11
location in space 7.1
polygon 7.5, 7.8
polyhedron 7.7
positive number 8.1
temperature 8.1
whole numbers 8.1–8.3
pound 12.3
powers of 10 3.13
predicting outcomes 14.10
prime factorization 8.7
prime number 8.7
prism 7.7
cube 7.7, 13.9
rectangular 7.7, 13.8–13.10
triangular 7.7
probability
making predictions 14.10–14.11
written as a fraction 14.10–14.11
Problem-Solving Guide 1.9, 2.10, 3.9, 5.8, 10.5
problem-solving strategies
analyzing the data 1.9, 2.3, 2.10, 3.9, 3.11–3.12, 6.5, 8.13, 10.5, 12.9, 14.2–14.9
checking for a reasonable answer 1.9, 2.3, 3.9, 6.5, 14.9
choosing a strategy or method 1.9, 2.3, 2.10, 3.9, 3.12, 4.9, 6.5, 6.10, 7.8, 7.13, 8.13, 9.13, 10.5, 10.9, 12.9, 13.11, 14.9
choosing the operation 2.3
determining a reasonable answer 1.9, 2.1, 3.8, 6.5, 14.9
drawing a figure, design, or diagram 7.5, 7.9, 7.11, 7.13
drawing a picture 3.12, 4.5, 7.8, 8.13
estimating 1.9, 3.7, 6.1, 6.5
evaluating the result 1.9, 2.3, 2.10, 3.9, 3.11–3.12, 6.5, 8.13, 10.5, 12.9, 14.9
identifying sufficient, insufficient, or extra data 3.11, 6.5
interpreting the remainder 4.3, 4.9
looking for a pattern 6.2
making a diagram 9.1, 13.9
making a table 10.9, 11.2
planning the strategy 1.9, 2.3, 2.10, 3.9, 3.11–3.12, 6.5, 8.13, 10.5, 12.9, 14.9
trying and checking 1.9
understanding the question 1.9, 2.3, 2.10, 3.9, 3.11–3.12, 6.5, 8.13, 10.5, 12.9, 14.9
using a calculator 1.5–1.6, 1.9, 1.10, 2.1, 2.6–2.10, 3.11–3.12, 4.3, 4.6, 4.9, 5.7, 6.2, 6.5, 6.8–6.10, 8.10, 14.7, 14.9
using a calendar 3.3
using data from a chart 1.3, 1.6, 1.8–1.9, 3.12, 4.6, 4.9, 6.4, 6.7–6.10, 7.7, 8.2, 8.13, 9.11, 11.6, 14.9
using data from a table 7.8, 3.13, 12.1–12.8, 13.6, 13.8, 14.2–14.3, 14.5, 14.8
using logical reasoning 7.8
writing an equation 1.9, 2.3, 2.10, 3.12, 7.8
product 3.1
estimating 3.7, 3.9, 6.1, 10.6
profit 3.12
projects
data arrays 14.1
dinner-party prices 2.1
geocache fraction clues 10.1
geometry city 7.1
recipe conversions 6.1
travel-itinerary map 12.1
water-park design 4.1
proper fraction 8.12
properties
Associative Property of Addition 2.6
Associative Property of Multiplication 3.1
Commutative Property of Addition 2.6
Commutative Property of Multiplication 3.1
Distributive Property of Multiplication 3.1, 3.6
Multiplication Identity Property of One 3.1
Zero Property of Addition 2.6
Zero Property of Division 4.2
Zero Property of Multiplication 3.1
proportion 11.3–11.4, 11.7
protractor 7.3
pyramid 7.7

Q

quadrilateral 7.6
quart 12.2
questionnaire 14.1
quotient 4.2
decimals in 6.6–6.8
estimating 4.4, 4.7–4.8, 5.2–5.8
four digits 4.8
one digit 4.3, 4.5, 5.1, 5.3, 5.5
three digits 4.7, 5.1, 5.6–5.8
two digits 4.1–4.6, 4.9–5.2, 5.4, 5.6
zero in 4.2–4.4, 4.7, 5.1–5.2, 5.7, 6.7–6.8

R

radius 7.9
random sample 14.1
range 4.6, 14.8
ratio 11.1
circumference to diameter 13.3
probability 14.10–14.11
proportions 11.3–11.5
ratio table 11.1–11.2
ray 7.1, 7.13
reasonable answer 1.9, 2.1–2.3, 2.10, 3.8–3.10, 6.5, 14.9
recipe 10.5, 11.3, 14.9
rectangle
area 13.1
perimeter 13.2
rectangular prism 7.7, 13.8–13.10
rectangular pyramid 7.7
reflection 7.11
regrouping
in addition 2.2, 2.5, 2.8, 3.14

regrouping, ***continued***
in decimals 2.5, 2.7–2.9, 2.11, 6.2, 6.6
in division 4.3, 4.7, 6.6
in multiplication 3.5–3.6, 3.8, 3.10, 6.2–6.3
in subtraction 2.2–2.5, 2.7–2.9
with money 6.6
remainder 4.3, 4.8–4.9, 5.5–5.6, 5.8
repeating decimal 10.9
retail price 3.12
rhombus 7.6
right angle 7.2
right triangle 7.4, 13.5
Roman numerals 1.9
rotation 7.11
rounding
decimals 1.8–1.9, 2.4, 2.7, 6.1, 6.5
estimating
differences 1.9, 2.1, 2.3, 2.7, 9.6
products 3.7, 3.9, 6.1, 10.6
quotients 5.2, 5.5
sums 1.9, 2.1, 2.4, 9.6
to nearest cent 6.4, 6.10, 11.12
to nearest dollar 1.9, 6.5, 6.10
to nearest half 9.6
to nearest hundred 1.4, 2.1
to nearest million 1.4, 1.9
to nearest pound 1.9
to nearest ten 1.4
to nearest tenth 1.8–1.9, 2.7, 6.3, 14.8
to nearest ten thousand 1.4
to nearest thousand 1.4, 3.13
using a number line 1.4, 1.8, 2.4
ruler 1.5, 7.3, 7.6, 7.9, 7.11–7.12, 8.4,
9.13, 10.8, 11.5, 12.1, 12.4, 12.10, 13.1, 13.3–13.4, 14.1–14.4, 14.6–14.7
rules for division 4.1–4.2

S

scale 9.13
balance 12.10
kitchen 12.3
map 9.13
thermometer 12.7, 8.1
scale drawing 11.5
scalene triangle 7.4
second 12.8
semicircle 7.9
similar figures 7.12
skip counting 3.2–3.3, 3.12
slide 7.11
solid figure 7.7
sphere 7.7
square
area 13.1
perimeter 13.2
square number 13.1, 13.5–13.8
square pyramid 7.7
square unit 13.1
standard form
in multiplication 3.8
in place value 1.1–1.2, 1.6
statistics 14.7
collecting, organizing, analyzing data 14.7
comparing data 14.2, 14.6
graphs
bar 14.2
circle 14.5
histogram 14.3
line 14.4, 14.6
line plot 14.7, 14.9
pictograph 14.2
outcomes 14.10
survey 14.1
tally 14.1–14.2, 14.7
straight angle 7.2
subtraction
basic facts 2.2
checking 2.3
count back 2.9
decimals 1.9, 2.7–2.8, 2.10–2.11
differences 2.1, 2.3, 2.7, 2.9, 9.6
range of numerical data 4.6
estimation in 1.9, 2.1, 2.7, 9.6
fractions 9.1, 9.8, 9.10
larger numbers 2.2
missing numbers 2.9
mixed numbers 9.2, 9.4–9.5, 9.12
money 1.9, 2.10
regrouping 2.1–2.3, 2.7–2.8
zeros in computation 2.1–2.2, 2.8
subtrahend 2.1
sum 2.2
surface area 13.8
symbol
approximately equal to (≈) 2.1
division (÷) 2.1
greater than (>) 1.3–1.4, 1.7–1.8, 2.2, 4.3, 4.5, 4.8, 5.1, 5.3–5.7, 8.2, 9.6–9.7, 11.8, 14.9
less than (<) 1.3–1.4, 1.8, 4.3, 4.5, 4.7–4.8, 5.1, 5.3–5.7, 8.2, 9.6–9.7
percent (%) 11.6
pi (π) 13.3
symmetry 7.10

T

tablespoon 12.2
tally 14.1–14.2, 14.7
teaspoon 12.2
temperature 12.7
ten billions place 1.2–1.3
ten millions place 1.2–1.3
tens place 1.1–1.3, 1.5–1.7, 3.6, 3.8, 4.3, 4.5, 4.7–4.8, 5.4, 5.6–5.7, 6.7
ten thousands place 1.1–1.3, 3.6, 4.8
tenths 1.5–1.8, 2.4–2.9, 2.11, 6.2–6.3, 6.6–6.7, 8.6, 14.
term 11.1
unknown 11.3–11.4
terminating decimal 10.9
thermometer 8.1, 12.7
thousands place 1.1–1.4, 3.6, 5.6
thousandths place 1.6–1.7, 2.4–2.5, 2.8, 2.11, 4.8, 6.2, 6.7, 8.6, 14.9
three-digit quotient 4.7, 5.1, 5.6–5.7
time
addition and subtraction of 12.8
calendar 3.3, 11.9
clock 12.8
elapsed 12.8
telling 12.8
units of 12.8
zones 12.9
ton 12.3
transformation 7.11
translation 7.11

trapezoid 7.6, 7.8
triangle 7.4–7.5
area of 13.6
triangular prism 7.7
triangular pyramid 7.7
turn 7.11
two-digit divisor 5.6–5.8
two-digit factor 3.7, 3.8, 6.2–6.3
two-digit quotient 4.1–4.6, 4.9–5.2, 5.4, 5.6
two-step problem 2.10, 3.7, 3.9, 3.11–3.12, 6.5, 10.3, 10.5–10.6

U

underestimate 1.9, 4.4
understanding the question 2.3, 2.10, 3.9
units
area 13.1, 13.5–13.8
capacity 12.2, 12.5
length 12.1, 12.4
volume 13.9–13.10
weight 12.3, 12.6
using data
from a chart 1.3, 1.6, 1.8–1.9, 4.6, 4.9, 8.13, 14.1
from a recipe 11.3

V

variable 2.3
Venn diagram 3.4, 8.8
vertex
of an angle 7.2–7.3
of a polygon 7.5
of a solid figure 7.7
volume 13.9
by counting 13.9
by multiplying 13.9–13.10
cubic inches, centimeters 13.9–13.10

W

weight
customary 12.3
metric 12.6
whole number
addition 2.1, 2.2, 2.4, 2.6, 3.9
comparing and ordering 1.3
division 4.1–4.3, 4.6–5.8, 6.6
estimation 1.9, 2.1, 2.3–2.4, 3.7, 3.9, 4.4, 4.7–4.8, 5.2–5.5, 5.6, 6.5
finding a fraction of 10.3, 10.7
integers 8.1–8.3
multiplication 3.1–3.14, 6.1–6.2, 6.5
place value 1.1–1.3, 2.4, 3.6, 3.9
regrouping 2.2–2.3, 3.5–3.6, 3.8, 3.14, 6.6
rounding 1.4, 1.9, 2.1, 2.3–2.4, 3.5, 3.9, 4.9, 5.2, 5.5, 6.5
subtraction 2.1–2.2
writing 1.1–1.3, 3.6
wholesale price 3.12
word forms of numbers
decimals 1.5–1.6, 2.8, 2.11
fractions 8.4, 8.6
money 1.5
whole numbers 1.1–1.2, 3.6

Y

yard 12.1

Z

zero
in addition 2.5, 2.8, 2.11
in decimals 1.7, 2.5, 2.8, 2.11, 6.2–6.4, 6.7–6.8
in division 4.2–4.4, 4.7–4.8, 5.1–5.2, 5.6–5.7, 6.7–6.8
in estimation 2.1
in integers 8.1
in multiplication 3.8, 6.2–6.4
in place value 1.1–1.2, 2.4–2.5, 6.2–6.3, 6.7–6.8
in quotients 4.2–4.4, 4.7, 5.1–5.2, 5.7, 6.7–6.8
in rounding 1.4, 5.2
in subtraction 2.2, 2.8, 2.11